D0919437

CCNP Security IPS 642-627 Official Cert Guide

David Burns
Odunayo Adesina, CCIE No. 26695
Keith Barker, CCIE No. 6783

Cisco Press

800 East 96th Street

Indianapolis, IN 46240

CCNP Security IPS 642-627 Official Cert Guide

David Burns

Odunayo Adesina, CCIE No. 26695

Keith Barker, CCIE No. 6783

Copyright© 2012 Pearson Education, Inc.

Published by:
Cisco Press
800 East 96th Street
Indianapolis, IN 46240 USA

All rights reserved. No part of this book may be reproduced or transmitted in any form or by any means, electronic or mechanical, including photocopying, recording, or by any information storage and retrieval system, without written permission from the publisher, except for the inclusion of brief quotations in a review.

Printed in the United States of America 1 2 3 4 5 6 7 8 9 0

First Printing October 2011

Library of Congress Cataloging-in-Publication data is on file.

ISBN-13: 978-1-58714-255-0

ISBN-10: 1-58714-255-4

Warning and Disclaimer

This book is designed to provide information about selected topics for the CCNP Security IPS 642-627 exam. Every effort has been made to make this book as complete and as accurate as possible, but no warranty or fitness is implied.

The information is provided on an "as is" basis. The authors, Cisco Press, and Cisco Systems, Inc., shall have neither liability nor responsibility to any person or entity with respect to any loss or damages arising from the information contained in this book or from the use of the discs or programs that may accompany it.

The opinions expressed in this book belong to the authors and are not necessarily those of Cisco Systems, Inc.

Feedback Information

At Cisco Press, our goal is to create in-depth technical books of the highest quality and value. Each book is crafted with care and precision, undergoing rigorous development that involves the unique expertise of members from the professional technical community.

Readers' feedback is a natural continuation of this process. If you have any comments regarding how we could improve the quality of this book, or otherwise alter it to better suit your needs, you can contact us through e-mail at feedback@ciscopress.com. Please make sure to include the book title and ISBN in your message.

We greatly appreciate your assistance.

Corporate and Government Sales

The publisher offers excellent discounts on this book when ordered in quantity for bulk purchases or special sales, which may include electronic versions and/or custom covers and content particular to your business, training goals, marketing focus, and branding interests. For more information, please contact: U.S. Corporate and Government Sales   1-800-382-3419   corpsales@pearsontechgroup.com

For sales outside the United States, please contact: International Sales   international@pearsoned.com

Trademark Acknowledgments

All terms mentioned in this book that are known to be trademarks or service marks have been appropriately capitalized. Cisco Press or Cisco Systems, Inc. cannot attest to the accuracy of this information. Use of a term in this book should not be regarded as affecting the validity of any trademark or service mark.

Publisher: Paul Boger

Associate Publisher: Dave Dusthimer

Executive Editor: Brett Bartow

Managing Editor: Sandra Schroeder

Development Editor: Kimberley Debus

Senior Project Editor: Tonya Simpson

Copy Editor: John Edwards

Manager, Global Certification: Erik Ullanderson

Business Operation Manager, Cisco Press: Anand Sundaram

Technical Editor: Brandon Anastasoff

Proofreader: Sarah Kearns

Indexer: Tim Wright

Compositor: Mark Shirar

Book Designer: Gary Adair

Americas Headquarters
Cisco Systems, Inc.
San Jose, CA

Asia Pacific Headquarters
Cisco Systems (USA) Pte. Ltd.
Singapore

Europe Headquarters
Cisco Systems International BV
Amsterdam, The Netherlands

Cisco has more than 200 offices worldwide. Addresses, phone numbers, and fax numbers are listed on the Cisco Website at **www.cisco.com/go/offices.**

CCDE, CCENT, Cisco Eos, Cisco HealthPresence, the Cisco logo, Cisco Lumin, Cisco Nexus, Cisco StadiumVision, Cisco TelePresence, Cisco WebEx, DCE, and Welcome to the Human Network are trademarks; Changing the Way We Work, Live, Play, and Learn and Cisco Store are service marks; and Access Registrar, Aironet, AsyncOS, Bringing the Meeting To You, Catalyst, CCDA, CCDP, CCIE, CCIP, CCNA, CCNP, CCSP, CCVP, Cisco, the Cisco Certified Internetwork Expert logo, Cisco IOS, Cisco Press, Cisco Systems, Cisco Systems Capital, the Cisco Systems logo, Cisco Unity, Collaboration Without Limitation, EtherFast, EtherSwitch, Event Center, Fast Step, Follow Me Browsing, FormShare, GigaDrive, HomeLink, Internet Quotient, IOS, iPhone, iQuick Study, IronPort, the IronPort logo, LightStream, Linksys, MediaTone, MeetingPlace, MeetingPlace Chime Sound, MGX, Networkers, Networking Academy, Network Registrar, PCNow, PIX, PowerPanels, ProConnect, ScriptShare, SenderBase, SMARTnet, Spectrum Expert, StackWise, The Fastest Way to Increase Your Internet Quotient, TransPath, WebEx, and the WebEx logo are registered trademarks of Cisco Systems, Inc. and/or its affiliates in the United States and certain other countries.

All other trademarks mentioned in this document or website are the property of their respective owners. The use of the word partner does not imply a partnership relationship between Cisco and any other company. (0812R)

About the Authors

David Burns has in-depth knowledge of routing and switching technologies, network security, and mobility. He is currently a systems engineering manager for Cisco, covering various U.S. Service Provider accounts. Dave joined Cisco in July 2008 as a lead systems engineer in a number of areas that include Femtocell, Datacenter, MTSO, and Security Architectures, working for a U.S.-based SP Mobility account. He came to Cisco from a large U.S.-based cable company, where he was a senior network and security design engineer. Dave has held various roles prior to joining Cisco during his ten-plus years in the industry, working in SP operations, SP engineering, SP architecture, enterprise IT, and also U.S. military intelligence communications engineering. He holds various sales and industry/Cisco technical certifications, including the CISSP, CCSP, and CCDP, as well as two associate-level certifications. Dave recently passed the CCIE Security Written and is currently preparing for the CCIE Security Lab. Dave is a big advocate of knowledge transfer and sharing and has a passion for network technologies, especially as they relate to network security. Dave has been a speaker at Cisco Live on topics including Femtocell (IP Mobility) and IPS (Security). Dave earned his bachelor of science degree in telecommunications engineering technology from Southern Polytechnic State University, Georgia, where he currently serves as a member of the Industry Advisory Board for the Computer & Electrical Engineering Technology School.

Odunayo Adesina, CCIE No. 26695 (Routing and Switching), is a systems engineer with Cisco in the U.S. commercial segment. In this role for over four years, Odunayo has worked with commercial customers in St. Louis, Missouri, to help develop their enterprise network architectures, which are typically a combination of borderless, collaboration, and virtualization solutions. He has more than 12 years of experience in the industry and holds various industry and Cisco certifications, including the CISSP No. 54152, CCSP, CEH, and VSP. He was one of the first few people who were CSS1 certified when the Cisco security certification was first developed. Prior to his role at Cisco, Odunayo worked with a large service provider as a network engineer, implementing and managing security, routing, and switching solutions, and later as a security specialist, driving ISO 27001 compliance, developing and enforcing security policies for the enterprise. He also worked with Cisco partners, where he implemented solutions across many industry verticals. Odunayo holds a bachelor of technology degree in electronics and electrical engineering from Ladoke Akintola University of Technology.

Keith Barker, CCIE No. 6783 R/S & Security, is a 27-year veteran of the networking industry. He currently works as a network engineer and trainer for Nova Datacom. His past experience includes EDS, Blue Cross, Paramount Pictures, and KnowledgeNET, and he has delivered CCIE-level training over the past several years. He is CISSP and CCSI certified, loves to teach, and keeps many of his video tutorials at http://www.youtube.com/keith6783. He can be reached at KBarker@NovaDatacom.com or by visiting http://www.NovaDatacom.com.

About the Technical Editor

Brandon Anastasoff has been a systems engineer with Cisco Systems since October 2007, when he moved from a lead network architect role in a major newspaper publishing firm. He has spent over 20 years in the industry and has been focused on security for the last ten, obtaining certifications inside and outside of Cisco with his CISSP, CCSP, and most recently the Security CCIE. After studying in the United Kingdom, Brandon took a year off in Saudi Arabia to see what a real job would be like before proceeding to college but found the lure of an income too irresistible and never went back for the degree. Brandon had to make a choice early in his career to either follow the art of computer animation or the up-and-coming PC networking boom, and he has never regretted the decision to enter networking. He moved from early versions of Windows and Macintosh OSs through Novell's Netware and then moved more into the infrastructure side, focusing mostly on Cisco LAN/WAN equipment. After Y2K, the focus became more security oriented, and Brandon became familiar with virus and Trojan analysis and forensic investigations. Today, Brandon is glad to be where he is and enjoys taking the opportunity to talk about security whenever the opportunity presents itself.

Dedications

"To fight and conquer in all your battles is not supreme excellence; supreme excellence consists in breaking the enemy's resistance without fighting."

—*Sun Tzu, the Art of War*

From David:

This book is dedicated to my wife and best friend in life, Lisa, whose love, encouragement, and support continue to drive my passion to learn, achieve, and serve; to our two boys, Will and Christian, who have an unending curiosity to learn, grow, and challenge the norm; to my extended family for their support, encouragement, and inspiration all these years; and finally to my fellow soldiers (present, past, and future) for their selfless service, integrity, honor, pride, and drive to do the right thing to protect us all—God Bless!

From Odunayo:

This book is dedicated to God for his many blessings; to my loving wife, Aramide, who always gives me great encouragement and support, especially as she did during the writing of this book; and to my parents, who have continually encouraged my brother, sister, cousins, and me and our families, in everything we've done. Also to the loving memories of my aunt, Olayemi Akere, and cousin, Korede Akindele, who were supportive and instrumental to my many successes.

Acknowledgments

We would like to thank many people for helping us put this book together:

The Cisco Press team: Brett Bartow, the executive editor, was the catalyst for this project, coordinating the team and ensuring that sufficient resources were available for the completion of the book. Kimberley Debus, the development editor, has been invaluable in producing a high-quality manuscript. Her great suggestions and keen eye caught some technical errors and really improved the presentation of the book. We would also like to thank the project editor team for their excellent work in shepherding this book through the editorial process.

The Cisco IPS 7.0 course development team: Many thanks to the IPS course development team members.

The technical reviewers: We would like to thank the technical reviewer of this book, Brandon Anastasoff, for his thorough, detailed review and very valuable input.

Our families: Of course, this book would not have been possible without the constant understanding and patience of our families. They have lived through the long days and nights it took to complete this project and have always been there to motivate and inspire us. We thank you all.

Each other: Last, but not least, this book is a product of work by three strangers (now friends) and colleagues, which made it even more of a pleasure to complete.

From Odunayo:

The Cisco Press team was very instrumental in the success of this book. The executive editor, Brett Bartow, did an outstanding job of coordinating the team, ensuring that timelines were met and that resources required in completing the book were available. The hard work of the development editor, Kimberley Debus, produced the brilliant formatting of the text and images, which are pivotal to the overall experience of the reader. And also Tonya Simpson, John Edwards, and Drew Cupp, for making sure the text is free of typos with dotted i's and crossed t's.

My St. Louis Cisco family, especially Mark Meissner, Deana Patrick, Cindy Godwin-Sak, Brian Sak, Josh Gentry, Corey Moomey, and Jeff Peterson, encouraged me through all the stages of this project and provided some of the hardware used for the practical sections of the book.

My coauthors David Burns and Keith Barker worked diligently toward the completion of this book. Keith Barker also ensured the integrity of the text as a technical reviewer with Brandon Anastasoff.

And last but not least, my family, colleagues, and friends showed tremendous support and excitement while looking forward to the book's completion; this I found very energizing.

From Keith:

Thanks to Dave Burns, Odunayo Adesina, Brett Bartow, and Andrew Cupp for the opportunity to be part of this project, and to all those who assisted in making my words look better, including Brandon Anastasoff, Kimberley Debus, and Tonya Simpson, as well as the other amazing folks at Cisco Press. A special shout-out to Jeremy Dansie for his assistance regarding this project.

Thanks to the viewers of my YouTube channel, Keith6783, for all your requests, encouragement, and kind feedback regarding the content there. It means a lot to me.

Finally, I want to thank my wife, Jennifer, for being a solid foundation for me and our family, and to my seven children, who continue to remind me how absolutely wonderful life can be.

Contents at a Glance

Contents

Command Syntax Conventions

The conventions used to present command syntax in this book are the same conventions used in the IOS Command Reference. The Command Reference describes these conventions as follows:

- **Boldface** indicates commands and keywords that are entered literally as shown. In actual configuration examples and output (not general command syntax), boldface indicates commands that are manually input by the user (such as a **show** command).

- *Italic* indicates arguments for which you supply actual values.

- Vertical bars (|) separate alternative, mutually exclusive elements.

- Square brackets ([ ]) indicate an optional element.

- Braces ({ }) indicate a required choice.

- Braces within brackets ([{ }]) indicate a required choice within an optional element.

Introduction

So, you have worked on Cisco security devices for a while, designing secure networks for your customers, and now you want to get certified. There are several good reasons to do so. The Cisco certification program allows network analysts and engineers to demonstrate their competence in different areas and levels of networking. The prestige and respect that come with a Cisco certification will definitely help you in your career. Your clients, peers, and superiors will recognize you as an expert in networking.

Cisco Certified Network Professional (CCNP) Security is the professional-level certification that represents the knowledge of security in routers, switches, network devices, and appliances. The CCNP Security demonstrates skills required to design, choose, deploy, support, and troubleshoot firewalls, VPNs, and IDS/IPS solutions for network infrastructures.

Although it is not required, Cisco suggests taking the Secure v1.0, Firewall v1.0, VPN v1.0, and IPS v7.0 courses before you take the specific CCNP Security exams. For more information on the various levels of certification, career tracks, and Cisco exams, visit the Cisco Certifications page at http://www.cisco.com/web/learning/le3/learning_career_certifications_and_ learning_paths_home.html.

Our goal with this book is to help you prepare and pass the IPS v7.0 test. This is done by having assessment quizzes in each chapter to quickly identify levels of readiness or areas that you need more help on. The chapters cover all exam topics published by Cisco. Review tables and test questions will help you practice your knowledge on all subject areas.

About the 642-627 IPS v7.0 Exam

The CCNP Security IPS v7.0 exam measures your ability to deploy Cisco IPS–based security solutions. The exam focuses on small- to medium-sized networks. The candidate should have at least one year of experience in the deployment and support of small- to medium-sized networks using Cisco products. A CCNP Security candidate should understand internetworking and security technologies, including the Cisco Enterprise Network Architecture, IPv4 subnets, IPv6 addressing and protocols, routing, switching, WAN technologies, LAN protocols, security, IP telephony, and network management. The new exam adds topics such as new features introduced in the v7.0 secure data center design, and updates IPv6, complex network security rules, troubleshooting, secure WAN design, and optimizing/managing the Cisco IPS security infrastructure device performance.

The tests to obtain CCNP Security certification include Implementing Cisco Intrusion Prevention System v7.0 (IPS) Exam #642-627, Securing Networks with Cisco Routers and Switches (SECURE) Exam #642-637, Deploying Cisco ASA VPN Solutions (VPN) Exam 642-647, and Deploying Cisco ASA Firewall Solutions (FIREWALL) Exam 642-617. All four tests are computer-based tests that have 65 questions and a 90-minute time limit. Because all exam information is managed by Cisco Systems and is therefore subject to change, candidates should continually monitor the Cisco Systems site for course and exam updates at http://www.cisco.com/web/learning/le3/learning_career_certifications_and_learning_paths_home.html.

You can take the exam at Pearson VUE testing centers. You can register with VUE at http://www.vue.com/cisco. The CCNP Security certification is valid for three years. To recertify, you can pass a current CCNP Security test, pass a CCIE exam, or pass any 642 or Cisco Specialist exam.

642-627 IPS v7.0 Exam Topics

Table I-1 lists the topics of the 642-627 IPS v7.0 exam and indicates the parts in the book where they are covered.

Table I-1   *642-627 IPS v7.0 Exam Topics*

Exam Topic	Part
Preproduction Design	
Choose Cisco IPS technologies to implement HLD (High-Level Design)	I
Choose Cisco products to implement HLD (High-Level Design)	I
Choose Cisco IPS features to implement HLD (High-Level Design)	I
Integrate Cisco network security solutions with other security technologies	II
Create and test initial Cisco IPS configurations for new devices/services	II
Complex Support Operations	
Optimize Cisco IPS security infrastructure device performance	II
Create complex network security rules to meet the security policy requirements	III
Configure and verify the IPS features to identify threats and dynamically block them from entering the network	III, IV
Maintain, update, and tune IPS signatures	IV, V
Use CSM and MARS for IPS management, deployment, and advanced event correlation	V
Optimize security functions, rules, and configuration	V–VII
Advanced Troubleshooting	
Advanced Cisco IPS security software configuration fault finding and repairing	II, VII
Advanced Cisco IPS Sensor and module hardware fault finding and repairing	II, VII

About the CCNP Security IPS v7.0 642-627 Official Cert Guide

This book maps to the topic areas of the 642-627 IPS v7.0 exam and uses a number of features to help you understand the topics and to prepare for the exam.

Objectives and Methods

This book uses several key methodologies to help you discover the exam topics on which you need more review, to help you fully understand and remember those details, and to help you prove to yourself that you have retained your knowledge of those topics. So, this book does not try to help you pass the exams only by memorization, but by truly learning and understanding the topics. The book is designed to help you pass the CCNP Security IPS v7.0 exam by using the following methods:

■ Helping you discover which exam topics you have not mastered

■ Providing explanations and information to fill in your knowledge gaps

■ Supplying exercises that enhance your ability to recall and deduce the answers to test questions

■ Providing practice exercises on the topics and the testing process through test questions on the CD

Book Features

To help you customize your study time using this book, the core chapters have several features that help you make the best use of your time:

■ **"Do I Know This Already?" quiz:** Each chapter begins with a quiz that helps you determine how much time you need to spend studying that chapter.

■ **Foundation Topics:** These are the core sections of each chapter. They explain the concepts for the topics in that chapter.

■ **Exam Preparation Tasks:** After the "Foundation Topics" section of each chapter, the "Exam Preparation Tasks" section lists a series of study activities that you should do at the end of the chapter. Each chapter includes the activities that make the most sense for studying the topics in that chapter:

— **Review All the Key Topics:** The Key Topic icons appear next to the most important items in the "Foundation Topics" section of the chapter. The Review All the Key Topics activity lists the key topics from the chapter, along with their page numbers. Although the contents of the entire chapter could be on the exam, you should definitely know the information listed in each key topic, so you should review these.

— **Complete the Tables and Lists from Memory:** To help you memorize some lists of facts, many of the more important lists and tables from the chapter are included in a document on the CD. This document lists only partial information, allowing you to complete the table or list.

— **Define Key Terms:** Although the exam is unlikely to ask a question such as "Define this term," the CCDA exams do require that you learn and know a lot of networking terminology. This section lists the most important terms from the chapter, asking you to write a short definition and compare your answer to the glossary at the end of the book.

■ **CD-Based Practice Exam:** The companion CD contains an exam engine that allows you to review practice exam questions. Use these to prepare with a sample exam and to pinpoint the topics where you need more study.

How This Book Is Organized

This book contains 24 core chapters—Chapters 1 through 24. Chapter 25 includes some preparation tips and suggestions for how to approach the exam. Each core chapter covers a subset of the topics on the CCNP Security IPS v7.0 exam. The core chapters are organized into parts. They cover the following topics:

Part I: Introduction to Intrusion Prevention and Detection, Cisco IPS Software, and Supporting Devices

■ **Chapter 1, "Intrusion Prevention and Intrusion Detection Systems":** This chapter covers evaluating and choosing approaches to intrusion prevention and detection.

■ **Chapter 2, "Cisco IPS Software, Hardware, and Supporting Applications":** This chapter covers Cisco IPS solution components available to satisfy policy and environmental requirements.

■ **Chapter 3, "Network IPS Traffic Analysis Methods, Evasion Possibilities, and Anti-evasive Countermeasures":** This chapter covers assessing IPS analysis methods, possibilities for evasion in an environment, and choosing the correct anti-evasion methods in a Cisco IPS solution.

■ **Chapter 4, "Network IPS and IDS Deployment Architecture":** This chapter covers choosing an architecture to implement a Cisco IPS solution according to policy environment requirements.

Part II: Installing and Maintaining Cisco IPS Sensors

■ **Chapter 5, "Integrating the Cisco IPS Sensor into a Network":** This chapter covers the most optimal method of integrating a Cisco IPS Sensor into a target network.

■ **Chapter 6, "Performing the Cisco IPS Sensor Initial Setup":** This chapter covers configuring the basic connectivity and networking functions of a Cisco IPS Sensor and troubleshooting its initial installation.

■ **Chapter 7, "Managing Cisco IPS Devices":** This chapter covers deploying and managing Cisco IPS Sensor management interfaces and functions.

Part III: Applying Cisco IPS Security Policies

■ **Chapter 8, "Configuring Basic Traffic Analysis":** This chapter covers deploying and managing Cisco IPS Sensor basic traffic analysis parameters.

■ **Chapter 9, "Implementing Cisco IPS Signatures and Responses":** This chapter covers deploying and managing the basic aspects of Cisco IPS signatures and responses.

■ **Chapter 10, "Configuring Cisco IPS Signature Engines and the Signature Database":** This chapter evaluates the Cisco IPS signature engines and the built-in signature database.

- **Chapter 11, "Deploying Anomaly-Based Operation":** This chapter covers deploying and managing Cisco IPS anomaly-based detection features.

Part IV: Adapting Traffic Analysis and Response to the Environment

- **Chapter 12, "Customizing Traffic Analysis":** This chapter covers deploying and managing custom traffic analysis rules to satisfy a security policy.

- **Chapter 13, "Managing False Positives and False Negatives":** This chapter covers deploying and managing Cisco IPS Sensor features and approaches that allow the organization to optimally manage false positives and negatives.

- **Chapter 14, "Improving Alarm and Response Quality":** This chapter covers deploying and managing Cisco IPS features that improve the quality of prevention and detection.

Part V: Managing and Analyzing Events

- **Chapter 15, "Installing and Integrating Cisco IPS Manager Express with Cisco IPS Sensors":** This chapter covers installing the Cisco IPS Manager Express (IME) software, integrating it with a Cisco IPS Sensor, and managing related faults.

- **Chapter 16, "Managing and Investigating Events Using Cisco IPS Manager Express":** This chapter covers the Cisco IME features to view, manage, and investigate Cisco IPS events.

- **Chapter 17, "Using Cisco IPS Manager Express Correlation, Reporting, Notification, and Archiving":** This chapter covers using Cisco IME features to correlate and report on Cisco IPS events and create notifications.

- **Chapter 18, "Integrating Cisco IPS with CSM and Cisco Security MARS":** This chapter covers configuring the Cisco IPS to integrate with Cisco Security MARS and choosing Cisco Security MARS features that enhance Cisco IPS event quality.

- **Chapter 19, "Using the Cisco IntelliShield Database and Services":** This chapter covers choosing the features of and using the Cisco IntelliShield services to gather information about event meaning and response guidelines.

Part VI: Deploying Virtualization, High Availability, and High-Performance Solutions

- **Chapter 20, "Using Cisco IPS Virtual Sensors":** This chapter covers deploying and managing Cisco IPS policy virtualization.

- **Chapter 21, "Deploying Cisco IPS for High Availability and High Performance":** This chapter covers deploying and managing features for Cisco IPS redundancy and performance optimization.

Part VII: Configuring and Maintaining Specific Cisco IPS Hardware

- **Chapter 22, "Configuring and Maintaining the Cisco ASA AIP SSM Modules":** This chapter covers performing initial configuration, installation, troubleshooting, and maintenance of the Cisco ASA AIP SSM hardware modules.

- **Chapter 23, "Configuring and Maintaining the Cisco ISR AIM-IPS and NME-IPS Modules":** This chapter covers performing the initial configuration, installation, troubleshooting, and maintenance of the Cisco ISR NME and AIM hardware modules.

- **Chapter 24, "Configuring and Maintaining the Cisco IDSM-2":** This chapter covers performing the initial configuration, installation, troubleshooting, and maintenance of the Cisco IDSM-2 module.

Part VIII: Final Exam Preparation

- **Chapter 25, "Final Preparation":** This chapter identifies tools for final exam preparation and helps you develop an effective study plan.

Part IX: Appendixes

- **Appendix A, "Answers to the "Do I Know This Already?" Quizzes":** This appendix includes the answers to all the questions from Chapters 1 through 24.

- **Appendix B, "CCNP Security IPS 642-627 Exam Updates: Version 1.0":** This appendix provides instructions for finding updates to the exam and this book when and if they occur.

- **Appendix C, "Memory Tables":** This CD-only appendix contains the key tables and lists from each chapter, with some of the contents removed. You can print this appendix and, as a memory exercise, complete the tables and lists. The goal is to help you memorize facts that can be useful on the exams. This appendix is available in PDF format on the CD; it is not in the printed book.

- **Appendix D, "Memory Tables Answer Key":** This CD-only appendix contains the answer key for the memory tables in Appendix C. This appendix is available in PDF format on the CD; it is not in the printed book.

642-627 IPS v7.0 exam topics covered in this part:

- Choose Cisco IPS technologies to implement HLD (High-Level Design)

- Choose Cisco products to implement HLD (High-Level Design)

- Choose Cisco IPS features to implement HLD (High-Level Design)

Part I: Introduction to Intrusion Prevention and Detection, Cisco IPS Software, and Supporting Devices

This chapter covers the following subjects:

- **Intrusion Detection Versus Intrusion Prevention:** Understanding the ability to view and alert versus viewing, alerting, and performing an action.

- **Intrusion Prevention Terminology:** The language and definition of the security control components and countermeasures.

- **Network Intrusion Prevention Approaches:** The options available to security administrators when deploying a network IPS in their environment.

- **Endpoint Security Approaches:** The options to protect various endpoints in a network infrastructure.

- **A Systems Approach to Security:** Security has multiple layers, and each layer has vulnerabilities that need to be protected.

CHAPTER 1

Intrusion Prevention and Intrusion Detection Systems

Networks have evolved rapidly over the last several years, and so have the methods with which we defend those networks. Traditionally, intrusion detection systems (IDS) have been deployed as a security control or countermeasure to monitor, detect, and notify any unauthorized access to, abuse of, or misuse of information systems or network resources. There is another security control method more commonly used today than in the past known as intrusion prevention systems (IPS). This chapter will cover evaluating and choosing approaches to intrusion prevention and detection.

This chapter begins with "Intrusion Detection Versus Intrusion Prevention," which is a review of the core concept of defense-in-depth security. Following the review, the chapter examines intrusion prevention terminology and intrusion prevention approaches, including other security controls and approaches.

"Do I Know This Already?" Quiz

The "Do I Know This Already?" quiz helps you determine your level of knowledge of this chapter's topics before you begin. Table 1-1 lists the major topics discussed in this chapter and their corresponding quiz questions. The answers to the "Do I Know This Already?" quiz appear in Appendix A.

Table 1-1 *"Do I Know This Already?" Foundation Topics Section-to-Question Mapping*

Foundation Topics Section	Questions
Intrusion Prevention Terminology	1, 2
Intrusion Detection Versus Intrusion Prevention Systems	3
Intrusion Prevention Approaches	4, 5
Endpoint Security Controls	6–9
A Systems Approach to Security	10

1. Which security control is a consequence of nonmalicious activity generally representing an error?

    a. True positive

    b. False positive

    c. True negative

    d. False negative

2. Which of the following terms is a weakness that can allow a compromise of the security or the functionality of a system?

    a. Exploit

    b. Vulnerability

    c. Threat

    d. Risk

3. Which of the following capabilities does an IPS have that an IDS does not?

    a. Detect

    b. Alert

    c. Prevent

    d. Monitor

4. Which of the following is not a factor that influences the addition of sensors?

    a. Performance capabilities of the sensor

    b. Exceeded traffic capacity

    c. Network implementation

    d. Performance capabilities of the host

5. Which of the following network intrusion prevention approaches observes network traffic compared to a baseline and acts if a network event outside the normal network behavior is detected?

    a. Anomaly-based network IPS

    b. Signature-based network IPS

    c. Policy-based network IPS

    d. Host-based IPS

6. Which of the following are limitations of endpoint security controls?

    a. Controls are useless if the host is compromised before endpoint security is applied.

    b. All hosts require an agent.

    c. Operating system dependent (might not be supported).

    d. No correlation is possible if a single agent is deployed.

    e. All of the above.

7. Cisco Security Agent uses API interception to control access to all of the following except for which one?

   a. Host itself

   b. Files

   c. Process

   d. Windows Registry

8. Which of the following is designed to prevent file-based malware threats and uses content scanning to identify known patterns of malware?

   a. Heuristics antimalware

   b. File-based antimalware

   c. Code emulation

   d. Pattern matching

9. Which of the following are endpoint security controls?

   a. Cryptographic data protection

   b. Antimalware agents

   c. Host-based firewalls

   d. Native operating system access controls

   e. All of the above

10. Which of the following requires a network-focused technology to provide a defense-in-depth security solution?

   a. Protection of the operating systems

   b. Protection of applications and the data they handle

   c. Detection and prevention of DoS attacks

   d. Controlling access to local host process

Foundation Topics

Intrusion Prevention Overview

All the CCNP Security exams consider CCNA Security materials as prerequisites, so the Cisco Press CCSP Exam Certification Guide series of books also assumes that you are already familiar with CCNA Security topics. However, the CCNP Security exams do test on features that overlap with CCNA Security. Additionally, most people forget some details along the way.

This book uses two methods to help you review CCNA-level Security topics. The first is an examination of concepts included in the CCNA Security certification. The second is a brief review of other CCNA-level Security features along with a deeper discussion of each topic.

To that end, the following sections begin with a review of intrusion prevention terminology. The following section details the key features and limitations of both intrusion detection and intrusion prevention systems. Finally, the last part of this chapter discusses security controls, approaches, and technologies.

Intrusion Detection Versus Intrusion Prevention

An *intrusion detection system (IDS)* is a security control or countermeasure that has the capability to *detect* misuse and abuse of, and unauthorized access to, network resources. An IDS, in most cases, is a dedicated device that monitors network traffic and detects malicious traffic or anomalies based on multiple criteria.

Figure 1-1 shows how an IDS is typically deployed. Notice the placement of the device.

Some of the most commonly detected attacks by a network IDS are as follows:

- Application layer attacks, such as directory traversal attacks, buffer overflows, or various forms of command injection.

- Network sweeps and scans (indicative of network reconnaissance).

- Flooding denial of service (DoS) attacks in the form of TCP SYN packets or large amounts of Internet Control Message Protocol (ICMP) packets. DoS attacks are those in which an attacker uses a large number of compromised systems to disrupt the operation of another system or device on a network. Attacks of this nature can impact the resources of a system and severely degrade performance.

- Common network anomalies on most Open Systems Interconnection (OSI) layers. Some of these common network anomalies detected by a network IDS include the following:
  - Invalid IP datagrams
  - Invalid TCP packets
  - Malformed application layer protocol units
  - Malformed Address Resolution Protocol (ARP) requests or replies

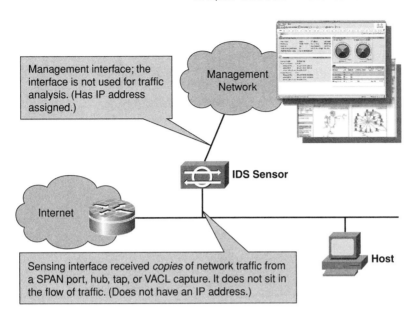

Management interface; the interface is not used for traffic analysis. (Has IP address assigned.)

Management Network

IDS Sensor

Internet

Sensing interface received *copies* of network traffic from a SPAN port, hub, tap, or VACL capture. It does not sit in the flow of traffic. (Does not have an IP address.)

Host

Figure 1-1   *Intrusion Detection System*

After an IDS detects an anomaly or offending traffic, it generates alerts, which are stored locally on the IDS and can be retrieved by a management system. The network security administrators monitor these alerts generated by the IDS and decide how to react. An IDS cannot stop an attack or malicious traffic alone.

A security control or countermeasure that has the capability to *detect* and *prevent* misuse and abuse of, and unauthorized access to, networked resources is an *intrusion prevention system (IPS)*.

Figure 1-2 shows how an IPS is typically deployed. Notice the placement of the device or sensor.

Intrusion Prevention Terminology

Before digging too deeply into intrusion prevention technology, we examine terminology that is important to understand. This section only focuses on terminology as it relates to intrusion prevention; there is a more inclusive list of information security terms in the glossary.

As discussed, an IPS or IDS detects and produces alerts because of a number of factors that include legitimate malicious activity, misconfiguration, environmental changes, and so on. Security controls are classified in one of the following terms:

■ **True positive:** A situation in which a signature fires correctly when intrusive traffic for that signature is detected on the network. The signature correctly identifies an attack against the network. This represents normal and optimal operation.

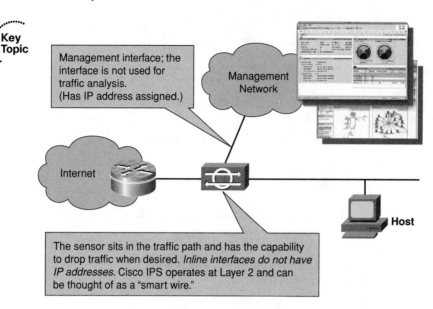

Figure 1-2   *Intrusion Prevention System*

■ **False positive:** A situation in which normal user activity triggers an alarm or response. This is a consequence of nonmalicious activity. This represents an error and generally is caused by excessively tight proactive controls or excessively relaxed reactive controls.

■ **True negative:** A situation in which a signature does not fire during normal user traffic on the network. The security control has not acted and there was no malicious activity. This represents normal and optimal operation.

■ **False negative:** A situation in which a detection system fails to detect intrusive traffic although there is a signature designed to catch the activity. In this situation, there was malicious activity, but the security control did not act. This represents an error and generally is caused by excessively relaxed proactive controls or excessively tight reactive controls.

Most security administrators will agree that addressing false negative and false positive issues is a bit of a balancing act. While tuning a system to be less restrictive to fix false positives, you can increase the likelihood of false negatives and vice versa. Security controls should only be tuned by those expertly trained to do so to optimize these decisions.

Preventive controls, such as IPS sensors, are often tuned to be less sensitive to prevent blocking legitimate traffic, while detective controls, such as IDS sensors, are tuned to be more sensitive, which often results in false positives. Some best practices often combine a sensitive detective control with a relaxed preventive control to gain insight to the preventive control and enable incident response. This is often advantageous if the preventive control is bypassed.

Some other critical terminology that is important to understand when dealing with intrusion prevention are *vulnerability*, *exploit*, *risk*, and *threat*.

A *vulnerability* is a weakness that compromises either the security or the functionality of a system. You'll often hear the following examples listed as vulnerabilities:

- **Insecure communications:** Any form of data or voice susceptible to interception, such as system passwords, personnel records, and confidential documents.

- **Poor passwords:** Often referred to as the first line of defense. Weak or easily guessed passwords are considered vulnerabilities.

- **Improper input handling:** Software that hasn't been through a good security and quality scan (which usually involves evaluating all possible input and results) can lead to a form of DoS or access denied or restricted to system resources.

An *exploit* is the mechanism used to leverage a vulnerability to compromise the security functionality of a system. You'll often hear the following examples listed as exploits:

- **Executable code:** Often referred to as more advanced form of an exploit, these are exploits written as executable code requiring programming knowledge and access to software tools such as a compiler.

- **Password-guessing tools:** There are tools built specifically for this function that can be easily found on the Internet designed to "guess" or "crack" passwords using knowledge of the algorithm used to generate the actual password or by attempting to access a system using combinations and permutations of different character sets.

- **Shell or batch scripts:** Scripts created to automate attacks or perform simple procedures known to expose the vulnerability.

A *threat* is defined as any circumstance or event with the expressed potential for the occurrence of a harmful event to an information system in the form of destruction, disclosure, adverse modification of data, or DoS. Examples of Internet threats that have been prevalent over the past few years include malware that utilizes HTML code or scripts that the cybercriminals place on legitimate websites. These programs generally redirect a user to a malicious user's exploit-infected website without the user noticing. Other examples of threats include network attacks against exposed application servers, malware targeting workstations, or even physical destruction (natural or unnatural).

A *risk* is the likelihood that a particular threat using a specific attack will exploit a particular vulnerability of an asset or system that results in an undesirable consequence. Security engineers, administrators, and management will often try to determine risk in their business continuity and disaster recovery planning. A simple equation often used to equate risk is to multiply threat by vulnerability and multiply the result by the asset value. This equation might sound simple, but the vulnerability and threat of an asset depend on a number of factors to include the presence and quality of the security controls deployed to guard an asset, the capability of the attacker, and the frequency of attacks.

Some other critical terms we'll reference throughout the study guide are as follows:

- **Risk rating (RR):** A rating based on numerous factors besides just the attack severity.

- **Deep-packet inspection:** Decoding protocols and examining entire packets to allow policy enforcement based on actual protocol traffic (not just a specific port number).

- **Event correlation:** Associating multiple alarms or events with a single attack.

- **Inline mode:** Examining network traffic while having the ability to stop intrusive traffic from reaching the target system.

- **Promiscuous mode:** Also known as *passive mode*, a way to passively examine network traffic for intrusive behavior.

- **Signature:** A rule configured in a network IPS or IDS device that describes a pattern of network traffic that matches a specific type of intrusion activity.

- **Signature engine:** An engine that supports signatures that share common characteristics (such as the same protocol, service, operating system, and so on). The Cisco IPS Sensor has multiple signature engines called *microengines*.

- **Atomic signature:** A signature that triggers based on the contents of a single packet.

- **Flow-based signature:** A signature that triggers based on the information contained in a sequence of packets between two systems (such as the packets in a TCP connection).

- **Anomaly-based signature:** A signature that triggers when traffic exceeds a baseline.

- **Behavior-based signature:** A signature that triggers when traffic deviates from regular user behavior.

- **Meta-event generator:** The capability to define metasignatures based on multiple existing signatures that trigger at or near the same window of time within a sliding time interval.

Intrusion Prevention Systems

As defined earlier, an IPS (also referred as a network IPS or NIPS) is a security control put in place to detect by analyzing network traffic and prevents by attempting to block malicious network traffic. There are different aspects in which a network IPS analyzes traffic, such as the following:

- Reassembles Layer 4 sessions and analyzes their contents

- Monitors packet and session rates to detect and/or prevent deviations from the baseline (or normal) network profiles

- Analyzes groups of packets to determine whether they represent reconnaissance attempts

- Decodes application layer protocols and analyzes their contents

- Analyzes packets to address malicious activity contained in a single packet

Network intrusion prevention systems provide proactive components that effectively integrate into the overall network security framework. A network IPS includes the deployment of sensors (also known as monitoring devices) throughout the network to analyze traffic as it traverses the network. An IPS sensor detects malicious and/or unauthorized activity in real time and takes action if/when required. There are various approaches to deploying IPS sensors, which are usually deployed at designated points that enable security managers to monitor network activity while an attack is occurring in real time. The security policy will often drive the designated points in the network where the sensors are to be deployed.

Network growth will often require additional sensors, which can easily be deployed to protect the new networks. A network IPS enables security managers to have real-time insight into their networks regardless of the growth caused by more hosts or new networks. Following are some common factors that often influence the addition of sensors:

- **Network implementation:** Additional sensors might be required to enforce security boundaries based on the security policy or network design.

- **Exceeded traffic capacity:** Additional bandwidth requirements might require an addition or upgrade of network link(s), thus requiring a higher-capacity sensor.

- **Performance capabilities of the sensor:** The current sensor might not be able to perform given the new traffic capacity or requirements.

Typically, network IPS sensors are tuned for intrusion prevention analysis. In most cases, the operating system of an IPS sensor is "stripped" of any unnecessary network services while essential services are secured. To maximize the intrusion prevention analysis for networks of all types, there are three essential elements to the IPS hardware:

- **Memory:** Intrusion prevention analysis is memory intensive. The memory directly affects the ability of a network IPS to detect and prevent an attack accurately.

- **Network interface card (NIC):** The network IPS must have the capability to connect into any network infrastructure. Network IPS NICs today include Fast Ethernet, Gigabit Ethernet, and 10 Gigabit Ethernet.

- **Processor:** CPU power to perform intrusion prevention protocol analysis and pattern matching is required for an effective intrusion prevention system.

Features of Network Intrusion Prevention Systems

A network IPS has four main features:

- A network IPS can detect attacks on several different types of operating systems and applications, depending on the extent of its database.

- A single device can analyze traffic for a large scale of hosts on the network, which makes network IPSs a cost-effective solution that decreases the cost of maintenance and deployment.

- As sensors observe events from and to various hosts and different parts of the network, they can correlate the events, hosts, and networks to higher-level information. In conjunction with the correlation, they can obtain deeper knowledge of malicious activity and act accordingly.

- A network IPS can remain invisible to the attacker through a dedicated interface that monitors only network traffic and is unresponsive to various triggers or stimuli.

Limitations of Network Intrusion Prevention Systems

The most commonly known limitations of network IPS are as follows:

■ The network IPS can require expert tuning to adapt the sensor to its network, host, and application environments.

■ The network IPS sensor is unable to analyze traffic on the application layer when traffic is encrypted either with IPsec or SSL (Secure Socket Layer).

■ The network IPS can be overloaded by network traffic if not properly sized. Thus, the IPS can easily fail to respond to real-time events in a timely manner if it is sized improperly.

■ The network IPS might interpret traffic improperly, which can lead to false negatives. This is often a result of the sensor's seeing traffic differently from how the end system or target sees the traffic.

Network Intrusion Prevention Approaches

There are three commonly used approaches to network intrusion prevention by security managers today. The security policy often helps security managers determine the approach in which they'll deploy in their networks. In some cases, you'll see more than one approach on one particular network. The three commonly used approaches are as follows:

■ **Signature-based:** A network IPS that analyzes network traffic and compares the data in the flow against a database of known attack signatures. A signature-based IPS looks at the packet headers and/or data payloads when analyzing network traffic. All signature-based IPSs require regular updates for their signature databases. Table 1-2 outlines signature-based features and limitations.

Table 1-2 *Signature-Based Features and Limitations*

Category	Feature	Limitation
Complexity	Simple for administrators to add new signatures, customize signatures, extend, and so on. Often the simplest of IPS approaches to deploy (depends on the environment).	Sensors require constant and quick updates of the signature database to ensure that the IPS can detect the most recent attacks. Can require expert tuning to be effective in complex and unsteady environments.
Susceptibility and Accuracy	Relatively low false positive rate (if the IPS is properly tuned and using well-designed signatures).	More susceptible to evasion through complex signatures that are designed to evade a signature-based IPS. Cannot detect unknown attacks of which there is no signature in the database.

Table 1-2 *Signature-Based Features and Limitations*

Category	Feature	Limitation
Reporting	Ability to name attacks and provide the administrator with additional information about a specific attack.	—

- **Anomaly-based:** A network IPS that analyzes or observes network traffic and acts if a network event outside normal network behavior is detected. The two types of anomaly-based network IPSs are *statistical anomaly detection* and *protocol verification*. Table 1-3 outlines anomaly-based features and limitations.

Table 1-3 *Anomaly-Based Features and Limitations*

Features	Limitations
Ability to act on both known and yet-unknown threats.	More susceptible to evasion through complex signatures that are designed to evade an anomaly-based IPS.
	Unable to name individual attacks.
	Statistical approach requires a learning period to establish a normal network profile.
	Statistical approach can cause false positives in unstable environments where it can be difficult or impossible to establish a model of a normal network traffic behavior.

- **Policy-based:** A network IPS that analyzes traffic and acts if it detects a network event outside a traffic policy. A traffic policy usually involves permitted or denied communications over a network segment similar to an enterprise-class firewall. Table 1-4 outlines policy-based features and limitations.

Table 1-4 *Policy-Based Features and Limitations*

Features	Limitations
Very focused on the target environment and triggers very few false positives; thus, very accurate and effective in most cases.	Requires the design of the policy from scratch, which in best practice should be as minimal as possible using as much detail as possible to provide the best protection.
Ability to act on both known and yet-unknown threats.	Unable to name individual attacks.

Endpoint Security Controls

Another form of intrusion prevention is the host IPS (HIPS). Often referred to as endpoint security controls, a HIPS consists of operating system security controls or security agent software installed on hosts that can include desktops PCs, laptops, or servers. Host IPSs in most cases extend the native security controls protecting an operating system or its applications. Endpoint security controls can monitor local operating system processes and protect critical systems resources. HIPSs fundamentally have two essential elements: a software package installed on the endpoint or agent to protect it and a management system to manage the endpoints or agents.

In most cases, operating systems today split the runtime functions of the operating systems into two concurrently running modes known as *Kernel mode* and *User mode*. Kernel mode is the software that has complete access to the operating system hardware; thus, all the software running in Kernel mode can act without restrictions. Generally, the software running in Kernel mode includes the hardware drivers, operating system scheduler, and the application programming interfaces (API). User mode is the software that requires kernel services to execute applications in the form of processes but don't have direct access to the hardware components of the operating system. There is required protection in the system hardware that separates the two modes so that the User mode applications cannot tamper with the Kernel mode software.

Access control enforcement for an operating system can be done using local system resources (native operating system access control) or remote system resources (RADIUS, TACACS, and so on). The local system of user or process privileges and permissions on the discretion of the logical owner/administrator is known as Discretionary Access Control (DAC). Another local system access control that extends the functionality by using the user's role in the organization is known as Role-Based Access Control (RBAC) capability. Access control lists (ACL) are often used to define which systems or networks have access and in which direction. Audit trails (system logs) can aid in the detection of system misuse and attacks to protected objects. The same access control mechanism that decides whether to permit or deny access usually provides this audit trail, showing successful and unsuccessful access attempts. Buffer and heap overflow protection is critical for local applications that contain input-validation vulnerabilities. Protection against buffer and heap overflow attacks is often embedded into hardware and operating systems that provide specialized protection against this specific class of threats. Table 1-5 summarizes the features and limitations of endpoint security.

Table 1-5   *Features and Limitations of Endpoint Security*

Features	Limitations
Identity association, meaning that the endpoint security control can provide the information about the attacker.	Platform flexibility (some operating systems might not support endpoint security controls).
System-specific or customized to protect the system it is protecting and resides on.	Inability to correlate whether a single endpoint or agent is deployed.

Table 1-5 *Features and Limitations of Endpoint Security*

Features	Limitations
Ability to see malicious network data; consequences of network attacks even if encrypted.	Every host requires an agent. Thus, the cost of endpoint security controls can become quite large in some environments and also be quite challenging to manage with only a single or a few administrators to manage the hosts.
Detection of the success of an attack and can take action after the system is stable.	If an attack is successful in accessing the host prior to the endpoint security reacting, the host is compromised.

Host-Based Firewalls

Endpoint security isn't complete without a form of host-based firewall. There are two basic implementations, which include packet filtering and socket filtering (also known as API call filtering):

- **Packet filtering:** Host firewalls use stateful and stateless packet filtering, and typically support dynamic applications such as HTTPS, FTP, and so on. Filtering is based on Open Systems Interconnection (OSI) Layer 3 and 4 information, so it can control connections based on host addresses, protocols, and port numbers. Similar in behavior to a network firewall.

- **Socket filtering (API call filtering):** Controlling application requests to either create an outgoing or accept an incoming connection by filtering network-related API calls. API call filtering is applications aware, so there is no need to require intelligence to support dynamic sessions.

API and System Call Interception

Secondary Security Reference Monitor (SSRM) is an operating system security extension that provides a "second opinion" or layered approach of security by extending and duplicating the functionality of the native operating security model. SSRMs are often third-party extensions for the operating system kernel. They use API interception to insert themselves into the access control path. API interception has a low performance impact while consuming less than 5 percent of additional CPU resources; therefore, most of today's HIPS products implement SSRM functionality. API interception (also called *API hooking*) is when an API call is intercepted and the SSRM registers itself as the replacement handler code for the API call it considers important enough to intercept. This allows the SSRM to enforce its own security policy. The SSRM can act as the host firewall, now controlling all applications' access to the network.

Cisco Security Agent

The Cisco HIPS is Cisco Security Agent (CSA), which complements the Cisco NIPS, protecting the integrity of applications and operating systems. Malicious activity is blocked before damage is done by using behavior-based technology that monitors application behaviors. CSA protects against known and new/unknown attacks. Residing between the kernel and applications, CSA enables maximum application visibility with little impact to the performance and stability of the underlying operating system. A few of the numerous network security benefits CSA offers are as follows:

■ Zero-update protection reduces emergency patching in response to vulnerability announcements, minimizing patch-related downtime and IT expenses.

■ Visibility and control of sensitive data protect against loss from both user actions and targeted malware.

■ Predefined compliance and acceptable use policies allow efficient management, reporting, and auditing of activities.

■ System is protected at all times, even when users are not connected to the corporate network or lack the latest patches. This is often referred to as "always vigilant" security.

As stated in the previous paragraph, host IPSs and network IPSs are complementary. Table 1-6 illustrates this point.

Table 1-6   *Host IPS (HIPS) and Network IPS (NIPS)*

Host IPS	Network IPS
CSA can inspect the behavior of applications (encrypted or nonencrypted).	Requires constant updates for new vulnerabilities.
CSA is a behavior-based HIPS.	Can prevent known attacks.
CSA does not need constant updates.	Can protect complete network.
CSA can protect the host (server, desktop, and so on) efficiently, communicate with IPSs, and stop known and unknown (Day Zero) attacks.	—
CSA cannot "name" the attack or protect unsupported platforms.	—

Antimalware Agents

Antivirus and antispyware are primarily designed to find file-based malware threats and scan the content to identify known patterns of malware. This tends to be a permissive security approach. File and memory content can both contain traces of known malware, and fortunately antimalware scanners can examine both. Some antimalware scanners can perform scanning using the following methods or approaches:

■ Using on-demand scanning when the user initiates a thorough system scan.

■ Using real-time scanning, which in some cases isn't as thorough as offline/on-demand, especially if executable code is populated in memory and the files being scanned are busy writing or reading from the file system.

■ Using scanning in a scheduled manner in which all files are scanned thoroughly on the endpoint.

Viruses, spyware, adware, Trojan horses, worms that use file-based infections, rootkit software, and general attack tools can all be detected using file-based antimalware software, as long as that type of malware is known (through the malware database) and can be located using the file and memory scanning.

Typically, the antimalware scans files and memory for known patterns of virus code. This is compared to a database of known malware signatures. In some instances for accuracy, a lot of antivirus scanners today require content matching through multiple, independent detectors for the same virus. Scanners that analyze content for suspicious coding tricks, runtime attributes, structure, and behavior associated with malicious code use heuristic antimalware. Heuristics are not that reliable for new viruses and often will use various techniques that weight malicious features to determine whether the code should be classified as malicious. A common antimalware scanning technique is known as *code emulation*. In code emulation, the antimalware software executes suspicious code in a simple virtual machine that is isolated or sandboxed from the rest of the system. The antimalware scanner can (or attempts to) determine the behavior and actions that the suspicious code performs. The learned behavior is then stored in a database of executable signatures that can detect known patterns of execution to detect the virus in the future.

Data Loss Prevention Agents

Another form of endpoint security is known as Data Loss Prevention (DLP) extensions. DLP controls mobile data distributed on users' systems to prevent users from accidentally or deliberately transferring sensitive data to uncontrolled systems. Examples of uncontrolled systems would be paper (using printers), open network systems (file sharing), and mobile storage (USB keys, portable hard disks, and so on). There are different forms of implementation when it comes to DLPs, but two common examples would be using content scanning to identify sensitive content (assuming that the content is labeled appropriately with a standardized labeling systems identifying sensitive material) and controlling transfer of data off the system using interception of users' and applications' actions.

Cryptographic Data Protection

One of the most discussed and well-known approaches to endpoint security today is file integrity checking to detect unauthorized changes to sensitive files or the system itself. Integrity-checking software calculates a secure fingerprint (HMAC [Hash Message Authentication Code]) for every important file on the system with a secret key. These fingerprints are created when the file(s) are known to be trusted and not modified from their original states. There are periodic rescans of the files and file fingerprints compared to a database of known good fingerprints, which identify whether they have been tampered with.

Integrity checkers rescan files in a specified interval or time, so they can only provide detection of attacks rather than provide real-time detection. It's important to note that integrity checkers can be compromised with the system, given that they are usually a user-mode application.

Encryption is also an important method to prevent data from being stolen or compromised physically from a system, disk drive, third-party add-on, or file system. The user holds the decryption keys with Windows EFS (Encrypting File System) that are transparently linked to user credentials and provide access to encrypted information. Lost cryptographic keys can lead to sensitive data loss, which is why many security policies require the creation of a backup decryption key. Key generation might be left to the user, which substantially weakens cryptography protection of data if operated poorly. If stolen, an attacker must attempt to decrypt protected information; however, this is very difficult to do if cryptographic implementation and key management are done properly.

A Systems Approach to Security

Multiple layers of protection increase the probability of detection and prevention of malicious activity. As we've discussed, there are multiple approaches to detection and prevention, but it's important to understand that what one security control detects, another type can overlook. Proper correlation results in more accurate or trustworthy data about system behavior or incidents when network and endpoint security controls are used together.

A defense-in-depth security solution attempts to protect assets by providing layers of security. Applying security controls at the network and host levels provides this defense-in-depth concept. Table 1-7 summarizes and compares the defense-in-depth technology approaches. It's important to understand that one isn't preferred over the other, but they both complement each other.

Key Topic

Table 1-7   *Defense-in-Depth: Host-Focused and Network-Focused Technology*

Host-Focused Technology	Network-Focused Technology
Protects the operating system	Detects and prevents DoS attacks
Controls access to local host resources	Detects and prevents network reconnaissance attacks
Protects applications and the data they handle	Detects and prevents attacks against many network-facing applications and operating systems

Exam Preparation Tasks

Review All the Key Topics

Review the most important topics from the chapter, noted with the Key Topic icons in the margin of the page. Table 1-8 lists a reference of these key topics and the page numbers on which each is found.

Table 1-8   *Key Topics for Chapter 1*

Key Topic Element	Description	Page Number
Figure 1-1	Intrusion Detection System	9
Paragraph	Security Controls Classifications	9
Figure 1-2	Intrusion Prevention System	10
Table 1-2	Signature-Based Features and Limitations	14
Table 1-3	Anomaly-Based Features and Limitations	15
Table 1-4	Policy-Based Features and Limitations	15
Table 1-5	Features and Limitations of Endpoint Security	16
Table 1-6	Host IPS and Network IPS	18
Table 1-7	Defense-in-Depth: Host-Focused and Network-Focused Technology	20

Complete the Tables and Lists from Memory

Print a copy of Appendix C, "Memory Tables" (found on the CD), or at least the section for this chapter, and complete the tables and lists from memory. Appendix D, "Memory Tables Answer Key," also on the CD, includes completed tables and lists to check your work.

Define Key Terms

Define the following key terms from this chapter, and check your answers in the glossary:

vulnerability, exploit, risk, threat, signature, anomaly

This chapter covers the following topics:

- **Choosing the Appropriate IPS Hardware:** The platforms, features, and where to place them in the network.

- **Understanding the IPS Sensor Software Architecture:** The packet flow, various engines, behavior, and user interface.

- **Choosing the Appropriate IPS Management Product:** The options available to manage the sensors and the capabilities of each option.

- **Knowing the Benefits of Security Intelligence Operations and IntelliShield Alert Manager:** Updates, correlation, and the ability to stay on top of the latest cyber-security risks globally.

CHAPTER 2

Cisco IPS Software, Hardware, and Supporting Applications

Overview

Cisco has a variety of intrusion prevention system (IPS) sensor platforms that satisfy different implementations or requirements. This chapter covers evaluating and choosing the appropriate platform, model, and management applications that fulfill these requirements.

This chapter begins with a deep dive into the fundamental differences among the various platforms available today, followed by a deep dive into the IPS sensor software architecture. The next section explores network management and discusses choosing the appropriate IPS management product. The chapter concludes with a look at the benefits of the Security Intelligence Operations and IntelliShield Alert Manager in staying in front of the threats being seen around the world.

"Do I Know This Already?" Quiz

The "Do I Know This Already?" quiz allows you to assess whether you should read the entire chapter. If you miss no more than one of these self-assessment questions, you might want to move ahead to the "Exam Preparation Tasks" section. Table 2-1 lists the major headings in this chapter and the "Do I Know This Already?" quiz questions covering the material in those headings so that you can assess your knowledge of these specific areas. The answers to the "Do I Know This Already?" quiz appear in Appendix A.

Table 2-1 *"Do I Know This Already?" Foundation Topics Section-to-Question Mapping*

Foundation Topics Section	Questions
Cisco Intrusion Prevention Hardware	1, 2, 5, 6
Cisco Intrusion Prevention Software	3, 4, 7
Cisco Intrusion Prevention Management Products	8
Cisco Security Intelligence Operations	9
Cisco Security Resources	10

1. Which of the following Cisco IPS sensors has a maximum throughput of 4 Gbps?

   a. IPS 4240

   b. IPS 4255

   c. IPS 4260

   d. IPS 4270

2. Which of the following modules are available for the Cisco ASA 5500 Series?

   a. AIP SSM-10

   b. AIP SSM-20

   c. AIP SSM-40

   d. AIP SSC-5

   e. All of these answers are correct.

3. In the Cisco IPS software architecture, which component of the sensor architecture provides the communications channel between the applications?

   a. IDAPI

   b. CollaborationApp

   c. SensorApp

   d. MainApp

4. Which of the following processors are supported on the Sensor app?

   a. Statistics Processor (SP)

   b. Layer 2 Processor (L2P)

   c. Time Processor (TP)

   d. Database Processor (DBP)

   e. All of these answers are correct.

5. How many Cisco IDSM-2 modules are supported in a single Catalyst 6500 Series switch?

   a. 8

   b. 6

   c. 4

   d. 2

6. What is the maximum throughput supported by an NME-IPS module on a Cisco 3845 Series router?

   a. 10 Mbps

   b. 20 Mbps

   c. 75 Mbps

   d. 100 Mbps

7. Which of the following protocols or methods of transport is supported by the SDEE pull communications model?

    a. IPsec

    b. HTTP

    c. HTTPS (SSL/TLS)

    d. UDP

    e. None of these answers are correct.

8. What is the maximum number of IPS devices the IME can provide support for?

    a. 5

    b. 10

    c. 100

    d. 1000

9. Which of the following are the major components of the Cisco Security Intelligence Operations (SIO)?

    a. Cisco SensorBase

    b. Cisco Threat Operations Center

    c. Cisco Web Portal

    d. Dynamic Updates

    e. None of these answers are correct.

10. Which of the following are online security resources?

    a. Cisco IPS signature search page

    b. Cisco IPS threat defense bulletins

    c. Security Intelligence Operations

    d. Cisco Threat Operations Center

    e. All of these answers are correct.

Foundation Topics

Cisco IPS Network Sensors

The Cisco IPS sensor platforms integrate in a variety of network topologies and architectures. The sensor platforms are divided into the following major groups, as illustrated in Figure 2-1:

■ Standalone IPS appliances in the form of Cisco IPS 4200 Series sensors

■ Cisco AIM-IPS, NME-IPS for Cisco Integrated Services Routers

■ Cisco Catalyst 6500 Series Intrusion Detection System (IDSM-2) Modules

■ Integrated Cisco ASA 5500 Series Advanced Inspection and Prevention Security Services Modules (AIP SSC-5, AIP SSM-10, AIP SSM-20, and AIP SSM-40)

Note: Figure 2-1 provides the Cisco IPS platforms and models that support Cisco IPS Sensor Software Version 7.0 or higher at the time of publication. Refer to www.cisco.com for the most current information.

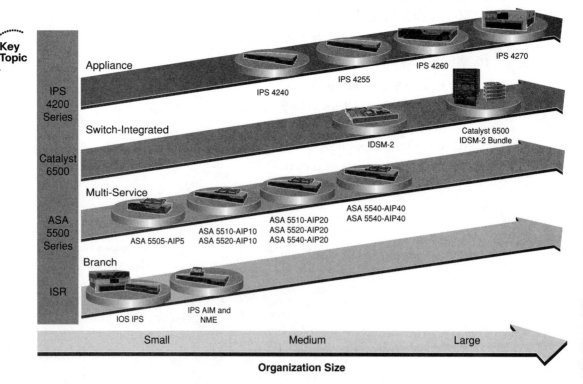

Figure 2-1   *Cisco IPS Sensor Family*

Cisco IPS 4200 Series Sensors

The Cisco IPS 4200 Series sensors are standalone network appliances for intrusion detection and prevention. The Cisco sensors integrate into customer networks in either inline forwarding mode or in promiscuous monitoring mode using Ethernet interfaces. The appliances deliver up to 4 Gbps IPS throughput (with the Cisco IPS 4270 appliance sensor).

Integration into any LAN-based network architecture is simplified with the appliance sensors because they don't require another network platform and can be easily moved around in a network if the need arises.

The Cisco IPS 4240 and 4255 sensors are fixed-configuration sensors that include a fixed number of LAN interfaces. The Cisco 4260 and 4270 sensors include a certain number of LAN interfaces by default, and offer the possibility to accommodate additional network interfaces, including 1000BASE-SX fiber-optic interfaces.

Figure 2-2 shows a matrix comparing the four available sensor appliance models with respect to their performance and interface type.

Features	Cisco IPS 4240 Sensor	Cisco IPS 4255 Sensor	Cisco IPS 4260 Sensor	Cisco IPS 4270 Sensor
Maximum Traffic Throughput	300 Mbps	600 Mbps	2 Gbps	4 Gbps
Sensing Interfaces	Four 10/100/1000-BASE-TX	Four 10/100/1000-BASE-TX	10/100/1000-BASE-TX	Four 10/100/1000-BASE-TX or four 1000BASE-SX or two 10GE-SX
Command and Control Interface	10/100BASE-TX	10/100BASE-TX	10/100/1000-BASE-TX	10/100/1000-BASE-TX
Optional Network Integration Interfaces?	None	None	Yes	Yes
Redundant Power Supply	No	No	Optional	Yes

Figure 2-2   *Cisco IPS 4200 Series Sensor Comparison*

The Cisco IPS 4200 Series sensor inspection maximum performance ranges from 300 Mbps (Cisco IPS 4240) to 4 Gbps (Cisco IPS 4270). The Cisco IPS 4240 and 4255 sensors (see Figure 2-3) feature a fixed monitoring interface configuration with four 10/100/1000BASE-TX interfaces. The Cisco IPS 4260 and 4270 sensors support optional monitoring interfaces that can be installed in addition to the default interface configuration. The 4260 sensor can accommodate an optional redundant power supply, while the

4270 has two factory-built-in power supplies. All Cisco 4200 IPS Series appliances support global correlation, anomaly detection, custom signatures, and four virtual sensors.

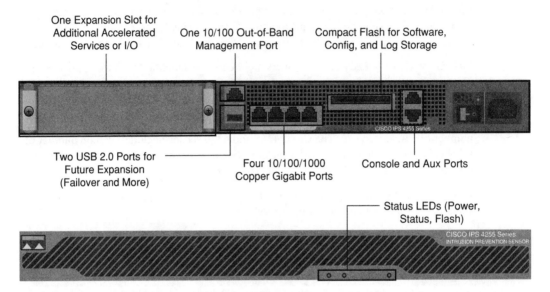

Figure 2-3   *Cisco IPS 4240 and 4255 Sensors*

Note: The virtual sensor concepts are covered in later chapters.

Cisco IPS 4240 Sensor

The Cisco IPS 4240 sensor is a 1-rack-unit (RU)-high, rack-mountable appliance that uses diskless architecture using compact flash storage. The sensor's front panel includes three indicator lights that can assist in hardware troubleshooting tasks. The three indicator lights are described as follows:

■ **Flash indicator light:** Off when the compact flash device is not being accessed. Blinks green when the compact flash device is being accessed.

■ **Power indicator light:** Off indicates no power. Green when the power supply is running.

■ **Status indicator light:** Blinks green while the power-up diagnostics are running or the system is booting. Solid green when the system has passed the power-up diagnostics. Solid amber when the power-up diagnostics have failed.

The back panel of the Cisco IPS 4240 sensor is made up of the following:

■ **One serial console port:** Can be used to configure initially or reconfigure using the command-line interface (CLI), if needed.

■ **Two USB ports:** Currently not used by Cisco IPS Software.

■ **One auxiliary port:** Currently not used by Cisco IPS Software.

- **External compact flash slot:** Currently not used by Cisco IPS Software.

- **One 10/100BASE-TX command and control network interface:** The Cisco IPS Software uses the command and control network interface to provide remote management access to the sensor.

- **Four 10/100/1000BASE-TX sensing interfaces:** The Cisco IPS Software uses sensing interfaces to forward traffic in inline mode or to monitor traffic in promiscuous mode. The interfaces are numbered from right to left. Table 2-2 provides more detail about the interfaces.

Table 2-2 *Cisco IPS 4240 Sensor Interfaces*

Key Topic

Position on Sensor	Label on Sensor	Function	Name
0	0	Sensing	GigabitEthernet 0/0
1	1	Sensing	GigabitEthernet 0/1
2	2	Sensing	GigabitEthernet 0/2
3	3	Sensing	GigabitEthernet 0/3
4	MGMT	Command and control	Management 0/0

The physical dimensions of the Cisco IPS 4240 sensor are as follows:

- **Height:** 1.72 in. (4.3688 cm)

- **Width:** 17.25 in. (43.815 cm)

- **Depth:** 14.5 in. (36.83 cm)

- **Weight:** 20.0 lb. (9.07 kg)

Cisco IPS 4255 Sensor

The Cisco IPS 4255 sensor is a 1-rack-unit (RU)-high, rack-mountable appliance that uses diskless architecture using compact flash storage. The sensor's front panel includes three indicator lights that can assist in hardware troubleshooting tasks. The three indicator lights are described as follows:

- **Flash indicator light:** Off when the compact flash device is not being accessed. Blinks green when the compact flash device is being accessed.

- **Power indicator light:** Off indicates no power. Green when the power supply is running.

- **Status indicator light:** Blinks green while the power-up diagnostics are running or the system is booting. Solid green when the system has passed the power-up diagnostics. Solid amber when the power-up diagnostics have failed.

The back panel of the Cisco IPS 4255 sensor is made up of the following:

- **One serial console port:** Can be used to configure initially or reconfigure using the command-line interface (CLI), if needed.

- **Two USB ports:** Currently not used by Cisco IPS Software.

- **One auxiliary port:** Currently not used by Cisco IPS Software.

- **External compact flash slot:** Currently not used by Cisco IPS Software.

- **One 10/100BASE-TX command and control network interface:** The Cisco IPS Software uses the command and control network interface to provide remote management access to the sensor.

- **Four 10/100/1000BASE-TX sensing interfaces:** The Cisco IPS Software uses sensing interfaces to forward traffic in inline mode or to monitor traffic in promiscuous mode. The interfaces are numbered from right to left. Table 2-3 provides more detail about the interfaces.

Key Topic

Table 2-3   *Cisco IPS 4255 Sensor Interfaces*

Position on Sensor	Label on Sensor	Function	Name
0	0	Sensing	GigabitEthernet 0/0
1	1	Sensing	GigabitEthernet 0/1
2	2	Sensing	GigabitEthernet 0/2
3	3	Sensing	GigabitEthernet 0/3
4	MGMT	Command and control	Management 0/0

The physical dimensions of the Cisco IPS 4255 sensor are as follows:

- **Height:** 1.72 in. (4.3688 cm)

- **Width:** 17.25 in. (43.815 cm)

- **Depth:** 14.5 in. (36.83 cm)

- **Weight:** 20.0 lb. (9.07 kg)

Cisco IPS 4260 Sensor

The Cisco IPS 4260 sensor, shown in Figure 2-4, is a 2-rack-unit (RU)-high, rack-mountable appliance that uses diskless architecture using compact flash storage. The sensor's front panel includes three indicator lights that can assist in hardware troubleshooting tasks.

The three indicator lights are described as follows:

- **Flash indicator light:** Off when the compact flash device is not being accessed. Blinks green when the compact flash device is being accessed.

- **Power indicator light:** Off indicates no power. Green when the power supply is running.

- **Status indicator light:** Blinks green while the power-up diagnostics are running or the system is booting. Solid green when the system has passed the power-up diagnostics. Solid amber when the power-up diagnostics have failed.

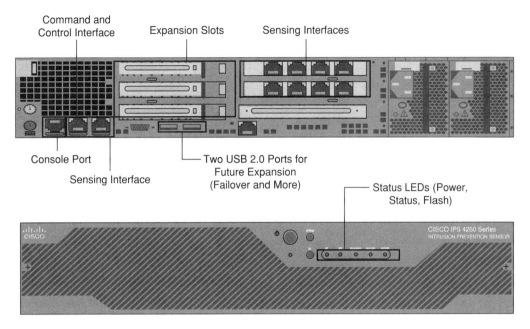

Figure 2-4 *Cisco IPS 4260 Sensor*

The back panel of the Cisco IPS 4260 sensor is made up of the following:

- **One serial console port:** Can be used to configure initially or reconfigure using the command-line interface (CLI), if needed.

- **Two USB ports:** Currently not used by Cisco IPS Software.

- **One auxiliary port:** Currently not used by Cisco IPS Software.

- **Two expansion slots:** These slots each can hold either four 10/100/1000BASE-TX sensing or two 1000BASE-SX fiber sensing interfaces, allowing a total of nine sensing interfaces. The 4GE bypass interface card also supports the hardware-bypass feature.

- **One 10/100BASE-TX command and control network interface (Mgmt0/0):** The Cisco IPS Software uses the command and control network interface to provide remote management access to the sensor.

- **One onboard 10/100/1000BASE-TX sensing interface:** The Cisco IPS Software uses sensing interfaces to forward traffic in inline mode or to monitor traffic in promiscuous mode. The interfaces are numbered from right to left.

- **Single- or dual-power connections to the power supplies:** You can install an optional redundant power supply.

The physical dimensions of the Cisco IPS 4260 sensor are as follows:

- **Height:** 3.45 in. (8.76 cm)

- **Width:** 17.14 in. (43.53 cm)

- **Depth:** 20.0 in. (50.8 cm)

- **Weight:** 40.0 lb. (18.1 kg) (when loaded)

Cisco IPS 4270 Sensor

As shown in Figure 2-5, the Cisco IPS 4270 (Model 4270-20) sensor is a 4-rack-unit (RU)-high, rack-mountable appliance that uses diskless architecture using compact flash storage. The sensor's front panel includes four indicator lights that can assist in hardware troubleshooting tasks.

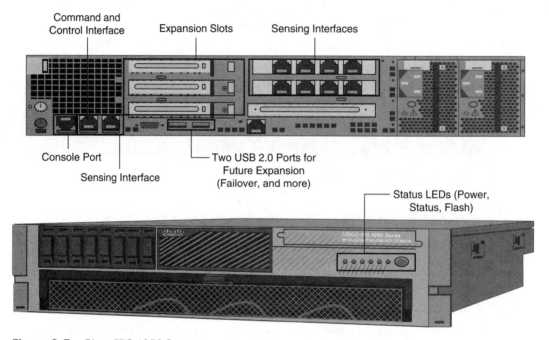

Figure 2-5   *Cisco IPS 4270 Sensor*

The four indicator lights are described as follows:

- **Management interface indicator light:** Indicates the status of the management port. Green indicates linked to the network, flashing green indicates linked with activity on the network, and off indicates no network connection.

- **Power status light:** Off indicates no power. Flashing amber indicates that power supply health is degraded, flashing red indicates that power supply health is critical, and green indicates that the power supply is running/on.

- **System indicator light:** Indicates overall system health. Green indicates that the system is on, flashing amber indicates that system health is degraded, flashing red indicates that system health is critical, and off indicates that the system is off.

- **UID indicator light:** Toggles the system ID indicator, which assists with chassis location in a rack. Blue signals activated, and off signals deactivated. The ID switch is activated by a switch on the front of the chassis.

The back panel of the Cisco IPS 4270 sensor is made up of the following:

- **One serial console port:** Can be used to configure initially or reconfigure using the command-line interface (CLI), if needed.

- **Two USB ports:** Currently not used by Cisco IPS Software.

- **One auxiliary port:** Currently not used by Cisco IPS Software.

- **Six expansion slots:** These slots each can hold either 10/100/1000BASE-TX sensing interfaces, 1000BASE-SX fiber sensing interfaces, or 10GE fiber interfaces, allowing up to a total of 16 sensing interfaces (depending on the interface type).

- **One 10/100BASE-TX command and control network interface (Mgmt0/0):** The Cisco IPS Software uses the command and control network interface to provide remote management access to the sensor.

- **Four 10/100/1000BASE-TX or four 1000BASE-SX sensing interfaces:** The Cisco IPS Software uses sensing interfaces to forward traffic in inline mode or to monitor traffic in promiscuous mode. The interfaces are numbered from right to left.

- Redundant connections to the power supplies

The physical dimensions of the Cisco IPS 4270 sensor are as follows:

- **Height:** 6.94 in. (17.6 cm)

- **Width:** 19 in. (48.3 cm)

- **Depth:** 26.5 in. (67.3 cm)

- **Weight:** 80.0 lb. (36.3 kg)

Sensing Interface Details

The Cisco IPS 4260 and 4270 sensors support three interface cards: the 4GE bypass interface card, the 2SX interface card, and the 10GE interface card.

10GE Interface Card

The 10GE interface card provides two 10000BASE-SX (fiber) interfaces. The part numbers are IPS-2X10GE-SR-INT and IPS-2X10GE-SR-INT=. The Cisco IPS 4260 supports one 10GE interface card, for a total of two 10GE fiber interfaces. The Cisco IPS 4270-20 supports two 10GE interface cards, for a total of four 10GE fiber interfaces. The card ports require a multimode fiber cable with an LC connector to connect to the SX interface of the IPS sensor. The 10GE interface card does not support hardware bypass.

4GE Bypass Interface Card

The 4GE bypass interface card provides four 10/100/1000BASE-T (4GE) monitoring interfaces. The part numbers are IPS-4GE-BP-INT and IPS-4GE-BP-INT=. The Cisco IPS 4260 sensor supports up to two 4GE interface cards, and the IPS 4270-20 sensor supports up to four 4GE interface cards, for a total of eight and 16 GE bypass interfaces, respectively. The 4GE bypass interface card supports hardware bypass.

2SX Interface Card

The 2SX interface card provides two 1000BASE-SX (fiber) interfaces. The part numbers are IPS-2SX-INT and IPS-2SX-INT=. The Cisco IPS 4260 sensor supports two 2SX interface cards, for a total of four SX interfaces. The Cisco IPS 4270-20 supports up to six 2SX interface cards, for a total of 12 SX interfaces. The 2SX card ports require a multimode fiber cable with an LC connector to connect to the SX interface of the sensor. The 2SX interface card does not support hardware bypass.

Cisco ASA AIP SSM and AIP SSC-5 Modules

The Cisco ASA Advanced Inspection & Prevention Security Services Modules (AIP SSM and AIP SSC) provide the intrusion detection and prevention security feature set for the Cisco ASA 5500 Series Adaptive Security Appliance.

AIP SSM modules run the same Cisco IPS Sensor Software Version 7.0 or higher software image as the sensor appliances, so they provide the same security features as the sensor appliance. The Cisco ASA AIP SSM is available in three models:

- AIP SSM-10

- AIP SSM-20

- AIP SSM-40

There is currently only one AIP SSC model, the AIP SSC-5.

The AIP SSC-5 (Security Services Card) modules are compatible with only the Cisco ASA 5505 devices. Typically these are targeted at small- and medium-sized businesses and branch deployments. Though the software for the AIP SSC-5 module is based on the same software as the AIP SSM modules, because of disk and memory limitations, not all the features are available in the AIP SSC-5.

Both inline monitoring and promiscuous mode on a single physical back plane interface inside the ASA are supported on the AIP SSM and AIP SSC-5 modules. The configuration of the security appliance must be used to designate which packets/connections should be monitored by the module as either promiscuous or inline. Table 2-4 compares the available AIP modules in further detail.

Key Topic

Table 2-4   *Cisco ASA 5500 AIP Module Comparison*

	Cisco ASA AIP SSC-5	Cisco ASA AIP SSM-10	Cisco ASA AIP SSM-10	Cisco ASA AIP SSM-20
Supported Platforms	ASA 5505	ASA 5510 ASA 5520	ASA 5520 ASA 5540	ASA 5520 ASA 5540
Maximum Traffic Throughput	75 Mbps (ASA 5505)	225 Mbps (ASA 5520)	500 Mbps (ASA 5540)	650 Mbps (ASA 5540)
Monitoring Interfaces	ASA backplane interface	ASA backplane interface	ASA backplane interface	ASA backplane interface

Table 2-4 *Cisco ASA 5500 AIP Module Comparison*

	Cisco ASA AIP SSC-5	Cisco ASA AIP SSM-10	Cisco ASA AIP SSM-10	Cisco ASA AIP SSM-20
Command and Control Interface	Backplane VLAN	10/100BASE-TX	10/100BASE-TX	10/100/1000BASE-TX
Global Correlation	No	Yes	Yes	Yes
Anomaly Detection	No	Yes	Yes	Yes
Customer Signature Support	No	Yes	Yes	Yes
Virtual Sensors	1	4	4	4

The AIP SSC-5 uses an ASA backplane VLAN as the command and control interface because the module doesn't have an external interface. The Cisco AIP SSC-5 can be initialized with a GUI using the Ethernet management port on the host Adaptive Security Appliance. Global correlation, anomaly detection, customer signatures, and multiple virtual sensors aren't supported because of memory and disk limitations in the ASA 5505.

The AIP SSC-5 provides up to 75 Mbps of IPS throughput and is typically recommended to be used in small- and medium-sized businesses (SMB) and branch deployments.

The AIP SSM-10, SSM-20, and SSM-40 modules are supported on the ASA 5510, ASA 5520, and ASA 5540. These modules all support global correlation, anomaly detection, customer signatures, and four virtual sensors. As stated previously, the AIP SSM modules provide complete IPS capabilities, including day-zero attack protection. All models have one external 10/100 or 10/100/1000 Ethernet interface for management and software downloads.

Cisco Catalyst 6500 Series IDSM-2 Module

The Cisco Catalyst 6500 Series IDSM-2, shown in Figure 2-6, provides full-featured intrusion prevention in a core network fabric device. The Cisco Catalyst 6500 Series IDSM-2 is designed specifically to address switched environments by integrating the IPS functionality directly into the switch. The IDSM-2 runs the same software image as the sensor appliances and can be configured to perform intrusion prevention. VLANs are used instead of interfaces because there are no external interfaces on the IDSM-2. The Catalyst 6500 switch supports up to eight IDSM-2 modules installed per chassis.

The Cisco IDSM-2 module can provide up to 600 Mbps of inspection performance. As mentioned previously, the Catalyst 6500 supports up to eight modules, which enables 4-Gbps total inspection throughput. Monitoring and command interfaces are achieved through VLAN because there is no external interface supported on the IDSM-2 module. Global correlation, anomaly detection, customer signatures, and up to four virtual sensors are supported by the IDSM-2 module.

- IDSM-2 has no physical interfaces (no console or LAN ports)
- Up to eight IDSM-2 per chassis scalable with etherchannel load balancing
- Catalyst 6500 backplane used for
    1. Initial console access (boot-strap)
    2. Management access via SSH, SDEE
    3. Data traffic IPS mode
    4. Data traffic IDS mode

Physical View

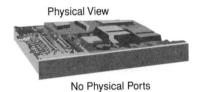

No Physical Ports

Logical View

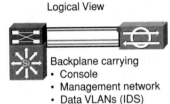

Backplane carrying
- Console
- Management network
- Data VLANs (IDS)
- Data VLANs (IPS)

Figure 2-6 *Cisco Catalyst 6500 IDSM-2 Module*

Cisco AIM-IPS and NME-IPS Supported on Cisco ISR Routers

The Cisco IPS Advanced Integration Module (AIM) sensor is designed for small- and medium-sized businesses and small branch office deployments. The Cisco IPS Network Module Enhanced (NME) is designed for small enterprises and large branch office deployments. Both modules are supported/compatible with Cisco ISR generations 1 and 2 routers, and they run the same software image as sensor appliances along with full-featured intrusion protection.

Both inline and promiscuous inspection modes are supported by the AIM-IPS and NME-IPS (as shown in Figure 2-7). The modules monitor traffic from any Cisco IOS Software router interface and also support generic routing encapsulation (GRE) and IPsec traffic inspection that has been decrypted at the router. Virtualization is not supported by either module.

The Cisco AIM-IPS module can be installed on the following Cisco ISR routers, providing up to 45 Mbps of intrusion protection services within the router:

- Cisco 1841 Series router

- Cisco 2801 Series router

- Cisco 2811 Series router

- Cisco 2821 Series router

- Cisco 2851 Series router

- Cisco 3825 Series router

- Cisco 3845 Series router

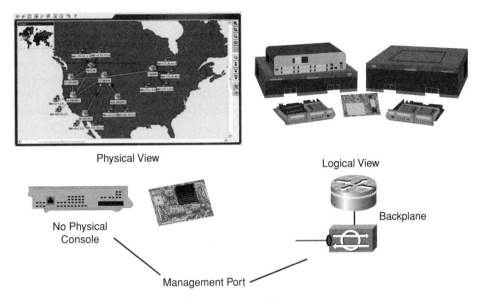

Physical View

Logical View

No Physical
Console

Backplane

Management Port

Figure 2-7   *Cisco AIM-IPS and NME-IPS Modules*

The Cisco NME-IPS module provides up to 75 Mbps of intrusion protection services within the following routers:

■ Cisco 2811 Series router

■ Cisco 2821 Series router

■ Cisco 2851 Series router

■ Cisco 3825 Series router

■ Cisco 3845 Series router

The Cisco NME-IPS module requires an adapter card for installation with the following routers:

■ Cisco 2911 router

■ Cisco 2921 router

■ Cisco 2951 router

■ Cisco 3925 router

■ Cisco 3945 router

The Cisco AIM-IPS and NME-IPS use router backplane interface to monitor traffic. The AIM-IPS module has no external interface, whereas the NME-IPS has one external Gigabit Ethernet port that is used as a command and control interface for out-of-band management. Both the Cisco AIM-IPS and NME-IPS modules support global correlation, anomaly detection, and custom signatures. Only one virtual sensor is supported by both the AIM-IPS and NME-IPS modules.

Cisco IPS Software Architecture

The Cisco IPS Sensor Software runs on all sensor platforms, providing traffic analysis, intrusion response, and device management functions in the Cisco IPS solution. As discussed in Chapter 1, "Intrusion Prevention and Intrusion Detection Systems," there are three different approaches to traffic analysis. Of the three, the Cisco IPS Software primarily uses the signature approach to traffic analysis and includes a rich signature database that is regularly and automatically updated (if configured) to detect and prevent current network-borne attacks. The analysis engine supports simple and flexible creation of customer signatures using signature engines, and includes powerful anti-evasion mechanisms to minimize false negatives.

Cisco IPS Software also supports policy-based and anomaly-based analysis methods. Protocol verification features examine network traffic for protocol compliance. An administrator can manually configure traffic rate thresholds to provide a simple rate-monitoring mechanism that can detect flooding attacks, although built-in signatures already address many flooding attacks. Cisco IPS Software can configure platform interfaces to support both inline and promiscuous mode integration into a network. The IPS sensor architecture can be seen in Figure 2-8.

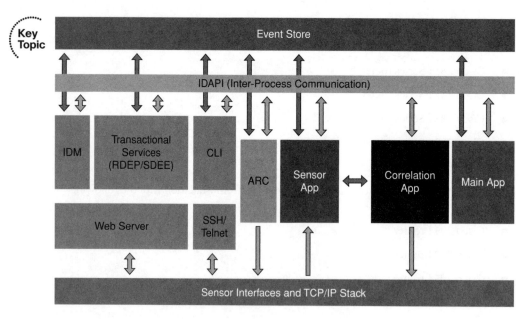

Figure 2-8 *Cisco IPS Software Architecture Overview*

The Cisco IPS Sensor Software Version 7.0 runs on a hardened version of Linux operating systems. The primary components of the sensor architecture are as follows:

■ **Intrusion Detection Application Programming Interface (IDAPI):** Provides the communication channel between applications.

- **CLI:** The CLI provides the sensor user interface for all direct node access, such as Telnet, SSH, and serial interface. It accepts command-line input and modifies the local configuration using IDAPI.

- **Event Store:** Provides storage for all events.

- **SensorApp:** SensorApp performs network traffic analysis. Signature engines are located inside the SensorApp, and the information about the violations is forwarded to the Event Store in the form of an alert. Packets flow through a pipeline of processors fed by a producer designed to collect packets from the network interfaces on the sensor. SensorApp supports the follow processors:

    - Statistics Processor (SP)

    - Database Processor (DBP)

    - Layer 2 Processor (L2P)

    - Time Processor (TP)

    - Signature Event Action Processor (SEAP)

    - Deny Filters Processor (DFP)

    - Slave Dispatch Processor (SDP)

    - Fragment Reassembly Processor (FRP)

    - Signature Analysis Processor (SAP)

    - Stream Reassembly Processor (SRP)

SensorApp also supports the following units:

    - Analysis Engine
    - Alarm Channel

- **MainApp:** Initializes the system, starts and stops the other applications, configures the operating system, and performs upgrades. It contains the following components:

    - **Event Store:** This is an indexed store used to store IPS events (error, status, and alert system messages) that is accessible through the CLI, Cisco IPS Device Manager (IDM), Cisco Adaptive Security Device Manager (ASDM), or Security Device Event Exchange (SDEE).

    - **ctlTransSource (Control Transaction Server):** This component allows sensors to send control transactions. This is used to enable the master blocking sensor capability of the Attack Response Controller (also known as the ARC and formerly known as the Network Access Controller [NAC]).

    - **LogApp:** This component writes all the application log messages to the log file and the application error messages to the Event Store.

    - **InterfaceApp:** This component handles bypass and physical settings and defines paired interfaces. Physical settings are speed, duplex, and administrative state.

    - **ARC:** The ARC was formerly known as the NAC (see the earlier bullet). The ARC manages remote network devices (firewalls, routers, and switches) to provide blocking capabilities when an alert event has occurred. The ARC creates and applies access control lists (ACL) on the controlled network device or uses the **shun** command (firewalls).

- **AuthenticationApp:** AuthenticationApp authorizes and authenticates users based on IP address, password, and digital certificates. It verifies that users are authorized to perform CLI, Cisco IDM, Cisco ASDM, or SDEE actions.

- **NotificationApp:** This component sends Simple Network Management Protocol (SNMP) traps when triggered by alert, status, and error events. NotificationApp uses the public domain SNMP agent. SNMP GETs provide information about the general health of the sensor.

- **Web Server (HTTP SDEE server):** Provides a web interface and communication with other IPS devices through the SDEE protocol using several servlets to provide IPS services. The IPS web server is accessible with IPS Device Manager and IPS Manager Express.

■ **Sensor Interfaces:** Sensor interfaces serve as the traffic inspection points. Sensor interfaces are also used for TCP resets and IP logging.

■ **CollaborationApp:** CollaborationApp shares information with other devices through a global correlation database to improve the combined efficacy of all the devices. It interfaces with the MainApp and SensorApp using various interprocess communication technologies including IDAPI control transactions, semaphores, shared memory, and file exchange. CollaborationApp exchanges information with Collaboration Manifest Server, Network Participation Server, and Collaboration Update Servers.

Traffic is inspected through the Cisco IPS sensor in the following steps and is also shown in Figure 2-9.

1. The Cisco IPS sensor first applies preprocessing for traffic entering the sensor. The appropriate virtual sensor is selected based on which interface or VLAN the traffic entered the sensor.

2. IPS reputation filters block access to IP addresses on stolen "zombie" networks or networks controlled entirely by malicious organizations. Traffic from known bad IP addresses is dropped.

3. The traffic is inspected for known vulnerabilities and exploits according to predefined signatures.

4. Anomaly detection examines the traffic for behavioral and protocol anomalies (if enabled on the IPS sensor).

5. Global correlation inspection raises the risk rating of events when the attacker has a negative reputation, allowing those events to be blocked more confidently and more often than an event without negative reputation.

6. The sensor applies the appropriate actions to the traffic flow in the last step in traffic analysis and processing. Results from a few signatures or several signatures correlated together produce sensor actions.

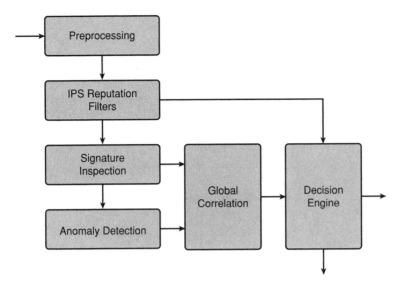

Figure 2-9 *IPS Sensor Packet Flow*

The Cisco IPS sensor produces various types of events including intrusion alerts and status events. Cisco IPS communicates these events to clients such as management applications using the Security Device Event Exchange (SDEE). The Cisco SDEE is a standardized IPS communication protocol developed by Cisco for the IDS Consortium at the International Computer Security Association (ISCA). The Cisco IPS Sensor Software Version 7.0 uses SDEE to deliver a standardized application programming interface (API) to the IPS sensor, which facilitates the integration of third-party management and monitoring solutions with the Cisco IPS solution. Users have a choice of third-party solutions to monitor events generated by Cisco IPS sensors.

The Cisco Intrusion Detection Event Exchange (CIDEE) specifies Cisco IPS extensions to SDEE. The CIDEE standard specifies all possible extensions that are supported by Cisco IPS. The extensions add information to the event format, so some items in an alert are specified by SDEE and some are CIDEE extensions. Event messages are sent to the SDEE upon request through the pull communications model. The management console pulls alerts at its own pace over HTTPS connections protected by SSL/TLS layers, as shown in Figure 2-10. Alerts remain on the sensor until the capacity of the Event Store is met in the Cisco IPS Sensor Software Version 7.0. Alarms are overwritten when the limit is met, and the oldest alarms are overwritten first.

Cisco IPS Management Products

There are a variety of management products offered by Cisco that integrate with Cisco IPS sensors based on the size of the IPS deployment, the required management processes, and the need for automation.

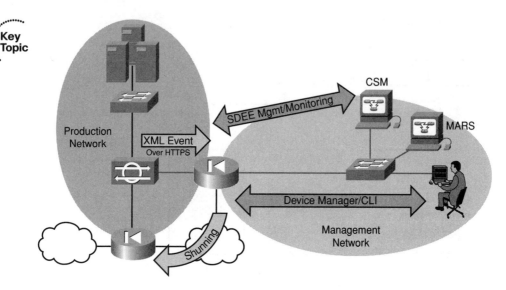

Figure 2-10 *Cisco IPS Sensor Management*

Cisco IPS Device Manager

The Cisco IPS Device Manager (IDM) is a web-based Java application that enables you to configure and manage your sensor using a GUI. IDM provides management for a single IPS device. The web server for the Cisco IDM application resides on the Cisco IPS sensor itself.

Following is a list of actions permitted remotely on the Cisco IDM over a secure (HTTPS) connection:

- Restart sensor

- Power down the sensor

- Configure the sensor

- Monitor sensor health and basic events

Cisco IPS Manager Express

The Cisco IPS Manager Express (IME), shown in Figure 2-11, is a Windows-based application that allows you to configure, manage, and monitor the sensor. Following is a more specific list of functions that the IME provides:

- Management for up to ten IPS devices. IME is an ideal solution for smaller and simpler deployments.

- Management of all the sensor models available today to include IPS 4200 Series appliances, AIP SSC and AIP SSM, IDSM-2, and AIM-IPS and NME-IPS modules.

- Integration with IDM, providing the same interface to configure sensor features.

- Includes a database into which it can pull IPS events from sensors using the SDEE protocol over an HTTPS connection.

- Monitoring of real-time and historical events through the Cisco IPS Manager Express Event Viewer, which is an integral part of IME.

- Customizable dashboards and gadgets. Live RSS feeds keep the administrator informed about the most recent security threats.

Figure 2-11   *Cisco IPS Manager Express (IME)*

Cisco Security Manager

The Cisco Security Manager (CSM) is an integral part of the Cisco Security Management Suite. CSM, also shown in Figure 2-12, delivers comprehensive policy administration and enforcement for the Cisco Self-Defending Network, and supports policy provisioning to Cisco firewalls/appliances, VPN devices, and IPS sensors.

CSM excels at efficiently managing networks of all sizes using powerful policy-based management techniques. Multiple views are provided by CSM into the application to accommodate different tasks and user experience levels. The Cisco Security Management Suite is effective at managing networks that scale from less than ten devices up to thousands of devices.

Cisco Security MARS

Cisco Security Monitoring, Analysis, and Response System (MARS) recognizes and correlates real network attacks and then defines how to stop or mitigate them. This simplifies audit compliance and reduces false positives by allowing the administrator to free network resources.

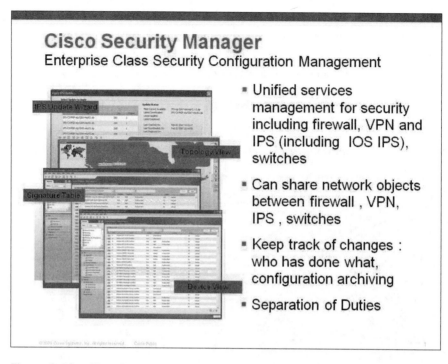

Figure 2-12 *Cisco Security Manager*

Cisco Security MARS aggregates and reduces large amounts of network and security data from popular network devices and security countermeasures. Using network intelligence, Cisco Security MARS effectively identifies network and application threats through sophisticated event correlation and threat validation. Attacks that are verified can be seen through a drill-down topology map to augment incident identification, investigation, and workflow. When and if an attack is discovered, Cisco Security MARS allows the operator to prevent, contain, and stop an attack in real time by pushing specific mitigation commands to network devices that can enforce the action requested. The system supports custom rule creation, incident investigation, threat notification, and various security posture and trend reports.

Some common benefits of Cisco Security MARS are as follows:

■ Provides quick and easy access to audit compliance reports

■ Reduces false positives

■ Provides precision with regard to recommendations for threat removal and mitigation, and the ability for operators and administrators to visualize the attack path and source of the threat

■ Defines the most effective mitigation responses

■ Not only provides security monitoring for Cisco devices but also devices from other vendors

Cisco Security Intelligence Operations and Cisco Security IntelliShield Alert Manager Service

Cisco Security Intelligence Operations (SIO) is an advanced security infrastructure that provides threat identification, analysis, and mitigation to continuously provide the highest level of security for Cisco customers. Cisco SIO does this by using a combination of threat telemetry, a team of global research engineers, and sophisticated security modeling/trending. Figure 2-13 shows a high-level global view of Cisco SIO.

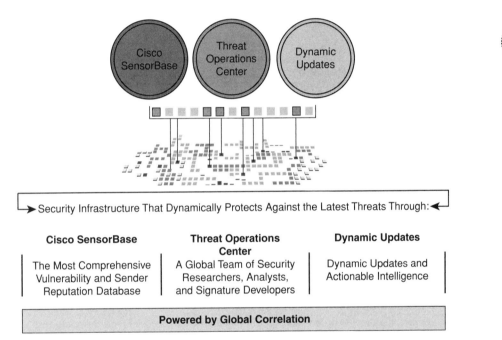

Figure 2-13 *Cisco Security Intelligence Operations*

The three major components of Cisco SIO are as follows:

- **Cisco SensorBase:** The world's largest threat-monitoring network that captures global threat telemetry data from a growing footprint of Cisco devices and services in real time. The SensorBase sources include

  - **Cisco IntelliShield:** A historical threat database including vulnerabilities and IPS signatures

  - **Globally deployed Cisco security devices collecting threat information**

  - **Third-party threat intelligence sources:** More than 500 third-party data feeds and 100 security news feeds around the clock

- **Cisco Threat Operations Center:** A global team of security analysts, engineers, and researchers and automated systems. The team of people and automated algorithms process Cisco SensorBase in real time, create machine-generated and manually generated rules, and provide actionable intelligence for protection against threats. The team of Threat Operations Center consists of several security teams spanning five global locations to include

- **Cisco Products Security Incident Response Team (PSIRT):** Evaluates and works across Cisco to mitigate vulnerabilities reported in Cisco products

- **Cisco IronPort Email and Web Threat Research Teams:** Provide the latest protection for SMTP and web-based attacks

- **Applied Intelligence:** Researches, documents, and tests potential mitigations for Cisco security advisories and responses, Microsoft security bulletins, and other vendor security advisories to help Cisco customers improve network security, protect infrastructure investments, and ensure business continuity

- **Cisco Malware Research Lab:** A centralized malware lab focused on researching the latest malicious activity

- **Strategic Assessment Technology Team (STAT):** Advanced, area-specific security research and product vulnerability testing

- **Intrusion Protection Signature Team:** Researches and develops vulnerability and exploit-specific signatures that are used by IPS product lines

- **IntelliShield Security Analysts:** Collect, research, and provide information about security events that have the potential for widespread impact on customer networks, applications, and devices

- **Infrastructure Security Research & Development (ISRD):** A research-oriented, business enablement function that maintains strong expertise in the area of security and creates security solutions for customers engaged in emerging industries and infrastructures

- **Remote Management Services (RMS):** Provides 24×7×365 remote monitoring and management of Cisco security devices that are deployed on operator networks

- **Dynamic updates:** Real-time updates automatically delivered to security devices, along with best-practice recommendations and other content dedicated to helping customers track threats, analyze intelligence, and ultimately improve their organization's overall security posture. Threat mitigation data is provided through

  - Security best-practice recommendations

  - Automatic rule updates for Cisco products, such as IPSs, firewalls, and web or email devices

  - IntelliShield vulnerability data and alert services

Cisco Security Intelligence Operations offers a web portal that provides access to a multitude of security-related information, such as early warnings, threat and vulnerability analysis, mitigation solutions, best-practice guides, and links to other useful resources. The IntelliShield security alerts also display information about the latest vulnerabilities on the web portal.

Note: To access this page, go to www.cisco.com/security.

The online security resources that are accessible through the Cisco SIO portal also include a Cisco intrusion prevention signatures search page and Cisco IPS threat defense bulletins.

The IPS search page allows operators and administrators to search through security alerts and IPS signatures based on selected search criteria.

The IPS threat defense bulletin supplies a rich source of information on threats, vulnerabilities, and protection provided by Cisco IPS solutions. New vulnerability and exploit protection details (such as signature severity, links to signature descriptions, protection dates, default actions, and so on) are included in the bulletins.

The Cisco Security Intelligence Operations information is published in many forms for the benefit of end customers, enterprises, governments, and the general public. Some examples of the other forms of Cisco Security Intelligence Operations information are as follows:

- Cyber risk reports

- Cisco annual security reports

- Cisco PSIRT security advisories and security responses

- Cisco IntelliShield alerts, including malicious code alerts, security activity bulletins, security issue alerts, threat outbreak alerts, and geopolitical security reports

- Service provider security best practices

- Security Intelligence best practices

- Cisco IPS active update bulletins

- Applied mitigation bulletins

- Cisco IronPort virus outbreak reports

- IntelliShield event responses

Cisco Security IntelliShield Alert Manager Service

The Cisco Security IntelliShield Alert Manager Service is a threat- and vulnerability-alerting service that allows organizations to easily access timely, accurate information about potential vulnerabilities in their environment. Organizations can customize their portal by defining the unique networks, systems, and applications that make up their infrastructure. The service then provides alerts that are filtered to deliver only relevant information, which enables security personnel to take quick action to protect their infrastructure.

The IntelliShield Alert Manager historical database is a fully indexed and searchable database that extends back over six years and contains more than 1700 vendors, 550 products, and 18,500 distinct versions of applications. This database is one of the most extensive collections of past threat and vulnerability data in the industry. Organizations can try out this service for 90 days for free by going to the IntelliShield Alert Manager web portal to register.

Summary

This section highlights the key topics discussed in this chapter:

- Cisco offers a variety of IPS network sensor appliances and modules.

- Cisco IPS modules are supported with the Cisco Adaptive Security Appliance, Cisco Catalyst 6500 Series switches, and Cisco ISRs.

- Security operators and administrators can manage Cisco IPS sensors using several Cisco management products.

- Cisco Security Intelligence Operations and IntelliShield Alert Manager Services provide an advanced security infrastructure.

References

For additional information, refer to these resources:

Cisco Security Operations Web Portal, at www.cisco.com/security.

Cisco IPS 4200 Series Sensors, at www.cisco.com/en/US/products/hw/vpndevc/ps4077/index.html.

Cisco Catalyst 6500 Series Intrusion Detection System (IDSM-2) Module, at www.cisco.com/en/US/products/hw/modules/ps2706/ps5058/index.html.

Cisco ASA Advanced Inspection and Prevention Security Services Module, at www.cisco.com/en/US/products/ps6825/index.html.

Cisco IOS Intrusion Prevention System (IPS), at www.cisco.com/en/US/products/ps6634/index.html.

IronPort Threat Operations Center, at www.ironport.com/toc.

Cisco Intrusion Prevention System Signature Search Pages, at http://tools.cisco.com/security/center/search.x?search=Signature.

Cisco IPS Threat Defense Bulletins, at http://tools.cisco.com/security/center/bulletin.x?i=57.

Exam Preparation Tasks

Review All the Key Topics

Review the most important topics from the chapter, noted with the Key Topic icons in the margin of the page. Table 2-5 lists a reference of these key topics and the page numbers on which each is found.

Table 2-5   *Key Topics for Chapter 2*

Key Topic Element	Description	Page Number
Figure 2-1	Cisco IPS 4200 Series Sensor Comparison	26
Table 2-2	Cisco IPS 4240 Sensor Interfaces	29
Table 2-3	Cisco IPS 4255 Sensor Interfaces	30
Table 2-4	Cisco ASA 5500 AIP Module Comparison	34
Figure 2-8	Cisco IPS Software Architecture Overview	38
Figure 2-10	Cisco IPS Sensor Management	42
Figure 2-13	Cisco Security Intelligence Operations	45

Definitions of Key Terms

Define the following key terms from this chapter, and check your answers in the glossary:

attack, global correlation

This chapter covers the following topics:

- **Various Network IPS Traffic Analysis Methods:** Different types of traffic and patterns require various methods of analysis to properly provide the necessary countermeasures.

- **Various Network Evasion Attacks:** Methods used to evade intrusion prevention systems or traffic-filtering techniques.

- **Choosing the Appropriate Anti-evasion Countermeasures:** Methods to counter the methods of evasion.

Network IPS Traffic Analysis Methods, Evasion Possibilities, and Anti-evasive Countermeasures

Overview

Cisco and third-party intrusion prevention system (IPS) sensors use a variety of techniques to analyze network traffic to optimally detect suspicious and malicious traffic. This chapter covers the methods that Cisco IPS supports, as well as the various evasion techniques used by attackers.

This chapter begins with the "Network IPS Traffic Analysis Methods" section, which is a high-level overview of the various analysis methods available today. Following the analysis methods, the chapter examines the evasion techniques and describes how to stay in front of the threats being seen around the world with anti-evasive countermeasures.

"Do I Know This Already?" Quiz

The "Do I Know This Already?" quiz allows you to assess whether you should read the entire chapter. If you miss no more than one of these ten self-assessment questions, you might want to move ahead to the "Exam Preparation Tasks" section. Table 3-1 lists the major headings in this chapter and the "Do I Know This Already?" quiz questions covering the material in those headings so that you can assess your knowledge of these specific areas. The answers to the "Do I Know This Already?" quiz appear in Appendix A.

Table 3-1 *"Do I Know This Already?" Foundation Topics Section-to-Question Mapping*

Foundation Topics Section	Questions
Network IPS Traffic Analysis Methods	1-4
Network IPS Evasion Attacks	5-8
Cisco IPS Anti-evasive Countermeasures	9-10

1. Which of the following is a common limitation of packet header matching as a method of IPS traffic analysis?

   a. True positive

   b. True negative

   c. False positive

   d. False negative

2. Which of the following is *not* a limitation of stateful content matching as a method of IPS traffic analysis?

   a. Performance impact

   b. False negatives if search is limited

   c. True positives because of lack of context

   d. False positives because of lack of context

3. Which of the following are benefits of using protocol decoding as a method of IPS traffic analysis?

   a. Reliably detect known application layer attacks

   b. Detect yet-unknown application layer attacks through application layer protocol verification

   c. Fewer false positives

   d. Improved performance for application layer analysis

   e. All of these answers are correct.

4. Which of the following network IPS traffic analysis methods is the most granular method?

   a. Protocol decoding

   b. Stateful content matching

   c. Packet content matching

   d. Packet header matching

5. Which of the following attacks is mainly detected through the IPS traffic analysis method known as traffic correlation?

   a. Denial of service (DoS) attacks

   b. Reconnaissance attacks

   c. Application layer attacks

   d. Composite attacks

6. Which of the following IPS evasion techniques describes where the attacker splits malicious traffic, hoping to avoid detection or filtering?

   a. Traffic fragmentation

   b. Traffic substitution and insertion

   c. Protocol-level misinterpretation

   d. Encryption and tunneling

7. Which of the following Unicode decoding methods is often referred to as a worst-case scenario when utilized?

   a. Ambiguous bits

   b. Alternate code pages

   c. Multiple directory delimiters

   d. Double encoding

8. Which of the following IPS evasion techniques causes the IPS sensor to ignore traffic that should *not* be ignored?

   a. Traffic fragmentation

   b. Traffic substitution and insertion

   c. Protocol-level misinterpretation

   d. Encryption and tunneling

9. Which of the following are examples of secure sessions used in encryption and tunneling?

   a. Secure Socket Layer (SSL)

   b. Secure Shell (SSH)

   c. Site-to-site IP Security (IPsec) Virtual Private Network (VPN) tunnel

   d. Client-to-LAN IPsec tunnel

   e. All of these answers are correct.

10. Which of the following Cisco IPS anti-evasion features is more suitable against resource exhaustion?

   a. Smart dynamic event summarization

   b. Full session reassembly

   c. Data normalization (deobfuscation)

   d. IP TTL and TCP checksum validation

Foundation Topics

Network IPS Traffic Analysis Methods

A network IPS sensor uses a number of different aspects to analyze network traffic. Some of the most common methods of network analysis include the following:

- Stateful content matching

- Protocol decoding

- Traffic correlation

- Rate analysis

- Packet header matching

- Packet content matching

- Statistical modeling

- Event correlation

Stateful Content Matching

The Cisco IPS sensor will fully reassemble a transport layer session between network endpoints to extract a stream of bytes exchanged through an application session. Using this stream of bytes, the sensor can perform more reliable matching when searching for payload data across the entire session, even if the content is split across many packets.

The sensor reassembles different pieces of data depending on the Open Systems Interconnection (OSI) layer:

- **OSI Layer 3:** The sensor reassembles the fragmented IP packets.

- **OSI Layer 4:** The sensor reassembles the TCP session in the correct manner, relying on sequence numbers to correctly sequence data. UDP session reassembly can rely on some application layer UDP sequencing to extract the correct byte stream.

Stateful content matching improves the quality of detection and doesn't allow attackers to easily evade the sensor using packet fragmentation and segmentation. This method is more demanding of the sensor, as the sensor must perform real-time, in-memory buffering of application data. The sensor can be instructed to only look into one portion of the byte stream (for example, only the first 100 bytes) to increase performance. This can lead to false negatives if the attacker is able to send malicious data later in the session, outside the inspection window. The sensor still does not fully understand the application layer protocol and content. Therefore, administrators might see false positives because the content that the sensor is looking for can appear in many different contexts in the application stream (for example, a user might be visiting a web page that contains certain malicious sequences inside a textual description, where they pose no harm). This could possibly cause the sensor to act on legitimate or nonharmful traffic.

Protocol Decoding

The most granular method of analysis is protocol decoding. The sensor takes an extra step and parses the application layer protocol from a reassembled byte stream provided by the stateful transport layer reassembly routines. The quality of detection is improved by this method in the following three ways:

- It improves performance, as the sensor needs to examine less traffic after it has decoded it.

- The sensor can perform protocol verification and reject protocol messages that do not conform to the standard behavior of the protocol. The sensor can detect or prevent both known and yet-unknown attacks that violate protocol standards (for example, buffer overflows that send too much data to a host, violating maximum lengths set forth in protocol standards).

- It reduces false positives by providing the context in which the sensor needs to look for suspicious or malicious patterns. For example, instead of searching through the entire TCP session's byte stream, the sensor can now search for malicious HTTP URLs exactly in the part of the HTTP request where the URL is located. This increases the accuracy of the sensor, ensuring that it won't make a wrong decision by finding offending content in the wrong context.

Traffic Correlation

A network IPS sensor sees a large amount of flows from different network endpoints, so the sensors have the advantage of being able to correlate packets of multiple network conversations. Suspicious or malicious activity can be identified through the network IPS sensors as they correlate different packets and determine their common properties.

IPS sensors use these real-time correlation abilities mainly to detect network reconnaissance attacks, where attackers send many packets to few or many other hosts to determine their reachability, to determine the presence of specific applications, or to enumerate all exposed network services offered by an endpoint. Worms use similar scanning techniques to find other systems to spread to, and they can be detected and stopped using the same correlation mechanisms on the network IPS sensors.

One fundamental limitation of packet correlation is that it takes a while before the sensor classifies and correlates packets to determine whether these packets constitute an interesting event. Until this threshold is met, all previous packets will already be on the way to their destination and therefore cannot be dropped or captured.

A good example of such a correlation would be a network sensor detecting more than ten different connection request packets from a single host, to multiple other hosts, on the same TCP destination ports, within 60 seconds. This can indicate that a host is performing a service scan of the network.

Rate Analysis

A network IPS can analyze network traffic to monitor the rate of packets of a particular protocol, the rate of packets between host pairs, the connection rates, or the rate of application layer requests and messages. These rate monitors work using a set of thresholds that determine maximums expected for normal network operation. This capability is referred to as *rate analysis*. The thresholds can be set manually by the administrator or preconfigured by the IPS vendor. Denial of service attacks often use flooding at various levels of the OSI model, so they can be detected using these mechanisms.

An example of rate analysis is an IPS sensor configured to monitor the UDP traffic rate between the attacker and the target host. The threshold for traffic rate is at 150 packets per second. After this threshold is met or exceeded, the sensor sounds an alarm and acts accordingly (results can vary depending on what actions or alarming thresholds are configured).

Packet Header Matching

The simplest method of traffic analysis is to address suspicious or malicious activity by analyzing a packet's header. An anomalous combination of TCP flags in a TCP segment is an example of this packet header matching method of analysis.

This method of analysis is used to

- Provide basic identification of network connections made by malware or accepted by malware-infested PCs (for example, a Trojan horse program that allows remote control of a system). The sensor can identify these connections based on the well-known transport layer ports these malware applications use. Identification of this nature is prone to errors, as there are some applications that can be legitimately using these ports.

- Detect malformed packets of OSI Layers 2–4 by performing low-level protocol verification of these protocols. Attackers can and often do use these malformed packets to crash protected systems or network devices by exploiting bugs in their TCP/IP stacks or packet-forwarding functions.

Packet Content Matching

Another method of analysis uses basic examination of packet payloads for each individual packet. The sensor uses this to

- Improve its identification of malware connections, if these connections use some well-known payload data patterns that can be identified in individual packets

- Detect unwanted applications in the network, such as messaging or gaming applications that use ports of standard applications

- Detect known application layer attacks that are embedded in the packet payloads, by looking for a specific sequence of payload bytes

Attackers often evade this method of analysis simply by spreading the characteristic or "signature" of suspicious or malicious traffic over two or more packets, thus bypassing this analysis because the sensor is examining each packet individually.

This method of analysis often causes false positives, as legitimate traffic might contain the same traffic pattern. Given that the sensor doesn't understand the context in which the payload will appear, it will trigger an event or act in error.

Statistical Modeling

A network IPS sensor can use an analysis technique and supervised learning to build a statistical model that describes certain traffic properties. Some examples can be traffic patterns, traffic rates, traffic composition, traffic intervals, and so on. This method typically aligns to the anomaly-based approach, which allows the sensor to detect any known or yet-unknown attacks that violate the learned "normal" behavior. Denial of service and similar flooding-based attacks are often detected by sensors using this approach. Statistical modeling is prone to higher rates of false positives in networks that cannot be adequately described with a statistical model. If an administrator is trying to address specific issues similar to reconnaissance detection problems, this method of analysis can work well with almost no false positives.

Typically, management stations and tools scan the network, legitimately opening several sessions a minute to different hosts, but often, infected servers or PCs try to open a much larger number of sessions. An IPS sensor would detect such anomalies and identify a worm attack.

Event Correlation

Finally, in addition to traffic correlation, the last method of analysis allows the sensor to provide event correlation where it correlates multiple detected events to present higher-level, consolidated information to the administrator, and possibly automatically act on such higher-level information using preventive actions.

Event correlation on the sensor is beneficial in detecting composite attacks more reliably. A composite attack usually consists of multiple individual events or attacks. The sensor is required to see multiple components of the attack to recognize it as an attack. This increases the reliability and confidence required to deploy preventive aggressive actions and provides more information about the network activity to the administrator.

Unlike other methods, the limitation isn't with false reporting but with performance degradation. The sensor isn't able to use very long windows of time in which to correlate events. Therefore, an attacker might be able to evade detection if the attacker performed an attack in a slow sequence, at the expense of attack efficiency. Although this might be the case, individual components of the attack are still likely to be detected or prevented.

Network IPS Evasion Techniques

As discussed in the previous section, there are a number of methods to analyze attacks, but to better analyze and choose anti-evasion countermeasures, it's important to understand the various evasion techniques used by attackers. Network attackers often use network IPS evasion techniques to attempt to bypass the intrusion detection, intrusion prevention, and traffic-filtering functions provided by network IPS sensors. Some commonly used network IPS evasion techniques include the following:

Key
Topic

■   Encryption and tunneling

■   Timing attacks

■   Resource exhaustion

- Traffic fragmentation

- Protocol-level misinterpretation

- Traffic substitution and insertion

Encryption and Tunneling

One common method of evasion used by attackers is to avoid detection simply by encrypting the packets or putting them in a secure tunnel. As previously discussed, IPS sensors monitor the network and capture the packets as they traverse the network, but network-based sensors rely on the data being transmitted in plain text. When and if the packets are encrypted, the sensor captures the data but is unable to decrypt it and cannot perform meaningful analysis. This is assuming that the attacker has already established a secure session with the target network or host. Some examples that can be used for this method of encryption and tunneling are as follows:

- Secure Shell (SSH) connection to an SSH server

- Client-to-LAN IPsec (IP Security) VPN (Virtual Private Network) tunnel

- Site-to-site IPsec VPN tunnel

- SSL (Secure Socket Layer) connection to a secure website

There are other types of encapsulation that the sensor cannot analyze and unpack that attackers often use in an evasion attack. For example, GRE (generic route encapsulation) tunnels are often used with or without encryption.

Timing Attacks

Attackers can evade detection by performing their actions slower than normal, not exceeding the thresholds inside the time windows that the signatures use to correlate different packets together. These evasion attacks can be mounted against any correlating engine that uses a fixed time window and a threshold to classify multiple packets into a composite event. An example of this type of attack would be a very slow reconnaissance attack sending packets at the interval of a couple per minute. In this scenario, the attacker would likely evade detection simply by making the scan unacceptably long.

Resource Exhaustion

A common method of evasion used by attackers is extreme resource consumption. For this subtle method, it doesn't matter whether such a denial is against the device or the personnel managing the device. Specialized tools can be used to create a large number of alarms that consume the resources of the IPS device and prevent attacks from being logged. These attacks can overwhelm what is known as the management systems or server, database server, or out-of-band (OOB) network. Attacks of this nature can also succeed if they only overwhelm the administrative staff, which does not have the time or skill necessary to investigate the numerous false alarms that have been triggered.

Intrusion detection and prevention systems rely on their capability to capture packets off the wire and analyze them quickly, but this requires the sensor to have adequate memory capacity and processor speed. The attacker can cause an attack to go undetected through the process of flooding the network with noise traffic and causing the sensor to capture unnecessary packets. If the attack is detected, the sensor resources can be exhausted and unable to respond within a timely manner.

Traffic Fragmentation

Fragmentation of traffic was one of the early network IPS evasion techniques used to attempt to bypass the network IPS sensor. Any evasion attempt where the attacker splits malicious traffic to avoid detection or filtering is considered a fragmentation-based evasion by

- Bypassing the network IPS sensor if it does not perform any reassembly

- Reordering split data if the network IPS sensor does not correctly order it in the reassembly process

- Confusing the network IPS sensor's reassembly methods, which might not reassemble split data correctly and result in missing the malicious payload associated with it

Following are two classic examples of fragmentation-based evasion:

- **TCP segmentation and reordering:** The sensor must correctly reassemble the entire TCP session, including possible corner cases, such as selective ACKs and selective retransmission.

- **IP fragmentation:** The attacker fragments all traffic if the network IPS does not perform reassembly. Most sensors do perform reassembly, so the attacker fragments the IP traffic in a manner that it is not uniquely interpreted. This action causes the sensor to interpret it differently from the target, which leads to the target being compromised.

In the same class of fragmentation attacks, there is a class of attacks involving overlapping fragments. In *overlapping fragments*, the offset values in the IP header don't match as they should, so one fragment overlaps another. The IPS sensor might not know how the target system will reassemble these packets, and typically different operating systems handle this situation differently.

Protocol-Level Misinterpretation

Attackers also evade detection by causing the network IPS sensor to misinterpret the end-to-end meaning of network protocols. In this scenario, the traffic is seen differently from the target by the attacker, causing the sensor either to ignore traffic that should not be ignored or vice versa. Two common examples are packets with bad TCP checksum and IP TTL (Time-to-Live) attacks.

A bad TCP checksum could occur in the following manner: An attack intentionally corrupts the TCP checksum of specific packets, confusing the state of the network IPS sensor that does not validate checksums. The attacker can also send a good payload with the bad checksum. The sensor can process it, but most hosts will not. The attacker follows with a bad payload with a good checksum. From the network IPS sensor, this appears to be a duplicate and will ignore it, but the end host will now process the malicious payload.

The IP TTL field in packets presents a problem to network IPS sensors because there is no easy way to know the number of hops from the sensor to the endpoint of an IP session stream. Attackers can take advantage of this through a method of reconnaissance by sending a packet that has a very short TTL that will pass through the network IPS fine, but be dropped by a router between the sensor and the target host when a TTL equals 0. The attacker can then follow by sending a malicious packet with a long TTL, which will make it to the end host or target. The packet looks like a retransmission or duplicate packet from the attacker, but to the host or target, this is the first packet that actually reached it. The result is a compromised host and the network IPS sensor ignored or missed the attack.

Traffic Substitution and Insertion

Another class of evasion attacks includes traffic substitution and insertion. Traffic substitution is when the attacker attempts to substitute payload data with other data in a different format. A network IPS sensor can miss such malicious payloads if it looks for data in a particular format and doesn't recognize the true meaning of the data. Some examples of substitution attacks include the following:

- Substitution of spaces with tabs, and vice versa; for example, inside HTTP requests

- Using Unicode instead of ASCII strings and characters inside HTTP requests

- Exploit mutation, where specific malicious shellcode (executable exploit code that forces the target system to execute it) can be substituted by completely different shellcode with the same meaning and thus consequences on the end host or target

- Exploit case sensitivity and changing the case of characters in a malicious payload, if the network IPS sensor is configured with case-sensitive signatures

Insertion attacks act in the same manner in that the attacker inserts additional information that does not change the payload meaning into the attack payload. An example would be the insertion of spaces or tabs into protocols that ignore such sequences.

Unicode provides a unique identifier for every character in every language to facilitate uniform computer representation of the world's languages. The Unicode Consortium manages Unicode and has been adopted by the majority of information technology industry leaders. Modern standards including Java, LDAP (Lightweight Directory Access Protocol), and XML require Unicode. Many operating systems and applications support Unicode. Also known as "code points," Unicode can be represented by $U+xxxx$, where x is a hexadecimal digit.

UTF-8 is the Unicode Transformation Format that serializes a Unicode code point as a sequence of 1 to 4 bytes, as defined by the Unicode Consortium. UTF-8 provides a way to encode Unicode points and still be compatible with ASCII, which is the common representation of text on the Internet.

Even though the Unicode specification dictates that the code points should be treated differently, there are times that the application or operation system can assign the same interpretation to different code points.

Cisco supports the following variations of its Unicode deobfuscation, although there are many different implementations of Unicode decoding (including some "free interpretations"):

- **Ambiguous bits:** Some decoder implementations ignore certain bits in the encoding. For example, an application will treat %A9 and %C9 identically, discarding the fifth bit in a UTF-8 two-octet encoding.

- **Alternate code pages:** Most Windows-based personal computers have extended Latin code pages loaded. Typically when an extended character is processed, it is normalized to an ASCII-equivalent character.

- **Self-referencing directories:** The directory name test/./app refers to the same path as test/app.

- **Double encoding:** The code point passes through two levels of encoding. The base encoding can be either a single-octet UTF-8 or Unicode %U encoding (without variation). The second encoding can encode each octet of the base encoding with any encoding method and variation. When utilized, a single character can be encoded in many unique ways, such as the following:

  - % can be represented in at least 140 ways.

  - x can be represented in at least 1000 ways on average.

  - U can be represented in at least 3260 ways.

- **Multiple directory delimiters:** Some operating systems will treat / and \ equivalently as directory delimiters. Repeated directory delimiters are also ignored.

- **Unencoded octets mixed with encoded octets in a UTF-8 sequence:** Any octet except the first octet in a UTF-8 sequence can be an unencoded value. A good example of this is the value 0x123, represented in UTF-8 as %E0%84%A3, but the 84, being an ASCII value, can also be represented with a UTF-8 value.

- **Microsoft base-36:** Older versions of Microsoft's UTF-8 decoder accept 36 characters (A–Z and 0–9) as valid hexadecimal characters in the UTF-8 encoding instead of the normal 16 characters (A–F and 0–9). This is often referred to as a decoder implementation error.

Table 3-2 summarizes the evasion methods, tools, and corresponding IPS anti-evasion features available on the Cisco IPS sensors.

Table 3-2   *Cisco IPS Evasion Tools and Anti-evasion Features*

Evasion Method	Evasion Tool	Cisco IPS Anti-evasion Features
Traffic fragmentation	Fragroute, fragrouter	Full-session reassembly in STRING and SERVICE engines
Traffic substitution and insertion	Metasploit, Nessus	Data normalization (deobfuscation) in SERVICE engines

Table 3-2 *Cisco IPS Evasion Tools and Anti-evasion Features*

Evasion Method	Evasion Tool	Cisco IPS Anti-evasion Features
Protocol-level mis-interpretation	No common tool available	IP TTL validation TCP checksum validation
Timing attacks	Nmap	Configuration intervals and use of CS-MARS and similar tools for correlation
Encryption and tunneling	Any encrypted protocol	GRE tunnel inspection
Resource exhaustion	Stick	Smart dynamic event summarization

Although they are covered in the table, the anti-evasion features are listed with additional detail, as follows:

■   Smart and dynamic summarization of events to guard against too many alarms for high event rates

■   IP TTL analysis and TCP checksum validation to guard against end-to-end protocol-level traffic interpretation

■   Full-session reassembly that supports the STRING and SERVICE engines that must examine a reliable byte stream between two network endpoints

■   Configurable intervals for correlating signatures, or the use of an external correlation that does not require real-time resources, such as Cisco Security Monitoring, Analysis, and Response System (MARS)

■   Data normalization (deobfuscation) inside SERVICE engines, where all signatures convert network traffic data into a normalized, canonical form, and typically do so by comparing the signature matching rules

■   Inspection of traffic inside GRE tunnels to prevent evasion through tunneling

We discuss the configuration of these features in later chapters.

Summary

This section highlights the key topics discussed in this chapter:

- The various methods used for traffic analysis using a network IPS sensor

- The various evasion techniques used by attackers to bypass detection and filtering while understanding the benefits and limitations of each method to assess the risk of evasion

- The various countermeasures and tools, and choosing the best approach based on the methods used by attackers

References

For additional information, refer to these resources:

IDS Evasion with Unicode, at www.securityfocus.com/infocus/1232.

IDS Evasion Techniques and Tactics, at www.securityfocus.com/infocus/1577.

Evading NIDS, Revisited, at www.securityfocus.com/infocus/1852.

Insertion, Evasion, and Denial of Service: Eluding Network Intrusion Detection, at www.insecure.org/stf/secnet_ids/secnet_ids.html.

Firewall/IDS Evasion and Spoofing, at http://nmap.org/book/man-bypass-firewalls-ids.html.

Intrusion Detection FAQ: IDS Evasion and Denial of Service Using RPC Design Flaws, at www.sans.org/security-resources/idfaq/rpc_evas.php.

Intrusion Detection Evasion: How Attackers Get Past The Burglar Alarm, at www.sans.org/reading_room/whitepapers/detection/intrusion-detection-evasion-attackers-burglar-alarm_1284.

Intrusion Detection FAQ: How Does Fragroute Evade NIDS Detection, at www.sans.org/security-resources/idfaq/fragroute.php.

The Unicode Standard, at www.unicode.org/standard/standard.html.

Exam Preparation Tasks

Review All the Key Topics

Review the most important topics from the chapter, noted with the Key Topic icons in the margin of the page. Table 3-3 lists a reference of these key topics and the page numbers on which each is found.

Table 3-3 *Key Topics for Chapter 3*

Key Topic Element	Description	Page Number
Paragraph	Common Methods of Traffic Analysis	54
Paragraph	Network IPS Evasion Techniques	57
List	Common Encryption and Tunneling Evasion Techniques	58
List	Different Variations of Unicode Decoding	61
Table 3-2	Cisco IPS Evasion Tools and Anti-evasion Features	61

Complete the Tables and Lists from Memory

Print a copy of Appendix C, "Memory Tables" (found on the CD), or at least the section for this chapter, and complete the tables and lists from memory. Appendix D, "Memory Tables Answer Key," also on the CD, includes completed tables and lists to check your work.

Definitions of Key Terms

Define the following key terms from this chapter, and check your answers in the glossary:

deobfuscation, evasion, encode, decode, reconnaissance attack, SSL, IPsec, VPN, GRE

This chapter covers the following topics:

- **Planning, Placement, and Deployment of a Network IPS:** Things to consider while designing and implementing network intrusion prevention and detection systems.

- **Choosing the Appropriate Network IPS Internet Edge Design:** Factors to consider when deploying a network intrusion prevention and detection system at the network edge.

- **Choosing the Appropriate Network IPS Wide-Area Network Design:** Factors to consider when deploying a network intrusion prevention and detection system in a wide-area network.

- **Choosing the Appropriate Network IPS Data Center Design:** Factors to consider when deploying a network intrusion prevention and detection system in a data center.

- **Choosing the Appropriate Network IPS Centralized Sensor Design:** Factors to consider when deploying a network intrusion prevention and detection system in a centralized campus.

CHAPTER 4

Network IPS and IDS Deployment Architecture

Overview

Network architectures are typically deployed to solve or meet specific technical requirements derived through business initiatives or needs. Network intrusion detection system (IDS) and intrusion prevention system (IPS) sensors are deployed in various architectures to enhance network-based protection of business assets and infrastructure. This chapter covers the common deployment scenarios and provides design guidelines for these scenarios.

The chapter begins with the "Sensor Deployment Considerations" section, which discusses the various scenarios and considerations you face when designing, planning, and implementing the Cisco IPS/IDS sensor. Following the deployment considerations, the chapter examines the IPS/IDS sensor implementation at the Internet edge, wide-area networks, data centers, and a centralized sensor deployment.

"Do I Know This Already?" Quiz

The "Do I Know This Already?" quiz allows you to assess whether you should read the entire chapter. If you miss no more than one of these ten self-assessment questions, you might want to move ahead to the "Exam Preparation Tasks" section. Table 4-1 lists the major headings in this chapter and the "Do I Know This Already?" quiz questions covering the material in those headings so that you can assess your knowledge of these specific areas. The answers to the "Do I Know This Already?" quiz appear in Appendix A.

Table 4-1   *"Do I Know This Already?" Foundation Topics Section-to-Question Mapping*

Foundation Topics Section	Questions
Sensor Deployment Considerations	1-3
Implementing IPS at the Internet Edge	4, 5
Implementing IPS in Wide-Area Networks	6, 7
Implementing IPS in Data Centers	8
Implementing IPS in a Centralized Deployment	9, 10

1. Which of the following sensor deployment locations should an administrator consider when deploying a network IDS or IPS sensor?

   a. At network perimeter chokepoints

   b. Near high-valued assets for added internal protection

   c. At any point inside the internal network to prevent internal threats

   d. Near hosts that are known to be vulnerable to known attacks

   e. All of these answers are correct.

2. Which of the following performance criteria should *not* be considered when deploying network IDS or IPS sensors?

   a. Throughput

   b. Connections per second

   c. Delay and jitter

   d. Memory

3. Policy virtualization is *not* required to inspect multiple different network segments. True or false?

   a. True

   b. False

4. Which of the following is a policy-facing network infrastructure and is particularly exposed to a large array of external threats?

   a. Internet edge

   b. Wide-area network (WAN)

   c. Data center

   d. Local-area network (LAN)

5. Which of the following interfaces are typically known as "trusted" interfaces when integrating a firewall with an IPS architecture?

   a. Outside

   b. Inside

   c. DMZ

   d. None of these answers are correct.

6. Which of the following is a network with geographically dispersed remote sites with access to the same services as users at central enterprise site(s)?

   a. Internet edge

   b. Wide-area network (WAN)

   c. Data center

   d. Local-area network (LAN)

7. Which of the following threats are addressed in the WAN edge IPS architecture or key areas?

    a. Malicious activity initiated by branch clients (that is, botnet participation)

    b. Attacks against vulnerabilities (man-in-the-middle attacks)

    c. Attacks against infrastructure (denial of service attacks)

    d. All of these answers are correct.

8. Which of the following hosts most of the critical applications and data for an enterprise or provider?

    a. Internet edge

    b. Wide-area network (WAN)

    c. Data center

    d. Local-area network (LAN)

9. Which two IPS topologies are supported in a centralized campus sensor deployment?

    a. RSPAN (Remote Switched Port Analyzer) VLAN

    b. Remote access

    c. Wide-area network (WAN)

    d. ERSPAN (Encapsulated RSPAN) GRE tunnel

10. Which of the following architectures involves deploying network IPS sensors to inspect traffic on ports that are located on multiple remote network switches?

    a. Internet edge

    b. Centralized campus

    c. Wide-area network (WAN)

    d. Data center

Foundation Topics

Sensor Deployment Considerations

Fundamentally, when deploying a network IDS or IPS, the following need to be considered:

- Security

- Prevention mode or detection mode

- Performance

- Virtualization requirements

Security Considerations

There are many scenarios where implementing a network IDS or IPS is suitable for addressing various threats in specific situations. As a best practice, security administrators typically deploy a network IDS or IPS in the following scenarios:

- At any point in the network, to protect hosts that are known to be vulnerable to known attacks. These "known attacks" include hosts that are unpatched, that are known to be misconfigured, and whose condition cannot be easily improved. Network IDSs and IPSs have the ability to alert the security administrator or prevent these systems from being compromised through known attacks.

- Near any high-valued assets, where the enterprise or provider requires as many protection layers as possible because the risks are high due to asset value.

- At any point inside the network infrastructure to protect the network infrastructure itself, and to provide protection to endpoints at the same time. A good example would be to protect your low-bandwidth WAN links and edge routers against scanning or flooding worms.

- At network perimeter chokepoints (inside enterprise or provider firewall systems that can be comprised of multiple network security devices) to provide a signature- or anomaly-based method to detect or prevent network attacks, in addition to classic policy-based controls implemented by other network security devices. The protection ability of the firewall system to detect or prevent threats that the base system cannot address is enhanced in this manner. The firewall systems can be either facing external networks (for example, the Internet) or can be used internally (for example, to protect data center applications).

- At network points where an enterprise or provider needs to identify attacks (by name) or determine attack trends. These types of deployments only provide detection rather than threat prevention, so they are only used for intelligence-gathering purposes and alarming.

Prevention Mode Versus Detection Mode

As discussed in previous chapters, when deploying an IPS sensor, fundamentally the security administrator and planners need to determine whether the intent is detection or prevention mode. Regardless, Cisco IPS sensors support both modes at the same time. Security administrators can configure certain rules (signatures) to perform aggressive response (blocking hosts, dropping packets, or both) and other signatures to only alert you or gather forensic data of suspicious activity.

Cisco recommends as a best practice where possible to deploy sensors in preventive mode. Preventive mode has the benefit of automated prevention of attacks and is typically used for most sensor rules or signatures, especially where enhanced network-based protection of infrastructure assets and applications is required. Administrators must be willing to invest some time for initial configuration and periodic retuning to achieve optimal preventive performance when using preventive mode. This mode requires that sensors are properly tuned to achieve the high accuracy needed to enable preventive actions.

Another mode often used by some administrators when deploying sensors is known as detection mode. Detection mode does not use aggressive responses, but instead alerts administrators or captures network traffic to provide intelligence about suspicious network activity (which might not necessarily be malicious). Detection mode is deployed in two well-known scenarios:

- **To monitor critical systems:** False positives often break legitimate network connectivity to critical assets, which administrators can't afford. That being said, it is often better to deploy sensors in detection mode as it will provide the intelligence needed to respond to incidents manually and provide a forensic trail that administrators can use to investigate incidents.

- **On network segments:** Administrators might need to boost sensor sensitivity to detect as much suspicious and malicious activity as possible. There is the risk of increased number of false positives. So administrators often deploy another sensor in combination running in preventive mode that is tuned for very low false positive rates, offsetting the primary sensor in detection mode.

Performance Considerations

Administrators need to ensure that the Cisco IPS sensor platform and model will provide adequate performance for the network environment in which it will operate. There are three common criteria or performance considerations that administrators can and should use when deploying an IPS or IDS sensor:

- **Connections per second:** Transaction-oriented server farms can require higher-than-normal connections over a given period of time, so an analysis of application session rates can be critical to avoiding potential bottlenecks.

Key
Topic

- **Delay and jitter:** Although Cisco IPS sensors do not guarantee low delay and jitter in their data path, administrators might want to consider bypassing the sensor with real-time application flows if acceptable to the security policy, or at least test the application performance to verify that it is not impacted. An example of an application that is sensitive to delay and jitter is high-definition videoconferencing.

- **Throughput:** The due diligence with regard to published performance numbers in comparison with the traffic patterns and properties of the test bed (lab) and production networks is critical in the analysis completed by administrators. Traffic patterns and properties that differ greatly in terms of packet rates and packet sizes typically would signify a need for an administrator to choose a higher-performing sensor to avoid performance bottlenecks.

Virtualization Requirements

Finally, it is important for administrators to evaluate virtualization. Cisco IPS sensors support virtualization in the form of policy virtualization. For example, there can be multiple virtual sensors running on a single Cisco IPS platform, where each of these sensors applies a different inspection policy based on the IP addresses of hosts communicating through the virtual sensor.

It's important not to confuse traffic isolation with policy virtualization for two reasons. First, policy virtualization is not required to inspect multiple different network segments. Second, a Cisco IPS provides traffic isolation with or without virtualization. Administrators only need virtual sensors, where they need to apply different policies to the same flows at different points in the network or if overlapping address spaces are necessary using the same physical sensor. Administrators should use these guidelines along with factors discussed in previous chapters to determine the best platform that supports.

Network IPS Implementation Guidelines

The following sections provide design guidelines for deploying network IDS and IPS sensors in various network designs. The most commonly used network designs, as illustrated in Figure 4-1, are as follows:

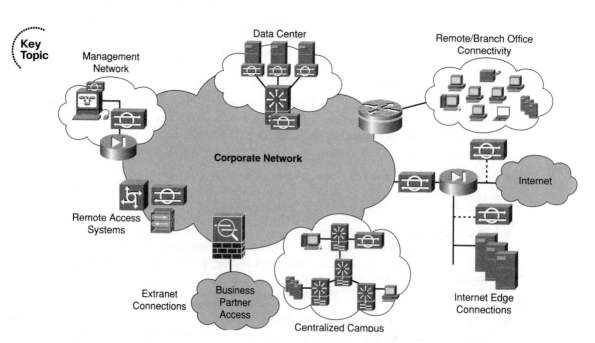

Figure 4-1   *Network IPS or IDS Deployment Areas*

- Enterprise or provider Internet edge

- Wide-area networks (WAN)

- Data center

- Centralized campus

Enterprise or Provider Internet Edge

The Internet edge is the part the service provider or an enterprise network infrastructure that provides connectivity to the Internet or other external (public) networks, and it acts as the gateway for the provider or enterprise to most external networks. As shown in Figure 4-2, the Internet edge is a public-facing network infrastructure and is particularly exposed to a large array of external threats, so comprehensive security measures usually need to be implemented at this point, including intrusion prevention and detection.

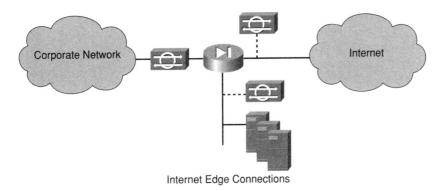

Internet Edge Connections

Figure 4-2 *Implementing a Network IPS at the Internet Edge*

Generally, basic control is to separate the less-trusted network from the internal enterprise or provider network into separate security domains. In the scenario described here, the less-trusted network is the Internet or business partner network. A firewall system (or in this case, the network security boundary) typically is a combination of network security controls. A network IDS or IPS is a common component inside a firewall system that controls access between the domains and enforces a desired access policy.

Figure 4-3 represents an example of a simple enterprise Internet edge architecture using a firewall system, which is comprised of a stateful filtering security appliance and an IPS appliance. It's important to note that in the figure the two components are separate, but they can be one and the same with the IPS Module (AIP SSM) supported in the Cisco ASA device (discussed in previous chapters). All the network security components are redundant.

In this particular example, there is no demilitarized zone (DMZ) network. The network IPS sensors are placed on the trusted (ASA inside interface) side of the stateful filtering component, which in this case is a Cisco Adaptive Security Appliance (ASA). The Cisco ASA filters much of the unwanted traffic from the Internet, while the IPS sensor only needs to analyze the remaining traffic for possible threats. This particular implementation example reduces the required processing power for the IPS sensors, and the sensors only report the most relevant events. In this example, the two IPS sensors are deployed in inline mode adjacent to the Cisco ASA devices and are redundant. For the IPS sensors to analyze the traffic correctly, they should receive symmetrical data flows. The ASA active/failover mechanism ensures that only one Cisco ASA is active at any given time. If the IPS were integrated into the Cisco ASA as mentioned earlier, it would greatly simplify the integration of active/active operation if deemed necessary.

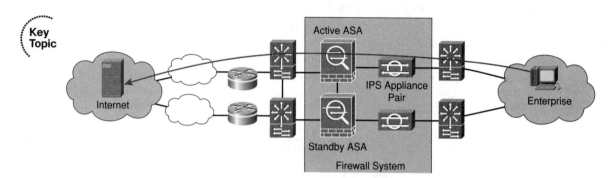

Figure 4-3 *Implementing a Network IPS at the Internet Edge Redundant System*

It's common and most recommended to deploy network IPS sensors on the more-trusted side of the stateful firewalling component as in the last example, but it might not be optimal for all organizations.

Another approach is to use network IDS or IPS analysis on the untrusted (outside) segment of a network deployment to monitor traffic "in the wild" or detect and prevent attacks and attempts before they hit the main firewall filtering components. Monitoring in this fashion is useful to detect new forms of attacks, new trends in attacking, and raw data, which can be correlated with other sensors. The network sensor that is deployed in this manner, unlike other sensors deployed on the trusted segment, isn't dedicated to monitoring specific applications or systems. Instead, the sensor is attempting to gather as much information as possible about something. This sensor is typically very sensitive and tuned to reduce only noise and very basic false positives; it is rarely deployed to provide true prevention.

Generally, network IPS monitoring is used on the trusted (inside) segment of a network to detect attacks that might pass from the untrusted to the trusted side, or to prevent suspicious or malicious network traffic from leaving the network. A sensor (or sensors) deployed in this manner are typically configured for prevention and tuned for manageably low rates of false positives. There are also scenarios where sensors are deployed both on the trusted and untrusted segments of a network using correlation techniques. The sensors correlate events so that they can indicate which attacks have penetrated other network security components between the two sensors.

There are some guidelines to consider when implementing a network IDS or IPS at the provider or enterprise Internet edge, including the following:

■ Redundancy by using IPS sensor pairs: Cisco IPS sensors lose visibility into the traffic flows with asymmetrical data paths, so to ensure symmetrical paths, it is good practice to fine-tune spanning tree parameters and deploy or implement the firewalls in active/standby mode. This can be achieved by deploying AIP SSM modules with ASA failover pairs or with separate ASA firewalls and IPS sensors, which depends ultimately on the bandwidth requirements.

■   Integration of IDS/IPS sensors into the Internet edge infrastructure on the trusted side of the core stateful filtering components, such as Cisco ASA devices: Another alternative method of integration is to use modules that integrate into the Cisco ASA for more flexible selection of inspected traffic.

■   Additionally or optionally placing an IDS/IPS sensor on the untrusted side of the Internet edge allows extensive visibility into external attack attempts that are otherwise stopped by the network firewall.

Wide-Area Network

A wide-area network (WAN), shown in Figure 4-4, provides users at geographically dispersed remote sites access to the same network services as users at the central site(s). In a WAN, network-borne threats commonly originate from branch offices or locations.

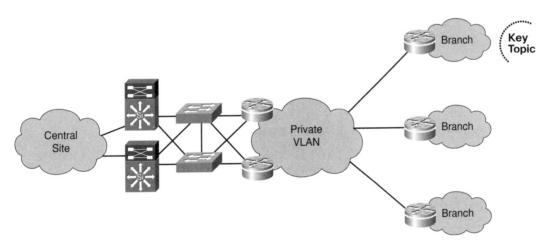

Figure 4-4   *General Wide-Area Network (WAN)*

Common threats addressed in the WAN are focused in three key areas:

■   Attacks against the infrastructure to include unauthorized access, privilege escalation, and denial-of-service (DoS) attacks

■   Malicious activity initiated by clients, such as malware proliferation, botnet participation, network and application abuse, and other malicious or noncompliant activity

■   WAN transport/transit vulnerabilities, including sniffing and man-in-the-middle (MITM) attacks

Mitigation is the critical component that network IPS sensors play in guarding against these common threats. In some cases, branch locations or offices use direct local Internet access, making the branch router part of the Internet edge. Implementations like this often require substantial firewall system functionality, including network IPS services.

One of the most common approaches or options from a WAN perspective is to deploy network IPS sensors centrally or on the "hub" site/location to filter traffic entering the central site from the branch/remote locations, as illustrated in Figure 4-5. Sensors deployed centrally not only protect the central site from the branch sites but also protect the branch sites from malicious traffic coming from the central site and the Internet. Traffic can be managed through configuration in the form of routing that direct branch to branch traffic through the central IPS sensors.

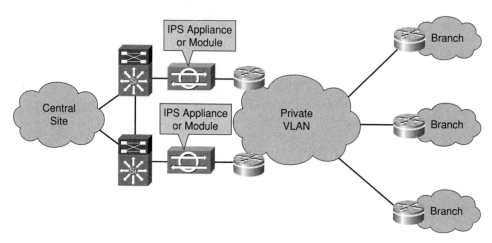

Figure 4-5   *Implementing an IPS in a WAN (Centralized)*

A centralized approach is much more cost effective and easy to manage, given that there are a small number of network sensors providing protection to all traffic. Commonly deployed Cisco IPS hardware to support a central site include the Cisco IPS 4200 Series appliance sensors, Cisco IDSM-2 modules, AIM-IPS or NME-IPS modules on aggregation WAN routers, and SSM-AIP inside Cisco ASA devices. (For more information on the hardware listed here, see Chapter 2, "Cisco IPS Software, Hardware, and Supporting Applications.")

Note: There are limitations that administrators need to factor in when deploying the AIM-IPS and NME-IPS modules in various places in the network.

Another approach or alternative for deploying IPS sensors in a WAN uses distributed network IPS sensors integrated into branch location or office WAN devices. This approach, illustrated in Figure 4-6, leverages the use of the Cisco AIM-IPS or NME-IPS modules for Cisco Integrated Services Routers. If the branch offices or locations use Cisco ASA firewall or VPN devices, the Cisco ASA SSM-AIP or AIP SSC modules can be leveraged as an integrated but distributed architecture.

An architecture using this approach should be considered when there is a need to protect WAN resources such as WAN links from flooding, or when remote sites or locations have direct/local Internet access through the use of split tunneling. The advantage of a distributed model is that the traffic directly between the branch locations is inspected at all times; so all traffic is inspected whether the traffic traverses the central site or not.

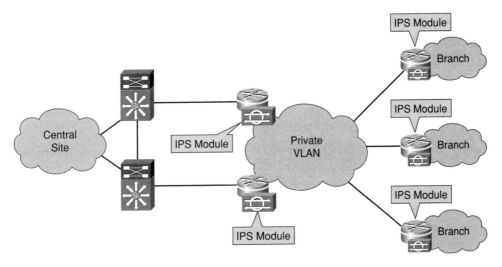

Figure 4-6 *Implementing an IPS in a WAN (Distributed)*

There are some guidelines to consider when implementing a network IDS or IPS in WANs:

- A combination of centralized and distributed IPSs enables the appropriate deployment model to be chosen according to the needs of a particular branch while maintaining consistent policy enforcement across the entire WAN.

- In a hub-and-spoke topology, where all remote site traffic is forced through the central (hub) site, a centralized IPS deployment is highly effective from an ease-of-management and -cost perspective. Unfortunately, in the centralized approach, branch-to-branch (also known as intrabranch) traffic is not analyzed, and monitoring requires additional design steps to force traffic through the network IPS. Traffic capacity of various paths should be considered in a design using route manipulation to provide traffic symmetry. Another consideration in the centralized design would be the IPS scalability and high availability.

- Monitoring requirements for branch locations need to be considered, especially if the branch offices or locations have direct or local Internet access through the use of split tunneling. If this is the case, the distributed approach should be considered.

Note: To ensure that the network IPS receives clear text, sensors should always be integrated on the trusted side of network VPN devices, after VPN termination and application optimization.

Implementing an IPS in Data Centers

Provider and enterprise data centers host most of the critical applications and data for that given provider or enterprise. Typically, the data center is inward facing, and most of its clients are on the internal enterprise network. The exception to the rule would be provider data centers, which typically are externally facing the clients, who can be consumers or businesses. In both scenarios, the data center is subject to external threats but must remain guarded against internal threats.

There are multiple approaches and layers used by network and security professionals to protect the data center server farms from internal threats and the previously mentioned external threats. A network IPS is a viable technology used in these approaches, whether the applications are directly or indirectly exposed to external networks.

In both Figures 4-7 and 4-8, network IPS sensors are placed between data center firewalls and data center server farms. Network IPS sensors can be implemented as appliances, physically connected to data center switches, integrated into these switches, or integrated into the data center security appliances or firewalls. As discussed in previous chapters, traffic modeling and proper planning are recommended, but typically data centers require more bandwidth. Where traffic modeling and proper planning have shown scalable performance and clustering capability for future growth, Cisco IPS 4270 and 4260 sensors might be best suited.

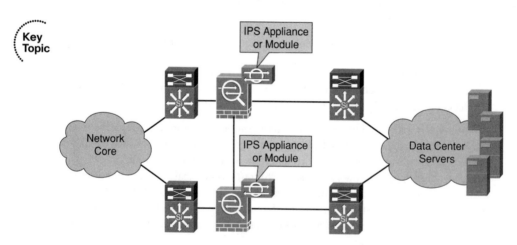

Figure 4-7   *Implementing an IPS in a Data Center*

There are some guidelines to consider when implementing a network IDS or IPS in a provider or enterprise data center:

- Data centers are typically designed for high-speed, highly available connectivity, so it's important to ensure that network IPS sensors do not impact these functions and integrate well with the surrounding network environment.

- Using logical VLAN interfaces on network sensors gives designers the flexibility to address different deployment requirements.

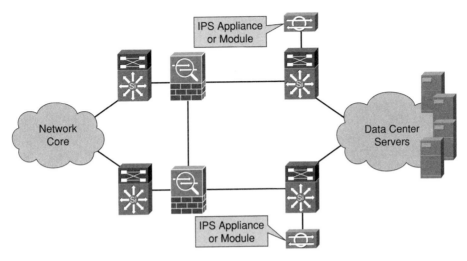

Figure 4-8   *Implementing an IPS in a Data Center Architecture Example*

- Scale performance well and maintain configuration simplicity by considering using dedicated network IPS sensors or virtual contexts for particular data center applications.

- Data centers are typically more controlled environments, so it might be easier to tune and deploy preventive actions. This is usually the case with a more centralized data center approach. In today's application-dependent networks, there can be more distributed data centers similar to the WAN model, so tuning and deploying preventive actions can become more challenging.

Centralized Campus

Another commonly used design with network IPS implementations is a centralized campus deployment. Because it's not always possible for a variety of reasons to connect or deploy a network sensor to every switch or segment in the network, a network sensor or sensor cluster can be deployed to inspect traffic on ports that are located on multiple remote network switches. In scenarios like this, it's common for security administrators to configure the sensor to operate in promiscuous mode, which results in the sensor receiving a copy of the traffic from remote networks rather than receiving the actual traffic it would normally see in inline mode. The Remote Switched Port Analyzer (RSPAN) feature is used to capture traffic on remote switchports and transport the captured traffic to the switch to which the IPS sensor is physically connected or integrated into through a module. RSPAN uses a Layer 2 VLAN to carry SPAN traffic between switches. RSPAN typically consists of an RSPAN source session, an RSPAN VLAN, and an RSPAN destination session. RSPAN source and destination sessions are configured separately on different switches, so it is possible to capture traffic at several different points in the network and send it to a single IPS sensor for inspection.

In Figure 4-9, traffic traverses ports that are configured for monitoring on switches A and B, and the traffic is captured and flooded to all ports belonging to the RSPAN VLAN. The traffic might be between the clients in the Finance department (connected to switch B) and servers (connected to switch A). Captured traffic or packets then traverse the LAN over RSPAN VLANs. The interswitch links are typically configured as VLAN trunks, permitting those VLANs to traverse the links. After the traffic is received on switch C, the switch copies the traffic from the RSPAN VLANs to the monitoring destination port to which the IPS sensor is connected. The sensor then inspects the traffic.

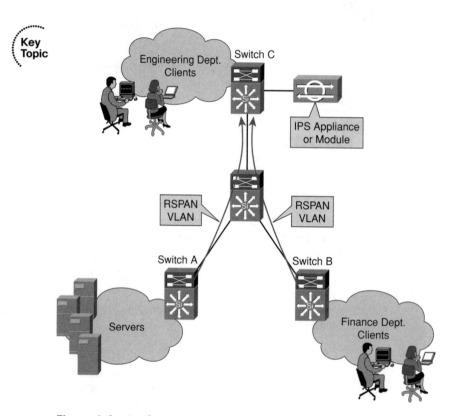

Figure 4-9   *Implementing an IPS in a Centralized Campus*

Another form of RSPAN is called Encapsulated RSPAN (ERSPAN). ERSPAN is similar to RSPAN, except that it enables traffic to be carried over multiple Layer 3 hops rather than Layer 2. It does this by using generic routing encapsulation (GRE) tunnels instead of Layer 2 VLANs to carry traffic between switches.

There are some guidelines to consider when implementing a network IDS or IPS in a centralized campus:

■   Carefully plan the RSPAN VLAN or ERSPAN GRE tunnel topology between traffic sources and the IPS sensor. VLAN access control lists (VACL) are commonly used in the RSPAN VLAN to limit traffic sent to the central network sensor.

■   Understand the limited response options because the sensor is placed away from traffic-capturing points. If prevention is desired, consider using blocking as an aggressive response, where the sensor can reconfigure an ACL on remote switches.

- Centralized campus architecture is typically deployed in a single campus and only for low-bandwidth applications to minimize infrastructure requirements to transfer copied traffic.

- Consider port capacity to which the sensor is connected to ensure that the volume of traffic captured doesn't exceed the capacity. If it does exceed the traffic capacity of the port, some traffic can be dropped and the sensor will not be able to inspect all the captured traffic.

- Ensure that the hardware and software (switch type/model and IOS image) support either RSPAN or ERSPAN features and the required number of sessions. Both the hardware and software limitations with regard to RSPAN and ERSPAN vary.

Design and Implementation Resources

A number of design and implementation guides are available on Cisco.com. The Cisco.com Design Zone for Security section covers many design and implementation guides that include guidelines on Cisco IPS technologies. Guidelines available today include the following:

Cisco SAFE Reference Guide, Enterprise Core, at www.cisco.com/en/US/docs/solutions/Enterprise/Security/SAFE_RG/chap3.html.

Cisco SAFE Reference Guide, Intranet Data Center, at www.cisco.com/en/US/docs/solutions/Enterprise/Security/SAFE_RG/chap4.html.

Cisco SAFE Reference Guide, Enterprise Campus (Centralized Campus), at www.cisco.com/en/US/docs/solutions/Enterprise/Security/SAFE_RG/chap5.html.

Cisco SAFE Reference Guide, Enterprise Internet Edge, at www.cisco.com/en/US/docs/solutions/Enterprise/Security/SAFE_RG/chap6.html.

Cisco SAFE Reference Guide, Enterprise WAN Edge, at www.cisco.com/en/US/docs/solutions/Enterprise/Security/SAFE_RG/chap7.html.

Cisco SAFE Reference Guide, Enterprise Branch, at www.cisco.com/en/US/docs/solutions/Enterprise/Security/SAFE_RG/chap8.html.

Cisco SAFE Security Solutions, at www.cisco.com/en/US/netsol/ns954/index.html#~one.

Cisco IPS 4200 Series Sensors Design Guides, at www.cisco.com/en/US/products/hw/vpndevc/ps4077/products_implementation_design_guides_list.html.

Summary

This section highlights the key topics discussed in this chapter:

- The various methods used for planning, placement, and deployment of network IPS sensors

- The various design considerations when selecting and deploying a network IPS solution

- The various resources and reference guides available on Cisco.com

Exam Preparation Tasks

Review All the Key Topics

Review the most important topics from the chapter, noted with the Key Topic icons in the margin of the page. Table 4-2 lists a reference of these key topics and the page numbers on which each is found.

Table 4-2   *Key Topics for Chapter 4*

Key Topic Element	Description	Page Number
Paragraph	Sensor Deployment Considerations	70
List	Performance Considerations	71
Figure 4-1	Most Commonly Used IPS Designs	72
Figure 4-3	Implementing a Network IPS at the Internet Edge Redundant System	74
Figure 4-4	Implementing a Network IPS in a WAN	75
Figure 4-7	Implementing a Network IPS in a Data Center	78
Figure 4-9	Implementing a Network IPS in a Centralized Campus	80

Definitions of Key Terms

Define the following key terms from this chapter, and check your answers in the glossary:

jitter, WAN, LAN, RSPAN, ERSPAN

642-627 IPS v7.0 exam topics covered in this part:

- Integrate Cisco network security solutions with other security technologies

- Create and test initial Cisco IPS configurations for new devices/services

- Optimize Cisco IPS security infrastructure device performance

- Advanced Cisco IPS security software configuration fault finding and repairing

- Advanced Cisco IPS Sensor and module hardware fault finding and repairing

Part II: Installing and Maintaining Cisco IPS Sensors

This chapter covers the following topics:

- **Planning and Deployment of Cisco IPS Sensors in Promiscuous Mode:** When and where to deploy a sensor to monitor and alert.

- **Planning and Deployment of Cisco IPS Sensors in Inline Interface Pair Mode:** When and where to deploy a sensor to monitor, alert, and act on.

- **Planning and Deployment of Cisco IPS Sensors in Inline VLAN Pair Mode:** When and where to deploy a sensor to monitor, alert, and act using VLAN pairs.

- **Planning and Deployment of Cisco IPS Sensors in Inline VLAN Group Mode:** When and where to deploy a sensor to monitor, alert, and act using VLAN groups.

- **Planning and Deployment of Cisco IPS Sensors in Selective Inline Analysis Mode:** When and where to deploy a sensor to monitor, alert, and act using the analysis of packets, flows, and state.

CHAPTER 5

Integrating the Cisco IPS Sensor into a Network

Overview

Cisco Network Intrusion Prevention System (IPS) sensors can be configured to provide prevention or detection. As discussed in previous chapters, prevention or IPS mode and detection or IDS mode both help defend against network attacks. This chapter covers the different modes of operation of integrating a Cisco IPS sensor into an enterprise or provider network.

The chapter begins with the integration mode more commonly used for offline detection and where packets are copied and analyzed, known as promiscuous mode. The following sections discuss the various prevention modes, all of which are modes that operate inline and can aggressively respond to defend against a network attack. Of the modes discussed in this chapter, the benefits and limitations are covered for each.

"Do I Know This Already?" Quiz

The "Do I Know This Already?" quiz allows you to assess whether you should read the entire chapter. If you miss no more than one of these ten self-assessment questions, you might want to move ahead to the "Exam Preparation Tasks" section. Table 5-1 lists the major headings in this chapter and the "Do I Know This Already?" quiz questions covering the material in those headings so that you can assess your knowledge of these specific areas. The answers to the "Do I Know This Already?" quiz appear in Appendix A.

Table 5-1 *"Do I Know This Already?" Foundation Topics Section-to-Question Mapping*

Foundation Topics Section	Questions
Deploying Sensors in Promiscuous Mode	1-5
Deploying Sensors in Inline Interface Pair Mode	6, 7
Deploying Sensors in Inline VLAN Pair Mode	8
Deploying Sensors in Inline VLAN Group Mode	9
Deploying Sensors in Selective Inline Analysis Mode	10

1. Which of the following is the main limitation of promiscuous mode on a Cisco IPS sensor?

   a. Complexity to deploy

   b. Lack of rich real-time preventive capability

   c. Impact to network performance

   d. Impact to network availability

2. Which of the following are promiscuous mode deployment options supported by the Cisco IPS sensor?

   a. SPAN or RSPAN

   b. VACL capture ports

   c. Router Selective Capture

   d. Cisco ASA Selective Capture

   e. All of these answers are correct.

3. Which of the following Cisco Catalyst switches is FSPAN supported on?

   a. Catalyst 6500 Series

   b. Catalyst 4900 Series

   c. Catalyst 3560-E Series

   d. Catalyst 3570-E Series

4. Which of the following Cisco Catalyst switches supports the VLAN access control list (VACL) capture feature?

   a. Catalyst 6500 Series

   b. Catalyst 4900 Series

   c. Catalyst 3560-E Series

   d. Catalyst 3570-E Series

5. Which of the following promiscuous mode features can be connected to the same analysis engine and is treated as the same traffic source?

   a. VLAN tag recognition

   b. Promiscuous delta

   c. Multi-interface analysis

   d. Integration with network devices

6. Which of the following is *not* a benefit of an inline interface pair deployment on a Cisco IPS sensor?

   a. Provides a set of preventive actions

   b. Can normalize traffic to improve accuracy and enhance protection

   c. Can impact network availability

   d. Oversubscription typically does not result in false negatives

7. Which of the following are features specific to the mode on a Cisco IPS sensor?

    a. UDLD support

    b. Interface shutdown on software failure

    c. Multi-interface analysis

    d. Hardware bypass

    e. All of these answers are correct.

8. Which of the following modes on a Cisco IPS sensor acts as a wire between two VLANs on the same interface?

    a. Interface pair mode

    b. VLAN pair mode

    c. VLAN group mode

    d. Selective inline analysis mode

9. No VLAN can be a member of more than one VLAN group subinterface in an inline VLAN group deployment. True or false?

    a. True

    b. False

10. Cisco IPS selective inline analysis mode is supported on which Cisco ASA model?

    a. ASA 5505 w/AIP SSC module

    b. ASA 5510 w/AIP SSM module

    c. ASA 5520 w/AIP SSM module

    d. ASA 5540 w/AIP SSM module

    e. All of these answers are correct.

Foundation Topics

Sensor Deployment Modes

When deploying a network intrusion detection system (IDS) or intrusion prevention system (IPS), the following modes are supported on Cisco IPS sensors:

- Promiscuous mode

- Inline interface pair mode

- Inline VLAN pair mode

- Inline VLAN group mode

- Selective inline analysis mode

Deploying Sensors in Promiscuous Mode

The simplest deployment mode for Cisco IPS sensors is typically promiscuous mode. Packets in promiscuous mode don't flow through the Cisco IPS sensor. The sensor receives a copy of network traffic and analyzes copied packets to determine whether they contain signs of suspicious or malicious activity. In addition to being simple to deploy, it typically doesn't impact network performance because the sensor sees only a copy of network traffic. The original packets are forwarded unmodified to their original destinations. In this deployment mode, if the sensor fails, there is no impact on network availability because the sensor is out of the packet path.

Promiscuous mode lacks rich real-time preventive capability, which is its main limitation. The Cisco IPS sensor can disconnect some network sessions creatively (for example, generating TCP reset packets) or dynamically modify access rules on a nearby inline device such as a router or a firewall. It's important to understand that this deployment mode lacks the capability to drop the original suspicious or malicious packets that are forwarded to their destinations. Promiscuous mode IPS sensors cannot modify copied traffic to normalize it. As a result, promiscuous IPS sensors are less accurate compared to inline methods, which can use normalization to remove ambiguous traffic properties and therefore enhance analysis. Figure 5-1 is an example of a commonly deployed sensor in promiscuous mode.

One of the simplest options for a promiscuous mode deployment is to use a hub or a network tap to copy network traffic to a sensor interface of the Cisco IPS sensor. By design, the Cisco IPS sensor receives all traffic that is forwarded over the hub if used on the edge segment or in transit. Taps are dedicated devices for capturing traffic that allow you to monitor edge segments or transit links in the same manner.

By design, a hub or network tap cannot oversubscribe the interface to which the sensor is connected, which is a benefit of this approach. Unfortunately, though, the IPS sensor itself can be oversubscribed if it cannot handle all the traffic forwarded to it. Other benefits of this approach include less complex network reconfiguration and the fact that network availability isn't impacted upon sensor failure. With benefits often come limitations:

- Potentially reducing network performance because of a lack of switched operation

- No support for full-duplex communications on hubs

- Lack of selective capture

- Capture of a subset of traffic type or packets

- Inability to support all media types and speeds

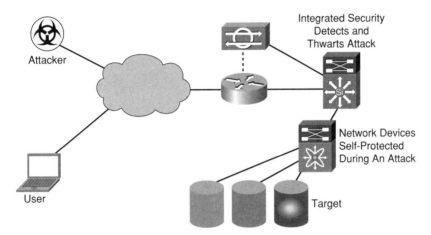

Figure 5-1   *IPS Promiscuous Mode Deployment*

The Cisco IPS 4200 Series sensors can use their sensing interfaces in promiscuous mode to connect to hubs or taps, so this mode of deployment is supported.

The second Cisco IPS sensor promiscuous mode deployment option is to use the SPAN (Switched Port Analyzer) function on LAN switches. This mode, as shown in Figure 5-2, has the advantage of already being present in the infrastructure in most networks. Most switches support SPAN in one form or another, but the SPAN function on a Cisco switch allows the user to flexibly select a subset of traffic either by port or VLAN that is copied to a dedicated port marked as the SPAN port. The SPAN port is typically where the sensing interface of the Cisco IPS sensor is connected.

Similar to a hub or network tap sensor deployment discussed earlier, the Cisco IPS sensor on a SPAN port doesn't impact network availability or performance. The SPAN option does limit the granularity, however, because the capture can't be performed on a per-port (TCP or UDP) basis or per-IP-address basis. The oversubscription of the SPAN port results in dropping packets at the SPAN port. If this occurs, incomplete traffic flows to the analyzing Cisco IPS sensor, creating a potentially large number of false negatives. Most switches (Cisco and others) have limited SPAN resources and thus cannot (in most cases) support many SPAN destination ports on the same switch.

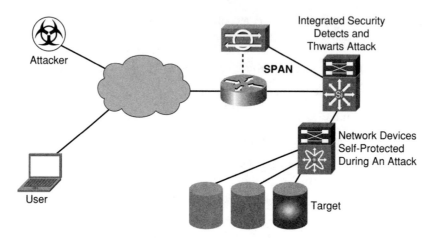

Figure 5-2   *IPS Promiscuous Mode Deployment - SPAN (Option)*

The Cisco IPS 4200 Series sensors and Cisco Intrusion Detection Services Module (IDSM-2) blade in Cisco Catalyst 6500 Series chassis support the promiscuous mode sensing interfaces using the SPAN deployment option.

SPAN or Remote SPAN (RSPAN) can be used for network traffic analysis for traffic passing through ports or VLANs by sending a copy of the traffic to one of the following:

■ Another switch that has been connected to a network analyzer, which can be an actual network analyzer or other monitoring/security device (RSPAN)

■ Another port on the switch (SPAN)

SPAN does not affect the switching of network traffic on the source ports or VLANs. SPAN copies (or mirrors) traffic received and/or sent on source ports or source VLANs to a destination port for analysis. Destination ports do not receive or forward traffic, except for traffic that is required for the SPAN or RSPAN session. The destination port must be dedicated for SPAN use. Only traffic that enters or leaves source ports or traffic that enters or leaves source VLANs can be monitored by using SPAN. Traffic routed to a source VLAN cannot be monitored. For example, if incoming traffic was being monitored and gets routed from another VLAN to the source VLAN, it cannot be monitored; however, if the traffic is received on the source VLAN and routed to another VLAN, it can now be monitored.

Figure 5-3 shows a SPAN deployment example with two Cisco IPS 4200 sensors connected to a single Cisco Catalyst switch. The switch is configured with two separate/independent SPAN sessions, with each session copying network traffic to its dedicated sensor.

SPAN session 1 monitors traffic in both directions (CLI term "both") on port GigabitEthernet 0/1 and copies it to the Cisco IPS sensor connected to GigabitEthernet 0/40. The SPAN destination port is configured to allow incoming traffic as well to allow TCP reset packets to be generated by the Cisco IPS sensor.

SPAN session 2 monitors all incoming traffic (CLI term "rx") on VLANs 12 and 13 and copies it to the Cisco IPS sensor connected to interface GigabitEthernet 0/41. The SPAN destination port is configured to maintain the original 802.1q tagging of packets when copying them to the Cisco IPS sensor so the sensor can display the source VLAN ID in its alarms.

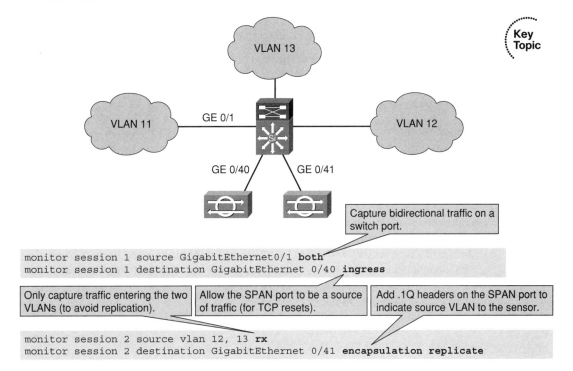

Figure 5-3   *IPS Promiscuous Mode Deployment - SPAN Examples*

Remote SPAN (RSPAN) allows LAN switches to forward copied or mirrored traffic to a VLAN instead of a destination port and use this VLAN to transport copied traffic to another switch. The destination switch copies it to its local SPAN destination port. RSPAN is typically used to centralize promiscuous mode analysis services and send captured traffic from remote LAN segments to a central Cisco IPS sensor farm, which can be used to analyze low-volume traffic flows using a low number of central sensors. In addition to the same benefits and limitations as normal SPAN capture, RSPAN has the benefit of possibly reducing the number of required sensors.

It is important to ensure that the path between the capture and analysis points is not oversubscribed so as to not drop traffic with RSPAN. Cisco IPS 4200 Series sensors, Cisco IDSM-2 in Cisco Catalyst 6500 Series chassis, and Cisco Catalyst switches support RSPAN capture when connected to SPAN ports using their promiscuous mode sensing interfaces.

The **monitor session** command is a global configuration command on a Cisco Catalyst switch stack or on a standalone Cisco Catalyst switch. The command is used to perform one of the following actions:

- Limit or filter SPAN source traffic to specific VLANs

- Start a new SPAN session

- Start a new RSPAN source or destination session

- Add or delete interfaces or VLANs to/from an existing SPAN or RSPAN session

- Start a flow-based SPAN or FSPAN session

- Start a flow-based RSPAN or FRSPAN source/destination session

- Enable ingress traffic on the destination port for a network security device, including a Cisco ASA or IPS sensor appliance

Note: The **no** keyword before the command removes the SPAN or RSPAN session and removes the source/destination interfaces or filters from the SPAN or RSPAN session, and for destination interfaces, the encapsulation options are ignored if the **no** command is used.

Flow-Based SPAN (FSPAN) is a feature that enables more granularity of captures on LAN switches using access control lists (ACL) that can select traffic that is copied to the SPAN destination port. FSPAN uses classic stateless ACLs, which can select captured traffic on a variety of Open Systems Interconnection (OSI) Layer 3 and Layer 4 criteria, such as IP addresses, ports, protocols, and so on. FSPAN has the same benefits and limitations of SPAN-based deployments. To use FSPAN, simply use the additional **filter** keyword in the SPAN session configuration command-line interface (CLI). Figure 5-4 shows an example of an FSPAN implementation.

```
ip access-list standard Capture_ACL
  permit ip any host 10.1.1.1
  permit ip host 10.1.1.1 any
!
monitor session 1 source vlan 11, 12 rx
monitor session 1 destination GigabitEthernet 0/40 ingress
monitor session 1 filter ip access-group Capture_ACL
```

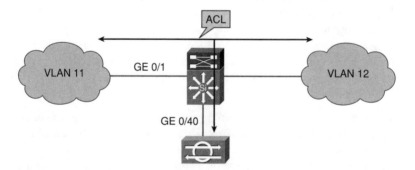

Figure 5-4   *IPS Promiscuous Mode Deployment - Flow-Based SPAN (Option)*

The Cisco Catalyst 3560-E and 3750-E switches and Cisco IPS 4200 Series sensors using the sensing interfaces in promiscuous mode on SPAN destination ports support the FSPAN feature, as shown in Figure 5-5.

```
ip access-list standard Capture_ACL
  permit ip any host 10.1.1.1
  permit ip host 10.1.1.1 any
!
vlan access-map CAPTURE-MAP 10
  match ip address Capture_ACL
  action forward capture
vlan access-map CAPTURE-MAP 20
  match ip address ANY-ACL
  action forward
vlan filter map CAPTURE-MAP vlan-list 10
!
interface GigabitEthernet 0/1
  switchport capture
```

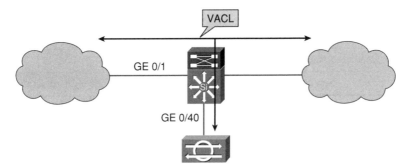

Figure 5-5   *Promiscuous Mode Deployment - VACL Capture Ports (Option)*

Another promiscuous mode deployment option supported on the Cisco Catalyst 6500 Series switches is the VLAN access control list (VACL) capture feature. The VACL feature
captures a subset of traffic in a VLAN and is functionally equivalent to the FSPAN feature. The VACL feature also allows the administrator to specify a stateless ACL to limit
the scope of capture. An administrator can specify which intra-VLAN traffic should be
copied to the VACL capture destination port by defining a VLAN access map in the Cisco
Catalyst 6500 Series switch. The destination port defined on the VLAN access map is
typically the interface on which the Cisco IPS sensor appliance is connected.

The **vlan access-map** command in global configuration mode creates a VLAN access map
or puts the administrator/user in VLAN access map command mode. The **no** command removes a mapping sequence or the entire map. Table 5-2 shows the parameters when using
the **vlan access-map** command.

Table 5-2   vlan access-map *Parameters*

Parameter	Description
name	VLAN access map tag
seq-number	Map sequence number; valid values are 0–65535 (optional)

The **match** command in VLAN access map configuration mode specifies the match clause by selecting one or more IP, IPX (Internetwork Packet Exchange), or MAC ACLs for a VLAN sequence for traffic filtering. The **no** command removes that matching clause.

Table 5-3 shows the parameters when using the **match** command.

Table 5-3   match *Parameters*

Parameter	Description
ip address *acl-number*	Selects one or more IP ACLs for a VLAN access map sequence; valid values are from 1 to 199 and from 1300 to 2699.
ip address *acl-name*	Selects IP ACL by name.
ipx address *acl-number*	Selects one or more IPX ACLs for a VLAN access map sequence; valid values are from 800 to 999.
ipx address *acl-name*	Selects an IPX ACL by name.
mac address *acl-name*	Selects one or more MAC ACLs for a VLAN access map sequence.

The **vlan filter** command in global configuration mode applies a VLAN access map. The **no** command clears the VLAN access maps from VLANs or interfaces. Table 5-4 shows the parameters when using the **vlan filter** command.

Table 5-4   vlan filter *Parameters*

Parameter	Description
map-name	VLAN access map tag.
vlan-list *vlan-list*	VLAN list; valid values are from 1 to 4094.
interface *interface*	Specifies the interface type; valid values are pos, atm, or serial.
interface-number	Interface number.

Cisco Integrated Services Routers (ISR) and Cisco ISR generation 2 (ISR G2) routers support built-in Cisco IPS modules, which support promiscuous mode operation. Similar to the configuration of FSPAN on the switches, the administrator configures a traffic-selecting ACL and the router then copies traffic selected by this ACL from specific interfaces to the built-in Cisco IPS module. An example of this can be seen in Figure 5-6. This allows very flexible traffic selection, doesn't impact network performance and availability, and is available on all routers with the Cisco IPS module. It's important to note that selecting too much traffic can oversubscribe the local Cisco IPS module.

The **ids-service-module monitoring** command in interface configuration mode, in addition to applying a standard or extended ACL to inline monitoring, configures a router interface for monitoring in promiscuous or inline mode. The **no** command clears the monitoring from the interface. Table 5-5 shows the parameters when using the **ids-service-module monitoring** command.

```
ip access-list standard Capture_ACL
  permit ip any host 10.1.1.1
  permit ip host 10.1.1.1 any
!
interface GigabitEthernet 0/1
  ids-service-module monitoring
    promiscuous
      access-list Capture_ACL
```

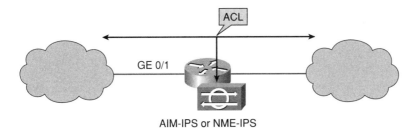

Figure 5-6 *Promiscuous Mode Deployment - Router Selective Capture (Option)*

Table 5-5 ids-service-module monitoring *Parameters*

Parameter	Description
promiscuous	Specifies that the module inspects traffic in promiscuous mode (optional)
inline	Specifies that the module inspects traffic in inline mode (optional)
access-list	Specifies a numbered or extended ACL to the inspected interface
number	ACL number

Cisco ASA (Adaptive Security Appliance) 5500 Series, Cisco ASA AIP SSC (Advanced In-spection and Prevention Security Services Card), and Cisco ASA AIP SSM (Advanced In-spection and Prevention Security Services Modules) all provide high-performance IPS analysis that is independent of the main processing on the Cisco ASA. Using the Modular Policy Framework (MPF) command-line interface, the Cisco ASA can selectively copy transit traffic to the Cisco IPS module. A key difference between FSPAN or VACL capture and Cisco ASA or Cisco router IPS module promiscuous mode integration is stateful traf-fic selection. Typically asymmetric capture leads to false negatives. The Cisco ASA avoids false negatives by specifying traffic copied to the Cisco IPS module through an ACL or other criteria. The only packet that must match in the flow is the first, while all subse-quent packets of the bidirectional flow are automatically copied to the Cisco IPS module. As previously mentioned, ACLs aren't the only method of specifying traffic. An example of an optional criteria supported on the Cisco ASA would be IP precedence or a dynamic protocol such as HTTP or FTP. It should be noted that traffic must transit the ASA to be directed to the AIP SSM, even in promiscuous mode.

ASA selective capture deployment mode, as shown in Figure 5-7, has the same benefits and limitations as other selective capture modes and is supported on all Cisco ASAs that support Cisco ASA AIP SSC and Cisco ASA AIP SSM IPS modules.

```
ip access-list standard Capture_ACL
  permit ip any host 10.1.1.1 eq 80
!
class-map IDS
  match access-group Capture_ACL
!
policy-map global_policy
  class IDS
    ips promiscuous fail-close
```

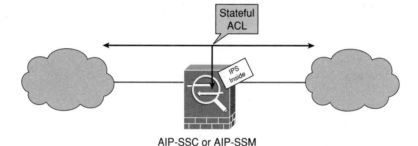

Figure 5-7 *Promiscuous Mode Deployment - ASA Selective Capture (Option)*

The **class-map** command in global configuration mode (without the **type** keyword) identifies the Layer 3 or 4 traffic to which the actions are meant to be applied using the MPF. The **no** command clears the class map from the global configuration. Table 5-6 shows the parameter when using the **class-map** command.

Table 5-6 class-map *Parameter*

Parameter	Description
class_map_name	The name of the class for the class map. The name can be a maximum of 40 alphanumeric characters. The class name is used for the class map and to configure a policy for the class in the policy map.

The **policy-map** command in global configuration mode assigns actions to the traffic identified with a Layer 3/4 class map when using the MPF. The **no** command removes the Layer 3/4 policy map from the global configuration. Table 5-7 shows the parameter when using the **policy-map** command.

Table 5-7   policy-map *Parameter*

Parameter	Description
policy_map_name	Specifies the name for this policy map up to 40 characters in length. All types of policy maps use the same name space, so the reuse of a name already used by another type of policy map isn't supported.

The **ips** command in class configuration mode diverts traffic from the Cisco ASA to the Cisco ASA AIP SSC or Cisco ASA AIP SSM module for inspection. The **no** command removes this command from the class configuration mode. Table 5-8 shows the parameters when using the **ips** command.

Table 5-8   ips *Parameters*

Parameter	Description
inline	Directs packets to the Cisco ASA AIP SSC or Cisco AIP SSM module. The packet might be dropped as a result of IPS operation.
promiscuous	Duplicates packets for the Cisco ASA AIP SSC or Cisco ASA AIP SSM module. The original packet cannot be dropped by the Cisco ASA AIP SSC or Cisco AIP SSM module.
fail-close	Blocks traffic if the Cisco ASA AIP SSC or Cisco ASA AIP SSM module fails.
fail-open	Permits traffic if the Cisco ASA AIP SSC or Cisco ASA AIP SSM module fails.
sensor [*sensor_name* | *mapped_name*]	Sets the virtual sensor name for this traffic. If virtual sensors are used, the Cisco AIP SSC or Cisco ASA AIP SSM module supports specifying a sensor name using this argument.

Multiple modes of deployment for promiscuous mode have been discussed in detail, but there are also some specific or notable features supported on the Cisco IPS. These features include the following:

- **Promiscuous delta:** An adjustable numeric value that influences reported event severity. This feature can be used to automatically lower the reported event confidence for promiscuous mode sensors.

- **VLAN tag recognition:** The ability to recognize VLAN tags received by the sensor and report them inside alarms to indicate the source of malicious or suspicious activity.

- **Integration with network devices:** As discussed in previous chapters, Cisco offers a variety of appliances and modules that allow flexible traffic selection at the traffic source without the need for additional filtering devices.

- **Multi-interface analysis:** The Cisco IPS sensor can use multiple LAN-sensing interfaces to capture traffic while presenting all aggregate traffic to the analysis engine as if it were coming from a single interface.

Deploying Sensors in Inline Interface Pair Mode

All Cisco IPS sensors are forwarding devices when deployed in inline mode. One of the simplest and most commonly deployed is the inline interface pair mode. In this mode, a sensor uses a pair of network interfaces to interconnect physical or logical (VLAN) networks and essentially acts as a wire between two network segments. All IPv4 and IPv6 traffic that is forwarded over the interface pair is inspected by Cisco IPS sensors, whereas all non-IP traffic passes through uninspected. Physical separation between networks is maintained in this mode and can't be bypassed by misconfiguration of the LAN switch.

Like the other modes, the inline interface mode has its benefits and limitations. The major benefits include the following:

- Improved accuracy and enhanced protection with the ability to modify traffic in real time (also known as normalization) to remove malicious traffic characteristics and ambiguities

- Rich preventive responses available with the sensor in traffic-forwarding mode (dropping of suspicious or malicious packets, blocking a traffic source or destination, and reliable TCP resets)

- Oversubscription of the sensor that doesn't lead to false negatives (network performance can be impacted, though)

The limitations include the following:

- Impact to network performance (especially if not correctly dimensioned)

- Impact to network reliability upon sensor failure (if path or device redundancy is not provided)

Inline interface pair deployment mode is supported on Cisco IPS 4200 Series sensors and the Cisco IDSM-2 module in the Cisco Catalyst 6500 Series switch chassis.

In Figure 5-8, there are two common examples of inline interface pair deployment mode.

In the first example (top picture in Figure 5-8), the Cisco IPS 4200 Series sensor forwards traffic between two physically unique infrastructures by connecting two physically distinct switches using two paired physical interfaces. All LAN frames are forwarded by the Cisco IPS sensor between the two switches. The switchports connecting the sensor can support either trunk or access mode. In the second example (bottom picture in Figure 5-8), the Cisco IPS 4200 Series sensor forwards traffic between logical domains on the same switch by connecting to a single switch using two paired physical interfaces. All traffic is forwarded by the Cisco IPS sensor between VLANs 11 and 12. VLANs 11 and 12 are configured on the LAN switchports connected to the Cisco IPS sensor, as seen in the excerpt in the figure.

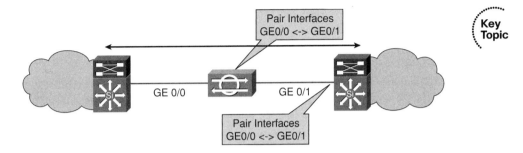

** A sensor connecting two physically separate networks or infrastructures

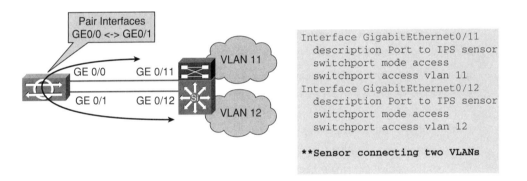

```
Interface GigabitEthernet0/11
    description Port to IPS sensor
    switchport mode access
    switchport access vlan 11
Interface GigabitEthernet0/12
    description Port to IPS sensor
    switchport mode access
    switchport access vlan 12

**Sensor connecting two VLANs
```

Figure 5-8 *Inline Interface Deployment Mode Examples*

Inline interface pair mode has the following notable features:

- **Support for UDLD (UniDirectional Link Detection):** UDLD traffic is passed through Cisco IPS sensors, which enables neighboring switches to quickly detect unidirectional links and reroute around the failure.

- **Hardware bypass:** Using hardware bypass, the Cisco IPS sensor in a failure allows the administrator to maintain network connectivity.

- **Interface shutdown on software failure:** The Cisco IPS sensor has the ability to shut down network interfaces on Cisco IPS Software failure and reroute traffic over redundant links or paths.

Note: Cisco IPS sensors also have some restrictions that include the following:

- A physical interface can be a member of only one inline interface pair.
- The command and control interface cannot be a member of an inline interface pair.

- Any combination of physical interface type of sensing interfaces is supported to include type, speed, or duplex. It is recommended that if using different media types, though, they are fully tested prior to deployment.

- Pairing a physical interface with itself in an inline interface pair is not supported.

Deploying Sensors in Inline VLAN Pair Mode

Another inline deployment mode commonly used by administrators, enterprises, and operators is known as inline VLAN pair mode. In this mode, the sensor acts as an 802.11q trunk port and also acts as a wire, performing VLAN translation between pairs of VLANs on this trunk interface/port. All traffic is inspected as it is received on each VLAN in each pair, and then can either forward the packets on the other VLAN in the pair or drop the packet if an intrusion attempt is detected. The sensor replaces the VLAN ID in the 802.1q header of each received packet with the ID of the egress VLAN on which the sensor forwards the packet. All packets are dropped if they are received on any VLANs that aren't assigned to the inline pair(s). Traffic can only use up to half the bandwidth made available by the trunk interface fundamentally because all packets cross the trunk interface twice (inbound and outbound over the same physical sensor interface).

Inline VLAN pair mode deployment is supported on Cisco IPS 4200 Series sensors and the Cisco IDSM-2 module in a Cisco Catalyst 6500 Series switch chassis.

Figure 5-9 displays an example of inline VLAN pair deployment mode with a snippet of a Cisco Catalyst switch configuration.

Interface GigabitEthernet 0/1 is configured as a trunk port, which is the port connected to the Cisco IPS appliance sensor. The Cisco IPS sensor acts as a relay or wire between VLANs 11 and 12, which are encapsulated using 802.1q. Devices or hosts on VLANs 11 and 12 are in the same IP subnet, so the sensor doesn't perform any OSI Layer 3 routing.

Inline VLAN pair mode has the following features:

- **Support for up to 255 different VLAN pairs:** The Cisco IPS sensor can be configured to simultaneously bridge up to 255 VLAN pairs on each sensing interface and the Cisco IDSM-2 Catalyst switch blade to bridge up to 255 VLAN pairs total.

- **Interface shutdown on software failure:** The Cisco IPS sensor has the ability to shut down network interfaces on Cisco IPS Software failure and reroute traffic over redundant links or paths.

Note: Cisco IPS sensors also have some restrictions with regard to inline VLAN pair deployment mode that include the following:

- Using the default VLAN as one of the paired VLANs in an inline VLAN pair is not supported.

- VLANs can only be a member of one inline VLAN pair for a given sensing interface, but a VLAN can be a member of more than one inline VLAN pair on more than one sensing interface.

- A VLAN can't be paired with itself.

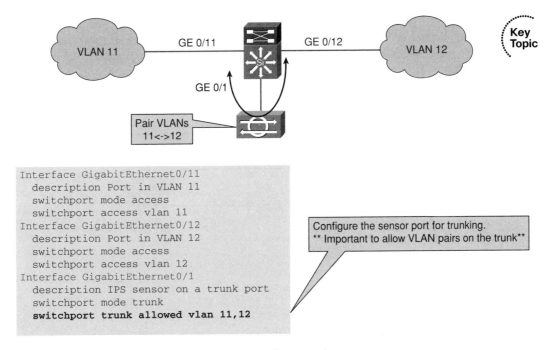

```
Interface GigabitEthernet0/11
  description Port in VLAN 11
  switchport mode access
  switchport access vlan 11
Interface GigabitEthernet0/12
  description Port in VLAN 12
  switchport mode access
  switchport access vlan 12
Interface GigabitEthernet0/1
  description IPS sensor on a trunk port
  switchport mode trunk
  switchport trunk allowed vlan 11,12
```

Configure the sensor port for trunking.
** Important to allow VLAN pairs on the trunk**

Figure 5-9 *Inline VLAN Pair Deployment Mode Example*

Deploying Sensors in Inline VLAN Group Mode

A commonly deployed inline mode, where a pair of sensing interfaces can be selectively divided or virtualized into multiple logical "wires," is known as inline VLAN group mode. In this mode, each logical wire or instance can be analyzed separately. Each physical interface in this mode can be divided into VLAN group subinterfaces, which consist of a group of VLANs on that physical interface or port. Cisco IPS sensors and modules support multiple virtual sensors on their analysis engines (the exact number supported varies by model and licenses purchased; see the datasheets available on Cisco.com). These virtual sensors can monitor traffic on one or more of these VLAN groups or subinterfaces simultaneously or separately. This gives an administrator the flexibility to apply multiple policies to the same sensor. This mode of inline deployment is often advantageous for enterprises or providers, because it allows them to use a sensor with a few interfaces as if it had many interfaces and gives them the ability to apply granular policies on trunked interfaces.

The Cisco IPS 4200 Series sensors support inline VLAN group mode.

Figure 5-10 is an example of a Cisco IPS sensor deployed in inline VLAN group mode between two Cisco Catalyst switches. Trunk interfaces are used to connect the Cisco IPS sensor to the switches, and VLANs 11, 12, 13, and 14 are the VLANs being trunked in this example. Two subinterfaces are configured/created on the physical interface pair. The first subinterface in this scenario is analyzing VLANs 11 and 12 by attaching them to a separate virtual sensor, which also means a separate analysis and response policy. The second subinterface in this scenario is analyzing VLANs 13 and 14 by attaching them to another virtual sensor, which again means a separate analysis and response policy compared to the other subinterface.

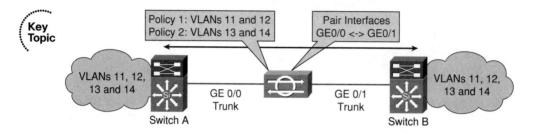

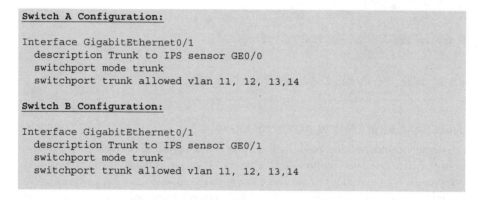

Figure 5-10 *Inline VLAN Group Deployment Mode Example*

Inline VLAN group mode has the following features:

- **Support for up to 255 VLAN groups per interface pair:** The Cisco IPS sensor can be configured to identify each VLAN group subinterface by using a number between 1 and 255. Subinterface 0 is a reserved subinterface number used to represent the entire unvirtualized physical or logical interface. Subinterface 0 cannot be created, deleted, or modified, and no statistics are reported for it.

- **Support for unassigned VLAN groups:** The Cisco IPS sensor supports an unassigned VLAN group that contains all VLANs that are not specifically assigned to another VLAN group. These VLANs can't be specified directly, but when VLANs are added or deleted from another VLAN group subinterface, the unassigned group is updated accordingly.

- **Support for native VLANs:** The Cisco IPS sensor supports packets of the native VLAN being associated with a particular VLAN group if interesting traffic is forwarded from this VLAN. Typically packets in the native VLAN of an 802.1q trunk do not have 802.1q encapsulation headers to identify the VLAN number to which the packets belong. Default VLAN variables are associated with each physical interface. Cisco recommends setting these variables to the VLAN number of the native VLAN or to 0.

■ **Interfaces can either be part of inline VLAN groups or pairs, but not both:**
The Cisco IPS sensor with an interface part of inline VLAN pairs cannot be used for VLAN groups.

Note: VLAN group subinterfaces associate a set of VLANs with an inline or physical interface. VLANs cannot be a member of more than one VLAN group subinterface.

Deploying Sensors in Selective Inline Analysis Mode

The most flexible method of inline mode is called selective inline analysis mode. This mode is available in the Cisco IPS sensor that is integrated in another network device, such as a Cisco Catalyst 6500 switch, Cisco ASA, or Cisco IOS router. The network device that the sensor is integrated into has the option of selectively forwarding a subset of traffic to the Cisco IPS sensor. If the Cisco IPS sensor does not trigger any configured aggressive response options following its analysis, the traffic is forwarded.

Selective inline analysis mode enables the enterprise or provider to granularly determine which traffic requires inline treatment, giving the flexibility to engineer the network for an optimal balance of performance and security. All other benefits of inline analysis mode are provided, but performance and availability limitations of an inline analysis can suffer if not engineered properly. The host chassis or device eliminates the limitations of high-availability and various load-balancing methods when using the selective inline analysis mode.

The Cisco ASA AIP SSC module, Cisco ASA AIP SSM module, Cisco ISR AIP-IPS and NME-IPS modules, and the Cisco ISR G2 AIM-IPS and NME-IPS modules all support the selective inline analysis mode.

The Cisco ISR and Cisco ISR G2 routers support router selective inline analysis mode in IOS Software, which can selectively forward packets selected by a stateless ACL to the IPS module. Cisco IPS modules support fail-closed and fail-open operation. When applying an ACL for selective inline analysis, administrators need to consider traffic flows in both directions to ensure optimal analysis. Table 5-9 lists the parameter used to configure a router interface for monitoring in promiscuous or inline mode. Figure 5-11 (top) shows an example of a Cisco IOS configuration that is redirecting a subset of traffic selected using an ACL to the built-in (installed) Cisco IPS module. All other traffic that is denied by the ACL in this example is forwarded without inspection.

Figure 5-11 (lower) shows a Cisco ASA with an IPS module using the MPF configuration to forward flows to the Cisco IPS module. The Cisco ASA IPS modules support both fail-close and fail-open operation. The Cisco ASA IPS modules are tightly integrated with the Cisco ASA failover capabilities and functionality.

Table 5-9 *Cisco IOS Configuration Reference*

Parameter	Description
ids-service-module monitoring [promiscuous | inline] access-list *<number>*	Configures a router interface for monitoring in promiscuous or inline mode, entering configuration mode, and applying a standard or extended ACL to inline monitoring.

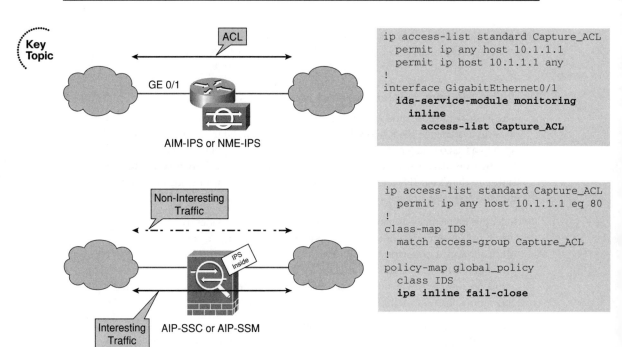

Figure 5-11 *Selective Inline Analysis Deployment Mode Scenarios*

The Cisco ASA uses the ACL or other criteria (similar to promiscuous mode) to specify traffic to be copied to the Cisco IPS module, but only has to match the first packet of a flow. All subsequent packets of the bidirectional flow are automatically copied to the Cisco IPS module. As discussed in promiscuous mode, there are other criteria that can be used for selecting traffic. The configuration scenarios seen in Figure 5-11 show a Cisco ASA MPF configuration needed to statefully redirect a subset of traffic selected using an ACL to the Cisco IPS module. All other traffic, not including the MPF class map, is forwarded without inspection. Table 5-10 lists the configuration commands shown in Figure 5-11 with the parameters or options available for each command.

Table 5-10 *ASA Configuration Reference*

Parameter	Description
class-map *class_map_name*	Applies class map actions after the Layer 3 or Layer 4 traffic type is defined in MPF.
policy-map *policy_map_name*	Specifies the name for this policy map up to 40 characters in length. All types of policy maps use the same name space, so you cannot reuse a name already used by another type of policy map.
ips [inline	promiscuous] [fail-close	fail-open] sensor [*sensor_name*	*mapped_name*]	Used in class configuration mode to divert traffic from the Cisco ASA to the Cisco IPS module being used by the administrator.

Design and Implementation Resources

There are a number of design and implementation guides available on Cisco.com. The Cisco.com Design Zone for Security section covers many design and implementation scenarios that include guidelines on Cisco IPS technologies. Guidelines available today include the following:

Cisco SAFE Reference Guide, Threat Control and Containment, at www.cisco.com/en/US/docs/solutions/Enterprise/Security/SAFE_RG/chap11.html.

Security and Virtualization in the Data Center, at www.cisco.com/en/US/docs/solutions/Enterprise/Data_Center/DC_3_0/dc_sec_design.html.

Cisco SAFE Security Solutions, at www.cisco.com/en/US/netsol/ns954/index.html#~one.

Cisco IPS 4200 Series Sensors Design Guides, at www.cisco.com/en/US/products/hw/vpndevc/ps4077/products_implementation_design_guides_list.html.

Configuring the Cisco Intrusion Prevention System Sensor Using the Command Line Interface 7.0, at www.cisco.com/en/US/docs/security/ips/7.0/configuration/guide/cli/cliguide7.html.

Summary

This section highlights the key topics discussed in this chapter:

- The various promiscuous deployment modes supported by the Cisco network IPS sensors

- The various inline deployment modes supported by the Cisco network IPS sensors

- The various resources and reference guides available on Cisco.com

Exam Preparation Tasks

Review All the Key Topics

Review the most important topics from the chapter, noted with the Key Topic icons in the margin of the page. Table 5-11 lists a reference of these key topics and the page numbers on which each is found.

Key Topic

Table 5-11 *Key Topics for Chapter 5*

Key Topic Element	Description	Page Number
Paragraph	Sensor Deployment Modes	90
Figure 5-1	IPS Promiscuous Mode Deployment	91
Figure 5-3	IPS Promiscuous Mode Deployment - SPAN Examples	93
Figure 5-4	IPS Promiscuous Mode Deployment - Flow-Based SPAN (Option)	94
Figure 5-7	Promiscuous Mode Deployment - ASA Selective Capture (Option)	98
Figure 5-8	Inline Interface Deployment Mode Examples	101
Figure 5-9	Inline VLAN Pair Deployment Mode Example	103
Figure 5-10	Inline VLAN Group Deployment Mode Example	104
Figure 5-11	Selective Inline Analysis Deployment Mode Scenarios	106

Definitions of Key Terms

Define the following key terms from this chapter, and check your answers in the glossary:

MPF, UDLD, SPAN, RSPAN

This chapter covers the following topics:

- **Cisco IPS Sensor Basic CLI Features:** An introduction to the sensor.

- **Cisco IPS Sensor Basic Configuration and Verification of Parameters:** Initialization, setup, and how to verify that the sensor is working as expected.

- **Cisco IDM Basic Features:** An introduction to managing the sensor through the web interface called IDM.

- **Cisco IPS Sensor Configuration and Verification of Interface Modes Using Cisco IDM:** Setting up and verifying the interface modes available on the sensor through the web interface called IDM.

- **Cisco IPS Sensor Basic Software Troubleshooting:** An introduction to troubleshooting the sensor software.

- **Cisco IPS Sensor Basic Hardware Troubleshooting:** An introduction to troubleshooting the physical components of the sensor.

- **Cisco IPS Sensor Restoration to Its Default Configuration:** Restoring the sensor to the factory defaults.

CHAPTER 6

Performing the Cisco IPS Sensor Initial Setup

Overview

Initializing the Cisco Network Intrusion Prevention System (IPS) sensors is the first and one of the most important steps in configuring and verifying forwarding capabilities and basic management of the sensor. This chapter will cover initial configuration, verification, and troubleshooting for deployment of the Cisco IPS sensor in an enterprise or provider network infrastructure.

This chapter begins with the initialization, configuration, and verification of the basic Cisco IPS sensor parameters. This is followed by an introduction to Intrusion Device Manager (IDM) features, configuration, and verification parameters. The chapter concludes with basic troubleshooting of the Cisco IPS hardware and the process of restoring the Cisco IPS sensor to its default configuration.

"Do I Know This Already?" Quiz

The "Do I Know This Already?" quiz allows you to assess whether you should read the entire chapter. If you miss no more than one of these self-assessment questions, you might want to move ahead to the "Exam Preparation Tasks" section. Table 6-1 lists the major headings in this chapter and the "Do I Know This Already?" quiz questions covering the material in those headings so that you can assess your knowledge of these specific areas. The answers to the "Do I Know This Already?" quiz appear in Appendix A.

Table 6-1   *"Do I Know This Already?" Foundation Topics Section-to-Question Mapping*

Foundation Topics Section	Questions
Accessing and Using the Cisco IPS Sensor CLI	1, 2
Initializing the Cisco IPS Sensor	3, 4
Introducing and Configuring the Cisco IPS Device Manager	5
Deploying and Configuring the Cisco IPS Sensor Interfaces	6, 7
Troubleshooting the Initial Cisco IPS Sensor Configuration	8, 9
Troubleshooting the Cisco IPS Sensor Hardware	10
Restoring the Cisco IPS Sensor Default Settings	11

1. The Cisco IPS Sensor Software version 7.0 permits multiple users to log in at one time. How many concurrent CLI users are supported?

   a. 3

   b. 5

   c. 10

   d. 15

2. Which of the following commands on the Cisco IPS sensor module is *not* used to access the CLI for a given sensor?

   a. session

   b. ssh

   c. telnet

   d. module

3. Which of the following key combinations ends configuration mode and returns the administrator/user to the EXEC prompt?

   a. Ctrl-Y

   b. Ctrl-Z

   c. Esc-C

   d. Esc-D

4. Which method of access can be used when initializing the Cisco IPS sensor appliance?

   a. Console port

   b. SSH

   c. Telnet

   d. HTTPS

5. Which of the following "gadgets" are present by default on the Cisco IDM home page?

   a. Sensor Health

   b. Licensing

   c. Interface Status

   d. CPU, Memory, & Load

   e. All of these answers are correct.

6. When configuring/creating inline interface pairs on the Cisco IPS sensor through the IDM, which of the following fields are required?

   a. Interface Pair Name

   b. Description

   c. Select Two Interfaces

   d. None of these answers are correct.

7. When configuring/creating inline a VLAN group on the Cisco IPS sensor through IDM, which of the following fields are required?

   a. Interface Name

   b. Subinterface Number

   c. VLAN Group

   d. Description

8. Which of the following is *not* a condition on the Cisco IPS sensor to fail-open with hardware bypass?

   a. Both of the physical interfaces support hardware bypass.

   b. Both of the physical interfaces are on a different interface card.

   c. The two interfaces are associated in hardware as a bypass pair.

   d. The speed and duplex settings on the physical interfaces are identical.

9. There is no command interrupt available for the **ping** and **trace** commands on the Cisco IPS 4200 sensor. True or false?

   a. True

   b. False

10. Which of the following are common reasons for sensor management inaccessibility on the Cisco IPS sensor?

   a. Management interface status down

   b. IP address conflict

   c. Access list misconfigured

   d. Network firewall between the sensor and the management workstation, and the firewall is blocking network traffic from the workstation

   e. All of these answers are correct.

11. Restoring default values resets the IP address, netmask, default gateway, and ACL configuration while the password and time are not reset. True or false?

   a. True

   b. False

Foundation Topics

Accessing and Using the Cisco IPS Sensor CLI

The Cisco IPS Sensor Software version 7.0 resembles the Cisco IOS Software command-line interface (CLI), but it has fewer Cisco IOS configuration commands. Administrators of the Cisco IPS sensor have full CLI capability to configure, administer, and troubleshoot with additional configuration modes and commands. You can access the CLI of a sensor appliance in one of three ways:

- SSH (Secure Shell)

- Telnet (disabled by default)

- Serial interface connection

When you first log in to the appliance, the default username is cisco and the default password is cisco. This first login will prompt you to change the default password. Cisco IPS Sensor Software version 7.0 permits up to ten concurrent users or sessions at one time.

IPS Modules

Similar to the IPS sensor appliance, administrators can access the CLI of a Cisco IPS module running Cisco IPS Sensor Software version 7.0 through SSH and Telnet. The **session** command from the host device also allows the administrator to access the IPS module. As discussed in previous chapters, the three Cisco host devices that support the Cisco IPS module running Cisco IPS Sensor Software version 7.0 are the Cisco ASA 5500 Series, Cisco ISR (generation 1 and 2) Series routers, and the Cisco Catalyst 6500 Series switches. Each platform has a slight variation of the **session** command, as shown here:

- AIP SSM and AIP SSC-5 example: asa# **session 1**

- IDSM-2 example: switch# **session** *slot_number* **processor** *processor_id*

- AIM IPS and NME IPS example: router# **service-module ids-sensor** *slot/port* **session**

To start an AIP SSM and AIP SSC-5 console session, follow these steps:

Step 1. Log in to the Cisco ASA adaptive security appliance.

Note: If in multicontext mode, use the change system command to get to the system-level prompt.

Step 2. Create a terminal session to the module:

```
asa# session 1
Opening command session with slot 1.
Connected to slot 1. Escape character sequence is 'CRTL-^X'.
```

You have 60 seconds to log in before the session times out.

Step 3.   Enter your username and password at the login prompt:

Note: The default username and password are both cisco.

```
login: cisco
Password:
***NOTICE***
<...part of output omitted...>
Aip-ssm#
```

Step 4.   Press Ctrl-Shift-6-x or enter **exit** to escape from a session to the Cisco ASA prompt.

To start a Cisco Catalyst 6500 Series IDSM-2 console session, follow these steps:

Step 1.   Log in to the Cisco Catalyst 6500 Series switch supervisor running Cisco IOS Software.

Step 2.   Create a session to the Cisco Catalyst 6500 Series IDSM-2:
```
switch# session slot 1 process 1
```

Step 3.   Enter your username and password at the login prompt.

Note: The default username and password are both cisco.

```
login: cisco
Password:
***NOTICE***
<...part of output omitted...>
idsm-2#
```

Step 4.   Press Ctrl-Shift-6-x or enter **exit** to escape from a session to the Cisco Catalyst 6500 switch prompt.

To start an AIM-IPS and NME-IPS console session, follow these steps:

Step 1.   Log in to the Cisco ISR (generation 1 or 2) router.

Step 2.   Check the status of the AIP-IPS module to make sure that it is running:
```
router# service-module ids-sensor 0/1 status
Service Module is Cisco IDS-Sensor0/1
Service Module supports session via TTY line 322
Service Module is in Steady state
Getting status from the Service Module, please wait...
Cisco Systems Intrusion Prevention system Network Module
 Software version: 7.x
<...part of output omitted...>
```

Step 3. Open a terminal session from the router to the AIM-IPS module:
```
router# service-module ids-sensor 0/1 session
Trying 10.1.1.2, 2322 ... Open
```

Step 4. Enter your username and password at the login prompt:

Note: The default username and password are both cisco.

```
login: cisco
Password:
***NOTICE***
<...part of output omitted...>
sensor#
```

Step 5. Press Ctrl-Shift-6-x to suspend and close a module session. (Entering **exit** only logs you out, but you remain in the session.)

Step 6. Disconnect from the module by entering the **disconnect** command:
```
router# disconnect
```

Step 7. Press **Enter** to confirm the disconnection:

```
Closing connection to 10.1.1.2 [confirm] <Enter>
router#
```

Command-Line Interface Features

The command-line interface (CLI) for the Cisco IPS Sensor Software version 7.0 features a few key components:

- **Command abbreviation:** The CLI recognizes shortened forms of many common commands. An administrator or user has to enter only enough characters for the sensor to recognize the command as unique. Examples include **sh ver**, which executes the **show version** command.

- **Tab completion:** If an administrator or user is unsure of the complete syntax for a command, he can enter a portion of the command and press Tab to complete the command. If multiple commands match for tab completion, nothing is displayed. The terminal repeats the line that was entered. Only commands available in the current mode are displayed by tab completion.

- **User interactive prompts:** The CLI displays user interactive prompts when the system displays a question and waits for user input. The default input is displayed within brackets. Press Enter to accept the default input.

- **Help:** Enter ? after any command to display command help. Help displays only commands available in the current mode.

- **Command history:** To recall the command entered in a mode, the administrator or user can use the up-arrow or down-arrow keys, or press Ctrl-P or Ctrl-N. The recall list does not report help and tab complete requests.

The CLI is not case sensitive, yet it does echo the text exactly as the administrator or user entered it. An example would be if the administrator or user typed the **SHOW VER** command and pressed Tab, the display would show **SHOW version**.

An interactive prompt "---More---" indicates that the terminal output exceeds the allotted display space. To display the next page of output, simply press the spacebar. To display the output one line at a time, press Enter. Press Ctrl-C to cancel the contents of the current command line and return to a blank command line without processing the command.

Features or functions can be disabled in most cases using the **no** form of a command. For example, the **service event-action-rules rule0** command adds/enables an event to the sensor, while the **no service event-action-rules rule0** command removes/disables the event from the sensor. To enable a disabled feature or function, use the command without the **no** keyword. Configuration commands that specify a default value in the configuration files can have a default form of the command. The default value is set when the default form of a command is used.

The Cisco IPS sensor CLI provides many editing capabilities; the editing keys available at the CLI of a Cisco IPS sensor are listed in Table 6-2.

Table 6-2 *Command-Line Interface Editing Keys*

Key
Topic

Key	Description
Tab	This key completes a partial command name entry. When you type a unique set of characters and press Tab, the system completes the command name. If you enter a set of characters that could indicate more than one command, the system beeps to indicate an error. Enter a question mark (?) immediately following the partial command (with no spaces). The system provides a list of commands that begin with that string.
Backspace	This key deletes the character to the left of the cursor.
Enter	At the command line, press Enter to process a command. At the —-More—- prompt on a terminal screen, press Enter to display the next line.
Spacebar	This key enables you to see more output on the terminal screen. Press the spacebar when you see the —-More—- prompt on a terminal screen to display the next screen.
Left arrow	This key moves the cursor one character to the left. When you issue a command that extends beyond a single line, you can press the left-arrow key repeatedly to scroll back toward the system prompt and verify the beginning of the command entry.
Right arrow	This key moves the cursor one character to the right.
Up arrow or Ctrl-P	This recalls commands in the history buffer, beginning with the most recent command. Repeat the key sequence to recall successively older commands.

Table 6-2 *Command-Line Interface Editing Keys*

Key	Description
Down arrow or Ctrl-N	This returns to more recent commands in the history buffer after recalling commands with the up-arrow key or Ctrl-P. Repeat the key sequence to recall successfully more recent commands.
Ctrl-A	This key moves the cursor to the beginning of the line.
Ctrl-B	This key moves the cursor left one character.
Ctrl-D	This key deletes the character at the cursor.
Ctrl-E	This key moves the cursor to the end of the command line.
Ctrl-F	This key moves the cursor forward one character.
Ctrl-K	This key deletes all characters from the cursor to the end of the command line.
Ctrl-L	This key clears the screen and redisplays the system prompt and command line.
Ctrl-T	This key transposes the character to the left of the cursor with the character located at the cursor.
Ctrl-U	This key deletes all characters from the cursor to the beginning of the command line.
Ctrl-V	This key inserts a code to indicate to the system that the keystroke immediately following should be treated as a command entry, not as an editing key.
Ctrl-W	This key deletes the word to the left of the cursor.
Ctrl-Y	This key recalls the most recent entry in the delete buffer. The delete buffer contains the last ten items that the user/administrator deleted or cut. The key will show each one at a time; thus to see all ten items, the user/administrator needs to repeat the key.
Ctrl-Z	This key ends configuration mode and returns you to the EXEC prompt.
Esc-B	This key moves the cursor back one word.
Esc-C	This key capitalizes the character at the cursor.
Esc-D	This key deletes from the cursor to the end of the word.
Esc-F	This key moves the cursor forward one word.
Esc-L	This key changes from the cursor to the end of the word to lowercase.
Esc-U	This key capitalizes from the cursor to the end of the word.

Command-Line Interface Uses

There are several tasks that the CLI can be used for:

- **Troubleshooting:** These include tasks such as verifying statistics and settings.

- **Administrative tasks:** These include tasks such as backing up and restoring the current configuration file.

- **Sensor initialization tasks:** These include tasks such as assigning the sensor IP address, specifying trusted hosts, and creating users accounts.

- **Configuration tasks:** These include tasks such as tuning signature engines and defining the ports where web servers are running.

Cisco IPS Device Manager (IDM) or Cisco Security Manager (also known as higher-level tools) are recommended to configure Cisco IPS sensor security policy and administer the sensor. That being said, you should use the CLI primarily to initialize the sensor and to perform advanced troubleshooting.

Command-Line Interface Modes

There are four primary command modes supported by the Cisco IPS sensor CLI, which provides access to a subset of commands:

- **Service mode:** This mode is a generic command mode used to edit the configuration of a service. A service is a related set of functionality provided by an IPS application. An IPS application can provide more than one service. You can enter service mode from global configuration mode by using the **service** *<service-name>* command, where *<service-name>* identifies the actual service that you are trying to access. The sensor(config-ser)# prompt denotes service mode, where "ser" represents the first three characters of the service name. See Table 6-5, later in this chapter, for specific commands.

- **Privileged EXEC mode:** Privileged EXEC mode is the first level of the CLI. Enter privileged EXEC mode by logging in to the CLI. The sensor# prompt denotes privileged EXEC mode. See Table 6-3 for specific commands.

- **Multi-instance service mode:** The signature definition service, event action rules service, and anomaly detection service are multi-instance services. Their respective configuration modes are

  - Anomaly detection mode

  - Signature definition mode

  - Event action rules mode

Enter these modes from global configuration mode by using the **service** *<service-name log-instance-name>* command. The sensor(config-log)# prompt denotes the multi-instance service mode, where "log" represents the first three characters of the logical instance name. See Table 6-6, later in this chapter, for specific commands.

- **Global configuration mode:** This mode is the second level of the CLI. Enter global configuration mode by first logging in to the CLI and then using the **configure terminal** command. The sensor(config)# prompt denotes global configuration mode. See Table 6-4, later in this chapter, for specific commands.

The **exit** command is used to exit any configuration mode or simply to close an active terminal session (which also terminates privileged EXEC mode). When you exit service mode, you are prompted to apply any modifications you have within the service mode or any subnodes contained within it. If you choose to apply the modifications by answering yes, the changes are applied to the service immediately.

Table 6-3 shows the commands in privileged EXEC mode.

Table 6-3   *Privileged EXEC Mode Commands (Administrator)*

Command	Description
anomaly-detection	Performs an action on the anomaly detection application
clear	Clears system settings or devices
clock	Sets system settings or devices
configure	Enters configuration mode
copy	Copies IP log, license key, or configuration files
erase	Erases a logical file
exit	Terminates the current CLI login session
iplog	Controls IP logging on the interface group
iplog-status	Displays a list of IP logs currently existing in the system
more	Displays a logical file
no	Removes or disables system settings
packet	Captures traffic on an interface, or displays a previously captured file or IP log
ping	Sends echo messages to the destination
reset	Shuts down the sensor applications and reboots the sensor
setup	Performs basic sensor applications and reboots the sensor
show	Displays system settings or history information
ssh	Configures SSH settings
terminal	Changes terminal configuration parameters
tls	Configures Transport Layer Security (TLS) settings
trace	Displays the route an IP packet takes to a destination

Note: User roles supported by the CLI include administrator, operator, service, and viewer. Privilege levels for each role are different; thus, the menus and available commands vary for each role. Users are discussed in later chapters.

Global configuration mode is the second level of the CLI. This mode enables you to perform global configuration tasks such as creating user accounts, configuring and reconfiguring SSH and TLS settings, upgrading and downgrading software and signature updates, reimaging the application partition, or entering other configuration modes. Table 6-4 lists various commands available in this mode.

Table 6-4   *Global Configuration Mode Commands*

Command	Description
banner	Defines a login banner
default	Resets settings to default
downgrade	Removes the last applied upgrade
end	Exits global configuration mode and returns to privileged EXEC mode
exit	Exits global configuration mode and returns to privileged EXEC mode
no	Removes configuration
password	Modifies current user password on the local sensor
privilege	Modifies user privilege
recover	Reimages the application partition from the recovery partition
service	Enters configuration mode for node services
show	Displays system settings or history information
ssh	Configures SSH settings
tls	Configures TLS settings
upgrade	Upgrades system software and signatures
username	Adds a user to the local sensor

Note: TLS (Transport Layer Security) is very similar to the SSL (Secure Sockets Layer) protocol.

Service mode is a generic command mode that allows you to enter configuration mode for various services. The service mode commands are listed in Table 6-5.

Table 6-5   *Service Mode Commands*

Command/Parameter	Description
analysis-engine	Enters configuration mode for global analysis engine options
anomaly-detection	Enters configuration mode for anomaly detection
authentication	Enters configuration mode for user authentication options

Table 6-5 *Service Mode Commands*

Command/Parameter	Description
event-action-rules	Enters configuration mode for event action rules
external-product-interface	Enters configuration mode for interfaces to external products
global-correlation	Enters configuration mode for global correlation configuration
health-monitor	Enters configuration mode for health and security monitoring
host	Enters configuration mode for host configuration
interface	Enters configuration mode for interface configuration
logger	Enters configuration mode for debug logger
network-access	Enters configuration mode for the network access controller
notification	Enters configuration mode for the notification application
signature-definition	Enters configuration mode for the signature definition
ssh-known-hosts	Enters configuration mode for configuring SSH known hosts
trusted-certificates	Enters configuration mode for configuring trusted certificates
web-server	Enters configuration mode for the web server application

Service signature definition mode is a global configuration command mode that allows you to perform such tasks as modifying signatures and using the **default** command to reset signature settings to the default settings. Table 6-6 lists the commands available in this mode.

Table 6-6 *Service Signature Definition Mode Commands*

Command/Parameter	Description
application-policy	Configures application policy enforcement parameters
default	Sets the value back to the system default setting
exit	Exits service configuration mode
fragment-reassembly	Configures IP fragment reassembly
ip-log	Configures IP log
no	Removes an entry or selection setting
show	Displays system settings and/or history information
signatures	Configures signature definitions
stream-reassembly	Configures TCP stream assembly
variables	Configures user- and system-defined variables
	Note: This text will not actually display when you ask for online help.

Initializing the Cisco IPS Sensor

To initialize the Cisco IPS sensor, you must first gain management access to the sensor through one of the following methods:

- **Console port:** Requires the use of the RS-232 cable provided with the sensor and a terminal emulation program such as HyperTerminal, Putty, and so on. As discussed in the previous section, for console access when an IPS module is involved, the **session** command is the equivalent to console access.

- **Secure Shell (SSH):** Requires an IP address that has been assigned to the command and control interface through the CLI **setup** command and uses a supported SSH client. The SSH server in the sensor is enabled by default.

- **Telnet:** Requires an IP address that has been assigned to the command and control interface through the CLI **setup** command. You must enable this IP address to allow Telnet access. Telnet is disabled by default.

- **HTTPS:** Requires an IP address that has been assigned to the command and control interface through the CLI **setup** command and uses a supported web browser. HTTPS is enabled by default but can be disabled.

Note: Sensor initialization can only be done through the console connection, and after network settings are configured, SSH and Telnet are available.

After you have access, initialization can begin. The **setup** command begins the sensor initialization process and initiates an interactive dialogue. The interactive dialogue includes the following initialization tasks:

- Assign the sensor a host name.

- Assign an IP address and a subnet mask to the command and control interface.

Note: If the IP address of the sensor is changed later, you can regenerate the certificate (self-signed X.509) of the sensor.

- Assign a default route.

- Add and remove access control list (ACL) entries that specify which hosts are allowed to connect to the sensor.

- Configure a Domain Name System (DNS) and HTTP proxy server for use with global event correlation.

- Configure the date and time.

- Configure the level of the participation of this sensor in the Cisco SensorBase.

- Enable or disable the Telnet server.

- Specify the web server port.

- Configure the sensor interfaces and virtual sensors.

- Configure threat prevention.

As discussed previously, the **setup** command is the command that starts the system configuration dialogue. You can manually enter the **setup** command to start the system configuration dialogue. The sensor automatically calls the **setup** command with the simplified setup mode when

- Sensor basic network settings have not yet been configured.

- You connect to the sensor using a console port.

The **setup** command leads to a configuration dialogue through the basic setup and the advanced setup of initial sensor parameters.

Basic setup functions require you to configure basic sensor management parameters, which include the host name, network options for the management interface, sensor participation in global event correlation and SensorBase network, and management of the sensor. The basic setup doesn't include configuring any sensing interface settings, operation mode of these interfaces, traffic analysis, or sensor response to suspicious or malicious traffic.

After you complete the basic setup mode, you can elect to save it and exit. To continue with interface and basic intrusion prevention configuration, proceed to the advanced setup mode. Table 6-7 lists the configurable settings presented by the **setup** command.

Table 6-7 *Basic* setup *Command Settings*

Setting	Description
Host name	The host name is a case-sensitive character string of up to 256 characters. Numbers, underscore ( ), and dash (-) are valid, but spaces are not acceptable. The default host name is sensor.
	Note: The CLI prompt of the current session and other existing sessions does *not* update with the new host name, but new login sessions following the change reflect the new host name in the prompt.
IP address, netmask, and gateway	The syntax for these values is $x.x.x.x/aa,y.y.y.y$, where $x.x.x.x$ specifies the sensor IP address, aa specifies the number of bits in the netmask, and $y.y.y.y$ specifies the default gateway. An example default value is 10.1.9.201/24,10.1.9.1.
Network access lists	The network ACL specifies networks that are allowed to access the sensor. If you answer yes when prompted to modify the network ACL, the current ACL entries are displayed. You are then is prompted to delete any existing entries, one at a time. Pressing Enter without entering a number retrieves the Permit prompt. To enable hosts or networks to access the sensor, they need to be defined in the ACL in the form of $x.x.x.x/aa$.

Table 6-7   *Basic* setup *Command Settings*

Setting	Description
DNS and HTTP proxy server settings	These settings are required for the sensor to contact the SensorBase network, and upload and download global event correlation information. Global correlation is discussed in later chapters.
System clock settings	Answering yes when prompted to modify the system clock settings enables you to configure Network Time Protocol (NTP), summertime settings, and the system time zone. **Note:** The Cisco IDM can be used to configure the system clock settings and sensor interfaces. The value shown in the brackets next to the prompt is the current value; to accept the default value, press Enter.
SensorBase network participation	If you agree to participate in the SensorBase network, Cisco will collect aggregated statistics sent to the IPS. This includes summary data on the Cisco IPS network traffic properties and how this traffic was handled by the Cisco IPS devices. All data is aggregated and sent by secure HTTP to the Cisco SensorBase network servers in periodic intervals. All data shared with Cisco will be anonymous and treated strictly confidential. SensorBase network participation is explained in later chapters. There are three ways to participate in the SensorBase network participation: ■ **Full:** All data is contributed to the SensorBase network. ■ **Partial:** Data is contributed to the SensorBase network, while some data considered potentially sensitive is filtered out and never sent. ■ **Off:** No data is contributed to the SensorBase network.

A summary of the administrator/user configuration is presented after the basic configuration setup is completed. The following options are presented:

0: Go to the command prompt without saving the configuration.

1: Return to setup without saving the configuration.

2: Save this configuration and exit setup.

3: Continue to the advanced setup.

Table 6-8 lists the configurable settings for the advanced setup.

Table 6-8 *Advanced* **setup** *Command Settings*

Setting	Description
Telnet server status	Can disable or enable Telnet services. The default is disabled.
Web server port	The web server port is the TCP port used by the web server (1 to 65,535). The default is 443. If you change the web server port, you must specify the port in the URL address of the web browser when you connect to Cisco IDM. The format is https://*sensor_ip_address*:*port*. (An example is https://10.1.1.9:1010.)
Virtual sensor configuration	The virtual sensor interactive prompts enable you to configure promiscuous interfaces and, if the platform supports it, inline functionality or inline pairs. This is typically configured using the Cisco IPS Device Manager and not the CLI.
Threat prevention configuration	There is a default event action override that denies high-risk network traffic with a risk rating of 90 to 100. Choosing this option gives you the ability to disable this feature. Threat prevention is usually configured using the Cisco IPS Device Manager and not the CLI.

A summary of the administrator/user configuration is presented after the advanced configuration setup is completed. The following options are presented:

0:   Go to the command prompt without saving the configuration.

1:   Return to setup without saving the configuration.

2:   Save this configuration and exit setup.

If option 2 is selected, the configuration is saved and the following warning is displayed:

```
Warning: Reboot is required before the configuration change will take effect
Configuration Saved.
Warning: The node must be rebooted for the changes to go into effect.
Continue with reboot? [yes]:
```

To make the configuration changes effective, you must press Enter to reboot the sensor.

Introducing and Configuring Cisco IPS Device Manager

The Cisco IPS Device Manager (IDM) is a web-based Java Web Start application that enables you to configure, manage, and monitor the Cisco IPS sensor. Both Microsoft Internet Explorer and Firefox web browsers are supported by the Cisco IDM. Figure 6-1 displays a sample screen shot of the IDM.

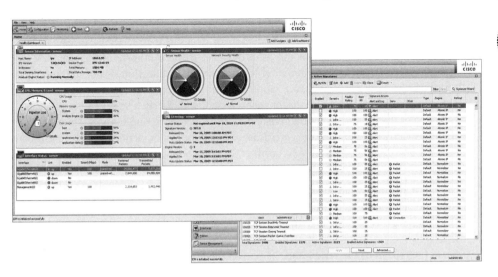

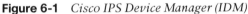

Figure 6-1 *Cisco IPS Device Manager (IDM)*

The Cisco IDM provides element management functionality for a single Cisco IPS sensor. The Cisco IDM GUI was designed to simplify the sensor configuration, management, and monitoring tasks. You can sort and view by signature ID, signature name, attack type, protocol, operating system, service, engine, and action to be performed.

A Custom Signature Wizard is a benefit of the Cisco IDM to assist you in creating new signatures. The wizard steps or guides you through the parameters that you must select to configure a custom signature, including selecting the proper signature engine.

The web server for the Cisco IDM provides transmission security and authentication using an encryption protocol known as TLS, which is enabled by default. TLS is closely related to the SSL protocol. You can disable the use of TLS, although it is highly recommended not to do this as the feature provides security for communications between the sensor and external systems. TLS is initiated by the client through a TCP connection to an HTTPS server on the target host; it provides cipher and secret key negotiation, session privacy and integrity, server authentication, and optional client authentication.

Note: HTTPS is HTTP over SSL or TLS. Cisco IDM can be used to configure the sensor to use certificates for secure communications to prove its identity to a client. The certificate is returned by the sensor when an administrator/user directs the web browser to connect with the Cisco IDM.

Log in to the Cisco IDM by opening a web browser and entering the HTTPS URL that uses the sensor IP address set up during the initialization discussed earlier in the chapter (for example, https://*sensor_ip_address*).

The Cisco IPS sensor presents you with its server certificate to prove its identity. Typically, the server certificate fails because the sensor issues its own server certificate or is a self-signed certificate. The sensor acts as its own Certificate Authority (CA), though it is not in the list of CAs trusted by most browsers as of this publication. There are three options when the security alert message appears while attempting to log in to the Cisco IDM. The first is to select No to disconnect the site immediately. The second is to select Yes to accept the certificate for the remainder of the web-browsing session. Third, you can click View Certificate to view the certificate and add the issuer identified in the certificate to the list of trusted CAs of the web browser (the web browser now trusts the sensor server certificate until it expires).

The easiest and most convenient option is to permanently trust the certificate issued. That being said, it's important to examine the fingerprint of the certificate through out-of-band (OOB) methods. Verifying or examining the certificate validity helps prevent you and your users from being a target or victim of an attacker posing as a sensor. Comparing the certificate fingerprint of the sensor and the one on the user's browser helps confirm the authenticity. You can view the certificate fingerprint of the sensor by logging in to the Cisco IPS sensor and using the **show tls fingerprint** command in CLI privileged EXEC mode.

Note: Installing and Using Cisco Intrusion Prevention System Device Manager 7.0 discusses certificate validation along with many other aspects of the Cisco IDM. You can find this document at http://www.cisco.com/en/US/docs/security/ips/7.0/configuration/guide/idm/idmguide7.html.

The final step in logging in to the Cisco IDM is entering the username and password into the GUI.

As shown in Figure 6-1, the Cisco IDM home pane contains various knobs and widgets. These knobs and widgets can quickly help the administrator/user determine the health of the sensor and get an overview of current network activity. The following gadgets are presented on the Cisco IDM home pane by default:

- Licensing

- Sensor Information

- Interface Status

- Sensor Health

- CPU, Memory, & Load

The Cisco IDM home pane can be customized by adding, removing, and renaming gadgets and dashboards. The available sensor gadgets can be displayed by clicking the **Add Gadgets** button. To display more sensor information, the gadgets can be dragged and dropped to a tab. Another dashboard on the home pane can be created to display more information by clicking the **Add Dashboard** button. The icons in the upper-right corner should be used to collapse the gadget, configure the display, or close the gadget. Follow these steps to add and customize a new dashboard:

Step 1.   Click the **Add Dashboard** button. A tab appears named Untitled.

Step 2.   Double-click the Untitled tab and enter the dashboard name on the tab.

Note: Steps 1 and 2 created/added the dashboard, whereas the proceeding steps are used to customize the dashboard.

Step 3. To add gadgets to a dashboard, click the **Home** button on the Cisco IDM toolbar and then click the **Add Gadgets** button. There are nine gadget icons that appear at the bottom of the home pane:

- **CPU, Memory, & Load:** Displays the current CPU, memory, and disk usage percentages.

- **Sensor Health:** Two meters are displayed. The Sensor Health meter indicates overall sensor health status, and the Network Security Health meter indicates overall network security status. The meters read Normal, Needs Attention, or Critical. Values or messages associated with the status can be displayed by clicking **Details**.

- **Sensor Information:** Displays the most important sensor information, including the installed IPS software version and the available memory and storage.

- **Interface Status:** Displays whether the interface is up or down and enabled or disabled, the speed and mode, and the received and transmitted packet counts for each interface.

- **Licensing:** Displays the licensing, signature version, and engine version of the sensor.

- **Global Correlation Reports:** Displays the alerts and the denied packets resulting from reputation data.

- **Global Correlation Health:** Displays the configuration status of global correlation and network participation.

- **Top Applications:** Displays the top-ten service ports that the sensor has observed over the past 10 seconds.

- **Network Security:** Displays graphs of the alert counts, the average threat rating and risk rating values, and the maximum threat rating and risk rating values over a configured time period. Every 10 seconds, the sensor aggregates these values and puts them into one of three risk categories that include red, yellow, or green. The risk value for each category in event action rules as a threshold arrangement can be configured.

Step 4. Click the tab of the dashboard that the administrator/user wants to customize, and then drag and drop the gadget he/she wants into the dashboard.

Step 5. To customize the gadget, click the Tool icon in the upper-right corner of the gadget window. The Configure Settings pane appears.

Step 6. Click the Double Arrow icon in the upper-right corner of the gadget window to hide the gadget and just display its title bar.

Step 7.   Click the X icon in the upper-right corner of the gadget window to close the gadget.

You can modify the Cisco IP sensor settings simply by opening the Cisco IDM Configuration pane by clicking the **Configuration** button on the Cisco IDM toolbar. For the most part, the majority of the Cisco IPS sensor features can be configured from here. There are four main configuration items in the Configuration pane of the Cisco IDM:

- **Sensor Management:** Configure various sensor device management functions.

- **Sensor Setup:** Reconfigure basic sensor settings.

- **Interfaces:** Configure individual sensing interfaces, as well as configure them in a particular operational mode.

- **Policies:** Configure and tune Cisco IPS security policies to achieve optimal traffic analysis and response functionality.

Note: While in the Sensor Setup pane above the main configuration items, you can observe the sets of settings of a particular configuration item.

The Cisco IDM supports the monitoring of the Cisco IPS sensor events. Click the **Monitoring** button to display the Cisco IPS sensor events, health and performance indicators, and traffic and operational statistics.

Online help is available at all stages of configuration or monitoring in the Cisco IDM. You can use the context-sensitive **Help** button on the Cisco IDM toolbar to access locally present help files on the sensor.

Deploying and Configuring Cisco IPS Sensor Interfaces

Key Topic

As discussed in previous chapters, the Cisco IPS sensor provides traffic isolation between different interfaces or interface pairs that include the following:

- **Inline interface pair mode:** In this mode, the Cisco IPS is directly in the traffic flow while the sensor receives traffic on one interface and forwards it through the other interface in the interface pair. Traffic through one interface pair is isolated from other interfaces.

- **Inline VLAN pair mode:** You can associate VLANs in pairs on a physical interface, which acts as an 802.1q trunk port. Packets received on one of the paired VLANs are analyzed and then forwarded to the other VLAN in the pair. The sensor performs VLAN bridging between pairs of VLANs on the trunk. Traffic is isolated by the physical interfaces of the sensor and 802.1q tagging.

- **Inline VLAN group mode:** You can divide each physical interface or inline interface into VLAN group subinterfaces, each of which consists of a group of VLANs on that interface. The analysis engine supports multiple virtual sensors, each of which can monitor one or more of these interfaces. Traffic is isolated by the physical interfaces and 802.1q tagging.

■ **Promiscuous mode:** In this mode, the sensor analyzes a copy of the monitored traffic rather than the actual forwarded packet. The sensor does not forward traffic received over interfaces.

The Cisco IDM allows you to set the administrative status of the sensing interfaces. By default, all sensing interface are disabled or shut down. Follow these steps to enable the sensing interfaces on a Cisco IPS device:

Step 1. Choose **Configuration > Interfaces > Interfaces**. The Interfaces pane displays a list of the existing physical interfaces on the sensor and the associated settings. The sensor automatically detects the interfaces and populates the interfaces list in the Interfaces pane.

Step 2. Select the interface and click **Enable**.

Note: The **Select All** button will select all interfaces simultaneously. To disable an interface, select it and click the **Disable** button. To edit values associated with an interface, select the interface and click the **Edit** button. The Edit Interface window opens.

Step 3. (Inline mode only) Enable at least two interfaces *if* the sensor is being deployed to do inline monitoring.

Step 4. Click **Apply** to apply the changes and save the revised configuration.

Note: All changes can be undone by clicking the **Reset** button at the bottom of the window. Reset refreshes the panel by replacing any edits that you made with the previously configured value.

Edit an interface by selecting from the Interfaces pane and clicking the **Edit** button. The Edit Interface window opens. The name of the interface is displayed to the right of the Interface Name label. Table 6-9 lists the properties associated with the selected interface.

Table 6-9 *Edit Interface Settings*

Setting	Description
Enabled	This is the state of the interface. Click the **Yes** radio button to enable the interface, or click the **No** radio button to disable it.
Media Type	This is the media type of the selected interface. The media type will be any of these: ■ **TX:** Copper media ■ **SX:** Fiber media ■ **XL:** Network accelerator card ■ **Backplane interface:** An internal interface that connects a monitoring module to the backplane of the parent chassis

Table 6-9   *Edit Interface Settings*

Setting	Description
Duplex	This is the duplex setting of the interface. Use the Duplex drop-down menu to choose one of these options: ■ **Auto:** Sets the interface to autonegotiate duplex ■ **Full:** Sets the interface to full duplex ■ **Half:** Sets the interface to half duplex
Speed	This is the speed setting of the interface. Use the Speed drop-down menu to choose one of these options: ■ **Auto:** Sets the interface to autonegotiate speed ■ **10 MB:** Sets the interface to 10 MB (for TX interfaces only) ■ **100 MB:** Sets the interface to 100 MB (for TX interfaces only) ■ **1000 MB:** Sets the interface to 1 GB (for gigabit interfaces only)
Default VLAN	Set this variable to the VLAN number of the native VLAN or to 0. If the default VLAN setting is 0, the following occurs: ■ Any alerts triggered by packets without 802.1Q encapsulation have a VLAN value of 0 reported in the alert. ■ Non-802.1Q-encapsulated traffic is associated with the unassigned VLAN group, and it is not possible to assign the native VLAN to any other VLAN group.
Use Alternate TCP Reset Interface	This is an option to have the sensor send TCP resets on an alternate interface when this interface is used for promiscuous monitoring and the reset action is triggered by the firing of a signature. Select the check box to enable this option.
Select Interface	This is the interface to be used as the alternate TCP reset interface. Use the drop-down menu to choose an interface. On all platforms other than the Cisco Catalyst 6500 Series IDSM-2, you can choose any interface except the interface that you are editing, or the command and control interface, as the alternate TCP reset interface.
Description	Enter a description of the interface in this field.

Creating Promiscuous Interfaces

You do not have to perform any action in the Interfaces pane to configure a sensing interface as a promiscuous interface. Any interfaces not selected as members of inline pairs or inline VLAN pairs are automatically considered as promiscuous, and will later be assigned to the analysis engine (virtual sensor).

Creating Inline Interface Pairs

You must configure an interface pair in Cisco IDM to use it in interface pair operational mode. Follow these steps to create an inline interface pair:

Step 1. Choose **Configuration** > **Interfaces** > **Interface Pairs**. The Interface Pairs panel is displayed.

Step 2. Click **Add** to open the Add Interface Pair window and add an interface pair.

Step 3. Enter a name in the Interface Pair Name field.

Step 4. Select the first interface from the Select Two Interface list, and then hold the Shift key while selecting the second interface of the pair.

Step 5. Optionally, add a description of the interface pair in the Description field.

Step 6. Click **OK**.

Creating Inline VLAN Pairs

You must configure an interface VLAN pair in the Cisco IDM to use it in inline VLAN pair operational mode. Follow these steps to create an inline VLAN pair:

Step 1. Choose **Configuration** > **Interfaces** > **VLAN Pairs**.

Step 2. Click **Add** to open the Add Inline VLAN Pair window and add an inline VLAN pair.

Step 3. Choose an interface from Interface Name drop-down list.

Step 4. Enter a subinterface number (1 to 255) for the inline VLAN pair in the Subinterface Number field.

Step 5. Specify the first VLAN (1 to 4096) for this inline VLAN pair in the VLAN A field.

Step 6. Specify the second VLAN (1 to 4096) for this inline VLAN pair in the VLAN B field.

Step 7. Optionally, add a description of the inline VLAN pair in the Description field.

Step 8. Click **OK**.

Creating Inline VLAN Groups

You must configure an inline interface pair in Cisco IDM and additional interface VLAN groups to use in inline VLAN group operational mode. Follow these steps to create an inline VLAN group:

Step 1. Choose **Configuration** > **Interfaces** > **VLAN Groups**.

Step 2. Click **Add** to open the Add VLAN Group window and add a VLAN group.

Step 3. Choose an interface from Interface Name drop-down list.

Step 4. Enter a subinterface number (1 to 255) for the VLAN group in the Subinterface Number field.

Step 5.   Under the VLAN Group section, specify the VLAN group for this interface by selecting one of the radio buttons:

- **Unassigned VLANs:** This lets you assign all the VLANs that are not already specifically assigned to a subinterface.

- **Specify VLAN Group (for example, 1, 5–8, 10–15):** This lets you specify the VLANs that he/she wants to assign to this subinterface. You can assign more than one VLAN (up to 4096) in this pattern: 1, 5–8, 10–15. This option lets you set up different policies based on the VLAN ID (VID). For example, you can make VLANs 1–5 go to one virtual sensor (VS0) and VLANs 6–10 go to another virtual sensor (VS1).

Note: You *must* enter the VIDs as they appear on the switch.

Step 6.   Optionally, you can add a description of the VLAN group in the Description field.

Step 7.   Click **OK**.

Step 8.   Assign the VLAN group to a virtual sensor.

Configuring a CDP Policy

All IP and non-IP traffic will pass through an inline interface pair until the interface pair is connected to the analysis engine of the sensor (the virtual sensor), which can cause it to drop some suspicious or malicious IP traffic. An exception to this rule is the Cisco Discovery Protocol (CDP), an option on the Cisco IPS sensor to configure passing or not passing CDP through the sensor. By passing CDP through the sensors, the network devices on opposite "sides" of the sensors will see each other as CDP neighbors, which can be beneficial for network manageability. Follow these steps to configure Cisco Discovery Protocol policy on the sensor:

Step 1.   Choose **Configuration > Interfaces > CDP Mode**.

Step 2.   From the CDP Mode drop-down list, choose either Drop CDP Packets (which is the default value) or Forward CDP Packets.

Step 3.   Click **Apply** to apply changes and save the revised configuration.

Configuring Traffic Flow Notifications

You can configure the sensor to monitor the flow of packets across an interface and send a notification if that flow changes (starts or stops) during a specified interval. The missed packet threshold can be configured within a specific notification interval and the interface idle delay before a status event is reported. Follow these steps to configure traffic flow notification:

Step 1.   Choose **Configuration > Interfaces > Traffic Flow Notifications**. The Traffic Flow Notifications panel is displayed.

Step 2.   In the Missed Packets Threshold field, enter the percent of packets that must be missed during a specified time before a notification is sent.

Step 3.   In the Notification Interval field, enter the number of seconds during which you want the sensor to check for the percentage of missed packets.

Step 4.   In the Interface Idle Threshold field, enter the number of seconds that an interface must be idle and not receiving packets before a notification is sent.

Note: The **Reset** option is there to refresh the panel by replacing any edits that were made previously with the saved values.

Step 5.   Click **Apply** to apply the changes and save the revised configuration.

Configuring Sensor Bypass

All Cisco IPS sensors support software bypass, which is covered later. There is a four-port GigabitEthernet card with hardware bypass as well that is only supported by the Cisco IPS 4260 and Cisco IPS 4270 sensor.

Hardware bypass complements software bypass and does not require any special configuration. The software bypass will bypass the packets through the sensor if set to On or Auto, assuming that the operating system of the sensor and the four-port GigabitEthernet network interface card (NIC) driver are functioning. The hardware bypass becomes active when the operating systems and the NIC driver are no longer running, which can result from different factors including loss of power, sensor reboot, or hardware failure. The four-port GigabitEthernet network interface card is configured not to use hardware bypass if the software bypass is set to Off or if the interfaces are paired in any other order.

Hardware bypass is only supported between ports 0 and 1, and between ports 2 and 3 on the four-port GigabitEthernet module. Fail-open hardware bypass is only supported on inline interface pairs and thus not supported on inline VLAN pairs. The conditions in which fail-open hardware bypass is available on an inline interface are as follows:

- Both interfaces are administratively enabled.

- Both of the physical interfaces support hardware bypass.

- Both of the physical interfaces are on the same interface card.

- The speed and duplex settings on the physical interfaces are identical.

- The two physical interfaces are associated in hardware as a bypass pair.

Tip: Switchports must be set to Autonegotiation on the medium-dependent interface crossover (MDIX) ports connected to a Cisco IPS 4260 or 4270 sensor. Both the sensor and switchports must be configured for autonegotiation of speed and duplex setting for hardware bypass to work. MDIX must be supported on switchports, which automatically reverses the transmit and receive lines if necessary to correct any cabling problems.

As discussed previously, there are several Cisco IPS modules available (including the Cisco ASA AIP SSM, Cisco ASA AIP SSC-5, AIM-IPS, and NME-IPS) that also support the bypass feature/function. The parent device/chassis periodically checks whether the Cisco IPS module operating system is operational. If the operating system of the sensor is functioning, and software bypass is set to On or Auto, the software bypass feature will pass the packets through the module without inspection. The parent device/chassis can be configured in two ways:

- **Fail-close:** The parent device blocks to-be-inspected traffic when the IPS module is not operational.

- **Fail-open:** The parent device/chassis continues to pass to-be-inspected traffic if the Cisco IPS module cannot be reached, and the traffic will not be inspected by the IPS module.

Troubleshooting the Initial Cisco IPS Sensor Configuration

Troubleshooting the initial configuration of the Cisco IPS sensor often starts with a common issue: the inaccessibility of the management interface of the sensor. Network issues or misconfigured sensor network settings often prevent accessing the sensor CLI through Telnet (if enabled), SSH, or HTTPS. To troubleshoot these issues, you must be connected to the sensor itself through its serial console (or using the **session** command if an IPS module).

Ping or traceroute are common tools when troubleshooting from a workstation to verify network connectivity. These same tools can be used from the sensor in addition to the **show interfaces** command or the **setup** command to verify network settings. Follow these steps to troubleshoot sensor management:

Step 1. Log in to the sensor CLI through a console or using the **session** command.

Step 2. Use the **show interfaces** command to verify that the sensor management interface is enabled.

Step 3. Use the **setup** command to make sure that the sensor IP address is unique.

Step 4. Use the **show interfaces** command to make sure that the management port is connected to an active network connection.

Step 5. Use the **setup** command to make sure that the IP address of the workstation that is trying to connect to the sensor is permitted in the ACL of the sensor.

Step 6. Make sure that the network configuration allows the workstation to connect to the sensor.

The **ping** and **traceroute** commands are tools that can be used to diagnose basic network connectivity. The sensor always sends ping and traceroute requests only over its management interface. The sensor uses a User Datagram Protocol (UDP)–based traceroute algorithm. Table 6-10 lists the **ping** parameters.

Table 6-10   ping *Parameters*

Command	Description
address	IP address of the system ping.
count	Number of echo requests to send. If no value is entered, four requests are sent. The valid range is 1 to 10,000. **Note:** No command interrupt is available for this command. (As mentioned before, pressing Ctrl-C will stop the AIM-IPS.)

Table 6-11 lists the **traceroute** parameters.

Table 6-11   traceroute *Parameters*

Command	Description
address	IP address of the system to which to trace the route.
number_of_hops	Number of hops to take. The default is four. Valid values range from 1 to 100. **Note:** No command interrupt is available for this command.

Another valuable tool/command is the **show interfaces** command, which allows you to verify that the link status is up. The management interface is the interface described as the command control interface.

A common reason for the management interface not coming up automatically is if a duplicate IP address on the network is detected. Use the **setup** or **more current-config** commands to make sure that the IP address of the sensor is unique and correct if necessary.

As discussed earlier, it's important to permit the client or workstation IP address(es) that you are using to access the sensor. This can be verified on the sensor using the **show settings network-settings** command. If the host or network IP address isn't defined in this access list, you won't be able to access the sensor.

Another common issue that often prevents access to the Cisco IPS sensor includes another device such as a firewall, router, or switch between the sensor and the workstation.

The Cisco IPS sensor appliance should forward Ethernet frames over an inline interface pair when the conditions listed here are met:

- The sensing interfaces are enabled.

- Interfaces on neighboring devices are enabled and properly configured.

- The sensing interfaces are assigned to an inline interface pair, an inline VLAN pair, or an inline VLAN group.

A virtual sensor does *not* need to be assigned to the interface pair for the traffic to be successfully forwarded.

Troubleshooting the Cisco IPS Sensor Hardware

Troubleshooting the Cisco IPS sensor hardware is necessary when troubleshooting the sensor, network connectivity issues, and so on. Typically, the Cisco IPS 4200 Series sensors are physically connected to network switches. The Cisco IPS modules do not use physical interfaces directly but are internally connected to their host device. The first step in troubleshooting hardware is to verify proper power prior to moving on to physical connectivity checks.

Three common steps apply when troubleshooting sensor interface issues:

1. Make sure that all cables are securely connected by checking the LED indicators and unplugging and plugging cables back in to make sure that they are properly connected.

2. Make sure that no cables are physically damaged and that they do not have bent pins or damaged connectors.

3. Check for configuration issues on neighboring devices.

Restoring the Cisco IPS Sensor Default Settings

You might be required to restore the sensor to its default configuration. Follow these steps to restore the default configuration to the Cisco IPS sensor:

Key
Topic

Step 1.   Choose **Configuration > Sensor Management > Restore Defaults**.

Step 2.   To restore the default configuration, click **Restore Defaults**.

Step 3.   In the Restore Defaults dialog box, click **OK**.

Note: Restoring default values resets the IP address, netmask, default gateway, and ACL configuration. The password and time are not reset. Manual and automatic blocks also remain in effect. A manual reboot is required.

Summary

This section highlights the key topics discussed in this chapter:

- Using a serial console or the **session** command to log in to a Cisco IPS sensor

- Using the **setup** command to initialize the Cisco IPS sensor

- Accessing and using the Cisco IDM as a web-based application that provides management for a single Cisco IPS sensor

■ Using the Cisco IDM to initially configure the Cisco IPS sensor interfaces in a desired operational mode

■ Using steps to troubleshoot the initial configuration and any issues related to the Cisco IPS sensor

■ If necessary, restoring the sensor to the default configuration

References

For additional information, refer to these resources:

Cisco SAFE Security Solutions, at www.cisco.com/en/US/netsol/ns954/index.html#~one.

Cisco IPS 4200 Series Sensors Design Guides, at www.cisco.com/en/US/products/hw/vpndevc/ps4077/products_implementation_design_guides_list.html.

Configuring the Cisco Intrusion Prevention System Sensor Using the Command-Line Interface 7.0, at www.cisco.com/en/US/docs/security/ips/7.0/configuration/guide/cli/cliguide7.html.

Installing and Using Cisco Intrusion Prevention System Device Manager 7.0, at www.cisco.com/en/US/docs/security/ips/7.0/configuration/guide/idm/idmguide7.html.

Exam Preparation Tasks

Review All the Key Topics

Review the most important topics from the chapter, noted with the Key Topic icons in the margin of the page. Table 6-12 lists a reference of these key topics and the page numbers on which each is found.

Table 6-12 *Key Topics for Chapter 6*

Key Topic Element	Description	Page Number
Paragraph	Accessing and Using the Cisco IPS Sensor CLI	114
Step list	AIP SSM and AIP SSC-5 Console Session	114
Step list	Cisco Catalyst 6500 Series IDSM-2 Console Session	115
Step list	AIM-IPS and NME-IPS Console Session	115
Table 6-2	Command-Line Interface Editing Keys	117
Bullet list	Command-Line Interface Modes	119
Table 6-7	Basic Setup Command Settings	124
Figure 6-1	Cisco IPS Device Manager	127
Paragraph	Deploying and Configuring the Cisco IPS Sensor Interfaces	130
Paragraph	Configuring Sensor Bypass	135
Step list	Restoring the Cisco IPS Sensor Default Settings	138

Definitions of Key Terms

Define the following key terms from this chapter, and check your answers in the glossary:

SSH, Telnet, HTTPS, TLS, IDM, NIC, MDIX

This chapter covers the following topics:

- **Cisco IPS Sensor Configuration and Verification Using the IDM:** Installation, setup, and verification that the sensor is working as expected using the web GUI.

- **Cisco IPS Sensor Configuration and Verification of the User Database and Remote Management Channels Using the IDM:** Navigating and verifying the user database and accessing the sensor through the web GUI.

- **Cisco IPS Sensor License Installation and Verification:** Installation, setup, and verification of the sensor licensing scheme.

- **Cisco IPS Sensor Software Upgrade and Recovery:** Managing, upgrading, and recovering the sensor software.

- **Cisco IPS Sensor Configuration, Installation, and Verification of IPS Signatures:** Managing and verifying the sensor signature database.

- **Cisco IPS Sensor Password Recovery:** Performing password recovery on the various sensor platforms.

- **Cisco IPS Sensor Management and Monitoring Using Both the CLI and the IDM:** Managing and monitoring the various sensor platforms through the command line or through the web GUI.

CHAPTER 7

Managing Cisco IPS Devices

Overview

Managing the Cisco Network Intrusion Prevention System (IPS) sensors is just as critical as initializing the sensors. This chapter will cover initial and periodic (or operational) management to ensure optimal performance.

This chapter begins with using the IPS Device Manager (IDM) for configuration, scheduling, and verification of the basic Cisco IPS sensor parameters. This is followed by an introduction to IPS Device Manager features, configuration, and verification parameters using the IDM. The chapter then discusses how to manage and configure the Cisco IPS sensor licenses, signatures, and software updates/upgrades using the IDM. The chapter concludes with basic troubleshooting of the Cisco IPS hardware and software followed by managing sensor health and password management using the IDM.

"Do I Know This Already?" Quiz

The "Do I Know This Already?" quiz allows you to assess whether you should read the entire chapter. If you miss no more than one of these self-assessment questions, you might want to move ahead to the "Exam Preparation Tasks" section. Table 7-1 lists the major headings in this chapter and the "Do I Know This Already?" quiz questions covering the material in those headings so that you can assess your knowledge of these specific areas. The answers to the "Do I Know This Already?" quiz appear in Appendix A.

Table 7-1 *"Do I Know This Already?" Foundation Topics Section-to-Question Mapping*

Foundation Topics Section	Questions
Managing Basic Cisco IPS Sensor Device Features	1, 2
Managing Users and Remote Management Channels	3, 4
Managing Cisco IPS Licensing	5
Upgrading and Recovering Cisco IPS Sensor Software	6
Updating Cisco IPS Signatures	7
Recovering System Passwords	8
Monitoring Cisco IPS Sensor Health and Performance	9–11

1. Telnet is not a secure access service; thus, it is disabled by default on the Cisco IPS Sensors. True or false?

   a. True

   b. False

2. Which of the following are options on the IDM GUI under the Sensor Setup pane?

   a. Network

   b. Time

   c. Reboot Sensor

   d. Shutdown Sensor

   e. All of these answers are correct.

3. Which of the following user roles permits the user access to the most features except reconfiguration of basic sensor settings?

   a. Administrator

   b. Operator

   c. Viewer

   d. Service

4. The Cisco IDM permits only one user to log in to a sensor at a time. True or false?

   a. True

   b. False

5. Which of the following is *not* a place an administrator or user can view the status of the license key?

   a. License notice at the CLI login

   b. IDM Licensing pane (**Configuration > Sensor Management > Licensing**)

   c. IDM Sensor Setup pane

   d. IDM Home window Licensing section on the Health tab

6. Which of the following are valid types of sensor images?

   a. Application image

   b. System image

   c. Recovery image

   d. Maintenance image

7. Which of the following is the time in which Trend Micro, in partnership with Cisco, pushes signature update out from signature creation?

   a. 30 minutes

   b. 60 minutes (1 hour)

   c. 90 minutes

   d. 120 minutes (2 hours)

8. Which of the following key combination(s) interrupts the boot process on the Cisco IPS Sensor to perform password recovery?

   a. Esc

   b. Ctrl-X-6

   c. Ctrl-R

   d. Ctrl-C

9. Which of the following are characteristics of the Unique Device Identifier (UDI)?

   a. It includes product version traceability.

   b. It can be retrieved through the CLI or SNMP MIB.

   c. It is guaranteed to be unique for all Cisco devices.

   d. It is a deliverable of the Cisco Product Evolution Program (PEP).

   e. All of these answers are correct.

10. Which of the following commands displays the current state of sensor devices?

   a. show events

   b. show statistics (this command needs the virtual-sensor argument)

   c. show inventory

   d. show interfaces

11. Which of the following meters are displayed on the Health Dashboard pane by default?

   a. Inspection Load

   b. CPU Usage

   c. Memory Usage

   d. Disk Usage

   e. All of these answers are correct.

Foundation Topics

Managing Basic IPS Sensor Device Features

The Cisco IPS Sensor Software version 7.0 includes the following basic management features:

- **Reconfiguring basic network settings:** These settings are typically configured during the initial sensor provisioning, but as network and infrastructure changes occur, reconfiguration might be necessary.

- **Configuring time and time zone:** The ability to configure the time, time zone, and daylight saving time (DST) is critical for many reasons, including logging, accurate monitoring and response, and so on.

- **Scheduling sensor reboots:** Typically required for maintenance or through a troubleshooting process.

- **Viewing the sensor local event log:** The ability to view the sensor's local event log to analyze events that can indicate suboptimal operation.

Reconfiguring Basic Network Settings

In most cases, the **setup** command was used during initial sensor setup to set basic sensor parameters. To reconfigure these parameters or set additional basic parameters, the administrator or user can use the Cisco IPS Device Manager (IDM).

The sensor must be initialized by using the CLI **setup** command before using the **Configuration > Sensor Setup** pane in the Cisco IDM to further configure the sensor. After the sensor is initialized, the administrator or user can communicate with the Cisco IDM, and the network and communication parameter values will appear on the Network panel of the Cisco IDM. The basic network settings and parameters can be modified from this panel, which can be accessed by choosing **Configuration > Sensor Setup > Network**. The fields and check boxes that can be seen on the Network panel are listed in Table 7-2.

Table 7-2 *Configuration Parameters Available on the Network Panel of the Cisco IDM*

Parameter	Description
Hostname	This is the name of the sensor. The hostname can be a string of 1 to 64 characters including letters (lowercase/uppercase), numbers, and special characters. The default is "sensor."
	Note: If the name contains a space or exceeds the 64 alphanumeric characters, you will receive an error message.
IP Address	This is the IP address of the sensor. The default is 192.168.1.2.
Network Mask	This is the mask corresponding to the IP address. The default is 255.255.255.0.
Default Route	This is the default gateway address. The default is 192.168.1.1.

Table 7-2 *Configuration Parameters Available on the Network Panel of the Cisco IDM*

Parameter	Description
Allow Password Recovery	Enables password recovery. The default is enabled.
Enable TLS/SSL	This enables Transport Layer Security (TLS) and Secure Sockets Layer (SSL) in the web server. The default is enabled.
Web Server Port	This is the TCP port used by the web server. The default is 443 for HTTPS. **Note:** If the value entered is outside the range of 1 to 65535, you will get an error message.
DNS/Proxy Setting	Lets you configure either an HTTP proxy server or Domain Name System (DNS) server to support global correlation. Global correlation is discussed in detail later in the certification guide. The following DNS/proxy settings are available: ■ **DNS Primary:** Lets the admin/user enter the primary DNS server IP address. ■ **DNS Secondary:** Lets the admin/user enter the secondary DNS server IP address. ■ **DNS Tertiary:** Lets the admin/user enter the tertiary DNS server IP address. ■ **HTTP Proxy Server:** Lets the admin/user enter a proxy server IP address. ■ **HTTP Proxy Port:** Lets the admin/user enter the port number for the proxy server. **Note:** If/when using DNS server, there must be at least one DNS server configured and reachable for global correlation updates to be successful. DNS queries are sent to the first server in the list, and when unreachable, go to the next in the configured list. **Caution:** The DNS server or HTTP proxy server *must* be configured at all times for global correlation to function, and DNS resolution is supported *only* for accessing the global correlation update server.
Enable Telnet	This enables or disables Telnet for remote access. Telnet is disabled by default; however, Secure Shell (SSH) is always running on the sensor (unlike Telnet, SSH is a secure service).

Configuring Time and Time Zone

The Cisco IP Sensor requires a reliable time source to time-stamp its errors or intrusion events. All events should have the correct Coordinated Universal Time (UTC) and local time stamp. Inaccurate time often leads to inaccurate and inefficiently analyzing and correlating events after suspicious or malicious activity. Sensor appliances have two methods to set their time:

■   Using Network Time Protocol (NTP) on the sensor appliance with a reliable NTP server.

■   Using the **clock set** command from the Cisco IPS CLI to manually set the time.

Cisco recommends configuring the sensor to get its time from an NTP time synchronization source when possible. NTP authentication requires the NTP server IP address, NTP server key ID, and the key value from the NTP server administrator. Unauthenticated NTP is supported as well and only requires the IP address of the NTP server. NTP typically is set up on the appliance during initialization, or it can be configured on the Time panel in the Cisco IDM.

IPS modules obtain their time from their parent devices (Cisco Catalyst 6500 Supervisor module, ISR/ISR G2 routers, or Cisco ASA 5500 appliances) in which they are installed, or from an NTP server. Cisco recommends synchronizing the parent device with a reliable NTP source followed by synchronizing the module to the parent device.

Saving a bad NTP configuration is not allowed by the Cisco IPS Sensor because of the nt-pdate utility of the sensor testing the NTP server reachability when an admin/user attempts to apply an NTP configuration. If an error is produced by the ntpdate utility, the sensor reruns the ntpdate with a debug option. The MainApp then parses the **debug** output and returns one of the following errors:

■   Sensor command and control interface are not activated.

■   Authentication failed – invalid NTP key value or ID.

■   Cannot connect to NTP server or NTP server is not running.

When configuring NTP basic settings, you have several implementation choices. NTP associations can be authenticated or unauthenticated. Typically you implement authentication for NTP when going over untrusted networks. Unauthenticated NTP can be used if the entire network path between the sensor and the NTP server is trusted. Another commonly configured option is DNS and proxy settings. If global event correlation is used, these options are necessary. If an HTTP proxy server is the only method of Internet access, you need to use a proxy server.

Note: Configuring a proxy server does *not* affect any other sensor HTTP connectivity features such as signature updates and so on.

NTP can also be configured using the Cisco IDM, which can be accessed by choosing the **Configuration > Sensor Setup > Time** panel. The date, time, time zone, and daylight saving time (DST) settings can also be configured using the Time panel, as shown in the following steps:

Step 1.   Click **Configuration** and choose **Sensor Setup > Time**. The Time panel is displayed.

Step 2.   Choose the current month, day, and year from the Sensor Local Date drop-down menus. The default is January 1, 1970.

Note: The Date and Time fields are disabled if the sensor does not support these fields or if the admin/user has configured NTP settings on the sensor.

Step 3.   Enter the current time in the Sensor Local Time fields in the format *hh:mm:ss*. This indicates the current time on the sensor. The default is 00:00:00.

Step 4.   Complete the following steps under Standard Time Zone:

- From the Zone Name drop-down menu, select a time zone or create one. The default is UTC.

- Enter the offset from UTC in minutes in the UTC Offset field. The default is 0. The field automatically populates if a predefined time zone name is selected.

Step 5.   To configure the NTP server at the time source, complete the following steps:

- Enter the IP address of the NTP server in the IP Address field.

- If authentication is required, select the Authenticated NTP radio button.

- Enter the key of the NTP server in the Key field.

- Enter the key ID of the NTP server in the Key ID field. The acceptable values for this field are from 1 to 65535.

Step 6.   If using unauthenticated NTP, select **Unauthenticated NTP**.

Step 7.   (Optional) If configuring summertime settings, select the Enable Summertime check box and then click **Configure Summertime**. The Enable Summertime check box is not selected, and the **Configure Summertime** button is disabled by default.

Step 8.   Click **Apply** to apply the configuration.

You can confirm the NTP configuration and see whether the sensor is synchronized with the NTP server by using the **show statistics host** command. NTP synchronization often takes a few minutes between the sensor and the NTP server.

The system clock can be displayed through the **show clock** command. The system clock indicates whether the time is authoritative or believed to be accurate. An asterisk in the output indicates that the time is not authoritative. With NTP set to on, the sensor time is believed to be accurate.

Scheduling Sensor Reboots

The Cisco IPS Sensor might require a reboot during the maintenance or troubleshooting process. Follow these steps to reboot the sensor:

Step 1.   Choose **Configuration > Sensor Management > Reboot Sensor**. The Reboot Sensor panel is displayed.

Step 2.   Click the **Reboot Sensor** button.

Step 3.   Click **OK** to shut down and restart the sensor.

Note: There is a 30-second delay during which users who are logged in to the CLI are notified that the sensor applications are going to shut down.

In some cases, it's necessary to shut down or power down the sensor, as shown in the following steps:

Step 1.   Choose **Configuration > Sensor Management > Shut Down Sensor**. The Shut Down Sensor panel is displayed.

Step 2.   Click the **Shut Down Sensor** button.

Step 3.   Click **OK** to shut down the sensor (applications and any open connections to the sensor will close).

Note: There is a 30-second delay during which users who are logged in to the CLI are notified that the sensor applications are going to shut down.

Viewing the Local Sensor Events Log

The Cisco IPS Sensor has a local event store that has a circular buffer (first in, first out). The event store permanently stores a certain number of events, which is dependent on the platform size. Events stored include both notable system events and IPS intrusion events. System events include things like operation errors, which can assist in troubleshooting. The steps to view system events (not intrusion events) generated by the sensor are as follows:

Step 1.   Navigate to the **Monitoring > Events** pane.

Step 2.   Select the filter choices in the Events pane. Filter choices can be based on things such as event severity, types of events, number of events per page, and time consideration.

Step 3.   Click the **View** button. An event view window will open displaying all events in the selected time frame or desired event properties.

When using the CLI, you can use the **more** command to display the entire sensor configuration. The **more begin**, **more exclude**, and **more include** commands limit the output of the **more** command. The configuration guide at Cisco.com provides more detail on the **more** command parameters.

Another common command used through the CLI is the **copy** command, which can be used to make a snapshot of the configuration. The **copy** command allows you to copy the current configuration to a backup configuration and restore the current configuration from a backup. The syntax and parameters for the **copy** command are covered in the configuration guide at Cisco.com. The **copy** command can also be used to transfer a configuration file to or from another host system using FTP or Secure Copy Protocol (SCP), or to copy log files to another host system.

Managing Users and Remote Management Channels

Typically, when managing the user database of a Cisco IPS Sensor and its remote management channels, there are a few main configuration and administration tasks to keep in mind:

- **Creating, deleting, and modifying local user accounts:** An administrative task in the local user database, which includes the creation, deletion, and modification of user accounts (including password management and privilege-level assignment).

- **Managing the sensor's authentication credentials:** The sensor uses its authentication credentials to authenticate itself to remote management systems and users. This involves the management of the sensor's Rivest, Shamir, and Adelman (RSA) key-pairs and X.509 certifications (RSA for SSH and X.509 for HTTPS).

- **Managing remote management access rules:** This includes the management of access rules that govern the availability of management protocols and limit management access to the sensor based on client IP addresses.

Sensor Local User Accounts

You must log in to the sensor using a locally configured user account to configure or view/pull events from the event store. Users can be created or deleted from either the CLI or the Cisco IDM. User accounts are associated with a role that determines the privileges of the user. There are four user roles supported on the Cisco IPS:

- **Administrator:** This user role has the highest level of privileges. The administrator role has unrestricted view access and can perform the following functions:
  - Enabling and disabling physical interfaces
  - Assigning physical monitoring interfaces to a virtual sensor
  - Modifying sensor address configuration
  - Adding and deleting users and modifying passwords
  - Modifying the list of hosts allowed to connect to the sensor
  - Adding and deleting users and modifying passwords
  - Tuning signatures
  - Managing blocking devices

- **Operator:** This user role has the second-highest level of privileges. The operator role can view all configuration and events and can perform the following functions:

  - Changing their own user passwords

  - Tuning signatures

  - Managing blocking devices

- **Viewer:** This user role has the lowest level of privileges. The viewer role can view configuration and events. Viewers can't modify any configuration data except their own passwords.

- **Service:** This is a special role that allows the user to log in to the native operating system shell.

Note: The service role should only be used under direction of Cisco TAC.

The service account role allows the Cisco Technical Assistance Center (TAC) to log in to the sensor's native operating system (which is Linux) shell for troubleshooting purposes. The role is intended to support troubleshooting only and is not intended to support configuration. Only one user account is permitted/allowed to have the service role. The service account does not exist by default on a sensor, so it must be created by the administrator for TAC to use during troubleshooting. Cisco recommends that this account be deleted after a troubleshooting session.

The user with the service role cannot log in to the Cisco IDM and does not have direct access to the sensor CLI. The service role logs directly into a Linux Bash shell when accessing the CLI. Root access to the sensor is possible only if you log in to the service account and use the **su** command to access the root account. If the password of the service account is set or reset, the password of the root account is automatically set to the same password. After the service account is removed, the password of the root account is locked.

Note: Cisco recommends against making modifications to the sensor through the service account except under direction from TAC. Modifications to the sensor through the service account are considered unauthorized modifications (that is, *not* supported) and require the sensor to be reimaged to guarantee proper operations.

Create a user account in the sensor's local user database by following these steps:

Step 1.   Navigate to the **Configuration > Sensor Setup > Users** pane.

Step 2.   Click **Add**. The Add User window opens.

Step 3.   Enter a username in the Username field. A valid username is a string of 1 to 64 characters long. It must begin with an alphanumeric character.

Step 4.   Select one of the options from the User Role drop-down menu: Administrator, Operator, Viewer, or Service.

Step 5.   Enter the password for the user in the Password field. A valid password is 6 to 32 characters long. All characters except a space and a question mark (?) are allowed.

Step 6.   Enter the password again in the Confirm Password field.

Step 7.   Click **OK**. The Users panel becomes active. The new user account is displayed in the Users panel. The Role column displays the role of the user, and the Status column displays the account status (active, expired, or locked).

Step 8.   Click **Apply** to apply your changes and save the revised configuration.

To delete an existing account from the user list, choose the account and click **Delete**. To edit an existing user account, choose the account from the users list and click **Edit**. The Edit User dialog box appears after clicking **Edit**, which enables you to change the user role and password. To undo any changes made, click **Reset**, which refreshes the panel by replacing any edits that you made with the previously configured value.

Managing the Sensor's Authentication Credentials

Cisco IPS Sensor Software version 7.0 supports creating and tuning password complexity policies that are enforced upon local accounts. Navigate to **Configuration** > **Sensor Management** > **Passwords** to access a variety of rules that can increase authentication strength for management connections.

Secure Shell (SSH) is the primary method used by the Cisco IPS Sensor to allow CLI access to remote terminal users. SSH requires the use of an RSA keypair, which authenticates the sensor to the remote administrative user. The SSH host public key of the sensor can be displayed by navigating to **Configuration** > **Sensor Management** > **SSH** > **Sensor Key**. The Sensor Key panel displays the sensor SSH host key fingerprint. The fingerprint can be used to validate the public key that is sent in the clear during initial SSH contact with the sensor. The SSH client will present an SSH public key fingerprint when connecting to the sensor for the first time. The fingerprint must match the fingerprint observed in the IDM. If the key gets corrupted for any reason, follow these steps to generate (or regenerate) a new sensor SSH host key:

Step 1.   Click **Generate Key**. A dialog box appears with a warning, asking if you want to continue.

Step 2.   Click **OK** to continue. A new host key is generated, and the old host key is deleted. You are then prompted to reboot the sensor.

Step 3.   Reboot the sensor.

Much like SSH host keys, the sensor uses an RSA key pair and an associated certificate to authenticate itself in HTTPS management sessions. A self-signed server certificate is generated by the sensor when it first starts. The Server Certificate panel in Cisco IDM displays MD5 fingerprints of the self-signed X.509 certificate. This certificate is verified using this fingerprint at the start of an HTTPS connection to verify that the connection is authentic. To display the server certificate of the sensor, navigate to **Configuration > Sensor Management > Certificates > Server Certificate**. If the certificate gets corrupted for any reason, follow these steps to generate a new self-signed X.509 server certificate:

Step 1.   Click the **Generate Certificate** button within the Server Certificate panel. A dialog box appears with a warning, asking if you want to continue.

Step 2.   Click **OK** to continue. A new server certificate is generated, and the old server certificate is deleted.

The **banner** login command can be used to create a login banner that is displayed before the user and password login prompts in Telnet and SSH sessions. The maximum length is 2500 characters. The configuration guide at Cisco.com provides more detail on the steps to configure the banner parameters.

Managing Remote Management Access Rules

Cisco recommends that you only enable the management interfaces that you plan on using to decrease the sensor's attack surface. HTTPS and Telnet access can be disabled or enabled from the Cisco IDM by navigating to **Configuration > Sensor Setup > Network**. SSH access cannot be disabled unless you disable all access to the sensor using IP address-based rules.

The **setup** command interactive dialog prompts you to permit hosts or networks to access the sensor. If hosts or networks are not permitted, no hosts are able to communicate with the sensor. All inbound packets on the command and control interface are denied in Cisco IPS Sensor Software version 7.0 except for the following:

- Packets on established connections

- Packets originating from addresses in the access list

- Packets originating from a Network Time Protocol (NTP) server

From the Cisco IDM, the admin/user can specify hosts and networks that have permission to access the sensor. Follow these steps to specify the hosts and networks permitted to access the sensor:

Step 1.   Navigate to **Configuration > Sensor Setup > Allowed Hosts/Networks**. The Allowed Hosts/Networks panel is displayed.

Step 2.   Click **Add** to add a host or network to the list. The Add Allowed Host window opens. Up to 512 hosts are allowed.

Step 3.   Enter the IP address of the host or network in the IP Address field. An error message is generated if the IP address is already included as part of an existing list entry.

Step 4.   Select the proper network mask from the Network Mask drop-down menu. An error message is generated if the network mask does not match the IP address.

Step 5.   Click **OK**. The new host or network appears in the allowed hosts list on the Allowed Hosts panel.

Verify remote management access using the appropriate clients already discussed, which includes a Telnet client, SSH client, and web browser for HTTPS.

Managing Cisco IPS Licensing

The Cisco IPS Sensor functions without a license key, but to obtain signature updates, a license key is required. A Cisco Services for IPS service contract is required to obtain the license. Trial license keys are available if needed as well. The license can be obtained from the Cisco.com licensing server, which is then delivered to the sensor. Another option to update the license is to use a license key provided in a local file (located on a server or PC).

The Cisco IPS device serial number is required to obtain the license key. The serial number can be displayed through the CLI with the **show version** command or through the Cisco IDM by navigating to the **Configuration > Sensor Management > Licensing Pane**. The status of the license key can be displayed from the Licensing panel of the Cisco IDM. You are informed of the license status when the Cisco IDM is started or when entering the CLI.

As stated previously, a Cisco Services for IPS service contract is required to download a valid license key and obtain the latest IPS updates. The IPS and ASA 5500 Series products that fall within this requirement include the following:

- IPS-4240
- IPS-4255
- IPS-4260
- IPS-4270-20
- AIM-IPS
- NME-IPS
- IDSM-2
- ASA5510-AIP10-K9
- ASA5520-AIP10-K9
- ASA5520-AIP20-K9
- ASA5540-AIP40-K9
- ASA5520-AIP40-K9
- ASA5540-AIP40-K9
- ASA-SSM-AIP-10-K9=
- ASA-SSM-AIP-20-K9=
- ASA-SSM-AIP-40-K9=

Install the license key directly from Cisco.com by following these steps:

Step 1.   Log in to the Cisco IDM with administrator privileges.

Step 2.   Navigate to **Configuration** > **Sensor Management** > **Licensing**. The Licensing pane displays the status of the current license.

Step 3.   Click the **Cisco.com** radio button to obtain the license from Cisco.com. The Cisco IDM contacts the license server at Cisco.com and sends the server the serial number to obtain the license key. This is the default method.

Step 4.   Click **Update License**, and in the Licensing dialog box, click **Yes** to continue. The Status dialog box informs you that the sensor is trying to connect to Cisco.com. An information dialog box confirms that the license key has been updated.

Step 5.   Click **OK**.

Install the license key directly from a local file by following these steps:

Step 1.   Go to http://www.cisco.com/go/license.

Step 2.   Fill in the required fields.

Step 3.   Download and save the license key directly to a hard drive or a network drive that the client running IDM can access.

Step 4.   Log in to IDM using administrator privileges.

Step 5.   Navigate to **Configuration** > **Sensor Management** > **Licensing**.

Step 6.   Click the **License File** radio button.

Step 7.   In the Local File Path field, specify the path to the license file or click **Browse Local** to browse to the file.

Step 8.   Browse to the license file and click **Open**.

Step 9.   Click **Update License**.

Install the license key from the CLI by following these steps:

Step 1.   Go to http://www.cisco.com/go/license.

Step 2.   Fill in the required fields.

Step 3.   Download and save the license key directly to a hard drive or a network drive that has a web server, FTP server, or Secure Copy Protocol (SCP) server.

Step 4.   Log in to the CLI using administrator privileges.

Step 5.   Copy the license key to the sensor using **copy source-url** *license_file_name* **license-key** *<password>*.

Step 6.   Verify that the sensor is licensed using the **show version** command.

The status of the license key can be found in three places:

■   License notice at CLI login

- IDM Licensing pane (**Configuration > Sensor Management > Licensing**)

- IDM Home window Licensing section on the Health tab

As you start the IDM or log in through the CLI, you are informed of the license status. This occurs regardless of whether you have a trial, invalid, or expired license key. If there is a valid license key, the option to click **Download** on the License pane is available to download a copy of the license key to the computer on which the IDM is running and save it to a local file.

Upgrading and Recovering Cisco IPS Sensor Software

There are a few different types of sensor images, which are listed as follows:

Key Topic

- **Recovery image:** The application image plus an installer to be used for recovery

- **Application image:** The image used for operating the sensor

- **System image:** The full IPS application and recovery image used for reimaging an entire sensor

- **Service Update image:** Signature update file

- **Service Pack image:** Normal sensor upgrade (service pack)

Note: If the sensor is unusable after installing an update and it reboots, the only way to recover the sensor is to reimage it from scratch.

Table 7-3 lists the Cisco IPS Sensor Software naming convention as seen on the sensor image name, shown later in Figure 7-1. This is important to know or reference when troubleshooting, installing, upgrading, or recovering the sensor software.

Table 7-3   *Cisco IPS Sensor Software Image Naming Convention*

Image Part/Section Name	Description
IPS	Specifies the product line.
K9	Indicates strong cryptography.
Major Version Level	Specifies major version—for example, 7.
Minor Version Level	Specifies minor version—for example, 0.
Service Pack Level	Specifies service pack level—for example, 2.
Repackage Level	Repackage level designator can be omitted.
Patch Level	Patch level designator can be omitted.
Signature Engine Level	Signature engine level designator—for example, E3.
Extension	The filename extension is .pkg.

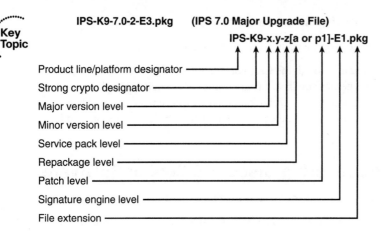

Figure 7-1   *Cisco IPS Sensor Software Image Naming Convention*

Application image updates can be applied from the Cisco IDM Update Sensor panel. The application image update can be downloaded from Cisco.com to an FTP, SCP, HTTP, or HTTPS server; then configure the sensor to download them from the server. Figure 7-2 illustrates the sensor signature filename.

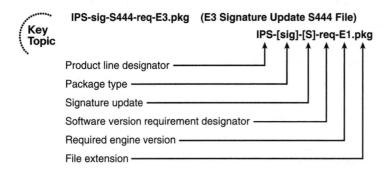

Figure 7-2   *Cisco IPS Sensor Software Signature Filename Structure*

Apply a service pack and signature update by following these steps:

Step 1.   Navigate to **Configuration > Sensor Management > Update Sensor**.

Step 2.   Choose one of the two options and complete the fields it activates:

- **Update Is Located on a Remote Server and Is Accessible by the Sensor:** Supply the following information for this option: URL (FTP, HTTPS, SCP, HTTP), username, and password.

- **Update Is Located on This Client:** This option pushes the update from the local client to the sensor. The path to the update file is in the Local

File Path field, or there's an option to navigate through the files on the local client.

Step 3.   Click **Update Sensor.** The Update Sensor window opens.

Step 4.   Click **OK.**

> **Note:**   During an update, the sensor applications are stopped, and while applying a service pack, the installer automatically reboots the sensor.

The **upgrade** command can be used through the CLI to apply a service pack, a signature update, an engine update, a minor version, or recovery partition file upgrades to the sensor. Upgrade the Cisco IPS Sensor through the CLI by following these steps:

Step 1.   Download the appropriate file to an FTP, SCP, HTTP, or HTTPS server that is accessible from the sensor.

Step 2.   Log in to the CLI using an account with administrator privileges.

Step 3.   Enter global configuration mode.

Step 4.   Upgrade the sensor from the CLI using the **upgrade** command string. An example is as follows:

```
sensor(config)# upgrade url/IPS-K9-7.0-2-E3.pkg
```

Step 5.   Enter the password when prompted.

Step 6.   Enter **Yes** to complete the upgrade.

> **Note:**   Updates and service packs usually force a restart of the IPS processes or even force a reboot of the sensor to complete the installation.

In some cases, the Cisco IPS Sensor application image becomes corrupted, in which case there are two ways to recover it:

■   **Use the** recover **command.** This method retains the sensor IP address, subnet mask, and default gateway settings.

■   **Select the Cisco IPS recovery image from the boot menu during bootup.** This method retains the sensor IP address, subnet mask, and default gateway settings and is useful if you are unable to access the CLI.

The **recover application-partition** command is used to perform an application reimage on the sensor. This command can be performed on the following IPS 4200 Sensor models: 4240, 4255, 4260, and 4270. It is recommended to upgrade the recovery image on the sensor with the most recent version so that it is ready if you need to recover the application image. Recover images are generated only for major and minor software releases and not for service packs or signature updates. The recover image file can be recognized by the *r* identifier in its name (for example, IPS-K9-r-1.1-a-7.0-2E3.pkg). The recovery image can be applied to the sensor through the CLI using the **upgrade** command.

Updating Cisco IPS Signatures

Attacks pose a threat to networks and are discovered every day (new, modified, and old). Cisco releases regular signature updates and critical updates for major attack events to enable the sensor to detect these attacks. There are also service packs to improve the intrusion prevention capabilities of the Cisco IPS Sensors.

Signature updates, major upgrades, minor upgrades, and service packs are all released independently from the other software files; thus, they have their own version capabilities. Typically, signature engine updates add new engines or engine parameters that are used by new signatures in later signature updates. Specific service packs are required for signature file engines.

Cisco and Trend Micro are partners that provide an additional signature update service that enables users to subscribe to this service, in which Trend Micro pushes signature updates to sensors within two hours of signature creation. As discussed earlier, the sensor *must* be properly licensed to accept the signature updates. Table 7-4 lists the structure of a typical IPS signature update filename using the following example: IPS-sig-S457-req-E2.pkg.

Table 7-4 *Cisco IPS Sensor Software Signature Filename Structure*

Image Part/ Section Name	Description
IPS	This specifies the product line.
Sig	This specifies the update type, which indicates the type of content contained in the file. The package type "sig" indicates that this is a signature update.
S	This is the signature version designator.
x	This is the signature update version.
Req	This is the minimum requirement designator.
W	This is the required engine version.
Extension	This is the filename extension.

Typically you will need to manually update the sensor or sensors from a remote server or from a local file. This can be done through the Cisco IDM Update Sensor panel, as discussed earlier in the steps to update the sensor software. Automatic updates can be configured on the sensor to have service pack or signature updates that reside on a local FTP or SCP server downloaded and applied to the sensor. The service pack or signature update needs to be downloaded from Cisco.com to the FTP or SCP server, and then the sensor needs to be configured to download them from the server. Follow these steps to configure automatic updates from a remote server:

Step 1. Log in to the Cisco IDM with administrator privileges.

Step 2. Navigate to **Configuration** > **Sensor Management** > **Auto/Cisco.com Update.**

Step 3. Enable automatic updates from a remote server by selecting the **Enable Auto Update from a Remote Server** check box. The following fields will need to be updated accordingly:

- **IP Address field:** Enter the IP address of the remote server where you have downloaded and stored updates.

- **File Copy Protocol drop-down list:** Choose the protocol used to connect to the remote server—for example, FTP or SCP.

- **Directory field:** Enter the path to the directory on the remote server where the updates are located. A valid value for the path is 1 to 128 characters.

- **Username and Password fields:** Enter the username and password on the remote server. A valid value for the path is 1 to 2047 characters. There is a Confirm Password field where you will need to enter the password to confirm it.

- **Hourly or Daily check box:** Select the frequency of the updates and follow the steps accordingly, depending on how often the admin/user decides to have the updates.

Step 4. Click **Apply** to apply the changes to the sensor and save them.

Another way to get automatic updates to the sensor is through Cisco.com. When enabling automatic updates, the sensor logs in to Cisco.com and checks the signature and signature engine updates. When the update is available, the sensor downloads the update and installs it. Configure automatic updates from Cisco.com by following these steps:

Step 1. Log in to the Cisco IDM with administrator privileges.

Step 2. Navigate to **Configuration** > **Sensor Management** > **Auto/Cisco.com Update.**

Step 3. Enable automatic updates from a remote server by selecting the **Enable Auto Update from a Cisco.com** check box. The following fields will need to be updated accordingly:

- The Cisco IDM prefills the Cisco.com URL field with the correct URL. A valid value for the path is 1 to 2047 characters.

- **Username and Password fields:** Enter the username and password on the remote server. There is a Confirm Password field where the admin/user will need to enter the password to confirm it.

- **Hourly or Daily check box:** Select the frequency of the updates and follow the steps accordingly, depending on how often the admin/user decides to have the updates.

Step 4.   Click **Apply** to apply the changes to the sensor and save them.

Select Details in the Sensor Health gadget to access signature update status information through **Home > Health Dashboard.** One of the following values appears according to the thresholds configured:

■   Normal

■   Needs Attention

■   Critical

Sensor health thresholds can be configured through the Sensor Health panel. There are two thresholds: Yellow Threshold (Needs Attention status) and Red Threshold (Critical status). Their default values are 30 days for yellow and 60 days for red.

In some cases, automatic update fails on the sensor, which requires some troubleshooting to resolve. Typically this is a result of settings being misconfigured, but you can use CLI commands such as the manual **upgrade** and **pack display** to troubleshoot communications between the sensor and the update server. The configuration guide found at Cisco.com provides more detail that is outside the scope of this book.

Recovering System Passwords

Most Cisco IPS Sensor platforms support password recovery; thus, the need for the service account isn't as common as in previous platforms or releases. Password recovery implementations vary according to the Cisco IPS Sensor platform requirements. Only the Cisco administrative account is permitted to perform password recovery. By default, password recovery is enabled; however, it can be disabled if required. The Cisco user password reverts back to cisco and must be changed after the next login. The following list describes the various Cisco IPS platforms and their supported password recovery methods:

■   **4200 Series sensors:** GRUB (Grand Unified Bootloader) prompt or ROMMON

■   **AIM-IPS:** Bootloader command

■   **AIP SSM & AIP SSC-5:** ASA CLI command

■   **IDSM-2:** Download image through the maintenance partition

Note: A terminal server or direct serial connection to the sensor to use the GRUB menu to recover the password is required on the 4200 Series sensors.

Follow these steps to recover the passwords on the 4200 Series sensor appliances:

Step 1.   Reboot the appliance. The GRUB menu appears. Use the arrow keys to select the desired entry and press Enter.

Step 2.   Press any key to pause the boot process.

Step 3.   Choose 2: **Cisco IPS Clear Password (cisco).**

The password is reset to cisco. You must change the password the next time you log in to the CLI.

The Cisco IPS 4240 and 4255 sensors also support password recovery from the ROM monitor CLI. To access the ROM monitor CLI, simply reboot the sensor from a terminal server or direct connection and interrupt the boot process by pressing Esc or Ctrl-R. When you are at ROM prompt, enter **confreg=0x7** and boot the sensor.

As discussed previously, you have the ability to disable password recovery if required (it is enabled by default). Follow these steps to disable password recovery from the CLI:

Step 1.   Log in to the CLI using administrative privileges.

Step 2.   Enter global configuration mode followed by host mode:

```
sensor# configure terminal
sensor(config)# service host
```

Step 3.   Disable password recovery:

```
sensor(config-host)# password-recovery disallowed
```

Note: If an admin/user tries to recover the password on a sensor that is disabled, the process proceeds with no errors or warnings; however, the password is not reset.

Follow these steps to disable password recovery from the Cisco IDM:

Step 1.   Log in to the Cisco IDM using administrative privileges.

Step 2.   Navigate to **Configuration** > **Sensor Setup** > **Network**.

Step 3.   Disable password recovery by deselecting the **Allow Password Recovery** check box.

Monitoring Cisco IPS Sensor Health and Performance

Cisco IPS Sensor platforms support health monitoring via Simple Network Management Protocol (SNMP). Monitoring sensor health and performance is critical to ensuring a secure network infrastructure. Cisco IPS Sensors all can be monitored and managed as discussed previously through the CLI and/or the IDM GUI.

Displaying and Troubleshooting the Sensor

All Cisco devices have a Unique Device Identifier (UDI) that enables the admin/user to easily and efficiently manage certified hardware versions within the provider's network. The characteristics of the UDI are as follows:

■   It is guaranteed to be unique for all Cisco devices.

■   It can be retrieved through the CLI or an SNMP MIB.

■   Methods of retrieving it are platform independent.

■   It includes product version traceability.

- It is a deliverable of the Cisco Product Evolution Program (PEP), a new architecture baseline for all Cisco products.

- It is made up of three values, which include product identifier (PID), version identifier (VID), and serial number (SN).

The UDI provides simplification of product identification and consistent product identification across products, and it gives you the ability to electronically inventory Cisco products accurately and reliably. The UDI can be displayed through the **show inventory** command on the Cisco IPS 4200 Series appliances. The output of the command varies depending on the sensor platform.

The **show version** command is used to display version information for all installed operating system packages and signature packages. It also displays the information listed here, which can be useful for troubleshooting the following information:

- Serial number

- License information

- Platform

- Memory usage

- Upgrade history

- IPS processes running on the system

- Recovery partition information (only available for the appliances)

Another very useful troubleshooting command is the **show statistics** *<sub-command>* command, which provides a snapshot of the current internal state of the sensor services and statistics. For specific parameters for this and other commands, see the configuration guide found at Cisco.com.

The **show interfaces** command displays statistics for all sensor interfaces. Statistics for all interfaces can be displayed simultaneously or for specific interfaces. The **clear** option clears statistics that can be reset, which can be very useful while troubleshooting.

Events are the data generated by the sensor applications. An example of events would include the alerts produced by the SensorApp or errors caused by an application. There are four types of events:

- **evError:** Application errors

- **evIdsAlert:** Intrusion detection alerts

- **evShunRqst:** Shun requests

- **evStatus:** Status changes, such as a software upgrade being completed

Events are stored in the sensor event store, where they remain until they are overwritten by newer events. An existing event isn't overwritten until 30 MB of newer events are generated. From the top-level prompt of the CLI, events can be displayed through the **show events** command. This command displays requested event types beginning at the requested start time. If a specific start time isn't entered, all events are displayed.

The one command that allows information to be transferred to a remote system is the **show tech-support** command, which captures all status and configuration information on the sensor. The output includes HTML-linked output from the following commands and is often very large:

- **cidDump**

- **show interfaces**

- **show statistics network-access**

Monitoring Sensor Health and Performance

The Sensor Health meter in the Sensor Health gadget enables the admin/user to access the sensor health. The Health meter indicates three possible health statuses:

- Green (normal)

- Yellow (needs attention)

- Red (critical)

The Health status is calculated based on configurable metrics. To view sensor health details, click **Details** in the Sensor Health meter. A new window opens, displaying individual metric status. The metric values are displayed together with yellow and red threshold values. Navigate to **Configure Sensor Health Metrics** in the Sensor Health meter details, or choose **Configuration > Sensor Management > Sensor Health**.

The Sensor Information gadget displays analysis engine status. Unless the analysis engine is initializing or being reconfigured, the status reads Running Normally.

The Health Dashboard, as shown in Figure 7-3, can be displayed by navigating to **Home > Health Dashboard** on the Cisco IDM.

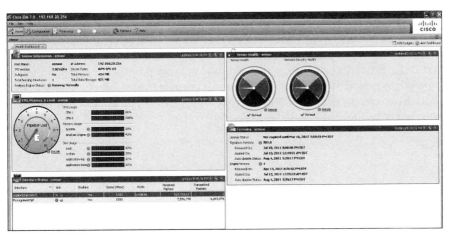

Figure 7-3 *Cisco IPS Sensor IDM Sensor Health Dashboard (Home > Health Dashboard)*

The CPU, Memory, and Load gadget allows the admin/user to quickly assess resource usage on the sensor. The gadget displays the following meters:

- **CPU Usage:** Indicates how much of the CPU of the sensor is being used.

- **Inspection Load:** Indicates how much traffic inspection capacity the sensor is using, which can be affected by a number of factors, including the rate of traffic that needs inspection, the type of traffic being inspected, the rate of new connections per second, the rate of attacks being detected, the custom signatures created, the active signatures, and the number of active connections being inspected.

- **Memory Usage:** Indicates the memory being used by the system and analysis engine.

- **Disk Usage:** This includes the application data and boot image (and includes the recovery image too).

There is also a Statistics panel, which shows statistics for the Analysis Engine, Event Server, Event Store, Host, Interface Configuration, Network Access, Logger, Notification, Transaction Source and Server, and Web Server. To display the Statistics panel from the Cisco IDM, navigate to **Monitoring > Support Information > Statistics**. The page can be refreshed by clicking **Refresh**.

Diagnostic information about the sensor can be obtained for troubleshooting purposes by running a diagnostics report. Navigate to **Monitoring > Support Information > Diagnostics Report** and click **Generate Report**. When the process is complete, a report is generated and the display is refreshed with the updated report. The report can be saved as a file to the terminal you are logged in from for further analysis.

Typically when troubleshooting, you will need to know various information about the sensor, such as the software version and hardware type. The System Information panel displays the TAC contact information, type of sensor, software version, status of applications, upgrades installed, and Cisco PEP information. To view this panel, navigate to **Monitoring > Support Information > System Information**.

Simple Network Management Protocol (SNMP) is an application layer protocol that facilitates the exchange of management information among network devices. SNMP enables you to manage network performance, find and solve network problems, and plan for network growth. A typical SNMP network management system (NMS) issues a request, and managed devices return responses. This behavior is implemented by using one of the following protocol operations:

- Get

- GetNext

- Set

- Trap

The Sensor Software implements the Get and Set SNMP operation, and the Get operation is used by the NMS to retrieve information from an agent. The Set operation is used by the manager to set the values of object instances within an agent.

SNMP is supported in the Cisco IPS Sensor Software. To configure the sensor so that it can be monitored by SNMP, follow these steps:

Step 1.   Navigate to **Configuration > Sensor Management > SNMP > General Configuration**. The SNMP General Configuration panel is displayed.

Step 2.   Select the **Enable SNMP Gets/Sets** check box to enable SNMP so that the SNMP NMS can issue requests to the sensor SNMP agent.

Step 3.   Configure the following substeps for the SNMP agent parameters, which are values that the NMS can/will request from the sensor SNMP agent:

- Enter the read-only community string in the Read-Only Community String field.

- Enter the read-write community string in the Read-Write Community String field.

- Enter the sensor contact user in the Sensor Contact field.

- Enter the location of the sensor in the Sensor Location field.

- Enter the sensor port for its SNMP agent in the Sensor Agent Port field. The default SNMP port number is 161.

- Select the protocol that the SNMP sensor agent will use from the Sensor Agent Protocol drop-down menu. The default protocol is User Datagram Protocol (UDP).

Step 4.   Click **Apply** to apply changes and save the revised configuration.

Summary

This section highlights the key topics discussed in this chapter:

- Navigate the Cisco IPS Sensor Software CLI and Device Manager to configure, manage, and monitor IPS devices.

- A valid license is required to obtain signature updates and use the global correlation features.

- Learn how to enable, disable, and utilize the password recovery feature in the Cisco IPS Sensor Software.

- The procedures to manage and monitor the Cisco IPS sensor through the IDM or SNMP.

References

For additional information, refer to these resources:

Cisco SAFE Security Solutions, at www.cisco.com/en/US/netsol/ns954/ index.html#~one.

Cisco IPS 4200 Series Sensors Design Guides, at www.cisco.com/en/US/products/hw/ vpndevc/ps4077/products_implementation_design_guides_list.html.

Configuring the Cisco Intrusion Prevention System Sensor Using the Command-Line Interface 7.0, at www.cisco.com/en/US/docs/security/ips/7.0/configuration/guide/cli/ cliguide7.html.

Installing and Using Cisco Intrusion Prevention System Device Manager 7.0, at www.cisco.com/en/US/docs/security/ips/7.0/configuration/guide/idm/idmguide7.html.

Configuring SNMP on the Cisco Intrusion Prevention System Device Manager 7.0, at www.cisco.com/en/US/docs/security/ips/7.0/configuration/guide/idm/idm_snmp.html.

Managing the Cisco Intrusion Prevention System Sensor via Cisco IDM 7.0, at www.cisco.com/en/US/docs/security/ips/7.0/configuration/guide/idm/ idm_sensor_management.html.

Monitoring the Cisco Intrusion Prevention System Sensor via Cisco IDM 7.0, at www.cisco.com/en/US/docs/security/ips/7.0/configuration/guide/idm/ idm_monitoring.html.

Exam Preparation Tasks

Review All the Key Topics

Review the most important topics from the chapter, noted with the Key Topic icons in the margin of the page. Table 7-5 lists a reference of these key topics and the page numbers on which each is found.

Table 7-5 *Key Topics for Chapter 7*

Key Topic Element	Description	Page Number
Bullet list	Managing Basic IPS Sensor Device Features	146
Table 7-2	Configuration Parameters Available on the Network Panel of the Cisco IDM	146
List	Configuring the Time Panel of the Cisco IDM	148
Section	Managing Users and Remote Management Channels	151
Section	Managing Cisco IPS Licensing	155
Bullet list	Upgrading and Recovering Cisco IPS Sensor Software	157
Figure 7-1	Cisco IPS Sensor Software Image Naming Convention	158
Figure 7-2	Cisco IPS Sensor Software Signature Filename Structure	158
Section	Updating Cisco IPS Signatures	160
Section	Recovering System Passwords	162
Section	Monitoring Cisco IPS Sensor Health and Performance	163
Figure 7-3	Cisco IPS Sensor IDM Sensor Health Dashboard	165

Definitions of Key Terms

Define the following key terms from this chapter, and check your answers in the glossary:

DST, UTC, URL, FTP, SCP, NTP, administrator, operator, viewer, service, UDI, VID, SNMP, NMS

642-627 IPS v7.0 exam topics covered in this part:

- Create complex network security rules to meet the security policy requirements

- Configure and verify the IPS features to identify threats and dynamically block them from entering the network

Part III: Applying Cisco IPS Security Policies

This chapter covers the following topics:

- **Cisco IPS Sensor Configuration and Verification and the Attachment of Sensing Interfaces to the Default Virtual Sensor:** Setting up and verifying the sensing interfaces.

- **Cisco IPS Sensor Configuration, Verification, and Monitoring of Inline Traffic Normalization:** Setting up, verifying, and monitoring the sensor for inline traffic normalization.

- **Cisco IPS Sensor Configuration and Verification of Promiscuous Mode Traffic Reassembly:** Setting up, verifying, and monitoring the sensor for traffic reassembly mode while out of line.

- **Cisco IPS Sensor Selection, Configuration, and Verification of TCP Session Tracking Mode:** Choosing, setting up, and verifying the sensor for TCP session tracking mode.

- **Cisco IPS Sensor Evaluation and Configuration of IPv6:** Setting up IPv6 on the sensor.

- **Cisco IPS Sensor Selection, Configuration, and Verification of the Bypass Mode Feature:** Choosing, setting up, and verifying that the sensor is supporting bypass mode.

CHAPTER 8

Configuring Basic Traffic Analysis

Overview

Configuring the Cisco Network Intrusion Prevention System (IPS) sensors involves attaching the sensing interfaces to the sensor analysis engine, tuning basic options, and applying low-level analysis options that apply to inspected traffic. This chapter covers this in some detail and enables optimal performance and analysis.

This chapter begins with configuring the default virtual sensor and assigning traffic sources. This is followed by an introduction, configuration, and verification of the inline traffic normalization on the Cisco IPS sensor. The chapter then discusses promiscuous mode traffic reassembly and describes how to configure the reassembly settings for both IP fragments and TCP streams. The chapter transitions into TCP session tracking, when it applies, and how to apply it to the Cisco IPS sensor. The chapter concludes with support and configuration for IPv6 and software bypass mode.

"Do I Know This Already?" Quiz

The "Do I Know This Already?" quiz allows you to assess whether you should read the entire chapter. If you miss no more than one of these self-assessment questions, you might want to move ahead to the "Exam Preparation Tasks" section. Table 8-1 lists the major headings in this chapter and the "Do I Know This Already?" quiz questions covering the material in those headings so that you can assess your knowledge of these specific areas. The answers to the "Do I Know This Already?" quiz appear in Appendix A.

Table 8-1 *"Do I Know This Already?" Foundation Topics Section-to-Question Mapping*

Foundation Topics Section	Questions
Configuring the Default Virtual Sensor	1, 2
Understanding Cisco IPS Sensor Inline Traffic Normalization	3, 4
Configuring Cisco IPS Sensor Promiscuous Traffic Reassembly Options	5
Configuring TCP Session Tracking	6
Understanding IPv6 Support in Cisco IPS Sensors	7–9
Selecting and Configuring Cisco IPS Sensor Bypass	10

1. A virtual sensor includes all policies except which of the following?

   a. Monitor policy

   b. Signature policy

   c. Event action policy

   d. Anomaly policy

2. A single virtual sensor named vs1 is the default virtual sensor on all IPS sensors. True or false?

   a. True

   b. False

3. Which two modes are available on the Cisco IPS sensor for traffic normalization from the Edit Virtual Sensor pane?

   a. Strict Evasion Protection

   b. Loose Evasion Protection

   c. Symmetric Mode Protection

   d. Asymmetric Mode Protection

4. Which of the following is *not* an available option in the Clear Flow States pane?

   a. Clear nodes

   b. Clear inspectors

   c. Clear database

   d. Clear alerts

5. The Cisco IPS sensor supports which of the following modes of IP fragment reassembly?

   a. BSD mode

   b. Linux mode

   c. NT mode

   d. Solaris mode

   e. All of these answers are correct.

6. Which of the following TCP session tracking modes is *not* supported on the Cisco IPS sensors?

   a. Virtual sensor

   b. Interface and VLAN

   c. VLAN only

   d. Interface only

7. Which of the following engines are used to inspect IPv6 traffic?

   a. ATOMIC IP

   b. ATOMIC IP ADVANCED

   c. ATOMIC IPv6

   d. All of these answers are correct.

8. Which of the following Cisco IPS Manager Express (IME) elements are supported for IPv6?

   a. Filtering

   b. Grouping

   c. Reporting

   d. All of these answers are correct.

9. Bypass mode is meant to be used only with inline implementations of IPS. True or false?

   a. True

   b. False

10. In which of the following bypass modes does traffic flow through the sensor, even if the monitoring process of the sensor is down?

   a. On

   b. Auto

   c. Off

   d. Disabled

Foundation Topics

Configuring the Default Virtual Sensor

The Cisco IPS Sensor defines the collection of all traffic analysis settings as a virtual sensor. The sensor can receive data input from one or many monitored data streams, including inline interface pairs, inline VLAN pairs, inline VLAN groups, and promiscuous interfaces. A single sensor policy or configuration is applied to all monitored data streams by default. This configuration is called a *virtual sensor*, which includes a signature policy, action policy, and anomaly detection policy that is applied to traffic as a whole. Keep the following important points in mind when configuring the default virtual sensor:

- To start IPS traffic analysis, apply the default virtual sensor to inline pairs, inline VLAN pairs/groups, or promiscuous interfaces.

- Each IPS sensor already has a default virtual sensor, vs0.

- The default virtual sensor (vs0) is comprised of a signature policy (sig0), event actions policy (rules0), and anomaly detection policy (ad0).

- The default virtual sensor can analyze a combination of traffic sources and still maintain isolation for each. Traffic sources cannot "leak" to another traffic source.

Assigning and Verifying Traffic Sources to the Default Virtual Sensor

Follow these steps to assign traffic sources to the default vs0 virtual sensor:

Step 1. Navigate to **Configuration > Policies > IPS Policies**. The upper half of the screen displays the list of virtual sensors, and by default, the vs0 is predefined.

Step 2. Select the vs0 virtual sensor.

Step 3. Click **Edit** to edit the virtual sensor, and the Edit Virtual Sensor window opens.

Step 4. The assignable interfaces or interface pairs are displayed that you can assign to a given virtual sensor. Choose the interface or interface pair from the Interfaces list.

Step 5. Click **Assign** or click **Remove** to remove an interface or interface pair from the list.

Step 6. Enter a description for the default virtual sensor in the Description field (optional).

Step 7. Click **OK**. The Edit Virtual Sensor window closes, and the Virtual Sensor window panel displays the interface(s) or interface pair(s) that you added to the virtual sensor.

Step 8. Click **Apply** to apply the changes.

Follow these steps to verify that the interfaces are correctly assigned to the virtual sensor:

Step 1. Navigate to **Monitoring > Sensor Monitoring > Support Information > Statistics**.

Step 2. Scroll down to the Virtual Sensor Statistics section.

Step 3. There is a Virtual Sensor Statistics section and Statistics for Virtual Sensor vs0, where the administrator can verify the interfaces assigned to the Virtual Sensor under the line starting with "List of interfaces monitored by this virtual sensor." This line lists the interfaces assigned to the virtual sensor.

Understanding Cisco IPS Sensor Inline Traffic Normalization

The Cisco IPS Sensor traffic normalizer is a function performed by the SensorApp application in inline mode. A function of the normalizer identifies and stops users from trying low-level evasive techniques to evade detection. The normalizer ensures low-level (mostly IP and TCP) protocol conformance, tracks session state, modifies ambiguously fragmented traffic to remove ambiguities, and properly orders segments to present normalized data to application layer inspectors.

The inline traffic normalizer enforces all anti-evasion checks to traffic incoming from inline traffic sources by operating in its Strict Evasion Protection mode. The normalizer operates in this mode by default, and it is the recommended mode by Cisco best practices. The normalizer can optionally be switched to Asymmetric Mode Protection. While in Asymmetric Mode Protection, most anti-evasion countermeasures are disabled, but the sensor is able to analyze asymmetric traffic. Also in this mode, the sensor only sees one direction of a session. Asymmetric Mode Protection of the traffic normalizer should only be used if asymmetric traffic flows are being inspected and remediation cannot be done by forcing symmetric traffic flows.

Follow these steps to configure the normalizer mode for vs0 or the default virtual sensor:

Step 1. Navigate to **Configuration > Policies > IPS Policies**. The screen displays the list of virtual sensors at the top of the display.

Step 2. Select the vs0 virtual sensor.

Step 3. Click **Edit**. The Edit Virtual Sensor window opens.

Step 4. Click **Advanced Options**.

Step 5. Choose the normalizer mode from the following:

- **Strict Evasion Protection:** The default mode that fully enforces TCP state and sequence tracking.

- **Asymmetric Mode Protection:** Disables most of the normalizer checks. Used typically when the entire stream cannot be inspected.

Clearing Flow States

The Cisco IPS sensor normalizer analyzes packets and builds a session state on the data it sees in each packet. The session state includes pieces of information required to track TCP/IP sessions, and ensures that they conform to the correct standards and that the packets seen on the wire actually belong to one session or another. Typically, pieces of data tracked by every device will include source and destination IP address, but sometimes this isn't the case. TCP connections have additional data, including ports, sequence number, TCP window size, time to live (TTL), and others. The Cisco IPS sensor can accurately enforce the TCP/IP state on traversing packets using this information, but if this information is missing, it can be difficult to tell when evasion techniques are being used to hide malicious activity.

Per-signature states can be built by the upper-layer signature engines, and a signature state of this type is typically the information stored for various detection algorithms. The information is built from seeing a complete connection as it traverses the device. The signature state can be larger than the packet that generated it (unlike a session state). A reason for this can be because a single packet can generate state for many different algorithms.

The Cisco IDM Clear Flow States pane enables you to clear the sensor database of some of or all its contents. The following options are available in the Clear Flow States pane:

- **Clear Alerts:** This is not recommended per Cisco best practices. This option clears the alerts database, including the alert nodes, meta inspector information, summary state, and event count structures. This option clears the alert database entirely.

- **Clear Nodes:** This option clears the overall packet database elements, including the packet nodes, TCP session information, and inspector lists. Clearing the nodes in the database causes the sensor to start fresh as if from a restart. All open TCP stream information is deleted, and new TCP stream nodes are created as new packets are received.

- **Clear Inspectors:** This option clears the inspector lists contained with the nodes. When you clear the inspector's database, the TCP and state information is retained. New inspection records are created as new packets are retrieved.

Follow these steps to clear flow states on the sensor:

Step 1. Log in to the Cisco IDM using an account with administrator privileges.

Step 2. Navigate to **Monitoring > Sensor Monitoring > Properties > Clear Flow States**.

Step 3. Select the radio button of the value you intend to clear:

- Clear Nodes

- Clear Inspectors

- Clear Alerts

- Clear All

Step 4. Select the **Specify a Single Virtual Sensor (otherwise all virtual sensors will be cleared)** check box to clear the flow state of one virtual sensor, or skip this step if all virtual sensors need to be cleared.

Step 5. From the drop-down list, select the virtual sensor for which you want to clear the flow state.

Step 6. Click the **Clear Flow State Now** button.

Configuring Cisco IPS Sensor Promiscuous Mode Traffic Reassembly Options

Traffic normalization cannot perform traffic normalizations for flows received on the sensing interfaces when operating in promiscuous mode. The sensor is receiving a copy of the original traffic stream; thus, it cannot modify the original packets to normalize them and drop or fix potential ambiguities. The sensor must be configured to interpret the received data in the same manner as the protected hosts, which will receive the original traffic stream. If packets and protocols are interpreted differently from the protected host, the attacker can introduce ambiguities inside traffic that the sensor will not be able to properly resolve. The sensor might treat much of the malicious traffic as legitimate for this reason. The sensor needs to be tuned for IP and TCP reassembly strategies to match these potential targets.

IP Fragment Reassembly

The sensor must reassemble IP fragments that it receives inside the copied traffic stream while in promiscuous mode. Typically, the main issue with IP fragmentation is the overlapping fragments, where two adjacent fragments do not reassemble neatly but contain a region of the reassembled packet that could come from the first or the second packet.

On the Cisco IPS Sensor, the method of assembly can be selected globally from one of the following four modes:

■ Linux mode

■ Solaris mode

■ BSD mode (typically used by IP stacks derived from the BSD UNIX TCP/IP implementation, which includes Mac OS X and many others)

■ NT mode (this is the default setting, and includes all Microsoft Windows TCP/IP stacks)

In a heterogeneous environment, consider migrating to inline mode, which does not require such reassembly methods as it normalizes overlapping fragments on the sensor. Follow these steps to configure IP fragment reassembly options:

Step 1. From the Cisco IDM, click the **Configuration** button.

Step 2. Navigate to **Policies > Signature Definitions**.

Step 3. Select sig0 and click **All Signatures**.

Step 4. From the All Signatures panel, click **Advanced** and click the Miscellaneous tab. The Miscellaneous panel is displayed.

Step 5. Under Fragment Reassembly, select the option next to IP Reassembly Mode and choose the operating system that you want to simulate when reassembling IP fragments. You can choose one of the following values: BSD, Linux, NT, and Solaris.

TCP Stream Reassembly

The sensor should be able to observe all TCP segments of a TCP session to reliably inspect it for malicious or suspicious traffic in promiscuous mode. Sometimes the sensor might not be able to observe the entire session, which includes situations where the IPS is overloaded and packets don't make it to the analysis engine. By default, the Cisco IPS sensor will require that it sees a full three-way handshake for all TCP sessions, and that it sees all packets of a TCP session. If the three-way handshake isn't seen, the sensor's promiscuous mode interfaces will ignore the TCP sessions that violate the requirements, which can lead to false negatives. This is why it is very important to size the Switched Port Analyzer (SPAN) ports, size the sensor, and provide symmetric routing to provide highly reliable detection. You can tune the TCP reassembly options and adjust the parameters for reassembly mode. The three reassembly modes include the following:

- **Loose:** There can be gaps in the sequence space and the session is still analyzed while many anti-evasion checks are disabled.

- **Strict:** The default setting and recommended by Cisco best practices. The sensor must see all packets of a session to reassemble.

- **Asymmetric:** Traffic is only in one direction and is enough to analyze, but most anti-evasion checks are disabled.

It is important to remember that Cisco recommends addressing and/or fixing the problem rather than tuning the reassembly options.

Follow these steps to configure TCP stream reassembly options:

Step 1. From the Cisco IDM, click the **Configuration** button.

Step 2. Navigate to **Policies > Signature Definitions**.

Step 3. Select sig0 and click **All Signatures**.

Step 4. From the All Signatures panel, click **Advanced** and click the Miscellaneous tab. The Miscellaneous panel is displayed.

Step 5. Under Stream Reassembly, select the TCP Handshake Required check box. Choose Yes if you want the sensor to only track sessions for which the three-way handshake is completed. If not, select No.

Step 6. Select TCP Reassembly Mode and choose one of the modes the sensor uses for reassembling TCP sessions:

- **Loose:** This option can consume excessive resources on the sensor, so it should be used only in environments where packets might be dropped.

- **Strict:** The default setting.

- **Asymmetric:** This option disables TCP window evasion checking and allows asymmetric traffic.

Step 7. Click **Apply** to apply the changes and save the revised configuration.

Configuring TCP Session Tracking

In some cases, the Cisco IPS Sensor will receive the same packet twice, which hinders the normalizer's (inline) ability to properly track flows. This can happen in environments where the same connection is forwarded through multiple VLANs or interfaces. The virtual sensor is configured to treat all packets equally by default, and considers them as coming from the same source even though they might be arriving on different interfaces or VLANs. This behavior can be modified by configuring a different session tracking mode to accommodate these specific environments and to maintain segregation of these flows, even though they belong to the same network session.

There are three commonly used session-tracking modes supported on the Cisco IPS Sensor:

- **Interface and VLAN:** Packets of the same network connection in the same VLAN or inline VLAN pair and on the same interface belong to the same session. Packets of the same network connection, but on different VLANs or interfaces, are tracked separately. This option is typically used when the same network connection crosses the sensor more than once.

- **VLAN Only:** Packets of the same network connection in the same VLAN or inline VLAN pair regardless of the interface belong to the same session. Packets of the same network connection but on different VLANs are tracked separately. This option is typically used when the same connection is present in multiple VLANs on the same interface or interface pair.

- **Virtual Sensor:** This is the default and almost always the best option to choose. Packets of the same network connection within a virtual sensor belong to the same session.

Follow these steps to configure TCP session-tracking mode for the default virtual sensor:

Step 1.   Navigate to **Configuration > Policies > IPS Policies.** The upper half of the screen displays the list of virtual sensors.

Step 2.   Select the default virtual sensor, vs0.

Step 3.   Click **Edit.** The Edit Virtual Sensor window opens.

Step 4.   Click **Advanced Options.**

Step 5.   From the Inline TCP Session Tracking Mode drop-down menu, select one of these possibilities:

- Interface and VLAN

- VLAN Only

- Virtual Sensor (default mode)

Understanding IPv6 Support in Cisco IPS Sensors

The Cisco IPS Sensor software provides protection for both IPv4 and IPv6 networks. With the depletion of IPv4 address space, implementation of IPv6 will become inevitable and will require appropriate security controls for communications using the IPv6 stack. The Cisco IPS Software has supported the IPv6 protocol since Release 6.2(1)E3. The Advanced Inspection and Prevention (AIP) Security Services Module (SSM) and AIP Security Services Card (SSC)-5 support IPv6 with ASA software version 8.2(1). Some Cisco IPS management applications also support IPv6. The Cisco IPS Manager Express (IME) supports filtering, grouping, and reporting elements for IPv6.

IPS software incorporates a dedicated set of signatures to fully analyze native and tunneled IPv6 traffic, including native IPv6 packets, Internet Control Message Protocol version 6 (ICMPv6), tunnel detection, tunnel inspection, and IPv6 fragments. The three engines that are used to inspect IPv6 traffic on the Cisco IPS Sensor are the following:

- ATOMIC IP

- ATOMIC IP Advanced

- ATOMIC IPv6

The Atomic IP Advanced engine enhances the detection capabilities of the Cisco IPS platforms with native IPv6 inspection capabilities. Some other IPS configuration elements that also support IPv6 include IPv6 Target Value Rating, event variables, event action filters, IP logging, and event actions.

The IPv6 normalizer engine can reassemble IPv6 fragments and forward the reassembled buffer inspection and actions by other engines and processors. There are a few differences that exist between the IPv4 and IPv6 normalizers:

- Modifying packets inline for the Normalizer engine signatures has no effect on IPv6 datagrams, whereas it does for IPv4.

- Signature 1202 allows 48 additional bytes beyond the maximum diagram size for IPv6 because of the longer IPv6 header fields.

- Signature 1206, which is IP Fragment Too Small, does not fire for IPv6 datagrams. Signature 1741 in the Atomic IP Advanced engine fires for IPv6 fragments that are too small.

The IPv6 dedicated signatures can be viewed by navigating to **Configuration > Policies > Signature Definitions > sign0 > All Signatures** and selecting Sig. Name from the Filter drop-down menu. All signatures that contain "v6" in their name are displayed. The signatures predominantly belong to the three signature engines that support IPv6 (listed previously).

It's important to understand that there are some limitations when implementing IPv6 IPS inspection:

- AIM-IPS and NME-IPS do not currently support IPv6 features.

- IPv6 inspection might work on the Intrusion Detection System Module (IDSM-2), but it is not officially supported. VLAN access control lists (VACL) on Catalyst switches do not support IPv6, but IPv6 with promiscuous mode using SPAN ports instead with lower capture granularity is another option.

- IPv6 is not supported on the management or command and control interface.

- IPv6 does not support event actions such as Request Block Host, Request Block Connection, and Request Rate Limit.

- The Anomaly Detection (AD) feature does not support IPv6 traffic.

Selecting and Configuring Cisco IPS Sensor Bypass

Key
Topic

Bypass is a feature that enables and ensures that packets continue to flow through the sensor, even if the sensor software fails. The Cisco IPS Sensor Software supports a software bypass mechanism. Typically the sensor analysis engine performs packet analysis. When the inline bypass is activated, the analysis engine is bypassed, thus allowing traffic to flow through the inline interfaces and inline VLAN pairs without inspection. Packets continue to flow through the sensor in inline bypass mode when the sensor processes are temporarily stopped for upgrades or when the sensor monitoring processes fail. Network traffic isn't impaired, but traffic inspection ceases.

Another use for bypass mode outside of the software failover mechanism would be for troubleshooting purposes or sensor upgrades.

Three software bypass modes are supported on the Cisco IPS sensor:

- **On:** Traffic bypasses the analysis engine and is not inspected. The inline traffic is *not* inspected in this mode.

- **Auto:** Traffic flows through the sensor for inspection unless the monitoring process of the sensor is down. If the monitoring process of the sensor is down, traffic bypasses the sensor until the sensor is running again. When the monitoring process of the sensor comes back up, the sensor then inspects the traffic again. Auto mode is useful during sensor upgrades to ensure that the traffic is still flowing while the sensor is being upgraded.

- **Off:** Disables bypass mode. Traffic flows through the sensor for inspection, and if the monitoring process of the sensor is down, traffic stops flowing.

Follow these steps to configure software bypass:

Step 1.   Navigate to **Configuration > Interfaces > Bypass**. The Bypass panel is displayed.

Step 2.   Choose one of the modes from the Bypass Mode drop-down menu:

- On

- Off

- Auto

Step 3.   Click **Apply** to apply changes and save the revised configuration.

Changes to the software bypass feature are reported by the sensor and these interface configuration events as status events: Traffic start or stop, Link up or down, and Missed packet percentage threshold exceeded.

There is also a hardware bypass feature supported on the Cisco IPS Sensor for the Cisco IPS-4260 and IPS-4270, which require the four-port GigabitEthernet card. If the sensor is powered off or reset, or if the network interface card (NIC) interfaces fail or are unloaded, paired interfaces enter fail-open state in their hardware (NIC).

Summary

This section highlights the key topics discussed in this chapter:

- A virtual sensor is a collection of signature, event action, and anomaly detection parameters.

- The traffic normalizer provides evasion protection when inline.

- Configure reassembly settings and use strict TCP reassembly when using promiscuous mode.

- The sensor TCP session tracking mode can be configured to adapt to specific environments.

- Bypass mode is used to avoid traffic disruptions, but there are security risks and limitations.

References

For additional information, refer to these resources:

Cisco SAFE Security Solutions, at www.cisco.com/en/US/netsol/ns954/index.html#~one.

Cisco IPS 4200 Series Sensors Design Guides, at www.cisco.com/en/US/products/hw/vpndevc/ps4077/products_implementation_design_guides_list.html.

Configuring the Cisco Intrusion Prevention System Sensor Using the Command-Line Interface 7.0, at www.cisco.com/en/US/docs/security/ips/7.0/configuration/guide/cli/cliguide7.html.

Installing and Using Cisco Intrusion Prevention System Device Manager 7.0, at www.cisco.com/en/US/docs/security/ips/7.0/configuration/guide/idm/idmguide7.html.

Configuring the Default Virtual Sensor on the Cisco Intrusion Prevention System Device Manager 7.0, at www.cisco.com/en/US/docs/security/ips/7.0/configuration/guide/idm/idm_policies.html#wpmkr2163359.

Managing the Cisco Intrusion Prevention System Sensor via Cisco IDM 7.0, at www.cisco.com/en/US/docs/security/ips/7.0/configuration/guide/idm/idm_sensor_management.html.

Monitoring the Cisco Intrusion Prevention System Sensor via Cisco IDM 7.0, at www.cisco.com/en/US/docs/security/ips/7.0/configuration/guide/idm/idm_monitoring.html.

Configuring Policies on the Cisco Intrusion Prevention System Sensor, at www.cisco.com/en/US/docs/security/ips/7.0/configuration/guide/idm/idm_policies.html.

Exam Preparation Tasks

Review All the Key Topics

Review the most important topics from the chapter, noted with the Key Topic icons in the margin of the page. Table 8-2 lists a reference of these key topics and the page numbers on which each is found.

Table 8-2   *Key Topics for Chapter 8*

Key Topic Element	Description	Page Number
Section	Configuring the Default Virtual Sensor	176
Section	Understanding Cisco IPS Sensor Inline Traffic Normalization	177
Paragraph	Clear Flow States from the Cisco IDM	177
Section	Configuring Cisco IPS Sensor Promiscuous Mode Traffic Reassembly Options	179
Section	Configuring TCP Session Tracking	181
Section	Understanding IPv6 Support in Cisco IPS Sensors	182
Section	Selecting and Configuring Cisco IPS Sensor Bypass	183

Definitions of Key Terms

Define the following key terms from this chapter, and check your answers in the glossary:

vs0, sig0, rules0, ad0, symmetric, asymmetric

This chapter covers the following topics:

- **Cisco IPS Signatures:** This covers the description types, features, and actions of signatures.

- **Configuring Basic Signature Properties:** This covers the basic configuration and verification of signature properties.

- **Configuring Signature Actions:** This covers the configuration and verification of signature actions.

- **Configuring Remote Blocking:** This covers the configuration and verification of the Cisco IPS using remote blocking devices to mitigate attacks.

- **Configuring Packet Capture and IP Logging:** This covers the configuration and verification of packet captures and IP logging using a Cisco IPS Sensor.

- **Understanding Threat and Risk Rating:** This covers the evaluation of the concepts and usage of threat and risk rating.

- **Understanding and Configuring Event Action Overrides:** This covers the configuration and verification of event action overrides.

- **Using Event Action Filters:** This covers the configuration and verification of event action filters.

- **Choosing an Action Configuration Strategy:** This covers the selection of the appropriate strategy for configuring the Cisco IPS Sensors and the expected results.

- **Examining Alerts in IPS Event Logs:** This covers the use of the CLI and Cisco IDM to view and analyze logs.

CHAPTER 9

Implementing Cisco IPS Signatures and Responses

Overview

The Cisco IPS sensors have built-in signatures that can be configured based on security requirements to mitigate attacks. A signature is a set of predefined rules the sensor uses to detect known attacks and malicious network activity based on the behaviors or characteristics exhibited by such suspicious activity. This chapter is focused on the configuration of the signatures and the actions the Cisco IPS can take when it detects such activity.

"Do I Know This Already?" Quiz

The "Do I Know This Already?" quiz allows you to assess whether you should read the entire chapter. If you miss no more than one of these self-assessment questions, you might want to move ahead to the "Exam Preparation Tasks" section. Table 9-1 lists the major headings in this chapter and the "Do I Know This Already?" quiz questions covering the material in those headings so that you can assess your knowledge of these specific areas. The answers to the "Do I Know This Already?" quiz appear in Appendix A.

Table 9-1 *"Do I Know This Already?" Foundation Topics Section-to-Question Mapping*

Foundation Topics Section	Questions
Cisco IPS Signatures	1–4
Configuring Signature Actions	5
Configuring Remote Blocking	6–7
Configuring Packet Capture and IP Logging	8–10
Understanding Threat and Risk Rating	11

1. Which of the following is *not* a signature type that can be used on the Filtering menu?

    a. Default signature

    b. Custom signature

    c. Tuned signature

    d. Malicious signature

2. What elements make up a signature engine?

    a. An analyzer and an inspector

    b. A parser and an inspector

    c. String patterns

    d. None of these answers are correct.

3. Which of the following can be used to collect or pull alerts from the Cisco IPS Sensor?

    a. IDM

    b. IME

    c. MARS

    d. All of these answers are correct.

4. What can be done to improve the performance of the IPS sensor with over 4500 built-in signatures, and still allow the IPS to function properly?

    a. Implement a policy with the top 10 signatures.

    b. Retire unused signatures.

    c. Disable all signatures.

    d. None of these answers are correct.

5. Which of the following is the most severe of the deny actions?

    a. Deny Packet Inline

    b. Deny Connection Inline

    c. Deny Attacker Inline

    d. Deny Attacker Victim Pair Inline

6. Which protocols can be used by an IPS appliance to manage a blocking device? Choose two.

    a. Telnet

    b. SSH

    c. RCP

    d. SFTP

7. Which of the following cannot be a blocking or shunning device?

    a. Cisco routers

    b. Cisco Catalyst 6500 FWSM

    c. Cisco ASA

    d. None of these answers are correct.

8. IP logging settings under the Miscellaneous tab that can be viewed through **Configuration > Policies > Signature Definitions > sig0 > Active Signatures > Advanced** is a global setting. True or false?

   a. True

   b. False

9. To view logs and analyze them with a network protocol analyzer, what extension should the logs be saved with when being downloaded through Cisco IDM?

   a. *.pdf

   b. *.log

   c. *.txt

   d. *.cap

10. Which of the following is *not* a component of risk rating?

   a. Attack Relevancy

   b. Target Asset Value

   c. Signature Accuracy

   d. None of these answers are correct.

Foundation Topics

Cisco IPS Signatures

IPS signatures are a set of rules used by Cisco IPS Sensors to detect known attacks, such as denial of service (DoS) attacks. The sensors analyze packets, and if malicious, a signature is triggered based on the way the IPS sensor has been configured to react. Cisco IPS Sensors have some critical signatures enabled by default to ensure that a level of security is maintained after the sensor is integrated into the network as steps toward compliance with the security policy.

Because of the nature of some attacks, signatures are also designed to have subsignatures. This implies that certain characteristics of the signature can be modified through the subsignature without changing the entire signature. Cisco IPS Sensor signatures are generally classified into three types:

- **Default signatures:** Created for known attacks

- **Tuned signatures:** Created by modifying built-in signatures to suit particular needs

- **Custom signatures:** Created based on your criteria

Although there are different types of signatures, they all have the same properties:

- **Signature Name:** The user-friendly name of the signature; it usually provides a short description of the attack that the signature is designed to detect or prevent.

- **Signature ID:** An integer that uniquely identifies the signature. The Cisco IPS assigns custom signatures an ID of 60000 and higher. If a signature has multiple subsignatures, each subsignature is assigned a subsignature ID unique in the context of the parent signature.

- **Signature Status:** Describes the signature as enabled or disabled, which can mean inspecting traffic or not and also as active or retired.

- **Signature Engine:** Defines the Cisco IPS inspection routines that the signature uses to match traffic.

- **Severity Rating:** Determines the default severity that is assigned to events causing the signature to trigger. The severity can be later adjusted to reflect other environmental conditions.

- **Fidelity Rating:** Describes the accuracy with which the signature matches attacks.

- **Triggering Conditions:** The most important part of the signature; this describes the network traffic properties that need to be present for the signature to trigger.

- **Summarization Strategy:** Describes how often the signature generates alarms.

- **Response Actions:** Taken by the sensor when the signature triggers.

Signature Engines

A signature engine, a component of the analysis engine of the sensor, inspects a particular aspect of network traffic and supports a category of signatures. Each Cisco IPS signature is created and controlled by a signature engine that is specifically designed for the type of traffic being monitored. For example, the STRING.TCP engine examines TCP connections searching for string patterns. It controls signatures such as the Signature 29619, Heap Feng Shui Code. This signature triggers on detecting a heap-spraying attack execution. This remote code execution exploit allows the attacker to insert arbitrary code into the system heap memory space, which can cause a denial of service. This signature is enabled by default by the Cisco IPS Sensor with the following parameters:

- **Severity rating:** High

- **Fidelity rating:** 95 (means that it is accurate in 95 percent of cases)

- **Response action:** Block

The Cisco IPS signature engines run simultaneously with one another, depending on the number of signatures that are enabled. Each engine is comprised of a parser, an inspector, and a set of parameters that have configurable ranges or sets of values. These configurable parameters enable you to tune signatures to work optimally in your network and to create unique signatures as the occasion demands.

Another example is the ATOMIC.IP engine, which inspects IP protocol headers and associated Layer 4 transport protocols (TCP, UDP, and ICMP) and payloads. It controls signatures such as the Signature 1006, IP Options-Strict Source Route, which by default detects packets containing the Strict Source Route option in the IP header. These packets are often used in spoofing attacks to bypass normal network routing. This signature is also enabled by default by the Cisco IPS Sensor with the following parameters:

- **Severity rating:** High

- **Fidelity rating:** 100

- **Triggering conditions:** IP Option 137 found in header

- **Summarization strategy:** Summarize if occurrences exceed 100 in 30 seconds

- **Response action:** Produce alert and log

Figure 9-1 shows the properties of Signature 1006.

Alerts

The Cisco IPS Sensor generates alerts by default for most signatures, after a signature is triggered because of matching malicious traffic. The alerting feature is a configurable signature action that can be disabled or left enabled, which is recommended. Alerts are stored in the sensor event store, which is a fixed-size indexed store. The Cisco IPS Device Manager (IDM), Cisco IPS Manager Express (IME), or Cisco Monitoring Analysis and Response System (MARS) can pull alerts from the sensor through the Security Device Event Exchange (SDEE) protocol, which allows a host or hosts to collect alerts as needed without significant tasking of the sensor processor.

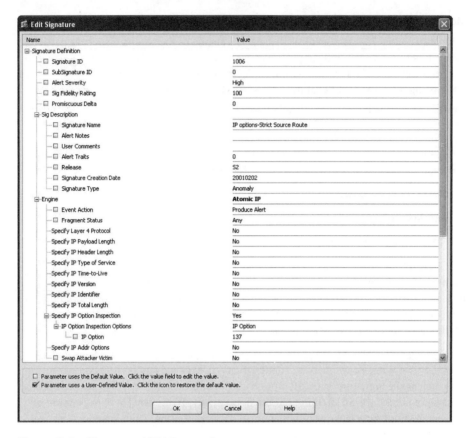

Figure 9-1   *Signature 1006 Properties*

There are two types of event requests used by the SDEE protocol for external monitoring applications (as mentioned previously) when interfacing with the sensor:

- **Query:** Issue a query request to retrieve the events in the event store at the time of the request.

- **Subscription:** Establish a live feed to view alerts as they occur.

Note: Multiple hosts can perform queries and subscribe to the live event feed simultaneously.

Based on the signature triggering an alert, a severity level is derived, and it can be any of the following:

- Informational

- Low

- Medium

- High

These severity levels do not affect the format of the alert as it stays consistent irrespective of the severity level. The format of an alert as it appears in the CLI conforms with the Cisco Intrusion Detection Event Exchange standards. The Cisco Intrusion Detection Event Exchange extends the SDEE and adds IPS specific elements that are used in Cisco IPS Sensor Software version 7.0 alerts.

Example 9-1 shows a CLI output of the **show events alert** command from a Cisco IPS Sensor running version 7.0 software where Signature 1334, TCP Drop – Segment Out of Order is triggered. The evIdsAlert indicates that this is an alert.

Example 9-1   show events alert max-threat-rating 40 *Command Output*

```
ips4240# show events alert max-threat-rating 40
evIdsAlert: eventId=1303689059967096434 severity=informational vendor=Cisco
  originator:
    hostId: ips4240
    appName: sensorApp
    appInstanceId: 411
  time: 2011/05/15 22:37:42 2011/05/15 16:37:42 GMT-06:00
  signature: description=TCP Drop - Segment Out Of Order id=1330 created=20050304
    type=anomaly version=S242
    subsigId: 12
    sigDetails: TCP Packet segment is out of order and cannot queue
    marsCategory: Penetrate/ProtocolAnomaly/TCPIP
  interfaceGroup: vs0
  vlan: 0
  participants:
    attacker:
      addr: locality=OUT 10.92.32.13
      port: 443
    target:
      addr: locality=OUT 192.168.1.70
      port: 62516
      os: idSource=learned relevance=relevant type=windows-nt-2k-xp
  actions:
    logPacketsActivated: true
    deniedPacket: true
    logAttackerPacketsActivated: true
    logVictimPacketsActivated: true
    logPairPacketsActivated: true
  ipLogIds:
    ipLogId: 1701800537
    ipLogId: 1701800534
    ipLogId: 1701800538
  riskRatingValue: attackRelevanceRating=relevant targetValueRating=medium 35
```

```
threatRatingValue: 0
interface: ge0_0
protocol: tcp
```

The following fields are used in Example 9-1:

- **vendor:** This is always Cisco for Cisco products as other vendors can use SDEE as well.

- **originator:** This contains the following subfields that provide information on the originator of the alert:
  - **hostID:** Name of the sensor that originated the alert
  - **appName:** Name of the application that originated the alert
  - **appInstanceId:** Numerical value that uniquely identifies this instance of the application that originated the alert

- **marsCategory:** This is the category of events to be used by Cisco MARS.

- **interfaceGroup:** This is the name of the interface group that received the traffic.

- **vlan:** This is the VLAN number that is associated with packets involved in the activity that triggered the alert. If this field is omitted or the value is 0, no VLAN information is available.

- **Participants:** This contains the following subfields, providing information about the attacker and target hosts:
  - **attacker:** Host or hosts that were involved in the attacking of the target hosts.
  - **addr: locality:** This is the IP address of the attacker and where the address is located within the network topology.
  - **target:** Host or hosts that are the target of an attacker or attackers.
  - **addr: locality:** This is the IP address of the target host and where this address is located within the network topology.

- **riskRatingValue:** This is the value that represents the calculated risk that is associated with the detected activity. This value is calculated with multiple factors and has a range between 0 and 100 with both numbers inclusive, where 0 is the lowest risk and 100 is the highest risk.

- **threatRatingValue:** This is the value that represents the risk rating minus the threat rating adjustment.

- **interface:** This provides traffic source information. The interface field holds a simple value such as ge0_0.

- **protocol:** This is the network protocol wherein the malicious content was discovered.

- **eventIDeventId:** This is a unique identification for the alert.

- **severity:** This is the severity level assigned to the signature that was triggered.

In some cases, the contents of the packet that triggered the alert are captured and displayed in the **show events alert** command output. The Cisco IPS Sensor Software version 7.0 contains more than 4500 built-in default signatures, of which approximately 1500 are enabled by default. These signatures will increase as new known threats are discovered; the Cisco IPS can automatically update its signatures or it can be done manually. You cannot rename or delete built-in signatures, but you can disable or retire signatures that are old or are not applicable. If you are not running an application on your network, a signature preventing attacks to such an application is not required. Retiring signatures conserves memory and improves the performance of the sensor.

Note: Sensor performance can be improved by retiring signatures that are not in use or that are not applicable. You can always reactivate retired signatures if the need arises.

The maximum number of signatures you can enable depends on the sensor platform; the sensor will notify you when the maximum has been reached. The fact that a sensor can hold more signatures than other sensors does not indicate better or faster performance. Judging sensors based on signatures can be deceiving, as different vendors build signatures in different ways. Consider these two points when choosing a sensor:

- Some vendors create many signatures to cover all variations, while other vendors use a lower number of more generic signatures that cover all of these variations.

- Generic signatures are often better and tend to be less susceptible to evasion, but they can cause more false positives.

The Cisco IPS Sensor does not rely on signatures alone to mitigate attacks. It also looks at behaviors and its global correlation by using SensorBase to mitigate attacks on all Cisco IPS–protected networks.

Configuring Basic Signature Properties

The signatures in the Cisco IPS Sensor can be accessed through the Cisco IDM by choosing **Configuration** > **Policies** > **Signature Definitions** > **sig0** and then clicking **All Signatures** to access the Signature Configuration panel. The **All Signatures** view is only visible when the Sig0 is expanded. By default, the signature configuration panel displays signatures that are listed by signature ID number. The All Signatures database view displays all signatures available in the sensor signature set; when each signature set is clicked on, it displays the list of signatures grouped under it in the view pane. Figure 9-2 shows the signature view in the left pane.

The signature sets are as follows:

- **Active Signatures:** Displays all nonretired signatures

- **Adware/Spyware:** Displays signatures that are designed to address adware and spyware issues

- **Attack:** Displays attack-based signatures that are grouped by attack types

- **Configurations:** Displays configuration-based signatures that mitigate attacks typically because of misconfiguration

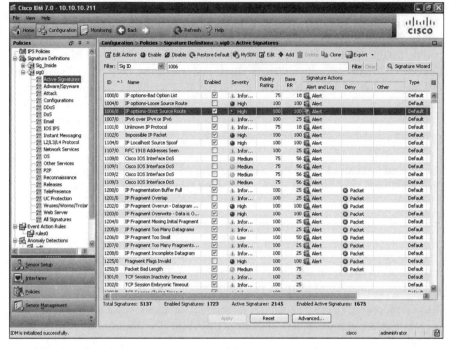

Figure 9-2 *Signature Configuration View*

- **DDoS:** Displays distributed denial of service (DDoS) signatures

- **DoS:** Displays denial of service signatures

- **Email:** Displays email signatures by protocol, such as Internet Message Access Protocol (IMAP) or Simple Mail Transfer Protocol (SMTP)

- **IOS IPS:** Displays signatures in the IOS IPS

- **Instant Messaging:** Displays instant messaging (IM) signatures grouped by IM application

- **L2/L3/L4 Protocol:** Displays signatures grouped by network protocol type, including Address Resolution Protocol (ARP), IP fragment, IP version 6 (IPv6), and others

- **Network Services:** Displays signatures that are based on network service protocols, such as DHCP

- **OS:** Displays signatures grouped by operating system type

- **Other Services:** Displays signatures based on application layer services, such as FTP, HTTP, and others

- **P2P:** Displays signatures based on different peer-to-peer file-sharing applications

- **Reconnaissance:** Display signatures based on discovery protocols, such as Internet Control Message Protocol (ICMP) sweeps

- **Releases:** Enables you to view signatures grouped by signature update releases

- **TelePresence:** Enables you to display TelePresence-based signatures

- **UC Protection:** Displays Cisco Unified Communications–based signatures

- **Viruses/Worms/Trojans:** Displays signatures based on malware that is defined as these three types

- **Web Server:** Enables you to display signatures based on web servers

- **All Signatures:** Displays all defined signatures

The Filter drop-down list in the configuration view pane can be used to display signatures in different ways, such as the types of attacks they detect or the services being inspected. When you change your selection in the Filter drop-down list, the Select Criteria menu changes to correspond to your selection. For example, if you choose Severity in the Filter drop-down list, the criteria field provides a drop-down menu with High, Medium, Low, and Informational options, respectively, as shown in Figure 9-3. You can also choose Sig Name as another example, which provides a field where you can type in the criteria. After you type in the criteria and click Filter, the configuration view pane refreshes to display only those signatures that match your sorting criteria.

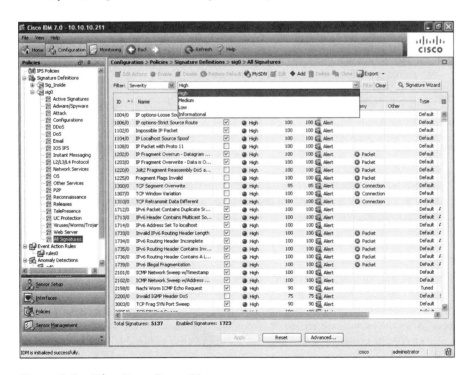

Figure 9-3 *Filter Drop-Down List*

The following options are available from the Filter drop-down list:

- **Sig ID:** Displays signatures by signature ID number

- **Sig Name:** Displays signatures by signature name

- **Enabled:** Displays all signatures that are enabled or actively running on the sensor

- **Severity:** Displays signatures based on their severity

- **Fidelity Rating:** Allows you to define a fidelity rating range of numbers, and then displays only those signatures within that fidelity range

- **Base Risk Rating:** Is a value between 0 and 100 that represents a numerical quantification of the risk associated with a particular event on the network

- **Action:** Displays signatures grouped by assigned signature actions

- **Type (Tuned,..):** Displays signatures based on type, such as tuned, custom, or default

- **Engine:** Displays signatures grouped by engine

Enabling and Disabling Signatures

Enabling a signature makes the signature inspect traffic; when it is disabled, it does not inspect traffic. The following steps walk you through enabling a signature:

Step 1.   Click **Configuration** and choose **Policies > Signature Definitions > Sig0 > Active Signatures.** The Signature Configuration panel is displayed.

Step 2.   Locate the signature that you want to enable.

Step 3.   A signature that is already enabled has a check mark in the check box. If the signature is disabled, the check box is empty.

Step 4.   If the signature is currently disabled, select the signature by clicking it.

Step 5.   Click **Apply** to apply your changes and save the updated configuration.

To disable a signature that is already disabled, deselect the check box in the Enabled column.

Tip: To enable multiple signatures at the same time, hold down the Ctrl or Shift key and click the signatures that you would like to enable; then right-click one of the selected signatures and click **Enable.**

Retiring and Activating Signatures

Signatures that are not being used or are no longer applicable to the network resources being protected should be retired to improve sensor performance. Retiring a signature removes it from the set of currently available signatures, which are part of the signature database. After the signature is retired, it is removed from memory but stored in flash. For a signature to function, the signature must be both activated and enabled.

You can activate signatures you have previously retired. When this is done, the sensor rebuilds its configurations and the signature is once again added to the set of currently active signatures. Follow these steps to retire or activate a signature:

Step 1.   Click **Configuration** and choose **Policies > Signature Definitions > Sig0 > All Signatures.** The Signature Configuration panel is displayed.

Step 2.   Select a signature that you want to retire or activate, and click **Edit** on the toolbar. The Edit Signature window opens.

Step 3.   Scroll down to the Status section and click the Retired field.

Step 4.   Select Yes or No from the drop-down list.

Alternatively, you can retire or activate a signature from the Signature Configuration panel by following these steps:

Step 1.   Select a signature that you want to retire or activate.

Step 2.   Right-click the signature.

Step 3.   Choose **Change Status To** and then choose **Active** or **Retired**.

Note: Retiring or activating signatures can take 30 minutes or longer.

Configuring Signature Actions

The Cisco IPS Sensor allows you to have various detective or preventive actions based on the signature. While some of these actions will only work in inline mode, others will only work with specific network protocols.

Cisco preconfigures many actions for specific signatures and provides additional configuration tools, allowing you to easily modify actions to many signatures at the same time.

Signature Detective Actions

The Cisco IPS supports detective actions based on matching network traffic, as outlined in Table 9-2.

Table 9-2   *Detective Signature Actions*

Key Topic

Signature Action	Description
Produce Alert	This action writes the event that is related to the trigger signatures to the event store as an alert.
Produce Verbose Alert	This action includes an encoded dump of the offending packet in the alert. This action causes an alert to be written to the event store, even if the Produce Alert action is not selected.
Log Attacker Packets	This action starts capturing packets that contain the IP address of the attacker. This action causes an alert to be written to the event store, even if the Produce Alert action is not selected.
Log Victim Packets	This action starts IP logging on packets that contain the IP address of the victim and sends an alert. This action causes an alert to be written to the event store, even if the Produce Alert action is not selected.

Table 9-2 *Detective Signature Actions*

Signature Action	Description
Log Pair Packets	This action starts IP logging on packets that contain the attacker and victim address pair. This action causes an alert to be written to the event store, even if the Produce Alert action is not selected.
Request SNMP Trap	This action sends a request to the Notification Application component of the sensor to send a Simple Network Management Protocol (SNMP) trap about this event. This action causes an alert to be written to the event store, even if the Produce Alert action is not selected.

Note: Log Attacker Packets, Log Victim Packets, and Log Pair Packets signature actions have configurable parameters. On a Cisco IPS Sensor, parameters regarding how long to capture packets are configured globally.

SNMP Traps

Cisco IPS Sensors from software version 6.0 and higher have a notification application that runs as a sensor service. This application enables the sensor to send notification of sensor alerts and system errors to an SNMP Network Management System (NMS). These SNMP notifications are called *traps*. In addition to enabling the sending of such traps, the notification application also enables the NMS to obtain basic health information from the sensor. SNMP is used by many network administrators to monitor and configure network devices and consolidate data into a single console.

The notification application runs as a thread within MainApp and uses the Net-SNMP agent, a public domain SNMP agent, to collect and store information about the sensor, translate the information into a form that is compatible with SNMP, and deliver it to an NMS through SNMP. Although the Net-SNMP agent currently supports SNMP version 3 (SNMPv3), the notification application currently does not.

Signature Preventive Actions

The Cisco IPS supports preventive (aggressive) actions based on matching network traffic, as outlined in Table 9-3.

Table 9-3   *Signature Preventive Actions*

Signature Action	Description
Deny Packet Inline	This action drops the offending packet that has caused the signature to trigger. This action is only applicable to virtual sensors in inline mode.
Deny Connection Inline	This action drops the offending packet and future packets of a particular TCP or UDP flow. This action is only valid when inline.
Deny Attacker Victim Pair Inline	This action drops the offending packet and future packets between the attacker and the victim addresses for a specified period of time. This action is only valid for sensors in inline mode.
Deny Attacker Service Pair Inline	This drops the offending packet and future packets from the attacker address and victim port pair for a specified period of time. This action is only valid for sensors in inline mode.
Deny Attacker Inline	This action drops the offending packet and future packets from this attacker address for a specified period of time. The sensor maintains a list of the attackers currently being denied by the system. Entries can be removed from this list or allowed to expire based on a timer, which is reset should a currently listed attacker issue another attack. This is only valid for inline modes.
Reset TCP Connection	This action sends spoofed TCP reset (RST) segments to terminate the offending TCP connection. This can be used with the deny packet to quickly free the connection-related resources of the target.
Request Block Connection	This action sends a request to a remote blocking device to block a connection.
Request Block Host	This action sends a request to a remote blocking device to block an attacker host.
Request Rate Limit	This action sends a request to a remote blocking device to start rate-limiting traffic from the attacker host.
Modify Packet Inline	This action is used by the sensor's IP and TCP normalization engines to change some packet property, such as clearing a TCP flag.

Notice that all the signature actions with "Inline" can only be carried out by sensors in inline mode and not in promiscuous mode. The inline mode sensor supports all the actions listed in Table 9-3, but the promiscuous mode sensor only supports those without the inline.

You can try to use the Reset TCP Connection action in promiscuous mode to attempt to block TCP-based attacks in real time. Note, however, that this is not always reliable in high-packet-rate flows; instead, you can use the Request Block Host and Request Block Connections actions to prevent some attacks in promiscuous mode.

To configure signature actions by tuning individual signatures, perform the following steps:

Step 1.   Using the Cisco IDM, navigate to the **Configuration > Policies > Event Action Rules > rules0** pane.

Step 2.   From the General tab, you can configure the following:

- **Deny Attacker Duration:** Number of seconds to deny attacker inline; the default is 3600 and the range is from 0 to 518400.

- **Block Action Duration:** The number of minutes to block a host or connection, with a default of 30 minutes and a range from 0 to 10000000.

- **Maximum Denied Attackers:** Limits the number of denied attackers possible in the system. The default is 10000, with a range from 0 to 100000000.

You can also enable the following options by selecting their check boxes:

- **Use Summarizer:** Enables the summarizer component. When disabled, all signatures are set to Fire All with no summarization. If you configure individual signatures to summarize, it will be ignored if this is not selected. This is enabled by default.

- **Use Meta Event Generator:** This is enabled by default, and if disabled, all meta signatures are disabled.

- **Use Threat Rating Adjustment:** When enabled, it adjusts the risk rating, and when disabled, the risk rating is equal to the threat rating.

- **Use Event Action Filters:** Enables the event action filter component when selected. This has to be selected to use any filter that is enabled.

- **Enable One Way TCP Reset:** This is for use with inline mode only. It enables a one-way TCP reset for deny packets' inline actions for TCP-based alerts. It sends a TCP reset to the victim of the alert, thus clearing the TCP resources of the victim.

Step 3.   Click **Apply** to apply your changes to the sensor, or click **Reset** to replace any edits that you made with the previously configured value.

Step 4.   Navigate to the active signatures through **Configuration > Policies > Signature Definitions > sig0 > Active Signatures.**

Step 5.   Locate the signature or signatures for which you want to review actions.

Step 6.   Determine the currently assigned actions in the Signature Actions column.

Step 7.   Identify the signature you want to modify, select the signature (or group of signatures), and select **Edit Actions.**

Step 8.   Select the check boxes for the actions that you want to assign to the signature. No check mark shows that no action is assigned. A gray check mark indicates that the action is assigned to some of the selected signatures. You can choose one or more of the following actions from the on-screen list:

- **Alert and Log Actions:** Produce Alert, Produce Verbose Alert, Log Attacker Packets, Log Victim Packets, Log Pair Packets, Request SNMP Trap

- **Deny Actions:** Deny Packet Inline, Deny Connection Inline, Deny Attacker Victim Pair Inline, Deny Attacker Service Pair Inline, Deny Attacker Inline

- **Other Actions:** Reset TCP Connection, Request Block Connection, Request Block Host, Request Rate Limit, Modify Packet Inline

Step 9.   Click **OK** to close the Edit Actions window. The Signature Configuration panel displays the actions that you selected for the signature that you configured.

Step 10.   Click **Apply** to apply your changes.

Managing Denied Attackers

The IP addresses of all the attackers that have been denied on the sensor are displayed in the Denied Attackers panel, along with the hit count for each denied attacker. The hit count for all IP addresses can be reset, and you can clear the list of denied attackers. The Denied Attackers panel is accessed through **Monitoring > Sensor Monitoring > Time Based Actions > Denied Attackers**. Click **Refresh** to refresh the list and also note the following clear and reset buttons:

- **Reset All Hit Counts:** Clears the hit count for the denied attackers

- **Clear List:** Clears the entire list of denied attackers

Detective Signature Action Implementation Guidelines

The guidelines outlined in Table 9-4 should be considered when using detective actions.

Table 9-4   *Detective Signature Action Implementation Guidelines*

Signature Action	When to Use
Produce Alert Request SNMP Trap	This is to be used for all active and enabled signatures to inform the administrator of the triggering based on malicious or suspicious action that has been detected.
Produce Verbose Alert	This is to be used instead of the Produce Alert actions as it always provides additional information concerning the true cause for the triggering of the signature.
Log Attacker, Victim, or Pair Packets	This is used to provide data for analysis to determine the exact nature of low-rate suspicious traffic or evasion events that would not significantly affect the sensor. It is also used to provide useful forensic data to assist in investigating incidents.

Preventive Signature Action Implementation Guidelines

The guidelines outlined in Table 9-5 should be considered when using preventive actions with Cisco IPS signatures. These signatures are more aggressive than the detective signatures.

Table 9-5   *Preventive Signature Action Implementation Guidelines*

Signature Action	When to Use
Deny Packet Inline	This is used to effectively prevent single-packet attacks and application layer attacks by dropping the packet containing the detected malicious packet.
Deny Connection Inline	This is used to prevent the initial attack and prevent an attacker's long-lived session from doing more damage after the initial attack.
Deny Attacker Inline	This is used to fully stop a confirmed attacker from performing any additional actions where there is one attacker per IP address.
Deny Attacker-Victim Pair Inline	This is used when you cannot configure full attacker denial because of false positives. This action is less likely to stop threats that spread in the network using many means such as scanning worms.
Deny Attacker-Service Pair Inline	This is used to prevent an attacker from further contacting a network-wide service. Although less effective than the Deny Attacker Inline action, it is more precise and can allow worm-infected clients to continue working using legitimate applications while still blocking malicious traffic.
Reset TCP Connection	This is used in promiscuous mode to attempt to prevent TCP-based attacks in real time. It is also used in inline mode as an addition to drop or block actions to free resources on the victim.
Request Block Connection	This is used in promiscuous mode to prevent an attacker's long-lived session from doing more damage. In inline mode, it is used for the same purpose as in promiscuous mode through a remote network chokepoint.
Request Block Host	This is used in promiscuous mode to fully stop an attacker for a period of time, preventing any further communication. This is a severe action that is most appropriate when there is minimal chance of a false alarm or spoofing. In inline mode, it is the same as stated previously for a remote network chokepoint. There is usually a slight delay as the sensor has to reconfigure the external network chokepoint.

Configuring Remote Blocking

The Cisco IPS uses the blocking feature to prevent packets from reaching their destination by using another Cisco device as the initiator at the request of the sensor. The blocking device must be reachable and accessible by the sensor for management purposes.

The sensor must be able to communicate with the blocking device and should have Telnet or Secure Shell (SSH) access configured. The sensor will connect to the blocking device through either of these protocols.

If SSH is used, the blocking device must support SSH, which means that it must have a software license that supports Data Encryption Standard (DES) or Triple Data Encryption Standard (3DES) encryption. After the sensor is configured with the details of the blocking device, the sensor attempts to log in to the blocking device. If the login is successful, a user connection is maintained between the sensor and the blocking device. This persistent connection allows the sensor to quickly modify the configured temporary blocking rules.

Using ACLs on a Router

On a blocking device, you can have only one active access control list (ACL) for each interface and direction combination. To accommodate other ACL entries apart from the ones that are generated by the sensor, you should configure the additional ACLs in the form of pre-block and post-block ACLs. These ACLs allow an administrator to include access rules that must be processed before and after the blocking rules are added by the sensor:

- **Pre-block ACLs:** These are used for permitting what you do not want the sensor to block and thus override the deny lines resulting from blocks. For example, when a packet is checked against an ACL, the first line that is matched determines the action. Therefore, if the first line matched is a permit line from the pre-block ACL, the packet is permitted, even though there could be a deny line from an automatic block that is listed later in the ACL.

- **Post-block ACLs:** These are used for additional blocking or permitting of traffic on an interface when there is an existing ACL that must be there after the block action. The sensor creates an ACL with the following entries and applies it to the specified interface and direction as required:

  - A permit line for the sensor IP address if it is currently blocked

  - A copy of all the configuration lines in the pre-block ACL

  - A deny line for each address being blocked by the sensor

  - A copy of all the configuration lines of the post-block ACL

If you do not have a post-block ACL, the sensor inserts **permit ip any any** at the end of the new ACL. The pre-block and post-block ACLs that you plan to use must be created on the blocking device before you specify them in Cisco IDM, and they must be names or numbered extended IP ACLs.

Note: When signature-induced blocking is not in effect, the ACL applied to the interface is a combination of the pre-block and post-block ACLs without any blocking entries inserted.

Configuration Tasks

A number of steps need to be performed to complete the configuration process for blocking. They are grouped here into tasks to make them easy to follow:

Step 1.   **Add the blocking device to the sensor known host list.** This involves importing an authentic copy of the public key of the blocking device to later reliably authenticate it in SSH connections. This is only required if you use SSH to communicate with the blocking devices, and it is optional.

Step 2.   **Configure the sensor global blocking properties.** This involves enabling blocking and defining blocking parameters, such as the maximum number of blocking entries, IP addresses to be blocked, and IP addresses that cannot be blocked.

Step 3.   **Create blocking device login profiles.** This task involves defining the username, password, and enable password for communication between the sensor and the blocking device for blocking.

Step 4.   **Define the blocking device properties.** This task involves defining the properties of the blocking device such as device type, IP address, login profile, and communication method.

Step 5.   **Configure properties of managed interfaces.** This involves selecting the blocking interfaces or VLAN and specifying the direction in which to apply the ACL and also defining pre-block and post-block ACLs. This step is optional and is not required for Cisco ASA devices.

Step 6.   **Assign a block action to a signature.** This task involves configuring a signature action to request blocking from an external device.

In Figure 9-4, the sensor initiates a connection to a Cisco router running IOS Software and logs in to configure it to block the attacker's IP address.

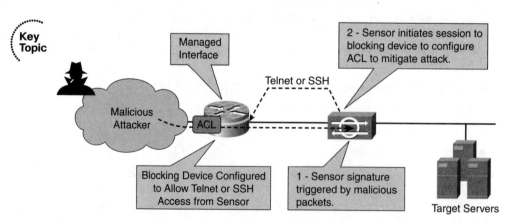

Figure 9-4   *Remote Blocking*

For Task 1, if you select SSH-DES or 3DES as the secure communication method, the sensor uses SSH password authentication to log in to the managed device. To configure the sensor to communicate with a blocking device using SSH, you must manually retrieve the SSH public key of the blocking device to the sensor. Follow these steps to add the blocking device to the sensor known hosts list:

Step 1. Navigate to **Configuration** > **Sensor Management** > **SSH** > **Known Host Keys.**

Step 2. Click **Add.** The Add Known Host Key window opens, as shown in Figure 9-5.

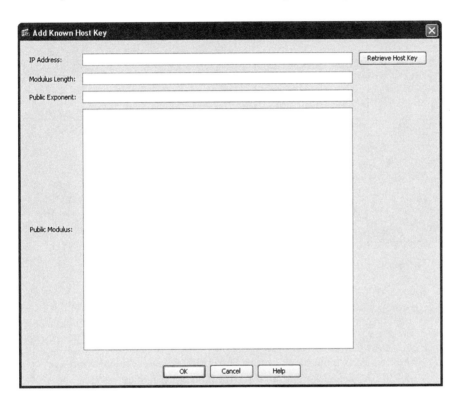

Figure 9-5 *Add Known Host Key Window*

Step 3. Enter the IP address of the managed (blocking) device, and click **Retrieve Host Key.**

Step 4. The sensor will retrieve the host key of the device. Verify the authenticity of this key by comparing it with a known authentic copy, and click **OK** to confirm that it is authentic.

In Task 2, you will be configuring the blocking settings, as shown in Figure 9-6.

Follow these steps to configure the sensor blocking properties:

Step 1. Navigate to **Configuration** > **Sensor Management** > **Blocking** > **Blocking Properties** to display the Blocking Properties panel.

Step 2. Verify that the **Enable Blocking** check box is selected. Blocking is enabled by default, so it should be selected.

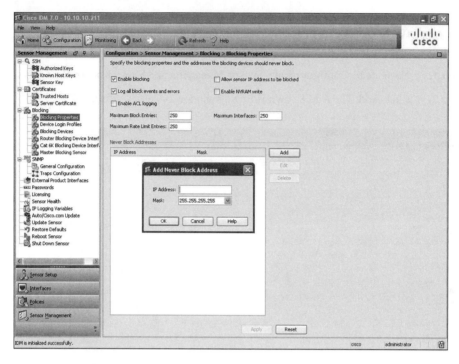

Figure 9-6   *Blocking Properties Window*

Step 3.   There is an **Allow Sensor IP Address to Be Blocked** check box as well, which should remain deselected. Selecting this box can allow the sensor to block it- self and not be able to communicate with the devices it is managing.

Step 4.   There is a Maximum Block Entries Field that has values ranging from 1 to 65,535. The default is 250 and is the recommended amount of entries to be blocked. After the sensor reaches it maximum, newer blocks will not occur.

Step 5.   Click the **Add** button to add a host or network to the list of addresses never to be blocked, which will appear under the Never Block Addresses section.

Step 6.   Enter the IP address of the host or network in the IP Address field.

Step 7.   Choose the network mask that corresponds to the IP address from the Mask drop-down menu.

Step 8.   Click **OK**. The new host or network appears in the Never Block Addresses list on the Blocking Properties panel.

Step 9.   Click **Apply** to apply your changes and save the updated configuration.

In Task 3, you will be specifying the username and password that the sensor will use when logging in to blocking devices. This is created under a login profile, where one login pro- file can be used for multiple devices, as shown in Figure 9-7.

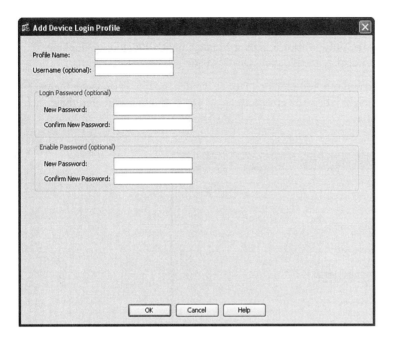

Figure 9-7 *Add Device Login Profile Window*

An example will be creating a login profile for routers that share the same username and password. Follow these steps to create a device login profile:

Step 1. Navigate to **Configuration** > **Sensor Management** > **Blocking** > **Device Login Profiles**. This displays the Device Login Profiles window.

Step 2. Click **Add** to add a profile, and the Add Device Login Profile window opens.

Step 3. Enter a name for your profile in the Profile Name field.

Step 4. Enter the username that will be used to log in to the blocking device in the Username field. This step is optional if a username is not required by the blocking device.

Step 5. Enter the password that is used to log in to the blocking device in the New Password field. Enter the same password in the Confirm New Password field.

Step 6. Enter the enable password that is used on the blocking device under the Enable Password section in the New Password field. This is optional if an enable password is not used. If this is entered, it will have to be confirmed by entering the same password in the Confirm New Password field.

Step 7. Click **OK** and the new device login profile appears in the list in the Device Login Profiles window.

Step 8. Click **Apply** to apply your changes and save the revised configuration.

In Task 4, you will define the properties of the blocking device by following these steps:

Step 1. Navigate to **Configuration > Sensor Management > Blocking > Blocking Devices** to display the Blocking Devices panel.

Step 2. Click **Add** and the Add Blocking Device window opens, as shown in Figure 9-8. You might receive an error message if you have not configured the device login profile.

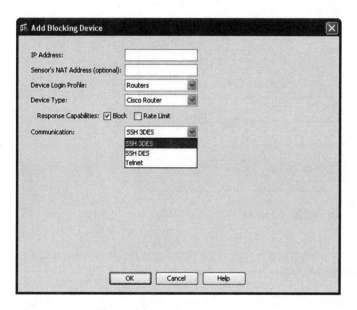

Figure 9-8   *Adding Blocking Devices*

Step 3. Enter the IP address of the blocking device in the IP Address field.

Step 4. Enter the sensor's Network Address Translation (NAT) address in the Sensor's NAT Address field. This is an optional field and should only be used if there is a NAT device between the management interface of the sensor and the management interface of the blocking device.

Step 5. Choose the device login profile from the Device Login Profile drop-down list. The login profile was created in Task 3 and is a prerequisite to this step.

Step 6. Choose the device type from the Device Type drop-down list. The options from the list are Cisco Router, PIX/ASA, and Cat 6K.

Step 7. Observe the Block and Rate Limit check boxes in the Response Capabilities section. The Block check box is selected, as the response action by the blocking device is to block.

Step 8. From the Communication drop-down list, choose the connection method that will be used for the management access. It is recommended that you use the SSH 3DES method.

Step 9.   Click **OK**.

Step 10.   Click **Apply** to apply your changes and save the updated configuration.

In Task 5, you will configure the properties of the managed interface by following these steps:

Step 1.   Navigate to **Configuration > Blocking > Router Blocking Device Interfaces**. Because a router was selected in Task 3, it only follows that the interfaces will be router interfaces. If the blocking device is not created in Task 3, an error message will be produced when attempting the next step.

Step 2.   Click **Add** and the Add Router Blocking Device Interface window opens.

Step 3.   Choose the IP address of the blocking device from the Router Blocking Device drop-down list.

Step 4.   Type in the blocking interface name in the Blocking Interface field.

Step 5.   As illustrated in Figure 9-9, select the direction in which you want to apply the blocking ACL, which can be in or out.

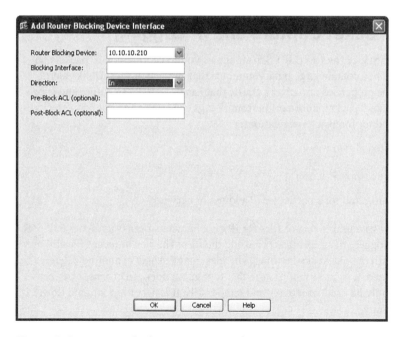

Figure 9-9   *Router Blocking Device Interface*

Step 6.   Enter the name of the pre-block ACL in the Pre-Block ACL field. This is optional.

Step 7.   Enter the name of the post-block ACL in the Post-Block ACL field. This is also an optional field.

Step 8.   Click **OK** and the new interface appears in the Router Blocking Device interface list. If the exact same information already exists, you will receive an error message.

Step 9.   Click **Apply** to apply your changes and save the revised configuration.

Task 6 is the last set of steps when configuring remote blocking. The key here is selecting a signature and modifying it such that the alert response is to block the malicious host. Follow these steps to modify the signature so that a block is performed when triggered:

Step 1.   Navigate to **Configuration > Policies > Signature Definition > sig0** to reveal the Signatures window.

Step 2.   From the Sig0 window, select a signature or a group of signatures and click **Edit Actions.** The Edit Actions window opens.

Step 3.   Select the Request Block Host, Request Rate Limit, or Request Block Connection action from the Other Actions section.

Step 4.   Click **OK**.

Step 5.   Click **Apply** to apply your changes and save the revised configuration.

Configuring Packet Capture and IP Logging

The IP logging feature of the Cisco IPS Sensor allows you to capture raw IP packets on the sensor itself. They contain large binary numbers that the sensor sees. Unlike alerts, which describe the properties of network traffic that has triggered a signature and showing at least one trigger packet, information from IP logs can be used to confirm attacks, to assess damage, and for forensic investigations.

IP logs are generated in two ways:

■   As a signature response action

■   Manually configured for a particular IP address or network

The sensor reserves a reusable ring of files for IP logging when it starts up. After 512 MB of data has been logged, the sensor starts reusing the files. The sensor reuses files by overwriting the file with the oldest closing time. The files on the sensor cannot be deleted as they are preallocated. It is important to note that IP logging does affect sensor performance and should only be used selectively and temporarily. It is best used for data flows with a low traffic rate.

IP log files can be retrieved from the sensor before or after they are closed. Retrieving an IP log file before it closes cannot guarantee that all the packets will be captured, but you can get a snippet of any packet. It is best done when the IP log file is closed. IP log files can be retrieved by the following methods:

■   Use the CLI **copy** command to copy the IP log files to another host using FTP or SCP.

■   Download the IP log files through the Cisco IDM.

After the files have been obtained, you can use a network protocol analyzer such as Wireshark to examine the data.

To configure IP logging, you will have to go through a number of steps, which have been broken into tasks for easy understanding:

Step 1.   Configure global sensor IP logging settings.

Step 2.   Configure individual signature actions.

Step 3.   Configure manual IP logging.

In Task 1, you will configure global sensor IP logging parameters by following these steps:

Step 1.   Navigate to **Configurations > Policies > Signature Definitions > sig0 > Active Signatures**. Click **Advanced** to reveal the Advanced window, and click the Miscellaneous tab, as shown in Figure 9-10.

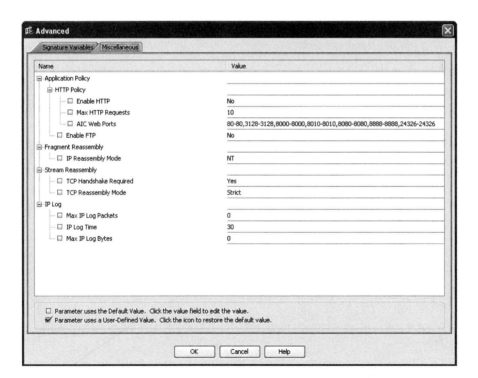

Figure 9-10   *Global Sensor IP Logging Settings*

Step 2.   Enter the maximum number of packets you want to be logged in a single IP logging session under IP Log in the Max IP Log Packets field.

Step 3.   In the IP Log Time field, enter the maximum duration that you want the sensor to log in a single IP logging session. The default is 30 seconds and a valid value is from 30 to 300 seconds.

Step 4.   In the Max IP Log Bytes field, enter the maximum number of bytes that you want to have logged in a single IP logging session.

Step 5.   Click **OK**.

Step 6.   Click **Apply** to apply your changes and save the updated configuration.

Note: If multiple thresholds are configured, the sensor will stop logging in a particular IP logging session when the first threshold is met.

Task 2 is quite straightforward. You will configure the sensor to generate an IP session log when a particular signature is triggered. When IP logging is configured as a response action for a signature and the signature is triggered, the sensor creates an IP log and other configured actions. The event alert triggering the IP log appears in the IP logging table and is closed after a configured threshold is met. Follow these steps to configure the signature action:

Step 1.   Navigate to **Configuration > Policies > Signature Definition > sig0** to reveal the Signatures window.

Step 2.   From the Sig0 window, select a signature or a group of signatures and click **Edit Actions**. The Edit Actions window opens, as shown in Figure 9-11.

Step 3.   Select one of the following as the event action for a signature:

- Log Attacker Packets
- Log Victim Packets
- Log Pair Packets

Step 4.   Click **OK**.

Step 5.   Click **Apply** to apply your changes and save the updated configuration.

Note: To verify the creation of IP logs and display a description of the available IP log contents, issue the **iplog-status** command.

In Task 3, you will configure logging manually for a particular IP address, by following these steps:

Step 1.   Navigate to **Monitoring > Sensor Monitoring > Time-Based Actions > IP Logging** to reveal the IP Logging configuration panel.

Step 2.   Click **Add** and the Add IP Logging window opens.

Step 3.   Click the Virtual Sensor drop-down list and choose the sensor on which you want to configure this IP logging action.

Step 4.   In the IP Address field, enter the IP address of the host from which you want IP logs to be captured. You receive an error message if you try to add a capture that already exists and is in the added or started state.

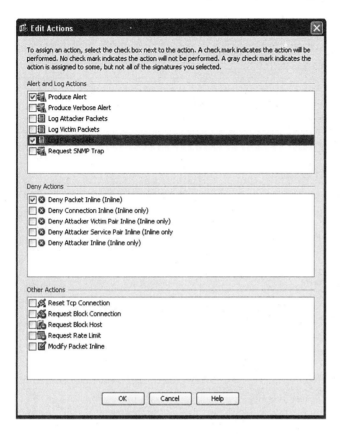

Figure 9-11   *Configuring Individual Signature Actions*

Step 5.   In the Duration field, shown in Figure 9-12, enter the number of minutes that you want IP logs to be captured. The default is 10 minutes, and it accepts a range from 1 to 60 minutes.

Step 6.   In the Packets field, enter the number of packets that you want to have captured. The Packets field is optional, and valid ranges are from 0 to 4294967295.

Step 7.   In the Bytes field, enter the number of bytes you want to have captured. This field is optional, and valid ranges are from 0 to 4294967295.

Step 8.   Click **Apply** to apply your changes and save the revised configuration. The IP address is then displayed on the IP Logging panel along with the following information:

- **Log ID:** This is the ID of the IP log.

- **Status:** This is the status of the IP log. Valid values are Added, Started, and Completed.

- **Alert ID:** This is the event alert, if any, that triggered the IP log.

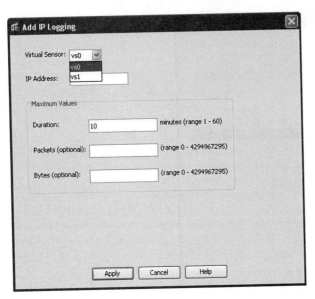

Figure 9-12 *Adding IP Logging Manually for a Specified IP Address*

- **Start Time:** This is the time stamp of the first captured packet.

- **Current End Time:** This is the time stamp of the last captured packet. There is no time stamp if the capture is not complete.

- **Packets Captured:** This is the current count of the packets captured.

- **Bytes Captured:** This is the current count of the bytes captured.

An existing log entry can be edited by selecting it in the list and clicking **Edit.** The Edit IP Logging window opens, where you can edit all the information in the previous Steps 4 to 7.

Downloading, Saving, and Stopping IP Logs

The IP Logging panel, which is viewed through **Monitoring > Sensor Monitoring > Time-Based Actions > IP Logging** and shown in Figure 9-13, has a **Download** button that allows IP logs to be downloaded and saved.

Follow these steps to download and save IP logs:

Step 1. Navigate to **Monitoring > Sensor Monitoring > Time-Based Actions > IP Logging.**

Step 2. Click **Download** and the Save As dialog box appears.

Step 3. Save the log with a .cap extension for later viewing with a network protocol analyzer application, such as Wireshark.

To stop logging, select a log ID from the IP Logging panel and click **Stop.** The Stop IP Logging window appears, prompting that you are sure you want to stop logging for the ID you selected. If you click **OK**, the logging entry is removed from the IP Logging panel.

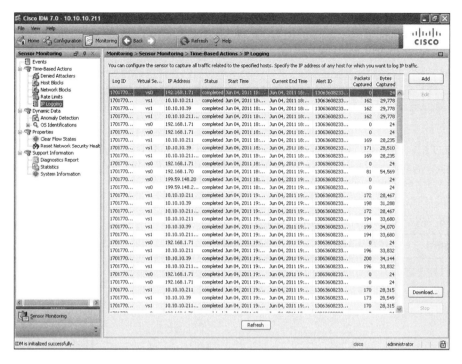

Figure 9-13   *Download and Stop Buttons in the IP Logging Panel*

Understanding Threat and Risk Management

The Cisco IPS delivers unique severity ratings that are assigned to all alerts generated from the Cisco IPS Sensors; this differentiates it from the regular alerts that are commonly used in the industry. The Cisco IPS uses a concept called *risk rating*, which provides the network security administrator with an indicator of the relative severity of the event in his or her network environment. The risk rating is assigned values in a range from 0 to 100, which is calculated dynamically each time a signature is triggered. The higher the value, the greater the security risk of the event associated to the alert.

Five inputs are used to calculate the risk rating for each triggering of a signature:

- **Potential Damage:** This is the damage that could be caused by the activity that is described by the signature.

- **Target Asset Value:** This is based on attacks against high-valued assets potentially being higher from a risk perspective.

- **Signature Accuracy:** When a signature is inaccurate and is fired, it lowers confidence in sensor decisions; thus, triggered inaccurately, this results in lower risk ratings.

- **Attack Relevancy:** This refers to the priority of attacks that cannot cause damage against their target. An example of this is launching a Windows-specific attack against a Linux host. This has little or no effect on the target and should be deprioritized because of its low risk.

- **Clues from Other Controls:** There can be other measures or controls within the network that increase the awareness of the Cisco IPS Sensor and allow it to react better to network events and threats.

Note: If global correlation is enabled on the Cisco IPS Sensor, it also influences the risk rating calculation. The global correlation feature is discussed in later chapters.

Table 9-6 lists the risk rating components and their corresponding variables used by the IPS sensor, such as the variable used by the IPS, how the IPS variable is derived based on signature configuration, and the value ranges.

Table 9-6 *Risk Rating System Components*

Component	IPS Variable	Source	Values
Potential Damage	Attack Severity Rating (ASR)	Preconfigured in a signature and tunable	Informational (25) Low (50) Medium (75) High (100)
Target Asset Value	Target Value Rating (TVR)	Manually configured	Zero (50) Low (75) Medium (100) High (150) Mission Critical (200)
Signature Accuracy	Signature Fidelity Rating (SFR)	Preconfigured in a signature and tunable	0–100
	Promiscuous Delta (PD)	Preconfigured in a signature and tunable	0–30
Attack Relevancy	Attack Relevancy Rating (ARR)	Collected or manually configured	Relevant (10) Unknown (0) Not Relevant (−10)
Clues from other controls	Watch List Rating (WLR)	Collected	0–100

The IPS variables are defined as follows:

- **Attack Severity Rating (ASR):** This is determined by the severity level that you configured for the signature.

- **Target Value Rating (TVR):** This is a user-configurable value that identifies the importance of a network asset through its IP address.

- **Signature Fidelity Rating (SFR):** This is an indication of the confidence that the signature writer has in the signature accuracy.

- **Promiscuous Delta:** This is a per-signature setting that lowers the risk rating of certain alerts in promiscuous mode.

- **Attack Relevancy Rating:** This is computed by comparing the targeted platform to the attack launched against it.

- **Watch List Rating:** This is used when information on malicious IP addresses is pulled from another application, such as the Cisco Security Agent Management Center, and used to increase the risk rating for events from the malicious hosts.

Risk Rating Calculation

Risk rating is calculated using the following formula:

$$RR = (ASR * TVR * SFR) / 10,000 + ARR - PD + WLR$$

The formula uses all the previously defined parameters, and the value of the risk rating is always an integer between 0 and 100.

In applying the formula, review this example, in which the signature that was triggered in a Cisco IPS Sensor in inline mode had an ASR of 75 and an SFR of 90. The target has a default TVR of 100 and an ARR of 10 and is not listed in another other application; thus, the WLR is 0.

Note: In inline mode, the PD is 0.

$$RR = (75 * 100 * 90) / 10,000 + 10 - 0 + 0$$
$$RR = 77.5$$
$$RR = 78 \text{ (It has to be an integer.)}$$

Threat Rating

Cisco IPS also supports another key threat determinant called the *threat rating*. This indicates the severity of an event in the local environment by also taking into account any preventive actions that the sensor took to reduce the risk for this event. You should use the threat rating to determine the level of residual risk following the prevention of malicious attacks by the sensor.

If the Cisco IPS Sensor is not configured with any preventive functions, the threat rating always equals the risk rating. The threat rating uses threat rating adjustments to lower the risk rating, and every preventive action that is assigned to a signature uses a specific threat rating adjustment that is hard-coded in the Cisco IPS Software. If multiple preventive actions are enabled for a signature, the risk rating is reduced by the largest adjustment of the configured actions.

The formula for calculating the threat rating is as follows:

Threat Rating = Risk Rating – Threat Rating Adjustment

Threat rating adjustment is enabled by default, and adjustments can be disabled on the General parameters tab. This can be accessed through **Configuration > Policies > Event Action Rules > rules0 > General** and is shown in Figure 9-14. Disabling the threat rating adjustment is not recommended.

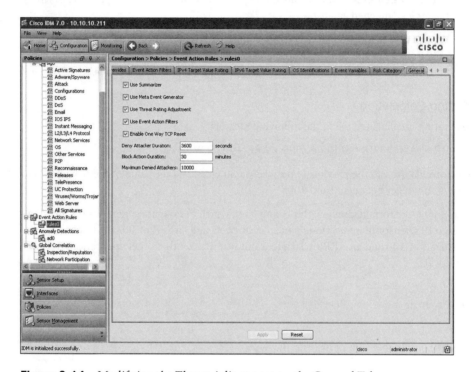

Figure 9-14   *Modifying the Threat Adjustment on the General Tab*

Risk rating is adjusted based on the values listed and the action taken to mitigate attacks. The result of the adjustment is called the threat rating. Table 9-7 shows some risk rating adjustment amounts as a result of the action taken to mitigate some attacks.

Table 9-7   *Risk Rating Adjustment*

Risk Rating Adjustment Amount	Action
45	deny-attacker-inline
40	deny-attacker-victim-pair-inline
35	deny-connection-inline

Understanding and Configuring Event Action Overrides

Event action overrides are a way to add event actions globally without having to configure each signature individually. If a signature event occurs and the risk rating for that event falls within the range for an event action, that action takes place for the event. For example, if you set a risk rating of 70 or more to generate an SNMP trap, you can set the risk rating range for Request SNMP Trap to 70–100.

There are some steps required to successfully configure event action overrides, which have been divided into tasks here for your convenience:

Step 1.   Globally enable event action overrides.

Step 2.   Tune risk categories.

Step 3.   Specify actions to be added in a risk category.

In Task 1, you will enable the event action overrides should they have been disabled previously. The following steps will guide you through the process:

Step 1.   Navigate to **Configuration** > **Policies** > **Event Action Rules** > **rule0** to reveal the rule0 panel.

Step 2.   Click the Event Action Overrides tab to display the Event Action Overrides panel.

Step 3.   Select the **Use Event Action Overrides** check box, as shown in Figure 9-15.

For events with a risk rating of 90 or more, the default setup might have enabled preventive actions, and in such case, the corresponding event action override is displayed.

In Task 2, you will tune risk categories, which are predefined as HIGHRISK, MEDIUMRISK, and LOWRISK. You can also define your own categories with custom ranges. It is good to keep the categories contiguous so that no range is left out, with 0 being the lowest and 100 being the highest.

Follow these steps to add, edit, or delete a risk category:

Step 1.   Navigate to **Configuration** > **Policies** > **Event Action Rules** > **rules0**. Click the Risk Category tab and click **Add**, and the Add Risk Level window opens.

Step 2.   In the Risk Name field, enter a name for the risk category.

Step 3.   In the Risk Threshold field, enter a number for the risk threshold between 0 and 100. This number represents the lower boundary of the risk for this level.

Step 4.   In the Active options, as shown in Figure 9-16, click the Yes radio button to make the risk category active.

Step 5.   Click **OK** and the new risk category appears in the list on the Risk Category tab.

Step 6.   To edit an existing risk category, select it in the list and click **Edit**.

Step 7.   Make the required changes.

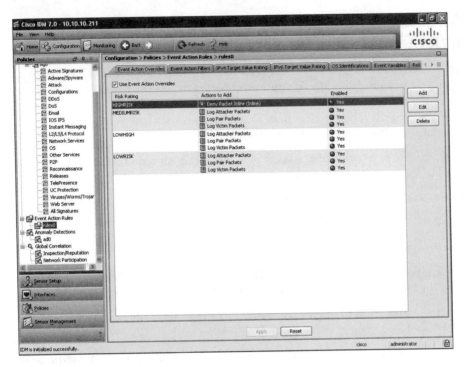

Figure 9-15   *Enabling Event Action Overrides*

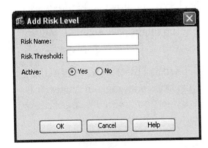

Figure 9-16   *Tuning Risk Categories*

Step 8.   Click **OK** and the edited risk category appears in the list on the Risk Category tab.

Step 9.   To delete a risk category, select the category in the list and click **Delete**. The risk category no longer appears in the list on the Risk Category tab.

Step 10.   Click **Apply** to apply your changes and save the revised configuration.

In Task 3, you will be specifying actions to be added in a risk category. The following steps take you through the configuration process:

Step 1.   Navigate to **Configuration > Policies > Event Action Rules** and choose **rules0**.

Step 2.   From the rules0 panel, click the Event Action Overrides tab.

Step 3.   Select the **Use Event Action Overrides** check box.

Step 4.   Click **Add** to create a new event action override, and the Add Event Action Override window opens.

Step 5.   Assign a risk rating range from the Risk Rating drop-down list.

Step 6.   From the Available Actions to Add list, select the event actions that this event action will correspond to.

Step 7.   As illustrated in Figure 9-17, select the Enabled check boxes for the actions you want to enable in the override.

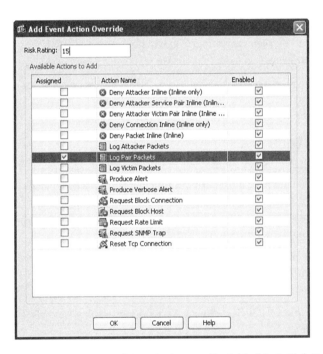

Figure 9-17   *Specifying Actions to Be Added in a Risk Category*

Step 8.   Click **OK** and the new event action override now appears in the list on the Event Action Overrides tab.

Step 9.   Ensure that the **Use Event Action Overrides** check box is still selected.

Step 10.   To edit an existing event action override, select it in the list, click **Edit**, and make any changes as required.

Step 11.   Click **OK** and the edited event action override appears on the Event Action Overrides tab.

Step 12.   Ensure that the **Use Event Action Overrides** check box is still selected.

Step 13.   To delete an event action override, select it from the list and click **Delete**. The event action override no longer appears in the list after the delete action.

> **Note:** You cannot delete the event action override for Deny Packet Inline because it is protected by the system. You can disable it if you do not want to use it.

Step 14. To enable or disable an event action override, select it from the list and click **Edit**.

Step 15. To disable an event action override, deselect the Enabled check box, and to enable an event action override, select the check box.

Step 16. Click **Apply** to apply your changes and save the updated configuration.

When implementing event action overrides on your Cisco IPS Sensor, consider the following:

■ Use event action overrides to simplify the creation of either detective or preventive actions for all signatures based on their risk rating. You will not have to configure each signature individually this way.

■ If you do not want to use event action overrides, you can disable the entire event action override component.

Using Event Action Filters

Event action filters allow you to remove one or more actions from any active signature based on various criteria as determined by your security requirements. This will typically help in fine-tuning your Cisco IPS Sensor when managing false positive events. In this context, you typically would remove one or some actions from a particular signature if it does not pose a risk and is triggered by a valid source IP address.

Event action filters are processed in the order in which they are listed, and you can move the filters up and down in the list. The event action filter works by removing certain actions from events. To create an event action filter, follow these steps:

Step 1. Navigate to **Configuration > Policies > Event Action Rules > rules0** and click the Event Action Filters tab.

Step 2. Click **Add** and the Add Event Action Filter window opens, as shown in Figure 9-18.

Step 3. In the Name field, enter a name for the event action filter.

Step 4. In the Enabled field, click the Yes radio button to enable the filter.

Step 5. In the Signature ID field, enter the signature IDs of all signatures to which this filter should be applied.

Step 6. In the Subsignature ID field, enter the subsignature IDs of the subsignatures that the filter is being applied to.

Step 7. In the Attacker IPv4 Address field, enter the IP address(es) of the source host(s).

Step 8. In the Attacker IPv6 Address field, enter the range set of attacker IPv6 addresses of the source host.

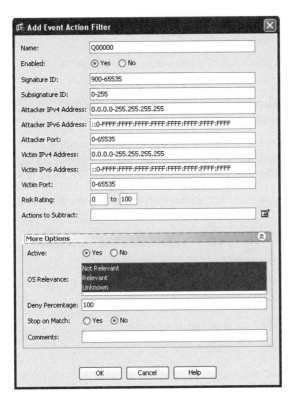

Figure 9-18   *Configuring an Event Action Filter*

Step 9.   In the Attacker Port field, enter the port number or range that is used by the attacker to send the offending packet.

Step 10.   In the Victim IPv4 Address field, enter the IP address(es) of the recipient host(s).

Step 11.   In the Victim IPv6 Address field, enter the range set of IPv6 addresses of the recipient host.

Step 12.   In the Victim Port field, enter the port number or range that is used by the victim host to receive the offending packet.

Step 13.   In the Risk Rating field, enter a risk rating range for this filter.

Step 14.   In the Actions to Subtract field, click the Note icon to open the Edit Actions dialog box.

Step 15.   Select the check boxes of the actions you want the filter to remove from the event. Click the More Options arrow at the bottom of the Add Event Action Filter window to reveal the fields for Steps 16–19.

Note: IPv6 does not support the Request Block Host, Request Block Connection, and Request Rate Limit event actions.

Step 16. In the Active field, select the Yes radio button to add this filter to the list so that it takes effect on the filtering events.

Step 17. In the OS Relevance field, choose whether you want to know if the alert is relevant to the operating system that has been identified for the victim.

Step 18. In the Deny Percentage field, enter the percentage of packets to deny from deny attacker features. The default is 100.

Step 19. In the Stop on Match field, select Yes if you want the event action filters to stop processing after the actions of the particular filter have been removed, or select No if you want it to continue processing additional filters.

Step 20. Click **OK** and the new event action filter appears listed on the Event Action Filters tab.

You can also click **Cancel** to discard your changes and close the Add Event Action Filter dialog box.

It is important to consider the following implementation guidelines when preparing to implement event action filters on the Cisco IPS Sensor:

■ Configure event action filters to tune false positives from specific flows.

■ Configure event action filters to remove specific actions for all signatures.

■ Configure event action filters for variable group addresses, which allows you to make changes to the variable when needed.

Choosing an Action Configuration Strategy

When configuring the Cisco IPS Sensor in a production network, it is very pivotal to employ one of the following four strategies for configuring signature actions for the entire signature set:

■ Configure actions in each individual signature through the user interface by selecting individual signatures or groups of signatures and assigning actions manually.

■ Use event action overrides, configuring all supporting parameters for risk rating calculation and adding detective or preventive actions that are based on the risk rating threshold.

■ Use event action overrides and add detective or aggressive actions to all triggering signatures.

■ Use a mixed strategy of several concurrent strategies.

Table 9-8 summarizes the response strategies for signature actions as well as their benefits and limitations.

Table 9-8 *Signature Action Configuration Strategy*

Strategy	Benefits	Limitations
Individual signature responses	Can select the best responses for a particular attack	Does not take into account environmental properties (TVR, ARR)
		Very time consuming
Event action override with risk rating thre sholds	Takes environmental properties into account	Can cause false negatives with under-threshold events
	Can automatically ignore some false positives	
	Easy to configure	
Event action override for all risk ratings	Provides full preventive policy for all signatures	Requires an extremely well-tuned sensor
	Uses environmental properties to monitor threat rating	Does not choose the best response for a particular attack

The benefit of the individual signature configuration is being able to select the most appropriate response for a particular signature. An example is a Deny Attacker Inline action for a reconnaissance scan. However, this approach does not take into account all environmental properties and will not produce good risk rating or threat rating values for event monitoring. This configuration can be very time consuming when you have many active signatures.

Using event action overrides with risk rating thresholds is easy to configure, takes into account all your environmental variables, and can automatically ignore some common false positives by deprioritizing them with a low Signature Fidelity Rating. The downside of this approach is the likelihood of false negatives with under-threshold events and not choosing the best response for a particular attack as it adds signatures across the board.

The third approach is adding detective or preventive actions across the board without considering the risk rating. This approach has the benefit of providing the best detection and prevention coverage as it reacts to all signatures being triggered. It does require a well-tuned sensor with few or no false positives, but it does not choose the best response for a particular attack.

Using a mixed-approach strategy is the most efficient approach. For example, you could use a combination of threshold-based event action overrides and a Deny Packet Inline action to all signature triggers with a risk rating above 10, with a reasonable amount of tuning on the Cisco IPS Sensor.

Examining Alerts in IPS Event Logs

Alerts are generated by the Cisco IPS SensorApp application when there is malicious or suspicious behavior exhibited by the packets it is analyzing. All alerts are stored in the sensor event store with sensor error messages, which can be used for troubleshooting.

The **show events alert** command displays IPS alert outputs through the sensor CLI when issued. The command will typically display the output from when the time the command is issued unless a start time is entered as well. The events are displayed in the live feed and can be halted by pressing Ctrl-C, while a user with administrator privileges can issue the **clear events** command to remove all the events from the event store. The **show events alert** command has some parameters that can be used with it apart from the start time. Example 9-2 shows other command options available with the **show events** command from the CLI.

Example 9-2   show ip ips all *Command Output*

```
ips4240# show events ?
<cr>
alert          Display local system alerts.
error          Display error events.
hh:mm[:ss]     Display start time.
log            Display log events.
nac            Display NAC shun events.
past           Display events starting in the past specified time.
status         Display status events.
|              Output modifiers.
```

There are more parameters, which you can find by choosing those listed previously and putting a question mark at the end of the command. The complete syntax with options will look like this:

>   show events [{alert [informational] [low] [medium] [high] [include-traits *traits*]
>   [exclude-traits *traits*] [min-threat-rating *min-rr*] [max-threat-rating *max-rr*] | error
>   [warming] [error] [fatal] | log | nac | status}] [*hh:mm:ss month day year*] | past
>   *hh:mm:ss*]

Table 9-9 provides information on the parameters.

Table 9-9   show events *Parameters*

Parameter	Description
alert [informational] [low] [medium] [high]	This command provides notification of some suspicious activity that can indicate that an attack is in progress or has been attempted.
include-traits	Displays alerts that have the specified traits.
exclude-traits	Does not display alerts that have the specified traits.
traits	Trait bit position in decimal (0–15).

Table 9-9 show events *Parameters*

Parameter	Description
min-threat-rating *min-rr*	Displays events with a threat rating greater than or equal to the *min-rr* value. The valid range is from 0 to 100, where 100 is the default.
max-threat-rating *max-rr*	Displays events with a threat rating less than or equal to the *max-rr* value. The valid range is from 0 to 100, where 100 is the default.
error [warming] [error] [fatal]	Displays error events.
log	Displays log events.
nac	Displays NAC shun events.
status	Displays status events.
hh:mm:ss month day year	This is the start time (24-hour format), month (by name), day (by date), and year (no abbreviation).
past	Displays events starting at the current time minus hh:mm:ss.

Example 9-3 shows sample output from the **show events alert** command for a date.

Example 9-3 show events alert *Command Output*

```
ips4240# show events alert 9:00:00 May 21 2011
evIdsAlert: eventId=1306360823391418606 severity=informational vendor=Cisco
  originator:
    hostId: ips4240
    appName: sensorApp
    appInstanceId: 411
  time: 2011/06/02 22:58:12 2011/06/02 16:58:12 GMT-06:00
  signature: description=ARP Reply-to-Broadcast id=7102 created=20021223
    type=anomaly version=S37
    subsigId: 0
    marsCategory: Penetrate/ArpPoisoning
  interfaceGroup: vs0
  vlan: 0
  participants:
    attacker:
      addr: locality=OUT 192.168.1.71
    target:
      addr: locality=OUT 192.168.1.71
      os: idSource=unknown relevance=relevant type=unknown
  actions:
    logPacketsActivated: true
    logAttackerPacketsActivated: true
```

```
   logVictimPacketsActivated: true
   logPairPacketsActivated: true
 ipLogIds:
   ipLogId: 1701756292
   ipLogId: 1701756292
   ipLogId: 1701756292
 riskRatingValue: attackRelevanceRating=relevant targetValueRating=medium 35
 threatRatingValue: 35
 interface: ge0_0
 protocol: IP protocol 0
```

Viewing Events in the Cisco IDM

To view IPS alerts using the Cisco IDM, follow these steps:

Step 1.   Choose **Monitoring > Sensor Monitoring** and choose **Events**, as shown in Figure 9-19.

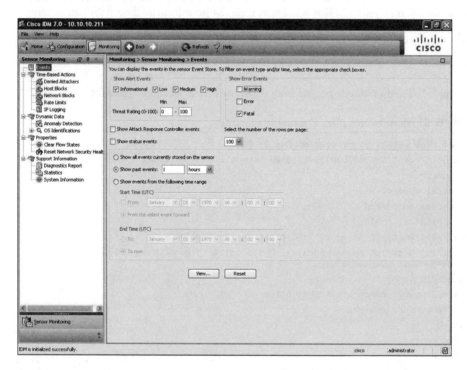

Figure 9-19   *Choosing Options to View IPS Alerts*

Step 2.   Do not select error events if you only want to see IPS alerts.

Step 3.   Complete the filter choices in the Events pane by choosing to view events based on criteria such as event severity, type of events, number of events per page, and time consideration.

Step 4.   Click the **View** button, and the Event Viewer window opens, as shown in Figure 9-20.

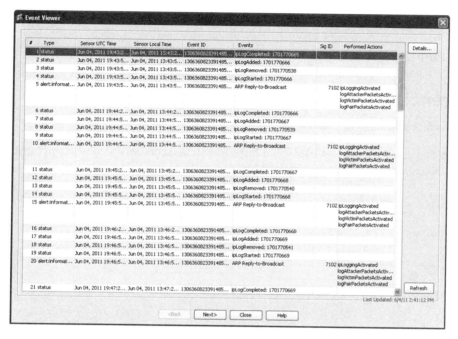

Figure 9-20   *Viewing Events in the Cisco IDM*

The Event Viewer has the following options within to aid the viewing and analysis of events, as shown in Figure 9-20:

- **Details:** This allows you to display individual event details.

- **Refresh:** This allows you to pull events again from the event store.

- **Back and Next:** These are navigation buttons that allow you to move back and forth through the pages.

Summary

This section highlights the key topics discussed in this chapter:

- The Cisco IPS signature is a set of rules that the sensor uses to detect malicious and suspicious activity.

- A signature engine is a part of the IPS sensor, and it supports a category of signatures.

- A Cisco IPS Sensor can dynamically reconfigure a remote Cisco device to block the source of an attack in real time.

- IP packets can be captured automatically or manually.

- The risk rating formula uses the ASR, TVR, SFR, ARR, PD, and WLR values to calculate a risk rating value.

- An event action override can be used to change the actions associated with an event.

- Event filtering enables you to reduce the number of false positives.

References

More information can be found at this URL:

Installing and Using Cisco IDM 7.0, at http://www.cisco.com/en/US/docs/security/ips/7.0/configuration/guide/idm/idmguide7.html.

Exam Preparation Tasks

Review All the Key Topics

Review the most important topics from the chapter, noted with the Key Topic icons in the margin of the page. Table 9-10 lists a reference of these key topics and the page numbers on which each is found.

Table 9-10 *Key Topics for Chapter 9*

Key Topic Element	Description	Page Number
Figure 9-2	Signature Configuration View	198
Table 9-2	Detective Signature Actions	201
Table 9-5	Preventive Signature Action Implementation Guidelines	206
Figure 9-4	Remote Blocking	208
Table 9-6	Risk Rating System Components	220
Table 9-8	Signature Action Configuration Strategy	229

Complete the Tables and Lists from Memory

Print a copy of Appendix C, "Memory Tables" (found on the CD), or at least the section for this chapter, and complete the tables and lists from memory. Appendix D, "Memory Tables Answer Key," also on the CD, includes completed tables and lists to check your work.

Definitions of Key Terms

Define the following key terms from this chapter, and check your answers in the glossary:

Signature, Security Device Event Exchange (SDEE), Attack Response Controller (ARC)

This chapter covers the following topics:

- **Using Cisco IPS Signature Engines and Configuring Common Signature Engine Parameters:** This section provides an overview of common Cisco IPS signatures.

- **Deploying ATOMIC Signature Engines:** This section covers the deployment, common, and engine-specific parameters of the ATOMIC signature engines.

- **Deploying STRING Signature Engines:** This section covers the deployment, common, and engine-specific parameters of the STRING signature engines.

- **Deploying SERVICE Signature Engines:** This section lists the different SERVICE signature engines and covers the deployment of a SERVICE engine and its common and engine-specific parameters.

- **Deploying FLOOD Signature Engines:** This section covers the deployment, common, and engine-specific parameters of the FLOOD signature engines.

- **Deploying SWEEP Signature Engines:** This section covers the deployment, common, and engine-specific parameters of the SWEEP signature engines.

- **Deploying the META Signature Engine:** This section covers the details of the META signature engine and its deployment.

- **Deploying the NORMALIZER Engine:** This section covers the NORMALIZER engine and provides information and guidelines if there is a requirement to tune the engine.

- **Deploying Other Engines:** This section covers Application Inspection and Control (AIC) engines and provides information on the benefits and disadvantages of the associated engines.

CHAPTER 10

Configuring Cisco IPS Signature Engines and the Signature Database

Overview

This chapter provides some insight into the engine architecture of Cisco Intrusion Prevention System (IPS) Sensors. Signature engines are categorized, and the built-in signature database is examined. The chapter also briefly covers how to configure and verify common signature engine parameters.

"Do I Know This Already?" Quiz

The "Do I Know This Already?" quiz allows you to assess whether you should read the entire chapter. If you miss no more than one of these self-assessment questions, you might want to move ahead to the "Exam Preparation Tasks" section. Table 10-1 lists the major headings in this chapter and the "Do I Know This Already?" quiz questions covering the material in those headings so that you can assess your knowledge of these specific areas. The answers to the "Do I Know This Already?" quiz appear in Appendix A.

Table 10-1 *"Do I Know This Already?" Foundation Topics Section-to-Question Mapping*

Foundation Topics Section	Questions
Using Cisco IPS Signature Engines and Configuring Common Signature Engine Parameters	1
Deploying ATOMIC Signature Engines	2
Deploying STRING Signature Engines	3
Deploying SERVICE Signature Engines	4

1. Which of the following is aided by Cisco IPS signature engines?

   a. Enables the creation of new signatures

   b. Enables the tuning of built-in signatures

   c. Uses their parameters to provide the configuration of signatures.

   d. All of these answers are correct.

2. Which of the following is unique about the ATOMIC signature engines?

   a. The ATOMIC signature engines support signatures that are triggered by the contents of multiple packets.

   b. The ATOMIC signature engines support signatures that are triggered by the contents of a single packet.

   c. The ATOMIC signature engines support signatures that are triggered by the output of multiple signatures.

   d. None of these answers are correct.

3. Which of the following is *not* a STRING signature engine?

   a. ATOMIC STRING

   b. STRING ICMP

   c. STRING TCP

   d. STRING UDP

4. At what OSI layer and above does the SERVICE engine analyze traffic?

   a. Layer 3

   b. Layer 2

   c. Layer 5 and higher

   d. Layer 1

Foundation Topics

Using Cisco IPS Signature Engines and Configuring Common Signature Engine Parameters

The following sections describe Cisco IPS signatures and signature engines and provide details on the configuration and verification of common signature engine parameters, trigger counting, and alarm summarization.

Signature and Signature Engines

A *signature* is a set of rules that your sensor uses to detect malicious or suspicious network activity, such as denial of service (DoS) attacks, while scanning network packets. A signature must be enabled to monitor network traffic.

A *Cisco IPS signature engine* is a component of the analysis engine of the sensor that inspects network traffic and supports signatures. Each Cisco IPS signature is supported and controlled by a particular signature engine that is specifically designed for the type of traffic being monitored. Cisco IPS signature engines enable network security administrators to tune and create signatures unique to their network environment, and also have a set of parameters that have allowable ranges or set of values.

Signature engines export their parameters to provide a programmable interface that is used for signature creation, where each has a name and value. Some parameters are common across all engines and therefore present in all signatures. These parameters define the general parameters of signatures, such as their name and alert summarization strategy. Some parameters are designed for a specific engine and are only applicable to signatures within that engine. Engine-specific parameters are used to describe network traffic that signatures should match.

The common signature parameters are listed in Table 10-2.

Table 10-2 *Common Signature Parameters*

Key Topic

Common Signature Parameters	Value	Description
Signature ID	■ 1000–59,000: Range for default signatures ■ 60,000–65,000: Range for custom signatures	This is the numeric value that is assigned to the signature.
Subsignature ID	0–255	This is used with the Signature ID to create a unique numerical identifier for a signature.

Table 10-2 *Common Signature Parameters*

Common Signature Parameters	Value	Description
Alert Severity	■ High ■ Medium ■ Low ■ Informational	This is the severity of the alert that is reported in the alarm.
Sig Fidelity Rating	0–100	This is the weight that is associated with how well this signature might perform in the absence of specific knowledge of the target. The Sig Fidelity Rating is one of the factors that are used in calculating the risk rating. The default value of each signature is assigned by the engineer who wrote the signature.
Promiscuous Delta	0–30	This value is deducted from the risk rating value when the sensor is in promiscuous mode. You should not change this parameter, which has a value of 0 for most built-in signatures.
Sig Description		When expanded, this displays the parameters that help you distinguish this signature from other signatures.
Signature Name	<string>	This is the alphanumeric name that is assigned to the signature.
Alert Notes	<string>	This corresponds to sig-string-info in the command-line interface (CLI). Alert Notes enables you to define extra information to be included in the alarm message.
User Comments	<string>	This corresponds to sig-comment in the CLI. The User Comments parameter is not reported in alerts and does not affect processing.
Alert Traits	0–65,535	Used to further categorize a signature. You can create your own grouping strategy to augment the traditional fields in the alert. Alert traits are limited to 16 user-configurable bits, meaning that 0–65,535 are valid values. The bits above 16 are reserved for use by IPS internals.

Table 10-2 *Common Signature Parameters*

Common Signature Parameters	Value	Description
Release	<string>	This is the signature release in which this signature became available.
Vulnerable OS List		This allows an administrator to configure a list of operating systems that are vulnerable to this attack.
MARS Category		This contains the list of the Cisco Monitoring, Analysis, and Response System (MARS) attack categories that are associated with the signature.
Engine		When expanded, this displays the engine-specific parameters for the signature. The engine-specific parameters apply only to the signatures within the engine.
Event Counter		When expanded, this displays the parameters that determine whether the signature fires. The Event Counter parameters enable you to configure how the sensor counts events. For example, you can specify that you only want the signature to fire if the activity it detects happens five times for the same address set within a specified period of time.
Event Count	1–65,535	The event count enables you to prevent the signature from firing until the number of specified events is seen during the specified alert interval in the specified Event Count Key. The default value is 1.
Event Count Key	■ Attacker address ■ Attacker address and victim port ■ Attacker and victim addresses ■ Attacker and victim addresses and ports ■ Victim address	This is used for counting multiple firings of the signature. This key influences signature firing by specifying the address sets on which the Event Count parameter is based.

Table 10-2   *Common Signature Parameters*

Common Signature Parameters	Value	Description
Alert Interval	2–1000	This is a modifier that adds a sliding-window time limit for the event count to be met.
Alert Frequency		When expanded, this displays the parameters for configuring how often the sensor sends an alert to the event store when the signature is firing. The Alert Frequency parameters enable you to control the number of alarms that are generated by a specific signature.
Summary Mode	■ **Fire Once:** Sends the first alert and then deletes the inspector ■ **Fire All:** Sends all alerts ■ **Summarize:** Sends an interval summary alert ■ **Global Summarize:** Sends a global summary alert	This is a technique that is used to limit alarm firings. The remaining configurable Alert Frequency parameters vary depending on the summary mode that you choose.
Summary Key	■ Attacker address ■ Attacker address and victim port ■ Attacker and victim addresses ■ Attacker and victim addresses and ports ■ Victim address	This is the storage type on which to summarize this signature. The summary key identifies the address set to use for counting events for event summarization.
Global Summary Threshold	1–65,535	This is the number of events that are required to automatically change the summary mode to Globally Summarize. When the alert rate exceeds this threshold within the summary interval, the sensor changes from sending a summary alert to sending a global summary alert.
Summary Interval	1–65,535	This defines the period of time in seconds that is used to control alarm summarization.

Table 10-2 *Common Signature Parameters*

Common Signature Parameters	Value	Description
Status		When expanded, this displays parameters for enabling, disabling, retiring, or activating the signature.
Enabled	■ **Yes:** Enables the signature ■ **No:** Disables the signature	This is used to enable or disable a signature.
Retired	■ **Yes:** Retires the signature ■ **No:** Activates the signature	This is used to disable aged signatures.

Trigger Counting

Trigger counting is a mechanism that signatures use to count the occurrence of traffic-matching events; it is also governed by the common engine parameters. Some signatures do not trigger immediately on the first occurrence of an event, as they require an event to repeat a particular number of times before it is considered malicious or suspicious. For example, a single failed login might not be suspicious, but five failed successive logins on the same host could indicate a password-cracking event or attack.

The following steps guide you in configuring trigger counting in signatures:

Step 1.   In the common parameters, configure the interval in which you want to count occurrences. After the passing of each interval, the signature removes previous occurrences and starts counting from scratch. A typical value for the counting interval is 60 seconds.

Step 2.   In the common parameters, configure the number of matches required to fire the signature. Configure this threshold in the Event Count parameter.

Step 3.   In the common parameters, configure the criteria on which the signature counts individual events. The Event Count Key parameter determines the counting criteria and can be set to the following values:

■ **Attacker address:** The signature maintains a separate counter for each attacker.

■ **Attacker address and victim port:** The signature maintains a separate counter for each attacker-service pair.

■ **Attacker and victim addresses:** The signature maintains a separate counter for each pair of communicating hosts.

- **Inside a single Layer 4 session:** The signature maintains a separate counter for each Layer 4 session.

- **Victim address:** The signature maintains a separate counter for each target.

Summary Key

The Summary Key parameter is similar to the Event Count Key parameter in trigger counting. The Summary Key parameter defines the addresses on which the signature will summarize its reporting, if configured to do so. It can have the following values:

- **Attacker address only:** Axxx

- **Attacker and victim addresses:** AxBx

- **Attacker address and victim port:** Axxb

- **Attacker and victim addresses and ports:** AaBb

Alarm Summarization

Summarization allows the sensor to adapt its alert rate based on the triggering rate. This is enabled by the IPS Sensor's dynamic summarization engine, which can automatically adjust the number of alarms resulting from malicious activity. The common summarization-related parameters of all engines provide the sensor with an option to adapt its alert rate based on the triggering rate of a signature. The Summary Mode common engine parameter controls the number of alarms that are generated by a specific signature.

The Summary Mode parameter can have one of the following values:

- **Fire Once:** The signature will generate a single alarm in a configurable summary interval time range for each unique Summary Key entry. This setting is generally not recommended.

- **Fire All:** The signature will generate an alarm each time the signature triggers. This is an optimal choice if the signature trigger rate is low.

- **Summarize:** The signature will send a summary alert once each interval for each unique key entry. This consolidates alarms for the address set specified in the Summary Key parameter. This mode also limits the number of alarms that are generated, which makes it difficult for an attacker to consume resources on the sensor or overwhelm the administrator with alerts.

- **Global Summarize:** This signature consolidates alarms for all address combinations (that is, without a summary key). The Global Summarize node specifies that you want the sensor to send an alert the first time that a signature fires on an address set and then send only a global summary alert that includes a summary of all the alerts for all address sets over a given time interval.

Dynamic Alarm Summarization

Dynamic summarization allows the sensor to dynamically change its summarization mode for each signature to adapt itself to the signature triggering rate. To take advantage of the dynamic alert summarization, you must configure the signature to initially use the Fire All or Summarize mode. When the signature is triggered, the Cisco IPS generates the alerts according to the original Summary Mode setting. If the number of alerts for the signature exceeds the value that is configured for the Summary Threshold parameter during a summary interval, the signature automatically switches to the next higher alert mode in which fewer alerts are generated. If the number of alerts of the signature exceeds the global summary threshold during the same summary interval, the signature switches to Global Summarize if not already at this level. At the end of the summary interval, the signature reverts to its original configured summary mode.

Deploying ATOMIC Signature Engines

ATOMIC signature engines support signatures that are triggered by matching the header or payload contents of a single packet. The ATOMIC signature engines examine single packets and do not need to maintain a state; thus, they do not store any persistent data across multiple data packets, but also cannot detect data that is spread across multiple packets.

The Cisco IPS Software uses the following ATOMIC signature engines:

- **ATOMIC ARP:** This engine is used to examine Address Resolution Protocol (ARP) packets. This engine is also used for detection of ARP spoofing attacks.

- **ATOMIC IP:** This engine is used to examine IP, TCP, UDP, and Internet Control Message Protocol (ICMP) headers and payloads.

- **ATOMIC IP Advanced:** The ATOMIC IP Advanced engine parses and interprets the IP version 6 (IPv6) header and its extensions, the IP version 4 (IPv4) header and its options, ICMP, ICMPv6, TCP, and UDP headers and payloads, and seeks out anomalies that indicate unusual or malicious activity.

- **ATOMIC IPv6:** This engine detects Cisco IOS Software vulnerabilities that are simulated by malformed IPv6 traffic.

- **FIXED TCP, FIXED UDP, and FIXED ICMP:** These are performance-optimized ATOMIC engines that perform a highly optimized pattern search, but only in a fixed portion of the packet headers and payload.

ATOMIC IP Signature Example

An example of a signature based on the ATOMIC IP engine is the Cisco IPS SYN/FIN Packet signature. The signature matches malformed TCP packets that have both the SYN and FIN bits set. The signature uses the following illustrative common and engine-specific parameters:

- **Signature Name (common):** TCP SYN/FIN packet

- **Signature ID (common):** 3041/0

- **Engine (common):** ATOMIC IP

- **Description (common):** Triggers when a single TCP packet with the SYN and FIN flags are set and is sent to a specific host. This indicates that a reconnaissance sweep of your network might be in progress. The use of this type of packet indicates an attempt to conceal the sweep. This can be the prelude to a more serious attack and is not acceptable as legitimate traffic.

- **TCP Flags (engine-specific):** SYN FIN (These two flags must be set.)

- **Mask (engine-specific):** SYN FIN ACK (These flags are inspected.)

- **Destination Port Range (engine-specific):** 1–1024

Implementation Guidelines for ATOMIC Signature Engines

To create new signatures or tune existing signatures using the ATOMIC signature engine, consider the following implementation guidelines:

- For custom signatures, use the ATOMIC signatures to match malicious activity that can be wholly classified by looking at a single packet. Avoid ATOMIC signatures for application layer matching, because attackers can easily evade it by splitting their malicious content across multiple packets.

- If the malicious payload can be found in the fixed-search portion of the packet, consider using FIXED engines as an alternative for ATOMIC engines. The same caveat applies for application layer inspection as with ATOMIC engines.

Deploying STRING Signature Engines

The STRING signature engines support regular expression pattern matching and alarm functionality for ICMP, UDP, and TCP. This signature matches patterns based on a reassembled stream of packets and not a single packet. The STRING signature considers the arrival order of packets in a TCP stream and handles pattern matching across packet boundaries. The Cisco IPS uses the following STRING signature engines:

- **STRING ICMP:** This engine searches ICMP packets for a string pattern.

- **STRING TCP:** This engine searches TCP connections for a string pattern.

- **STRING UDP:** This engine searches UDP flows for a string pattern.

- **MULTI STRING:** This engine searches through multiple independent connections to find multiple strings.

STRING TCP Signature Example

An example of a signature based on the STRING TCP engine is the Cisco IPS IOS FTPd MKD Command Buffer Overflow signature. This signature matches FTP sessions that include binary data in the argument of the **MKD (make directory)** FTP command. Some of the common and engine-specific parameters are as follows:

- **Signature Name (common):** IOS FTPd MKD Command Buffer Overflow

- **Signature ID (common):** 6973/0

- **Engine (common):** STRING TCP

- **Description (common):** Buffer Overflow in MKD

- **Service Ports (engine-specific):** 21

- **Direction (engine-specific):** To service (This indicates that the string should be matched in the direction from the client to the server.)

- **Regex String (engine-specific):** ^[mM][kK][dD]\x20[^\x0a\x0d]*[\x7f-\xff] (This specifies the data pattern to look for inside the TCP session, which is the **MKD** command followed by binary data.)

Implementation Guidelines for STRING Signature Engines

To create new signatures or tune existing signatures using the STRING signature engines, consider the following:

- For custom signatures, use the STRING engines to provide application layer inspection if no granular SERVICE engine is available for a particular application layer protocol. Configuring the STRING engines for application layer inspection requires considerable expertise and can easily lead to performance issues and false positives or negatives if improperly designed.

- Consider using MULTI STRING engines to detect composite attacks, as you cannot reliably detect such attacks by only inspecting a connection. However, MULTI STRING engine signatures can bog down sensor resources, and due care should be taken when designing them.

Deploying SERVICE Signature Engines

The SERVICE signature engines reassemble OSI Layer 4 sessions, decode application layer protocols, and analyze protocol and data units in the decoded stream. This provides inspection for numerous network protocols, such as Domain Name System (DNS), FTP, and HTTP.

The Cisco IPS Sensor Software uses the following SERVICE signature engines:

- **SERVICE DNS:** This engine examines TCP and UDP DNS packets.

- **SERVICE FTP:** This engine examines FTP traffic.

- **SERVICE Generic:** This is an emergency response engine that supplements the STRING and STATE engines, and is only used by Cisco engineering to quickly create complex signatures for which there are no other engines available.

- **SERVICE H225:** This engine examines H.225 call-signaling and call setup traffic.

- **SERVICE HTTP:** This engine examines HTTP traffic.

- **SERVICE IDENT:** This engine examines traffic of the IDENT protocol.

- **SERVICE MSRPC:** This engine examines Microsoft Remote Procedure Call (RPC) traffic.

- **SERVICE MSSQL:** This engine examines traffic used by Microsoft SQL Server.

- **SERVICE NTP:** This engine examines Network Time Protocol (NTP) traffic.

- **SERVICE P2P:** This engine examines peer-to-peer (P2P) traffic on all ports.

- **SERVICE RPC:** This engine examines UNIX remote procedure call (RPC) traffic.

- **SERVICE SMB Advanced:** This engine examines Microsoft SMB and Microsoft RPC over SMB traffic.

- **SERVICE SNMP:** This engine examines Simple Network Management Protocol (SNMP) traffic.

- **SERVICE SSH:** This engine examines Secure Shell (SSH) traffic.

- **SERVICE TNS:** This engine examines Transparent Network Substrate (TNS) traffic. TNS is an industry-standard database network protocol, used mostly by Oracle products.

SERVICE HTTP Signature Example

An example of a signature based on the SERVICE HTTP engine is the Cisco IPS Dot Dot Slash in Uniform Resource Identifier (URI). The signature matches HTTP requests that include an attempt to traverse directories on the web server file systems indicated by the "../" pattern in the HTTP request URI. The common and engine-specific parameters of the signature are as follows:

- **Signature Name (common):** Dot Dot Slash in URI

- **Signature ID (common):** 5256/0

- **Engine (common):** SERVICE HTTP

- **Description (common):** ../ in URI

- **De Obfuscate (engine-specific):** Yes (This specifies that the engine should convert all data to a normalized ASCII form before analyzing it.)

- **Service Ports (engine-specific):** #WEBPORTS (This is a customizable variable that, by default, includes the following TCP ports: 80, 3128, 8000, 8010, 8080, 8888, and 24326.)

- **URI Regex (engine-specific):** [.][.][/\\] (This specifies the data pattern to look for inside the URI container—two dots followed by a forward slash or a backslash.)

Implementation Guidelines for SERVICE Signature Engines

To create new signatures or tune existing signatures using the SERVICE signature engines, consider the following:

- For custom signatures, it is always recommended that you use SERVICE engines to provide application layer inspection if the SERVICE engines support the protocols that you need to inspect and provide appropriate granularity. Note that using SERVICE engines for a signature will typically result in fewer false positives and higher performance, because the sensor performs a more localized search in the protocol stream.

- If no SERVICE engine is available, or if the included SERVICE engine does not provide the required granularity, consider using STRING engines instead.

Deploying FLOOD Signature Engines

The FLOOD signature engines detect attacks in which the attacker is directing a flood of traffic to either a single host or, generally, over the sensor. Signatures of FLOOD engines measure the traffic rate and compare it to fixed per-signature thresholds to detect and react to denial of service attacks.

The following FLOOD signature engines are included in the Cisco IPS Sensor Software:

- **FLOOD NET:** Used to examine an excessive number of packets sent over the sensor (or received by the sensor in promiscuous mode).

- **FLOOD HOST:** Used to examine an excessive number of Internet Control Message Protocol (ICMP) or User Datagram Protocol (UDP) packets sent to an individual target host.

FLOOD Signature Example

An example of a signature based on the FLOOD HOST engine is the Cisco IPS DNS Flood Attack. The signature examines UDP packets from port 53 (DNS replies) and triggers if the rate of such packets is more than 500 per second. Such a high rate of DNS replies is indicative of a DNS cache-poisoning attempt. The signature uses the following common and engine-specific parameters:

- **Signature Name (common):** DNS Flood Attack

- **Signature ID (common):** 4004/0

- **Engine (common):** FLOOD HOST

- **Description (common):** This signature detects a DNS flood that could lead to potential DNS cache-poisoning, reflection, or amplification attacks.

- **Src Ports (engine-specific):** 53

- **Dst Ports (engine-specific):** 1–65,535

- **Rate Ports (engine-specific):** 500

Implementation Guidelines for FLOOD Signature Engines

To create new signatures or tune existing signatures using the FLOOD signature engines, consider the following:

- In a default Cisco IPS configuration, most FLOOD signatures are disabled, as the threshold rates vary in different networks. It is important to tune these signatures based on your security requirements by setting the appropriate thresholds.

- The FLOOD NET signature engine supports the pseudolearning function, where it can report the traffic rate that is observed across the sensor in specified time intervals. This is done by enabling the FLOOD NET-based signatures and setting the Rate parameter to 0.

Deploying SWEEP Signature Engines

The SWEEP signature engines detect attacks in which one system makes connections to multiple hosts or a single host on multiple ports. The SWEEP engines are used to detect network reconnaissance.

There are two SWEEP signature engines available in the Cisco IPS Sensor:

- **SWEEP:** This engine detects host sweeps, port scans, and service sweeps.

- **SWEEP Other TCP:** This engine analyzes traffic between two hosts, looking for the abnormal packets that are typically used to fingerprint a victim.

SWEEP Signature Example

An example of a signature based on the SWEEP engine is the Cisco IPS TCP FIN Port Sweep. This signature examines TCP FIN packets to each host and triggers if more than five packets to different ports are seen within an inspection interval, which indicates a possibility of a port scan.

The signature uses the following common and engine-specific parameters:

- **Signature Name (common):** TCP FIN Port Sweep

- **Signature ID (common):** 3005/0

- **Engine (common):** SWEEP

- **Description (common):** Triggers when a series of TCP FIN packets have been sent to a number of privileged ports on a specific host. This is indicative of a reconnaissance sweep of the network.

- **Unique (engine-specific):** 5 (This specifies the threshold number of unique port connections between the two hosts.)

- **TCP Flags (engine-specific):** FIN (This must be set.)

- **Mask (engine-specific):** SYN FIN ACK (These are inspected.)

- **Storage Key (common):** Attacker and victim addresses

Implementation Guidelines for SWEEP Signature Engines

To create new signatures or tune existing signatures using the SWEEP signature engines, consider the following:

- SWEEP engine signatures typically require tuning after initial sensor deployment because there can be legitimate hosts scanning the network and creating a pattern similar to reconnaissance.

- Cisco IPS Sensors support an anomaly detection function that is similar to SWEEP engines. However, the anomaly detection is not based on fixed thresholds but rather dynamically creates these thresholds and tunes itself to avoid false positives.

Deploying the META Signature Engine

The META engine correlates other signatures into a higher-level meta-event. Using the META engine can reduce the number of alerts that are generated by attacks from aggressive network activity. Multifactor attacks exploit a number of different vulnerabilities and can trigger several different signatures, which generate many alerts. The META engine enables you to disable the component signatures of such attacks so that they do not generate alerts, but you receive a meta-alert that the activity is happening.

The main difference between the META engine and other signature engines is its input. While regular engines take network traffic as input, the META engine takes signature events as input, even events of other META signatures to provide nested event correlation.

META Correlation Example

An example of a signature based on the META engine is the Cisco IPS Worm Activity – Brute Force. This signature observes three individual signatures and triggers if they all trigger within 60 seconds because of the same attacker IP address. The signature uses the following common and engine-specific parameters:

- **Signature Name (common):** Worm Activity – Brute Force

- **Signature ID (common):** 13491/0

- **Engine (common):** META

- **Description (common):** This signature detects a Trojaned Windows host attempting to spread through brute-force methods. The signature tracks multiple account lock messages, attempted access to ADMIN$, and attempts at writing to the system32 directory from a single host. This signature combines signatures 5602-0, 5605-0, and 5589-0 into a single meta-signature. The signatures must be enabled and active for this signature to fire. This signature can be used to help isolate infected hosts on the network.

- **Component List (engine-specific):** Signatures 5605, 5589, and 5602 (Windows Account Locked, ADMIN$ Hidden Share Access Attempt, and Windows System32 Directory File Access, respectively)

- **All Components Required (engine-specific):** Yes

- **Components List in Order (engine-specific):** No

- **Meta Key (engine-specific):** Attacker address

- **Meta Reset Interval (engine-specific):** 60 seconds

Implementation Guidelines for META Signature Engines

To configure META signatures, follow these steps:

Step 1.   Select the component signatures that are part of the META signature. You can specify that all the signatures are required to be fired or a subset of the signatures, which effectively creates AND and OR conditions.

Step 2.   Specify the key on which you will base correlated component events.

Step 3.   Configure the time period in seconds during which the component events must occur if this signature is to fire. Valid values range from 0 to 3600.

Step 4.   You can specify whether the component signatures must fire in a specific order for the signature to fire using the Components List in Order parameter.

Step 5.   Ensure that signatures used to trigger the meta-signature are all enabled.

Step 6.   Optional: You can remove configured actions from component signatures so that meta-signatures alone will produce actions.

Deploying the NORMALIZER Engine

The NORMALIZER engine is not a general signature engine, but it provides the configuration interface to both normalizers. This is contained in the Cisco IPS Sensor Software as an IP traffic normalizer and a TCP traffic normalizer and removes ambiguities and anomalies from IP and TCP packets through the Modify Packet Inline action. You cannot use the NORMALIZER engine to create new signatures, but you can tune all the signatures in the NORMALIZER engine and therefore influence the operation of the IP and TCP normalizers.

NORMALIZER Engine Example

An example of a signature based on the NORMALIZER engine is the Cisco IPS TCP Segment Overwrite. This signature triggers if packets of the same TCP session exhibit data overlaps with different data at the same place in the TCP sequence number space. The signature uses the following common parameters:

- **Signature Name (common):** TCP Segment Overwrite

- **Signature ID (common):** 1300/0

- **Engine (common):** NORMALIZER

- **Description (common):** This signature fires when one or more TCP segments in the same stream overwrite data from one or more segments located earlier in the stream.

Implementation Guidelines for the NORMALIZER Engine

When tuning NORMALIZER signatures, consider the following implementation guidelines:

- You should not tune NORMALIZER signatures unless some of your network traffic exhibits protocol violations that cannot be fixed by changing endpoint settings. When tuning NORMALIZER signatures, it is important to make only minimal changes and only create exceptions for specific legitimate flows.

- Changing NORMALIZER signatures can significantly impair and impact the sensor's upper-layer reassembly and analysis functions. **It is important to exercise extreme care when tuning any of the NORMALIZER signatures.**

Deploying Other Engines

The Application Inspection and Control (AIC) engines, such as AIC HTTP and AIC FTP, provide Layer 4–7 packet inspection for HTTP and FTP. By tuning the built-in AIC engine signatures, you can create granular policies for HTTP and FTP similarly to what you can achieve with the **inspect policy maps** command on the Cisco ASA security appliance.

The AIC HTTP provides granular control over HTTP sessions to prevent abuse of the HTTP protocol. It allows administrative control over applications that try to tunnel over specified ports. AIC also provides a way to inspect FTP traffic and control the commands being issued.

Both the AIC HTTP and AIC FTP engines are disabled by default. When enabling them, examine their signatures and enable the signatures that you consider necessary. Most of their signatures are disabled as well. When enabled, there is a large performance penalty as the overall throughput of the sensor is reduced.

AIC Signature Engine Example

An example of a signature based on the AIC HTTP engine is the Cisco IPS Request Method Not Recognized. This signature observes HTTP requests and matches requests containing an unknown HTTP request method. The signature uses the following common parameters:

- **Signature Name (common):** Request Method Not Recognized

- **Signature ID (common):** 12676/0

- **Engine (common):** AIC HTTP

- **Description (common):** The HTTP RFC provides a list of request methods such as GET, POST, and so on. You can also enter new request methods. If a method is seen that is not listed as a recognized method, this signature will take the associated action.

Implementation Guidelines for AIC Engines

When using the AIC signatures, consider using AIC signatures instead of or in addition to your classic application layer security controls to enforce a strong access control policy.

Note: More information on the signature engines is available at the link in the "References" section, later in this chapter. It is highly recommended that you read through it.

Summary

This section highlights the key topics discussed in this chapter:

- A signature engine is a component of the sensor that supports a category of signatures. The Cisco IPS signature engines enable you to tune built-in signatures and create new signatures.

- The signature engines use their parameters to provide configuration of signatures. Some parameters are common across all engines, such as Signature ID, Alert Severity, and Sig Description. Other parameters are unique to a specific engine.

- The ATOMIC signature engines support signatures that are triggered by the contents of a single packet.

- The STRING ICMP, STRING TCP, and STRING UDP are STRING signature engines.

- The SERVICE engines analyze traffic at and above OSI Layer 5. They analyze the Layer 5 and above payload in a manner similar to the live service.

- The FLOOD signature engines detect attacks in which the attacker is directing a flood of traffic to either a single host or the entire network.

- The SWEEP engines are commonly used to detect network reconnaissance. The SWEEP Other TCP signature engine supports signatures that trigger when a mixture of TCP packets with different flags set are detected on a network.

- The META engine provides event correlation on the sensor and can dramatically reduce the number of alerts and provide high-level information.

- The NORMALIZER engine provides an interface to the IPS IP and TCP normalizer engines.

- You can tune the built-in AIC engine signatures to create granular policies for HTTP and FTP.

References

More information can be found at the following URL:

Signature Engines, at www.cisco.com/en/US/docs/security/ips/7.0/configuration/guide/ime/ime_signature_engines.html.

Exam Preparation Tasks

Review All the Key Topics

Review the most important topics from the chapter, noted with the Key Topic icons in the margin of the page. Table 10-3 lists a reference of these key topics and the page numbers on which each is found.

Table 10-3   *Key Topics for Chapter 10*

Key Topic Element	Description	Page Number
Table 10-2	Common Signature Parameters	239

Complete the Tables and Lists from Memory

Print a copy of Appendix C, "Memory Tables" (found on the CD), or at least the section for this chapter, and complete the tables and lists from memory. Appendix D, "Memory Tables Answer Key," also on the CD, includes completed tables and lists to check your work.

Definitions of Key Terms

Define the following key term from this chapter, and check your answer in the glossary:

signature

This chapter describes the functions and operations of anomaly detection in the sensor. This covers the following:

- **Anomaly Detection Components:** The ingredients that go into the recipe called anomaly detection.

- **Configuring Anomaly Detection:** Putting the anomaly detection system to work and customizing for the needs of your network.

- **Verifying Anomaly Detection:** Making sure that anomaly detection is working and creating the results intended.

CHAPTER 11

Deploying Anomaly-Based Operation

Overview

The anomaly detection built in to the Cisco Intrusion Prevention System (IPS) has the ability to identify some self-propagating worms in the network. This allows the sensor to take actions to prevent spreading of a worm across the entire network. In this chapter, we will learn what the anomaly detection system is capable of doing and discover how to configure it and verify that it is working.

"Do I Know This Already?" Quiz

The "Do I Know This Already?" quiz allows you to assess whether you should read the entire chapter. If you miss no more than one of these self-assessment questions, you might want to move ahead to the "Exam Preparation Tasks" section. Table 11-1 lists the major headings in this chapter and the "Do I Know This Already?" quiz questions covering the material in those headings so that you can assess your knowledge of these specific areas. The answers to the "Do I Know This Already?" quiz appear in Appendix A.

Table 11-1 *"Do I Know This Already?" Foundation Topics Section-to-Question Mapping*

Foundation Topics Section	Questions
Anomaly Detection Overview	1–3
Configuring Anomaly Detection	4
Verifying Anomaly Detection	5

1. Which of the following is not a valid anomaly detection mode?

   a. Detect

   b. Inactive

   c. Standby

   d. Learn

2. Which type of worms are not detected directly by the anomaly detection system?

   a. ICMP-based worms

   b. UDP-based worms

   c. TCP-based worms

   d. File sharing–based worms

3. What is the most typical way that a worm would propagate, if it was identified by the anomaly detection system?

   a. Instant Messenger redirection

   b. Peer-to-peer file sharing

   c. A single host scanning to many IP addresses

   d. Server-based file infestation

4. What is the default configured action for host-related anomaly detection–related signatures?

   a. Deny attacker in line

   b. TCP reset

   c. Deny the attacker in line and generate an alert

   d. Generate an alert

5. Which of the following is true regarding a histogram?

   a. It must be set manually.

   b. It must be set dynamically.

   c. It must be given 24 hours initially to be built.

   d. It must be given 48 hours initially to be built.

Foundation Topics

Anomaly Detection Overview

One of the really cool features of anomaly-based intrusion prevention is the capability of the IPS sensor to learn statistical profiles of normal network traffic, and then compare that database of normal traffic to any deviation that might arise and identify the deviation.

The IPS anomaly detection feature is a statistical anomaly-based system. Its purpose is to identify and prevent scanning network worms. A scanning network worm spreads by blindly scanning a network to find victims and then compromising those victims through network attacks. These attacks are typically against exposed network services.

The method that anomaly detection uses is quite amazing. It will first dynamically learn the network patterns for a given network or even specific segments of your network. After it has learned a baseline, it can then identify yet unknown worms as they attempt to spread through the network based on scanning activity that is above the baseline. With the ability to identify specific infected hosts that are scanning and looking for the next victim, the IPS can alert us when worm activity is going beyond individual infections and trying to grow.

Note: Anomaly detection focuses on scans from individual computers or devices that are trying to infect other devices. Worms that propagate through email, instant messaging, or file sharing could be identified by other IPS signatures, but not anomaly detection specifically.

Scanning Worm Details

One of the things that differentiates a worm from a typical virus is that a worm is self-propagating. A worm will attack a vulnerable host, infect it, and then use that host as a base station to discover and attack other vulnerable hosts. Before it can infect another host, it needs to find the next victim. The worm finds other hosts by scanning the network looking for a vulnerability. A scanning worm locates vulnerable hosts by generating a list of IP addresses to probe and then contacts the hosts, through scanning. It is this scanning behavior that the anomaly detection system is using to identify the propagation of worms on the network.

A computer on the network that is searching or scanning for an inordinate number of services or hosts, without getting any responses, is very likely infected with a worm and can be categorized as a scanner. The scanner finds new hosts by scanning the network using TCP, UDP, and other protocols that the creator of the worm decided to use. To be considered a scanner from the anomaly detection point of view, an individual host would be generating events on the same destination TCP or UDP ports from a single IP address to an excessive number of destination IP addresses. This could also apply to other types of traffic, such as Internet Control Message Protocol (ICMP).

Note: If a worm is able to discover services and/or IP addresses that are on the network passively, and doesn't need to initiate scanning of any type, the anomaly detection system would not pick up on that behavior, as it does not involve scans coming from an IP address.

The anomaly detection feature can detect and react to the following situations:

- When a single worm-infected source comes on the network and starts scanning for other victims

- When multiple hosts are infected and the network starts on its initial path to a major infection of multiple network devices that could be catastrophic

Anomaly Detection Components

It's important to understand the components that are used by the anomaly detection system. By understanding the individual ingredients that go into this function, you'll be able to better implement and troubleshoot it.

The definition of a scanner is a single IP address that is scanning on the same TCP or UDP destination port for too many destination IP addresses. Each of the following events is considered a scan event by the anomaly detection system:

- For TCP connections, a scan event means a nonestablished TCP connection. This is simply where a TCP synchronization request has been sent and there's been no TCP acknowledgment within 15 seconds. A scanner is very likely not going to get an acknowledgment to all of its TCP synchronization requests because it is doing blind scanning; it doesn't know which hosts have which services, and that's what it's trying to find out. In its scans, it's very likely to attempt to connect to devices or IP addresses that don't even exist on the network.

- For UDP, there are no acknowledgment or synchronization requests. This makes it less accurate to detect compared to TCP. As a result, a scan event for UDP consists of one-way UDP flows where UDP packets have been sent and there's been no return UDP packet for at least 15 seconds. An infected host that scans using UDP will be generating many unidirectional flows on the same destination port for multiple IP addresses, because it again might not know exactly which services are available on which hosts.

- For other protocols besides TCP or UDP, a scan consists of multiple unidirectional flows for a particular protocol, without any return traffic for 15 seconds.

Some of the previous conditions can occur occasionally in a network that is not under attack. So how does the anomaly detection system know, or believe, that a device on the network is a scanner? The answer is simple: The anomaly detection considers a host to be a single scanner when it contacts a number of destinations (scanning events) that exceed the scanner threshold. The scanner threshold is a value that can be dynamically discovered or statically configured by the administrator. We will discuss more about the threshold and how it is determined later in this chapter.

Histograms

We've identified what classifies a device as a scanner; it's when the number of scan events exceeds the threshold. That identifies a single host as a scanner. But what if we have multiple scanners that might lead to a bigger problem: What if the worm is propagating? The answer to this challenge is the histogram.

A *histogram* is a chart representing a frequency distribution. Anomaly detection builds a separate histogram for each configured service in a zone. There are three zones by default: the internal zone, the external zone, and the illegal zone. The histograms for each of the zones track the source and destination IP addresses. Histograms identify tolerable thresholds for scans, such as up to ten hosts issuing 20 scans each or up to 100 hosts issuing two scans each. When scanning goes above any of the thresholds, the anomaly detection interprets this as a worm. The intent here is to identify whether we have a worm that's propagating across our network. Fortunately, the anomaly detection system can dynamically learn from the live network what the baseline should be, and then it looks for anomalies from that baseline (hence the term *anomaly detection*).

Zones

There are three zones used with anomaly detection. Each zone will typically have different traffic patterns, and as a result, thresholds in each zone are very likely to be different. It is the IP addresses that define which networks are part of which zones. By default, all IP addresses are assigned to the external zone. The internal zone should be configured with the IP address range of our internal networks. You can also configure the illegal zone with IP addresses and/or address ranges that aren't valid. The benefit of the illegal zone, which identifies invalid addresses, is that you shouldn't have any scans going to IP addresses in that zone because there aren't any real hosts there; therefore, the thresholds for the illegal zone can be much lower than the internal or external zones. The external zone accounts for all the IP addresses that are not included in the internal or the illegal zone.

Learning

When the IPS system is put in place, it will initially conduct a learning process to derive a set of scanner and histogram thresholds based on what it believes to be the normal network; this learning mode is usually the first 24 hours after the IPS appliance has been put in place. After learning mode is completed, the sensor will move into detection mode. In detection mode, the sensor still builds statistical network profiles and looks for worm attacks. If the sensor believes there is an attack in process, it will temporarily suspend learning so that the scans that are occurring during the attack won't become part of a modified knowledge base or baseline. It is recommended to run the IPS in learning mode for longer than 24 hours, preferably a full week, to get a representative sampling of data.

Note: A brand-new sensor will not have a baseline of current network activity for approximately 24 hours. After the initial knowledge base or baseline has been learned, it can then go into detection mode, while still learning and adapting the baseline.

Anomaly detection is consistently monitoring the network, looking for worms and scanners. If the scanner threshold is crossed, it means that a specific host has been identified as a scanner and the alert is triggered. When a histogram threshold is crossed, the anomaly detection system will fire off the multiple scanner signatures; for a short duration of time (which is called the *worm timeout*), learning is suspended so that the anomalous traffic isn't included as part of the normal baseline. Also during an attack, anomaly detection is going to lower the scanner threshold to more rapidly identify single scanners so that they can be also identified. When the attack is over, those thresholds will go back up to their previous levels.

Signatures Related to Anomaly Detection

Signatures 13,000 through 13,008 are related to anomaly detection. Each of these signatures has two subsignatures. A subsignature of 0 identifies a single scanner. A subsignature of 1 identifies that a zone-based histogram was crossed and that a serious problem of the worm infecting the network might be pending.

The following actions can be assigned to any of these signatures: produce alert, deny attacker inline, log attacker packets, log pair packets, deny attacker service pair inline, request Simple Network Management Protocol (SNMP) trap, request block host, or any of the other actions associated with sensor responses to a signature being matched.

Configuring Anomaly Detection

When configuring anomaly detection, you must determine whether to use its learning mode or manually set all scanner thresholds and histograms. You can decide to learn once and use the initial knowledge base or to learn continuously. You can also specify whether the sensor should automatically accept a newly learned profile or save it to review it manually.

You will also need to manually configure a few parameters including the internal and illegal zone addresses. Doing this will assist in minimizing false positives and false negatives.

By configuring source and destination IP addresses that the anomaly detection system should ignore in its calculations, you can avoid a network management station from being included in or triggering histograms and alerts.

You can optionally set scheduler parameters to specify when the sensor is going to write the current knowledge base to local storage and specify the default learning interval. By default, it's every 24 hours at 10 a.m.

Default Anomaly Detection Policy ad0

The default anomaly detection policy is called ad0, and it cannot be deleted. You can add a new anomaly detection policy or clone an existing anomaly detection policy.

To customize anomaly detection for your network, use IDM, as shown in Figures 11-1 and 11-2.

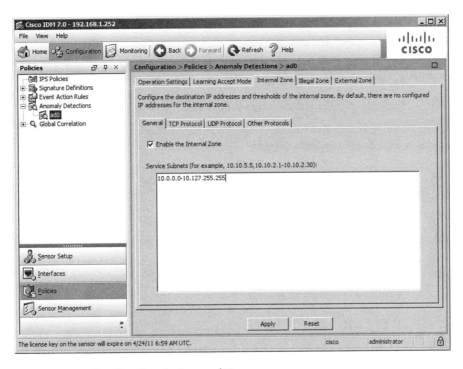

Figure 11-1 *Configuring the Internal Zone*

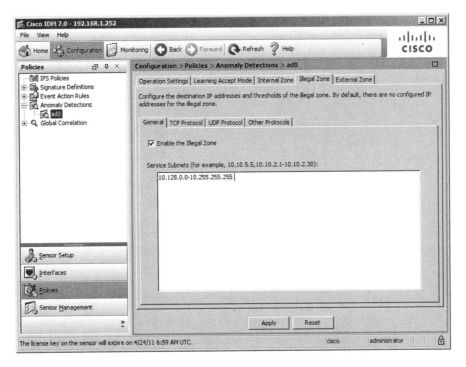

Figure 11-2 *Configuring the Illegal Zone*

The steps for configuring the zones are as follows:

Step 1.   Log in to Cisco IPS Device Manager (IDM).

Step 2.   Choose **Configuration > Policies > Anomaly Detections > ad0**, and click the **Internal Zone** tab.

Step 3.   Verify that the **Enable the Internal Zone** check box is selected.

Step 4.   In the **Service Subnets** section, specify all ranges that make up the internal network. Separate multiple ranges with a comma. Click **Apply** to save any changes.

Note: In our example, the internal networks are 10.0.0.0–10.127.255.255, as shown in the graphic.

Step 5.   Click the **Illegal Zone** tab, and verify that the **Enable the Illegal Zone** check box is selected.

Step 6.   In the **Service Subnets** section, specify address ranges that are unused in your network but would get routed across the sensor. Click **Apply** to save any changes.

Note: In our example, the unused network range of 10.128.0.0–10.255.255.255 will be specified for the illegal zone, as we shouldn't have any scans destined toward this unused space.

Step 7.   Click **Apply** to save your configuration changes.

You can optionally specify which services will be explicitly tracked by anomaly detection, as shown in Figure 11-3. By doing this, anomaly detection will build a separate profile for each tracked service. This will result in making anomaly detection more accurate.

To add specific services, follow these steps:

Step 1.   Log in to Cisco IPS Device Manager (IDM).

Step 2.   Choose **Configuration > Policies > Anomaly Detections > ad0**, and click the **Internal Zone** tab.

Step 3.   While in any of the protocol tabs **TCP Protocol, UDP Protocol,** or **Other Protocols,** click the **Add** button and add ports that a worm might typically use.

Note: In the destination port settings, you can specify that you want to override the default histograms and scanner thresholds. You would only use these settings if you were seeing false positives or false negatives with the default anomaly detection policy.

Step 4.   To change the scanner threshold, select the **Override Scanner Settings** check box and enter the new threshold. To change the histogram, click **Add** and specify the new values for **High, Medium,** and **Low.** When done, click the **OK** buttons to close the submenus, and then click the **Apply** button to save your changes.

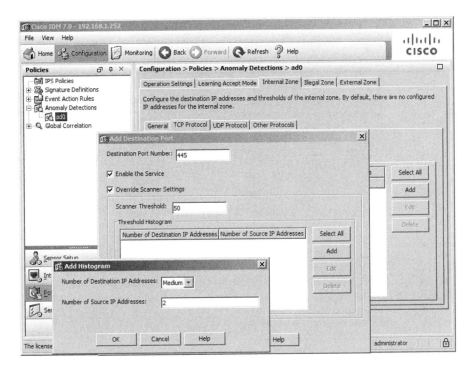

Figure 11-3 *Specifying Specific Services for Histograms*

The default thresholds are as follows:

- Scanner threshold: 200 scanners

- Histogram thresholds:

    - **Low:** 10 source IP addresses and five destination IP addresses

    - **Medium:** Three source IP addresses and 20 destination IP addresses

    - **High:** One source IP address and 100 destination IP addresses

You can specify whether the sensor will automatically create a new knowledge base and how often. You can specify whether the knowledge base will be rotated, which means that it will be created and loaded, or specify save only, which means that you would manually load the knowledge base after reviewing it. These options are shown in the following figures.

Figure 11-4 shows the option of automatically updating the knowledge base, using the periodic option, every 24 hours, at 10:00 a.m., and telling the sensor to implement the new knowledge base each time it is created.

Figure 11-5 shows the option of automatically updating the knowledge base as well, except the schedule for the new knowledge base is set to Calendar Schedule, and the new knowledge base will be updated and implemented based on the days and time.

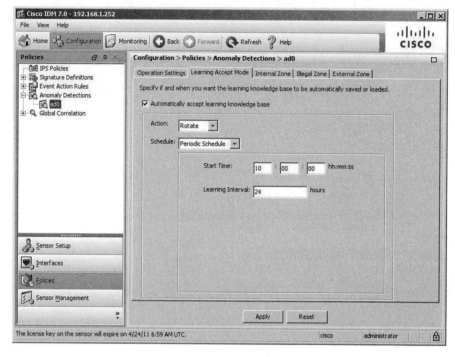

Figure 11-4 *Configuring Learning Accept Mode Periodic Schedule*

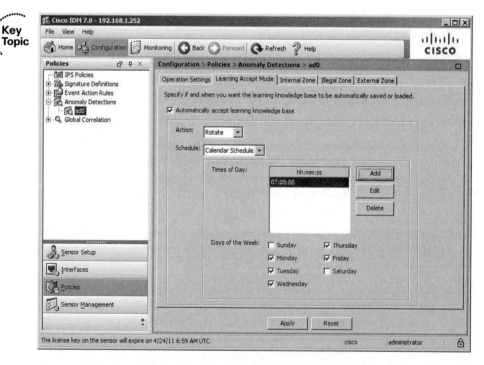

Figure 11-5 *Configuring Learning Accept Mode Calendar Schedule*

To configure the learning accept mode for anomaly detection, follow these steps:

Step 1.   Log in to Cisco IPS Device Manager (IDM).

Step 2.   Choose **Configuration > Policies > Anomaly Detections > ad0**, and click the **Learning Accept Mode** tab.

Step 3.   To have anomaly detection automatically update the knowledge base, simply select the **Automatically accept learning knowledge base** check box.

Step 4.   From the **Action** drop-down menu, select **Rotate** for new knowledge bases to be created and loaded according to the schedule we define. From the **Action** drop-down menu, select **Save Only**, if you want a new knowledge base created, but not automatically loaded.

Step 5.   From the **Schedule** drop-down list, you can choose to have a **Calendar Schedule** or a **Periodic Schedule**.

Note: To configure the periodic schedule, you don't need to do anything, as this is the default. If for some reason it was changed, you can change it back by specifying the start time in hours, minutes, and seconds using the 24-hour time format.

Step 6.   For the periodic schedule, click **Add** to enter the starting time and select the check boxes next to the **Days of the Week** you would like to use for your knowledge base to consider as part of the histograms.

Step 7.   Click the **Apply** button to save the configuration.

When anomaly detection detects an outbreak, a lower threshold is set to qualify a host as a scanner, to identify individual scanners faster. The duration of this time is called the worm timeout. After the timeout is over, the scanner threshold returns to its normal value. If the default timeout is not long enough to pinpoint all infected hosts in the network, you might want to increase this value.

You might also want to specify certain source and destination IP addresses that you want the sensor to ignore when building its knowledge base. When specified, anomaly detection does not include the source and destination IP addresses in the knowledge base, so the thresholds are not affected by these IP addresses. This is a good idea for management stations that would be specifically making many scans out into the network. Examples of changing these settings can be seen in Figure 11-6.

To modify the worm timeout, or ignore specific IP addresses from inclusion in the histograms, follow these steps:

Step 1.   Log in to Cisco IPS Device Manager (IDM).

Step 2.   Choose **Configuration > Policies > Anomaly Detections > ad0**, and then select the **Operation Settings** tab.

Step 3.   In the **Worm Timeout** field, enter the number of seconds that sensor should wait for detection to time out before restoring the scanner threshold. The default is 600 seconds.

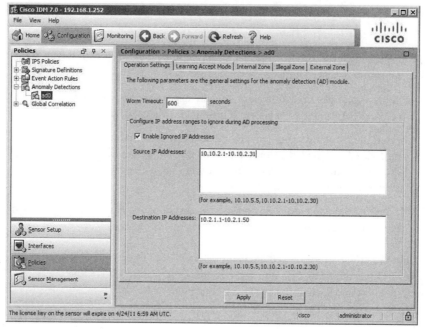

Figure 11-6 *Configuring Anomaly Detection Operation Settings*

Step 4.   To enable a list of ignored IP addresses, select the **Enable Ignored IP Addresses** check box.

Step 5.   In the **Source IP Addresses** and **Destination IP Addresses** fields, enter the IP addresses or range of addresses that you want anomaly detection to ignore.

Note: The addresses listed in the ignored IP address fields will not be used in the calculation of the histograms and knowledge base. In our example, we have management stations on the 10.10.2.0/27 subnetwork.

Step 6.   Click the **Apply** button to save the configuration.

A brand-new sensor will need to build its initial knowledge base. This can take 24 hours to complete, depending on when the sensor was powered on. If you want to specify the learn mode specifically, you can configure it as shown in Figure 11-7.

A new sensor will begin learning automatically, but if you want to specify the learn mode explicitly, complete the following steps:

Step 1.   Log in to Cisco IPS Device Manager (IDM).

Step 2.   Choose **Configuration > Policies > IPS Policies**.

Step 3.   Highlight the virtual sensor (such as vs0) by clicking that virtual sensor, and then click **Edit**. Near the bottom of the screen, in the **Anomaly Detection** section, use the drop-down menu labeled **AD Operational Mode** and select **Learn**.

Step 4.   Click **OK** to close the submenus, and click **Apply** to save changes.

Note: Anomaly detection will default to learn mode for a new sensor; after the initial knowledge base is built and applied, it will continue learning and be in detect mode.

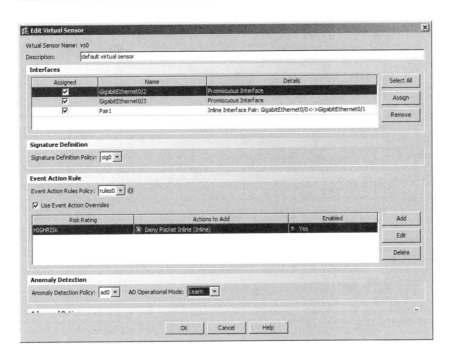

Figure 11-7   *Configuring Anomaly Detection Learn Mode*

After the initial knowledge base is built, the sensor will have the ability to identify scanners or groups of devices performing scanning activity based on the thresholds and histograms. All of this work would be wasted if you didn't have some way of identifying and responding to the worm. So, the last task is to edit or modify the anomaly detection–specific signatures and configure the actions that would be appropriate. By default, these signatures are only going to generate an alert without any countermeasures. You might want to enable countermeasures on the sensor to stop infected hosts from sending traffic across the network. These countermeasures should be associated with the anomaly detection–related signatures that have a subsignature of 0, which represents individual scanners. These signatures and configuring their actions are shown in Figures 11-8 and 11-9.

To assign specific actions to anomaly detection signatures, follow these steps:

Step 1.   Log in to Cisco IPS Device Manager (IDM).

Step 2.   Choose **Configuration** > **Policies** > **Signature Definitions** > **sig0** > **Active Signatures**.

Step 3.   Scroll down in the signature list until you see that signatures 13000 through 13008 are visible. These are the signatures related to anomaly detection.

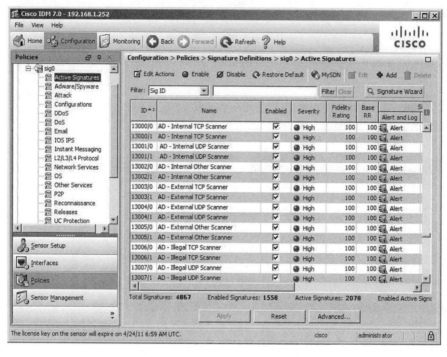

Figure 11-8   *Viewing Anomaly Detection Signatures*

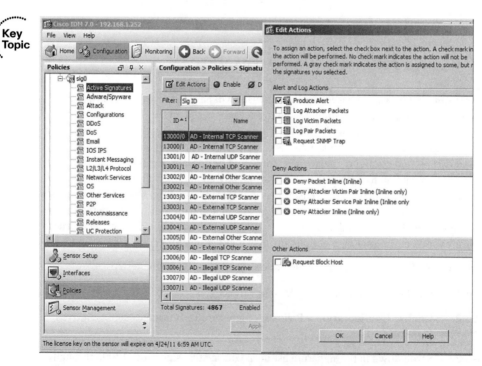

Figure 11-9   *Configuring Anomaly Detection Signature Actions*

Step 4. Click once on a signature to highlight it, and then click the **Edit Actions** button in the upper-left corner of the screen.

Step 5. Select the check boxes next to the **Alert and Log Actions** that should be added. The example in Figure 11-9 shows the default actions assigned to these signatures of **Produce Alert**.

Note: Actions should be assigned only to the signatures that have a subsignature of 0, which indicates an individual host. The subsignature of 1 is for histogram-related signatures and doesn't directly relate to any specific host, but rather a group of computers.

Step 6. Click **OK** to exit the submenu, and click **Apply** to save the configuration changes.

Verifying Anomaly Detection

To configure or verify that periodic knowledge bases are being generated, use the monitoring tools, as shown in Figure 11-10. It is also from this location that we can view the threshold of a specific knowledge base (KB), compare knowledge bases, and manipulate, upload, and download knowledge bases.

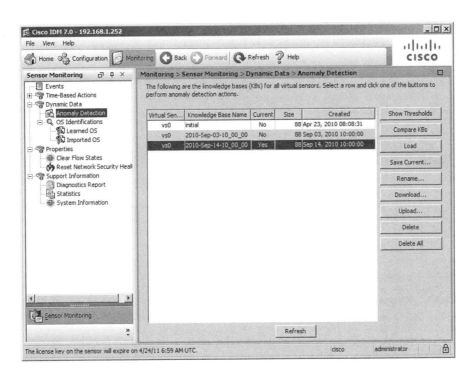

Figure 11-10 *Working with Knowledge Bases*

To view or work with the knowledge base, follow these steps:

Step 1.   Log in to Cisco IPS Device Manager (IDM).

Step 2.   Choose **Monitoring > Sensor Monitoring > Dynamic Data > Anomaly Detection.**

Step 3.   Select one of the knowledge bases by clicking it.

Step 4.   Select one of the buttons on the right to **Show Thresholds, Compare KBs, Load a KB, Make the KB the current KB, Rename a KB, Download a KB, Upload a KB,** or **Delete a KB.**

Note: If the sensor is configured to only save the KB but not to load it, the Load option (shown in the example) would be used to select and load the knowledge base.

You can verify which mode the sensor is in on the Edit Virtual Sensor screen, as shown in Figure 11-11.

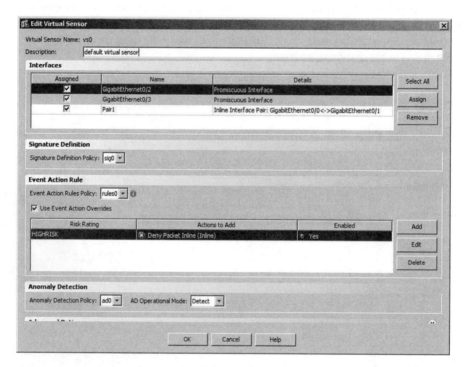

Figure 11-11   *Verifying Detect Mode*

The sensor should automatically switch to detection mode after the first initial learning. To verify this, follow these steps:

Step 1.   Log in to Cisco IPS Device Manager (IDM).

Step 2.   Choose **Configuration > Policies > IPS Policies**.

Step 3.   Highlight the virtual sensor (such as vs0) by clicking that virtual sensor, and then click **Edit**. Near the bottom of the screen, in the **Anomaly Detection** section, verify that **Detect** is selected from the **AD Operational Mode** drop-down menu.

Step 4.   Click **OK** to close the submenus, and click **Apply** to save any changes.

Note: If no changes are made, the **Apply** button will be grayed out, indicating that no changes need to be applied.

Verifying Anomaly Detection at the Command Line

The **show statistics anomaly-detection** command can be issued from the command-line interface, and it will reveal whether an anomaly has been detected, as well as reveal the source of the worm infestation. When an attack is in process, the sensor will turn off learning temporarily. The reason for this is to not skew the knowledge base (that is being dynamically created) by having artificially high numbers of scans considered as part of the norm.

We can view the current status of anomaly detection from the command line, as shown in Example 11-1.

Example 11-1   *Verifying Anomaly Detection from the Command Line*

```
Keith-IPS-IDS# show statistics anomaly-detection
Statistics for Virtual Sensor vs0
 Attach in progress
 Detection - ON
 Learning - OFF
 Next KB rotation at 07:00:00 GMT-07:00 Fri Apr 15 2011
 Internal Zone
 TCP Protocol
    Service 80
        Source IP: 10.1.9.42 Num Dest IP: 204
        Source IP: 10.1.9.47 Num Dest IP: 315
        Source IP: 10.1.9.72 Num Dest IP: 125
 UDP Protocol
 Other Protocol
 External Zone
 TCP Protocol
 UDP Protocol
 Other Protocol
 Illegal Zone
 TCP Protocol
 UDP Protocol
 Other Protocol
```

When implementing anomaly detection, consider a few guidelines. When the sensor is building its initial knowledge base, ensure that the network is in a normal operating state so that it can get an honest sample of what the network really looks like. You might want to have anomaly detection in the learning stage for longer than the 24 initial hours, and also possibly on a work day instead of the weekend.

Making the illegal zone as large as possible as far as IP address ranges go will assist in identifying scanners that are scanning to IP address ranges that are not being used. The larger the range, the more effective this zone will be because of its lower thresholds.

All the anomaly detection signatures are enabled by default; however, there are no actions besides alert. You might want to consider enabling an action associated with the subsignature zero-individual host-related signatures, such as deny attacker inline.

If your network has asymmetrical routing, where traffic goes in one direction but comes back through a different path, anomaly detection will think that everything is a scan. As a result, if you have asymmetrical routing, you should turn off anomaly detection by going to the virtual sensor and setting anomaly detection mode to inactive.

Troubleshooting Anomaly Detection

If the anomaly detection is not detecting scanning attacks while they are occurring on the network, this would represent a false negative. To troubleshoot, check the following:

- Verify that other IPS signatures are triggering. If the sensing interfaces are somehow disconnected from the network, or disassociated with the virtual sensor, that would be one reason that anomaly detection as well as any other signatures might not be firing.

- Make sure that the initial knowledge base has been built.

- Make sure that the operational mode is set to detect on the virtual sensor for anomaly detection.

- If the initial knowledge base does not reflect normal traffic, you might want to set it back to learning mode for it to learn a real sample of normal network traffic.

Summary

This section highlights the key topics discussed in this chapter:

- Anomaly detection automatically identifies worms as they attempt to spread, while at the same time, they can be configured to ignore legitimate scanners.

- Scan thresholds and histograms make up the primary worm-detection tools.

- You can assign effective preventive actions to a properly configured anomaly detection engine, such as deny attacker inline.

- From the anomaly detection pane, you can monitor and manage the knowledge base(s) used for anomaly detection.

References

More information can be found at the following URL:

Installing and Using Cisco IDM 7.0 – Configuring Anomaly Detection, at www.cisco.com/en/US/docs/security/ips/7.0/configuration/guide/idm/idm_anomaly_ detections.html.

Exam Preparation Tasks

Review All the Key Topics

Review the most important topics from the chapter, noted with the Key Topic icons in the margin of the page. Table 11-2 lists a reference of specific key topics and the page numbers on which each is found.

Table 11-2   *Key Topics for Chapter 11*

Key Topic Element	Description	Page Number
Figure 11-2	Configuring Zones	263
Figure 11-3	Configuring Specific Services	265
Figure 11-5	Configuring Learning Accept Mode	266
Figure 11-6	Configuring Worm Timeout and Ignored Addresses	268
Figure 11-9	Configuring the Anomaly Detection Signatures	270

Definitions of Key Terms

Define the following key terms from this chapter, and check your answers in the glossary:

anomaly detection, ad0, scanner, histogram, knowledge base

642-627 IPS v7.0 exam topics covered in this part:

- Configure and verify the IPS features to identify threats and dynamically block them from entering the network

- Maintain, update, and tune IPS signatures

Part IV: Adapting Traffic Analysis and Response to the Environment

In this chapter, you learn how to create and manage custom signatures. By learning how to create custom signatures, you will be able to meet these objectives:

- **Understanding Custom Signatures:** When the default signatures don't provide all the matching that needs to be done, you can create your own.

- **Using the Custom Signature Wizard:** This wizard will walk you through a series of questions that it will use to create the final signature based on your responses.

- **Creating Custom Signatures Without the Wizard:** For advanced users or individuals who need to create a signature that the wizard doesn't have the ability to create.

Customizing Traffic Analysis

Overview

There are thousands of signatures that we can use that are built into the Cisco Intrusion Prevention System (IPS). But what if a situation arises where we need to identify traffic that is not specifically identified by one of the built-in signatures? In this chapter, we're going to describe the methods and techniques for creating custom signatures for our networks.

"Do I Know This Already?" Quiz

The "Do I Know This Already?" quiz allows you to assess whether you should read the entire chapter. If you miss no more than one of these self-assessment questions, you might want to move ahead to the "Exam Preparation Tasks" section. Table 12-1 lists the major headings in this chapter and the "Do I Know This Already?" quiz questions covering the material in those headings so that you can assess your knowledge of these specific areas. The answers to the "Do I Know This Already?" quiz appear in Appendix A.

Table 12-1 *"Do I Know This Already?" Foundation Topics Section-to-Question Mapping*

Foundation Topics Section	Questions
Understanding Custom Signatures	1–2
Using the Custom Signatures Wizard	3–5

1. Which of the following would require a custom signature?

    a. Default signature that matches desired traffic, but is retired

    b. Tuned signature that matches desired traffic, but is disabled

    c. Network traffic matching for an in-house application

    d. Operating system–specific signatures

2. Which engine would most likely be used to detect a string of text that can cross multiple TCP segments?

   a. Atomic

   b. Sweep

   c. Chained

   d. TCP String

3. What is the most effective way to identify a string of text that can have multiple variations?

   a. Use multiple subsignatures, beginning with 0

   b. Use multiple subsignatures, beginning with 1

   c. Use regular expressions

   d. Use the variable string-matching attributes

4. Which of the following are not options under the Advanced Options in the wizard?

   a. Event count, to determine how many events will trigger an alert

   b. Summarization threshold for the initial event

   c. Global summarization for the signature

   d. The service port to listen to for the signature to match

5. What is the best way to verify that a custom signature is working?

   a. Specify the Fire All summarization method for the signature

   b. Use event action override to manually trigger the signature

   c. Generate network traffic and use the Monitor feature

   d. Launch an attack against the sensor

Foundation Topics

Understanding Custom Signatures

There are several reasons where we might need to create custom signatures. If we boil it all down, the main reason for creating custom signatures is to identify traffic that is not addressed, for whatever reason, in the default signature set.

Table 12-2 shows the Cisco IPS signature engines that we can use to create custom signatures. If we don't know exactly which signature engine to use, there is a wizard that can assist us in determining the correct one.

Table 12-2   *Traffic Analysis Method and the Inspection Engines in That Class*

Traffic Analysis Method	Cisco IPS Inspection Engines
Packet header matching	Atomic
Packet content matching	Atomic
Stateful content matching	String
Protocol decoding	Service
Rate analysis	Flood
Traffic correlation	Sweep
Event correlation	Meta

Creating Custom Signature Guidelines

When creating custom signatures, follow this general process:

Key
Topic

Step 1.   Identify what the network attack or exploit is going to look like. This means getting a sample or a description of the network traffic that will be generated by this attack.

Step 2.   Create a custom signature that is looking for the exact traffic pattern or network traffic that is being generated by this attack.

Step 3.   Test the signature in a nonproduction network environment, to verify that this signature actually works and matches on the malicious traffic it is intended to match on.

Step 4.   Implement the tested signature in a production environment, but do not use the aggressive actions that are available such as deny attacker. The purpose here is to identify any false positives that might arise before we start denying innocent traffic. If the false positives do arise, we would want to tune the signatures that we've created until the false positives, and/or false negatives, are eradicated.

Step 5.   After we know that the signature is working and that false positives and false negatives are not occurring, we can then assign the appropriate action to the signature as an IPS response, such as deny attacker.

Selecting Criteria to Match

When configuring our custom signature, options available for matching include

- Specific information that would be found in the protocol headers.

- Data patterns, found virtually anywhere in the packet or session.

- Thresholds and counters that can be used across multiple packets.

- Correlation to detect complex attacks, such as three individual signatures firing off within a short time frame, could represent one custom signature to indicate that the attack is under way. The meta engine would be used for a signature like this.

Regular Expressions

Regular expressions are a way to communicate or describe patterns inside a packet, and are quite often used when creating application layer rules for payload matching.

The benefit of using a regular expression is that it is an efficient way to describe a string of text or patterns that can have many variations. If we did not use regular expressions, we might have to create dozens of signatures to match a single string of text, based on its containing uppercase or lowercase characters, spaces, and so on. By using regular expressions, we can use special characters to represent variables inside the string of text that we were looking for.

Regular expressions use metacharacters, listed in Table 12-3, to assist in identifying variations of text.

Table 12-3   *Metacharacters Used in Regular Expressions*

Symbol	Meaning
?	Repeat 0 or 1 times
*	Repeat 0 or more times
+	Repeat 1 or more times
{x}	Repeat exactly x times
period (.)	Any one character except \n or \t
[abc]	Any character listed
[^abc]	Any character not listed
[a-z]	Any character listed inclusively in range
		OR of two regular expressions
\	This allows specifying a character that would otherwise be interpreted as special. It means take the next character literally, and that the next character should not be thought of as being any type of metacharacter.

The following provides examples of the special characters:

■   a* matches any number of occurrences of the letter *a*, including none.

■   a+ requires that at least one letter *a* be in the string to be matched.

■   ba?b matches the string *bb* or *bab*.

■   ** matches any number of asterisks (*).

To use multipliers with multiple-character patterns, you enclose the pattern in parentheses. (ab)* matches any number of the multiple-character string *ab*. Some examples of regular expressions are shown in Table 12-4.

Table 12-4   *Examples of Regular Expression Patterns*

To Match	Regular Expression
Hacker or hacker	[Hh]acker
Either hot or cold	hot|cold
Hacker using any case	[hH][aA][cC][kK][eE][rR]
Either hot or cold using any case	[hH][oO][tT]|[cC][oO][lL][dD]
Variations of bananas, banananas, banananananas	Ba(na)+s
moon or soon	(m|s)oon
Cisco or Francisco or csco	[Cc]?sco

Using the Custom Signature Wizard

Probably one of the easiest ways to create a custom signature it is to use the Custom Signature Wizard, and one of the most overlooked things to do is to make a plan before starting the wizard, regarding what we will specifically be looking for in our new custom signature.

As an example of demonstrating the use of a Custom Signature Wizard, we will create a signature that is looking for the word *hacker*, in uppercase or lowercase, if it is seen being used in a Telnet session. Knowing exactly what protocols Telnet uses will be critical in creating the new custom signature.

There are three ways of creating this signature:

■   Using the signature wizard and the specific engine to use.

■   Using the signature wizard and not specifying the specific engine.

■   Creating the new signature from scratch, without using any wizard.

Each of these methods includes configuration of the same general elements:

- The name and number of the signature

- The matching criteria that this signature will use or the matching network traffic

- The Signature Fidelity Rating and Attack Severity Rating

- Optionally the event counts (how many times to see the match) before triggering the signature match and summarization settings

We discuss each of these.

Signature Wizard, Specifying the Engine

To use the signature wizard, begin by clicking the **Signature Wizard** button, as shown in Figure 12-1.

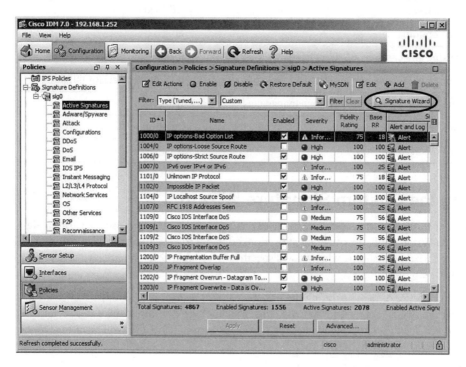

Figure 12-1 *Signature Definitions Page*

To create a custom signature, follow these steps:

Step 1.   In IDM, choose **Configuration > Policies > Signature Definition > sig0 > Active Signatures**, and then click the **Signature Wizard** button.

The welcome screen for the wizard provides the option for selecting the exact engine to use for the creation of this signature, as shown in Figure 12-2.

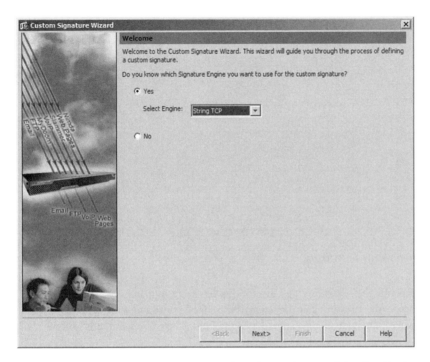

Figure 12-2   *Custom Signature Wizard, Welcome Screen, Selecting Engine*

Step 2.   If the specific engine to use is known, click the **Yes** radio button and select the engine that will be used from the drop-down list. After making the choice, click **Next** to continue.

> **Note:**   If the exact signature engine is not known, clicking **No** will facilitate the wizard prompting for additional information. This will determine the final engine to be used. We will cover that option later in the chapter.

The Signature Identification page of the wizard will ask for the name and number of the new signature that is being created, as shown in Figure 12-3.

Step 3.   On the Signature Identification screen, enter the **Signature ID** and **SubSignature ID** to be assigned to this signature. The first custom signature will default to 60,000 with a subsignature of 0. You can also assign a **Signature Name**, **Alert Notes**, and **User Comments**, which will all be properties of the new custom signature. Click **Next** to continue.

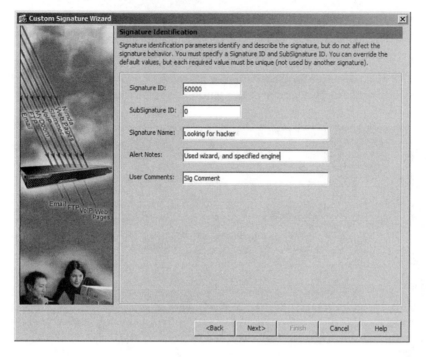

Figure 12-3 *Signature Identification*

To enter the regular expression for this signature to match on, as well as other properties of this signature, such as the service port and what action to take when this signature is matched, use the Engine Specific Parameters screen, as shown in Figure 12-4.

Step 4.   On the Engine Specific Parameters screen, enter the **Regex String** to be used for matching as well as the **Event Action** and **Service Ports**. Click **Next** to continue the wizard.

Note: The default action assigned to a custom signature is Produce Alert. You can modify that now for this signature, or you can change it later by editing the properties of this signature. The Regex String used in the example will match on a Telnet session (destined for TCP:23) if the word *hacker* is seen in uppercase or lowercase in the TCP session. Because the String TCP engine was selected earlier in the wizard, the wizard is assuming the L4 protocol of TCP.

To specify the Signature Fidelity Rating (SFR) and the Attack Severity Rating (ASR) of the signature, use the Alert Response screen of the wizard, as shown in Figure 12-5.

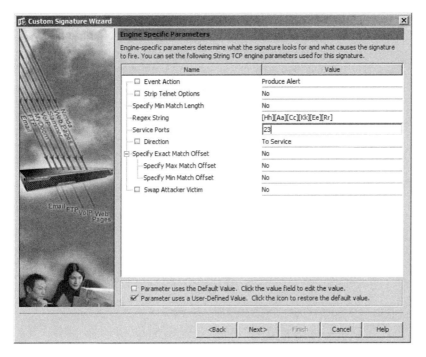

Figure 12-4 *Engine Specific Parameters for the String TCP Engine*

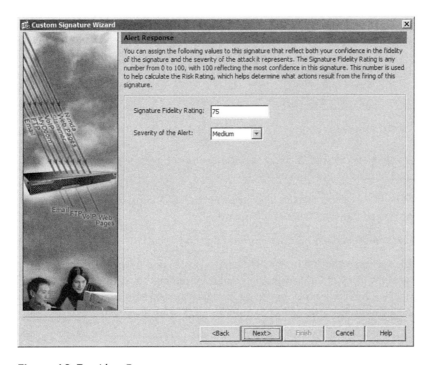

Figure 12-5 *Alert Response*

Step 5.   On the Alert Response screen, enter the **Signature Fidelity Rating** value for the new signature as well as the **Severity of the Alert.** Click **Next** to continue.

Note: The default Fidelity Rating for a custom signature is 75. The default Attack Severity Rating is Medium. These two factors will be used during a signature match, as part of the overall risk rating calculation.

To complete the configuration, click the **Finish** button, as shown on the Alert Behavior screen in Figure 12-6.

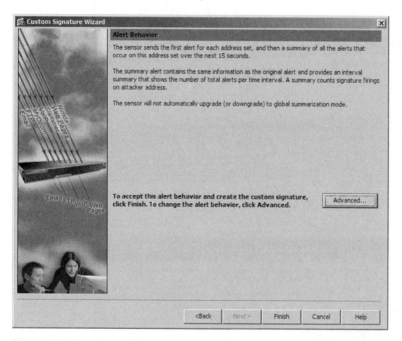

Figure 12-6   *Wizard Finish*

Step 6.   To complete the wizard, using the defaults for the alert behavior, click **Finish** and then click **Apply** to save the changes.

If the signature defaults for alert behavior are not acceptable, click the **Advanced** button, as shown in Figure 12-7.

Step 7.   Click the **Advanced** button to modify the alert behavior.

The **Advanced** button brings up the Event Count and Interval screen, to indicate how many matches make up a single event, with the default being 1. Clicking **Next** will bring up the Alert Summarization screen. To modify the default summarization methods, use the Alert Summarization screen, as shown in Figure 12-8.

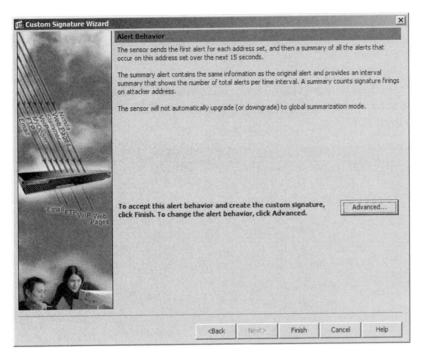

Figure 12-7   *Wizard, Advanced Options*

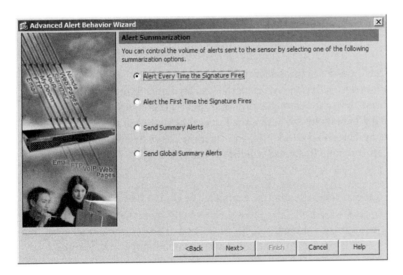

Figure 12-8   *Alert Summarization*

Step 8.   Click the radio button next to the summarization method desired for this signature. Selecting **Alert Every Time the Signature Fires** is preferable for the testing of new signatures, as this will assist in seeing the alerts based on a single signature match occurring. Click **Next** to continue the wizard.

Note: The alert summarization method can be tuned later, based on the summarization desired after testing.

To modify the default for summarization, based on the signature being matched multiple times, use the Alert Dynamic Response screen, as shown in Figure 12-9.

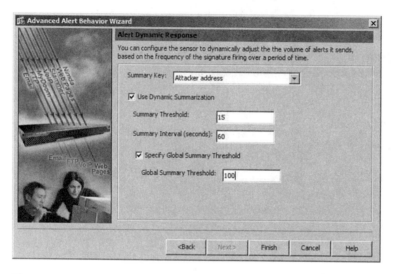

Figure 12-9   *Alert Dynamic Response*

Step 9.   From the drop-down list, select the **Summary Key** that will determine what the summaries are based on. Select the **Use Dynamic Summarization** check box to use dynamic summarization, and specify the values desired in the **Summary Threshold** and **Summary Interval** fields. Select the **Specify Global Summary Threshold** check box, and enter the desired value. Click **Finish** from the Alert Dynamic Response window to continue.

Note: The summarization values used in this example will log the first 15 signature matches from the same attacker within a 60-second window (because the Alert Every Time option was used for this signature in Figure 12-8). At the end of the 60-second window, the IPS will generate one summary event that indicates the total number of signature matches from that specific attacker for that 60-second window. If the number of attacks exceeds 100 in that same 60-second window (the global summary threshold), at the end of 60 seconds, the IPS will generate a global summary that specifies the total number of attacks from all source addresses, within that 60-second window. This display is based on selecting **Alert Every Time the Signature Fires** in the Alert Summarization step shown previously in Figure 12-8.

To complete the wizard, click the **Finish** button, which will return you to the Alert Behavior screen, as shown in Figure 12-10.

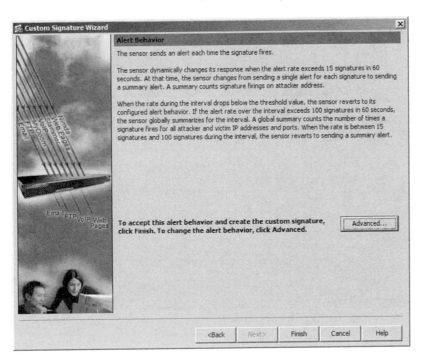

Figure 12-10   *Alert Behavior Finish*

Step 10.   Clicking the **Finish** button from the Alert Behavior window will close the wizard.

After a new signature is created, it can be viewed from the Active Signatures window, as shown in Figure 12-11.

Step 11.   After the wizard completes, a list of signatures is shown. Click **Apply** to save the custom signature that was just created. To navigate back to this screen and see just the custom signatures created, choose **Configuration > Policies > Signature Definitions > sig0 > Active Signatures**. From the **Filter** drop-down list, select **Type**. From the **Filter** drop-down list (just to the right), select **Custom**. This will filter the output and show only the custom signatures on the sensor.

Verifying the Custom Signature

To test the signature, we can use a Telnet session and send the string of *hacker*, as shown in Figure 12-12.

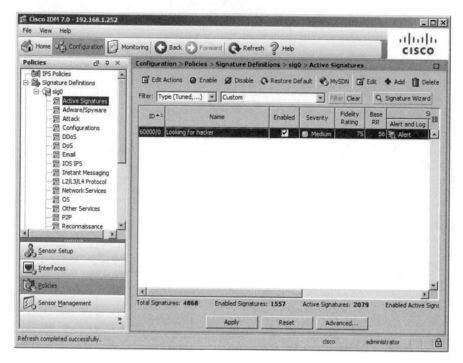

Figure 12-11 *Custom Signature*

Key
Topic

```
Telnet-Enabled-Router#
Telnet-Enabled-Router#
Telnet-Enabled-Router#
Telnet-Enabled-Router#
Telnet-Enabled-Router#
Telnet-Enabled-Router#
Telnet-Enabled-Router#
Telnet-Enabled-Router#
Telnet-Enabled-Router#
Telnet-Enabled-Router#
Telnet-Enabled-Router#
Telnet-Enabled-Router#
Telnet-Enabled-Router#
Telnet-Enabled-Router#
Telnet-Enabled-Router#
Telnet-Enabled-Router#
Telnet-Enabled-Router#
Telnet-Enabled-Router# hacker
                             ^
% Invalid input detected at '^' marker

Telnet-Enabled-Router# █
```

Figure 12-12 *Testing Custom Signatures*

To test the signature, follow these steps:

Step 1. Open a Telnet session using a Telnet program, and after connecting to a remote device where the IPS can see the conversation (either inline or promiscuous mode), type in the word **hacker**.

Note: Open a new Telnet session for this test. The sensor, because of the default TCP reassembly options on the sensor, might not record an existing Telnet session that was established before the signature was active. Even though the word *hacker* isn't a valid command on the remote Telnet device, the string was still sent, and the new custom signature should have been triggered as a match.

To view the alert generated by the signature match, use the Monitoring feature, as shown in Figure 12-13.

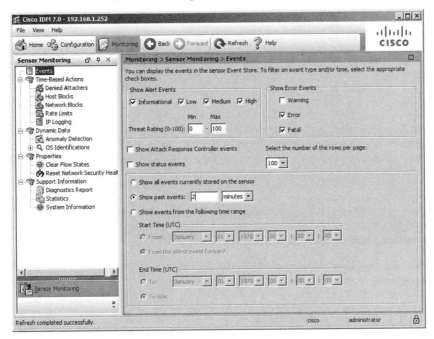

Figure 12-13 *Viewing Alerts For the Past Two Minutes*

Step 2.   Using IDM, navigate to **Monitoring > Sensor Monitoring > Events.** Click the **View** button to view past events.

Note: From the Monitoring Events screen, select the time frame of events as well as the levels of alerts to be seen. In Figure 12-13, the past two minutes were selected to focus on recent events, instead of seeing the hundreds of events that might be shown with the default of the past hour.

The event viewer will display all the alerts that match the criteria from the previous screen when the **View** button was clicked, as shown in Figure 12-14. This displays the event generated by our custom signature being triggered.

Step 3.   From the Event Viewer window, the recent alerts are shown. Select a specific event by clicking it to select it, and then click the **Details** button to see the specific details of that alert.

The details of a selected alert can be seen in the Details window for that alert, as shown in Figure 12-15.

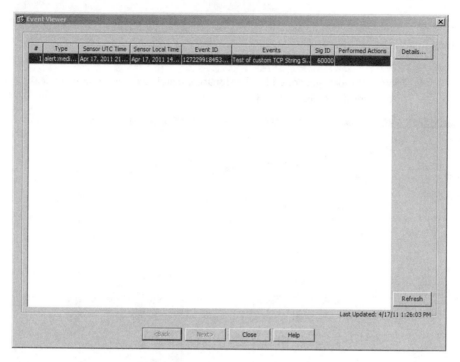

Figure 12-14   *Viewing Alerts Within the Last Two Minutes That Show the Custom Signature Was Triggered*

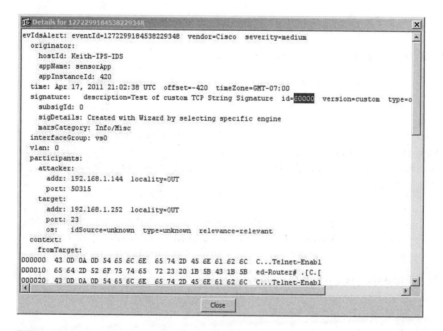

Figure 12-15   *Viewing Details of the Alert*

Step 4.   View the details of the alert, generated by our custom signature, including the Signature ID, time stamps, addresses involved, the sensor that generated the alert, and other details, as shown in Figure 12-15. Click **Close** in both windows to exit the event viewer.

Note: On many TCP-based signature matches, the sensor will also record the first 256 characters of the traffic that triggered this alert. It is referred to in 12-15 as the context information, which is shown in the alert.

Signature Wizard, Without Specifying the Engine

To start the wizard, click the **Signature Wizard** button, as shown in Figure 12-16.

Step 1.   In IDM, choose **Configuration > Policies > Signature Definition > sig0 > Active Signatures** and click the **Signature Wizard** button.

On the welcome screen of the wizard, select **No** when asked if you know the exact signature engine to be used, as shown in Figure 12-17.

Step 2.   Click the **No** radio button, regarding the question "Do you know which Signature Engine you want to use for the custom signature?" Click **Next** to continue.

The wizard will ask additional questions to assess which is the best engine to use. These questions are on the Protocol Type screen, as shown in Figure 12-18.

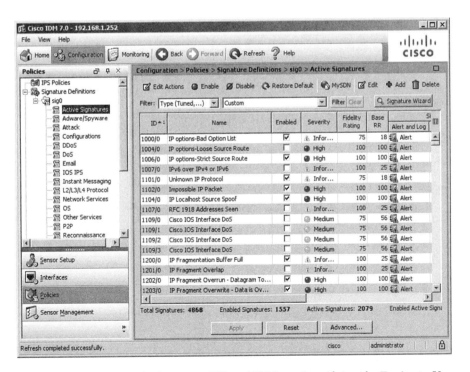

Figure 12-16   *Using the Signature Wizard Without Specifying the Engine to Use*

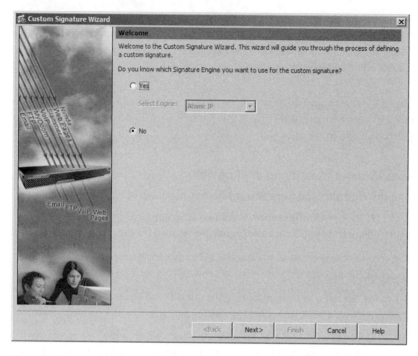

Figure 12-17   *Welcome Page, Not Specifying the Engine to Use*

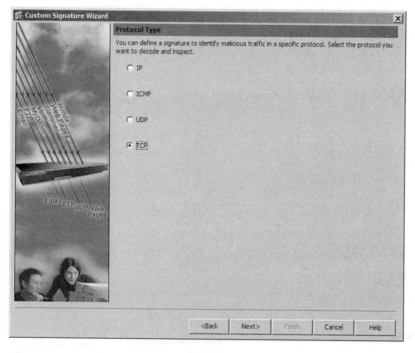

Figure 12-18   *Protocol Type Input Screen*

Step 3.   Click the **TCP** radio button. Click **Next** to continue.

Note: In this example, you will create another custom signature, still looking for hacker, within a Telnet session. In a production environment, you would not need multiple signatures matching on the exact same string in the exact same traffic. In this chapter, multiple ways to create a custom signature are being demonstrated, with the same target of hacker in a TCP session to port 23 for each of them.

The next part of the wizard is asking for more details to narrow down which engine will be used, as shown in the TCP Traffic Type screen in Figure 12-19.

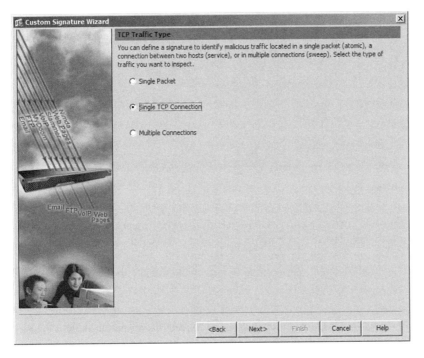

Figure 12-19   *TCP Traffic Type*

Step 4.   Click the **Single TCP Connection** radio button. Click **Next** to continue.

Note: It is common for Telnet to send each character, as it is typed, as a single packet. For this reason, you want to have your custom signature search across the TCP session, looking for the string *hacker*, instead of trying to match the string in a single packet.

The wizard next asks about the service type the signature should be watching on, as shown in Figure 12-20.

Step 5.   Select the **Other** radio button. Click **Next** to continue.

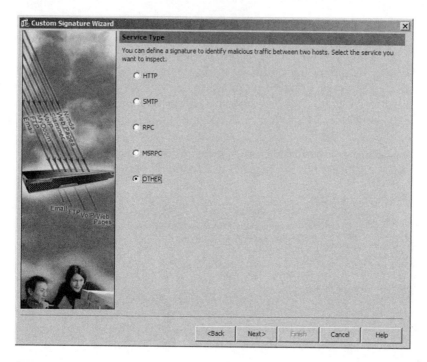

Figure 12-20 *Service Type*

Note: Because port 23 (Telnet) wasn't listed as part of the wizard, the Other option will allow you to manually specify the port number in an upcoming screen. The wizard screens will vary based on the information you provided in the previous screen. For example, if you had selected an ICMP-related protocol, the wizard would not ask about TCP services, as shown in Figure 12-20.

To configure the name, number, and description of the custom signature, use the Signature Identification page, as shown in Figure 12-21.

Step 6. Enter the **Signature ID**, **SubSignature ID**, **Signature Name**, **Alert Notes**, and **User Comments**. Click **Next** to continue.

Enter the details regarding the regular expressions, as well as the ports this signature should listen to, in the Engine Specific Parameters shown in Figure 12-22.

Step 7. On the Engine Specific Parameters screen, enter the **Event Action**, **Regex String**, and **Service Ports** as properties for this custom signature. Click **Next** to continue.

The Signature Fidelity Rating and the Attack Severity Rating can be entered on the Alert Response page, as shown in Figure 12-23.

Step 8. On the Alert Response page, enter the values to be assigned for **Signature Fidelity Rating** and **Severity of the Alert** (Attack Severity Rating). Click **Next** to continue.

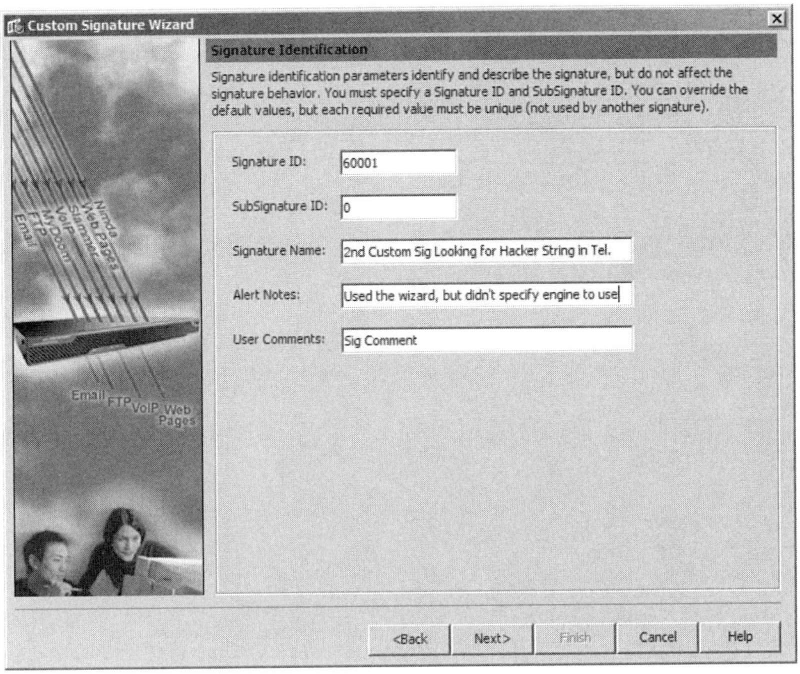

Figure 12-21 *Signature Identification*

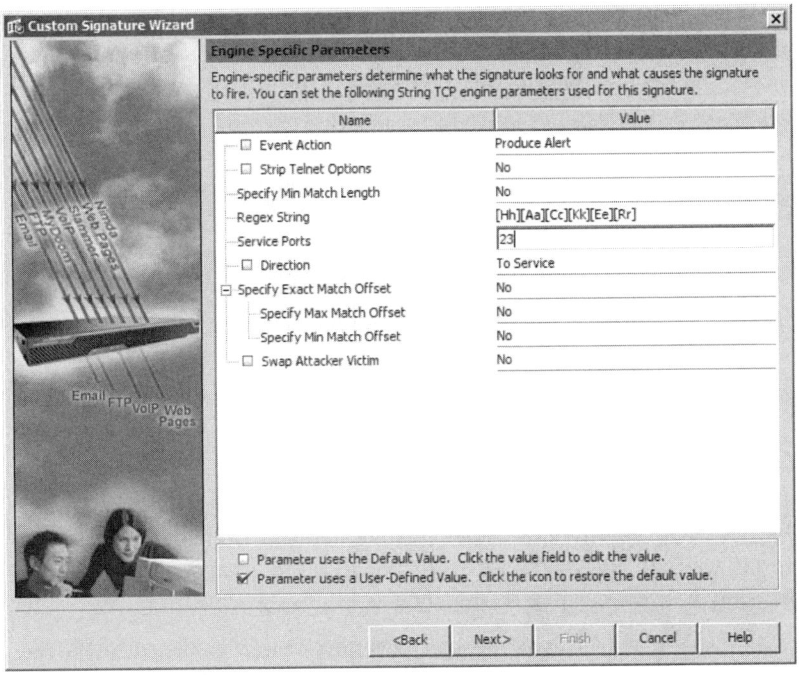

Figure 12-22 *Engine Specific Parameters*

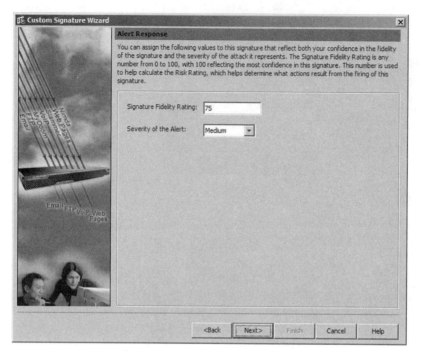

Figure 12-23   *Alert Response*

Note: Because the signature is custom, the creator can assign any value here. If the signature is very detailed, and is unlikely to generate false positives, a Fidelity Rating of 100 would be reasonable. If the attack is not likely to cause any damage or harm, the severity would be appropriately set to Low or Medium.

Step 9.   Click the **Advanced** button, shown in Figure 12-24.

Note: In this step, you are creating a signature similar to the original custom signature. As a result, you will configure the advanced options here as well.

To configure how many times the sensor must match on the signature before generating an alert, use the Event Count and Interval screen, shown in Figure 12-25.

Step 10.   The **Event Count** can be left to the default of 1. If you wanted (for some reason) to only trigger the alert if the signature was matched two or three times within a specific time frame set by the **Use Event Interval** option, you could increase the event count to do exactly that.

With the event count set to 1, you can tell the signature to fire each time the signature is matched using the Alert Summarization screen, as shown in Figure 12-26.

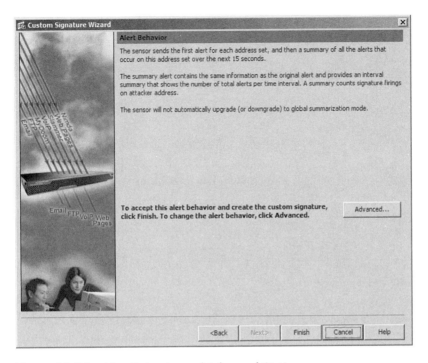

Figure 12-24 *Alert Behavior and Advanced Options*

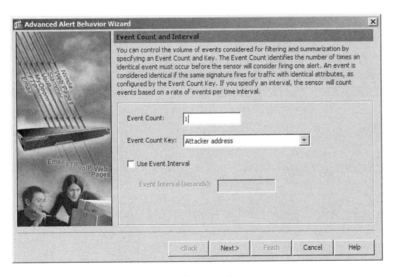

Figure 12-25 *Event Count and Interval*

Step 11. To tell the IPS that you want to see each alert when the signature is matched, select the **Alert Every Time the Signature Fires** radio button. Click **Next** to continue.

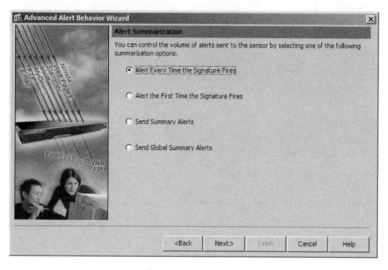

Figure 12-26   *Alert Summarization*

Note: This is the initial summarization for the signature. You can still set summarization so that after a specific number of alerts within a given time frame, the IPS can still summarize the alerts.

To enable additional summarization options, use the Alert Dynamic Response window, as shown in Figure 12-27.

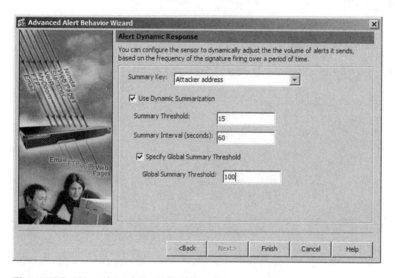

Figure 12-27   *Alert Dynamic Response*

Step 12.   From the drop-down list, select the **Summary Key** that will determine what the summaries are based on. Select the **Use Dynamic Summarization** check box to use dynamic summarization, and specify the values desired in the **Summary Threshold** and **Summary Interval** fields. Select the **Global Summary Threshold** check box, and enter the desired value. Click **Finish** in the Alert Dynamic Response window to continue.

This returns you to the final page of the wizard, as shown in Figure 12-28.

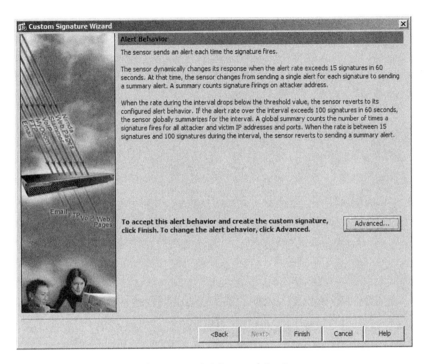

Figure 12-28   *Alert Behavior and Advanced Options*

Step 13.   Click **Finish** to close the wizard.

After creating the custom signature, verify the signature before saving the configuration, as shown in Figure 12-29.

Step 14.   From this screen, you can review the details of the signature by selecting the signature and clicking the **Edit** button. Click **Apply** to save the custom signature.

Note: To test the signature, you could use the exact same methods used for the first custom signature you created. Refer to Figure 12-12 for the testing steps.

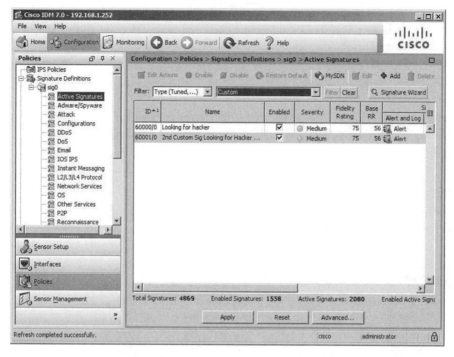

Figure 12-29 *Viewing Custom Signatures*

Creating Custom Signatures, Without the Wizard

The wizard doesn't have to be used to create a custom signature. To create a custom signature without the wizard, use the Configuration window, as shown in Figure 12-30.

Step 1.   In IDM, choose **Configuration > Policies > Signature Definition > sig0 > Active Signatures** and click the **Add** button.

All the fields of the new custom signature are presented for configuration, as shown in Figure 12-31.

Step 2.   Enter the values for the fields **Engine, Regex String, Service Ports, Summary Mode,** and any other options to be configured for the custom signature. Click **OK** to close the screen.

> **Note:**   In this example, you are replicating most of the values used for the first two custom signatures, for which you used the wizard.

After the properties of your custom signature have been set, you still need to apply the changes. You can do that from the Active Signatures window, as shown in Figure 12-32.

Step 3.   Review the signature created if desired, and/or modify the signature by highlighting the signature and clicking **Edit**. To apply the changes, click the **Apply** button.

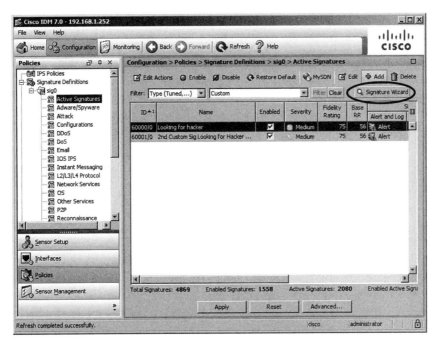

Figure 12-30   *Creating a Custom Signature Without the Wizard*

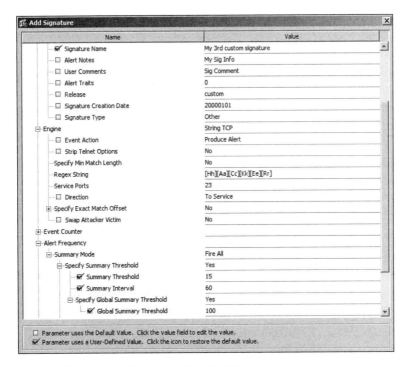

Figure 12-31   *Add Signature Details Window*

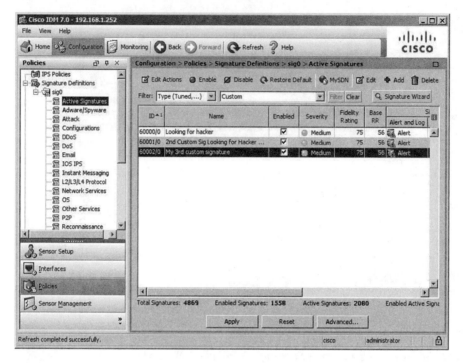

Figure 12-32 *Applying Custom Signatures*

To verify the signatures, use the same verification process used for the first signature. Refer to Figure 12-12 for those steps.

Summary

In this chapter, you learned about the need for custom signatures for matching on network traffic that isn't addressed by the built-in signatures on the sensor. You also learned how to create a custom signature with and without the wizard, and the best practices for verifying the new custom signature.

References

For additional information, refer to these resources:

Cisco Systems, Inc. Cisco Intrusion Prevention System: Introduction, at www.cisco.com/go/ips.

Cisco Systems, Inc. Cisco Intrusion Prevention System: Using the Signature Wizard, at www.cisco.com/en/US/docs/security/ips/7.0/configuration/guide/idm/ idm_signature_wizard.html.

Exam Preparation Tasks

Review All the Key Topics

Review the most important topics from the chapter, noted with the Key Topic icons in the margin of the page. Table 12-5 lists a reference of these key topics and the page numbers on which each is found.

Table 12-5 *Key Topics for Chapter 12*

Key Topic Element	Description	Page Number
Section	Creating Custom Signatures Guidelines	283
Table 12-3	Metacharacters Used in Regular Expressions	284
Figure 12-12	Testing Custom Signatures	294

Definitions of Key Terms

Define the following key terms from this chapter, and check your answers in the glossary:

custom signature, regular expression

A Cisco Intrusion Prevention System (IPS) is suspicious and not trusted when there are many false alarms. This chapter discusses methodologies to tune and tweak the sensor to manage and reduce the number of false positives and false negatives. In this chapter, you learn the following:

- **Identifying False Positives and False Negatives:** Understanding when the sensor is setting off alarms, when it shouldn't be, or missing malicious traffic when it should be firing off alarms is a critical first step in tuning the sensor for the network.

- **Tuning to Reduce False Positives:** Reducing or eliminating the erroneous alerts generated by the sensor.

- **Tuning to Reduce False Negatives:** By adapting the sensor to the current network and tuning the sensor to detect malicious traffic that can otherwise slip through without an alarm going off on the sensor.

CHAPTER 13

Managing False Positives and False Negatives

Overview

"One size fits all" doesn't fit regarding IPS. Each network is different. Default signatures might work for some networks, while custom signatures are needed for others, and yet others might need to disable or tune the default signatures for the desired effects in their network. This chapter is all about making sure that false positives and false negatives can both be reduced by tuning the sensor for a given network.

"Do I Know This Already?" Quiz

The "Do I Know This Already?" quiz allows you to assess whether you should read the entire chapter. If you miss no more than one of these self-assessment questions, you might want to move ahead to the "Exam Preparation Tasks" section. Table 13-1 lists the major headings in this chapter and the "Do I Know This Already?" quiz questions covering the material in those headings so that you can assess your knowledge of these specific areas. The answers to the "Do I Know This Already?" quiz appear in Appendix A.

Table 13-1   *"Do I Know This Already?" Foundation Topics Section-to-Question Mapping*

Foundation Topics Section	Questions
Understanding the Techniques for Tuning Out False Positives and Negatives	1–2
Implementing Tuning Techniques for Reducing False Positives and Negatives	3–5

1. An attacker is slowly scanning the network, even though the sensor has active signatures and is not generating an alert. What can cause this?

   a. Slow scans are not malicious.

   b. Default signature matches desired traffic and is enabled.

   c. Signature is too strict.

   d. Signature is too loose.

2. Question 1 would be an example of what?

    a. True positive

    b. True negative

    c. False positive

    d. False negative

3. What is one of the first general phases when tuning out false positives on a new IPS implementation?

    a. Disable any signatures with an ASR of 75 or higher.

    b. Do nothing; all the defaults will be perfect.

    c. Use event action filters to remove harmful actions.

    d. Use event filters to add sensor responses.

4. What is the default IP Reassembly option for the sensor?

    a. BSD

    b. Solaris

    c. Linux

    d. NT

5. How would you tune to correct a false positive?

    a. Disable the signature.

    b. Use event action filters.

    c. Make the match criteria stricter.

    d. All the above.

Foundation Topics

Identifying False Positives and False Negatives

As a general rule, *false* indicates something that is not desired, whereas *true* indicates a desired behavior, at least toward the IPS and signature matching. Let's review some definitions.

False Positives

False positives are events where the sensor reacts or responds to traffic that is not malicious. This would represent an error in the network environment the sensor is in. For two different networks, the attack might be a false positive in one and correct in the other. It depends on what type of traffic is permitted or acceptable on each network. A false positive can be caused by signatures that are too general in their attack-matching criteria and fire off on both malicious and nonmalicious traffic.

False Negatives

False negatives are events where the sensor doesn't fire off any alerts, or produce any actions, even when the sensor has seen malicious traffic. One network's malicious traffic can be a different network's acceptable traffic. This would represent an error from an IPS perspective and can be caused by a signature that is too specific in its matching criteria. This could also be caused by evasion techniques the attacker is using or by signatures being disabled that might have been able to identify the attack. Table 13-2 shows some examples of false positives.

Table 13-2 *Examples of Common False Positives*

Signature Type	Malicious Traffic	False Trigger
ICMP Network Sweep w/Echo	ICMP reconnaissance	Network mapping tools being run by management host
Failed Login	Brute-force attack or password guessing	Valid user forgot password and was making several attempts
UDP Flood	UDP DoS attack	Video or voice calls, using lots of UDP

You can see how a signature might not fire and create a false negative based on how the specific signature was written. An example is the Internet Control Message Protocol (ICMP) network sweep signature 2100.

The ICMP network sweep signature triggers when an echo request is sent to at least five unique destination IP addresses within 60 seconds. If an attacker scans the network slowly—for example, trying only four hosts per minute—the signature will not fire. By tuning this signature, you can control the matching criteria that will cause the sensor to react with an alert, or any other actions associated with this signature.

Tuning Consequences

Sensor tuning is a balancing act between making the sensor too sensitive, which results in false positives, and configuring the sensor to be too insensitive, which results in false negatives. One thing that can be observed is that decreasing false positives usually results in increased false negatives and vice versa.

Tuning Process Prioritization

Tuning the sensor is an ongoing process and will likely never by 100 percent perfect or complete, especially if network traffic and policies change over time. Prioritizing tuning efforts to get the highest return for time spent, these guidelines should be followed:

■ Tune the signatures that are most relevant to the network and business needs for the current network. These would include the false positives and false negatives regarding traffic to and from critical assets in the company, to assist in making signatures regarding this traffic as true as possible.

■ Tune signatures that have a high Attack Severity Rating (ASR) before spending time on signatures with lower ASRs. This will assist in making sure that the default signatures that have been identified as serious threats can be trusted in the current networks so that when an alert fires off, it is believed. Ideally, all alerts should be believed.

Tuning to Reduce False Positives

False positives are events where the sensor responds with an alert or other action, even though the traffic that triggered the alert is not malicious. There are two main categories of false positives:

■ Legitimate traffic that is very similar to the network attack the signature was looking for. The primary way to correct this is to tune the signature to make it less sensitive, when possible, so that it doesn't trigger on the nonmalicious traffic but still matches on malicious traffic.

■ Events that can be an attack, depending on where in the network they occurred. For example, a signature looking for TCP attempting to connect on port 23 (Telnet) might be acceptable on an internal network but might indicate an attack if being sourced from the outside or demilitarized zone (DMZ) portions of your network. In cases like this, the signature can be disabled for sensors monitoring the inside network and enabled for sensors monitoring the DMZ or outside networks. In cases where the traffic is allowed, the signature can be disabled for sensors that are analyzing traffic on that portion of the network. If traffic is allowed for some hosts on a given network but not others, the appropriate approach would be to use the event action filters.

When tuning to reduce false positives, priority should be given to inline sensors over sensors acting in promiscuous mode because an inline sensor could harm the network by stopping legitimate traffic because of a false positive. A sensor in promiscuous mode seeing the same alert will be less able to harm the traffic because it is limited to TCP resets and block requests.

Do No Harm, Initially

When a brand-new sensor is put on the network, it is very likely that there could be false positives. If these false positives don't have a negative impact on the network, it isn't really a big deal in terms of production network traffic. However, if the default signatures and default actions include denying traffic as a consequence of a false positive, the new IPS sensor would have a negative impact on a network. When tuning to reduce false positives, it makes sense to follow these phases:

■ Select the signature set and rules that will be used with a specific sensor.

Note: It is very important to keep track of which signature sets are being used as well as which virtual sensor is using which rules. Applying changes to the rules or signatures of a signature set or a rule set that doesn't belong to the sensor could cause misconfigurations for the sensors who are using those items.

■ Remove all default aggressive actions from all signatures. Use the event action filters, and subtract all aggressive action. This is faster than modifying individual signatures and removing all aggressive actions.

■ Add verbose alerts (which capture the first packet that triggered the alert) using event action overrides.

■ Add logging packets between the attacker and the victim, using event action overrides. Having the subsequent capture of packets can assist the analyst in better understanding the traffic that triggered and immediately followed the attack.

Note: Adding logging and/or verbose alerts will cause CPU utilization to increase and might not be a viable option depending on how busy the sensor already is. Use logging with caution. For many TCP-based signatures, additional information from the first 256 bytes of the packet that triggered the signature is included with the alert and is referred to as the *context data*. This context data is included in many TCP-based signatures, even without verbose alerts enabled, and can be used to assist in learning more about the traffic that triggered the signature.

■ Allow the sensor to analyze traffic, and then observe the alerts generated to see whether they are false positives or valid alerts; then tune the signatures as needed.

■ After the signatures are tuned, remove the event action filters that removed the aggressive actions, and remove the event action overrides that produced the verbose alerts.

■ Periodically, revisit the sensor to tune as needed. Realistically, new false positives showing up will alert you to the need for tuning.

Note: The duration of the initial and ongoing tuning depends on the specific network the sensor is in. Allow the sensor to analyze enough traffic to allow proper tuning. For example, a company that generates most of its traffic from Monday through Friday, with additional transactions at the end of every month, would not be properly tuned by analyzing just the traffic from a single weekend.

Learning About the Signatures and Why They Triggered a False Positive

Many times you will see an alert generated by a signature and need to know more about the signature to determine whether it is a false positive and know how to tune it. The Cisco IPS signature database descriptions on Cisco.com include a section on possible benign triggers for each signature that can assist in determining whether and how the signature should be tuned. There is a direct link from IPS Manager Express to the Cisco Security Intelligence Operations site, or it can be accessed directly through a browser. Sometimes when a false positive is triggered and you know it is not malicious traffic, you might want to disable that specific signature, or at least use an event action filter regarding the IP addresses involved for legitimate traffic, until you take the time to investigate and learn more about the signature.

Selecting and Verifying Signatures and Rules in Place

Now that you understand the overall process for tuning to reduce false positives, let's walk through examples of this step by step, starting by verifying which signature set and rules the sensor will be using, as shown in Figure 13-1.

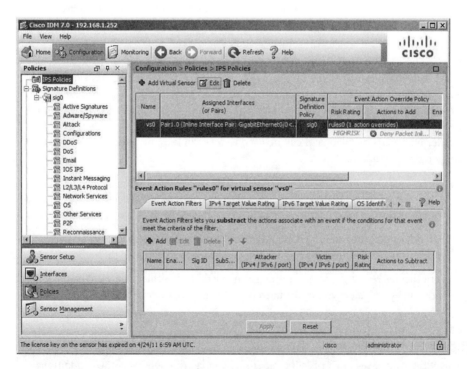

Figure 13-1 *Viewing Virtual Sensor Policies*

To verify which signature sets and which rules a virtual sensor is using, follow these steps:

Step 1. Open IPS Device Manager (IDM), and navigate to **Configuration > Policies > IPS Policies.**

Step 2. Select the virtual sensor from the list that you want to work with, and click it to highlight it. In the example, default virtual sensor vs0 is selected.

Step 3. Click the **Edit** button.

Step 4. From the new pop-up **Edit Virtual Sensor** window, view or change the signature and/or rules from the **Signature Definition Policy** and **Event Action Rules Policy** drop-down lists, as shown in Figure 13-2.

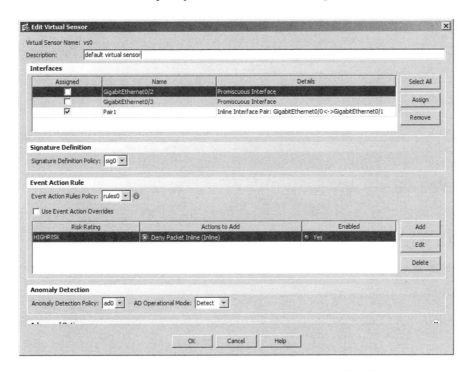

Figure 13-2 *Verifying or Editing the Signatures and Rules Used by the Sensor*

Note: If you want to use a different signature or rule set, it needs to be created before assignment to any sensor.

Removing All Aggressive Actions

Until you know exactly which signatures might be generating false positives, err on the side of caution initially with your sensor. To do this, you want to tell the sensor to avoid any negative reactions until you have identified false positives and know exactly what their responses are, and tuned signatures appropriately to avoid the false positives. There are a couple of different approaches that you could use to remove all the aggressive responses from the sensor. You could search for and individually remove every aggressive reaction such as "deny a packet inline," or you could go to one simple location to accomplish the same result. To do this, you would modify the rules in use by that virtual sensor, as shown in Figure 13-3.

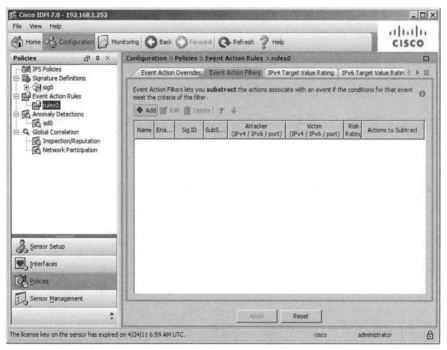

Figure 13-3 *Editing the Event Action Filters*

To implement event action filters, so that during the initial tuning of your sensor you don't cause traffic to be stopped, follow these steps:

Step 1.   Open IPS Device Manager (IDM), and navigate to **Configuration** > **Policies** > **Event Actions Rules** > **rules0**. Click the **Event Action Filters** tab.

> **Note:** You would select the rules set in use by your virtual sensor, as shown in Figure 13-2.

Step 2.   Click the **Add** button, and the **Add Event Action Filter** pop-up window will appear.

Step 3.   Click the small Notepad icon, to the far right of **Actions to Subtract**. This will invoke the pop-up window labeled **Edit Actions**.

Step 4.   From here, select the check boxes to choose all the options under **Deny Actions** and **Other Actions**, as shown in Figure 13-4. Click **OK** to exit the submenus.

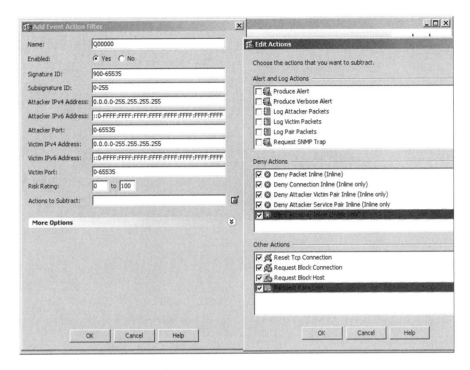

Figure 13-4   *Removing All Aggressive Responses*

> **Note:**   Accepting the defaults for the details of which signatures this filter will apply to results in applying the filter to all signatures for any IP addresses.

Step 5.   Click **Apply** to save your changes, as shown in Figure 13-5.

Adding Verbose Alerts and Logging

Adding verbose alerts and possibly IP logging will give you additional information or insight into the actual traffic patterns that triggered the signatures. By looking at this additional information, you can better understand why potentially nonmalicious traffic triggered a signature. The verbose alert option will include a copy of the initial packet that triggered the signature. Logging between the IP addresses of the attacker and the victim can allow further analysis of the traffic that is occurring between those two devices. As a general rule, logging is going to take more overhead and shouldn't be left on as a default for all signatures.

There is an easy way and a difficult way to enable verbose alerts and logging for all signatures. The hard way is to go to every single signature and modify the actions for each of the signatures. This is hard because there are thousands of signatures. An easier way is to use an event action override, as shown in Figure 13-6.

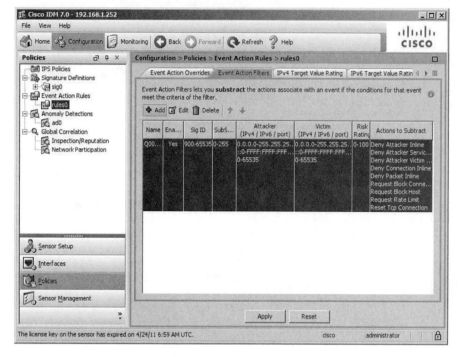

Figure 13-5 *Applying the Changes for the New Filter*

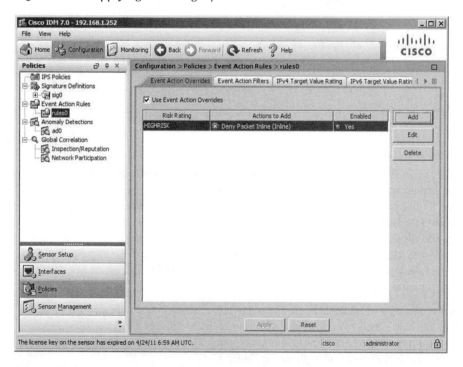

Figure 13-6 *Using Event Action Overrides*

To implement event action overrides, so that additional data about false positives is collected during the initial tuning of the sensor, follow these steps:

Step 1.   Open IPS Device Manager (IDM), and navigate to **Configuration** > **Policies** > **Event Actions Rules** > **rules0**. Click the **Event Action Overrides** tab.

Note: Select the rules set in use by your virtual sensor, as shown in Figure 13-2.

Step 2.   Click the **Edit** button, and the **Edit Event Action Override** pop-up window will appear. This will edit actions added for any risk rating of HIGHRISK.

Step 3.   Select the check boxes from the **Assigned** column, next to **Log Pair Packets** and **Produce Verbose Alert**. Deselect the Enabled check box for **Deny Packet Inline**, as shown in Figure 13-7.

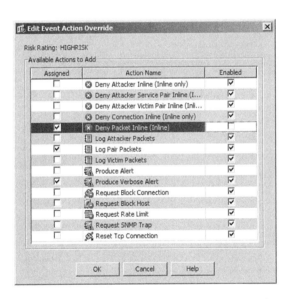

Figure 13-7   *Modifying Event Action Overrides*

Note: Deny Packet Inline for HIGHRISK is a default and must be assigned. Disabling it, however, is an option and can be done for peace of mind. Your event action filter (set up earlier) would not allow the Deny Packet Inline to take place, but it's nice to have it disabled in the overrides while tuning.

Step 4.   Click **OK** to close the window.

Step 5.   Click **Apply** to save the changes, as shown in Figure 13-8.

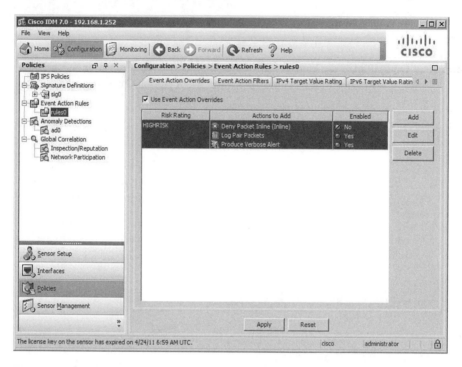

Figure 13-8   *Viewing and Applying the Changes to the Event Action Overrides*

Note: Repeat the previous process for MEDIUMRISK and LOWRISK events as well, if you want to collect the additional information on false positives that fall into those risk ratings, as shown in Figure 13-9. The priority would be to collect at a minimum the HIGH-RISK first, if there is not time to tune everything.

Using the Alert Data and Logging to Tune Out False Positives

In an earlier section, custom signatures were created to identify the word *hacker* that was part of a TCP session. In fact, three custom signatures, all looking for that same string, were created as part of the examples. You can leverage those signatures to test and verify that your event action overrides are logging, as well as demonstrate tuning out a false positive. In a Telnet session to the sensor (Telnet being a very bad idea in general, but useful for demonstration), you create a user named hacker, as shown in Figure 13-10.

There is nothing inherently wrong with the username, but it just happens to match your custom signatures. To get more information on the matches, you would use the monitoring features used previously to view the alerts, as shown in Figure 13-11.

To view the alerts, do the following: From the **Monitoring** tab, select **Events**, select how far back the sensor should show alerts for (in Figure 13-11, we are using 1 minute), and then click the **View** button.

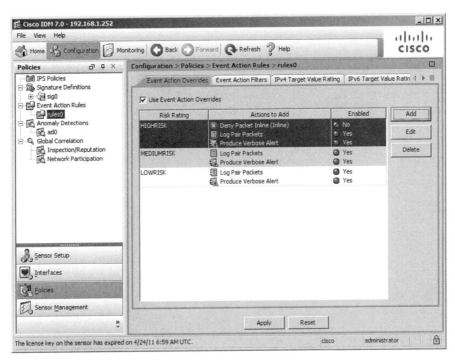

Figure 13-9 *Adding Logging and Verbose Alerts to the HIGHRISK, MEDIUMRISK, and LOWRISK categories*

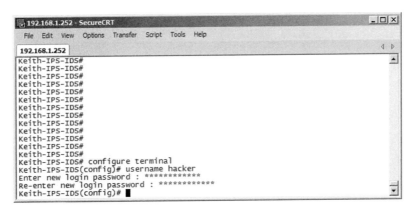

Figure 13-10 *Administrator Creating a Username of hacker*

> **Note:** You might need to scroll down to see the **View** button, which is not shown in Figure 13-11.

The Event Viewer window shows all the alerts from the past 1 minute, based on your input on the prior screen. The details from the alerts are shown in Figure 13-12.

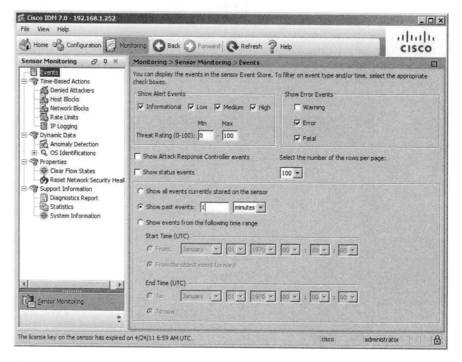

Figure 13-11 *Using the Monitoring Features to View Alerts*

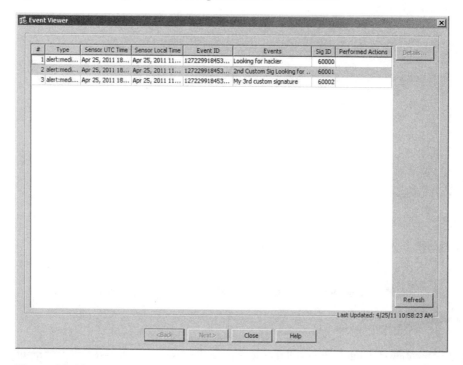

Figure 13-12 *Event Viewer Window*

To view the details of the event(s), highlight the event and click **Details** to open a new Details window. The details of the alert include the source, destination, signature number, and so on. If you scroll down, you will also see the details of what the attacker (which was me in this case) was sending through Telnet, including the password set for the hacker user account, as shown in Figure 13-13.

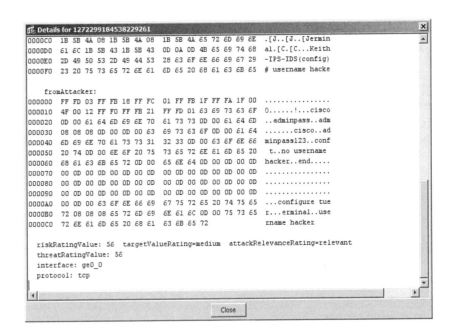

Figure 13-13 *Viewing the Details of the Alert*

In addition to the verbose alert, you also would have logging information for packets between the attacker (my workstation) and the victim (the destination of the Telnet session). You can see the logs in the Monitoring feature of the sensor, as shown in Figure 13-14.

To see the log files, follow these steps:

Step 1.   Open IPS Device Manager (IDM), and navigate to **Monitoring > Sensor Monitoring > Time-Based Actions > IP Logging**.

Step 2.   Click the log file you would like to analyze, and click the **Download** button to download the packet capture file to your computer.

Step 3.   After the file is downloaded to a local computer, Wireshark (installed on the same local PC) can be used to look at the details of the capture, as shown in Figure 13-15.

Note: Saving the file with a .pcap extension is not required but will better indicate the type of file it is for the protocol analyzer, such as Wireshark. In Figure 13-15, Wireshark is showing the file (named IPS Senor.pcap) that was downloaded from the sensor.

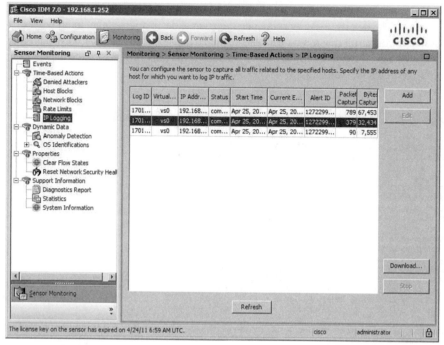

Figure 13-14 *Viewing Log Files*

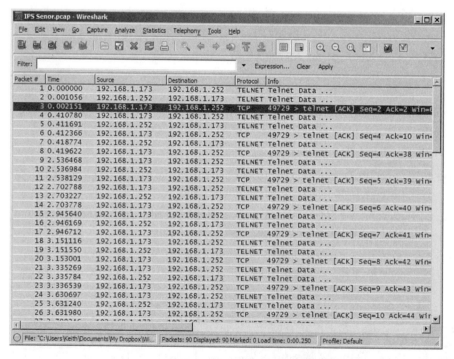

Figure 13-15 *Viewing Log Files on a Local PC with Wireshark*

Tuning the Signatures Based on Your Network

Now that a false positive is being triggered by someone creating a username called hacker, you can reduce this false positive by removing the source IP address or destination IP address that was involved in the signature match. You would do this by using an event action filter. Note that if you create a username called hacker, and you are allowing Telnet traffic where the username hacker might be logging in, that would also trigger it. In this case (which is just an example), where you want to trigger on the word *hacker* but not if it's someone trying to log on or telnet to a specific device, you can set the filter to not trigger on those signatures based on the destination IP address that you saw in the alerts. An example of event action filters is shown in Figure 13-16. Following Figure 13-16 are the steps to create a new custom filter.

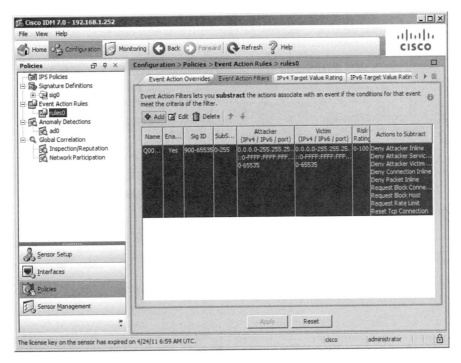

Figure 13-16 *Adding an Event Action Filter*

To implement a new event action filter so that the custom signatures 60000 through 60003 won't be triggered if the destination is 192.168.2.252, follow these steps:

Step 1. Open IPS Device Manager (IDM), and navigate to **Configuration > Policies > Event Actions Rules > rules0**. Click the **Event Action Filters** tab.

Step 2. Click the **Add** button, and the **Add Event Action Filter** pop-up window will appear.

Step 3. Click the small Notepad icon, to the far right of **Actions to Subtract**. This will invoke the pop-up window labeled **Edit Actions**.

Step 4.   From here, select the check boxes to choose all the actions you want to re-move based on Figure 13-17. Click **OK** to exit the submenus.

Note: In the example, signatures 60000–60003 will *not* produce any action or event when the destination IP address is 192.168.2.252 because of the filter just implemented.

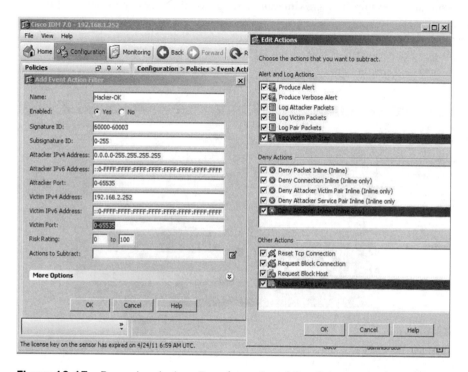

Figure 13-17   *Removing Actions Based on a Set of Conditions to Reduce False Positives*

Step 5.   Click the **Apply** button to save your changes, as shown in Figure 13-18.

Removing the Preliminary Overrides and Filters

After the sensor has been in place for a few weeks and the false positives have been identi-fied and corrected, you are ready to restore, or rather remove, the initial event action over-rides that were producing verbose alerts and logging. You would also remove the event action filters that are preventing any aggressive responses that you initially put in while you were tuning the sensor.

You have taken a look at the process of initializing and tuning the sensor and should note that this work is never truly ever done. Periodic work for tuning and tweaking the sensor will be required as the network changes over time.

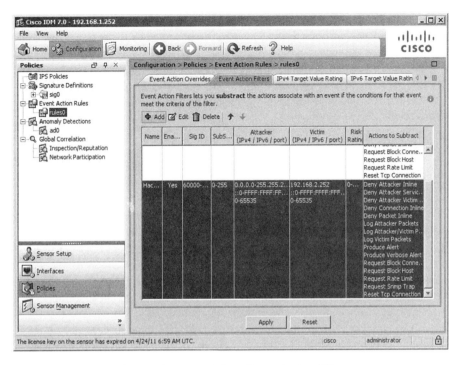

Figure 13-18   *Applying Changes Made to Event Action Filters*

Tuning the Sensor to Reduce False Negatives

A false negative occurs when the sensor does nothing when malicious traffic is present. It doesn't send an alert, it doesn't write home, it doesn't call—nothing. This is probably the trickiest aspect of identifying false negatives. A false negative would be primarily discovered through a secondary means such as a firewall reporting something or independent penetration tests that can be successful and at the same time are not detected or prevented by the sensor.

One practice for verifying that the IPS is doing its job is to create a baseline in a controlled environment regarding what the sensor should be able to detect. This would most likely be done with network tools such as vulnerability scanners that generate specific traffic that indeed looks like attacks that the sensor should recognize. Periodically, the scanners should run tests against all sensors to verify that any tuning or configuration that has been done has not desensitized the sensors to the point where they are not catching malicious traffic.

Note: Many companies have policies that strictly address scanning activity on the network. Make sure that senior management and the policies in place do not prohibit these types of tests if you plan on implementing them.

Tuning for false positives consists of defining the testing criteria for the success of a sensor and then using the network tools, which can be off-the-shelf or customized, to test the sensor to verify that it is catching the traffic that it should. Based on the analysis of how well the sensor did in identifying the malicious traffic generated by the scanner, you would tune or tweak the sensor until there are no false negatives. This basically means that the sensor is able to identify and detect everything that is thrown at it from your network scanner tool. As new attacks present themselves, and are publicly known, you would want to incorporate these simulated attacks into your scanning tools and verify that the sensor can detect them.

The primary reasons for false negatives include the following:

- The signature-matching criteria are too specific and do not match the malicious traffic.

- There is no signature for the particular malicious traffic.

- The sensor is not monitoring the portion of the network where the malicious traffic is happening.

- The attacker is using tools that are evasive enough in nature to not trigger the sensor.

The tuning and configuration to address these issues are fairly straightforward. If the signature-matching criteria are too specific, you could change the triggering conditions for specific signatures to make those signatures slightly more generic, which allows them to trigger on a wider set of criteria-matching parameters. In the situation where there is no existing signature, you can simply create a new one. If the sensor is not currently inline with the traffic you want to monitor, you could put it inline in that part of your network or mirror the data over to a promiscuous-mode interface on the sensor. If the attacker is using tools that are evading the sensor regardless of how you tune the sensor, you might need to rely on an outside or additional security control in addition to the sensor.

There thousands of signatures in the default signature set on the sensor. Some parameters of signatures are looking for strings of text using regular expressions. Other parameters are looking for the number of events to a given destination address. When all the matching criteria match traffic the sensors are looking at, it will trigger the alert. By modifying a signature and making it more generic (by specifying the matching criteria to be a little bit looser), you also run the risk of tuning a signature to the point where it will now be a false positive because it could match on all traffic, or at least more traffic that might not be malicious. Your goal here is to reduce false negatives. As you tune, test everything that you create to verify that it's working correctly and not creating false positives.

Tuning a Specific Signature

Key Topic

As an example, let's say that you ran your scanning tools and discovered that a ping flood of 50 ICMP packets on the network did not trigger any signatures. In your network, if 50 pings would be considered a malicious attack, if your IPS did not signal an alert, it would be a perfect example of a false negative. You could find and tune the signature for an ICMP flood, as shown in Figure 13-19.

To tune a signature, follow these steps:

Step 1.   Open IPS Device Manager (IDM), and navigate to **Configuration > Policies > Signature Definitions > sig0 > Active Signatures**.

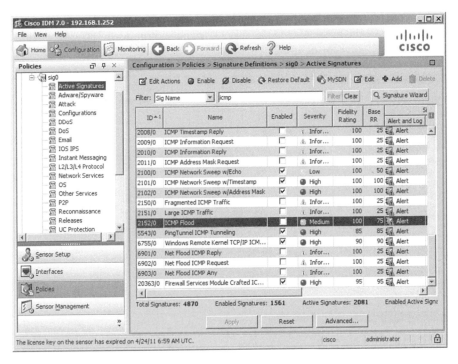

Figure 13-19 *Tuning Signatures for False Negatives*

Step 2.   In the **Filter** drop-down list, select **Sig Name**. In the filter entry field to the right of **Sig Name**, type in **icmp** and click the **Filter** button to the right.

Note: This will show all signatures with the word *ICMP* in the name.

Step 3.   Scroll down until you find the signature to be modified (in this example, the signature 2152 is used). Click the signature to highlight it. Notice that by default, the signature is not enabled, which would be one reason for the false negative.

Step 4.   Click the **Edit** button to edit the properties of this default signature. The pop-up window shown in Figure 13-20 will appear.

Step 5.   Edit the parameters to be changed. A green check mark will be placed in the check boxes where a nondefault value has been entered. In this example, the value of **Rate** is changed from its default value down to 49. Other parameters that might be considered are the summarization method, actions to be taken, and so on. Click **OK** to close this window, and then click **Apply** to save the changes.

Promiscuous Mode IP Reassembly

If you are missing alerts—or, in other words, are experiencing false negatives—it could be because your sensor is not correctly reassembling IP fragments. The IP reassembly mode should be set to the mode that most accurately reflects the traffic that will be seen by this sensor. To configure the reassembly mode, select it from the drop-down list, as shown in Figure 13-21.

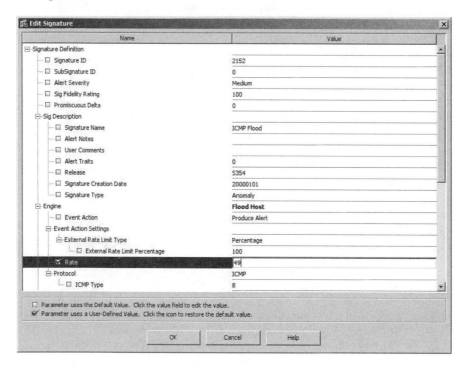

Figure 13-20 *Editing Signature Properties*

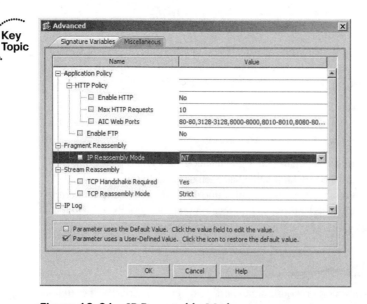

Figure 13-21 *IP Reassembly Mode*

To modify the reassembly mode, follow these steps:

Step 1.   Open IPS Device Manager (IDM), and navigate to **Configuration > Policies > Signature Definitions > sig0 > Active Signatures**.

Step 2.   On lower-right of side of the window, click the **Advanced** button. This will open the **Advanced** window.

Step 3.   Select the **Miscellaneous** tab. Next to **IP Reassembly Mode,** click the down arrow and select the desired mode.

Note: Options include BSD, Linux, NT, and Solaris. The default is NT, which relates to Windows computers. Select the type of devices most likely to be generating traffic on your network.

Step 4.   Click the **OK** button to close the window, and then click **Apply** to save the changes.

TCP Reassembly Mode

If you are experiencing false negatives regarding signatures that should be matching for TCP sessions, you should be aware that by default the sensor will only analyze TCP sessions for which it has seen a proper three-way handshake. This means that if you have asymmetrical routing, where only some of the packets go through the sensor and the return packets come back a different path, the sensor by default would not analyze these TCP sessions. To change this default behavior, you would choose a different stream reassembly mode, as shown in Figure 13-22.

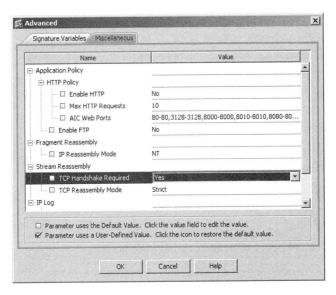

Key Topic

Figure 13-22   *TCP Stream Reassembly and Handshaking Settings*

To change the TCP stream reassembly options, follow these steps:

Step 1.   Open IPS Device Manager (IDM), and navigate to **Configuration > Policies > Signature Definitions > sig0 > Active Signatures**.

Step 2.   Click the **Advanced** button.

Step 3.   Click the **Miscellaneous** tab. Select the **TCP Handshake Required** and **TCP Reassembly Mode** options desired. If the **TCP Handshake Required** is set to yes (the default), the sensor will only track sessions for which a three-way handshake has been completed (and seen by the sensor).

Note: The options for TCP reassembly mode are Asymmetric, Strict, and Loose, with the default being Strict. In Strict mode, if a packet is missed for any reason, all packets after the missed packet in the session are not processed. Loose allows a dropped packet and will still process the rest. Asymmetric will work, even though it can only see one flow instead of bidirectional flows for the session.

Step 4.   Click the **OK** button to close the window, and then click **Apply** to save the changes.

Note: The default TCP reassembly mode of Strict was set as the default to protect against the sensor being overwhelmed. If you change the default and ask the sensor to analyze all TCP sessions for which it has not seen every TCP segment, it will increase the load on the sensor and should be monitored to make sure that you're not overtaxing it.

Normalizer Tuning

One possibility, although very slim, would be that the sensor itself is normalizing traffic to remove ambiguities from transit traffic that could allow an attacker to evade detection. It is not recommended to do so, but any signatures within the normalizer engine that have the action of modify packet could be changed and have the action of modify packet removed. An example of modifying a signature to remove the action of modify packet inline can be seen in Figure 13-23.

To remove the modify packet inline action from a signature, follow these steps:

Step 1.   Open IPS Device Manager (IDM), and navigate to **Configuration > Policies > Signature Definitions > sig0 > Active Signatures**.

Step 2.   In the **Filter** box, enter the number of the signature you want to modify and click the **Filter** button. Select the signature from the list by clicking it to highlight it; then click **Edit**.

Step 3.   In the **Event Action** field, click to bring up the actions submenu.

Step 4.   From here, place a check mark next to the actions you would like to have done, or click an existing check mark to remove that action. Click **OK** to close the windows, and then click **Apply** to save the changes.

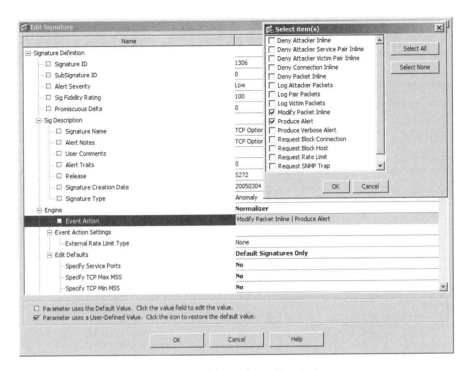

Figure 13-23 *Modifying the Modify Packet Inline Action*

Application-Layer Decoding and Deobfuscation

Obfuscation is an attempt to conceal an attack or to make the attack difficult to interpret and be correctly detected by an IPS. An example is sending a string of text that when interpreted by the victim causes damage to that destination host, but when seen by an IPS is not seen as damaging. The result, if successful by the attacker, would be a false negative at the IPS.

By default, deobfuscation is on for Service.HTTP engine signatures. Leaving this feature on will reduce your false negatives. Be very careful that any regular expressions used instead of a custom signature or a tuned signature are written correctly so that they would match on the expected traffic. An example of a signature that is enabled for deobfuscation can be seen in Figure 13-24.

Using the same process as shown in Figure 13-23 when editing the properties of a signature, select the **Yes** option to use deobfuscation for signatures that support it. Figure 13-24 shows signature 3253, which uses the Service HTTP engine and supports deobfuscation.

Encrypted Traffic

One of the benefits of encrypting your traffic is that you can hide the contents of the payload. This is also one of the negatives of encrypting your traffic when considering what will be seen by the IPS. The IPS can't inspect the encrypted portion of a packet. When possible, place the sensor's interfaces so that it will be able to see the traffic after it has been decrypted. An example of this would be to place the sensor behind the Virtual Private Network (VPN) firewall so that traffic coming in from VPN users is decrypted at the firewall before being seen by the sensor on the inside interface.

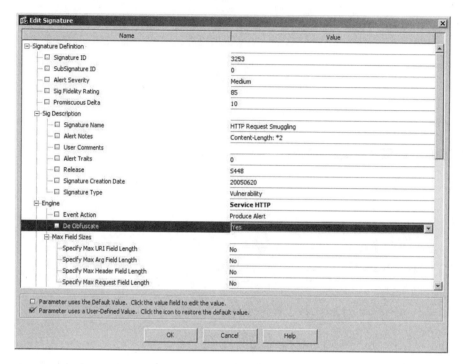

Figure 13-24 *De Obfuscate Option for Some Signatures*

Summary

In this chapter, we reviewed the concepts of false positives and false negatives, and described how to tune the sensor to minimize both of these.

References

For additional information, refer to these resources:

Cisco Systems, Inc. Cisco Intrusion Prevention System: Introduction, at www.cisco.com/go/ips.

Cisco Systems, Inc. Cisco Intrusion Prevention System: Configuring Policies, at www.cisco.com/en/US/docs/security/ips/7.0/configuration/guide/idm/idm_policies.html.

Cisco Systems, Inc. Cisco Intrusion Prevention System: Defining Signatures, at www.cisco.com/en/US/docs/security/ips/7.0/configuration/guide/idm/idm_signature_definitions.html.

Exam Preparation Tasks

Review All the Key Topics

Review the most important topics from the chapter, noted with the Key Topic icons in the margin of the page. Table 13-3 lists a reference of these key topics and the page numbers on which each is found.

Table 13-3 *Key Topics for Chapter 13*

Key Topic Element	Description	Page Number
Paragraph	Do No Harm, Initially	315
Figure 13-3	Editing Event Action Filters	318
Figure 13-13	Viewing Alert Details	325
Figure 13-14	Viewing Log Files	326
Paragraph	Tuning a Specific Signature	330
Figure 13-21	IP Reassembly Mode	332
Figure 13-22	TCP Stream Reassembly	333

Definitions of Key Terms

Define the following key terms from this chapter, and check your answers in the glossary:

tuned signature, false positive, false negative, tuning

Understanding how the IPS sensor can dynamically respond to an attack and also understanding the individual factors that go into the formula for risk rating are critical for optimizing the IPS sensor responses. In this chapter, you will learn the following:

- **Identifying and Adjusting Risk-Rating Components:** The ingredients that go into the recipe affecting risk rating, and how you can modify these as you tune the sensor.

- **Operating System Fingerprinting:** Understanding the relevance between a specific attack and the operating system of the victim will allow the sensor to increase the risk rating for a given signature match, depending on which operating system the victim is running.

- **Global Correlation and Reputation-Based Filtering:** Leveraging experiences other sensors are having can assist your local sensor to take extra precautions against potential external threats by being forewarned about them.

CHAPTER 14

Improving Alarm and Response Quality

Overview

To improve overall response quality, event action overrides and the elevated risk ratings that trigger them should be implemented. Understanding the components that go into the formula for the risk rating, and knowing how to modify those components, is critical to optimizing the sensor in protecting your network and its most critical resources.

"Do I Know This Already?" Quiz

The "Do I Know This Already?" quiz allows you to assess whether you should read the entire chapter. If you miss no more than one of these self-assessment questions, you might want to move ahead to the "Exam Preparation Tasks" section. Table 14-1 lists the major headings in this chapter and the "Do I Know This Already?" quiz questions covering the material in those headings so that you can assess your knowledge of these specific areas. The answers to the "Do I Know This Already?" quiz appear in Appendix A.

Table 14-1 *"Do I Know This Already?" Foundation Topics Section-to-Question Mapping*

Foundation Topics Section	Questions
Identifying and Understanding the Risk-Rating Components	1–3
Configuring Passive Operating System Fingerprinting	4
Describing Global Correlation	5

1. Which of the following factors of the risk rating are properties of a signature?

   a. Event count

   b. SFR

   c. TVR

   d. WLR

2. What would be required to utilize WLR in the risk-rating calculation?

   a. At least one external product interface

   b. Event action filters

   c. Event action overrides

   d. At least one custom signature

3. What would be the primary reason for tuning the SFR, ASR, and TVR parameters?

   a. To reduce false positives

   b. To reduce false negatives

   c. To modify the risk rating

   d. To modify the event action overrides

4. Which of the following is *not* a method that IPS can use to know the correlation between IP address and which operating system it is running?

   a. Passive operating system fingerprinting

   b. Posture notifications

   c. Static configuration

   d. Dynamic DNS

5. You want to use global correlation to influence the risk rating and reputation filters to deny suspicious source IP addresses. The feature is configured but not working. What is likely the problem?

   a. Default gateway isn't configured.

   b. Event action overrides aren't configured.

   c. DNS isn't configured.

   d. Signatures are by default disabled, until administratively enabled.

Foundation Topics

Identifying and Adjusting Risk-Rating Components

There are two primary methods for instructing the sensor to respond to an attack or signature match. The first option is to hard code, or assign, a specific response action to the individual signature itself. The other option is to allow the sensor to add actions based on a specific risk rating that has been achieved based on a signature match. Assigning a specific action to the signature is very standard, and you've done it before in this book. You've also done event action overrides in Chapter 13, "Managing False Positives and False Negatives," which will assist with minimizing false positives and false negatives. In the following sections, we are going to focus on the risk-rating components. These concepts apply to a sensor that is operating in promiscuous mode or inline mode.

Formula for Risk Rating

The formula for the risk rating is as follows:

$$RR = (ASR*TVR*SFR/10,000) + ARR - PD + WLR$$

Regardless of the calculation, if the final risk rating is over 100, it will be rounded down to 100. A description of the risk-rating components is shown in Table 14-2.

Table 14-2   *Risk-Rating Components*

Key Topic

Acronym	Definition
RR	Risk Rating. This is the final risk-rating result.
ASR	Attack Severity Rating. This is assigned as a property of the signature to indicate how serious an attack, in the mind of the person who created the signature, is happening when this signature is matched. The numeric value is hidden. You are presented with the options of High, Medium, Low, and Informational, which behind the scenes have a numeric value associated with them (shown later in Table 14-3).
TVR	Target Value Rating. This is configured in the set of rules that is assigned to a virtual sensor. The more critical the device is, based on its IP address, the higher the Target Value Rating will be and, as a result, the higher the final risk rating will be. There are values associated with each of the labels that can be assigned (shown later in Table 14-4).
SFR	Signature Fidelity Rating. This is assigned as a property of the signature to indicate how accurate the signature is, in the mind of the person who created the signature, regarding the matching ability of this signature.

Table 14-2 *Risk-Rating Components*

Acronym	Definition
ARR	Attack Relevancy Rating. This is configured as a property of a signature. If the person who wrote the signature indicates that the signature match is only relevant if the operating system is UNIX, and the IPS sensor knows that the destination address for a signature match is also UNIX, it will increase the value of the risk rating.
PD	Promiscuous Delta. If the sensor has a signature match learned on one of its promiscuous mode interfaces, and if the given signature that was matched includes a Promiscuous Delta value, the risk rating will be reduced by that value.
WLR	Watch List Rating. If the Cisco Security Agent manager has been configured, and has notified the sensor that a specific IP address is under attack, the Watch List Rating will be added to the risk rating.

Using Attack Severity and Signature Fidelity Ratings

An Attack Severity Rating (ASR) is assigned as a property of the signature to indicate how serious an attack is, in the mind of the person who created the signature. The numeric values associated with each of the ratings are shown in Table 14-3.

Table 14-3 *Attack Severity Rating Values*

Alert Severity	Value
High	100
Medium	75
Low	50
Informational	25

A Signature Fidelity Rating (SFR) is assigned as a property of the signature to indicate how accurate the signature is, in the mind of the person who created the signature. These values can be tuned from their defaults to increase or decrease their value as they go into the risk-rating calculation. Fidelity has a value from 0 to 100, and Severity has a value of High, Medium, Informational, or Low. To modify a signature's ASR or SFR, open the signature for editing, as shown in Figure 14-1.

To tune a signature, follow these steps:

Step 1.   Open IPS Device Manager (IDM), and navigate to **Configuration** > **Policies** > **Signature Definitions** > **sig0** > **Active Signatures**.

Step 2.   Scroll down or use the filter list to find the signature to be modified. Click the signature to be modified to select it.

Note: In the example, custom signature 60000 is being modified.

Key
Topic

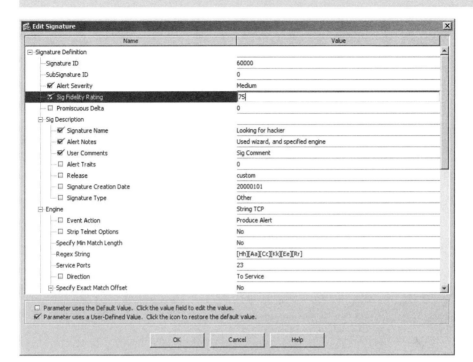

Figure 14-1 *Tuning Signatures' ASR and SFR Settings*

Step 3.   Click the **Edit** button to edit the properties of the signature. The **Edit Signature** window will open.

Step 4.   From here, modify the **Alert Severity** and/or **Sig Fidelity Rating** to the desired values. The higher these values are set, the higher the resulting risk rating will be. Click **OK** to close this window, and click **Apply** to save the changes.

Target Value Ratings

Another big factor in the calculation of the overall risk rating is the Target Value Rating. The purpose of knowing and understanding the individual components that make up the risk rating is so that you can manipulate them as needed, and take advantage of event action overrides that will add actions based on a signature match resulting in a risk rating of a specific level or higher. TVRs are assigned a value, based on the category, as shown in Table 14-4.

Table 14-4 *Target Value Ratings Assignments*

Target Value Rating	Value
Mission-critical	200
High	150

Table 14-4   *Target Value Ratings Assignments*

Target Value Rating	Value
Medium	100
Low	75
No value	50

Note: The default is Medium, with a value of 100.

When configuring TVRs, it is recommended to specify as many as possible in an environment. The more devices that are identified as being critical or not so critical, the more accurate and effective your IPS appliance will be when leveraging event action overrides. To assign IP addresses or ranges to a specific class, edit the rules in use, as shown in Figure 14-2.

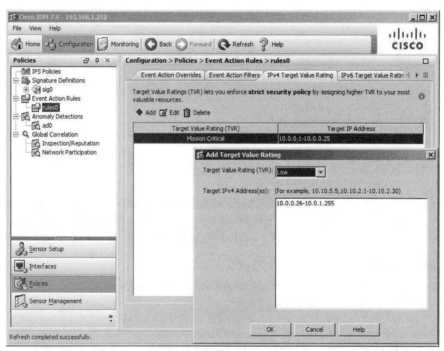

Figure 14-2   *Configuring Which IP Addresses Belong to Which Target Value Ratings*

To assign devices to specific Target Value Ratings, follow these steps:

Step 1.   Open IPS Device Manager (IDM), and navigate to **Configuration > Policies > Event Action Rules > rules0**.

Note: In this example, rules0 was selected as the rule set to modify. If the virtual sensor was assigned a different rules set, you would choose the one assigned to the sensor you are configuring.

Step 2.   Click the **IPv4 Target Value Rating** tab.

Step 3.   Click the **Add** button. The **Add Target Value Rating** window opens.

Step 4.   From here, from the **Target Value Rating (TVR)** drop-down list, select the category (as shown in Table 14-4) and enter the address range for that category. Click **OK** to close this window, and click **Apply** to save the changes.

Attack Relevancy Rating

When the sensor detects a signature match, it will look at the Attack Relevancy Rating associated with that signature, and it can modify the risk rating. An example would be if the signature itself specified an Attack Relevancy Rating for Macintosh, and the signature that fired was triggered on an attack destined to an IP address that the sensor knew was indeed a Macintosh, the Attack Relevancy Rating function would increase the overall risk rating by 10 points. If in the signature it specified relevancy to any general operating system, the sensor would add 10 points to the risk rating regardless of knowing whether the final destination IP address in the attack that triggered the signature was a Macintosh. This is because the sensor assumes that general operating system applies to all possible attacked IP addresses.

If there is a signature match that specifies, in the signature, that the Attack Relevancy Rating applies to UNIX, and the sensor does not know the specific operating system associated with the destination IP address of an attack, the sensor will ignore the Attack Relevancy Rating, using a value of 0.

In summary, if the Attack Relevancy Rating is relevant, 10 points may be added to the Risk Rating. To change the operating system for which a signature is relevant (regarding the ARR value), modify the signature as shown in Figure 14-3.

To tune a signature, follow these steps:

Step 1.   Open IPS Device Manager (IDM), and navigate to **Configuration > Policies > Signature Definitions > sig0 > Active Signatures**.

Step 2.   Scroll down or use the filter list to find the signature to be modified. Click the signature to highlight it.

Step 3.   Click the **Edit** button to edit the properties of this default signature. The **Edit Signature** window opens.

Step 4.   From here, modify the **Vulnerable OS List** by clicking it, which will bring up a **Select item(s)** pop-up menu. Select the operating systems that this signature is relevant to by selecting the check box next to that OS. Click **OK** to close the windows, and click **Apply** to save the changes.

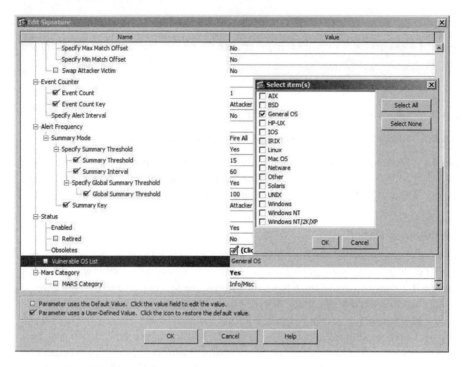

Figure 14-3   *Tuning Signatures' ARR Settings*

Watch List Rating

If you have configured your sensor to work with the Cisco Security Agent (CSA) manager, you can increase the value of the risk rating based on information from the Cisco Security Agent manager regarding a device that is specifically under attack. The default number that is added to the risk rating based on watch list reports is 25, and the valid range is from 0 to 35. This setting will be illustrated in the next section.

Operating System Fingerprinting

For the Attack Relevancy Rating to significantly shape your overall risk rating, the IPS sensor needs to know which operating systems are associated with which IP addresses. When a signature match occurs and the property of the signature says that it is relevant to a UNIX operating system, and the IPS also knows that the destination IP address associated in the attack is a UNIX operating system, it can increase the risk rating by 10 points. The sensor can learn or be configured with information regarding which operating systems are associated with which IP addresses, from one of three sources:

■ **The passive operating system fingerprinting function (POSFP):** Using this method, the sensor is going to analyze TCP packets that are being sent through the network, and based on what it knows about how specific operating systems use TCP, dynamically map the operating system when possible to the IP address. If there hasn't been much traffic or if the sensor, based on what it knows, is not able to determine the operating system, the operating system won't be dynamically added to it.

- **Manual operating system mappings:** This is just what it sounds like. You manu-ally specify which IP addresses are associated with which operating systems.

- **Imported information from the management center for the Cisco Security Agents:** Because the manager for the Cisco Security Agents knows exactly which IP addresses are associated with which operating systems, you could leverage that infor-mation on the IPS appliance.

To enable passive OS fingerprinting and specify which IP addresses the IPS should be willing to dynamically learn for, enable the feature, as shown in Figure 14-4.

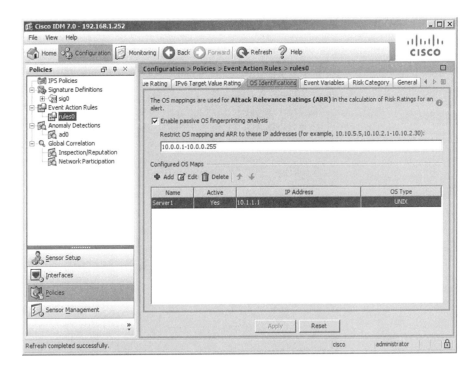

Figure 14-4 *Enabling Passive OS Fingerprinting Analysis*

To enable passive OS fingerprinting, follow these steps:

Step 1. Open IPS Device Manager (IDM), and navigate to **Configuration > Policies > Event Action Rules > rules0.** Click the **OS Identifications** tab.

Note: You might need to use the scroll arrows near the upper right to see the all the tabs, including the one in Step 1.

Step 2. Select the **Enable passive OS fingerprinting analysis** check box, and specify which range of IP addresses the IPs should be analyzing. By default, all IP ad-dresses are specified.

Step 3.   To add a static mapping, click **Add** and specify the IP address and OS type of that IP address. Then click **OK** and click **Apply** to close the submenus and save the configuration.

Note: In the example in Figure 14-4, the sensor has been configured to only learn through POSFP for addresses in the 10.0.0.0/24 network. The example also shows a specific device at 10.1.1.1 that has been hard coded as being a UNIX OS at that address.

To import OS identifications from the Cisco Security Agent manager, you must manually configure the CSA manager as an external product interface, as shown in Figure 14-5.

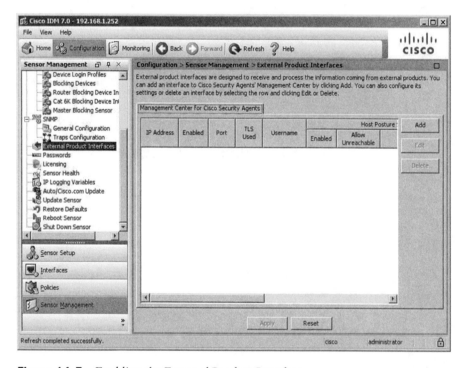

Figure 14-5   *Enabling the External Product Interface*

To enable interaction between the CSA manager and the IPS sensor, follow these steps:

Step 1.   Open IPS Device Manager (IDM), and navigate to **Configuration > Sensor Management > External Product Interfaces**.

Step 2.   Click **Add**. The **Add External Product Interface** window opens.

Step 3.   Provide the information for interaction with the CSA Manager, as shown in Figure 14-6. Click **OK** and then click **Apply** to close the window and save the configuration.

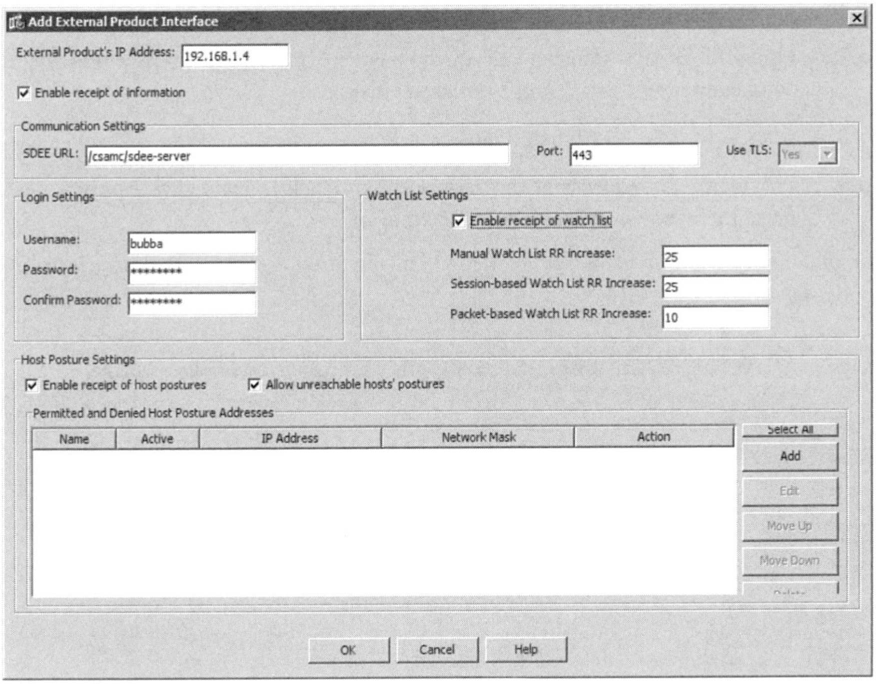

Figure 14-6   *Entering the Details for the Integration with CSA Manager*

Note: Host posture is the information the IPS appliance uses to identify the operating system associated with an IP. This information would affect the ARR component of the overall risk-rating formula.

The watch list is indicating that the device is under an attack, as known by the Cisco Security Agent, which was reported to the CSA manager. The watch list is how this information is communicated to the sensor. This would affect the WLR component of the overall risk-rating formula.

For the external product interface with the CSA manager to be successful, you would also need to configure the IP address of the CSA manager as a trusted host, as shown in Figure 14-7.

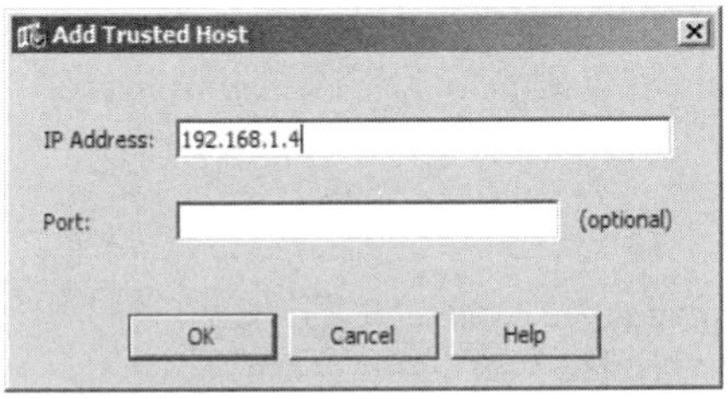

Figure 14-7   *Configuring the CSA Manager Address as a Trusted Host*

To enable the CSA manager address to be a trusted host, follow these steps:

Step 1.   Open IPS Device Manager (IDM), and navigate to **Configuration > Sensor Management > Certificates > Trusted Hosts**.

Step 2.   Click **Add**. The **Add Trusted Host** window will open.

Step 3.   Provide the **IP Address** of the CSA manager. Click **OK** and click **Apply** to close the window and save the configuration.

To see the imported and dynamically learned OS information, use the Monitoring section of IDM, as shown in Figure 14-8.

Figure 14-8   *Verifying What OS-to-IP Mappings Have Been Learned or Imported*

To see what OS-to-IP mappings have been learned, follow these steps:

Step 1.   Open IPS Device Manager (IDM), and navigate to **Monitoring > Sensor Monitoring > Dynamic Data > OS Identifications > Learned OS**.

Step 2.   Clicking **Imported OS** would reveal any posture mappings learned from the external product interface devices, namely, the CSA manager–provided mappings.

Note: The IP identified in the example in the mapping is the command and control interface of the sensor itself. The sensor is inline between the PC and the sensor's own interface.

Global Correlation and Reputation-Based Filtering

Using global correlation, the IPS sensor will periodically receive threat updates from the Cisco sensor-based network. This includes information about known threats, which include serial attackers, botnets, malware outbreaks, and similar large-scale events. The IPS can use this information to prevent serious attackers before they even get a chance to attack your network. By participating, not only does your sensor receive information, but you also provide information that is used for global correlation.

There are two mechanisms that the IPS sensor is going to use to correlate:

- Reputation filters, which can deny hosts that are blacklisted. When enabled, this will occur before the sensor further analyzes the traffic from the denied would-be attacker(s). There is a "test mode" so that implementers can verify that the filtering is acceptable and doesn't negatively affect legitimate traffic. This information can be reported through reputation filter hit statistics.

- Global correlation, which can influence the risk rating. With a higher risk rating, it is more likely that configured event action overrides would provide the correct sensor responses. The tables and calculations from the SensorBase network are complex, rely on statistical information, and can change over time.

Reputation Filters

Reputation filters provide the first level of defense regarding denying packets based on IP addresses that are provided by the SensorBase blacklist. No signature inspection or anomaly detection function is wasted on these packets, as they are denied before any other type of inspection is done. If the sensor is configured to participate, it will send data about the attacker back to the SensorBase network. With the test mode for reputation filters, instead of denying traffic at the sensor, it will simply report the potential denies as well as statistics. This allows the testing of reputation filters before completely buying in.

Global Correlation

By enabling global correlation, the IPS sensor can be aware of network traffic that has a reputation for malicious activity, and by increasing risk ratings, potentially protect the network from these sources. When global correlation is enabled, this sensor will periodically update reputation data. For this to work, the sensor needs to resolve a fully qualified domain name, which means that it will not work unless Domain Name System (DNS) is configured on the sensor. If the sensor is participating with global correlation, data will be sent every 10 minutes using a secure HTTPS connection. Information sent includes IP addresses and port numbers, signature IDs, some basic information about the sensor configuration, and so forth. No data content, private IP addresses, or payload information is sent.

To participate in the SensorBase network information, verify that the sensor is configured to use DNS, as shown in Figure 14-9.

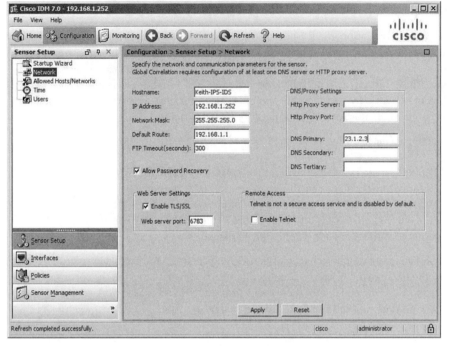

Figure 14-9   *Verify That DNS Is Configured on the Sensor*

To configure or verify the DNS configuration on the sensor, follow these steps:

Step 1.   Open IPS Device Manager (IDM), and navigate to **Configuration > Sensor Setup > Network**.

Step 2.   Supply a functional **DNS Primary** address.

Step 3.   Click **Apply** to save the configuration.

To enable the global correlation and reputation features, select the options for those, as shown in Figure 14-10.

To enable the global correlation and reputation filtering features, follow these steps:

Step 1.   Open IPS Device Manager (IDM), and navigate to **Configuration > Policies > Global Correlation > Inspection/Reputation**.

Step 2.   Click the **On** radio button under Global Correlation Inspection, and from the drop-down list, select **Aggressive**, **Standard**, or **Permissive**.

Note: The default mode of Global Correlation is off. When enabled, the Aggressive option will have the most impact on the risk rating (increasing it the most), compared to Standard or Permissive.

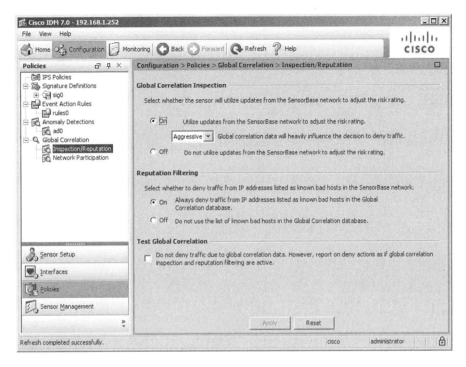

Figure 14-10   *Global Correlation and Reputation Filtering Options*

Step 3.   Click the **On** radio button under Reputation Filtering to use this feature.

Step 4.   Select the **Test Global Correlation** check box to gather statistics without actually denying because of the reputation filter or modifying the risk rating because of the Global Correlation Inspection settings.

Step 5.   Click **Apply** to save the configuration.

Note: You will be prompted to agree to sending information from the local IPS to the SensorBase, as shown in Figure 14-11.

The SensorBase relies on information that is collected from sensors located around the globe. You can decide how much your sensor contributes to the SensorBase information by choosing your Network Participation level, as shown in Figure 14-12.

To view or modify the sensor's participation level with SensorBase, follow these steps:

Step 1.   Open IPS Device Manager (IDM), and navigate to **Configuration** > **Policies** > **Global Correlation** > **Network Participation**.

Step 2.   Click the radio button next to **Off**, **Partial**, or **Full** for the option you want to select.

Step 3.   Click **Apply** to save the configuration.

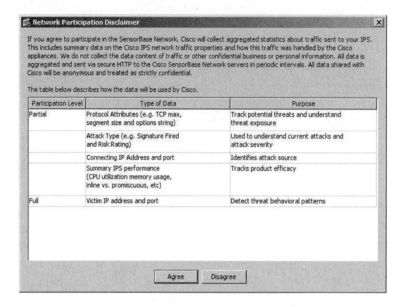

Figure 14-11   *Network Participation Agreement*

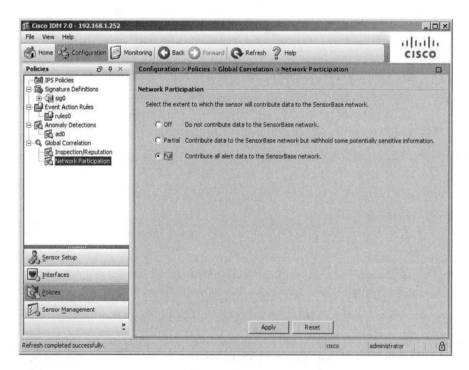

Figure 14-12   *Selecting the Network Participation Level*

Summary

In this chapter, we identified the individual components that go into the formula for the risk rating and described how that risk rating is related to event action overrides. We also discussed how the CSA manager information can be used to affect the risk rating regarding OS identification and watch lists. Reputation filters can deny suspect IP addresses, whereas global correlation can affect the risk rating by increasing its value.

References

For additional information, refer to these resources:

Cisco Systems, Intrusion Prevention Systems (IPS), at www.cisco.com/go/ips.

Cisco Systems, Installing and Using Cisco Intrusion Prevention System Device Manager 7.0, at www.cisco.com/en/US/docs/security/ips/7.0/configuration/guide/idm/idmguide7.html.

Exam Preparation Tasks

Review All the Key Topics

Review the most important topics from the chapter, noted with the Key Topic icons in the margin of the page. Table 14-5 lists a reference of these key topics and the page numbers on which each is found.

Table 14-5   *Key Topics for Chapter 14*

Key Topic Element	Description	Page Number
Table 14-2	Formula for Risk Rating and Risk-Rating Components	341
Figure 14-1	Editing ASR and SFR Signature Properties	343
Figure 14-2	Configuring Target Value Ratings	344
Figure 14-4	Configuring Passive OS Fingerprinting (POSFP)	347
Figure 14-8	Viewing Learned OS-to-IP Mappings	350
Figure 14-9	Enabling DNS for Global Correlation to Work	352
Figure 14-10	Configuring Global Correlation and Reputation Filtering	353

Definitions of Key Terms

Define the following key terms from this chapter, and check your answers in the glossary:

RR, ASR, TVR, SFR, ARR, PD, WLR

642-627 IPS v7.0 exam topics covered in this part:

- Configure and verify the IPS features to identify threats and dynamically block them from entering the network

- Maintain, update, and tune IPS signatures

- Use CSM and MARS for IPS management, deployment, and advanced event correlation

- Optimize security functions, rules, and configuration

Part V: Managing and Analyzing Events

This chapter covers the following topics:

- **Cisco IPS Manager Express Overview:** Provides a brief overview of the Cisco IPS Manager Express (IME) and describes how it simplifies the management of Cisco IP sensors.

- **Installing Cisco IPS Manager Express (IME):** Walks you through the installation process and provides information on actions that can prevent a successful install.

- **Integrating Cisco IPS Manager Express with Cisco IPS Sensors:** Covers the steps required to manage a Cisco IPS sensor using IME by adding the IPS sensor with the appropriate parameters.

- **Tuning the Cisco IPS Sensor Through Cisco IPS Manager Express:** Covers the steps required to modify or create new risk categories based on risk levels identified on the network.

- **Customizing the Cisco IPS Manager Express Dashboards:** Provides steps on creating and customizing the IME dashboard to display important information about the sensor and the network.

CHAPTER 15

Installing and Integrating Cisco IPS Manager Express with Cisco IPS Sensors

Overview

Cisco Intrusion Prevention System (IPS) Manager Express (IME) is an intuitive, user-friendly application designed to simplify the configuration, tuning, management, and troubleshooting of Cisco IPS sensors. Although it possesses these feature-rich capabilities (including monitoring), it is designed for small- and medium-sized businesses that manage less than ten devices. This reduces the time required to configure and integrate Cisco IPS devices into the network and gives the ability to manage the devices from a single window.

This chapter begins with an overview of Cisco IPS Manager Express, highlighting its key features. By the end of this chapter, you should be able to carry out the following:

■   Install the Cisco IME software

■   Use and customize the Cisco IME user interface

■   Integrate Cisco IME with a Cisco IPS sensor

■   Tune the Cisco IPS signatures through Cisco IME

"Do I Know This Already?" Quiz

The "Do I Know This Already?" quiz allows you to assess whether you should read the entire chapter. If you miss no more than one of these self-assessment questions, you might want to move ahead to the "Exam Preparation Tasks" section. Table 15-1 lists the major headings in this chapter and the "Do I Know This Already?" quiz questions covering the material in those headings so that you can assess your knowledge of these specific areas. The answers to the "Do I Know This Already?" quiz appear in Appendix A.

Table 15-1   *"Do I Know This Already?" Foundation Topics Section-to-Question Mapping*

Foundation Topics Section	Questions
Cisco IPS Manager Express Overview	1, 2
Installing Cisco IPS Manager Express	3
Integrating Cisco IPS Manager Express with IPS Sensors	4–6
Tuning the Cisco IPS Sensor Through Cisco IPS Manager Express	7
Customizing Cisco IPS Manager Express Dashboards	8–10

1. What is the maximum number of sensors supported by Cisco IPS Manager Express?

    a. 5

    b. 10

    c. 8

    d. 12

2. Which of the following is *not* a troubleshooting tool built into Cisco IME?

    a. Ping

    b. Debug

    c. DNS Lookup

    d. Traceroute

3. Which operating system does the Cisco IME application run on or support?

    a. Solaris

    b. MAC OS

    c. Windows

    d. UNIX

4. Which of these are *not* required to add a sensor to Cisco IME?

    a. Sensor IP address

    b. Sensor name

    c. Sensor login username and password

    d. Sensor location

5. When connecting to a Cisco IPS sensor through Cisco IME, what happens if you reject the certificate offered by the sensor?

    a. Connection is refused by the sensor

    b. Sensor powers down

    c. Sensor stops forwarding traffic

    d. Sensor logs the action as an attack

6. Why does Cisco IME prompt if the times on sensor and management host are more than 5 minutes apart?

    a. Cisco IME wants the clock on the management host to be changed.

    b. Cisco IME wants the time on the Cisco IPS to be changed.

    c. Cisco IME notifies you for informational purposes only.

    d. Cisco IME wants to ensure that event times are synchronized between the sensor and management host where IME is installed.

7. Which of the following risk categories is *not* predefined in Cisco IME?

    a. LOWRISK

    b. HIGHRISK

    c. LOWHIGHRISK

    d. MEDIUMRISK

8. How many default dashboards come preconfigured with Cisco IME?

    a. 2

    b. 4

    c. 6

    d. 8

9. Under which of the following can you add additional dashboards?

    a. **Home > Devices**; then click **Add Dashboard.**

    b. **Home > Dashboards**; then click **Add Dashboard.**

    c. **Home > Devices**; then click **Add Gadgets** and type the dashboard name.

    d. **Home > Dashboards**; then click **Add Gadgets** and type the dashboard name.

10. How many default gadgets are built into Cisco IME?

    a. 5

    b. 8

    c. 10

    d. 12

    e. 14

Foundation Topics

Cisco IPS Manager Express Overview

Cisco IPS Manager Express is a management application designed to simplify the configuration of IPS sensors for deployments of up to ten devices. This is suited more for small- and medium-sized organizations but does not in any way reduce the feature-rich capabilities of the application. Cisco IME has dashboards for monitoring that provide information on the software version, signature updates, sensor health, and alarms based on actions requiring attention. It also provides information on security intelligence. Cisco IME works in single application mode, where all configurations are done from the host where the application is installed.

Some of the tasks carried out with Cisco IME are as follows:

- **Cisco IPS sensor policy configuration:** Cisco IME provides an intuitive user interface that allows you to configure sensors and easily deploy policies within a few clicks.

- **Tightly integrated application functions:** Cisco IME has been purposely built with internal cross-linkages that allow you to drill down on an event and link it to a policy or signature within a sensor. The tight integration simplifies security policy configuration and reduces the chance of mistakes.

- **Monitor events and device health:** Cisco IME monitors the sensor and provides all the information in one interface, such as health, memory utilization, signatures, software, performance, and events.

- **Dashboards:** Cisco IME customizable dashboards provide information about the sensor that include alerts and memory and processor utilization. It also has drag-and-drop gadget capabilities, allowing you to customize the application so that you can view what you consider to be most important after you launch the Cisco IME.

- **Monitor real-time and historical events:** Cisco IME is equipped with advanced event-monitoring features to speed troubleshooting and to aid the analysis of events. Within the Event Viewer, which provides information about an event or a triggered signature, you can assign a color, assign a group, or filter events using more than ten parameters. The multilevel grouping function allows four levels of tiered grouping. While monitoring the events in real time, an attack can be blocked directly from the Event Viewer using one-click blocking.

- **Troubleshoot managed devices:** Cisco IME provides some tools to test connectivity through pings and to carry out Domain Name System (DNS) lookups, whois, and traceroute to aid fault analysis.

- **Generate reports using the Reporting tool:** Cisco IME has extensive built-in reporting capabilities that allow the generation of customized reports or predefined templates, such as the reporting tool in Cisco IME. This enables you to customize your reports based on specific time periods and choose between pie charts or bar graphs. The reports include IP addresses, and if you have DNS configured, it can resolve those IP addresses to host names. Generated reports can be printed, emailed, or saved to PDF or RTF files for future viewing or archiving.

■ **Information on new threats through live RSS feeds:** Cisco IME has the capability to check from other reputable security organizations' websites and provide this information to security administrators. This is done using the prebuilt custom RSS feeds, which enable you to view information about the latest security threats. This helps you improve the security of your network as the information feeds provide updated information on the latest threats and how to mitigate them. It also helps improve the security of your network. Custom RSS feeds from other reputable information security sources can be added as well, which Cisco IME pulls down periodically as configured.

■ **Demo mode:** Cisco IME provides a demonstration mode that is not connected to a real sensor. The demo provides a firsthand opportunity to try out some of the features within Cisco IME without fear of impacting a production network. It is launched using a shortcut named "Cisco IME-Demo" that is placed on the desktop during installation. It shows ten simulated sensors running different software versions and displays CPU, memory, and load information, along with simulated health dashboards, the ability to test various sensor configurations, and the ability to see the event monitoring of simulated attacks.

Cisco IME Versus Cisco IDM

Like Cisco IME, Cisco IPS Device Manager (IDM) is also used to manage IPS sensors. However, the Cisco IDM resides locally on the sensor and is not installed locally on a PC. The Cisco IDM is accessed by connecting through a web browser to the IP address of the sensor using Secure Sockets Layer (SSL).

Cisco IDM is also used to configure and tune the sensor signatures, but it is not as robust as the Cisco IME. While the Cisco IME can manage up to ten IPS devices, Cisco IDM can only manage one and hence does not scale well. Cisco IDM also does not have an event dashboard, integrated troubleshooting tools, or reporting or RSS feed integration.

The following features are supported by both Cisco IME and IDM:

■ Startup Wizard

■ Policy table configuration

■ Signature configuration

■ Device dashboard

Cisco IME and IDM both store events locally on the PC and sensor, respectively. Cisco IDM has limited storage of such events because it is resident on the IPS device. The Cisco IME offers more storage, but for just ten devices, as it is stored on the PC on which it is installed, whereas IDM only views alerts that are stored on the IPS sensor.

Note: Although both Cisco IME and IDM are limited both in events and features, Cisco Security Manager (CSM) offers advanced configuration and management capabilities for enterprise-class networks. It allows you to automatically schedule and manage the distribution of policies and signature updates. CSM also cross-collaborates with the Cisco Security Monitoring, Analysis, and Response System (Cisco Security MARS) for event and anomaly investigation with insight into policy deployment changes. CSM is a robust management platform installed on a server, and you connect to the application to manage the IPS Devices; thus, the policies are centrally stored.

Installing Cisco IPS Manager Express

Now we are getting into the fun part: the installation of Cisco IME. This is a simple task, and the first thing to do is ensure that the minimum hardware and software requirements for the installation are met, as outlined in Table 15-2.

Table 15-2 *Advantages and Limitations of Deploying an IPS in Inline Mode*

System Requirements	Description
Hardware	■ IBM PC-compatible 2-GHz or faster processor ■ Color monitor with at least 1024 × 768 resolution and video card capable of 16-bit colors ■ 100-GB hard disk drive (HDD) ■ 2 GB RAM
Operating systems	■ Windows Vista Business and Ultimate (32-bit only) ■ Windows XP Professional (32-bit only) ■ Windows 2003 server

Note:

■ Cisco IME supports only the 32-bit U.S. English and Japanese versions of Windows.

■ Cisco IME does not support Windows OS virtualization.

■ If you have a version of Cisco IPS Event Viewer (IEV) installed, the Install Wizard prompts you to remove it before installing IME.

■ Make sure you close any open instances of IME before upgrading to IME 7.0.

■ You must be an administrator to install IME.

■ Cisco IME 7.0 coexists with other instances of the MySQL database. If you have a MySQL database installed on your system, you do *not* have to uninstall it before installing IME 7.0

IME supports the Cisco IPS hardware platforms listed in Table 15-3.

Table 15-3   *Cisco IPS Hardware Supported by IME*

IPS Appliance	ASA Module	Router Module	Switch Module
IPS 4240	AIP SSC-5	AIM-IPS	IDSM-2
IPS 4255	AIP SSM-10	NME-IPS	—
IPS 4260	AIP SSM-20	—	—
IPS 4270-20	AIP SSM-40	—	—

IME supports the Cisco IPS versions with the features listed in Table 15-4.

Table 15-4   *Cisco IPS Versions and Features*

Features	Cisco IPS Versions					IOS IPS
	7.0	6.2	6.1	6.0	5.1	12.3(14)T7 and 12.4(15)T2
IPv6	Yes	Yes	—	—	—	—
Sensor configuration	Yes	Yes	Yes	—	—	—
Sensor Health dashboard	Yes	Yes	Yes	—	—	—
Events dashboard	Yes	Yes	Yes	Yes	Yes	Yes
Event monitoring	Yes	Yes	Yes	Yes	Yes	Yes
Reporting	Yes	Yes	Yes	Yes	Yes	Yes
Supports up to 10 devices	Yes	Yes	Yes	Yes	5 Devices	Yes
Up to 100 EPS	Yes	Yes	Yes	Yes	Yes	Yes

For more information, visit www.cisco.com/en/US/docs/security/ips/7.0/configuration/ guide/ime/ime_getting_started.html.

Installing Cisco IME

The installation steps described here are for Cisco IME version 7.0.2 because that is what you will be tested on. Version 7.0.3 is also available, which you can upgrade to later. Before installing this version of Cisco IME, it is recommended that you uninstall any previous versions of IME. If not, the Install Wizard will detect the previous installation and request that you remove the older version and stop the current installation.

Caution: Do not install Cisco IME on top of existing installations of CSM and vice versa. You must uninstall the previous for the later.

To proceed with the installation of Cisco IME, follow these steps:

Step 1.   Remove the old version of Cisco IME, if any exist.

Step 2.   Download the new version of Cisco IME software by typing **http://www. cisco.com/go/ime** in your browser; this takes you to the Cisco IME product page. Click **Download Software**, as shown in Figure 15-1 (the download requires Cisco.com access).

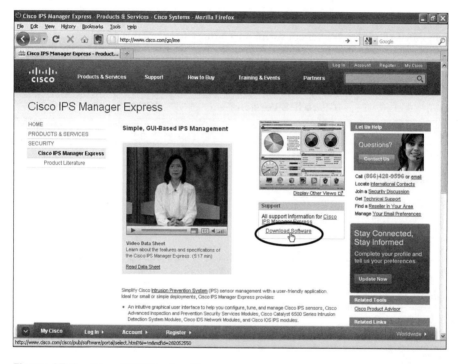

Figure 15-1   *Cisco IME Product Page*

Step 3.   As shown in Figure 15-2, select the 7.0 folder, choose version 7.0.2, and click the **Download Now** button. Walk through the download process and save the IME-7.0.2.exe file to your desktop. Double-click to begin the install process.

Step 4.   Follow through the installation process by agreeing to license agreements, accepting the default install location, and clicking **Next** where necessary to complete the installation.

Step 5.   As shown in Figure 15-3, the installation is complete. You will notice two new icons on your desktop: The Cisco IME icon will launch the software in live mode, and the Cisco IME-Demo icon will launch the software in demo mode.

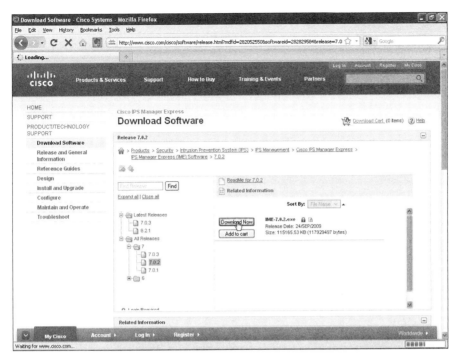

Figure 15-2 *Cisco IME Download Page*

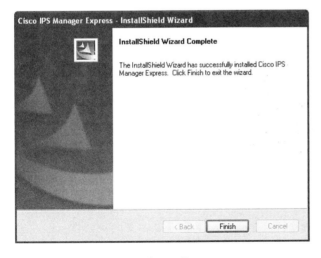

Figure 15-3 *Completed Installation*

Integrating Cisco IPS Manager Express with Cisco IPS Sensors

To add a sensor to Cisco IPS Manager Express, follow these steps:

Step 1. Launch the Cisco IME application by clicking the Cisco IME icon. After Cisco IME starts, a video opens, as shown in Figure 15-4. The video highlights key features within Cisco IME in a quick summary. To disable the video from opening, deselect the **Show feature presentation video at startup** check box.

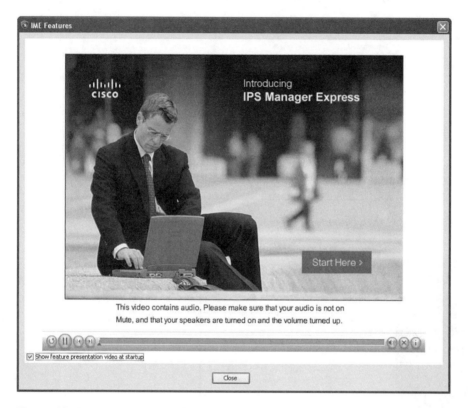

Figure 15-4   *Cisco IME Introduction Video*

Tip: Video help is always available to walk you through various steps within the application, depending on which dashboard or view you have open, but you can also view all video help available by choosing **Help > Show Video Help**.

Note: Video help requires that you have the Adobe Flash Player installed.

After you close the video, it reveals the Cisco IME home view, which is the default view when the application is launched.

Step 2. From the home view, choose **Devices > Device List** and then click **Add**.

Step 3.   Fill in the required fields in the **Add Device** dialog box, as shown in Figure 15-5:

- Enter the sensor name.

- Enter the sensor IP address.

- Enter the login username and password.

- To change the default web server port, enter a new port number (port 443 for https is recommended).

- Choose the event start time by either selecting the **Most Recent Alerts** check box or by entering a start date and time in the Start Date and Start Time fields.

- Under Exclude Alerts of the Following Severity Level(s), optionally select the check boxes of the levels you want to exclude.

- Click **OK** to add the sensor to Cisco IME.

Key Topic

Figure 15-5   *Adding an IPS Sensor to Cisco IME*

Step 4.   If you are connecting through HTTPS for the first time, you will be presented with a certificate from the sensor, as shown in Figure 15-6. Verify and accept the sensor certificate. Cisco IME will store the certificate locally for subsequent connections.

Caution: If you reject the certificate, the sensor will refuse your connection.

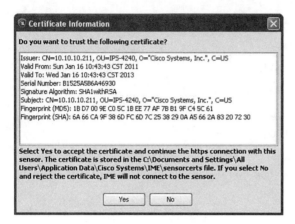

Figure 15-6 *Accept Sensor Certificate*

Note: During the initial setup of the IPS sensor, the IP address of the host running Cisco IME must be added under the allowed hosts section of the setup procedure; otherwise, Cisco IME will not be able to communicate with the sensor. This is covered in more detail in later chapters.

Note: Cisco IME compares the time configured on the host it is running on with the time on the sensor to make sure that they are synchronized. If they are not, Cisco IME will notify you through a warning, as shown in Figure 15-7, so that you can remediate that and ensure that the times read the same.

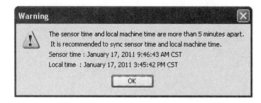

Figure 15-7 *Synchronize Time Between Sensor and Cisco IME Host*

Step 5. After connectivity has been established, check the sensor health and network security health to make sure that they are both normal and green. In Figure 15-8, sensor health is Critical because the signature update has not occurred for 458 days and the license has expired.

Step 6. To remedy the license issue in Step 5, choose **Configuration Sensor Name > Sensor Management > Licensing** and apply a license, as shown in Figure 15-9. Licenses can be updated through Cisco.com or locally. In this case, we have the license locally stored on the host.

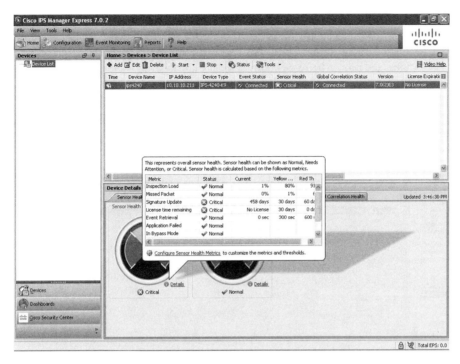

Figure 15-8   *Critical Sensor Health Because of License and Signature Age*

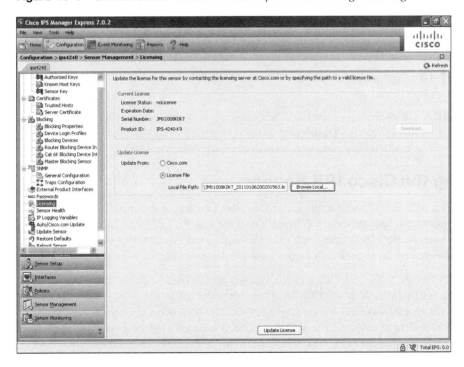

Figure 15-9   *Applying the Sensor License*

Step 7.   To remedy the signature age issue, navigate to **Configuration Sensor Name >
Sensor Management > Auto/Cisco.com Update.** Select **Enable Signature and
Engine Updates from Cisco.com,** supply the Cisco.com credentials, enter a start
time, and choose between hourly and daily updates; this is shown in Figure 15-10.

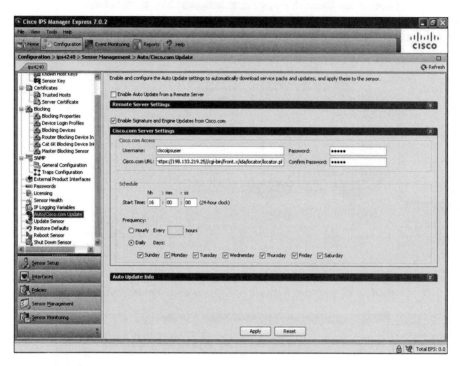

Figure 15-10   *Configuring Automatic Signature Updates*

Step 8.   With the issues resolved, check the sensor health by choosing **Home >
Dashboards > Dashboard** and selecting the Health Dashboard. The sensor
health is now green and normal, as shown in Figure 15-11.

Tuning the Cisco IPS Sensor

To tune the Cisco IPS sensor, navigate to the Risk Category view, located in
Configuration Sensor Name > Policies. Under the specific rule listed under the Event Action Rules section, by default rule0, click the Risk Category tab. Other event action rules
can be created as the need arises apart from the default rule.

When you are on the Risk Category tab, you will see the predefined risk categories: HIGH-
RISK, MEDIUMRISK, and LOWRISK. These are under the Risk Category Name column
with risk thresholds of 90, 70, and 1, respectively. The HIGHRISK is assigned a risk range of
90–100 and threat color red, the MEDIUMRISK is assigned a risk range of 70–89 and threat
color yellow, while the LOWRISK is assigned a risk range of 1–69 and a threat color of
green. These risk thresholds can be modified to suit the demands of your information/net-
work security policies; for example, HIGHRISK can be changed to a risk threshold of 85.

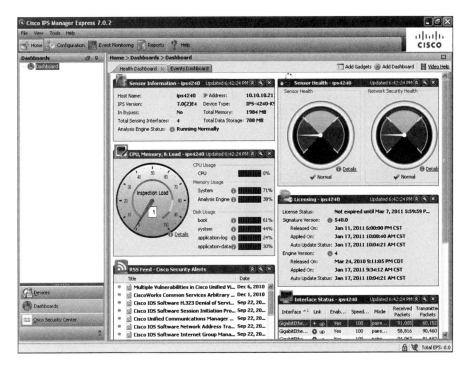

Figure 15-11   *Sensor and Network Health Are Now Normal*

The red, yellow, and green threshold statistics represent the state of the security of the network, with red being most critical and showing high-profile attacks being detected. You can create a new category based on your requirements. After it is defined, it will appear as a new risk category based on the risk range and risk threshold you assign.

To create a new risk category, follow these steps:

Step 1.   From **Configuration Sensor Name** > **Policies** > **IPS Policies** and under the specific rule under the Event Action Rules, select the risk category and click **Add**.

Step 2.   In the Add Risk Level dialog box shown in Figure 15-12, enter the risk name you choose (for this example, we will use the name LOWMEDIUMRISK), enter the risk threshold (we will use 30), and ensure that Active is set to Yes. Click **OK** and then **Apply** to push the configuration to the sensor.

Figure 15-12   *Add Risk Level Dialog Box*

Step 3.   The new risk category LOWMEDIUMRISK appears with a risk threshold of 30, as shown in Figure 15-13.

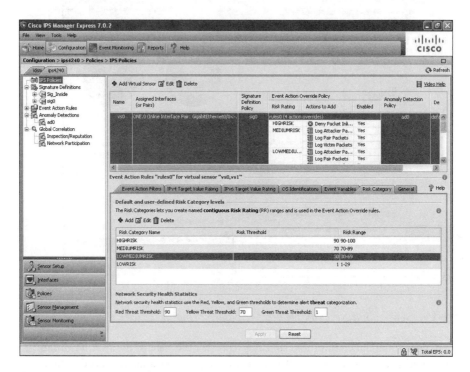

Figure 15-13   *New Risk Category*

Note: Default risk categories cannot be deleted; however, they can be marked as inactive if they are not needed.

Using and Customizing the Cisco IPS Manager Express User Interface

In this section, with Cisco IME successfully installed and tuned, you will be customizing the Cisco IME user interface. This gives you the flexibility of modifying the look and feel to your taste or needs. A good thing about this is that after you customize the interface, it will remain the same after you close and reopen Cisco IME.

Figure 15-14 shows the default view in Cisco IME.

The following are details of key areas in the default Home view of Cisco IME:

■   **Home view:** In the initial view into Cisco IME, you will find the Devices pane, the Dashboard pane, and the Cisco Security Center pane. It also contains access to video help in the upper-right corner, and it displays the events per second (EPS) received in the lower-right corner. The EPS is updated every 5 seconds, and Cisco IME handles a maximum of 100 EPS:

- **Devices:** This shows a listing of managed devices that have been added and are managed by Cisco IME. It displays the attributes for each of the managed devices: Time, Device Name, IP Address, Device Type, Event Status, Sensor Health, Global Correlation Status, Version, and License Expiration. There is also a subview section below with device details such as Sensor Health, Sensor Information, CPU, Memory and Load, Licensing, Interface Status, and Global Correlation Health.

- **Dashboards:** This shows all the customized dashboards.

- **Cisco Security Center:** This shows the configured RSS feeds.

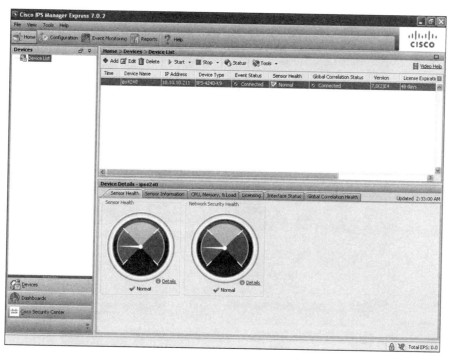

Figure 15-14 *Default Home View of the Cisco IME*

- **Configuration:** When a particular sensor is selected, this launches a session and appears as a tab in the configuration view. Other subconfiguration elements such as Sensor Setup, Interfaces, Policies, Sensor Management, and Sensor Monitoring are visible.

- **Event monitoring:** Launches the IME native event management view, where events can be filtered based on packet parameters, rating and action parameters, and other parameters. Events can also be grouped by criteria and colored. There are some standard event views that are basic view, dropped attacks, grouped severity, and real-time colored. There is also a **New** add button above the views that allows the addition of custom views.

■ **Reports:** Launches the IME native reporting view.

Customizing Cisco IME: Dashboards

The dashboards contain various gadgets that provide information on sensors, including sensor health, sensor status, security alerts, and event statistics.

The Dashboard view features two default dashboards:

■ **Health Dashboard:** Contains gadgets with information about selected sensor health, status, licenses, and utilization, as shown in Figure 15-15.

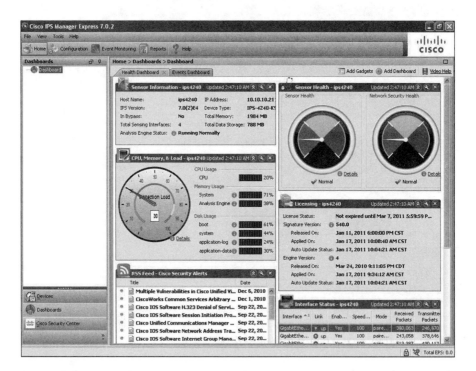

Figure 15-15 *Health Dashboard*

■ **Events Dashboard:** Contains gadgets with graphs and statistics about attackers, victims, and signatures, as shown in Figure 15-16.

You can add and customize your own dashboard and add gadgets based on the items you would like to track within the sensor.

To add a dashboard, choose **Home > Dashboards** and click **Add Dashboard**. A blank untitled dashboard appears and is named **CCNP Security** in this example.

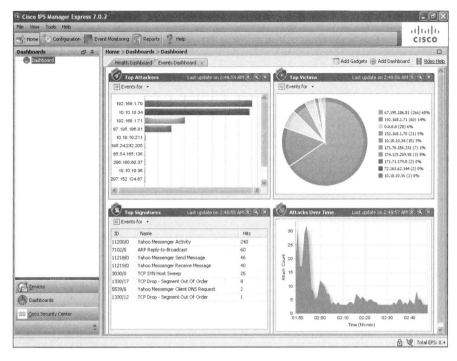

Figure 15-16 *Events Dashboard*

Based on your security standards and requirements, you can customize the metrics that are used to determine the health of the IPS in the Sensor Health pane. This can be done by choosing **Configuration Sensor Name > Sensor Management > Sensor Health**.

A metric must be selected, or it will not show up in the health status results. You can accept the default configuration or edit the values.

The IPS produces a health and security event when the overall health status of the IPS changes.

The fields outlined in Table 15-5 are found in the Sensor Health pane.

Table 15-5 *Event Retrieval Metrics*

Event Retrieval Metric	Explanation
Inspection Load	Lets you set a threshold for inspection load and whether this metric is applied to the overall sensor health rating
Missed Packet	Lets you set a threshold percentage for missed packets and whether this metric is applied to the overall sensor health rating
Memory Usage	Lets you set a threshold percentage for memory usage and whether this metric is applied to the overall sensor health rating

Table 15-5   *Event Retrieval Metrics*

Event Retrieval Metric	Explanation
Signature Update	Lets you set a threshold for when the last signature update was applied and whether this metric is applied to the overall sensor health rating
License Expiration	Lets you set a threshold for when the license expires and whether this metric is applied to the overall sensor health rating
Event Retrieval	Lets you set a threshold for when the last event was retrieved and whether this is applied to the overall sensor health rating
Application Failure	Lets you choose to have an application failure applied to the overall sensor health rating
In Bypass Mode	Let you choose to know whether bypass mode is active and have that apply to the overall sensor health rating
Active Interface Down	Lets you choose to know whether one or more enabled interfaces are down and have that apply to the overall sensor health rating
Global Correlation	Lets you choose whether the global correlation health metrics contribute to the overall sensor health rating
Network Participation	Lets you choose whether the network participation health metrics contribute to the overall sensor health rating

Adding Gadgets

With the CCNP Security dashboard successfully added, the next step is to add gadgets to the dashboard. To know which gadgets are available and which to choose, navigate to **Home > Dashboards** and click **Add Gadgets**. The available gadgets are displayed, as shown in Figure 15-17. Double-click a gadget icon or drag and drop a gadget to add it to the dashboard. After the gadgets are added, click **Add Gadgets** again to hide them.

Cisco IME provides you with 14 built-in gadgets:

- **Sensor Information:** Displays the most important sensor information, such as device type, IPS version, analysis engine status, host name, and IP address.

- **Sensor Health:** Displays two meters: the Sensor Health meter and the Network Security Health meter. They indicate the overall system health and overall network security health, respectively. The meters have three color scales—green, yellow, and red—to depict Normal, Needs Attention, and Critical.

- **Licensing:** Displays the license status and signature and engine versions of the sensor.

- **Interface Status:** Displays the status of the interfaces, whether enabled, whether up or down, mode, packets transmitted, and received.

- **Global Correlation Reports:** Display the alerts and denied packets resulting from reputation data and traditional detection techniques.

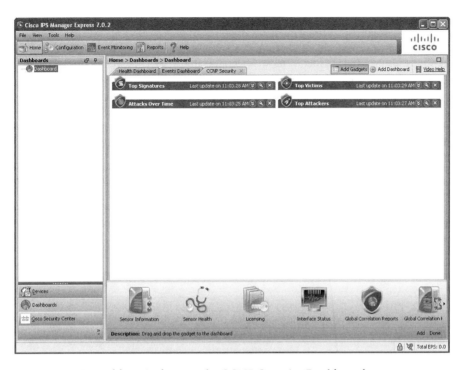

Figure 15-17 *Adding Gadgets to the CCNP Security Dashboard*

■ **Global Correlation Health:** Displays the status of global correlation and the network participation status, counters, and connection history.

■ **Network Security:** Displays graphs of the event count and the average threat rating and risk rating values, including the maximum threat rating and risk rating values over a configured time period. The sensor aggregates these values and puts them in one of three categories: green, yellow, or red.

■ **Top Applications:** Displays the top ten service ports that the sensor has observed over the past 10 seconds.

■ **CPU, Memory & Load:** Displays the current sensor CPU, memory, and disk usage. If the sensor has multiple CPUs, multiple meters are presented.

■ **RSS Feed:** A generic RSS feed gadget. By default, the data is fed from Cisco security advisories. You can customize and add more RSS feeds.

■ **Top Attackers:** Displays the top number of attacker IP addresses that occurred in the last configured time interval. You can configure the top number of attacker IP addresses for 10, 20, and 30. You can configure the time interval to cover the last hour, last 8 hours, or last 24 hours. You can also filter this information.

■ **Top Victims:** Displays the top number of victim IP addresses that occurred in the last configured time interval.

- **Top Signatures:** Displays the top number of signatures that occurred in the last configured time interval. You can also filter this information.

- **Attacks Over Time:** Displays the attack counts in the last configured interval. Each
set of data in the graph is the total alert counts that IME received during each minute.
You can configure the time interval to cover the last hour, last 8 hours, or last 24
hours. You can also filter this information.

Customizing Cisco IME: Cisco Security Center

Cisco IME also has RSS feed capabilities, which help ensure that you have the latest security information on threats and vulnerabilities.

By default, three RSS feed channels are set up to poll information from the Cisco Security
Center website. You can add other RSS feeds by choosing **Home > Cisco Security Center
> RSS Feeds** and clicking the **Add a New Channel** icon, as shown in Figure 15-18.

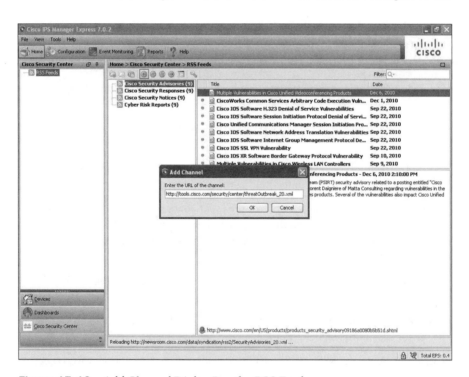

Figure 15-18   *Add Channel Dialog Box for RSS Feeds*

The RSS feed view is equipped with some tools for customizing the feeds. These tools allow you to

- Add, delete, and move a category

- Add, delete, reload, rename, and move a channel

- Change preferences, which allow you to change the RSS feed refresh interval

The following steps walk you through the RSS configuration process:

Step 1. Locate the website with the RSS feed that you want to add and copy the URL.

Step 2. Choose **Home > Cisco Security Center > RSS Feeds** and click the **Add a New Channel** icon on the RSS feeds toolbar.

Step 3. In the Add Channel dialog box, shown in Figure 15-18, paste the URL of the channel from which you would like to receive RSS feeds, and click **OK**.

The RSS feed appears in the left side of the RSS view, and the content appears in right side, as shown in Figure 15-19.

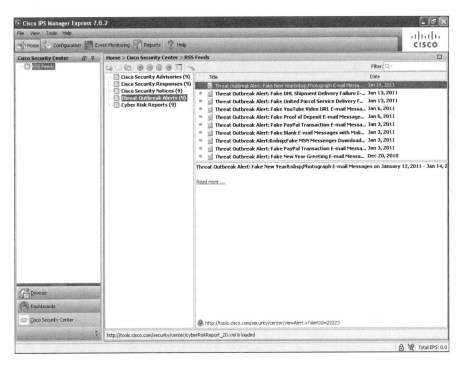

Figure 15-19 *RSS Feed Added*

Step 4. To view a particular RSS feed, select it in the list and click it. The item information appears in the lower-right pane.

Step 5. To create another category for this RSS feed, click the **Add a New Category** icon, and in the Add Category dialog box, assign a new category name. For this example, this channel is named Threat Outbreak, as shown in Figure 15-20.

Step 6. To move a channel to another category, click the **Move the Channel to Another Category** icon, and in the Move Channel dialog box, select the category you would like to move it to. You could also do this by right-clicking the channel and selecting Move Channel from the options, as shown in Figure 15-21.

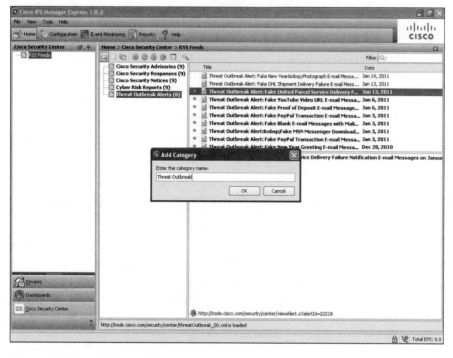

Figure 15-20   *Adding a New Category*

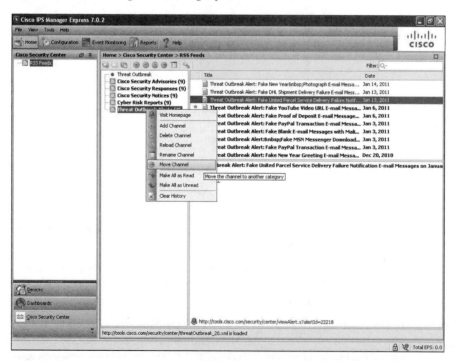

Figure 15-21   *Moving a Channel to the Category Created in Step 5*

Step 7.   To configure the RSS feed preferences, click **Change User Preferences**, as shown in Figure 15-22.

Figure 15-22   *RSS Feed Preferences*

Set the following preferences:

■   Select the Allow Duplicate Channel Creation check box to allow the creation of duplicate channels.

■   The News Items Remain on Cache drop-down box allows you to choose how many news items you would like to remain in the cache. The available options are 10, 30, 50, 100, 300, and 1000.

■   The Refresh Every Minutes box enables you to choose the RSS feeds' refresh frequency.

■   To change the default browser, click the **Use Following Browser** radio button, type in the browser command line in the Browser Command-Line field, and click **OK**.

Summary

The following key topics were discussed in this chapter:

■   Cisco IME is an intuitive management application for small and medium IPS sensor management.

■   Cisco IME supports up to ten sensors.

■   Cisco IME supports up to 200 events per second (EPS).

■   Cisco IME supports most Cisco IPS platforms.

■   Cisco IME installation requires Microsoft Windows operating systems.

■   Cisco IME should not be installed on a system with an existing Cisco Security Manager (CSM) installation. CSM must be uninstalled first.

References

For additional information, refer to this resource:

Installing and Using Cisco Intrusion Prevention System Manager Express 7.0, at www.cisco.com/en/US/docs/security/ips/7.0/configuration/guide/ime/imeguide7.html.

Exam Preparation Tasks

Review All the Key Topics

Review the most important topics from the chapter, noted with the Key Topic icons in the margin of the page. Table 15-6 lists a reference of these key topics and the page numbers on which each is found.

Table 15-6   *Key Topics for Chapter 15*

Key Topic Element	Description	Page Number
Table 15-2	Installing Cisco IPS Manager Express	366
Figure 15-5	Adding IPS Sensor to Cisco IME	371
Paragraph	Tuning the Cisco IPS Sensor	374
Paragraph	Customizing Cisco IME: Dashboards	378
Table 15-5	Event Retrieval Metrics	379
Paragraph	Customizing Cisco IME: Cisco Security Center	382

Complete the Tables and Lists from Memory

Print a copy of Appendix C, "Memory Tables" (found on the CD), or at least the section for this chapter, and complete the tables and lists from memory. Appendix D, "Memory Tables Answer Key," also on the CD, includes completed tables and lists to check your work.

Definitions of Key Terms

Define the following key terms from this chapter, and check your answers in the glossary:

threat, attack, global correlation

This chapter covers the following topics:

- **Managing IPS Events Using Cisco IPS Manager Express:** This covers the Cisco IME user interface tools to manage the event database.

- **Investigating IPS Events Using Cisco IPS Manager Express:** This covers the use of Cisco IME to drill down and investigate event details.

- **Acting on IPS Events Using Cisco IPS Manager Express:** This covers tuning of event actions in Cisco IME events.

- **Exporting, Importing, and Archiving Events:** This covers saving and pulling information from archives and also moving information between databases.

CHAPTER 16

Managing and Investigating Events Using Cisco IPS Manager Express

Overview

Cisco Intrusion Prevention System (IPS) Manager Express (IME) has built-in tools designed to help you manage events within Cisco IME, create customized views based on malicious activity, and help track or investigate incidents to determine the best line of action to take, in remediating such. This chapter will be focused on the use of these management tools.

"Do I Know This Already?" Quiz

The "Do I Know This Already?" quiz allows you to assess whether you should read the entire chapter. If you miss no more than one of these self-assessment questions, you might want to move ahead to the "Exam Preparation Tasks" section. Table 16-1 lists the major headings in this chapter and the "Do I Know This Already?" quiz questions covering the material in those headings so that you can assess your knowledge of these specific areas. The answers to the "Do I Know This Already?" quiz appear in Appendix A.

Table 16-1 *"Do I Know This Already?" Foundation Topics Section-to-Question Mapping*

Foundation Topics Section	Questions
Managing IPS Events Using Cisco IPS Manager Express	1–4
Investigating IPS Events Using Cisco IPS Manager Express	5
Acting on IPS Events Using Cisco IPS Manager Express	6
Exporting, Importing, and Archiving Events	7

1. Which of the following is not a predefined event view?

  a. Dropped Attacks view

  b. Basic view

  c. Grouped Severity view

  d. Grouped Security view

2. Under which views are custom views listed?

   a. Event Views

   b. Report Views

   c. My Views

   d. My Custom Views

3. Which of the tabs are under the View settings?

   a. No tabs

   b. Filter View, Group View, Color View

   c. Filter, Group By, Color Rules, Fields, General

   d. Filter, My Groups, Color Rules, Fields, General

4. When tuning an IPS sensor using the Filter drop-down box when an event is highlighted, what filtering options are available?

   a. Reputation, Risk Rating

   b. Severity, Risk Rating

   c. None

   d. Add To Filter, Create Filter

5. How many tabs are available in the Event details section?

   a. 5

   b. 8

   c. 7

   d. 4

6. Cisco IME has capabilities that allow you to modify sensor policies and perform actions based on the properties of an individual event. Which of the following is *not* a capability?

   a. Stop attackers

   b. Edit IPS sensor signatures

   c. Create event action filters

   d. Create IPS sensor signatures

7. Which of the following is *not* used when maintaining the Cisco IME database?

   a. Import

   b. Export

   c. Compress

   d. Archive

Foundation Topics

Managing IPS Events Using Cisco IPS Manager Express

Cisco IME has built-in monitoring capabilities designed to improve analysis and aid troubleshooting based on events received. The Monitoring pane contains predefined event views that can be filtered and customized based on different user requirements or information criteria. These predefined views cannot be modified and saved or deleted. Events in IME can be real-time or historical and are retrieved from the IME event database. The left side of the Event Monitoring window is a view tree, and the right side contains the view.

Cisco IME simplifies the following monitoring tasks:

■ Monitoring real-time and historical IPS events to aid the investigation of malicious or suspicious network activities for up to ten sensors

■ Modify views to filter out different event variables and further customize, based on your requirements

■ Group and color events to easily identify certain event types or patterns of suspicious activity

■ Save and delete events and event sets to archive or retrieve information

Event Monitoring Views

The IME Event Monitoring views can be accessed by choosing **Event Monitoring > Event Monitoring**.

The view tree consists of the following predefined views:

■ Basic view

■ Dropped Attacks view

■ Grouped Severity view

■ Real-time Colored view

■ Customized views that you create and are listed under My Views in the view tree

The Event Viewer pane consists of three parts, as shown in Figure 16-1 (right side) and described in the following list.

■ **Settings tab:** You can specify what events are shown and how you want to see events. You can specify filters, grouping, coloring, which fields you want to display, and the name of the filter. You can use color so that certain specific data stands out. For example, if you are looking for events from a certain attacker IP address, you can highlight the events with the severity level as high and then apply a certain color to those events. To collapse the Settings tab, click **View Settings** and click again to expand.

■ **Events table:** Displays the events. You can interface with events by selecting a row and then performing various actions using the toolbar or the right-click menu.

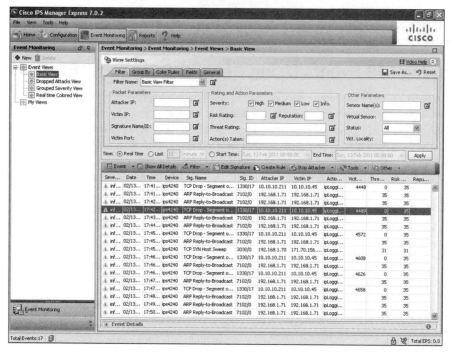

Figure 16-1   *Event Monitoring View*

- **Event details:** Select a single row in the Events table, and the details for that event are displayed in the Event Details section of the pane. The Event Details section might be collapsed; simply click **Event Details** to expand the view.

Table 16-2 provides details on the default event views and how to navigate to them. These views give a quick snapshot of events on the network.

Key Topic

Table 16-2   *Monitoring Event Views*

Event View	Navigation	Description
Basic view	To display events in the Basic view, choose **Event Monitoring > Event Monitoring > Event Views > Basic View**.	The Basic View filter is applied to the Basic view, which causes Cisco IME to display new events of all four severities. It does not have any grouping or coloring rules applied by default, so events are viewed in a free-flowing form. Figure 16-1 has Basic View highlighted.
Dropped Attacks view	To display events in the Dropped Attacks view, choose **Event Monitoring > Event Monitoring > Event Views > Dropped Attacks View**.	The Dropped Attacks filter is applied to get the Dropped Attacks view. The criterion for selection is based on event severities such as High, which have been set to drop packets. It also has grouping rules configured by signature, attacker, and victim IP address and threat rating.

Table 16-2 *Monitoring Event Views*

Event View	Navigation	Description
Grouped Severity view	To display events in the Grouped Security view, choose **Event Monitoring > Event Monitoring > Event Views > Grouped Security View.**	The Grouped Severity view is similar to the Dropped Attacks view as it uses the same grouping and coloring settings. The difference is that it uses the Basic filter; thus, it displays all new events and not only the dropped packets.
Real-time Colored view	To display events in the Real-time Colored view, choose **Event Monitoring > Event Monitoring > Event Views > Real Time Colored View.**	This view also has the Basic filter applied to it. In this view, Cisco IME displays new events of all four severities. It has no groupings as well, but severities appear colored, with High severity in red and Medium severity in blue.

Creating and Customizing Event Views

Custom event views can be created to meet your criteria for security events through filters, which allow you to specify the conditions required. Follow these steps to create a custom view:

Step 1. Click **New** above the Event View tree.

Step 2. In the New View dialog box, type in the name of your custom view and click **OK.** Figure 16-2 illustrates a custom view named CVIEW.

The two-step process creates your custom view, which is listed under My Views. A new filter, which by default has empty fields, is automatically created as well. The only configured options are the check boxes for High, Medium, Low, and Informational severities.

After creating your custom view, go to the View Settings section.

View Settings

Conditions in the View Settings section can be used to filter events in Cisco IME. To access the settings, choose **Event Monitoring > Event Monitoring > View Settings.** The settings are located under the following tabs:

- Filter
- Group By
- Color Rules
- Fields
- General

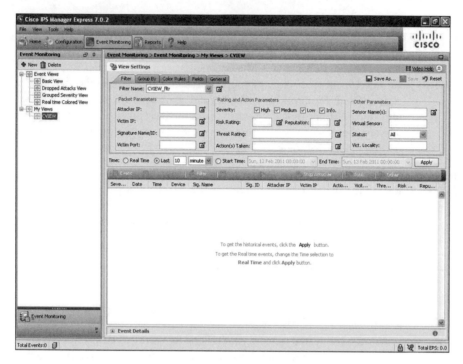

Figure 16-2   *Custom View CVIEW and New Event Filter CVIEW_fltr*

Table 16-3 shows the parameters available in each of the tabs in the View Settings section (shown in Figure 16-2).

Table 16-3   *Tabs and Parameters Available in the View Settings Section*

Tabs	Parameters
Filter	Packet parameters:
	■ Attacker IP
	■ Victim IP
	■ Signature Name/ID
	■ Victim Port
	Rating and action parameters:
	■ Severity (High, Medium, Low, Info)
	■ Risk Rating
	■ Reputation
	■ Threat Rating
	■ Action(s) Taken

Table 16-3 *Tabs and Parameters Available in the View Settings Section*

Tabs	Parameters
	Other parameters:
	■ Sensor Name(s)
	■ Virtual Sensor
	■ Status
	■ Vict. Locality (Victim Locality)
Group By (Events can be grouped based on five criteria.)	■ Group By Condition ■ Grouping Preferences ■ Single Level ■ Show Group Columns ■ Show Count Columns
Color Rules (Rule matching is done from top to bottom.)	■ Add colors to event filters
Fields (Add or remove fields that will be showed in the Event Display.)	■ List of Available Fields ■ Show Fields in the Following Order
General	■ View Description

Customizing Event Views

The Filter tab provides options that allow you to choose parameters you want real or historical events to be classified by. A filter name view_name_fltr appears under the Filter tab. In the previous section, the view created is CVIEW and the filter name is CVIEW_fltr. After you click the **Real Time** radio button or apply a time range, you will start to see events from the IP displayed in the Event Viewer.

Modify the filter parameters based on the values in Table 16-4 and observe the changes. You can also modify other parameters based on your desired outputs.

Table 16-4 *Modify Filter Tab Parameters*

Parameter	Value
Rating and action parameters	Severity: Check High and Medium Risk Rating: > 49
Other parameters	Sensor Name: ips4240

In the example shown in Figure 16-3, the parameters have been set to only see events with High and Medium severities with a risk rating greater than 49 from the sensor with host name ips4240.

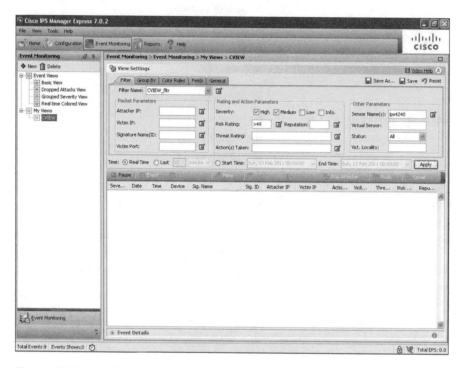

Figure 16-3 *Applying Parameters in Table 16-4*

The Group By tab provides options to modify the grouping rules. This can viewed by choosing **Event Monitoring > Event Monitoring > My Views >** *view_name* **>View Settings** and clicking the Group By tab.

As an example, under the Group by Condition section, select the **Group events based on the following criteria** check box. This immediately activates the Group By drop-down box; choose **Device** as an option and then **Severity** as the next option.

The Color Rules tab provides options to color events based on all the parameters available on the Filter tab. To add or modify a rule, choose **Event Monitoring > Event Monitoring > My Views >** *view_name* **> View Settings > Color Rules** and click **Add** for a new rule or **Edit** for an existing rule.

As an example, you can use the parameters and values shown in Table 16-5 to create two filters for different reputation values.

Table 16-5 *Modify Color Filter Parameters*

Parameter	Value for Red	Value for Orange
Filter Name	Red	Orange
Severity (Check box)	High	High
Reputation	< 0	>=0
Foreground	Red	Light Orange
Font Type	Bold	Bold

When creating a color filter, make sure to select the Enable check box.

Figure 16-4 shows the parameters for a red filter.

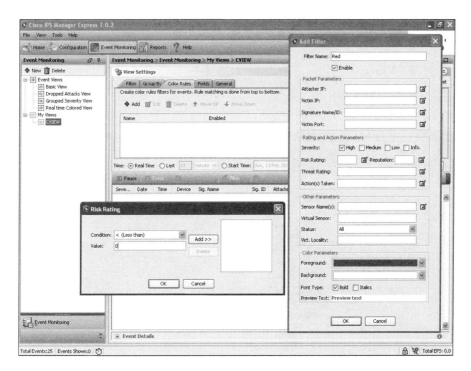

Figure 16-4 *Parameters for a Red Color Filter*

To view the impact of all the customization that has been done in this section, choose **Event Monitoring** > **Event Monitoring** > **My Views** > *view_name* > **View Settings** and select a time range that you would like it to be applied to. Choose the start time and end time, and then click **Apply**. This will show events that have been filtered, grouped, and colored.

Tuning and Creating IME Filters from the Event Display

There are some buttons that will appear grayed out in the event display right under the Time section. These allow you to create or modify filters based on events streaming through the Event Display.

To copy individual values directly from the event display to filter, complete the following steps:

Step 1.   Choose **Event Monitoring > Event Monitoring > My Views >** *view_name* **> Filter**. Select an event in the Event Display. You might have to click the **Pause** button to select a specific event, depending on the rate at which events are streaming through. After an event is selected, the buttons are no longer grayed out.

Step 2.   Click the drop-down arrow on the **Filter** button, which gives you the options Add To Filter and Create Filter.

Step 3.   Point your cursor to Add To Filter and choose one of the following, as shown in Figure 16-5:

- Attacker IP

- Victim IP

- Signature ID

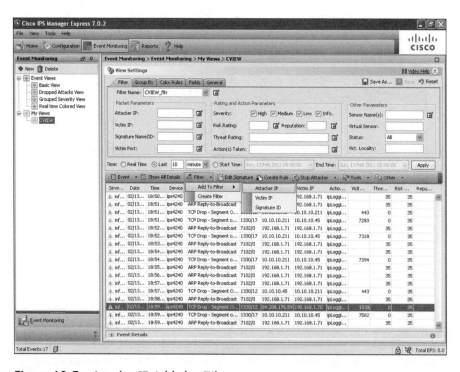

Figure 16-5   *Attacker IP Added to Filter*

The chosen option is automatically copied to the Packet Parameters section on the filter tab.

Step 4.   Choose the desired time setting and click **Apply** to apply the modified filter.

To create a filter from an event in the Event Display, complete the following steps:

Step 1.   Choose **Event Monitoring** > **Event Monitoring** > **My Views** > *view_name* > **Filter.** Select an event in the Event Display. The properties of this event will be used to create your filter.

Step 2.   Click the drop-down arrow on the Filter button, which gives you the options Add To Filter and Create Filter.

Step 3.   Choose the Create Filter option. The Create a Filter From Event dialog box opens, as shown in Figure 16-6.

**Key
Topic**

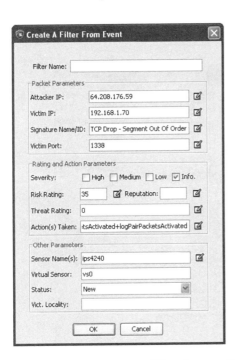

Figure 16-6   *Creating a Filter from an Event*

Step 4.   Enter the filter name as other parameters are already populated.

Step 5.   Review and/or modify the filter parameters and click **OK**. A new filter is created.

Step 6.   You will still be in the same view as in Step 1. Go to the Filter Name drop-down list and choose the new filter. This populates the values on the Filter tab.

Step 7.   Choose the desired time settings and click **Apply** to view the newly filtered events.

Note: To revert to the previous filter view, click **Reset** in the upper-right corner of IME.

Saving and Deleting Events

IME also has built-in functionality to allow you to save or delete events.

To save events in IME, follow these steps:

Step 1. Choose **Event Monitoring > Event Monitoring > My Views** > *view_name* and select an event so that the toolbar is no longer grayed out.

Step 2. Click the drop-down box on the **Other** button on the toolbar, or you can right-click an event and move the cursor over the **Other** button as well. This reveals the options shown Figure 16-7:

- Save

- Delete

- Copy

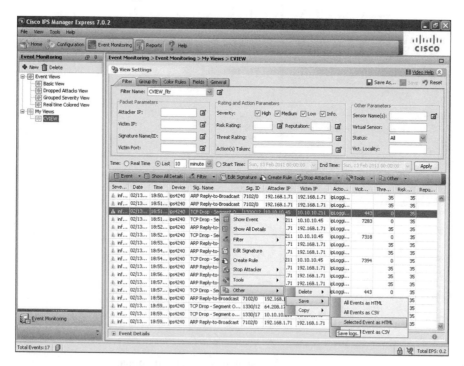

Figure 16-7 *Saving Cisco IME Events*

Step 3. Select Save, as shown in Figure 16-7, and you have the following options to choose from:

- All Events as HTML

- All Events as CSV

- Selected Event as HTML

- Selected Event as CSV

Step 4.   In the Save dialog box, type a filename and click the **Save** button.

The file can be viewed at a later time using the appropriate application.

Similar steps can be carried out to clear events from the database. This is completed by moving your cursor over the Clear drop-down box, which shows the following options:

- **Clear All:** Deletes all events in the database.

- **Clear Selected:** Deletes only the selected event or events.

The Copy drop-down option allows you to copy all or just selected events and paste them into desired documents or cases.

Investigating IPS Events Using Cisco IPS Manager Express

Cisco IME has built-in tools to allow you to drill down into events to determine the impact on your network; these tools also provide the information required to take the necessary action to protect resources.

These tools include event information stored in the IME database, a link to the Cisco.com Cisco Security IntelliShield Alert Manager Service, the ability to display raw dumps of malicious traffic, and the ability to investigate attacks using network reconnaissance tools.

Just as you have applied filters to historical events stored in the database within IME, as described in previous sections, you can also explore and drill down into events to get critical information. This information can be viewed by choosing **Event Monitoring > Event Monitoring > My Views >** *view_name* **> Event Details**, as shown in Figure 16-8.

The drop-down box on the Event Details provides the options shown in Table 16-6. You need to select an event to view the details, which provide seven options (or seven tabs, if viewed on the Event Details tab below the Event Window).

Table 16-6   *Event Details*

Event Details	Explanation
Event Summary	Summarizes all the information about that event.
Explanation	Provides the description and related signature information about the signature associated with this event.
Related Threats	Provides the related threat with a link to more detailed information on the Cisco Security Intelligence Operations (SIO) website.
Actions Taken	Lists which event actions were deployed.

Table 16-6 *Event Details*

Event Details	Explanation
Trigger Packets	Displays information about the packet that triggered the event.
Context Data	Displays the packet context information.
Notes	Lets you take action on this event by assigning a designation for it (New, Assigned, Acknowledged, Closed, or Deleted). Add any notes in the Notes field and click **Save Note** to save it.

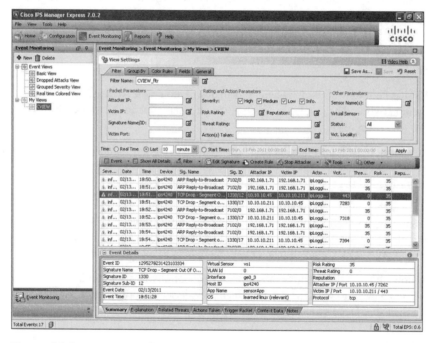

Figure 16-8 *Event Details Tab*

The Cisco.com link in the Related Threats pane provides a URL to Cisco Security Intelli-Shield, as shown in Figure 16-9.

This site provides more details about the IPS signature and worm information. The IPS can be configured to capture malicious traffic for specific signatures, which can be viewed natively through Cisco IME. It also includes the reconnaissance tools such as ping, whois, Nslookup, and traceroute to learn more about attackers.

As you investigate events, it might be necessary to have all the details of an event in one pane through the Event Details window, as shown in Figure 16-10.

Table 16-7 describes more of the tools available in IME to investigate events.

Figure 16-9   *Basic Cisco IntelliShield Service Information from the Related Threats Tab*

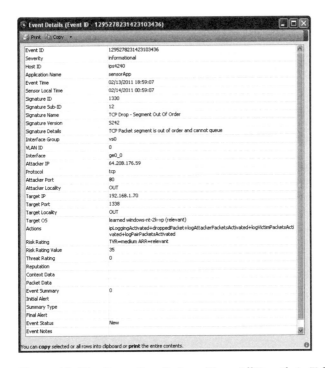

Figure 16-10   *Event Details from Show All Details in Table 16-7*

Key
Topic

Table 16-7   *More Tools to Investigate IPS Events*

Task	Details
Access all event details	To access all event details, navigate to **Event Monitoring > Event Monitoring > My Views >** *view_name*, right-click an event, and choose Show All Details. The Event Details window opens, showing all captured details of an event (see Figure 16-10).
Access and use Intelli-iShield information	The Related Threats tab in the Event Details window (choose **Event Monitoring > Event Monitoring > My Views >** *view_name*) provides a link to more detailed information for a selected event. This opens the browser and displays basic IntelliShield service information on Cisco.com. Each threat is identified with a name and related summary details, as listed here: ■ Threat Type ■ IntelliShield ID ■ Version ■ First Published Date ■ Last Published Date ■ Port Information Three indicators (Urgency, Credibility, and Severity) are represented by numerical values ranging from 1 to 5.
Access and use network reconnaissance tools	Cisco IME has built-in tools for further event analysis and investigation. These tools are ■ Ping ■ Traceroute ■ Resolve ■ Whois These can be accessed through **Event Monitoring > Event Monitoring > My Views >** *view_name* by clicking an event and clicking the Tools drop-down box or by right-clicking an event and choosing tools and any of the options.
Display trigger packet and context data	Cisco IME has the ability to automatically detect and integrate with Wireshark or Ethereal network analyzers if installed on the PC that IME is installed on. If Cisco IME fails to automatically locate and integrate with the application, it can be manually configured by choosing **Tools > Preferences > General > Network Sniffer Application Location**. When invoked, Wireshark displays the contents of the offending packet, allowing you to explore and analyze the detailed IP packet information.

Acting on IPS Events Using Cisco IPS Manager Express

Cisco IME has capabilities that allow you to modify sensor policies and perform actions based on the properties of an individual event. These capabilities include the following:

- **Edit IPS sensor signatures:** Directly edit signatures that have triggered specific events so that they can be tuned, as shown in Figure 16-11.

Figure 16-11   *Edit Signature by Double-Clicking the Signature*

- **Create event action filters:** Directly create event action filters to tune the actions for a specific signature, as shown in Figure 16-12.

- **Stop attackers:** Deny attackers inline or request a block through a device managed by the IPS sensor, as shown in Figure 16-13.

Figure 16-12   *Add Event Action Filter*

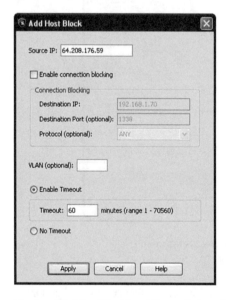

Figure 16-13   *Blocking Through Another Device*

Table 16-8 walks you through the previous processes.

Table 16-8 *Acting on IPS Signatures*

Task	Details
Edit Signature	Edit a signature by navigating to **Event Monitoring > Event Monitoring > My Views >** *view_name* and right-clicking an event whose signature you would like to tune. From the drop-down box, choose the Edit Signature option. This takes you to the **Configuration >** *sensor_name >* **Policies > Signature Definitions > sigx > Active Signatures** pane, where you can edit the signature. The signature is already highlighted within the pane for easy identification.
Edit Signature Properties	As a continuation from the previous step, the signature is already highlighted in the pane. Double-clicking the highlighted signature opens the Edit Signature dialog box, where you can edit all the signature parameters. While still in the **Configuration >** *sensor_name >* **Policies > Signature Definitions > sigx > Active Signatures** pane, you will notice two tabs below the Signature window: Explanation and Related Threats. These provide more details about the signature, as shown in Figure 16-11.
Create Rule	You can also create event action rule filters from a selected event from an event view such as **Event Monitoring > Event Monitoring > My Views >** *view_name*. Right-click an event and select the Create Rule option, which takes you to **Configuration >** *sensor_name >* **Policies > IPS Policies > Add Event Action Filter**. In the Add Event Action Filter dialog box, almost all the information is prepopulated by Cisco IME, as shown in Figure 16-12.
Stop Attacker	From the Event view, choose **Event Monitoring > Event Monitoring > My Views >** *view_name*. You can stop an attacker by right-clicking an event and choosing the Stop Attacker option, which gives the following blocking options: ■ **Using Inline Deny:** This takes you to the **Configuration >** *sensor_name >* **Sensor Monitoring > Time-Based Actions > Denied Attackers > Add Denied Attacker** pane, where you will confirm the action. ■ **Using Block on Another Device:** This takes you to the **Configuration >** *sensor_name >* **Sensor Monitoring > Time-Based Actions > Host Blocks > Add Host Block** pane, where you will put additional information where necessary in the Add Host Block dialog box, as shown in Figure 16-13, and apply the information. After it is applied, the information appears in the Host Block pane.

Key Topic

Exporting, Importing, and Archiving Events

Cisco IME installs and uses its own database to store event data. This makes it possible to parse through current or historical data and apply actions as necessary. It also allows some maintenance tasks to be carried out on the database to ensure that it is optimized:

- **Export:** This option is used when you want to import information from Cisco IME into another application such as a CSV file.

- **Import:** This option is used when porting over data from another application into Cisco IME.

- **Archive:** This option removes saved or old events from the database to improve performance, as shown in Figure 16-14.

Table 16-9 provides information on these options.

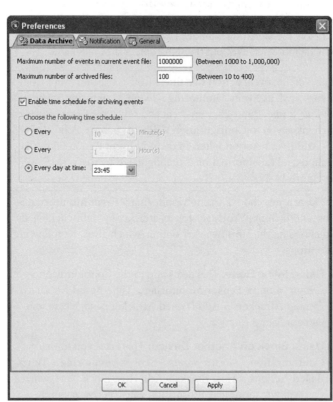

Figure 16-14 *Archive Preferences*

Table 16-9 *Exporting, Importing, and Archiving Events*

Key
Topic

Task	Details
Export	To export event data into a CSV file: ■ Navigate to **File > Export**. ■ In the Export Alarm Data dialog box, select the start and end time as events in this time range will be exported. ■ Select the name and location for the output file and click **OK** to continue. Cisco IME displays progress and notifies you on completion.
Import	To import previously exported data or data from another instance of IME: ■ Choose **File > Import**. ■ Browse to the file to be imported and click **OK** to proceed. Cisco IME will notify you on completion.
Archive	To configure and enable event data archiving, choose **Tools > Preferences > Data Archive**. It is prepopulated with recommended values. You can modify them if you want. The only other actions you need to carry out are the following: ■ Select the **Enable time schedule for archiving events** check box. ■ Choose the time schedule and click **OK** to apply the preferences.

Summary

This section highlights the key topics discussed in this chapter:

■ Cisco IME helps you analyze and manage IPS events.

■ Cisco IME helps you investigate event details and provides more information through Cisco.com.

■ Cisco IME provides options for creating custom event views or predefined event views.

■ Cisco IME simplifies Cisco IPS sensor configuration modification and helps you block attacks.

■ Cisco IME lets you export, import, and archive event data.

Exam Preparation Tasks

Review All the Key Topics

Review the most important topics from the chapter, noted with the Key Topic icons in the margin of the page. Table 16-10 lists a reference of these key topics and the page numbers on which each is found.

Key Topic

Table 16-10 *Key Topics for Chapter 16*

Key Topic Element	Description	Page Number
Table 16-2	Monitoring Event Views	392
Table 16-3	Tabs and Parameters Available in the View Settings	394
Figure 16-6	Creating a Filter from an Event	399
Table 16-7	More Tools to Investigate IPS Events	404
Table 16-8	Acting on IPS Signatures	407
Figure 16-14	Archive Preferences	408
Table 16-9	Exporting, Importing, and Archiving Events	409

Complete the Tables and Lists from Memory

Print a copy of Appendix C, "Memory Tables" (found on the CD), or at least the section for this chapter, and complete the tables and lists from memory. Appendix D, "Memory Tables Answer Key," also on the CD, includes completed tables and lists to check your work.

Definitions of Key Terms

Define the following key terms from this chapter, and check your answers in the glossary:

Cisco Security Intelligence Operations, Cisco IntelliShield Service

This chapter covers the following topics:

■ **Overview:** In this section, we review how the Cisco IME is used for event correlation, generating reports based on events, notification of events, and archiving of such events.

■ **Configuring Event Reporting in Cisco IME:** This section covers the use of built-in and customized reports, and how they can be shared and archived for viewing later.

■ **Using Notifications in Cisco IME:** This section covers the use of email notifications that are sent to administrators based on configured thresholds.

Using Cisco IPS Manager Express Correlation, Reporting, Notification, and Archiving

Overview

Cisco IPS Manager Express (IME) has built-in tools that allow the creation of reports that are based on events stored in the database. It also has features that enable it to provide real-time notifications to alert administrators of critical events. These events must be defined in the notification policy.

This chapter provides information on the reporting and notification capabilities of Cisco IME based on events from IPS sensors. These capabilities include using built-in and custom reports to extract information from the Cisco IME database, and configuring custom notifications in Cisco IME.

"Do I Know This Already?" Quiz

The "Do I Know This Already?" quiz allows you to assess whether you should read the entire chapter. If you miss no more than one of these self-assessment questions, you might want to move ahead to the "Exam Preparation Tasks" section. Table 17-1 lists the major headings in this chapter and the "Do I Know This Already?" quiz questions covering the material in those headings so that you can assess your knowledge of these specific areas. The answers to the "Do I Know This Already?" quiz appear in Appendix A.

Table 17-1 *"Do I Know This Already?" Foundation Topics Section-to-Question Mapping*

Foundation Topics Section	Questions
Configuring Event Reporting in Cisco IME	1–4
Using Notifications in Cisco IME	5

1. How many built-in report categories are available in the Reporting tree of Cisco IME?

    a. 8

    b. 6

    c. 10

    d. 12

2. If you select the **Resolve Addresses Using DNS** check box and IP addresses are still showing in the report, what is the likely cause of the problem?

   a. The IPS has not been rebooted.

   b. DNS is not configured on the IPS.

   c. Cisco IME host is not configured for DNS.

   d. None of these answers are correct.

3. Which of the following is *not* a way in which reports can be shared?

   a. PDF

   b. Printing

   c. PPT

   d. RTF

4. You can customize your Events Dashboard so that it contains "Top N" gadgets, which are essentially results of built-in reports. How many of these gadgets are available?

   a. 6

   b. 10

   c. 8

   d. 4

5. Which of the following is *not* a required email setting to enable notification?

   a. SMTP port

   b. From Address

   c. Recipient Address(es)

   d. Mail Server

Foundation Topics

Configuring Event Reporting in Cisco IME

Cisco IME stores events in a database, and this information is used for the built-in and custom reports. The reports are only limited by the size of the database. The reports can be saved as *.PDF or *.RTF files to be archived, shared with others, or printed.

IME Reporting

Cisco IME makes provisions for creating different reports that you can customize using different filters. The report consists of a bar or pie chart and tabular data used to construct the graphs. The reporting tool is accessible through the Reports pane. There are six categories or types of reports, as shown and explained in Table 17-2.

Table 17-2   *Cisco IME Report Categories*

Report	Details
Top Attacker	Shows top attacker IP addresses for a specified time. You specify the maximum number of attacker IP addresses.
Top Victim	Shows top victim IP addresses for a specified time. You specify the maximum number of victim IP addresses.
Top Signature	Shows top signatures fired for a specified time. You specify the maximum number of signatures.
Attacks Over Time	Show the attacks over a specified time.
Filtered Events vs. All Events	Displays a set of events against the total events for a specified time period.
Global Correlation	Displays the global correlation reports since the sensor has been running.

There are six report categories that, when expanded, display a total of 18 predefined reports. There are also user-defined reports that are created by clicking the **New** button or by tuning an existing predefined report and clicking the **Save As** button to save the report as a customized report. After they are saved, the reports are listed under the My Reports category. The Reports window is divided into two parts: the Report tree (left pane) and the Report Settings pane (right side), as shown in Figure 17-1.

These items are described as follows:

■ **The Report tree** shows the reports list in the form of a tree and contains a set of predefined reports (such as Basic Top Attacker) and user-defined or custom reports under the My Reports node.

■ **The Report Settings** pane contains the report and the settings that are used to generate it.

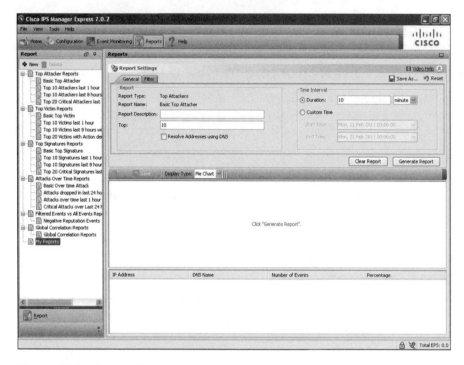

Figure 17-1 *Reports Pane*

When you select a report in the list and click **Generate Report**, the corresponding report containing a graph and a table is displayed in the lower half of the Report Settings pane. The Reports Setting pane contains two tabs, General and Filter, where you can customize the report.

Note: The Filter tab field supports IP version 4 (IPv4) and IP version 6 (IPv6) addresses.

Configuring and Generating Reports

You can customize your report by configuring the number of items you want to have in your report and what the time interval should be. You can also use Domain Name System (DNS) to resolve the IP addresses and use filters to further refine the type of information you want the report to contain.

To configure and generate a sample report, follow these steps:

Step 1.   In the Report tree, click **New**, and then in the New Report dialog box, enter the name of the new report, choose the type of report from the drop-down list, and then click **OK**, as shown in Figure 17-2. The new report will show up under My Reports in the Report tree.

Step 2.   Select your report, and on the General tab, configure the settings for your report:

■ In the Report Description field, enter a description for this report.

■ In the Top field, enter how many top events you want to see in this report.

- Select the **Resolve Addresses Using DNS** check box, if you want to use the DNS address resolution.

- Configure the time interval for this report. Either enter the duration or a custom time.

Figure 17-2 *New Report Dialog Box*

Step 3. On the Filter tab, from the Filter Name drop-down menu, choose the filter name. Or, to add a filter, click the **Note** icon.

Step 4. Click **Generate Report**. Your report shows up in the bottom half of the Report Settings pane, displaying the statistics in graph and table form.

Step 5. To customize the display, choose Bar or Pie Chart in the Display Type drop-down menu.

Step 6. Click **Print** to print the report, or click **Save** to save the report in PDF or RTF format, as shown in Figure 17-3.

Step 7. To see events for a single IP address, choose the IP address from the Events For drop-down list.

Event Dashboards

You can customize your Events Dashboard so that it contains "Top N" gadgets, which are essentially results of built-in reports. There are four such gadgets available, as described in Table 17-3.

Table 17-3 *"Top N" Gadgets*

Gadget	Details
Top Attackers	Displays the number of events for each top attacker IP address over a specified time
Top Victims	Displays the number of events for each top victim IP address over a specified time
Top Signatures	Displays the top number of signatures over a specified time
Top Applications	Displays the top ten Layer 4 protocols that the sensor has discovered

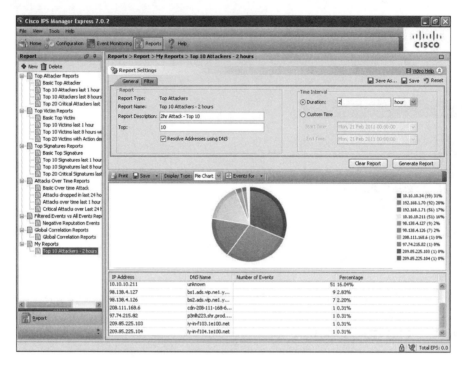

Figure 17-3 *Sample Generated Report View*

Using Notifications in Cisco IME

Cisco IME can be configured to send email notifications to administrators based on certain events. This is based on the events meeting certain criteria that are configured globally in IME and can be modified based on frequency and content.

Caution: Enabling email notifications can generate a large volume of email messages.

To configure email notifications in Cisco IME, follow these steps:

Step 1.   Choose **Tools > Preferences** and select the Notification tab, as shown in Figure 17-4.

Step 2.   Select the **Enable Email/Epage Notifications** check box to enable IME to send notifications.

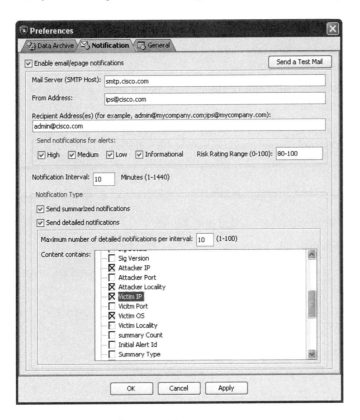

Figure 17-4 *Notification Tab*

Step 3.   Enter the email settings:

■ **Mail Server (SMTP Host):** SMTP server address; for example, smtp.cisco.com

■ **From Address:** Address from which the message is sent to the SMTP server; for example, ips@cisco.com

■ **Recipient Address(es):** Email address(es) to which notifications will be sent by the SMTP server; for example, admin@cisco.com

Step 4.   Configure the Send Notifications for Alerts values:

■ **High, Medium, Low, Informational:** Select severities for which notifications should be generated.

■ **Risk Rating Range (0-100):** Enter a risk rating range for which notifications should be generated.

Step 5.   Enter the notification interval. Notifications will be sent only once in the configured interval.

Step 6.   Select the notification type:

- Select the **Send Summarized Notifications** check box if you want to receive summarized notifications.

- Select the **Send Detailed Notifications** check box if you want to receive detailed notifications.

Step 7.   Configure the maximum number of detailed notifications per interval, and select which information from events you want to be included in notifications.

Summary

This section highlights the key topics discussed in this chapter:

- Cisco IME allows you to use built-in reports.

- Cisco IME allows you to customize reports and also share such reports as PDF or RTF documents.

- Cisco IME allows you to globally create email notifications for critical events.

References

More information on Cisco IME can be found at the following URL:

Installing and Using Cisco Intrusion Prevention System Manager Express 7.0, at www.cisco.com/en/US/docs/security/ips/7.0/configuration/guide/ime/imeguide7.html.

Exam Preparation Tasks

Review All the Key Topics

Review the most important topics from the chapter, noted with the Key Topic icons in the margin of the page. Table 17-4 lists a reference of these key topics and the page numbers on which each is found.

Table 17-4   *Key Topics for Chapter 17*

Key Topic Element	Description	Page Number
Table 17-2	Cisco IME Report Categories	415
Step list	New Report	416
Step list	Configuring Email Notifications	418

Complete the Tables and Lists from Memory

Print a copy of Appendix C, "Memory Tables" (found on the CD), or at least the section for this chapter, and complete the tables and lists from memory. Appendix D, "Memory Tables Answer Key," also on the CD, includes completed tables and lists to check your work.

Definitions of Key Terms

Define the following key terms from this chapter, and check your answers in the glossary:

Mail server (SMTP host), From address, Recipient address

This chapter covers the integration of Cisco Security Manager and Cisco Security MARS with the Cisco IPS sensors for configuration and monitoring purposes, with a focus on the following:

- **Configuring Integration with Cisco Security Manager:** This covers the steps required to integrate the Cisco IPS sensor with Cisco Security Manager.

- **Configuring Integration with Cisco Security MARS:** This covers the steps required to integrate the Cisco IPS sensor with Cisco Security MARS.

CHAPTER 18

Integrating Cisco IPS with CSM and Cisco Security MARS

Overview

Cisco IME is used in small to medium networks that do not want to manage more than ten IPS sensors. In larger enterprise networks, IME cannot suffice, and IPS sensors are often integrated with Cisco Security Manager (CSM) for enhanced provisioning and with Cisco Security Monitoring, Analysis, and Response System (MARS) for event monitoring and analysis. In this chapter, we will focus on the integration between Cisco IPS and the two management applications.

"Do I Know This Already?" Quiz

The "Do I Know This Already?" quiz allows you to assess whether you should read the entire chapter. If you miss no more than one of these self-assessment questions, you might want to move ahead to the "Exam Preparation Tasks" section. Table 18-1 lists the major headings in this chapter and the "Do I Know This Already?" quiz questions covering the material in those headings so that you can assess your knowledge of these specific areas. The answers to the "Do I Know This Already?" quiz appear in Appendix A.

Table 18-1   *"Do I Know This Already?" Foundation Topics Section-to-Question Mapping*

Foundation Topics Section	Questions
Configuring Integration with Cisco Security Manager	1, 2
Configuring Integration with Cisco Security MARS	3–5

1. Which of the following devices is *not* managed by Cisco Security Manager 4.0?

   a. Cisco Intrusion Prevention System

   b. Cisco Adaptive Security Appliance

   c. Cisco Security Monitoring, Analysis, and Response System (MARS)

   d. Integrated Services Router (ISR)

2. Which of the following is *not* a prerequisite for managing an IPS sensor through CSM?

   a. IP address and mask, default router, and sensor name

   b. FTP access

   c. HTTPS access

   d. Administrative username and password

3. Which of the following are features of Cisco MARS?

   a. Event correlation

   b. Threat detection and mitigation

   c. Reporting and incident querying

   d. All of these answers are correct.

4. CS-MARS pulls events using the Security Device Event Exchange (SDEE) over SSL (HTTPS). True or false?

   a. True

   b. False

5. What capability in CS-MARS and CSM allows them to integrate into each other in a collaborative manner?

   a. Cross-launch

   b. Cisco application programming interface

   c. Centralized management

   d. Server definition

Foundation Topics

Configuring Integration with Cisco Security Manager

The Cisco Security Management Suite is a framework of products and technologies designed to simplify and automate the tasks associated with security management operations; these tasks include configuration, monitoring, analysis, and response for the Cisco Self-Defending Network. This chapter focuses on the following key components of the suite:

- **Cisco Security Manager:** An enterprise-class security management software application designed for scalable operational, management, and policy control for a wide variety of devices, including Adaptive Security Appliances (ASA), IPS appliances and service modules, Integrated Services Routers (ISR), and some service modules for Catalyst 6500s.

- **Cisco Security MARS:** An appliance-based, all-inclusive solution that provides insight into events to help administrators monitor, identify, isolate, and remedy security issues or incidents.

One key benefit of the Cisco Security Management Suite is that products can be deployed separately from one another, and when other components are added on, they can be integrated into existing deployments of applications within the suite.

Cisco Security Manager 4.0 Features and Benefits

Cisco Security Manager 4.0, as mentioned previously, manages firewalls, routers, intrusion prevention systems (IPS), intrusion detection systems (IDS), and Virtual Private Networks (VPN). Table 18-2 highlights some key features that make it the robust management solution that it is.

Table 18-2   *CSM 4.0 Features and Benefits*

Key Topic

Features	Details
Scalable network management	Centrally administer security policies and device settings from a single point once and then apply it to all devices, a group of devices, or a single device. The policy is stored centrally within the application's database.
Provisioning of multiple security technologies	Manage VPNs across firewalls and routers. Also manage IPSs on routers, in switches, and in IPS appliances.
Event and policy correlation	Monitor and correlate events on IPS and firewall devices.

Table 18-2   *CSM 4.0 Features and Benefits*

Features	Details
Provisioning of platform-specific policies	Manage platform-specific configuration of these features on different device types: ■ Routing and bridging ■ IEEE 802.1X ■ Secure Device Provisioning (SDP) ■ Network Admission Control (NAC) on routers ■ Device access security ■ DHCP ■ QoS ■ Authentication, Authorization, and Accounting (AAA) ■ Multicast on firewall devices
VPN Wizard	Facilitates simplified configuration of site-to-site, hub-and-spoke and full-mesh VPNs across different VPN device types.
Multiple management views	Device, policy, and map views enable you to manage your security in a way that meets your needs.
Reusable policy objects	Create reusable objects to represent network addresses, device settings, and VPN parameters and use them instead of manually entering values.
Device grouping capabilities	Create device groups to represent organizational structure and apply policies according to the groups.
Policy inheritance	Centrally specify which policies are mandatory and enforced in the organization. New devices automatically acquire mandatory policies.
Role-based administration	Enable appropriate access controls for different operators based on their roles.
Workflow	Optionally allow the division of responsibility and workload between network and security operators and provide a change management approval and tracking mechanism.
Single, consistent user interface for managing common firewall features	Use a single rule table for all platforms (Cisco IOS Firewall, Cisco PIX Firewall, Cisco ASA Adaptive Security Appliance, and Cisco Firewall Services Module [FWSM]).

Table 18-2   *CSM 4.0 Features and Benefits*

Features	Details
Intelligent analysis of firewall policies	With the conflict-detection feature, analyze and report rules that overlap or conflict with other rules. The access control list hit count feature allows checking in real time if specific rules are being hit by packets.
Sophisticated rule table editing	Use inline editing, with the ability to cut, copy, and paste rules and to change their order in the rule table.
Firewall policies discovery from the device	Import policies that exist on the device into Cisco Security Manager for future management.
Flexible deployment options	Deploy configurations directly to a device or to a configuration file. Cisco Security Manager can also use the CiscoWorks Auto Update Server, Cisco Networking Service Configuration Engine, or Aladdin Token Management Server (TMS) for device configuration deployment.
Rollback	Roll back to previous configuration if necessary.
FlexConfig (template manager)	With an intelligent command-line interface (CLI), config-editor, manage features that are available on a device but that are not natively supported by Cisco Security Manager.

Cisco Security Manager version 4.1 is also available for download, even though the test covers version 4.0. New features in version 4.1 are as follows:

- **Reporting:** Provides enterprise-class integrated firewall, IPS, and VPN reporting functionality for improved visibility into security devices. Custom reports can also be created using advanced filters for immediate viewing or delivery through email.

- **Advanced troubleshooting:** Provides excellent troubleshooting or operation issues using packet capture, ping, traceroute, and other tools in addition to event-to-policy linkages and Cisco packet tracer tools.

- **Guided IPsec configuration:** Provides significantly streamlined and guided IPsec VPN configuration for partner/extranet VPN scenarios.

- **Policy support:** Provides new policy export and import features to address larger enterprise needs of transferring policies across multiple instances of CSM, to ensure multi-instance scalability and deployment.

Cisco Security Manager version 4.1 also supports the latest ASA 8.4 features set, including bridge groups, Kerberos Constrained Delegation (KCD), and Internet Key Exchange version 2 (IKEv2).

Managing Cisco IPS Sensors Using Cisco Security Manager

Cisco Security Manager provides different methods for device management. The only limitations to device management might be the hardware or software versions of the devices to be managed if not supported by Cisco Security Manager 4.0. Table 18-3 lists the supported devices and IPS software versions.

Table 18-3 *CSM 4.0–Supported IPS Hardware and Software Versions*

Supported IPS Hardware	Supported IPS Software
Cisco IPS 4200 Series sensors	Cisco IPS Software 5.1
Cisco ASA 5500 AIP SSM	Cisco IPS Software 6.0
Cisco ASA 5500 AIP SSC-5	Cisco IPS Software 6.1
Cisco Catalyst 6500 IDSM-2 module	Cisco IPS Software 6.2
Cisco IPS AIM for Cisco ISR/ISR G2 routers	Cisco IPS Software 7.0
Cisco IPS NME for Cisco ISR/ISR G2 routers	Cisco IPS Software 7.1 (with 4.0.1)
Routers running the IOS IPS feature including ISR/ISR G2 models	

Note: Cisco Security Manager Professional Edition is required to manage the Cisco Catalyst 6500 Series Router IDSM-2. IPS signature updates are supported only on Cisco IPS Software version 5.1(5) E1 and later.

The devices can be added to CSM during inventory, policy discovery, or configuration deployment. However, the devices have to be configured with some basic access settings so that they can be managed remotely with CSM, which uses the default protocols commonly used for each device type. Table 18-4 highlights some prerequisites to consider when managing an IPS device.

Key Topic

Table 18-4 *Prerequisites: Managing IPS Through CSM*

Task	Details
Configure the IPS device with at least a minimal network configuration	■ Sensor name ■ IPS address and network mask ■ A default router
To allow CSM to log in to an IPS device	■ Enable Transport Layer Security (TLS)/Secure Socket Layer (SSL) to allow HTTPS access if not already enabled. ■ Define the IP address of the CSM server as an allowed host in the configuration of the sensor.

Table 18-4 *Prerequisites: Managing IPS Through CSM*

Task	Details
Also verify that	■ A username and password that CSM will use as login credentials are configured on the IPS device and allow provisioning access (at least the operator role). ■ There is functioning network connectivity between IPS device and Cisco Security Manager.

Configuration procedures needed to accomplish the steps on the IPS sensor have been covered earlier, in Chapter 5, "Integrating the Cisco IPS Sensor into a Network."

Adding Sensors to Cisco Security Manager

One of the easiest ways to add a device into CSM is to add the device from the network, by following these steps:

Step 1.   In Device view, select **File > New Device** or click the **New Device (+)** button above the device selector to open the New Device Wizard, as shown in Figure 18-1.

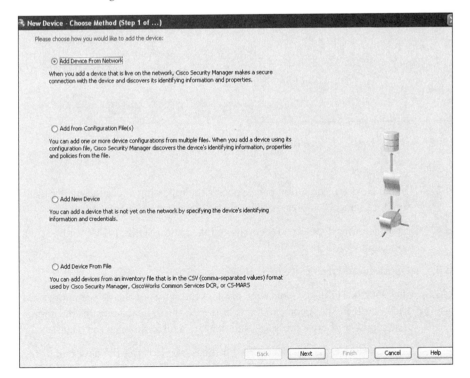

Figure 18-1 *Adding a Device to CSM*

Step 2. Select the **Add Device from Network** radio button and click **Next**. The Device Information page appears, as shown in Figure 18-2.

Provide the IP and login credentials; the CSM will then log you in to the device and obtain the information needed.

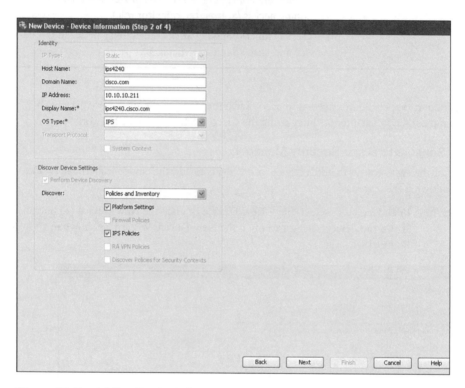

Figure 18-2 *Adding Device Information in CSM*

Step 3. On the Device Information page, specify the following key values under Identity: host name, IP address, display name, transport protocol, and so on.

Step 4. Enter the primary device credentials and then enter SDEE, HTTP, Rx-boot mode, and SNMP as required.

Step 5. (Optional) Add the device to a group.

Step 6. Click **Finish**. The Task status page displays the status of the device import and discovery. If the data you entered is incorrect, the system generates the appropriate number of error messages and displays a table showing the pages.

Step 7. Click **Close** to close this page. This button is enabled after the device import and discovery are completed.

After the IPS sensor has been added to the CSM inventory, it can be managed with CSM.

Configuring Integration with Cisco Security MARS

Cisco Security MARS offers features for improved threat redetection and mitigation, including event correlation. Table 18-5 lists some of the features and benefits.

Table 18-5 *Cisco MARS Features and Benefits*

Feature	Detail
Accurate threat detection and mitigation	Cisco Security MARS eases the process of identifying and mitigating threats.
Event correlation	Events from IPS sensors can be correlated with events from other devices on the network to identify attack patterns across the broader network.
Reporting and incident querying	Extensive reporting and incident-querying capabilities that are built into Cisco Security MARS provide detailed insight into network status and events.
Long-term event logging	CS-MARS can collect and store a vast amount of logs and event information, which can be stored over extended periods and used for investigations or analysis.

Note: As of this writing, the end of sale of Cisco Security MARS has been announced; the last day to order the appliance was June 3, 2011. However, existing customers will continue to receive support until June 30, 2016, after which it will be deemed to be obsolete. Find more details at this URL: www.cisco.com/en/US/prod/collateral/vpndevc/ps5739/ps6241/eol_c51-636888.html.

Although Cisco IME offers database storage for up to ten devices, there is no limit on the number of devices that can send log messages to the CS-MARS device. However, it is important to know the total number of events per second being generated from those devices and the appropriate CS-MARS box installed to support the devices to ensure that all logs are captured. Each CS-MARS box also has a storage capacity that must be put into consideration, depending on the desired age of events before they are archived.

Cisco MARS supports all the hardware and software versions in Table 18-3 with the addition of Cisco IDS Software 4.0.

CS-MARS pulls events using the Security Device Event Exchange (SDEE) over SSL (HTTPS). When it pulls events in this form or other forms from devices, it is first normalized so that it is compatible with the MARS internal format. This is important so as to correlate events with other data.

MARS can display trigger packet information for the first event that fires a signature on a Cisco IPS device, if the signature actions are configured correctly. MARS is also able to pull the IP log information from IPS sensors and display it within its user interface.

MARS provides IPS signature update reporting as well as IPS threat and risk rating monitoring. MARS also provides dynamic signature updates to sensors based on events received if it has an updated signature locally to mitigate a specific threat.

When adding a device to MARS, there are some tasks that need to have been completed on the managed device before you can enable MARS to monitor it. Table 18-6 highlights these requirements.

Table 18-6   *Prerequisites: Monitoring IPS Through MARS*

Task	Details
Configure the IPS device with at least a minimal network configuration	■ Sensor name ■ IPS address and network mask ■ A default router
To allow MARS to log in to IPS device and pull events	■ Enable Transport Layer Security (TLS)/Secure Socket Layer (SSL) to allow HTTPS access if not already enabled. ■ Define the IP address of MARS as an allowed host in the configuration of the sensor.
Also verify that	■ A username and password that MARS will use as login credentials are configured on the IPS. ■ There is functioning network connectivity between the IPS device and MARS.

Configuration procedures needed to accomplish the steps on the IPS sensor have been previously covered in Chapter 5.

Add a Cisco IPS Sensor to MARS

The steps for adding different IPS sensor device models to MARS are similar but differ in certain steps, depending on the sensor being added. When adding an IPS module to MARS, the parent device (ASA, ISR, ISR G2, or Catalyst 6500 switch) is first added. After the parent device has been added, the remaining steps are practically the same for the sensors.

To add an IPS 4200 Series sensor in Cisco Security MARS, follow these steps:

Step 1.   Choose **Admin > System Setup > Security and Monitor Devices > Add**.

Step 2.   Select Cisco IPS 7.x from the Device Type list, as shown in Figure 18-3.

Step 3.   Enter the following:

■ Host name of the sensor in the Device Name field

■ IP address in the Reporting IP field

■ Username associated with the administrative account on the reporting device

■ Password that is associated with the username specified in the Login field

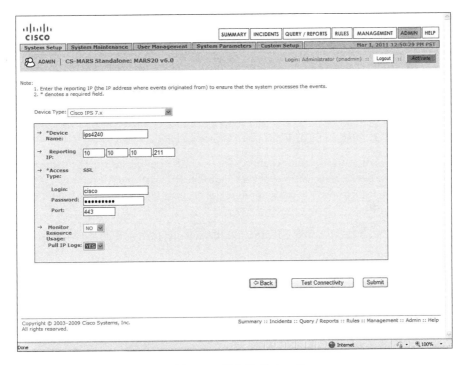

Figure 18-3 *MARS GUI: Adding an IPS 4240 Appliance*

Step 4. In the Port field, enter the TCP port the Web server running on the sensor listens on. The default is HTTPS, which is port 443.

Step 5. Choose No in the Monitor Resource Usage drop-down box.

Step 6. Select Yes in the Pull IP Logs field. This applies to the entire sensor including virtual sensors.

Step 7. Click **Test Connectivity** to verify the configuration and discovery of virtual sensors.

Step 8. Click **Discover** to discover any defined virtual sensors. MARS is unaware of any changes made to the sensor after this discovery. Anytime a change is made, you must click **Discover**.

Step 9. To define the monitored networks for each virtual sensor, select the Virtual Sensor Name check box and click **Edit**. The IPS Module page appears.

Step 10. (Optional) To select the networks that are attached to the device, click the Select a Network radio button:

- Select a network from the Select a Network drop-down list.

- Click **Add** to move the specified network into the monitored Networks field.

- Repeat as needed.

Step 11. (Optional) To define the attack path, follow these steps:

- Enter the network address in the Network IP field.

- Enter the corresponding network mask value in the Mask field.

- Click **Add.**

- Repeat as needed.

Step 12. (Optional) Repeat Steps 9 through 11 for each virtual sensor.

Step 13. Click **Submit** to save your changes. This records your changes in the database, and the device information appears under the Security and Monitoring information list. However, it does not load the changes into the working memory of MARS.

Step 14. Click **Activate** to enable MARS to start analyzing events for this device.

To add a Cisco IDS/IPS module to the parent device, perform the following tasks:

Step 1. Define the parent device as any of the following if not already existing:

- Cisco router

- Cisco switch

- Cisco ASA

Step 2. Configure the IDS/IPS module to enable SDEE traffic and to enable Cisco Security MARS to access the SDEE events that are stored on the module. This also allows MARS to receive trigger packets and IP log information.

Step 3. Add the IDS/IPS module to the parent device previously defined in the web interface of Cisco Security MARS, as shown in Figure 18-4, by following these steps:

- Choose **Admin > System Setup > Security and Monitor Devices.**

- From the drop-down list of devices, select the parent device to which you want to add the IPS module and click **Edit.**

- Click **Add Module** and a module window opens, allowing you to input the connectivity and login credentials for the IDS module.

The rest of the tasks are the same for the IPS sensor added previously.

Event Feed Verification

After these are configured properly, MARS should start to receive events from the IPS. To test, you can enable signatures 2000 and 2004. These signatures monitor Internet Control Message Protocol (ICMP) messages (pings). After it is enabled, ping a host on the subnet protected by the Cisco IPS device. Events should be generated, and you can verify that events appear in MARS. After this is done, disable signatures 2000 and 2004.

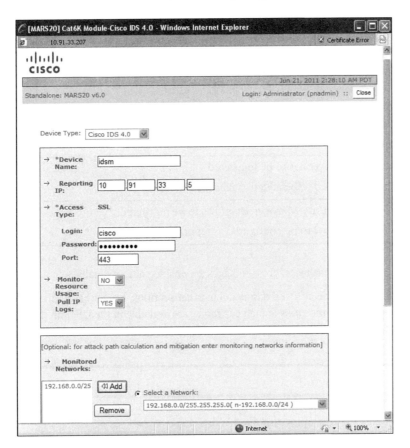

Figure 18-4 *Adding an IDS Module in a Catalyst 6500 Switch to Cisco MARS*

Cisco Security Manager (CSM) and MARS Cross-Launch Capability

There is a significant degree of collaboration between CSM and MARS. You can use the cross-launch capabilities built into both applications, which allow you to cross-launch CSM from MARS and MARS from CSM. This adds value because launch points are created in both applications for each other so that MARS creates queries that include a launch point for CSM. When CSM is launched, you can carry out the following:

■ Edit an IPS signature

■ Add an event action filter to an IPS configuration in Cisco Security Manager

And when you use CSM to cross-launch MARS, you can query events that were originated by the signatures in CSM.

To carry out cross-launching between the two applications, some prerequisites, listed in Table 18-7, need to be fulfilled.

Table 18-7   *Prerequisites: Cross-Launch Capability Between MARS and CSM*

Task	Details
In IPS	■ Enable Transport Layer Security (TLS)/Secure Sockets Layer (SSL) to allow HTTPS access if not already enabled. ■ Define the IP address of MARS as an allowed host in the configuration of the sensor. ■ Ensure that MARS can pull events using SDEE.
In CSM	■ The MARS server has to be registered. ■ IPS devices need to be added as managed devices.
In MARS	■ The Cisco Security Manager server has to be registered. ■ IPS devices need to be configured as reporting devices.

After you have completed these tasks, cross-linkages are enabled automatically.

The tasks in Table 18-7 have been covered in detail in other sections; hence the summary here. More detailed steps for the cross-launch capability are available in the URLs in the "References" section, later in this chapter.

Summary

This section highlights the key topics discussed in this chapter:

■ Managing Cisco IPS sensors with CSM provides

  ■ A single point of management for large deployments of IPS sensors

  ■ IPS configuration archiving and rollback

  ■ Automated IPS updates

  ■ Policy inheritance and sharing

■ Monitoring Cisco IPS sensors with CS-MARS provides

  ■ Event correlation

  ■ Improved threat identification and mitigation

  ■ Flexible reporting and incident querying

■ Cisco Security MARS and Cisco Security Manager cross-launch capabilities simplify configuration management and security monitoring for enterprise networks.

References

More information on CSM and MARS can be found at the following URLs:

User Guide for Cisco Security Manager 4.0, at www.cisco.com/en/US/docs/security/ security_management/cisco_security_manager/security_manager/4.0/user/guide/ CSMUserGuide_wrapper.html.

Device Configuration Guide for Cisco Security MARS 6.x, at www.cisco.com/en/ US/docs/security/security_management/cs-mars/6.0/device/configuration/guide/ GbkDcgMars.html.

Exam Preparation Tasks

Review All the Key Topics

Review the most important topics from the chapter, noted with the Key Topic icons in the margin of the page. Table 18-8 lists a reference of these key topics and the page numbers on which each is found.

Table 18-8 *Key Topics for Chapter 18*

Key Topic Element	Description	Page Number
Table 18-2	CSM 4.0 Features and Benefits	425
Table 18-4	Prerequisites: Managing IPS Through CSM	428
Table 18-6	Prerequisites: Monitoring IPS Through MARS	432
Table 18-7	Prerequisites: Cross-Launch Capability Between MARS and CSM	436

Complete the Tables and Lists from Memory

Print a copy of Appendix C, "Memory Tables" (found on the CD), or at least the section for this chapter, and complete the tables and lists from memory. Appendix D, "Memory Tables Answer Key," also on the CD, includes completed tables and lists to check your work.

Definitions of Key Terms

Define the following key terms from this chapter, and check your answers in the glossary:

Cisco Security Manager (CSM); Cisco Security Monitoring, Analysis, and Response System (CS-MARS or MARS); event correlation; Security Device Event Exchange (SDEE)

This chapter covers information on how the Cisco Intelli-Shield database and services aid organizations to identify, prevent, and/or mitigate attacks, as well as the following:

- **Using Cisco Security Intelligence Operations:** This provides an overview of the Cisco Security Intelligence Operations cloud service and its value.

- **Using the Cisco IntelliShield Alert Manager Service:** This provides the steps required to customize the Cisco IntelliShield Alert Manager Service based on individual requirements.

CHAPTER 19

Using the Cisco IntelliShield Database and Services

Overview

The Cisco Security Intelligence Operations (SIO) site, the Cisco IntelliShield database, and the Cisco Security IntelliShield Alert Manager provide the intelligence that organizations need to identify, prevent, and mitigate attacks; this enables them to take a more proactive approach to security. This also helps in analyzing information obtained based on suspicious or malicious activity in your infrastructure and making the best decisions thereafter.

"Do I Know This Already?" Quiz

The "Do I Know This Already?" quiz allows you to assess whether you should read the entire chapter. If you miss no more than one of these self-assessment questions, you might want to move ahead to the "Exam Preparation Tasks" section. Table 19-1 lists the major headings in this chapter and the "Do I Know This Already?" quiz questions covering the material in those headings so that you can assess your knowledge of these specific areas. The answers to the "Do I Know This Already?" quiz appear in Appendix A.

Table 19-1 *"Do I Know This Already?" Foundation Topics Section-to-Question Mapping*

Foundation Topics Section	Questions
Using Cisco Security Intelligence Operations	1–3
Using Cisco Security Alert Manager Service	4–6

1. Which of the following is *not* a core section of the Security Intelligence Operations portal?

    a. Risk rating

    b. Latest threat information

    c. Cisco products and services

    d. Resources

2. The Cisco Security IntelliShield Alert Manager Service is for Cisco devices and applications only. True or false?

   a. True

   b. False

3. What can you subscribe to for up-to-date information on IPS signature updates, vulnerability, and threat information?

   a. Alert Manager notifications

   b. Cisco Security Alert

   c. IPS Threat Defense Bulletin

   d. Cisco product notifications

4. You can customize the Cisco Security IntelliShield Alert Manager based on which of the following?

   a. How notifications are sent

   b. How much information is sent

   c. Who receives the notifications

   d. All of these answers are correct.

5. Which of the following users cannot log in to the Cisco Security IntelliShield Alert Manager?

   a. Registered user

   b. Virtual user

   c. Administrator

   d. All of these answers are correct.

6. Notifications are received out-of-band or in-band through which of the following?

   a. Email

   b. Pager

   c. a. and b.

   d. Pop-up window

Foundation Topics

Using Cisco Security Intelligence Operations

The Cisco Security Intelligence Operations (SIO) is a cloud-based service that connects global threat information, reputation-based services, and sophisticated analysis to Cisco network security devices to provide stronger protection with faster response times. It also has a site designed to provide Cisco customers with access to critical security information such as best practices, early warnings, threats, and vulnerabilities.

The Security Intelligence Operations site, whose home page is shown in Figure 19-1, is composed of the following core sections and subsections:

- **Latest Threat Information:** This contains information on security threats, alerts, and outbreaks, including cyber-risk reports, IPS threat defense bulletins, and virus information.

- **Resources:** This section contains both technical and business resources, which vary from white papers and best-practice documents to security reports, case studies, and programs.

Figure 19-1 *Cisco Security Intelligence Operations Home Page*

- **Cisco Products and Services:** This section includes security vulnerability advisories on Cisco products from the Product Security Incident Response Team (PSIRT), as well as security services, solutions, and products available from Cisco to improve the security of your network.

- **Cisco Emergency Response:** This section provides contact information should a vulnerability be discovered in Cisco products.

- **Notification Registration:** This section provides registration information and steps for notification on outbreaks that can be delivered through email, text messages, or RSS feeds and information on the IntelliShield Alert Manager.

- **Security Alerts:** This section contains a table with the latest security alerts that are listed with their Common Vulnerability Scoring System (CVSS) values, their names, and the last time they were published. The names are links to more detailed information about the vulnerability.

- **URL Reputation Lookup:** This bar allows you to look up the reputation of a web domain or IP address by querying the Cisco SenderBase.

From the core sections listed here, we will be looking into some key subsections and the value they add to customers.

Security Alerts

When you open the SIO URL, the Security Alerts table is there by default; it includes three columns for the CVSS Score, Name, and Last Published, respectively. It is designed to provide critical information on recent security alerts.

The fields contained in the Name columns are URLs and, when clicked, open into a new page to provide detailed vulnerability information that is provided by the IntelliShield service.

There is also a View Alerts drop-down box that is set to Most Recent by default. It provides other options, as shown in Figure 19-2, such as

- Top Alerts

- Alerts, Sorted by Vendor (Cisco, Microsoft, Apache, Red Hat, and HP)

In the Security Alerts view, if you click the **View More** link at the bottom of Figure 19-2, it opens up a page showing the following columns with information:

- Common Vulnerability Scoring System (CVSS) Score

- Cisco IPS Signatures

- Cisco Product Security Incident Response Team (PSIRT) Advisories

- Cisco Application Mitigation Bulletin

- Affected Cisco Products

Key
Topic

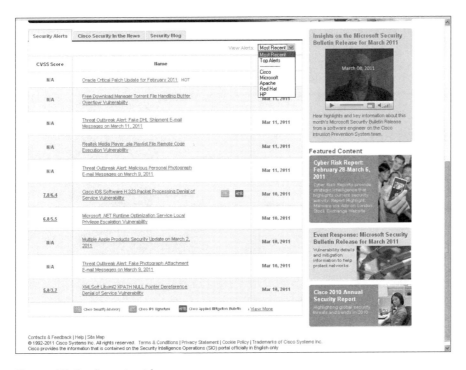

Figure 19-2 *Security Alerts*

Threat Analysis and Reporting

The Virus Watch (formerly Track and Analyze) section of the portal provides a graphical representation of global threat activity in terms of virus activity source. It can be reached through **Latest Threat Information** > **Virus Watch**. When the **Virus Watch** link is clicked, it redirects you to the Cisco IronPort SenderBase Security Network page.

The page is divided into four graphical panes, shown in Figure 19-3, which provide the following:

- **Virus Activity Source:** Provides a graphical view of virus activity sources.

- **Current Virus Outbreak Level:** Displays the current outbreak level using three color indicators:

  - **Red:** Virus outbreak in progress

  - **Orange:** Virus outbreak during the previous 24 hours

  - **Green:** No virus outbreaks during the previous 24 hours

- **Most Recent Virus Outbreaks:** Lists the virus name and the date published.

- **IronPort Virus Outbreak Leadtime:** Lists the lead time for the last five outbreaks.

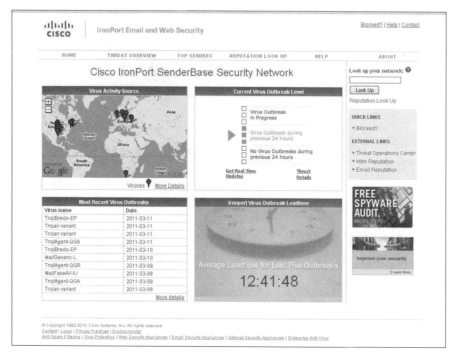

Figure 19-3   *Virus Watch View*

Resources

The Resources tab on the SIO portal drops down into Technical Resources and Business Resources, as shown in Figure 19-4. While the technical resources are focused on security best practices, the business resources are focused on security programs.

These sections have a lot of great content that is described as follows:

- **Security Programs:** Provide content in the form of podcasts, videos, articles, and general security topics.

- **Design Zone for Security:** This is a collection of designs that have been tested and validated in line with best practices, and it also provides the configuration used. These are aimed at ensuring that security engineers have enough content to guide them in the design, implementation, and operation of Cisco products and technologies.

- **Technical Resources:** This provides a link to a plethora of resources; some are listed as follows:

  - Cisco Security Text Alerts

  - Cisco Security Blog

  - Service Provider Security Best Practices

  - Security Multimedia Library

  - Cisco Applied Mitigation Bulletins

  - Cisco Event Responses

- Technical White Papers
- Security Case Studies
- Security Intelligence Operations (Best Practices and RSS Feeds)

■ **Best Practices White Papers**

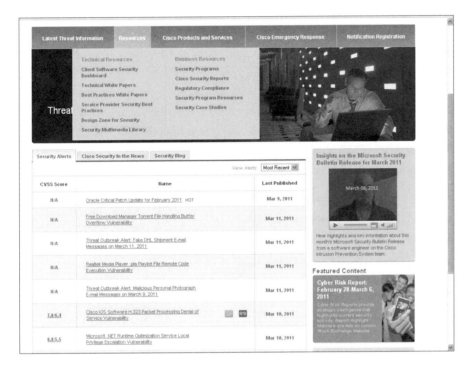

Figure 19-4 *Security Resources*

The links to the content in this section are divided into four groups, as outlined in Table 19-2.

Table 19-2 *SIO Best Practices Page*

Group	Content
Security Operations	■ Best Practices and Configuration Guides ■ Security Management ■ Attack Identification and Mitigation Techniques
Network Security	■ Best Practices and Configuration Guides ■ Attack Identification and Mitigation Techniques
Host Security	■ Attack Identification and Mitigation Techniques
Application Security	■ Best Practices and Configuration Guides ■ Attack Identification and Mitigation Technologies

Key
Topic

The page also contains links to content with practical solutions aimed at helping engineers identify and mitigate threats, including the following:

- IPS Testing

- CVSS Usage Within Cisco

- Cisco IPS Mitigation Capabilities

- Protect Against Worms, Fighting Spyware

- Identifying and Correlating Attack Indicators, DNS Best Practices, Network Protections, and Other Threats.

Products and Services Updates

The Products and Services Updates page can be accessed from the SIO page through **Cisco Products and Services > Product & Services Updates.**

This page has links to the following:

- Security-related and general services on Cisco.com, such as

  - Cisco IPS Signature Archive

  - Cisco IPS Threat Defense Bulletins

  - Cisco PSIRT Advisories and Responses

- Subscription pages for IntelliShield Alert Manager and virus alerts

IPS Threat Defense Bulletin

The Cisco IPS Threat Defense Bulletin, shown in Figure 19-5, describes updates to the Cisco IPS product line. The bulletins are issued frequently, and they contain information about vulnerabilities, the risk rating, and the signatures required to mitigate them.

Although different bulletins can contain different sections, the following are examples of the kinds of information listed in the IPS Bulletin:

- Release Summary

- New Vulnerability and Exploit Protections

- Retired Signatures

- Sensor Update Information

- New Product Announcements

- End of Life/End of Sale Announcements

- Links to security-related resources

- Threat Defense Bulletin subscription links

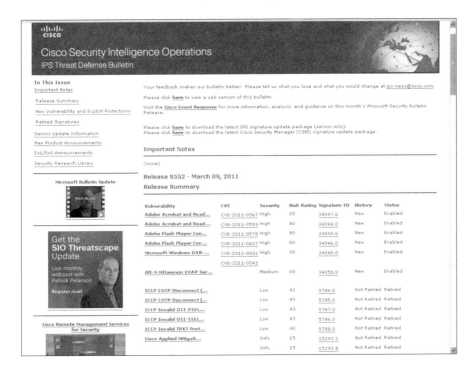

Figure 19-5 *Threat Defense Bulletin*

You can subscribe to receive Cisco threat defense bulletins as soon as they are published by email. To subscribe, follow these steps:

Step 1.   Go to the SIO page: http://tools.cisco.com/security/center/home.x.

Step 2.   Choose **Latest Threat Information > Cisco IPS Threat Defense Bulletin** and click the latest bulletin.

Step 3.   Scroll to the bottom of the Cisco IPS Threat Defense Bulletin and click **Subscribe**.

Step 4.   Fill in all the required information and click **Submit**. An email will be sent to the email address specified, informing you that your subscription status has been modified.

Using Cisco IntelliShield Alert Manager Service

The Cisco Security IntelliShield Alert Manager (SIAM) Service provides a comprehensive solution for delivering the security in mission-critical environments to prevent and remediate attacks. It provides the credible security intelligence that IT security staff needs and removes the challenge of having to sift through independent reports that are increasing by the day based on thousands of threats and vulnerabilities taking their toll on networks around the world.

The Cisco SIAM Service filters through the multitude of alerts from reporting organizations to provide strategic targeted security intelligence that customers can use to proactively respond to potential IT threats. You can customize based on the following:

- How much information is sent

- Who receives the notifications

- How the notifications are sent

The Cisco SIAM Service is an important component of the Cisco Self-Defending Network and threat control and containment strategies, which use multiple layers of defense. Unlike antivirus solutions that focus only on network endpoints, the service provides a single, comprehensive clearinghouse for the latest threat and vulnerability information across the enterprise network.

The Cisco Security IntelliShield Alert Manager Service consists of the following:

- **Web Portal:** Serves as the customer interface. The portal is secure and completely customizable, allowing organizations to receive only information on the specific networks, systems, and applications used by the organization. Organizations can also configure the portal to send notifications using email, pager, cell phone, and SMS-capable devices. A real-time XML feed is also available that allows Cisco customers to integrate IntelliShield Alert Manager content into their own applications.

- **Back-End Intelligence Engine:** The infrastructure that collects threat data and takes each new threat and vulnerability report through a rigorous verification, editing, and publishing process. Cisco Security IntelliShield Alert Manager intelligence experts review and analyze each threat to confirm the threat characteristics and product information and deliver the alert in a standardized, easy-to-understand format. Each threat is objectively rated on urgency, credibility of source, and severity of exploit, allowing easier comparison and faster decision making. New threats and vulnerabilities can be updated several times as a situation evolves.

- **Historical Database:** One of the most extensive collections of past threat and vulnerability data in the industry. The fully indexed and searchable database extends back over six years and contains more than 1700 vendors, 5500 products, and 18,500 distinct versions of applications.

- **Built-In Workflow System:** Provides a mechanism for tracking vulnerability remediation. The system allows IT management to see which tasks are outstanding, to whom the task is assigned, and the current status of all remediation efforts.

- **Vulnerability Alert:** Uses the Common Vulnerability Scoring System (CVSS) industry-standard rating system. Organizations also have access to a CVSS calculator that provides the ability to adjust and personalize scoring metrics to generate a more accurate reflection of their individual environments.

- **Outbreak Alert:** Covers the latest data regarding web-based threats and malicious emails, including spam, phishing, and botnet activity. This new alert is an effort to continually enhance the value of the service delivered and provide customers with valuable content to stay current with the evolving threat landscape.

Now we will delve into the Cisco IntelliShield Alert Manager portal.

Home Page

After you successfully log in to the Cisco IntelliShield Alert Manager Service portal through https://intellishield.cisco.com using your username and password, you will be presented with your home page, which you can customize based on your requirements, as shown in Figure 19-6.

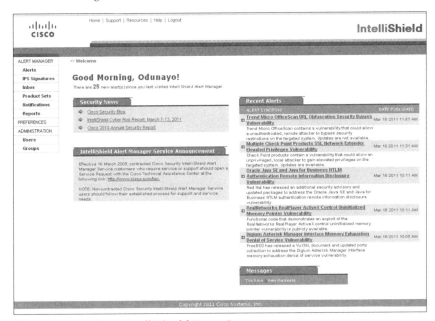

Figure 19-6 *Cisco IntelliShield Home Page*

The home page is divided into several areas, showing security news, recent alerts, messages, and a navigation page. There are also some useful links on the home page in these different areas, as described in Table 19-3.

Table 19-3 *Cisco IntelliShield Alert Manager Home Page Links*

Areas	Links and Description

Top Tab	These are root links, as they contain links to other functions within the page. They are located at the top of the page and lined up horizontally:
	
	■ **Home:** This link contains a URL that takes you to the home page.
	
	■ **Support:** This URL takes you to these two tabs:
	  ■ Contact Information: For the services you are subscribed to
	  ■ Frequently Asked Questions (FAQ)
	
	■ **Resources:** A list of security-related resources on Cisco.com, such as the SIO portal and online articles.
	
	■ **Help:** Online help.
	
	■ **Logout:** To manually exit IntelliShield Alert Manager. The inactivity logout occurs after 30 minutes.

Key Topic

Table 19-3 *Cisco IntelliShield Alert Manager Home Page Links*

Areas	Links and Description

Navigation Pane	Links to various Cisco IntelliShield Alert Manager screens reside here. It is located on the left of the page, and the screens are arranged vertically:
	
	■ Alert Manager:
	  ■ Alerts
	  ■ IPS Signatures
	  ■ Inbox
	  ■ Product Sets
	  ■ Notifications
	  ■ Reports
	■ Preferences
	■ Administration
	  ■ Users
	  ■ Groups

Security News	This section displays recent security-related topics on Cisco.com that are updated daily, such as the IntelliShield Cyber Risk Report and the Cisco SIO blog.
Recent Alerts	This section displays the five most recent IntelliShield alerts and includes the alert headline and a brief summary of the alert.
Messages	This section lists the number of new messages that have not been read in your inbox and can be accessed by clicking a new message.
Marketing Messages	This section is updated with recent marketing events.

Alerts

The Cisco IntelliShield alerts provide you with information pertaining to critical assets on your network and deliver information solely based on those assets to warn you against potential threats. This page, shown in Figure 19-7, contains alerts from May 2000, with over 20,000 alerts to date.

The Alerts page, which is accessed through **Alerts Manager** > **Alerts**, contains a list of alerts and a search menu with input fields. Table 19-4 outlines the fields in the alert list.

Table 19-4 *Alerts List Fields*

Alert List Field	Description
IntelliShield ID	The alert number that is automatically generated. There are no duplicate IDs.
Headline	A descriptive title of the alert.

Table 19-4   *Alerts List Fields*

Alert List Field	Description
Published EST	The date the alert was last published. You will also find the date the alert was originally published.
Version	The alert version number, which increases with published alerts.
Urgency, Credibility, and Severity	These show the importance or impact from an urgency perspective, how true the information is from a credibility point of view, and the severity.
Base, Temporal, and Version for CVSS	Base and temporal are only available for new or updated vulnerability alerts.
Notify	Click this link to access the Manual Notification page. From this page, you can notify security personnel about an alert and assign a task.
IPS Sig	This link provides information about specific IPS signatures related to the alert, if they exist.

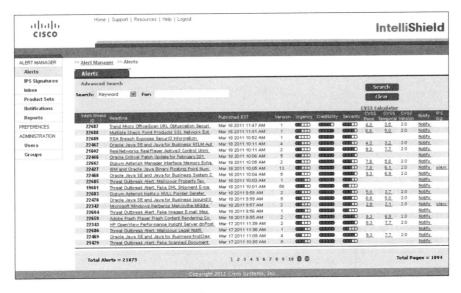

Figure 19-7   *Cisco IntelliShield Alerts Page*

To view the details of a particular alert, click the headline of the alert, which opens a separate browser window, at which time you will be at **Alert Manager > Alerts > Alerts Headline**. Clicking the headline with IntelliShield ID No. 22685, "Threat Outbreak Alert: "Malicious Property Tax E-mail Messages," pops up into an alert page providing more details on the alert, as shown in Figure 19-8 (which includes a sample email).

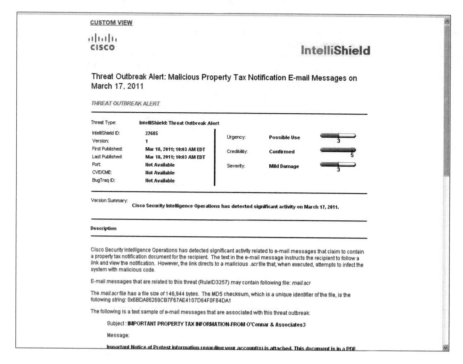

Figure 19-8 *Threat Outbreak Alert*

IPS Signatures

The Cisco IntelliShield Alert Manager Service also allows you to research Cisco IPS signatures; you can view the details, search for, and filter. The IPS Signature page is accessed through **Alert Manager > IPS Signatures**; it contains the fields listed in Table 19-5.

Table 19-5 *Cisco IPS Signature Fields*

IPS Signature Field	Description
Signature ID	Unique signature ID
Signature Name	Name describing the signature
Alarm Severity	Severity of the alarm produced by the signature
Release	Release designation
Release Date	Signature release date
Alert	Link to alert information related to signature

To view the signature details, click the signature name, and it will open in a new browser window, as shown in Figure 19-9.

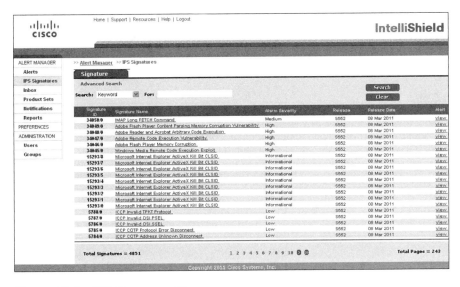

Figure 19-9 *IPS Signatures View*

Inbox

The inbox stores messages or tasks to be carried out on a particular alert. The tasks or messages can be sent manually from the Alerts page, or they can be set up as automatic notifications through the Notifications page. You can also add a task or message depending on your user role while in the inbox.

All users have access to a personal inbox, shown in Figure 19-10, where personal messages or assigned tasks are received. Group administrators have access to a group inbox, where group administrators can view messages and tasks for users within their group.

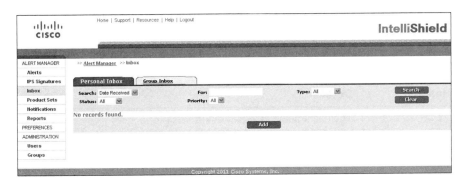

Figure 19-10 *Personal Inbox View*

To add a message or task to an inbox, follow these steps:

Step 1.   Click the inbox link in the left navigation pane.

Step 2. Click **Add** from either the Personal Inbox or the Group Inbox, depending on where you want the message to be sent.

Step 3. Complete all required fields.

Product Sets

The Cisco IntelliShield Alert Manager gives you the flexibility to choose to receive alerts that pertain to the products and applications on your network. These alerts are narrowed down to the specific products and are not generic.

The product sets can be accessed through **Alert Manager > Product Sets,** where you can search and filter out products and also generate a product set report (see Figure 19-11).

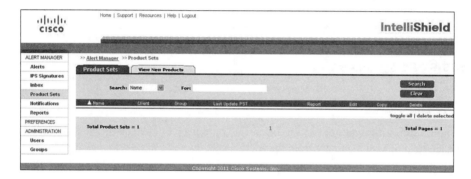

Figure 19-11 *Product Sets View*

The product set report is based on an individual product, which can be accessed by clicking the **Report** link to view the particular product set.

The product set report headings are outlined in Table 19-6.

Table 19-6 *Product Set Report Headings*

Report Heading	Details
Client	The client name associated with the product set
Group	The group name associated with the product set
Displayed On	The current date
Product Set	The name of the product set

To view the details of a particular product set, click the name of the product set, which takes you to the View Profile tab. This tab contains the information shown in Table 19-7.

Table 19-7 *View Profile Tab Details*

Advantage	Limitation
Client	The client name associated with the product set
Group	The group name associated with the product set
Product Set Name	The product set name
Date Created	The date the product set was created
Description	A brief summary of the product set type
Date Last Updated	When the product set was last updated

The included and excluded products in the product set profile are viewable in the inclusions and exclusions lists, respectively.

You can further customize the Cisco IntelliShield Alert Manager.

Follow these steps to add a product set:

Step 1.   Click the **Product Sets** link in the left navigation panel.

Step 2.   Click **Add**.

Follow these steps to add profile details:

Step 1.   Select a group from the Group drop-down list.

Step 2.   Type in the product name in the Product Set Name field.

Step 3.   You can type a brief description, which is optional.

Step 4.   Click **Save & Continue** to go to the next screen, or click **Cancel** to return to the product set list without saving your information.

Follow these steps to add products to a profile:

Step 1.   If you clicked **Save & Continue**, you will be on the Edit Profile Details tab, where you can add products to your product set.

Step 2.   Click the Add Products to Profile tab.

Step 3.   Select a product type.

Step 4.   Type in a name in the Vendor Name field. The field is not case sensitive.

Step 5.   Select **Starts With** or **Contains**:

- Choose **Start With** if you only know a partial name, and type in the first few letters of the vendor you are looking for.

- If you only know a few letters within the name, select **Contains**, which is the default selection.

Step 6.   Type a name in the Product Name field. The field is not case sensitive.

Step 7.   Click **Search**. The results of your search will appear in the Vendor list.

Step 8.   Click **Clear** to remove all search criteria.

Step 9.   After you have narrowed the search, you are ready to select the products to add to your product set, which must be added in the following order:

■ Vendor

■ Product

■ Version

■ Service Pack/Platform

Step 10.   Select a vendor by double-clicking the vendor name (you can select multiple vendors by pressing the Ctrl key as you select each one).

Step 11.   When you are done with the selections, click the View Profile Report tab.

Step 12.   Click **Back** to return to the Product Sets List page.

New Product Sets

Because of the dynamic trends of the industry and the need to upgrade existing products or add new products to meet demands and also take advantage of new features, the changes to the network and applications also need to be made within the Cisco Intelli-iShield Alert Manager to ensure that it delivers useful information consistently. To add new products to a product set, the product set must be in existence. Add or remove products from an existing set by following these steps:

Step 1.   Click the **Product Sets** link in the left navigation panel.

Step 2.   Click the New Product Released tab.

Step 3.   To include or exclude new products in an existing product set, select the following items in this order:

■ Group

■ Product Set

Step 4.   Select a group from the Group drop-down list.

Step 5.   Select a product set to include or exclude new products. The new and updated products are listed under the following headings:

■ Vendor

■ Product

■ Version Release

■ SP/Platform

■ Date Created

■ Include

■ Exclude

Select the Include or Exclude check boxes to add or remove a product.

Step 6.   Click **Submit** to save your changes, or click **Back** to return to the Product Sets List page without saving.

Notifications

Notifications can be set up within the Cisco IntelliShield Alert Manager Service to manually or automatically notify individuals. These notifications are set up based on certain thresholds, such as risk rating, and can be delivered in-band to your IntelliShield account or out-of-band through email to the inbox, pager, or cell phone. Access the Notifications page through **Alert Manager** > **Notifications**, as shown in Figure 19-12.

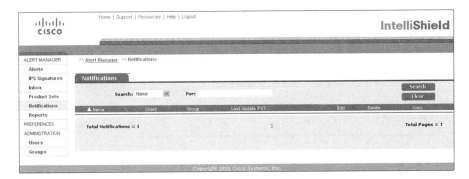

Figure 19-12   *Notifications View*

Follow these steps to create notifications:

Step 1.   Click the **Notifications** link in the left navigation pane and click **Add**.

Step 2.   Create a notification profile:

- Type in the notification name.

- Select a group from the Group drop-down list.

- Select whether you want the notifications to be active or inactive.

- Enter a default originating email address—for example, email@cisco.com.

- Enter a brief message in the Message field.

Step 3.   Select alert characteristics:

- Select the **Generate Notifications for All Alerts** check box if you want to receive all IntelliShield alerts. If this is chosen, other options are not necessary.

  or

- Select the **Generate Notifications by Alert Templates** check box to select required templates.

Step 4.   Select which notifications are sent using filters.

Step 5.   Select **Recipients**.

Reports

Reports are available within the Cisco IntelliShield Alert Manager Service for administrators to download for information on active products and delivered alerts. There are five report types available, as shown in Figure 19-13.

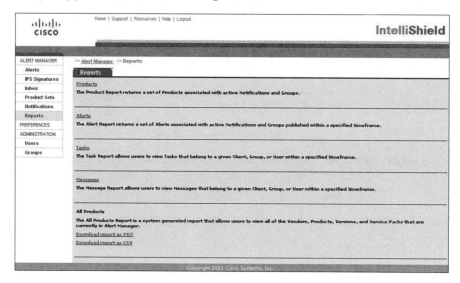

Figure 19-13   *Reports View*

The report types are described in Table 19-8.

Table 19-8   *Report Types*

Report Type	Description
Products	This report contains products that are generating notifications for a specified group or users; the report shows products with active notifications.
Alerts	This report contains alerts generating notifications for a specified group or user that are published within a specified time frame in association with active notifications.
Tasks	This report allows tasks that belong to a specified group or user in a specified time frame to be viewed by users.
Messages	This report allows users to view messages that belong to a specified group or user in a specified time.
All Products	This report allows users to view all the products in Alert Manager.

Preferences

The Cisco IntelliShield Preferences section allows you to change the following:

- User passwords

- Security questions

- Notification options

- Account information

Users

The Users section is where the IntelliShield account administrator can create users. There are two types of users:

- A registered user can log in to search the IntelliShield database and effect changes to groups and notifications.

- A virtual user does not have login credentials and can only receive notifications that a registered user has set up.

Groups

Cisco IntelliShield Alert Manager is group-based, and all users must belong to at least a group. Users can be members of multiple groups to inherit permissions of the different groups.

IntelliShield Alert Manager Service Subscription

The Cisco IntelliShield Alert Manager Service is subscription-based. However, there is a free 90-day trial and product information available on Cisco.com.

Summary

This section highlights the key topics discussed in this chapter:

- The Cisco IntelliShield Operations site is designed to provide detailed information and access to critical security-related information.

- The Cisco IntelliShield Alert Manager Service is a customizable threat and vulnerability service providing you with just the information you need based on the devices and applications you run in your organization.

- You can subscribe to receive the free Cisco IPS threat defense bulletins through email.

- A free 90-day trial of the Cisco IntelliShield Alert Manager is available on Cisco.com.

References

More information can be found at the following URLs:

Cisco Security Intelligence Operations, at http://tools.cisco.com/security/center/home.x.

Cisco Security IntelliShield Alert Manager Service, at www.cisco.com/en/US/products/ps6834/serv_group_home.html.

Cisco Security IntelliShield Alert Manager 90-Day Free Trial, at https://intellishield.cisco.com/security/alertmanager/trial.do?dispatch=4.

Cisco Security IntelliShield Demo, at www.cisco.com/warp/public/437/services/alertmgr/alertmgr_30daytrial.html.

Exam Preparation Tasks

Review All the Key Topics

Review the most important topics from the chapter, noted with the Key Topic icons in the margin of the page. Table 19-9 lists a reference of these key topics and the page numbers on which each is found.

Table 19-9 *Key Topics for Chapter 19*

Key Topic Element	Description	Page Number
Figure 19-2	Security Alerts	445
Table 19-2	SIO Best Practices Page	447
Figure 19-5	Threat Defense Bulletin	449
Table 19-3	Cisco IntelliShield Alert Manager Home Page Links	451

Complete the Tables and Lists from Memory

Print a copy of Appendix C, "Memory Tables" (found on the CD), or at least the section for this chapter, and complete the tables and lists from memory. Appendix D, "Memory Tables Answer Key," also on the CD, includes completed tables and lists to check your work.

Definitions of Key Terms

Define the following key terms from this chapter, and check your answers in the glossary:

Security Intelligence Operations (SIO), Cisco Security IntelliShield Alert Manager (SIAM)

642-627 IPS v7.0 exam topics covered in this part:

■ Optimize security functions, rules, and configuration

Part VI: Deploying Virtualization, High Availability, and High-Performance Solutions

This chapter covers the following topics:

- **Sensor Virtualization Overview:** This provides information on the virtual sensor and the benefit it brings to the network from a deployment standpoint.

- **Adding, Editing, and Configuring Virtual Sensors:** This section provides guidelines for configuring virtual sensors.

- **Verifying Virtual Sensor Operation:** This section provides the steps required to verify the proper operation of the virtual sensor after configuration.

CHAPTER 20

Using Cisco IPS Virtual Sensors

Overview

The Cisco Intrusion Prevention System (IPS) sensors allow the creation of multiple virtual IPS sensors within the same IPS hardware such that different policies can be applied to different groups of inline and promiscuous interfaces. This chapter focuses on configuring instances of virtual IPS sensors and describes how policies, signatures, and interfaces are applied to them.

"Do I Know This Already?" Quiz

The "Do I Know This Already?" quiz allows you to assess whether you should read the entire chapter. If you miss no more than one of these self-assessment questions, you might want to move ahead to the "Exam Preparation Tasks" section. Table 20-1 lists the major headings in this chapter and the "Do I Know This Already?" quiz questions covering the material in those headings so that you can assess your knowledge of these specific areas. The answers to the "Do I Know This Already?" quiz appear in Appendix A.

Table 20-1 *"Do I Know This Already?" Foundation Topics Section-to-Question Mapping*

Foundation Topics Section	Questions
Sensor Virtualization Overview	1–3
Adding, Editing, and Configuring Virtual Sensors	4
Verifying Virtual Sensor Operation	5

1. Which of the following does *not* support sensor virtualization?

   a. Cisco IPS 4240

   b. Cisco ASA SSP-10

   c. Cisco ASA AIP SSC-5

   d. Cisco IPS 4270

2. What is the maximum number of virtual sensors supported on devices that support virtualization?

a. 3

b. 10

c. 5

d. 4

3. Which of the following is *not* a benefit of sensor virtualization?

a. Applying different configurations to different traffic sets

b. Monitoring two networks with overlapping IP addresses

c. Persistent store is limited

d. Monitoring both inside and outside of a firewall or NAT device with the same sensor hardware

4. What policy or policies are required to be configured in a virtual sensor?

a. Signature policy

b. Event action rules policy

c. Anomaly detection policy

d. All of these answers are correct.

5. When a virtual sensor has been configured, what is the best way to ensure that it is working as configured?

a. Restart the virtual sensor

b. Delete the sensor and start again

c. Verify the configuration and operation

d. All of these answers are correct.

Foundation Topics

Sensor Virtualization Overview

The IPS sensor can receive data inputs from one or many monitored data streams. These monitored data streams can either be physical interface ports or virtual interface ports. A single sensor policy or configuration is applied to all monitored data streams.

A virtual sensor is a collection of data that is defined by a set of configuration policies and applied to a set of packets through groups of interfaces.

A virtual sensor can monitor multiple segments, and you can apply a different policy or configuration for each virtual sensor within a single physical sensor. You can set up a different policy per monitored segment under analysis. You can also apply the same policy to different virtual sensors and assign interfaces, inline interface pairs, inline VLAN pairs, and VLAN groups to a virtual sensor.

A virtualized IPS sensor allows you to have multiple IPS engines that are independent of each other but are able to share the same hardware. This feature is supported from version 6.0 of the software.

Note: The default virtual sensor is vs0 and cannot be deleted. You also cannot change its signature definition, event action rules, or anomaly detection policies.

Virtual IPS

The virtual IPS has many benefits. Foremost, it allows network security engineers to scale more as they can easily bring up another IPS sensor instance without physically adding new gear to the network. This is important, as this reduces the number of physical devices they have to manage. These sensors are alike and have the following information displayed:

- Virtual sensor name

- Assigned interface or pairs

- Signature definition policy

- Event actions rules overrides

- Anomaly detection policy

- Description of the virtual sensor

It is important to know that not all sensors support virtualization. Table 20-2 lists the Cisco IPS sensors that support virtualization, along with the number of contexts.

Table 20-2   *Cisco IPS Sensors Supporting Virtualization*

IPS Sensor	Number of Virtual Sensors
Cisco IPS 4240, 4255, 4260, and 4270	4
Cisco ASA AIP SSM-10, 20, and 40	4

Table 20-2 *Cisco IPS Sensors Supporting Virtualization*

IPS Sensor	Number of Virtual Sensors
Cisco ASA SSP-10, 20, 40, and 60	4
Cisco Catalyst 6500 Series IDSM-2 (does not support this on VLAN groups or inline interface pairs)	4

Note: AIM-IPS, NME-IPS, and AIP SSC-5 (for the ASA 5505) do not support multiple sensor instances. They have only the default sensor.

There are a number of benefits and restrictions imposed when running multiple sensor instances, as outlined in Table 20-3.

Table 20-3 *Benefits and Restrictions of Sensor Virtualization*

Benefits	Restrictions
■ You can apply different configurations to different sets of traffic. ■ You can monitor two networks with overlapping IP spaces. ■ You can monitor both the inside and outside of a firewall or NAT device with the same sensor hardware.	■ You must assign both sides of asymmetric traffic to the same virtual sensor. ■ Using VACL capture or SPAN is inconsistent with regard to VLAN tagging, which causes problems with VLAN groups. ■ Persistent store is limited.

Virtualization does have some issues with captures; there are some requirements to make sure that traffic captures work appropriately:

■ The virtual sensor must receive traffic that has 802.1q headers (other than traffic on the native VLAN of the capture port).

■ The sensor must see both directions of traffic in the same VLAN group in the same virtual sensor for any given sensor.

Adding, Editing, and Configuring Virtual Sensors

Before adding a sensor, it is best to carry out the following tasks:

■ Enable physical interfaces that you need to assign to the virtual sensor.

■ Optionally, create VLAN pairs or VLAN groups or both using these interfaces.

■ Create new policies that you will assign to the new virtual sensors that include the following:

■ Signature definition policy

■ Event action rules policy

■ Anomaly detection policy

The default signature policy is called Sig0. Any sensor that does not support more than one IPS sensor instance will have the Add option grayed out.

To add a virtual sensor, follow these steps:

Step 1.   Log in to Cisco IPS Manager Express (IME).

Step 2.   Choose **Configuration** > *sensor_name* > **Policies** > **IPS Policies**, and then click **Add Virtual Sensor**, as shown in Figure 20-1.

Step 3.   In the Virtual Sensor Name field, enter a name for the new virtual sensor.

Step 4.   In the Description field, enter a description for the new virtual sensor.

Step 5.   To assign the interface to the virtual sensor, select the check box next to the interface you need and click **Assign**.

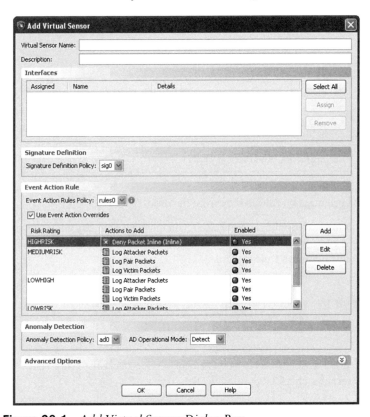

Figure 20-1   *Add Virtual Sensor Dialog Box*

Note: Only the available interfaces are listed in the interfaces list. If other interfaces exist but have already been assigned to a sensor, they do not appear in the list.

Step 6.   Choose a signature definition policy from the drop-down list.

Unless you want to use the default sig0, you must have already added a signature definition policy by choosing **Configuration** > *sensor_name* > **Policies** > **Signature Definitions** > **Add**, as shown in Figure 20-2.

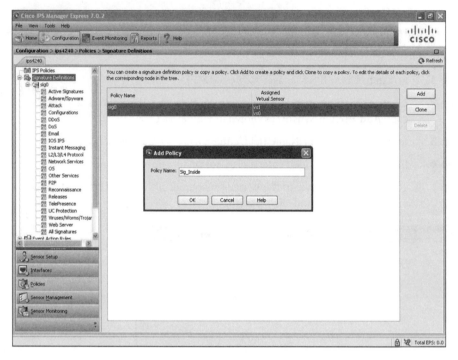

Figure 20-2 *Adding a New Signature Definition Policy*

Step 7. Choose an event action rules policy from the drop-down list.

Unless you want to use the default rules0, you must have already added an event action rules policy by choosing **Configuration** > *sensor_name* > **Policies > Event Action Rules > Add**.

Note: You must select the Use Event Action Overrides check box or none of the event action overrides will be enabled, regardless of the value you set.

Step 8. To add an event action override to this virtual sensor, select the **Use Event Action Overrides** check box and then click **Add**:

- Choose the risk rating from the Risk Rating drop-down list.

- Under the Assigned column, select the check boxes next to the actions you want to assign to this event action override.

- Under the Enable column, select the check boxes next to the actions you want to be enabled.

- Click **OK**.

Tip: To discard your changes and close the Add Event Action Override dialog box, click Cancel.

Step 9. Choose an anomaly detection policy from the drop-down list.

Unless you want to use the default ad0, you must have already added an anomaly detection policy by choosing **Configuration** > *sensor_name* > **Policies** > **Anomaly Detections** > **Add**.

Step 10. Choose the anomaly detection mode (Detect, Inactive, or Learn) from the drop-down list. The default is Detect.

Step 11. Click the double-arrow icon to change the default values under Advanced Options:

- Choose how the sensor tracks inline TCP sessions (by interface and VLAN, VLAN only, or virtual sensor). The default is virtual sensor, which is almost always the best option to choose.

- Choose the Normalizer mode (by strict evasion protection or asymmetric mode protection).

Tip: To discard your changes and close the Add Event Action Override dialog box, click Cancel.

Step 12. Click **OK**.

The virtual sensor appears listed in the IPS Policies pane, as shown in Figure 20-3.

The next step is to edit a virtual sensor. This is a two-step process:

Step 1. Select the virtual sensor in the list and click **Edit** through **Configuration** > *sensor_name* > **Policies** > **IPS Policies**, as shown in Figure 20-4.

Step 2. Make changes as needed and click **OK**.

The edited virtual sensor appears in the list in the upper half of the IPS Policies pane.

If a virtual sensor is no longer of use, it can be removed. This is a one-step process: Simply select the sensor and click **Delete**. The virtual sensor no longer appears in the upper half of the IPS Policies pane.

Click **Apply** to apply your changes and save the configuration.

Note: You cannot delete the default virtual sensor vs0.

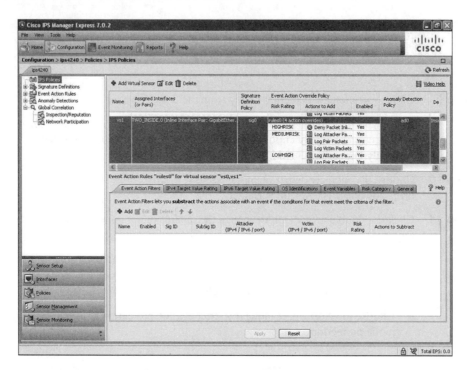

Figure 20-3 *Virtual Sensor in IPS Policies Pane*

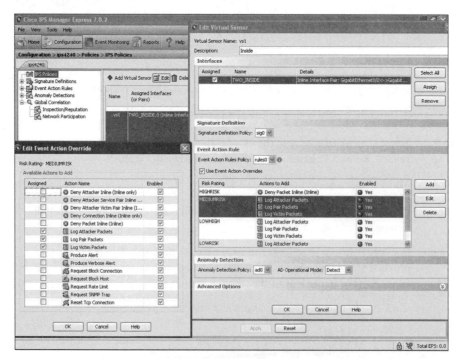

Figure 20-4 *Editing a Virtual Sensor*

Verifying Virtual Sensor Operation

After configuring devices generally, it is imperative that verification is done to ensure that all expectations are met and that the device operates as expected. This is one of the keys to excelling in configuration-based scenarios.

To verify a virtual sensor operation, you can do the following:

■ Verify interface configuration and virtual sensor assignment.

■ Verify virtual sensor statistics.

■ Verify alerts.

To verify the interface configuration and virtual sensor assignment, complete the following tasks:

■ Ensure that interfaces are enabled through **Configuration** > *sensor_name* > **Interfaces** > **Interfaces**, as shown in Figure 20-5.

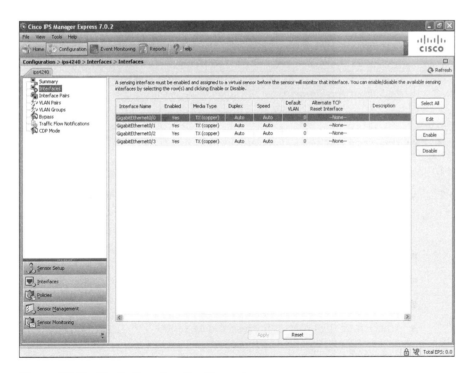

Figure 20-5   *Verify Interface Configuration*

■ Ensure that interfaces are properly configured.

■ Ensure that interfaces are assigned to the correct sensor through **Configuration** > *sensor_name* > **Interfaces** > **Summary**, as shown in Figure 20-6.

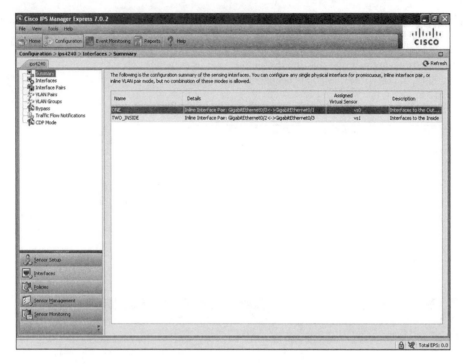

Figure 20-6   *Verify Sensor Assignment*

To verify the virtual sensor statistics, complete the following tasks:

Step 1.   Make sure that packet counters are increasing with traffic through the sensor.

Step 2.   Verify statistics through **Configuration** > *sensor_name* > **Sensor Monitoring** > **Support Information** > **Statistics**, as shown in Figure 20-7, to make sure that the values are increasing consistently:

■ Check for nonzero values.

■ Check total packets processed since reset.

■ Check total IP packets processed since reset.

■ Check total IPv4 packets processed since reset.

To verify alerts, complete the following tasks:

Step 1.   Check that alerts are being generated by the virtual sensor:

■ Enable signatures 2000 and 2004 for ICMP Echo Reply and ICMP Echo Request, respectively.

■ Ping an IP address that will make Internet Control Message Protocol (ICMP) traffic traverse the virtual sensor as the case might be.

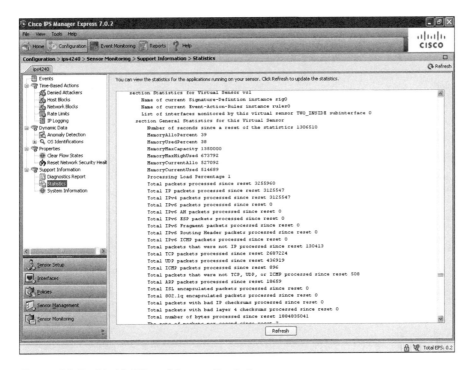

Figure 20-7   *Verify Virtual Sensor Statistics*

Step 2.   Navigate to **Configuration** > *sensor_name* > **Sensor Monitoring** > **Events** > **View**, as shown in Figure 20-8:

- In the viewer window, verify the signature IDs.

- Click **Details** to see the event details.

- Check that the correct sensor generated the event.

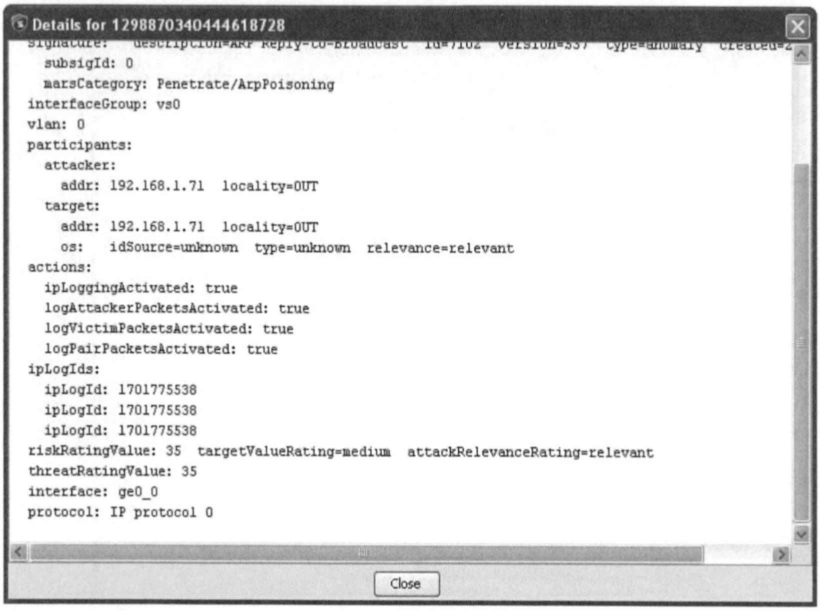

Figure 20-8   *Verify Alerts*

Summary

This section highlights the key topics discussed in this chapter:

■   The virtual IPS sensors mentioned in this chapter reside on physical sensors, and they are not virtual machines.

■   The virtual IPS sensor is a packet-processing policy whose engine has been virtualized.

■   All Cisco IPS sensors support virtualization except the Cisco ASA AIP SSC-5, AIM-IPS, and NME-IPS.

■   The IPS sensors that support virtualization support a maximum of four sensors.

■   You can separate signature sets, event rules, and anomaly detection policies for each virtual sensor.

References

More information can be found at the following URL:

Installing and Using Cisco IME 7.0 – Configuring Policies, at www.cisco.com/en/US/docs/security/ips/7.0/configuration/guide/ime/ime_policies.html#wp2003869.

Exam Preparation Tasks

Review All the Key Topics

Review the most important topics from the chapter, noted with the Key Topic icons in the margin of the page. Table 20-4 lists a reference of these key topics and the page numbers on which each is found.

Table 20-4   *Key Topics for Chapter 20*

Key Topic Element	Description	Page Number
Table 20-2	Cisco IPS Sensors Supporting Virtualization	469
Step list	Adding a Virtual Sensor	471
Paragraph	Verifying Virtual Sensor Operation	475

Complete the Tables and Lists from Memory

Print a copy of Appendix C, "Memory Tables" (found on the CD), or at least the section for this chapter, and complete the tables and lists from memory. Appendix D, "Memory Tables Answer Key," also on the CD, includes completed tables and lists to check your work.

Definitions of Key Terms

Define the following key terms from this chapter, and check your answers in the glossary:

virtual sensor, vs0, sig0, rules0, ad0

This chapter covers the following topics:

- **High-Availability Solutions for Cisco IPS Deployment:** This section covers the deployment guidelines for having Cisco IPS sensors operate in the redundant fashion.

- **Routing-Based Sensor High Availability:** This section provides deployment guidelines when routing is integrated into the sensor's high availability.

- **Cisco ASA-Based Sensor High Availability:** This section covers steps to take to ensure that the IPS sensors are highly available should one of the appliances experience failure; they will still continue to provide the service they were implemented for.

- **Cisco IPS Sensor Performance Overview:** This section provides information on the performance of IPS sensors from a throughput perspective as that is important to adequately scale the IPS for networks.

- **Increasing Performance Using Load Sharing:** This section provides information on how to improve sensor performance when the traffic is shared across multiple IPS sensors.

- **Increasing Performance Using Traffic Reduction:** This section provides information on how to improve sensor performance by ensuring that only critical traffic is being monitored.

CHAPTER 21

Deploying Cisco IPS for High Availability and High Performance

Overview

The Cisco Intrusion Prevention System (IPS) sensors are required to improve the security of the networks and also to provide a highly available service with adequate network performance. These factors are put into consideration when designing and deploying security networks as they must be fault tolerant and provide optimum performance.

"Do I Know This Already?" Quiz

The "Do I Know This Already?" quiz allows you to assess whether you should read the entire chapter. If you miss no more than one of these self-assessment questions, you might want to move ahead to the "Exam Preparation Tasks" section. Table 21-1 lists the major headings in this chapter and the "Do I Know This Already?" quiz questions covering the material in those headings so that you can assess your knowledge of these specific areas. The answers to the "Do I Know This Already?" quiz appear in Appendix A.

Table 21-1 *"Do I Know This Already?" Foundation Topics Section-to-Question Mapping*

Foundation Topics Section	Questions
High-Availability Solutions for Cisco IPS Deployment	1–5

1. What is the first thing you must do before deploying and configuring IPS sensors?

    a. Assign IP addresses

    b. Make sure that the network is running

    c. Ensure that there is a firewall

    d. Have a well thought-out design

2. What is the maximum number of IPS sensors supported on a switch in an EtherChannel bundle?

    a. 6

    b. 12

    c. 8

    d. 16

3. Which of the following does not enable sensor high availability?

    a. EtherChannel-based high availability

    b. Promiscuous mode–based high availability

    c. STP-based high availability

    d. Routing-based high availability

4. In what mode does an IPS sensor situate itself in the path of data traffic such that all the traffic passes through it?

    a. Horizontal mode

    b. Inline mode

    c. Promiscuous mode

    d. None of the answers are correct.

5. Which of the following are used to redirect traffic to the IPS sensor in promiscuous mode?

    a. VACL

    b. PBR

    c. SPAN

    d. All of the answers are correct.

Foundation Topics

High-Availability Solutions for Cisco IPS Deployments

High availability is an approach within a system design to limit or avoid service disruption when a component or groups of components fail.

Cisco IPS sensors are mostly deployed in inline mode because of the level of effectiveness at that level, where network traffic flows through the sensor for inspection and malicious packets are dropped. High-availability design options always need to be considered for critical network traffic, so if a failure occurs, traffic will be rerouted through a secondary sensor to provide the same or a comparable level of performance and security services.

Note: Cisco IPS sensors do not synchronize traffic session state information between themselves. However, when traffic is rerouted to a secondary Cisco IPS appliance, the secondary sensor will not drop packets of existing traffic sessions. The analysis engine will only analyze the network traffic of new sessions that are being established through the sensor. This behavior is different from the typical behavior of a Cisco firewall device in high availability.

Cisco IPS sensors can also be deployed in promiscuous mode, where network traffic is copied to the sensor. The original traffic does not flow through the sensor itself, and the sensor uses other devices for enforcement after it determines the packets it is receiving are malicious. If there is an IPS sensor failure, the original traffic flows unobstructed and uninspected, which can represent an undesirable level of risk. Having a secondary promiscuous sensor will ensure that the traffic is inspected at all times.

There are two general approaches to handling Cisco IPS sensor failures:

■   Using Cisco IPS bypass features

■   Using various failover techniques that use multiple redundant sensors

The software bypass features are supported by all Cisco IPS sensors where traffic is still being forwarded if there is a software (analysis engine) failure. There are some configuration-based dependencies when applying the software bypass and only one applies at a time. They are listed as follows:

■   Traffic always bypasses inspection and is never inspected (software bypass mode on).

■   Traffic will stop flowing through the sensor if the IPS sensor analysis engine is stopped or it fails (software bypass mode off).

■   Traffic flows through the sensor for inspection unless the analysis engine of the sensor is down. If the analysis engine is down, traffic continues to flow through the sensor but is not inspected (software bypass mode auto).

The auto mode is the recommended mode, depending on the level of risk that is acceptable in line with the security policy; this varies from organization to organization. In addition to software bypass, some Cisco IPS appliances with a four-port Gigabit Ethernet card

(Cisco IPS 4260 and IPS 4270) also support hardware bypass, which enables the card to forward traffic if the sensor hardware fails. When software or hardware traffic inspection bypass is on or active, network traffic is not being inspected and the sensor cannot address malicious or suspicious traffic, which implies that the network threat countermeasures are impaired and not effective.

Cisco IPS sensors are recommended to be deployed in a redundant fashion to satisfy high-availability requirements; however, certain mechanisms have to be in place for this deployment to be successful.

Note: Cisco IPS sensors do not support any native failover or clustering technology but rely on network mechanisms that are external to the IPS sensors to divert traffic from the primary to the secondary sensor upon failure.

The mechanisms include the following:

- **Routing-based sensor high availability:** Network routers and their routing protocols verify sensor health and are able to redirect traffic off a failed sensor.

- **Cisco ASA adaptive security appliance–based sensor high availability:** The failover functionality can detect a failed Cisco IPS module in a Cisco ASA and appropriately redirect traffic to the redundant device.

Note: Cisco IPS sensors do not support automatic configuration replication between sensors. If the primary and secondary IPS sensors need to operate using identical configurations, the configurations must be replicated manually.

Switching-Based Sensor High Availability

Cisco IPS sensors appear transparent and behave as smart wires to other network devices. In this way, it is possible to deploy network-based high availability methods where devices connected to IPS sensors track their state and are able to reroute traffic in case of a sensor failure. When network switches are used to provide sensor high availability, you have two design options:

- **EtherChannel-based high availability:** Multiple sensors are connected to the same network switch in an EtherChannel bundle, and up to eight IPS sensors can be connected to the bundle, which then performs load balancing across all connected sensors.

- **STP-based high availability:** Multiple sensors are connected to multiple switches and multiple redundant paths are created, in which case Spanning Tree Protocol (STP) verifies these paths and reroutes traffic in case of a failure. Such STP-based high availability can also be extended to use per-VLAN load sharing if Per-VLAN Spanning Tree (PVST) is used.

Figure 21-1 depicts the logical connectivity for EtherChannel-based high availability and STP-based high availability, as explained previously.

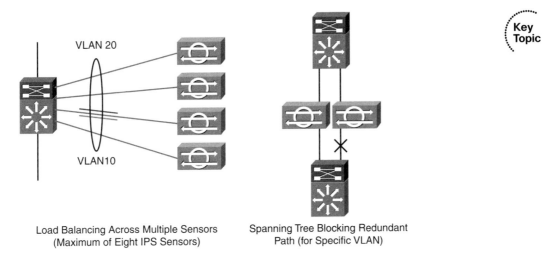

Load Balancing Across Multiple Sensors
(Maximum of Eight IPS Sensors)

Spanning Tree Blocking Redundant
Path (for Specific VLAN)

Figure 21-1 *Switching-Based High Availability Mechanisms*

EtherChannel-Based High Availability

EtherChannel bundling makes IPS sensors highly available and increases their aggregate throughput. While the sensors are all active, they are completely independent of each other and do not support any native active-active operation. With the bundling successfully done, it is important to know and guarantee the path through which traffic flows and to ensure that the flow is symmetric. If the flow is nonsymmetric, the Cisco IPS will analyze one-way traffic, which results in reduced security. It is very important to ensure that the same IP flow is always analyzed by the same sensor. To ensure that this is optimal, the IP source-destination-hash-based EtherChannel balancing algorithm is used. This load-balancing algorithm performs an exclusive OR (XOR) operation over the source and destination IP addresses of the flow and sends the traffic over the EtherChannel bundle. The resulting number determines the outgoing member link; therefore, the IPS sensor will analyze the packet and forward it in inline VLAN pair mode.

To configure the EtherChannel load-balancing algorithm, use the **port-channel load-balance src-dst-ip** command on the Cisco Catalyst switch in global configuration mode, and use the **show etherchannel load-balance** command to verify your configuration. The output of the **show** command is shown in Example 21-1.

Example 21-1 *EtherChannel Configuration Verification*

```
rack-6503# show etherchannel load-balance
EtherChannel Load-Balancing Configuration:
  src-dst-ip
  mpls label-ip
```

```
EtherChannel Load-Balancing Addresses Used Per-Protocol:
Non-IP: Source XOR Destination MAC address
 IPv4: Source XOR Destination IP address
 IPv6: Source XOR Destination IP address
 MPLS: Label or IP
```

Cisco IPS sensors must operate in inline VLAN pair mode or promiscuous mode when they are part of an EtherChannel bundle. The two modes are described in the following sections.

Inline Mode Redundant IPS Sensor Deployment Using a Single Switch

EtherChannel-based high availability (HA) for inline mode can be implemented using a single trunked LAN connection between the switch and each IPS sensor that is used for incoming and outgoing traffic. VLAN pairs will be configured on all links in the Ether-Channel bundle and all sensors that are attached to the switch. When traffic arrives at the switch, the EtherChannel load-balancing algorithm will determine the sensor to which traffic should be sent between the VLAN pair, ensuring symmetric forwarding.

In the event of a physical failure leading to bad ports on the switch or on the IPS sensor, that inline path is removed from the EtherChannel bundle. If there is a software failure, traffic could become black-holed, as there are no keepalives over links in the EtherChan-nel bundle. The Cisco IPS sensor, however, will automatically block traffic on their sens-ing network interfaces after their analysis engine fails as configured. This will allow the switch to sense the failure of the engine and remove the trunk port from the EtherChan-nel bundle.

Promiscuous Mode Redundant IPS Sensor Deployment Using a Single Switch

EtherChannel-based HA for promiscuous mode sensors can simply be achieved by con-necting multiple sensors to the EtherChannel ports and configuring the EtherChannel bundle as the destination Switched Port Analyzer (SPAN) or capture port. If the port on one IPS sensors fails, the traffic will continue to be sent to the EtherChannel bundle and the other IPS will continue to inspect the traffic being received; however, if the switchport fails, the EtherChannel will remove that link from the SPAN or capture destination bundle. Cisco IPS sensors in promiscuous mode will have no effect on network traffic when their analysis engine fails, as traffic will still continue to be sent to the EtherChannel bundle for inspection, but all traffic will go uninspected during that period.

EtherChannel-Based High-Availability Implementation Guidelines

When designing a Cisco IPS solution, it is important to consider the following so that the desired goal is met:

- You can use multichassis EtherChannel with switches that support stacking or virtu-alization. This way, the EtherChannel is not terminated on one switch alone, and if one member of the stack or virtual switch fails, the network traffic still continues to flow through the IPS sensors that are connected to the other members of the stack or other virtualized switch over the available EtherChannel bundle.

■ EtherChannel-based high availability is the recommend HA solution for IPS sensors because it also allows load sharing among up to eight IPS sensors. Load sharing is not easily achieved with other IPS HA or high-performance approaches. It is easy to determine the traffic path and flow when using EtherChannel as compared to STP and routing-based failover.

■ Traffic must be symmetrical so that an IPS sees an entire traffic flow, which ensures it sees everything completely; otherwise, the Cisco IPS will not see the complete traffic and cannot inspect it adequately, leading to reduced security. If traffic symmetry cannot be ensured, the IPS normalize mode could be set to asymmetric, which, however, is not recommended.

STP-Based High Availability

In STP-based high availability, multiple inline IPS sensors are installed along different paths where all the neighboring switches are configured to use STP. As stated earlier, inline IPSs are like smart wires: They are transparent to the switches, which allows them to be connected between two STP-capable switches forming multiple paths between different VLANs. STP will automatically block all paths between the two VLANs except one, which will have one IPS sensor in that path, as well as making that IPS sensor the active sensor. If this IPS sensor fails, this path will become blocked, and STP will recalculate the topology by selecting a path through one of the redundant sensors. Taking advantage of the nature of STP, port priorities can be configured on switches to make specific ports blocked ports to achieve a desired traffic flow and topology.

Devices participating must pass Bridge Protocol Data Unit (BPDU) frames between the switches as this carries information such as ports, costs, and priorities so that data ends up where it is intended. BPDU messages are also exchanged to detect loops in a network topology in which, when detected, certain ports are blocked so there is only one path. The Cisco IPS forwards Layer 2 multicast frames such as BPDUs, which are needed for the high-availability goal. Use of enhanced STP variants such as PVST+ and Rapid-PVST+ is recommended for faster switchover, which by default is in the order of tens of seconds with normal STP. PVST also allows some load sharing between IPS sensors, in which each sensor in a cluster can forward traffic for a distinct VLAN.

STP-Based High-Availability Implementation Guidelines

When designing a Cisco IPS solution using STP-based high availability, it is good to bear some guidelines in mind for a successful solution:

■ Deploy Rapid PVST+ to achieve faster switchover during failure situations, as classic STP operation results in longer switchover times.

■ Employ due care when tuning the STP parameters to achieve a desired STP operation, as errors could affect the network adversely.

- Spanning tree–based failover can be deployed when IPS sensors use
  - Inline interface pairs
  - Inline VLAN pairs
  - Inline VLAN groups

Note: Spanning tree–based failover cannot be used with IPS sensors with interfaces in promiscuous mode, as BPDUs need to be exchanged through the IPS sensors so that STP can adapt to topology changes should an IPS sensor fail.

Routing-Based Sensor High Availability

The routing-based high availability is another method to provide network-based HA. It is achieved by running a routing protocol over paths where the IPS sensors are installed in inline or promiscuous mode. This method can provide both active-active and active-standby HA, depending on how the routing protocol is configured.

When a routing protocol learns multiple paths to a specific destination network, the router chooses the path with the lowest metric to the destination. It will use the alternative route should the preferred route cease to exist, and this is the concept of *active-standby*, where the preferred route is through the primary IPS sensor and the alternative or less preferred route is through a secondary IPS sensor.

If the router receives multiple paths with the same metric to a destination network and installs them into its routing table, traffic will be load-balanced across the paths, in which case we would have an active-active scenario if we had an IPS sensor in each path.

The logical diagram in Figure 21-2 depicts the active-standby scenario, where traffic is going through a primary IPS sensor. It is in the path of the preferred route, and the metric has been modified to force the traffic through the preferred IPS sensor.

In the active-active scenario, however, the symmetry of traffic flow must be maintained, which is usually a huge challenge in routing-based high-availability designs. Alternatively, the IPS normalize mode could be set to asymmetric, but this is not recommended.

The active-active and active-standby IPS sensor HA scenarios are easily achievable because of the Cisco IPS sensor "smart wire" behavior, which forwards all the multicast and broadcast traffic required by the dynamic routing protocol to function properly.

Routing-Based Sensor High-Availability Implementation Guidelines

When designing a routing-based IPS sensor solution, it is important to bear the following guidelines in mind:

- The router has to run a routing protocol over redundant links where the IPS sensors are deployed.

- Routing protocol-based failover can be deployed when IPS sensors use the following:
  - Inline interface pairs

- Inline VLAN pairs (requires a routing protocol in each VLAN pair)
- Inline VLAN groups (requires a routing protocol in each VLAN)

Key
Topic

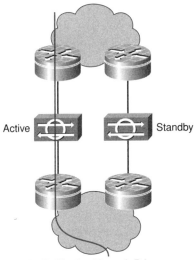

Active   Standby

Traffic Flowing Through Primary
Path with the Active IPS Sensor

Figure 21-2   *Routing-Based Sensor High Availability*

- Active-standby IPS sensor deployment is recommended because using the normalizer asymmetric mode should be avoided.

- Use routing protocols with fast convergence, such as Enhanced Interior Gateway Routing Protocol (EIGRP) or Open Shortest Path First (OSPF), when the options are available, to achieve desired switchover times.

Cisco ASA-Based Sensor High Availability

The Cisco ASA has a slot where it hosts the Advanced Inspection and Prevention Security Services Module (AIP SSM). When the Cisco ASA is configured in a failover cluster, it can also use the AIP SSM in it. In an active-standby Cisco ASA failover design, traffic always flows into and out of a single active Cisco ASA and its integrated AIP SSM, whereas in an active-active Cisco ASA failover design, both devices and their integrated AIP SSMs are processing traffic at the same time. The Cisco ASA periodically checks the health status of the IPS module using an internal heartbeat mechanism. When it detects a failure, the Cisco ASA declares itself as failed and is taken out of service by the failover mechanism. When this occurs, the standby Cisco ASA can take over in the case of an active-standby scenario or a single Cisco ASA continues to forward traffic in the case of the active-active scenario.

Figure 21-3 depicts two Cisco ASAs with integrated AIP SSMs in an active-standby deployment.

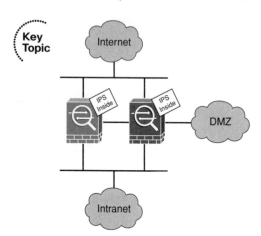

Figure 21-3 *Cisco ASAs with AIP SSM in High-Availability Configuration*

Note: The Cisco ASA AIP SSMs in the Cisco ASA have to be configured manually with identical configurations. They do not currently support configuration synchronization when in failover mode and are seen as 1 ASA + 2 IPS.

In the active-standby mode, the failover mechanism ensures that only one Cisco ASA is active and processes traffic so that the traffic flow is symmetric at all times. In the active-active Cisco ASA failover, the failover mechanism contains various functions to resolve possible asymmetric flows if they occur. Otherwise, traffic flows through the IPS modules, which are allowed to be symmetric while they operate at the same time and share the traffic load.

Note: The Cisco ASA AIP SSM does not use its TCP normalize code and does not completely track and enforce session state. Instead, the IPS module depends on the Cisco ASA to perform these functions and deliver a normalized stream to the AIP SSM.

Cisco ASA–Based Sensor High-Availability Implementation Guidelines

When designing a Cisco ASA-based IPS sensor solution, it is important to bear the following guidelines in mind. This HA solution is straightforward from a design and deployment perspective:

- When adding IPS modules into an existing Cisco ASA failover pair deployment, no topology changes are required because the IPS module connects internally to the Cisco ASA.

- Cisco ASA failover with IPS modules can be implemented as inline or promiscuous mode.

Cisco IPS Sensor Performance Overview

This section covers standalone performance characteristics of available sensor platforms. You can use these numbers, outlined in Table 21-2, to choose the optimal sensor based on your requirements.

Table 21-2   *Cisco IPS Standalone Performance Overview*

Model	Maximum Performance
IPS-SSP-60	10 Gbps
IPS-SSP-40	5 Gbps
IPS-SSP-20	3 Gbps
IPS-SSP-10	2 Gbps
IPS 4270	4 Gbps
IPS 4260	2 Gbps
IPS 4255	600 Mbps
IPS 4240	300 Mbps
IDSM-2	600 Mbps (single module)
AIP SSM-40	650 Mbps
AIP SSM-20	500 Mbps
AIP SSM-10	225 Mbps
AIP SSC-5	75 Mbps
NME-IPS	75 Mbps
AIM-IPS	45 Mbps

Performance Issues

When an IPS sensor is not adequately scaled for a network, it can lead to performance issues where the sensor, if in inline or promiscuous mode, can start to get overwhelmed because of the design issue. The events in Table 21-3 can take place if a sensor is not sized properly for a network.

Table 21-3 *Performance Issues*

IPS Sensors—Inline Mode	IPS Sensors—Promiscuous Mode
IPS sensor packet drop: This happens if the engine inspection capabilities are exceeded. The network is still secure because the packets are dropped and not forwarded, but the network can degrade because of retransmissions; thus, the IPS sensor can become a bottleneck.	**Span port capacity exceeded:** When this happens, the network switch can start to drop packets destined for the sensor; thus, the packets are not inspected by the IPS sensor. **IPS sensor packet drop:** In this case, the risk is higher as the packets are a copy of the original traffic flowing. If the packet is dropped by the IPS, the original packet continues without a copy being inspected, which could potentially be a malicious packet. However, a bottleneck is not created as the IPS sensor is not directly in the path of the data traffic.

Detecting Performance Issues

It is important to put measures in place to proactively detect performance issues early, before they start to degrade the network or expose it to risk. The following are some of the steps you can take to detect performance issues:

- Configure traffic flow notifications where the sensor is configured to monitor the flow of packets across an interface and send notifications if problems appear. You can configure the following:

  - **Missed Packets Threshold:** The percentage of packets that must be missed during a specified time before a notification is sent.

  - **Notification Interval:** The interval that the sensor checks for the missed packet percentage.

- **Display interface statistics:** You can also display interface statistics and missed packet percentage using the Cisco IDM, Cisco IME, or CLI.

- **Inspect performance-related gadgets:** You can manually inspect performance-related gadgets, such as

  - CPU, Memory, and Load Sensor gadget

  - Sensor Health gadget

- **Switch capture ports:** You should check SPAN or capture ports to detect dropped packets either manually or through Simple Network Management Protocol (SNMP).

Configuring Traffic Flow Notifications

The sensor can be configured to monitor the flow of packets across an interface and send notification if the packet flow changes, starts, or stops during a specified interval. To configure this within a notification interval and also configure the interface idle delay before a status is reported, follow these steps:

Step 1. Log in to Cisco IDM using an account with administrator privileges.

Key
Topic

Step 2. Navigate to **Configuration > Interfaces > Traffic Flow Notification.**

Step 3. Specify your desired value for the percentage of missed packets that will trigger a notification in the Missed Packets Threshold field.

Step 4. In the Notification Interval field, specify the interval during which the sensor will monitor missed packets and compare its results to the configured threshold.

Step 5. In the Interface Idle Threshold field, specify the number of seconds that an interface is allowed to be idle (not receiving packets) before a notification is generated.

Figure 21-4 shows the Traffic Flow Notifications pane, with fields being modified as described in Steps 1–5.

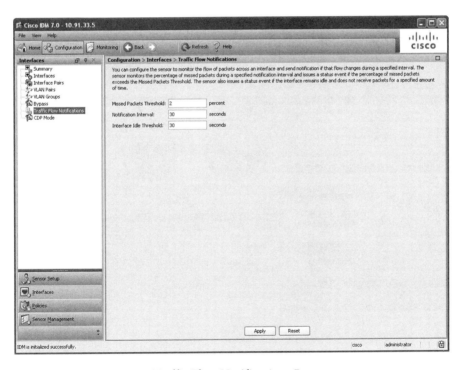

Figure 21-4 *Cisco IDM Traffic Flow Notifications Pane*

Inspecting Performance-Related Gadgets

The CPU, Memory, and Load gadgets can also be helpful when detecting performance issues. You can access the CPU, Memory, and Load gadgets using Cisco IDM through **Home > Health Dashboard > CPU, Memory & Load** or through Cisco IME through **Home > Device Details > CPU, Memory & Load.**

The gadget displays inspection load on a scale from 0 to 100 percent, and inspection load is affected by the following factors:

■ Rate of traffic needing inspection

■ Type of traffic that is being inspected

■ Number of active connections that are being inspected

■ Rate of new connections per second

■ Rate of attacks that are being detected

■ Signatures that are active on the sensor

■ Custom signatures that are created on the sensor

Periodically checking on the health of the IPS sensor through the gadgets will indicate possible performance issues; the steps to remediate them are discussed later in this chapter.

Figure 21-5 shows the Health Dashboard with IPS sensor gadgets, as previously described.

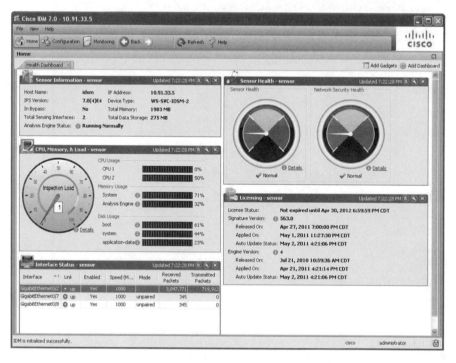

Figure 21-5 *IPS Sensor Gadgets*

You can also check whether an IPS sensor is dropping traffic by inspecting the Sensor Health gadget. Using Cisco IDM, navigate to **Home > Health Dashboard > Sensor Health**, and if you are using Cisco IME, go through **Home > Device Details > Sensor Health**. Click **Details** to view the missed packet percentage.

Checking Switch SPAN Interfaces for Dropped Packets

Packets can be dropped when they are being copied over a SPAN port to the sensing interface of a sensor if the traffic is too heavy when deployed in promiscuous mode. This goes back to ensuring that the IPS sensor is scaled adequately to meet the network demands. This also poses a security risk, as some packets will not be inspected by the IPS sensor, and they will be forwarded to their destinations undetected. This often occurs when multiple SPAN sources are sending captures to one destination port. On a Cisco switch, the **show monitor** command can be issued to determine which ports are the source and which port is the destination. After the destination port has been determined from the output of the command, issuing a **show interface** command for the specific interface will show interface statistics; the Total Output Drops statistic can then be examined to determine the severity of the issue.

Example 21-2 shows the output of the **show monitor** command showing the source and destination ports.

Example 21-2   show monitor *Command Output*

```
Switch# show monitor
Session 1
--------
Type      : Local Session
Source Ports   :
 Both    : Gi0/1
Destination Ports  : Gi0/2
 Encapsulation  : Native
   Ingress  : Disabled

Switch#
```

Example 21-3 shows the output of the **show interface** command for interface gigabitEthernet 0/2, which is the destination port.

Example 21-3   show interface *Command Output*

```
Switch# show interface gigabitEthernet 0/2
GigabitEthernet0/2 is up, line protocol is down (monitoring)
 Hardware is Gigabit Ethernet, address is 0018.7364.7102 (bia 0018.7364.7102)
 MTU 1500 bytes, BW 1000000 Kbit, DLY 10 usec,
  reliability 255/255, txload 1/255, rxload 1/255
 Encapsulation ARPA, loopback not set
 Keepalive set (10 sec)
 Full-duplex, 1000Mb/s, media type is 10/100/1000BaseTX
 input flow-control is off, output flow-control is unsupported
 ARP type: ARPA, ARP Timeout 04:00:00
 Last input 2w1d, output 00:05:08, output hang never
 Last clearing of "show interface" counters never
```

```
Input queue: 0/75/0/0 (size/max/drops/flushes); Total output drops: 0
Queueing strategy: fifo
Output queue: 0/40 (size/max)
5 minute input rate 0 bits/sec, 0 packets/sec
5 minute output rate 9000 bits/sec, 2 packets/sec
 489194 packets input, 162368075 bytes, 0 no buffer
 Received 424707 broadcasts (102782 multicasts)
 0 runts, 0 giants, 0 throttles
 0 input errors, 0 CRC, 0 frame, 0 overrun, 0 ignored
 0 watchdog, 102782 multicast, 0 pause input
 0 input packets with dribble condition detected
 6387456 packets output, 1934670598 bytes, 0 underruns
 0 output errors, 0 collisions, 0 interface resets
 0 babbles, 0 late collision, 0 deferred
 0 lost carrier, 0 no carrier, 0 PAUSE output
 0 output buffer failures, 0 output buffers swapped out
```

Scaling SPAN Sessions

The issue described previously can be remediated to improve the security of the network by configuring an additional SPAN session or configuring multiple interfaces.

To configure an additional SPAN session, you will map each SPAN source to a SPAN destination to reduce the SPAN source traffic. However, each new SPAN destination will require another port on the switch and on the IPS sensor. You can use the following steps as guidelines:

Step 1. Create an additional SPAN session:

- Assign some of the source SPAN interfaces from the existing SPAN session to the new SPAN session and as source interfaces.

- Assign an unallocated switch interface to the new SPAN session as a SPAN destination interface.

Step 2. Connect an unallocated IPS interface to the destination interface of the new SPAN session.

Step 3. Assign the IPS interface that was used in the previous step to the same IPS virtual sensor as the interface that is associated with the existing SPAN session.

After these steps have been carried out, the data is shared, which eliminates the possibility of dropped packets or reduces it to an acceptable minimum.

You can also configure multiple interfaces between the sensor and the switch, and bundle these interfaces into an EtherChannel bundle that is configured as a SPAN destination port. You must ensure that all the sensing interfaces are associated with the same IPS virtual sensor.

Increasing Performance Using Load Sharing

An effective way of increasing sensor performance is to use multiple sensors and distribute the traffic inspection task across all of them. The simplest and often most cost-effective option is to use EtherChannel load sharing with the help of a network switch and its EtherChannel traffic load-balancing algorithms. These same guidelines apply for EtherChannel Load Balancing (ECLB) high-availability designs (which were covered briefly in earlier parts of this chapter). However, we will be looking at ECLB in chassis-based deployments using the Cisco Catalyst 6500 Series switch and the Cisco Intrusion Detection Services Module (IDSM-2).

ECLB with Cisco Catalyst 6500 Series Switch and IDSM-2

ECLB can be implemented in the 6500 Series switch with the IDSM-2, as supervisor engines in the 6500 Series switch recognize IDSM-2 blades that are running Cisco IPS 5.x and greater as EtherChannel devices. This allows you to install up to eight IDSM-2 devices in the same chassis. The IDSM-2 and EtherChannel operate in three sensing modes:

- **EtherChannel and promiscuous mode:** The two data ports in the IDSM-2 operate independently of each other when the IDSM-2 is operating in promiscuous mode. If you configure the switch so that a data port has two or more IDSM-2 blades in a group, the switch distributes and thus balances the traffic between the modules. In the case where a data port goes to the err-disable state or if the IDSM-2 is shut down, powered down, or reset, the channel will have to be rebalanced.

- **EtherChannel and inline mode:** When you configure multiple Catalyst 6500 Series IDSM-2 devices for inline mode, you can load-balance the traffic between the modules by putting data port 1 of each IDSM-2 into one channel group and data port 2 of each IDSM-2 into another channel group.

- **EtherChannel and inline VLAN pair mode:** When the IDSM-2 is in inline-on-a-stick mode, the two data ports operate independently of each other. The same restrictions apply as for promiscuous mode.

Another load-sharing option is to split the network traffic using equal-cost routing (ECR) or dedicated load-balancing devices and install separate IPS sensors on each traffic path. This method reduces the amount of traffic that is monitored by each sensor. Policy-based routing (PBR) can also be used to split the traffic, but it is important that the traffic flows be symmetric. This load-sharing method using network splits can be cost-effective, but it is very complex and cumbersome to implement and might not be the best high-availability solution for your network.

Guidelines for Increasing Performance Using Load-Sharing Implementation

It is important to consider the following when implementing IPS sensor load balancing:

- EtherChannel IPS load balancing is easy to implement, and it provides high availability. It is a recommended solution when deploying IPS sensor HA.

- Load balancing across multiple network paths is more complex to implement when compared to ECLB, and it needs to be well thought out from a design perspective before implementing. It might require the use of a load balancer, such as the ACE module for the 6500 Series switch, or an external load balancer appliance, such as the Cisco ACE 4710.

Increasing Performance Using Traffic Reduction

Traffic reduction is improved by placing the IPS sensor closer to critical asset zones on the network. This varies from scenario to scenario, as the IPS sensor can either be deployed at the Internet edge, distribution, or core of the network switching infrastructure. Using the Internet edge as an example, placing the IPS sensor inline on the outside of the firewall will expose the sensor to a lot of irrelevant interactions and attacks from the Internet. Placing the IPS sensor on the inside of firewall will reduce the amount of traffic passing through the IPS. It is even possible that some of the attacks can be thwarted by the firewall, and the traffic reaching the IPS sensor inline is reduced.

The same applies to an IPS sensor in promiscuous mode, where traffic is spanned to the sensor. The IPS sensor will drop traffic if it gets overwhelmed, and some packets can go undetected, thus introducing some risk.

An example of optimizing sensor and network performance is to move sensors out of aggregate choke points where they analyze large amounts of traffic; they are usually centralized to network points closer to the resources that are being protected. This usually increases the number of sensors required to cover the new choke points, but each IPS sensor is analyzing specific low-volume traffic, which is easier to tune and operate.

Cisco ASA IPS Modules—Inline Operation

You can configure the ASA to only forward specific traffic to the AIP SSM or AIP SSC for inspection. This is achieved by using the Cisco Modular Policy Framework (MPF), where you can configure a Cisco ASA to selectively send traffic to the AIP module operating in inline or promiscuous mode. You can also specify that all traffic be inspected by the AIP module, and if the total traffic exceeds the IPS module inspection capacity, you can modify the MPF configuration in such a way that only critical traffic is inspected. This approach reduces the traffic the IPS module will have to analyze, and it is guaranteed to perform optimally.

Cisco ASA IPS Modules—Promiscuous Operation

A selective capture can also be used to ensure that only part of the traffic flowing through a Cisco ASA is sent to the AIP module in promiscuous mode. This way, the AIP module is not overwhelmed and critical data is analyzed.

The same concept applies when using the Cisco IPS Advanced Integration Module (AIM): When inline or in promiscuous mode, select traffic can be directed to it.

Cisco Catalyst Switches—VACL Capture

When an IPS is connected to a Cisco Catalyst switch, you can perform selective capture by setting the appropriate VLAN access control lists (VACL). The VACLs capture only a subset of traffic off the switch backplane and copy it to the sensor that is connected on a capture port, instead of a SPAN port. The sensor in this case only receives a copy of the packets that are suitable for analysis and completely ignores the rest of the traffic.

Summary

This section highlights the key topics discussed in this chapter:

- Before implementing an IPS sensor high-availability solution, it should be well thought out and should be as simple as possible.

- To achieve Cisco IPS sensor high availability, the following high-availability mechanisms should be considered:

  - Switching-based failover

  - Routing-based failover

  - Cisco ASA-based failover

- Performance issues and bottlenecks should be avoided by sizing the IPS sensors adequately and ensuring that the network topology design is a good fit.

- Load balancing and traffic reduction help improve the performance of a Cisco IPS sensor.

References

For additional information, refer to these resources:

Configuring IPS Bandwidth Using EtherChannel Load Balancing, at www.cisco.com/en/US/products/hw/vpndevc/ps4077/products_configuration_example09186a0080671a8d.shtml.

IPS Deployments in Enterprise Data Centers, at www.cisco.com/en/US/prod/collateral/vpndevc/ps5729/ps5713/ps4077/prod_white_paper0900aecd806e724b.html.

Configuring VACL Capture, at www.cisco.com/en/US/docs/security/ips/7.0/configuration/guide/cli/cli_idsm2.html#wp1181521.

Reference Documents (IPS Section), at www.cisco.com/en/US/docs/solutions/Enterprise/Security/SAFE_RG/appxA.html.

Exam Preparation Tasks

Review All the Key Topics

Review the most important topics from the chapter, noted with the Key Topic icons in the margin of the page. Table 21-4 lists a reference of these key topics and the page numbers on which each is found.

Table 21-4   *Key Topics for Chapter 21*

Key Topic Element	Description	Page Number
Figure 21-1	Switching-Based Sensor High Availability	485
Figure 21-2	Routing-Based Sensor High Availability	489
Figure 21-3	Cisco ASA with AIP SSM in High Availability	490
Table 21-3	Performance Issues	492
Step list	Traffic Flow Notification Configuration Steps	493

Complete the Tables and Lists from Memory

Print a copy of Appendix C, "Memory Tables" (found on the CD), or at least the section for this chapter, and complete the tables and lists from memory. Appendix D, "Memory Tables Answer Key," also on the CD, includes completed tables and lists to check your work.

Definitions of Key Terms

Define the following key term from this chapter, and check your answer in the glossary:

high availability

642-627 IPS v7.0 exam topics covered in this part:

- Optimize security functions, rules, and configuration

- Advanced Cisco IPS security software configuration fault finding and repairing

- Advanced Cisco IPS sensor and module hardware fault finding and repairing

Part VII: Configuring and Maintaining Specific Cisco IPS Hardware

This chapter covers the following topics:

- **Overview of the Cisco ASA AIP SSM and AIP SSC Modules:** This section provides information on the Cisco ASA IPS SSM and AIP SSC modules, including memory, flash, and the device models they fit into.

- **Initializing the Cisco ASA AIP SSM and AIP SSC Modules:** This section covers the steps required to install the IPS module hardware into the Cisco ASA or router and the configuration steps required to ensure that they can be managed after being successfully installed.

- **Redirecting Traffic to the Cisco AIP SSM and AIP SSC:** This section covers the configuration steps required to ensure that traffic is sent to the IPS so that it can be analyzed.

- **Troubleshooting the Cisco ASA AIP SSM and AIP SSC Modules:** This section covers configuration verification steps and provides direction to take when the IPS is not behaving as expected.

CHAPTER 22

Configuring and Maintaining the Cisco ASA AIP SSM Modules

Overview

The Cisco ASA 5500 Series Advanced Inspection and Prevention (AIP) Security Services Module (SSM) and Security Services Card (SSC) Module allow you to combine firewall services and intrusion prevention services in the same chassis. This solution is critical in helping organizations meet compliance mandates by securing critical assets and the network. This chapter focuses on the configuration and maintenance specific to the Cisco ASA IPS modules.

"Do I Know This Already?" Quiz

The "Do I Know This Already?" quiz allows you to assess whether you should read the entire chapter. If you miss no more than one of these self-assessment questions, you might want to move ahead to the "Exam Preparation Tasks" section. Table 22-1 lists the major headings in this chapter and the "Do I Know This Already?" quiz questions covering the material in those headings so that you can assess your knowledge of these specific areas. The answers to the "Do I Know This Already?" quiz appear in Appendix A.

Table 22-1 *"Do I Know This Already?" Foundation Topics Section-to-Question Mapping*

Foundation Topics Section	Questions
Overview of the Cisco ASA AIP SSM and AIP SSC Modules	1–4
Initializing the Cisco ASA AIP SSM and AIP SSC Modules	5–9
Redirecting Traffic to the Cisco AIP SSM and AIP SSC Modules	10–12
Troubleshooting the Cisco ASA AIP SSM and AIP SSC Modules	13

1. Which of the following is a benefit of implementing the AIP SSM or AIP SSC in such a way that all traffic passes through it?

   a. Original packets still flow to the intended destination.

   b. Original traffic is analyzed and stopped if it contains any malicious data.

   c. Original traffic is compressed to improve performance.

   d. All of these answers are correct.

2. How many modes can you configure the Cisco ASA AIP modules to operate in?

    a. 1

    b. 2

    c. 3

    d. 4

3. What are the names of the modes of operation that the Cisco ASA AIP operates in?

    a. Inline, outline, and parallel modes

    b. Outline mode only

    c. Inline mode only

    d. Inline and promiscuous mode only

4. The Modular Policy Framework and access control lists are used to redirect traffic to the AIP module in the Cisco ASA. True or False?

    a. True

    b. False

5. Which command is used when configuring the ASA 5505 with an AIP-SSC to allow a VLAN management access to the AIP SSC?

    a. nameif management

    b. allow-ssc-mgmt

    c. hw-module module 1 recover boot

    d. None of these answers are correct.

6. Which command is used to initiate the upgrade or recovery of the AIP mode?

    a. nameif management

    b. allow-ssc-mgmt

    c. hw-module module 1 recover boot

    d. None of these answers are correct.

7. Which command is used to set the parameters required before the upgrade of an AIP module can be carried out successfully?

    a. hw-module module 1 recover configure

    b. allow-ssc-mgmt

    c. hw-module module 1 recover boot

    d. None of these answers are correct.

8. Which command is used to initiate a session from the Cisco ASA to the AIP module through the CLI?

  a. telnet

  b. session 1

  c. rcp

  d. None of these answers are correct.

9. Which command is used to initiate a menu-driven configuration process to configure basic and advanced features of the AIP module through the CLI?

_____

10. What failure modes are available when configuring the AIP module?

  a. fail-safe

  b. fail-close

  c. fail-open

  d. None of these answers are correct.

11. What steps are required when configuring the Modular Policy Framework for use with an AIP module?

  a. Create a class of traffic that describes network traffic that is diverted to the AIP.

  b. Associate an IPS redirection policy with the class of traffic.

  c. Apply the policy to an interface or globally.

  d. All of these answers are correct.

12. What is missing from the Modular Policy Framework configuration?

```
policy-map outside-policy

ips inline fail-open
service-policy outside-policy interface outside
```

  a. access-list

  b. class (used to define the traffic class)

  c. access-class

  d. None of these answers are correct.

13. Which of the following is used to determine the software version of the AIP module in the Cisco ASA?

  a. show version

  b. show module

  c. show service-policy

  d. show running-configuration

Foundation Topics

Overview of the Cisco ASA AIP SSM and AIP SSC Modules

The Advanced Inspection and Prevention (AIP) Security Services Module (SSM) and AIP Security Services Card (SSC) are designed to provide additional security services to the Cisco ASA Firewall in the same chassis. The modules run a Cisco IPS software image, and although they can be configured in the same way as the standalone IPS appliance, they provide IPS services by internally redirecting traffic to the module.

The Cisco AIP SSM and AIP SSC can be configured using the Cisco ASA adaptive security appliance command-line interface (CLI), Cisco Adaptive Security Device Manager (ASDM), Cisco Security Manager (CSM), Cisco IPS Device Manager (IDM), and Cisco IPS Manager Express (IME).

Table 22-2 outlines the four types of advanced intrusion prevention security services modules/card available. Note that these are designed for specific Cisco ASA models.

Table 22-2 *Security Services Modules and Card*

Security Services Modules/Card	ASA Model
Security Services Card 5 (SSC-5)	ASA 5505
Security Services Module 10 (SSM-10)	ASA 5510
	ASA 5520
Security Services Module 20 (SSM-20)	ASA 5510
	ASA 5520
	ASA 5540
Security Services Module 40 (SSM-40)	ASA 5520
	ASA 5540

Figure 22-1 shows the AIP SSC module for the ASA 5505 on the left and the AIP SSM-10 for the ASA 5510 and ASA 5520 on the right. The AIP SSMs have the same form factor.

The AIP SSMs are designed to run without adding processor load to the CPU of the ASA but rather to offload some processing from the ASA. The AIP SSMs have dedicated hardware with flash-based memory, a CPU, RAM, and an out-of-band/1000 Gigabit Ethernet management interface (only on SSM modules).

Table 22-3 shows the hardware matrix with throughput of the various AIP SSMs, AIP SSC, and the Cisco ASA models that allow you to choose a particular combination or platform based on your needs.

Figure 22-1 *AIP SSC and AIP SSM*

Table 22-3 *Cisco ASA / AIP Hardware Matrix*

Module	RAM	Flash Memory	Throughput / ASA Model
SSC-5	512 MB	512 MB	75 Mbps – ASA 5505
SSM-10	1 GB	256 MB	150 Mbps – ASA 5510
			225 Mbps – ASA 5520
SSM-20	2 GB	256 MB	300 Mbps – ASA 5510
			375 Mbps – ASA 5520
			500 Mbps – ASA 5540
SSM-40	4 GB	2 GB	450 Mbps – ASA 5520
			650 Mbps – ASA 5540

Although the Cisco ASA AIP SSM and AIP SSC run the same code with the IPS 4200 Series appliance, there are a few features and functionality that set them apart. Table 22-4 compares the modules with the appliance.

Table 22-4 *Comparing the ASA AIP SSM, SSC, and IPS 4200 Series*

Features	AIP SSM	AIP SSC	IPS 4200 Series
Sensing interface	1	0	More than 1
Inline mode interface requirement	Does not require interfaces to be inline	Does not require interfaces to be inline	Requires at least two interfaces to be in inline mode
Inline VLAN pairs or inline pairs	Not supported	Not supported	Supported

Table 22-4 *Comparing the ASA AIP SSM, SSC, and IPS 4200 Series*

Features	AIP SSM	AIP SSC	IPS 4200 Series
Alternate TCP reset interface	Not supported	Not supported	Supported
Sensor virtualization	Supported from ASA code 8.0	Not supported	Supported
Console access	Not supported	Not supported	Supported
Command-line execution	Through Cisco ASA	Through Cisco ASA	Directly
Clock settings	Automatically synchronize with ASA clock	Automatically synchronize with ASA clock	Configured manually
Clock set command	Not supported	Not supported	Supported

Inline Operation

The Cisco ASA AIP modules can operate in one of two possible modes: inline or promiscuous.

The AIP SSM is usually deployed in inline mode. This mode ensures that all data flowing through the Cisco ASA goes through the AIP SSM. Therefore, any malicious packet will not successfully make it through the Cisco ASA to critical assets on your network without inspection by the Cisco IPS. Figure 22-2 depicts the topology of an AIP SSM in a Cisco ASA being inline.

You can configure a security policy on the Cisco ASA using the Modular Policy Framework (MPF) to identify traffic that should be redirected to the Cisco ASA AIP.

Figure 22-2 depicts the ASA with an IPS module in inline mode, where the sensor is in the path of traffic flowing through it.

Figure 22-3 depicts the ASA with an IPS module in promiscuous mode.

Promiscuous Operation

When deployed in promiscuous mode, the Cisco ASA AIP module is not directly in the path of traffic through the ASA. The Cisco ASA internally copies packets and sends a duplicate stream of traffic to the AIP module.

Although the AIP is not in the path of the traffic, the ASA must be able to allow traffic to be copied. That makes the diagram an unusual setup in that SPAN ports, hubs, and so on would need to be used with an ASA in transparent mode.

Like in the inline mode, you can configure a security policy on an adaptive security appliance, using the MPF class maps, to identify traffic that should be copied to the Cisco ASA AIP.

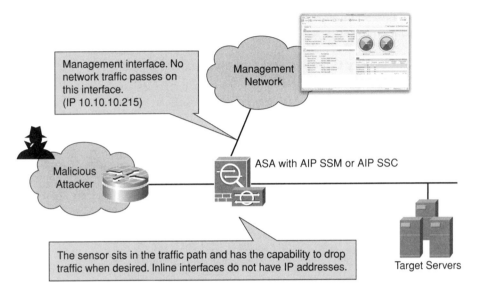

Figure 22-2 *IPS Inline Operation*

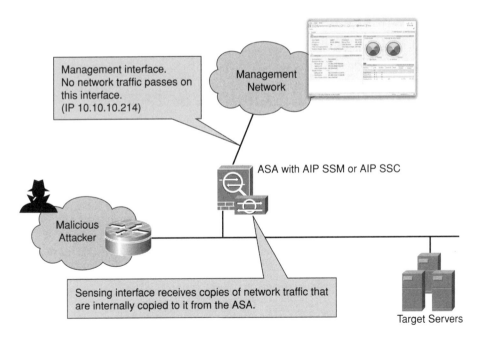

Figure 22-3 *IPS Promiscuous Operation*

Single-Mode Cisco ASA with Multiple Virtual Sensors

The Cisco ASA AIP SSM running software versions 6.0 and later can run multiple virtual sensors, which allows you to configure multiple security policies on the AIP SSM. You can assign each context or single-mode ASA to one or more virtual IPS sensors, or you can assign multiple security contexts to the same virtual sensor. The MPF configuration dictates which traffic flow is passed to which virtual sensor.

Cisco ASA with Security Contexts and Virtual Sensors

When security contexts are used, one or more contexts can be assigned to a virtual IPS sensor. Security contexts can share the same virtual sensor.

Deployment Guidelines—ASA AIP SSM and SSC

It is important to plan ahead when deploying the ASA AIP SSM and SSC. The following guidelines can help in the planning of the deployments:

■ Deploy Cisco ASA devices with AIP modules where an all-in-one security solution is needed.

■ Deploy configuration in line with security policy and best practices.

■ Deploy Cisco ASA redundant pairs with AIP modules for high availability.

■ Select appropriate Cisco ASA and AIP modules based on current and future traffic requirements, based on expected growth rate.

■ Redirect only high-risk traffic to the module, and if in doubt, redirect all traffic based on the zone in question.

■ Deploy AIP modules in inline mode by default to ensure stronger protection as malicious traffic is stopped while it goes through the IPS.

Initializing the Cisco ASA AIP SSM and AIP SSC Modules

The AIP SSM and AIP SSC are designed to provide additional security services to the Cisco ASA. The Cisco ASA might not come preinstalled with the AIP SSM or AIP SSC, and you might have to install the modules if ordered separately.

The following steps walk you through the hardware installation process

Step 1.   Power off the Cisco ASA.

Step 2.   Locate the ground strap kit and put it on your wrist; make sure that it touches your skin.

Step 3.   Remove the two screws at the left back end of the chassis, and remove the slot cover.

Step 4.   Insert the AIP into the slot.

Step 5.   Screw the AIP securely into the Cisco ASA chassis.

Step 6.   Power on the Cisco ASA.

Step 7.   Check the indicators. If the AIP SSM is properly installed, the POWER LED is solid green and the STATUS LED flashes green. If the AIP SSC is installed properly, the STATUS LED flashes green.

Step 8. Verify that the AIP is online by issuing the **show module** command.

Step 9. Initialize the AIP.

Step 10. Install the most recent software.

Step 11. Configure the AIP to receive traffic.

Apart from the LED indicators in Step 7, there are still other LEDs that are covered in the following table. These LEDs also help determine whether there are faults through visual inspection, in which we have more uses in the AIP SSM than in the AIP SSC. Table 22-5 shows the states of the AIP SSC LED indicators.

Table 22-5 *States of the AIP SSC LED Indicator*

LED	Color	State	Description
STATUS	Green	Flashing	The system is booting.
		Solid	The system has passed the power-up diagnostics.

As shown in Table 22-6, the AIP SSMs have more LED indicators and also have an Ethernet port for out-of-band (OOB) management.

Table 22-6 *States of the AIP SSM LED Indicators*

LED	Color	State	Description
PWR	Green	On	The system has power.
STATUS	Green	Flashing	The system is booting.
		Solid	The system has passed the power-up diagnostics.
LINK/ACT	Green	Solid	There is an Ethernet link.
		Flashing	There is Ethernet activity.
SPEED	Green	Solid	There is a 100-MB connection.
	Amber		There is a 1000-MB or 1-GB connection.
	Off		There is a 10-MB connection.

Apart from the external Ethernet connectivity that is available for OOB management, there is also an internal control channel and an internal data channel that facilitate configuration and connectivity to the data backplane within the ASA. Table 22-7 provides a breakdown of the channels.

Table 22-7 *Cisco AIP SSM and AIP SSC Data Channels*

Module	Channel	Description
AIP SSM	Internal control channel	10/100-Mbps interface used to access the module through the CLI through the Cisco ASA CLI

Table 22-7 *Cisco AIP SSM and AIP SSC Data Channels*

Module	Channel	Description
	Internal data channel	1-Gbps interface used to internally redirect packets that should be inspected by the module
	Out-of-band (OOB) management channel	Interface used for managing and updating the software on the module
AIP SSC	Internal control channel	10/100-Mbps interface used for management access and software updates
	Internal data channel	10/100-Mbps interface used to internally redirect packets that are to be inspected by the module

Initial Configuration of the AIP SSM and AIP SSC

In the last section, you learned about the hardware and management differences between the AIP SSM and AIP SSC. You learned that the AIP SSC has no OOB management interface, which makes it different from a hardware perspective and management perspective as well. In the following steps, you will see how the AIP SSC is configured and how it is set up for management.

By default, VLAN 1 in the ASA 5505 is enabled for the AIP SSC management, and only one VLAN can be assigned for such management. The VLAN is configured to access the internal management IP address of the AIP SSC over the backplane.

Note: The default management IP address on the Cisco ASA is 192.168.1.1/24.

Note: The management IP address, hosts, and gateway configuration are written to the AIP SSC configuration and not the Cisco ASA configuration. You can view these configuration settings from the Cisco ASA 5505 using the **show module details** command. You can also run the **setup** command from the AIP SSC CLI to configure the parameters.

The following list walks you through the initial configuration process of the AIP SSC:

Step 1. Log in to the Cisco ASA 5505, and enter privileged mode.

Step 2. Enter configuration mode by typing the following:
```
configure terminal
```

Step 3. Verify the current management interface. By default, this is VLAN 1.

Step 4. Allow the management of the AIP SSC from the management interface if different from VLAN 1:
```
interface VLAN number
allow-ssc-mgmt
```

Step 5. Configure the AIP SSC management interface:
```
hw-module 1 ip ip_address netmask gateway
```
Make sure that the address is on the same subnet as the Cisco ASA VLAN interface.

Step 6.   Set the hosts allowed to access the management IP address of the AIP SSC:

```
hw-module module 1 allow-ip ip_address netmask
```

Step 7.   Verify the settings:

```
show running-config
```

Step 8.   Exit and save the configuration.

Example 22-1 shows a sample configuration where VLAN 2 becomes the management VLAN.

Example 22-1   *Example AIP SSC Initial Configuration*

```
asa5505(config)# interface vlan 1
asa5505(config-if)# no allow-ssc-mgmt

asa5505(config-if)# interface vlan 2
asa5505(config-if)# nameif inside
asa5505(config-if)# ip address 10.10.10.214 255.255.255.0
asa5505(config-if)# security-level 100
asa5505(config-if)# allow-ssc-mgmt
asa5505(config-if)# no shutdown
asa5505(config-if)# management-only

asa5505(config-if)# hw-module module 1 ip 10.10.10.215 255.255.255.0 10.10.10.1
asa5505(config)# hw-module module 1 allow-ip 10.10.10.200 255.255.255.255

asa5505(config)# interface ethernet 0/1
asa5505(config-if)# switchport access vlan 2
asa5505(config-if)# no shutdown
```

The initial configuration steps for the AIP SSM are just about the same, except that in this case, you can just session into the AIP SSM and assign an IP address to the OOB interface. You can also type the **setup** command to go through the basic configuration:

Step 1.   Log in to the Cisco ASA.

Key
Topic

Step 2.   Session to the module:

```
session 1
```

You have 60 seconds to log in before the session times out.

Step 3.   Enter your username and password at the login prompt.

The default username and password are both cisco. You are prompted to change them the first time you log in to the module, and you are prompted for the new password twice for verification.

Step 4.   Go to configuration mode by entering the **configure terminal** command.

Step 5.   Enter the **service host** command.

Step 6.   Enter the **network-settings** command.

Step 7.   Enter the **host-ip** *ip_address/netmask, default_gateway* command:

`host-ip 10.10.10.214/24,10.10.10.1`

This assigns the IP, which in this case is 10.10.10.214 with a /24 netmask and a default gateway address of 10.10.10.1.

Step 8.   Verify the configuration using the **show settings** command.

Note: To suspend the AIP SSM session and return to the Cisco ASA CLI, press Ctrl-Shift-6-X.

Tip: These configuration steps can also be achieved using the **setup** command. This will walk you through the entire steps for basic and advanced configuration.

Software Update of the AIP SSM and AIP SSC

After you have successfully brought the AIP module online, the next step is to ensure that it is running the latest software so that you can take advantage of the improvements and features in the current release. Loading IPS software to the AIP SSM is a short process, as outlined in these steps:

Step 1.   Log in to the Cisco ASA.

Step 2.   Enter enable mode.

Step 3.   Specify recovery parameters using the **hw-module module 1 recover configure** command:

  ■ TFTP server IP and image filename and path

  ■ IP address of the module during the image transfer

  ■ Default gateway in cases when the TFTP server is more than a hop away

Step 4.   Enter the **hw-module module 1 recover boot** command to transfer the image from the TFTP server to the AIP and restart it.

Step 5.   Enter the **debug module-boot** command to monitor the download process.

Step 6.   Enter the **show module 1** command to check status at intervals.

Step 7.   Enter the **show module 1 details** command to view more detailed information.

Caution: If the AIP recovery needs to be stopped, you must issue the **hw-module 1 recover stop** command within 30 to 45 seconds after starting the AIP SSC recovery. Waiting any longer can lead to unexpected consequences.

The configuration steps and upgrade process for the AIP SSM in the Cisco ASA are shown in Example 22-2.

Check the status of the module by using the **show module** command to see the version of the IPS software on the AIP SSM.

Example 22-2 *Cisco AIP SSM and AIP SSC Software Update*

```
ciscoasa# show module

Mod Card Type Model Serial No.
--- -------------------------------------------------- ------------------- ------------
 0 ASA 5510 Adaptive Security Appliance ASA5510 JMX1233L1MK
 1 ASA 5500 Series Security Services Module-10 ASA-SSM-10 JAF1232AGKJ

Mod MAC Address Range Hw Version Fw Version Sw Version
--- -------------------------------------------- ------------ ------------- ----------------
 0 0021.d8cb.cae8 to 0021.d8cb.caec 2.0 1.0(11)4 8.0(5)
 1 0021.d871.886b to 0021.d871.886b 1.0 1.0(11)4 7.0(3)E4

Mod SSM Application Name Status SSM Application Version
--- -------------------------------- ---------------- --------------------------
 1 IPS Up 7.0(3)E4

Mod Status Data Plane Status Compatibility
--- ------------------- ---------------------- -------------
 0 Up Sys Not Applicable
 1 Up Up
```

Verify reachability to the server hosting the TFTP application or service and ensure that the service is running.

Tip: If a host-based firewall is running on the server hosting the TFTP application, ensure that UDP port 69 is allowed as this port is used by the TFTP service. The same applies if the upgrade is done across a network-based firewall. Finally, ensure that the TFTP service is running.

```
ciscoasa# ping 10.10.10.43
Type escape sequence to abort.
Sending 5, 100-byte ICMP Echos to 10.10.10.43, timeout is 2 seconds:
!!!!!
Success rate is 100 percent (5/5), round-trip min/avg/max = 1/1/1 m
```

Configure each parameter required using the context-sensitive help (?) if needed.

```
ciscoasa# hw-module module 1 recover configure ?

 gateway Configure gateway IP address
 ip Configure port IP address
```

```
url Configure image URL
vlanid Configure port vlan id
<cr>
```

```
ciscoasa# hw-module module 1 recover configure ip 10.10.10.214
ciscoasa# hw-module module 1 recover configure url tftp://10.10.10.43/IPS-
   SSM_10-K9-sys-1.1-a-7.0-4-E4.img
ciscoasa# debug module-boot
```

Use the **show history** command to verify what has been configured so far.

```
ciscoasa# show history
 enable
 show module
 ping 10.10.10.43
 hw-module module 1 recover configure ip 10.10.10.214
 hw-module module 1 recover configure url tftp://10.10.10.43/IPS-SSM_10-K9-
    sys-1.1-a-7.0-4-E4.img
 debug module-boot
 show history
```

Another option would be to use the menu-driven **hw-module module 1 recover config-ure** command to be prompted for the required configuration.

```
ciscoasa# hw-module module 1 recover configure
Image URL [tftp://10.10.10.43/IPS-SSM_10-K9-sys-1.1-a-7.0-4-E4.img]:
Port IP Address [10.10.10.214]:
VLAN ID [0]:
Gateway IP Address [0.0.0.0]:
```

To have the IPS image copied over to the AIP SSM, use the following command:

```
ciscoasa# hw-module module 1 recover boot
```

```
The module in slot 1 will be recovered. This may
erase all configuration and all data on that device and
attempt to download a new image for it.
Recover module in slot 1? [confirm]
```

```
ciscoasa#
Slot-1 0> Cisco Systems ROMMON Version (1.0(11)4)
#0: Fri Mar 21 17:35:35 PDT 2008Slot-1 1> Platform ASA-SSM-10
Slot-1 2> GigabitEthernet0/0
Slot-1 3> Link is UP
Slot-1 4> MAC Address: 0021.d871.886b
Slot-1 5> ROMMON Variable Settings:
Slot-1 6> ADDRESS=10.10.10.214
```

```
Slot-1 7> SERVER=10.10.10.43
Slot-1 8> GATEWAY=0.0.0.0
Slot-1 9> PORT=GigabitEthernet0/0
Slot-1 10> VLAN=untagged
Slot-1 11> IMAGE=IPS-SSM_10-K9-sys-1.1-a-7.0-4-E4.img
Slot-1 12> CONFIG=
Slot-1 13> LINKTIMEOUT=20
Slot-1 14> PKTTIMEOUT=4
Slot-1 15> RETRY=20
Slot-1 16> tftp IPS-SSM_10-K9-sys-1.1-a-7.0-4-E4.img@10.10.10.43
Slot-1 17>!!!!!!!!!!!!!!!!!!!!!!!!!!!!!!!!!!!!!!!!!!!!!!!!!!!!!!!!!!!!!!!!!!!!!!!!!!
Slot-1 18>!!!!!!!!!!!!!!!!!!!!!!!!!!!!!!!!!!!!!!!!!!!!!!!!!!!!!!!!!!!!!!!!!!!!!!!!!!
<truncated output>
.
.
.
Slot-1 105>!!!!!!!!!!!!!!!!!!!!!!!!!!!!!!!!!!!!!!!!!!!!!!!!!!!!!!!!!!!!!!!!!!!!!!!!!!
Slot-1 106> !!!!!!!!!!!!!!!!!!!!!!!!!!!!!!!!!!!!!!!!!!!!!!!!!!!!!!!!!!!!!!!!!!!!!!!!
Slot-1 107> Received 29435436 bytes
Slot-1 108> Launching TFTP Image...
Slot-1 109> Cisco Systems ROMMON Version (1.0(11)4)
#0: Fri Mar 21 17:35:35 PDT 2008Slot-1 110> Platform ASA-SSM-10
Slot-1 111> Launching BootLoader...

ciscoasa# show module

Mod Card Type Model Serial No.
--- ----------------------------------------------- ------------------ -----------
 0 ASA 5510 Adaptive Security Appliance ASA5510 JMX1233L1MK
 1 ASA 5500 Series Security Services Module-10 ASA-SSM-10 JAF1232AGKJ

Mod MAC Address Range Hw Version Fw Version Sw Version
--- ----------------------------------- ----------- ----------- ---------------
 0 0021.d8cb.cae8 to 0021.d8cb.caec 2.0 1.0(11)4 8.0(5)
 1 0021.d871.886b to 0021.d871.886b 1.0 1.0(11)4 7.0(4)E4

Mod SSM Application Name Status SSM Application Version
--- ------------------------------- ---------------- -------------------------
 1 IPS Up 7.0(4)E4

Mod Status Data Plane Status Compatibility
--- ---------------- -------------------- -------------
 0 Up Sys Not Applicable
 1 Up Up
```

The **hw-module module recover** command is a very important command in loading images to the AIP. Examples of the use have been provided in prior paragraphs and tables.
The syntax is **hw-module module 1 recover** {**boot** | **stop** | **configure** [**url** *tftp_url* | **ip**
port_ip address | **gateway** *gateway_ip_address* | **vlan** *vlan_id*]}.

Note: This would only be required for the initial installation of the IPS software. Subsequent updates should be installed as upgrades through the AIP interface using either the CLI or GUI to ensure that the configuration is not lost as in the previous process.

Basic Configuration of the AIP SSM and AIP SSC

After successfully updating the IPS software of the AIP, you can do a basic configuration of the AIP using the **setup** command, as shown in Example 22-3.

Example 22-3   *Basic Configuration Using the* **setup** *Command*

```
ciscoasa# session 1
Opening command session with slot 1.
Connected to slot 1. Escape character sequence is 'CTRL-^X'.


login: cisco
Password:
Last login: Mon Mar 28 05:18:42 on pts/0
***NOTICE***
This product contains cryptographic features and is subject to United States
and local country laws governing import, export, transfer and use. Delivery
of Cisco cryptographic products does not imply third-party authority to import,
export, distribute or use encryption. Importers, exporters, distributors and
users are responsible for compliance with U.S. and local country laws. By using
this product you agree to comply with applicable laws and regulations. If you
are unable to comply with U.S. and local laws, return this product immediately.

A summary of U.S. laws governing Cisco cryptographic products may be found at:
http://www.cisco.com/wwl/export/crypto/tool/stqrg.html

If you require further assistance please contact us by sending email to
export@cisco.com.

sensor# setup


 --- Basic Setup ---

 --- System Configuration Dialog ---

At any point you may enter a question mark '?' for help.
User ctrl-c to abort configuration dialog at any prompt.
Default settings are in square brackets '[]'.
```

```
Current time: Mon Mar 28 05:33:56 2011

Setup Configuration last modified: Mon Mar 28 05:21:46 2011

Enter host name[aipssm10]: aipssm10
Enter IP interface[192.168.1.2/24,192.168.1.1]: 10.10.10.214/24,10.10.10.1
Modify current access list?[no]: yes
Current access list entries:
Permit: 0.0.0.0/0
Permit:
Use DNS server for Global Correlation?[no]: yes

 DNS server IP address[]: 68.94.156.1
Use HTTP proxy server for Global Correlation?[no]:
Modify system clock settings?[no]: yes
 Modify summer time settings?[no]:
 Modify system timezone?[no]: yes
 Timezone[GMT-06:00]:
 UTC Offset[-360]:

 Use NTP?[no]:
Participation in the SensorBase Network allows Cisco to
collect aggregated statistics about traffic sent to your IPS.
SensorBase Network Participation level?[off]: full

If you agree to participate in the SensorBase Network, Cisco will
collect aggregated statistics about traffic sent to your IPS.
This includes summary data on the Cisco IPS network traffic properties
and how this traffic was handled by the Cisco appliances. We do not
collect the data content of traffic or other sensitive business or
personal information. All data is aggregated and sent via secure HTTP
to the Cisco SensorBase Network servers in periodic intervals. All data
shared with Cisco will be anonymous and treated as strictly confidential.
The table below describes how the data will be used by Cisco.
Participation Level = "Partial":
 * Type of Data: Protocol Attributes (e.g. TCP max segment size and
 options string)
 Purpose: Track potential threats and understand threat exposure
 * Type of Data: Attack Type (e.g. Signature Fired and Risk Rating)
 Purpose: Used to understand current attacks and attack severity
 * Type of Data: Connecting IP Address and port
 Purpose: Identifies attack source
 * Type of Data: Summary IPS performance (CPU utilization memory usage,
```

```
  inline vs. promiscuous, etc)
  Purpose: Tracks product efficacy
Participation Level = "Full" additionally includes:
  * Type of Data: Victim IP Address and port
  Purpose: Detect threat behavioral patterns


Do you agree to participate in the SensorBase Network?[no]: yes


The following configuration was entered.

service host
network-settings
host-ip 10.10.10.214/24,10.10.10.1
host-name aipssm10
telnet-option disabled
access-list 0.0.0.0/0
access-list 192.168.1.0/24
ftp-timeout 300
no login-banner-text
dns-primary-server enabled
address 68.94.156.1
exit
dns-secondary-server disabled
dns-tertiary-server disabled
http-proxy no-proxy
exit
time-zone-settings
offset -360
standard-time-zone-name GMT-06:00
exit
summertime-option recurring
offset 60
summertime-zone-name GMT-06:00
start-summertime
month march
week-of-month second
day-of-week sunday
time-of-day 02:00:00
exit
end-summertime
month november
week-of-month first
day-of-week sunday
time-of-day 02:00:00
exit
```

```
exit
ntp-option disabled
exit
service global-correlation
network-participation full
exit


[0] Go to the command prompt without saving this config.
[1] Return to setup without saving this config.
[2] Save this configuration and exit setup.
[3] Continue to Advanced setup.

Enter your selection[3]: 2
Warning: Global correlation inspection and reputation filtering have been disabled
because there is not a current license installed. Obtain a new license from
http://www.cisco.com/go/license.

--- Configuration Saved ---

Complete the advanced setup using CLI or IDM.
To use IDM, point your web browser at https://<sensor-ip-address>.

sensor#
```

Access the AIP SSM and AIP SSC Through the Cisco IDM or ASDM

After completing the basic configuration of the AIP SSM or AIP SSC, you can continue the configuration for the advanced setup through the setup menu or use Cisco IDM or ASDM. The Cisco ASDM uses the Cisco IDM to configure the AIP module, and it has to be running at least version 6.0. It is important that the basic configuration be completed before using the GUI as the AIP will only be reachable through an IP address following completion of the basic configuration. To access the Cisco IDM through the Cisco ASDM, click the Intrusion Prevention tab on the home pane. The IP address that is referenced by the AIP SSM Management IP Address field in the window refers to the IP address on the AIP SSM or AIP SSC module configured during the basic configuration setup dialog. The Cisco ASDM can only manage an AIP that is in the same chassis as the ASA.

At the prompt, enter the management IP address; specify the username and password and click **Continue** to start the IDM interface, as shown in Figure 22-4. You can also access the IDM directly by pointing your web browser to https://*sensor_ip_address*.

After you are logged in successfully, the Cisco IDM Health Dashboard pane appears, as shown in Figure 22-5.

The Health Dashboard provides a high-level view of the state of the sensor and almost looks like the Cisco IME presentation of the Health Dashboard. It also provides the information outlined in Table 22-8.

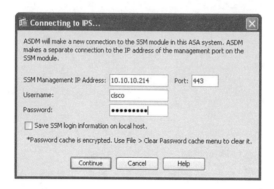

Figure 22-4   *Access the Cisco IDM Through the Cisco ASDM*

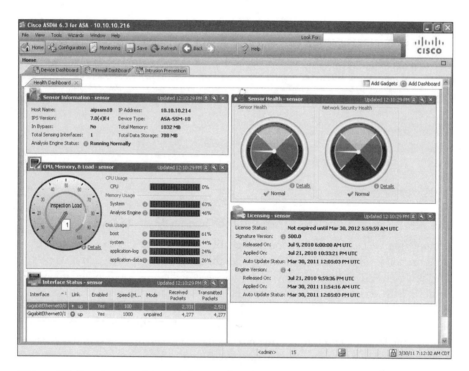

Figure 22-5   *IDM Health Dashboard Through ASDM*

Table 22-8   *Cisco IDM System Information*

System Information	Description
Sensor information	Displays the host name, the IPS software version, whether bypass mode is enabled or disabled, the IP address, the device type, the amount of memory, the amount of data storage, and the number of sensing interfaces.
System resources status	Displays the CPU and memory usage of the sensor.

Table 22-8   *Cisco IDM System Information*

System Information	Description
Interface status	Displays the status of the management and sensing interfaces. Choose the entry in the interface status table to view the received and transmitted packet count for each interface.
Sensor health status	Displays a graphical view of the health of the sensor. The Details link displays detailed information about the sensor.
Network security health	Displays a graphical view of network health. The Details link displays the number of alerts for each virtual sensor.
Licensing information	Displays information about the license on the sensor, signature, version, and engine version.

Just like you can customize the gadgets in Cisco IME, you can also customize the gadgets in Cisco IDM based on what you would like to be displayed. The gadgets that are available are as follows:

■ Global Correlation Reports

■ Global Correlation Health

■ Top Applications

■ CPU, Memory & Load

Redirecting Traffic to the Cisco ASA AIP SSM and AIP SSC Modules

After accessing the AIP module successfully, the next step will be to create a traffic redirection policy using the Cisco MPF on the Cisco ASA. The traffic redirection policy helps to choose which traffic streams you would like to pass to the AIP SSM or SSC for inspection and analysis. The traffic redirection policy can be configured using the Cisco ASDM or through the CLI.

The following tasks are required for a traffic redirection policy when configuring through the CLI:

■ Identify and create a class of traffic matching the network traffic to be passed on to the module.

■ Associate the class of traffic to an IPS redirection action in a policy.

■ Choose some modes in the policy:

   ■ Specify the mode of operation for traffic: Inline or promiscuous mode

   ■ Specify the mode on failure: Fail-close or fail-open mode

■ Apply the policy to an interface or globally to every interface.

The following steps configure redirection through the Cisco ASDM:

- Create a service policy rule.
- Identify and create a traffic class.
- Apply IPS redirection.

Traffic Redirection Policy Configuration Using the Cisco ASDM

This will be the first task from the Cisco ASDM mentioned in the previous bulleted steps that needs to be carried out. Follow these steps to create a new service policy using the Cisco ASDM:

Step 1. Click **Configuration** on the Cisco ASDM toolbar.

Step 2. Choose Firewall from the Navigation pane.

Step 3. Choose Service Policy Rules from the Firewall menu, and the Service Policy Rules menu is displayed.

Step 4. Click the Add drop-down box and choose Add Service Policy Rule.

Step 5. The Add Service Policy Rule Wizard opens.

Step 6. Click the **Interface** radio button to create a service policy rule for a specific interface, or click the **Global – Applies to All Interfaces** radio button to create a global service policy rule for all interfaces. In the following figure, the outside interface is selected.

Step 7. In the Policy Name field beneath the radio button, enter a name for the service policy rule.

Step 8. Click **Next**. The Traffic Classification Criteria page is displayed.

Figure 22-6 shows the Add Service Policy Rule window step of the Service Policy Wizard. In this phase, a new service policy is being created.

After the service policy rule has been created, the next step is to define a traffic class for the identified traffic. This is in the second step of the wizard, and it's a two-step process:

Step 1. Click one of the following radio buttons to determine how the traffic class criteria will be created:

Create a New Traffic Class: If you choose this option, you enter a name for the new class map in the Create a New Traffic Class field and select the check box that specifies the traffic match criteria for the traffic flow. The criteria include the following:

- Default Inspection Traffic
- Source and Destination IP Address (uses ACL)
- Tunnel Group
- TCP or UDP Destination Port
- RTP Range
- IP Diffserv Code Points (DSCP)
- IP Precedence
- Any Traffic

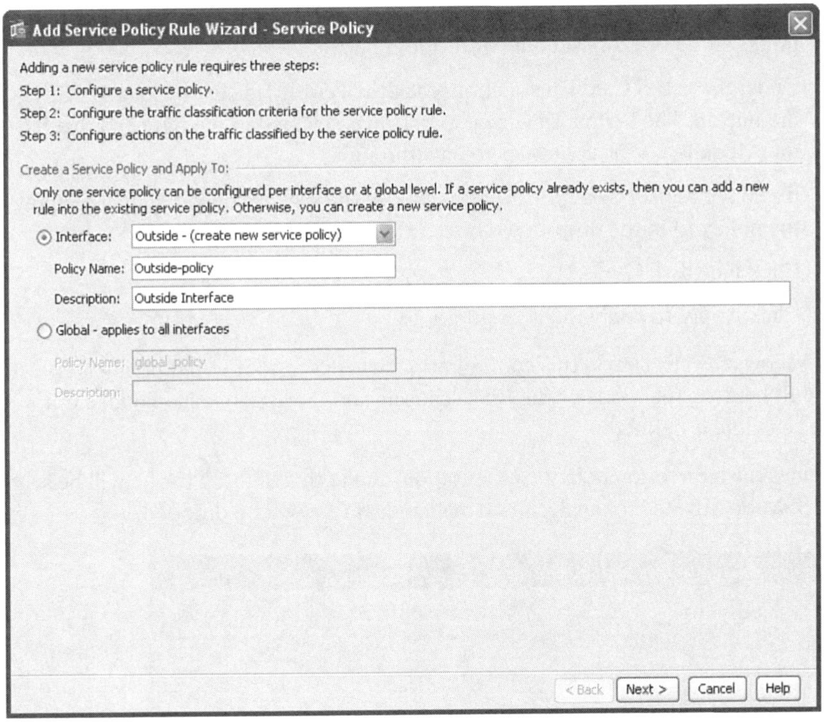

Figure 22-6 *Add Service Policy Phase Rule Step of the Wizard*

Use an Existing Traffic Class: If you choose this option, you will choose an existing class map from the drop-down list. If there is no class map defined, this option is not available.

Use Class-Default as the Traffic Class: If you choose this option, you will be matching all traffic. This is because it uses the class-default class. This class is created by default by the Cisco ASA and placed at the end of the policy. You can apply actions to this class if desired, and this option is chosen in Figure 22-7, which means that all traffic going into the ASA is redirected to the AIP for inspection.

Step 2. Click **Next** to advance to the last phase of this configuration wizard, which is the rule actions.

Figure 22-7 shows the wizard in the second step, where the traffic that is of interest is specified.

In the final phase of the configuration, you will be applying the redirection action to the traffic flow. Follow these steps to complete the configuration:

Step 1. Click the Intrusion Prevention tab.

Step 2. Select the **Enable IPS for this traffic flow** check box.

Step 3.   Under the Mode section, choose the operation mode by selecting either the Inline Mode or Promiscuous Mode radio button.

Step 4.   Under the If IPS Card Fails section, click the Permit Traffic or Close Traffic radio button. The Permit Traffic radio button is selected in the figure so that if the AIP fails, traffic continues to pass through.

Step 5.   In the IPS Sensor Selection section, choose the sensor you would like to apply the policy to in the drop-down box.

Step 6.   Click **Finish**.

Step 7.   Click **Apply** to apply the configuration.

Figure 22-8 shows the last step in this configuration, where the configured policy is applied to the IPS sensor, the mode of the IPS is chosen, and the action it should take if it experiences a failure is defined.

This concludes the redirection policy configuration, and at this time, all traffic will be sent to the AIP SSM or AIP SSC for analysis and malicious traffic will be dropped.

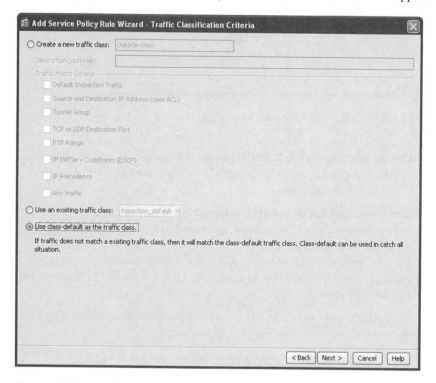

Figure 22-7   *Traffic Classification Criteria Phase of the Wizard*

Tip: To view the configuration in CLI format before it is applied to the device when using the ASDM, choose **Tools > Preferences > General** and choose **Preview commands before sending them to device**. This helps you learn the CLI syntax should you find yourself having to configure it through this method.

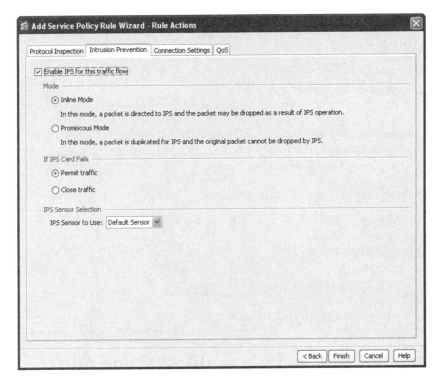

Figure 22-8   *Rule Actions*

Traffic Redirection Policy Configuration Using the CLI

Configuring the IPS redirection policy through the CLI is similar to the configuration through the Cisco ASDM. This is a five-step configuration process:

Step 1. Create a class map using the **class-map** command and specifying matching criteria. The class-default was used in the Cisco ASDM configuration step.

Step 2. Create a policy map using the **policy-map** command, and refer to the traffic class in Step 1 using the **class** command.

Step 3. For the class created in Step 2, specify the IPS redirection action using the **ips** command and also the operation mode: fail-open or fail-close.

Step 4. Apply the policy map to an interface or globally using the **service-policy** command.

Step 5. It is always good to save your configuration.

With the previous steps defined, the CLI configuration output follows. Example 22-4 shows how the configuration looks when configured through the Cisco ASDM.

Example 22-4 *Redirection Policy CLI Configuration*

```
policy-map outside-policy
 class class-default
 ips inline fail-open
service-policy outside-policy interface outside
```

The configuration will look a little different if the traffic being matched as defined using the **class-map** command is specified using an ACL and that was all you wanted to be redirected to the IPS. The configuration is shown in Example 22-5.

Example 22-5 *Redirection for Specific Traffic Using an ACL*

```
access-list out_mpc line 1 extended permit ip 0.0.0.0 0.0.0.0 host 11.0.0.129
class-map outside-class
 match access-list out_mpc
policy-map outside-policy
 class outside-class
 ips inline fail-open
service-policy outside-policy interface outside
```

Troubleshooting the Cisco ASA AIP SSM and AIP SSC Modules

It is very important to be able to verify and validate configuration after it is completed. Likewise, it is important to be able to troubleshoot issues that can arise because of hardware issues. The AIP SSM and AIP SSC modules run the same software as the 4200 Series IPS sensors, so the same troubleshooting methodology applies. There are, however, some procedures that differ for the AIP modules because they are hosted in another device chassis. The following steps are recommended when troubleshooting:

Step 1.   Verify that the module is reachable, and if it is, connect to the ASA and issue the **show module 1 details** command to ensure that the IPS services are operating correctly.

Step 2.   If the IPS is unreachable, you might consider resetting and reloading the AIP module.

When the reachability issues have been resolved, the next steps are as follows:

Step 3.   Verify the MPF configuration on the Cisco ASA and make sure that it is applied to the desired interface(s).

Step 4.   Check for Cisco ASA failover issues.

Following are some more troubleshooting commands:

■   hw-module module 1 reload

■   hw-module module 1 reset

- show module
- show module 1 details
- show service-policy ips
- show failover

Summary

This section highlights the key topics discussed in this chapter:

- The Cisco ASA can be configured in single mode with multiple virtual sensors.
- The Cisco ASA can have more than one security context assigned to a virtual sensor.
- Traffic redirection is configured using the Modular Policy Framework (MPF) and can be done using the Cisco ASDM or the CLI.
- The **session** command is used to connect to the AIP SSM module in the Cisco ASA for initial configuration.
- Use the **hw-module module 1 recover** command to load IPS software to the AIP SSM.

References

More information can be found at the following URLs:

Cisco ASA AIP SSM and SSC Datasheets, at www.cisco.com/en/US/prod/collateral/ vpndevc/ps6032/ps6094/ps6120/ps6825/product_data_sheet0900aecd80404916.html.

Cisco ASA AIP SSM and AIP SSC Installation Guide, at www.cisco.com/en/US/docs/ security/ips/6.0/installation/guide/hwSSM.html.

Configuring the Cisco AIP SSM / Intrusion Prevention System Sensor Using the Command Line Interface 7.0, at www.cisco.com/en/US/docs/security/ips/7.0/ configuration/guide/cli/cli_ssm.html.

Exam Preparation Tasks

Review All the Key Topics

Review the most important topics from the chapter, noted with the Key Topic icons in the margin of the page. Table 22-9 lists a reference of these key topics and the page numbers on which each is found.

Table 22-9 *Key Topics for Chapter 22*

Key Topic Element	Description	Page Number
Table 22-2	Security Service Modules and Card	508
Step list	Installing the Cisco AIP SSM and AIP SSC	512
Step list	AIP SSC Initial Configuration	514
Step list	AIP SSM Initial Configuration	515
Step list	AIP SSM and AIP SSC IPS Software Update	516
Step list	Creating a Service Policy Rule—Phase 1	526
Step list	Configuring Traffic Redirection Using the CLI	529

Complete the Tables and Lists from Memory

Print a copy of Appendix C, "Memory Tables" (found on the CD), or at least the section for this chapter, and complete the tables and lists from memory. Appendix D, "Memory Tables Answer Key," also on the CD, includes completed tables and lists to check your work.

Definitions of Key Terms

Define the following key term from this chapter, and check your answer in the glossary:

MPF

This chapter covers the following topics:

- **Overview of the Cisco ISR AIM-IPS and NME-IPS:** This section provides information on the two modules and lists their physical attributes, including their modes of operation, and compares them to the IPS appliance.

- **Initializing the Cisco ISR AIM-IPS and NME-IPS:** This section covers the steps required to physically install the modules in the routers and carry out the initial configuration to make sure that the module is reachable remotely.

- **Redirecting Traffic to the Cisco ISR AIM-IPS and NME-IPS:** This section covers the steps required to redirect traffic that is to be analyzed to the IPS modules.

- **Troubleshooting the Cisco ISR AIM-IPS and NME-IPS:** This section covers the steps and lines of action to take after configuration has occurred and the modules are not functioning as expected.

CHAPTER 23

Configuring and Maintaining the Cisco ISR AIM-IPS and NME-IPS Modules

Overview

The Cisco Intrusion Prevention System (IPS) Advance Integration Module (AIM) and Network Module Enhanced (NME) provide IPS services for Cisco Integrated Services Routers (ISR). This is to ensure that a level of security is maintained, even at the branches where the ISRs are deployed, thus improving the security of the network.

"Do I Know This Already?" Quiz

The "Do I Know This Already?" quiz allows you to assess whether you should read the entire chapter. If you miss no more than one of these self-assessment questions, you might want to move ahead to the "Exam Preparation Tasks" section. Table 23-1 lists the major headings in this chapter and the "Do I Know This Already?" quiz questions covering the material in those headings so that you can assess your knowledge of these specific areas. The answers to the "Do I Know This Already?" quiz appear in Appendix A.

Table 23-1 *"Do I Know This Already?" Foundation Topics Section-to-Question Mapping*

Foundation Topics Section	Questions
Overview of the Cisco ISR AIM-IPS and NME-IPS	1–4
Initializing the Cisco ISR AIM-IPS and NME-IPS	5–7
Redirecting traffic to the Cisco ISR AIM-IPS and NME-IPS	8
Troubleshooting the Cisco ISR AIM-IPS and NME-IPS	9–11

1. How many external interfaces does the AIM-IPS have?

   a. 1

   b. 3

   c. 2

   d. None

2. Which of the following is a router interface to the AIM-IPS?

   a. interface GigabitEthernet 0/0

   b. interface GigabitEthernet 0/1

   c. interface IDS-Sensor 0/**n** (where n is the slot number)

   d. None of these answers are correct.

3. What are the names of the modes of operation that the Cisco AIM-IPS and NME-IPS operate in?

   a. Inline, outline, and parallel modes

   b. Outline mode only

   c. Inline mode only

   d. Inline and promiscuous modes only

4. The AIM-IPS and NME-IPS modules do not require two interfaces to be inline. True or false?

   a. True

   b. False

5. Which command allows you to view all the modules installed in the Cisco ISR and the details including serial numbers and slot installed?

   a. show run

   b. show inventory

   c. show interfaces

   d. None of these answers are correct.

6. Which command is used to view the working condition of the AIM-IPS or NME-IPS?

   a. service-module ids-sensor 0/0 status

   b. service-module ids-sensor 0/1 session

   c. Answers A and B

   d. None of these answers are correct.

7. Which command is used to virtually console into the AIM-IPS or NME-IPS?

   a. service-module ids-sensor 0/1 telnet

   b. service-module ids-sensor 0/1 session

   c. service-module ids-sensor 0/1 ssh

   d. All of these answers are correct.

8. Which of the following is *not* a valid IPS service module command on a Cisco ISR?

    a. ids-service-module monitoring

    b. access-list

    c. ids-service-module capture

    d. None of these answers are correct.

9. What protocol is used by the router to monitor the status of the AIM-IPS and NME-IPS? _____

10. Which of the following does a router do when it stops receiving keepalives from the AIM-IPS or NME-IPS?

    a. Issues a reload to the IPS module

    b. Applies a fail-open or fail-close option

    c. Stops sending traffic to the module and sets the IPS module to the error state

    d. Monitors the module until the heartbeat is reestablished

    e. All of these answers are correct.

11. Which command is used to reset the password of an AIM-IPS or NME-IPS when the module is running from the bootloader?

    a. get password

    b. clear password

    c. password

    d. reset password

Foundation Topics

Overview of the Cisco ISR AIM-IPS and NME-IPS Modules

The Cisco ISR AIM-IPS is made for small- and medium-sized businesses (SMB) and small branch offices, whereas the NME-IPS is for small enterprises and large branch offices. The Cisco IPS Sensor Software running on the Cisco AIM-IPS and NME-IPS provides advanced, enterprise-class IPS functions to meet the ever-increasing security needs of branch offices.

The Cisco ISR AIM-IPS and NME-IPS can be configured using the ISR command-line interface (CLI), Cisco Security Manager (CSM), Cisco IPS Device Manager (IDM), and Cisco IPS Manager Express (IME).

Figure 23-1 shows a picture (from left to right) of the AIM-IPS and the NME-IPS.

Figure 23-1 *AIM-IPS and NME-IPS*

Table 23-2 shows the routers (ISR and ISR G2) supported by the AIM-IPS and the NME-IPS and some supported key features.

Table 23-2 *Cisco AIM-IPS and NME-IPS Router Support and Features*

Features	Cisco AIM-IPS	Cisco NME-IPS
ISR support	Cisco 1841 Router	Cisco 2811 Router
	Cisco 2801 Router	Cisco 2821 Router
	Cisco 2811 Router	Cisco 2851 Router
	Cisco 2821 Router	Cisco 3825 Router
	Cisco 2851 Router	Cisco 3845 Router
	Cisco 3825 Router	Cisco 2911 Router
	Cisco 3845 Router	Cisco 2921 Router
	(Only ISRs)	Cisco 2951 Router
		Cisco 3925 Router
		Cisco 3945 Router
Requires adapter card	No	Yes for ISR G2
Maximum performance	45 Mbps	75 Mbps
Monitoring interface	Backplane interface	Backplane interface
Management interface	Internal Gigabit Ethernet port	External Gigabit Ethernet port
Global correlation	Yes	Yes
Anomaly detection	Yes	Yes
Custom signature support	Yes	Yes
Virtual sensors	1	1

The Cisco AIM-IPS and NME-IPS have their own dedicated CPUs and DRAMs for all IPS functions. They offload the router CPU from processor-intensive tasks, such as deep packet inspection and analysis from the ISR/ISR G2.

Although the Cisco AIM-IPS and NME-IPS run the same code with the IPS 4200 Series appliance, there are a few features that set them apart. Table 23-3 highlights the similarities and differences among the AIM-IPS, NME, and 4200 Series appliance.

Table 23-3 *Comparing the AIM-IPS and NME-IPS with the IPS 4200 Series*

Features	AIM-IPS	NME-IPS	IPS 4200 Series
Inline mode interface requirement	Does not require interfaces to be inline	Does not require interfaces to be inline	Requires at least two interfaces to be in inline mode
Inline VLAN pairs or inline pairs	Not supported	Not supported	Supported

Table 23-3 *Comparing the AIM-IPS and NME-IPS with the IPS 4200 Series*

Features	AIM-IPS	NME-IPS	IPS 4200 Series
Alternate TCP reset interface	Not supported	Not supported	Supported
Sensor virtualization	Not supported	Not supported	Supported
Console access	Not supported	Not supported	Supported
Command-line execution	Through Cisco ISR	Through Cisco ISR	Directly
L3 interface monitoring	Supported	Supported	Supported

The Cisco AIM-IPS and NME-IPS can operate in one of two possible modes:

■   Inline

■   Promiscuous

Inline Operation

The AIM-IPS and NME-IPS are usually deployed in inline mode, where they reside in the data-forwarding path through the router; thus, malicious packets will first go through the IPS, where they are inspected, analyzed, and stopped.

You can configure monitoring for all traffic passing through the specific interfaces, or you can also define traffic to be monitored using an access control list (ACL).

Figure 23-2 shows a logical diagram with an ISR with an AIM or NME module installed and configured to be in inline mode.

Figure 23-3 depicts an ISR with an AIM-IPS or NME-IPS installed and configured to be in promiscuous mode.

Promiscuous Operation

When deployed in promiscuous mode, the Cisco AIM-IPS and NME-IPS are not in the path of traffic as in inline operation. The Cisco router internally copies packets and sends a duplicate stream of traffic to the AIM-IPS or NME-IPS module.

As in the inline mode, you can configure monitoring on the Layer 3 interface or specify traffic not to be monitored by defining the traffic using ACLs with permit statements.

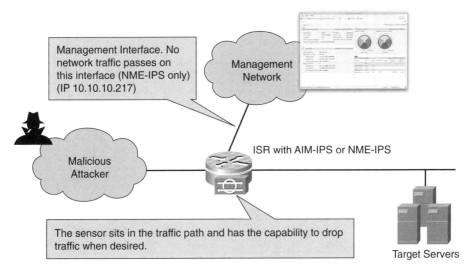

Figure 23-2 *IPS Inline Operation*

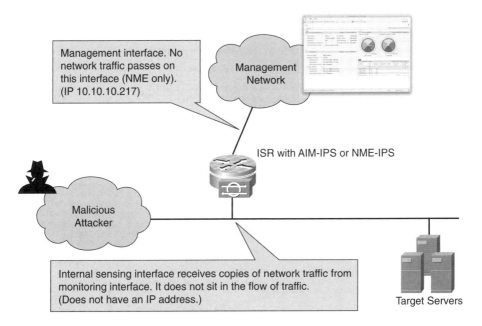

Figure 23-3 *IPS Promiscuous Operation*

AIM-IPS and Router Communication

The ISR has a backplane that facilitates communication between the AIM-IPS and the router. The following configurable interfaces are defined to facilitate such communication, including management and configuration as the case might be:

1. **IDS-Sensor 0/0 or 0/1:** This is the router interface to the AIM-IPS as is visible in the router configuration and configurable through the CLI. It is the logical interface

that the AIM-IPS uses to communicate with the router, as shown in Figure 23-4. Because there are two AIM slots in ISR routers, this could be 0/0 or 0/1.

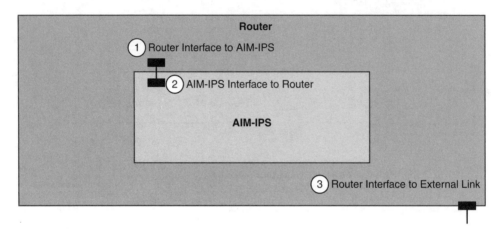

Figure 23-4   *AIM-IPS and Router Communication*

2. **GigabitEthernet 0/1:** This is the AIM interface to the router and acts as the sensing interface of the AIM-IPS. It is visible to the AIM-IPS module but not visible in the router configuration. This is the interface that is assigned to the virtual sensor in the module.

3. The Layer 3 interfaces of the router can be configured so that traffic flowing into and out of the interfaces can be inspected by the AIM-IPS.

NME-IPS and Router Communication

Similar to the AIM-IPS, the NME-IPS also has interfaces that it uses to connect to the backplane of the router for communication. In the ISR G2, the backplane is a Multi Gigabit Ethernet Fabric (MGF). The interfaces are as follows and are shown in Figure 23-5.

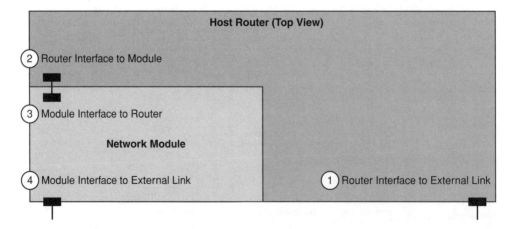

Figure 23-5   *NME-IPS and Router Communication*

1. The Layer 3 interfaces of the router can be configured so that traffic entering and leaving the interface can be inspected by the NME-IPS as well.

2. **ids-sensor n/0:** This is the router interface to the NME-IPS, where the number *n* is a designation of the router slot where the NME is located. This interface is configurable through the router CLI and visible in the router configuration.

3. **GigabitEthernet 0/1:** This is the NME-IPS interface to the router and acts as the sensing interface. It is visible to the NME-IPS but not to the router and is not in the router configuration. This is the interface assigned to the virtual sensor in the module.

4. **Management 0/1:** This is the NME-IPS external management interface. This interface can be assigned an IP address, netmask, and gateway using the **setup** command.

Initializing the Cisco ISR AIM-IPS and NME-IPS

You might be configuring an AIM-IPS or NME-IPS that is already in a router, and you might have to install the hardware itself and configure it. This section walks you through the entire process from the hardware installation to the basic configuration of the AIM-IPS and NME-IPS. The AIM-IPS is installed on the router motherboard, so the cover of the router has to be taken off to do that. The NME-IPS, on the other hand, is a module that is inserted into the slot of the router, so it is an easier process. Figure 23-6 depicts a view of the motherboard and the AIM-IPS being installed in Slot 1.

Follow these steps to install the AIM-IPS hardware:

Caution: Ensure that you wear an electrostatic discharge (ESD) preventive wrist strap, and make sure that it makes contact with your skin before installing the AIM-IPS or NME-IPS. Connect the equipment end of the strap to the router. Handle the AIM-IPS and NME-IPS at the edges only to prevent damage to its components.

Step 1.   Power off the router and disconnect the power cable from its power source.

Step 2.   Disconnect all network interface cables from the rear panel of the router.

Step 3.   Place the router on a flat surface, and use a Phillips screwdriver to remove the screws at the rear of the top cover. Set the screws aside in a safe place.

Step 4.   Lift the cover to a 45-degree angle and remove when it is free.

Step 5.   Install the machine-thread metal standoffs.

Step 6.   Insert the connector on the AIM into the connector on the motherboard.

Step 7.   Insert and tighten the machine-thread metal screws through the AIM into the metal standoffs.

Step 8.   Replace the cover and then reinsert and tighten the screws.

Step 9.   Reconnect all the cables removed previously.

Step 10.   Power on the router.

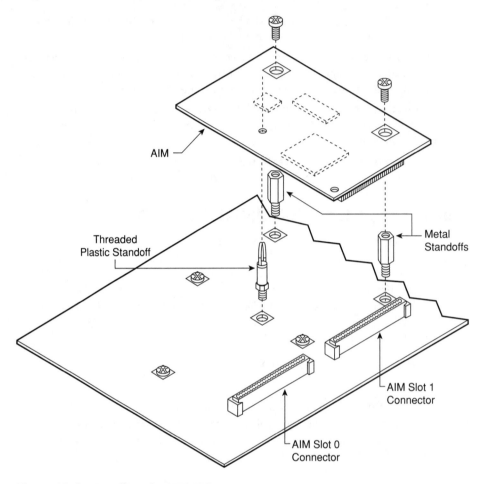

AIM

Threaded
Plastic Standoff

Metal
Standoffs

AIM Slot 1
Connector

AIM Slot 0
Connector

Figure 23-6 *Installing the AIM-IPS*

Installing the NME-IPS is a lot simpler than the AIM-IPS installation. Follow these steps to install the NME-IPS:

Note: The ISR G2 requires an adapter card for the NME-IPS to be installed. This is also stated in Table 23-2.

Step 1. Power off the router and disconnect the power cable from its power source.

Step 2. Disconnect network cables to ensure that you have access to the slot where you plan to install the NME-IPS.

Step 3. Remove the blank module panel from the chassis slot where you plan to install the NME-IPS.

Step 4. Align the NME-IPS with the guides in the router chassis, insert gently into the slot until it is inserted completely, and screw in place.

Step 5.   Reconnect all the cables removed previously.

Step 6.   Power on the router.

After the router has been powered on, it is important to ensure that the router has detected the module and lists the hardware in its inventory. The following steps walk you through some postinstallation commands:

Step 1.   Log in to the router.

Step 2.   Enter privileged EXEC mode by typing the **enable** command at the router prompt.

Step 3.   Verify that the AIM-IPS is part of the router inventory by issuing the **show inventory** command.

Step 4.   Verify the module status by issuing the **service-module ids-sensor 0/1 status** command (assuming that the AIM is in slot 0 and port 0) with the following output:

```
Service Module is Cisco IDS-Sensor0/1
Service Module supports session via TTY line 322
Service Module is in Steady state
Service Module is in fail close
Cisco Systems Intrusion Prevention System Network Module
  Software version:  7.0(4)E4
  Model:             AIM IPS
  Memory:            443508 KB
  Mgmt IP addr:      10.89.148.196
  Mgmt web ports:    443
  Mgmt TLS enabled:  true
```

Initial Configuration of the AIM-IPS and NME-IPS

The AIM-IPS and NME-IPS do not have external console ports, and the only way to access and carry out the initial basic configuration is through the host router CLI through a virtual console. Console access to the AIM-IPS or NME-IPS is enabled when you issue the **service-module ids-sensor** *slot/port* **session** command on the router.

The **session** command starts a reverse Telnet connection using the IP address of the IDS-Sensor interface. The IDS-Sensor interface is between the router and the AIM-IPS or NME-IPS. You can choose to make this not routable to eliminate security concerns. The recommendation is that you make it a nonroutable IP address so that the IPS is not exposed to threats because this is the virtual console. This is done by creating a loopback interface that is local to the router and configuring the IP address of the IDS-Sensor to be an unnumbered interface referencing the loopback interface. Follow these steps:

Step 1.   Log in to the router.

Step 2.   Enter privileged EXEC mode by issuing the **enable** command.

Step 3. Confirm the module slot number in the router using the **show run** command. You can use the **show run | include ids-sensor** command to get the information faster without having to go through the entire router configuration. The | and **include** are used to filter the configuration to list only lines with "ids-sensor."

Step 4. Create a loopback interface to be used as the unnumbered interface.

Step 5. Issue the **ip unnumbered interface loopback** *n* command, where *n* is the loopback interface number.

Step 6. Enter a route to send traffic to the IP address of the AIM-IPS or NME-IPS to the IDS-Sensor interface:

```
ip route sensor_ip_address 255.255.255.255 ids-sensor 0/1
```

Step 7. Session to the AIM-IPS or NME-IPS:

```
service-module ids-sensor 0/1 session
```

Step 8. Log in at the sensor login prompt with the default username and password.

Step 9. Issue the following commands to assign an IP address to the AIM-IPS or NME-IPS, or use the **setup** command:

```
configure terminal
service host
network-settings
host-ip ip_address/mask,gateway
exit
```

Step 10. Press **Enter** to apply the changes or enter **no** to discard them.

Step 11. Exit the session to the AIM-IPS or NME-IPS.

Step 12. After you are back to the router session, save your configuration.

Because the NME has an external interface for management, you can connect it to the network and manage it directly without going through the router after an initial IP address has been assigned.

Redirecting Traffic to the Cisco AIM-IPS and NME-IPS

After the initial configuration of AIM-IPS or NME-IPS has been completed, you can now move on to determining the traffic that you would like to monitor by following these steps:

Step 1. Log in to the router.

Step 2. Enter privileged EXEC mode on the router:

```
enable
```

Step 3. You can optionally configure a monitoring access list on the router:

```
access-list 101 permit tcp any eq www any
```

This is an access list for HTTP traffic.

Step 4.   Enable monitoring on the interface in either inline or promiscuous mode and associate the access list:

```
interface monitored_interface
  ids-service-module monitoring [inline | promiscuous]
access-list 101
exit
This controls what traffic is sent to the AIM-IPS or NME-IPS
```

Step 5.   For inline mode, specify how the router handles traffic inspection during a module failure:

```
interface ids-sensor 0/1
  service-module [fail-close | fail-open]
```

Step 6.   Exit and save your configuration.

Note: The default mode when the service module fails is fail-open.

To verify that traffic is being forwarded to the AIM-IPS or NME-IPS on the IDS-Sensor interface, execute a **show interfaces summary** command.

Troubleshooting the Cisco AIM-IPS and NME-IPS

The Cisco AIM-IPS and NME-IPS run the same software as the IPS 4200 Series sensors; thus, the same IPS troubleshooting commands are applicable. However, because of the form factors of the AIM-IPS and NME-IPS, there are some specific commands that are applicable only to the AIM-IPS and NME-IPS. These will be covered in the following sections:

■   Heartbeat Operation

■   Rebooting, Resetting, and Shutdown Procedures

■   Password Recovery Procedure

■   IPS Module Interoperability

Heartbeat Operation

To ensure the continuous operation of the AIM-IPS and NME-IPS in routers, the router exchanges certain keepalives with the module using the Router Blade Configuration Protocol (RBCP). If a failure occurs on the IPS module, the RBCP heartbeat responses do not return from the module to the host router. The router carries out the following actions to first try to restore the IPS service on the module that, when not successful, switches to the configured failure mode:

■   Router issues a **reload** command through RBCP to the IPS.

■   Router applies a fail-open or fail-close to the IPS as configured.

- Router stops sending traffic to the module and sets the IPS module to error state.

- Router continues to monitor the module until the heartbeat is reestablished.

In rare cases, the SensorApp can stop processing traffic, but the router will continue to receive RBCP keepalives from the AIM-IPS or NME-IPS application. In this case, packets are processed according to the bypass settings set on the AIM-IPS or NME. To reset the heartbeat of the AIM-IPS or NME-IPS, follow these steps:

Step 1.   Log in to the router.

Step 2.   Enter privileged EXEC mode on the router by typing **enable**.

Step 3.   Verify the status of the heartbeat reset by issuing this command:
```
service-module ids-sensor 0/1 status
```
The output will look like this:
```
Service Module is Cisco IDS-Sensor0/1
Service Module supports session via TTY line 322
Service Module is in Steady state
Service Module is in fail close
Cisco Systems Intrusion Prevention System Network Module
  Software version:  7.0(4)E4
  Model:             AIM IPS
  Memory:            443508 KB
  Mgmt IP addr:      10.89.148.196
  Mgmt web ports:    443
  Mgmt TLS enabled:  true
```

Step 4.   To disable the heartbeat on the AIM-IPS or NME-IPS, issue this command:
```
service-module ids-sensor 0/1 heartbeat-reset disable
```

Step 5.   To reenable the heartbeat on the AIM-IPS or NME-IPS, issue this command:
```
service-module ids-sensor 0/1 heartbeat-reset enable
```

Note: It helps to verify the *slot/port* number by viewing the configuration before configuring the IDS-Sensor.

Rebooting, Resetting, and Shutdown Procedures

You might have cause to reboot, reset, or shut down the AIM-IPS or NME-IPS module during a troubleshooting effort should it experience problems and you want to restore service. The following steps walk you through the process:

Caution: Data loss occurs only if you issue the **reset** command without first shutting down the AIM-IPS or NME-IPS.

Step 1. Log in to the router.

Step 2. Enter the privileged EXEC mode by issuing **enable**.

Step 3. To gracefully halt and reboot the operating system on the AIM-IPS or NME-IPS, issue this command:

```
service-module ids-sensor 0/1 reload
```

You are prompted whether you want to proceed with the reload. Press Enter to proceed.

Step 4. To reset the hardware on the AIM-IPS or NME-IPS, issue this command:

```
service-module ids-sensor 0/1 reset
```

The router will display a warning message, and you will be prompted whether you want to reset. Press Enter to proceed.

Step 5. To shut down applications running on the AIM-IPS or NME-IPS, issue this command:

```
service-module ids-sensor 0/1 shutdown
```

The following output is displayed after the command is executed:

```
Trying 10.10.10.217, 2129 . . . Open
%SERVICEMODULE-5-SHUTDOWN2:Service module IDS-Sensor1/0 shutdown
complete
```

Password Recovery Procedure

You might have cause to recover a password for the AIM-IPS or NME-IPS. This requires console access, which is basically issuing the **session** command from the router to the AIM-IPS or NME. The following steps walk you through the process:

Step 1. Log in to the router.

Step 2. Enter privileged EXEC mode.

Step 3. Confirm the AIM-IPS or NME-IPS module slot number in your router:

```
show run | include ids-sensor
interface IDS-Sensor0/1
```

Step 4. Session into the AIM-IPS or NME-IPS by issuing this command:

```
service-module ids-sensor slot/port session
```

Substituting for *slot/port* gives the following command:

```
service-module ids-sensor 0/1 session
```

Step 5. Press Ctrl-Shift-6-x to switch to the router CLI.

Step 6. Reset the AIM-IPS or NME-IPS from the router console by issuing this command:

```
service-module ids-sensor 0/1 reset
```

Step 7. Press Enter to return to the router console.

Step 8. When prompted for boot options, enter *** quickly.

You are now in the bootloader and the prompt changes:

```
ServicesEngine boot-loader#
```

Step 9.   Clear the password by issuing this command:

```
clear password
```

The AIM-IPS or NME-IPS reboots, and after it has rebooted, the password is reset to the default of username cisco and password cisco, which you can now change.

IPS Module Interoperability

You can have multiple WAN or Ethernet interfaces working at the same time in a router, but unfortunately the Cisco ISR supports only one AIM-IPS or NME-IPS (module) at a time. Thus, you cannot have two AIM-IPSs for high availability within the same router. The router sees the IPS modules in the following hierarchy:

- **First:** Cisco NME-IPS

- **Second:** Cisco AIM-IPS

- **Third:** Cisco NM-CIDS (which is now obsolete)

For example, if you install all modules, the NME-IPS will disable the other two modules, as it is the highest in the hierarchy. The AIM-IPS will do the same if it is the highest at the time in the hierarchy. If the modules are of the same capability, the first module to be discovered is enabled and others are disabled.

After a module has been disabled, you cannot bring it up, enable it, or configure it. To bring it up, you need to remove the more-capable module and restart the router (the router will be powered off to remove the module). Disabled modules are listed in the inventory of the router, though, and can be seen by issuing the **show diag** command; the state of the module is reported as disabled.

If the most capable module slot and port do not match the **interface ids-sensor** *slot/port* configuration command, the most capable module is disabled with the following warning:

```
The module in slot x will be disabled and configuration ignored.
```

The correct slot and port number are displayed so that you can change their configuration.

Summary

This section highlights the key topics discussed in this chapter:

- The Cisco AIM-IPS and NME-IPS provide IPS services for ISR routers.

- Both modules use the router backplane interface to monitor traffic.

- The modules do not have physical console ports, so you have to configure the IDS-Sensor interface to session into the IPS module.

- The modules can be in inline or promiscuous mode.

- When in inline mode only, you can configure bypass mode in the router configuration.

- Interface monitoring to capture traffic can be for promiscuous or inline mode.

- An access list can be used to specify the traffic to be sent for inspection by the IPS module.

- The Cisco ISR only supports one IPS module per router.

References

More information can be found at the following URL:

Installing Cisco Intrusion Prevention System Appliances and Modules 7.0, at www.cisco.com/en/US/docs/security/ips/7.0/installation/guide/hwguide7.html.

Exam Preparation Tasks

Review All the Key Topics

Review the most important topics from the chapter, noted with the Key Topic icons in the margin of the page. Table 23-4 lists a reference of these key topics and the page numbers on which each is found.

Table 23-4 *Key Topics for Chapter 23*

Key Topic Element	Description	Page Number
Table 23-2	Cisco AIM-IPS and NME-IPS Router Support and Features	539
Table 23-3	Comparing the AIM-IPS and NME-IPS with the IPS 4200 Series	539
Step list	AIM-IPS and NME-IPS Hardware Postinstallation Checks	545
Step list	Initial Basic Configuration of the AIM-IPS and NME-IPS	545
Step list	Configuring Monitoring on the Router Interface	546
Step list	Heartbeat Operation	548
Step list	Rebooting, Resetting, and Shutdown Procedures	549
Step list	Password Recovery Procedure	549

Complete the Tables and Lists from Memory

Print a copy of Appendix C, "Memory Tables" (found on the CD), or at least the section for this chapter, and complete the tables and lists from memory. Appendix D, "Memory Tables Answer Key," also on the CD, includes completed tables and lists to check your work.

Definitions of Key Terms

Define the following key terms from this chapter, and check your answers in the glossary:

promiscuous mode, inline mode

This chapter covers the following topics:

■ **Overview of the Cisco IDSM-2 Module:** This section provides information on the hardware and performance characteristics of the IDSM-2.

■ **Initializing the Cisco IDSM-2:** This section provides guidelines on initial configuration steps required to establish communication with the IDSM-2.

■ **Redirecting Traffic to the Cisco IDSM-2:** This section provides configuration steps required to send traffic to the IDSM-2 for analysis.

■ **Maintaining the Cisco IDSM-2:** This section contains information required to ensure that the code levels are up to date and also provides guidelines for system upgrades and recovery.

■ **Troubleshooting the Cisco IDSM-2:** This section contains steps required to verify the IDSM-2's configuration and systems status to address detected problems.

CHAPTER 24

Configuring and Maintaining the Cisco IDSM-2

Overview

The Cisco Intrusion Detection Services Module 2 (IDSM-2) for Cisco Catalyst 6500 Series switches provides intrusion prevention services for the switches. The Cisco IDSM-2 runs the same software as the Cisco IPS 4200 Series sensors but with some differences, which you will delve into through this chapter.

"Do I Know This Already?" Quiz

The "Do I Know This Already?" quiz allows you to assess whether you should read the entire chapter. If you miss no more than one of these self-assessment questions, you might want to move ahead to the "Exam Preparation Tasks" section. Table 24-1 lists the major headings in this chapter and the "Do I Know This Already?" quiz questions covering the material in those headings so that you can assess your knowledge of these specific areas. The answers to the "Do I Know This Already?" quiz appear in Appendix A.

Table 24-1 *"Do I Know This Already?" Foundation Topics Section-to-Question Mapping*

Foundation Topics Section	Questions
Initializing the Cisco IDSM-2	1–3
Maintaining the Cisco IDSM-2	4, 5
Troubleshooting the Cisco IDSM-2	6

1. How many external physical interfaces does the Cisco IDSM-2 have?

   a.   1

   b.   3

   c.   2

   d.   None

2. How many internal interfaces does the Cisco IDSM-2 have?

   a. 3

   b. 6

   c. 4

   d. 8

3. What are the names of the modes of operation that the Cisco IDSM-2 operates in?

   a. Inline, outline, and parallel

   b. Outline only

   c. Inline only

   d. Inline and promiscuous only

4. What are the names of the partitions on the Cisco IDSM-2?

   a. _____

   b. _____

5. Which switch command allows you to view all the modules installed in the Cisco IDSM-2 and the details including serial numbers, slot installed, firmware version, and sensor software version?

   a. show run

   b. show module

   c. show inventory

   d. None of these answers are correct.

6. Which command is used to view password recovery status on the Cisco IDSM-2?

   a. show settings | include password

   b. service password

   c. show configuration | include password

   d. None of these answers are correct.

Foundation Topics

Overview of the Cisco IDSM-2

The Cisco IDSM-2 is a services module for the Cisco Catalyst 6500 Series switch, planned for the core or distribution layer of an enterprise network. The IDSM-2 can be scaled to support multigigabit environments, and more than one IDSM-2 can be installed in the Cisco Catalyst 6500 Series chassis. Network uptime is very crucial in enterprise networks. The IDSM-2 supports Online Insertion and Removal (OIR), which does not require the Cisco Catalyst 6500 Series switch to be shut down before the IDSM-2 is inserted or re-moved, unlike other modules we have covered.

The Cisco IDSM-2, shown in Figure 24-1, can be configured through the command-line interface (CLI), Cisco Security Manager (CSM), Cisco IPS Device Manager (IDM), and Cisco IPS Manager Express (IME).

Figure 24-1 *Cisco IDSM-2*

Table 24-2 shows the Cisco IDSM-2-supported key features.

Table 24-2 *Cisco IDSM-2-Supported Key Features*

Feature	IDSM-2
Performance (passive/ promiscuous)	600 Mbps
	6000 new TCP connections per second
	6000 HTTP transactions per second
	60,000 concurrent connections
Performance (inline)	500 Mbps
	5000 new TCP connections per second
	5000 HTTP transactions per second
	50,000 concurrent connections
	Supports up to 500,000 concurrent connections
Multigigabit scalability	The 1-RU IDSM-2 can scale up to eight modules per chassis
	Provides a maximum of 4 Gbps
	No slot restriction

Table 24-2 *Cisco IDSM-2-Supported Key Features*

Feature	IDSM-2
Hot-swap modules	IDSM-2 insertion/removal never affects the Cisco Catalyst switch
Multiple capture technologies	Switch Port Analyzer (SPAN)/Remote SPAN (RSPAN)
	VLAN access control list (VACL) capture combined with shunning
	TCP resets in passive mode
Single device management	CLI
	SSH
	Cisco IDM
Enterprise management	Cisco Security Manager
	Cisco IPS Manager Express

The Cisco IDSM-2 can be installed together with other service modules, such as the Firewall Service Module (FWSM). The modules installed are independent of one another, despite the fact that they are integrated into the same Cisco Catalyst 6500 switch.

The Cisco IDSM-2 has eight internal ports, but only four of these ports are used:

- **Port 1 (System 0/1 in Cisco IPS Sensor Software version 7.0):** This is the TCP reset port for promiscuous mode and not used for inline IPS.

- **Port 2 (Gigabit Ethernet 0/2 in Cisco IPS Sensor Software version 7.0):** This is the command and control port.

- **Ports 7 and 8 (Gigabit Ethernet 0/7 and Gigabit Ethernet 0/8 in Cisco IPS Sensor Software version 7.0):** These are the monitoring ports, which can be a SPAN destination or VACL capture port for promiscuous mode. These ports can also be configured as a port pair to support inline mode.

The Cisco IDSM-2 runs the same code as the IPS 4200 Series appliance, but there are some differences because the Cisco IDSM-2 is a module in a switch. Table 24-3 highlights the similarities and differences between the IDSM-2 and the 4200 Series appliance.

Key
Topic

Table 24-3 *Comparing the IDSM-2 with the IPS 4200 Series*

Feature	IDSM-2	IPS 4200 Series
Sensor virtualization with inline VLAN groups	Not supported	Supported
Subdividing inline interfaces or VLAN groups	Not supported	Supported

Table 24-3   *Comparing the IDSM-2 with the IPS 4200 Series*

Feature	IDSM-2	IPS 4200 Series
Clock	Synchronizes its clock with the switch, and there is no **clock set** command	Clock configured locally, with **clock set** command available
Sensing interfaces	Has only two	Has more than two
Physical console access	Not supported	Supported
Recovery	Has a maintenance partition	No maintenance partition

The IDSM-2, like other sensors, needs to have the correct time on it, as it is heavily dependent on time sources. If the time is wrong, the time stamps on logs will be wrong as well, which will hinder correct analysis and correlation of data for an attack.

The IDSM-2 obtains its time from the following:

■ **Host switch:** The Cisco IDSM-2 automatically synchronizes its clock with the GMT time on the switch. This is the default behavior; however, the time zone and summertime settings are not synchronized. You must configure the time zone settings correctly on both and also ensure that the time on the switch is accurate as well.

■ **Network Time Protocol (NTP) server:** This method is recommended for all devices to ensure the highest degree of accuracy. You can configure the Cisco IDSM-2 to used NTP during initialization, or you can set up NTP through the Cisco IDM time panel.

The Cisco IDSM-2 can operate in two possible modes:

■ Inline

■ Promiscuous

Based on your selection of mode, the IDSM-2 exhibits certain behaviors on the features available. Table 24-4 shows the differences in behavior of features in promiscuous and inline modes.

Table 24-4 *Cisco IDSM-2 Features—Promiscuous Versus Inline Mode*

Feature	Promiscuous Mode	Inline Mode
Traffic visibility	Traffic is redirected to the IDSM-2 through VACL capture, SPAN, or RSPAN	Resides in the data-forwarding path
Maximum number of VLANs (802.1Q tagging)	Unlimited	One VLAN pair
Failover protection	■ No disruptive effect on the host switch in the event of a failure ■ No performance degradation as Cisco IDSM-2 is not in the forwarding path	■ Uses a software bypass capability that prevents the Cisco IDSM-2 from becoming a failure point ■ Can monitor Cisco IDSM-2 health through Simple Network Management Protocol (SNMP)
Cisco Catalyst IOS support	Yes, 12.2 (18) SFX4	Yes, 12.2 (18) SXE **Note:** 12.2 (18) SXE with a Supervisor 720 supports only one IDSM-2 inline between two VLANs
Cisco Catalyst 7600 support	Yes, 12.2 (18) SFX4 only	No
Supported signature actions	■ Log attacker packets ■ Log pair packets ■ Log victim packets ■ Produce alert ■ Produce verbose alert ■ Request block connection ■ Request block host ■ Request SNMP trap ■ Reset TCP connection	■ Deny attacker inline ■ Deny connection inline ■ Deny packet inline ■ Log attacker packets ■ Log pair packets ■ Log victim packets ■ Produce alert ■ Produce verbose alert ■ Request block connection ■ Request block host ■ Request SNMP trap ■ Reset TCP connection

Inline Operation

When configured for inline operation, the Cisco IDSM-2 requires two lines of configuration on the Cisco Catalyst 6500 Series switch, which specifies the two VLANs for which traffic is being analyzed. The IDSM-2 will be in the path of the traffic flow of the two VLANs being monitored. Figure 24-2 depicts a Cisco Catalyst 6500 switch with the IDSM-2 in inline mode.

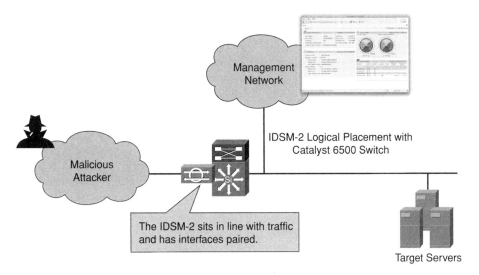

Figure 24-2 *Cisco IDSM-2 Inline Operation*

Promiscuous Operation

When deployed in promiscuous mode, the Cisco IDSM-2 receives packets that are directed toward its monitoring ports (ports 7 and 8). The traffic is redirected using VACL capture or by setting one of the ports as a SPAN or RSPAN destination. Figure 24-3 illustrates the traffic flow in a promiscuous mode scenario.

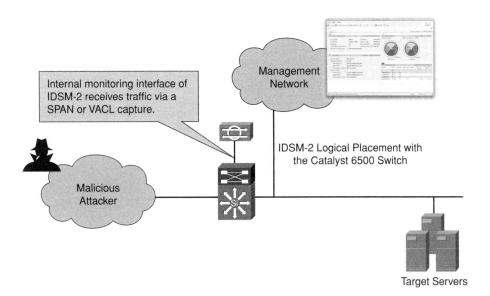

Figure 24-3 *Cisco IDSM-2 Promiscuous Operation*

SPAN provides a means by which traffic from a port can be copied to a destination port, where the spanned port is the source port that usually has traffic that is of interest that the Cisco IDSM-2 can monitor. Traffic being copied from the spanned port can be transmit (Tx), receive (Rx), or both. The Cisco Catalyst 6500 Series switches support a maximum of two Rx SPAN sessions per chassis and a maximum of four Tx SPAN sessions per chassis. For SPAN sessions copying both Rx and Tx traffic, you can have a maximum of two SPAN sessions per chassis. When using SPAN, you need to remember the following rules:

■   The total spanned traffic cannot exceed the maximum throughput of the Cisco IDSM-2, which is 600 Mbps.

■   The limitation on the number of SPAN sessions limits the number of ports that can be monitored by the Cisco IDSM-2.

VACL takes advantage of hardware resources of the Policy Feature Card (PFC) on the Supervisor engine of the switch. With VACL capture, traffic matching an ACL is copied and sent to a configured capture port, which in this case is the monitor port of the Cisco IDSM-2. The VACL capture requires more steps and precision than the SPAN configuration, but the VACL provides granularity regarding the particular subset of traffic to be copied and sent to the Cisco IDSM-2. In essence, this limits the amount of traffic to be processed and potentially analyzed.

Initializing the Cisco IDSM-2

To protect your network using the Cisco IDSM-2, you will go through similar steps to those in other sections for the respective sensors. There are three major tasks that must be carried out to facilitate the initialization:

■   Install the Cisco IDSM-2 in the Cisco Catalyst 6500 switch and verify module status.

■   Initialize the IDSM-2 module and go through the initial configuration using the **setup** command.

■   Configure the switch to allow command and control access to the IDSM-2.

Installing the Cisco IDSM-2

Following is a walk-through of the hardware installation process of the Cisco IDSM-2, as shown in Figure 24-4.

Caution: Do not touch the printed circuit boards or connector pins on the module, and always use the ejector levers when installing or removing the module. A partially seated module will not work and may cause the system to halt and later crash.

Step 1.   Familiarize yourself with the regulatory and safety information for the Cisco IDSM-2.

Step 2.   Choose a slot for the module. The supervisor will be installed in slot 1, and a redundant can be installed in slot 2. Any other slot will do, just in case there is a requirement for redundancy in the future.

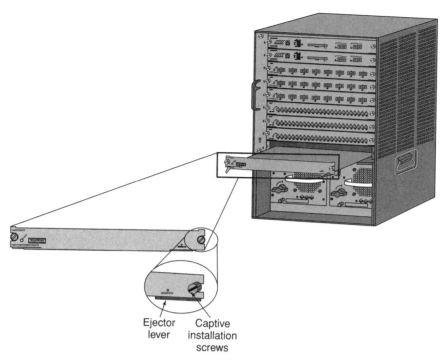

Ejector lever   Captive installation screws

Figure 24-4   *Cisco IDSM-2 Installation into the Cisco Catalyst 6500 Series Switch*

Step 3.   Loosen the installation screws that secure the filler plate to the desired slot. You might need a screwdriver to loosen the screw.

Step 4.   Remove the filler plate.

Step 5.   Hold the module with one hand, and place your other hand under the module for good support.

Step 6.   Place the module in the slot by aligning the notch on the sides of the module carrier with the groove in the slot.

Step 7.   Keeping the module at a 90-degree orientation to the backplane, carefully slide it into the slot until the notches on both ejector levers engage the chassis sides.

Step 8.   Using the thumb and forefinger of each hand, simultaneously pivot in both ejector levers to fully seat the module in the backplane connector.

Step 9.   Use a screwdriver to tighten the installation screws on the left and right sides of the module.

The Cisco Catalyst 6500 Series switches support Online Insertion and Removal (OIR), which means that they are hot-swappable. When the switch detects that a module has been installed, removed, or replaced, it runs discovery and diagnostic processes and resumes system operation for the module in question. Messages are sent to the console when such an event occurs and are visible to the logged-in user if connected directly to the switch or through a terminal server. If connected through Telnet, the messages do not appear by default.

The next step is to verify the module status by issuing the **show module** command, with the output shown in Example 24-1.

Example 24-1 show module *Command Output*

```
rack-6503(config)# do show module
Mod Ports Card Type                           Model               Serial No.
--- ----- ------------------------------- ------------------- -----------
 1    2   Supervisor Engine 720 (Active)    WS-SUP720-3B        SAD090108S1
 2    8   Intrusion Detection System        WS-SVC-IDSM-2       SAD081407EY
 3   48   48-port 10/100 mb RJ45            WS-X6148-45AF       SAL08321X2H


Mod MAC addresses                      Hw    Fw          Sw            Status
--- -------------------------------- ------ ----------- ------------- -------
 1  0011.21a1.6f7c to 0011.21a1.6f7f  4.1   8.1(3)      12.2(18)SXF5 Ok
 2  000f.905c.606e to 000f.905c.6075  4.0   7.2(1)      4.1(4)S91     Ok
 3  0012.0150.3c0c to 0012.0150.3c3b  1.1   5.4(2)      8.5(0.46)RFW Ok


Mod Sub-Module              Model              Serial        Hw    Status
---- ------------------------ ------------------- ----------- ------- -------
 1  Policy Feature Card 3   WS-F6K-PFC3B       SAD085205MA   1.1   Ok
 1  MSFC3 Daughterboard     WS-SUP720          SAD085208Z5   2.2   Ok
 2  IDS 2 accelerator board WS-SVC-IDSUPG      ADEI4131283   2.3   Ok
 3  IEEE Voice Daughter Card WS-F6K-FE48-AF    SAL08311DZU   1.1   Ok


Mod Online Diag Status
---- -------------------
 1  Pass
 2  Pass
 3  Pass
rack-6503#
```

The Cisco IDSM-2 is in slot 2 in the output, where the Cisco switch is a Cisco Catalyst 6503. From the output, you can see the module status has a **Pass** and the other sections respectively read an **Ok**.

Note: The status may read **other** or **unknown** when the IDSM-2 is first installed and it is going through the boot-up process, which usually takes about 5 minutes. After the diagnostics processes are completed by the IDSM-2, the status changes to **Ok**.

Initial Configuration of the Cisco IDSM-2

The Cisco IDSM-2 runs the same code as the Cisco IPS 4200 Series sensors; thus, the initialization for both platforms are the same. The main difference is the method of accessing the CLI for the Cisco IDSM-2 initialization. The following steps walk you through the process:

Step 1. Use the **session** command to initiate a session with the Cisco Catalyst 6500 Series IDSM-2 from the switch CLI. The Cisco IDSM-2 is installed in the slot from the **show module** output; hence the following command:

rack-6503# **session slot 2 processor 1**

Step 2. Log in to the Cisco IDSM-2 using the default username cisco and password cisco.

Step 3. Follow the prompts to change the default password.

Step 4. Run the **setup** command and respond to interactive prompts to complete the initial configuration.

Step 5. Apply the configuration changes.

Example 24-2 shows the initial configuration output from the Cisco IDSM-2.

Example 24-2 *Initial Configuration*

```
rack-6503# session slot 2 processor 1
The default escape character is Ctrl-^, then x.
You can also type 'exit' at the remote prompt to end the session
Trying 127.0.0.21 ... Open


login: cisco
Password: cisco
You are required to change your password immediately (password aged)
Changing password for cisco
(current) password:
New password:
Retype new password:
***NOTICE***
This product contains cryptographic features and is subject to United States
and local country laws governing import, export, transfer and use. Delivery
of Cisco cryptographic products does not imply third-party authority to import,
export, distribute or use encryption. Importers, exporters, distributors and
users are responsible for compliance with U.S. and local country laws. By using
this product you agree to comply with applicable laws and regulations. If you
are unable to comply with U.S. and local laws, return this product immediately.

A summary of U.S. laws governing Cisco cryptographic products may be found at:
http://www.cisco.com/wwl/export/crypto/tool/stqrg.html


If you require further assistance please contact us by sending email to
export@cisco.com.


***LICENSE NOTICE***
```

```
There is no license key installed on the WS-SVC-IDSM2-BUN.
The system will continue to operate with the currently installed
signature set.  A valid license must be obtained in order to apply
signature updates.  Please go to http://www.cisco.com/go/license
to obtain a new license or install a license.


    --- Basic Setup ---

    --- System Configuration Dialog ---

At any point you may enter a question mark '?' for help.
User ctrl-c to abort configuration dialog at any prompt.
Default settings are in square brackets '[]'.




Current time: Thu Apr 21 21:34:49 2011

Setup Configuration last modified: Thu Apr 21 21:13:40 2011

Enter host name[sensor]: idsm
Enter IP interface[192.168.1.2/24,192.168.1.1]: 10.91.33.5/24,10.91.33.1
Modify current access list?[no]: yes
Current access list entries:
  No entries
Permit: 0.0.0.0/0
Permit:
Use DNS server for Global Correlation?[no]: yes
  DNS server IP address[]: 64.102.6.247
Use HTTP proxy server for Global Correlation?[no]:
Modify system clock settings?[no]: yes
  Modify summer time settings?[no]:
  Modify system timezone?[no]: yes
    Timezone[UTC]:
    UTC Offset[0]:
  Use NTP?[no]:
Participation in the SensorBase Network allows Cisco to
collect aggregated statistics about traffic sent to your IPS.
SensorBase Network Participation level?[off]: full

If you agree to participate in the SensorBase Network, Cisco will
collect aggregated statistics about traffic sent to your IPS.
This includes summary data on the Cisco IPS network traffic properties
and how this traffic was handled by the Cisco appliances.  We do not
```

```
collect the data content of traffic or other sensitive business or
personal information.  All data is aggregated and sent via secure HTTP
to the Cisco SensorBase Network servers in periodic intervals.  All data
shared with Cisco will be anonymous and treated as strictly confidential.
The table below describes how the data will be used by Cisco.
Participation Level = "Partial":
  * Type of Data: Protocol Attributes (e.g. TCP max segment size and
    options string)
    Purpose: Track potential threats and understand threat exposure
  * Type of Data: Attack Type (e.g. Signature Fired and Risk Rating)
    Purpose: Used to understand current attacks and attack severity
  * Type of Data: Connecting IP Address and port
    Purpose: Identifies attack source
  * Type of Data: Summary IPS performance (CPU utilization memory usage,
    inline vs. promiscuous, etc)
    Purpose: Tracks product efficacy
Participation Level = "Full" additionally includes:
  * Type of Data: Victim IP Address and port
    Purpose: Detect threat behavioral patterns


Do you agree to participate in the SensorBase Network?[no]: yes


The following configuration was entered.

service host
network-settings
host-ip 10.91.33.5/24,10.91.33.1
host-name idsm
telnet-option disabled
access-list 0.0.0.0/0
ftp-timeout 300
no login-banner-text
dns-primary-server enabled
address 64.102.6.247
exit
dns-secondary-server disabled
dns-tertiary-server disabled
http-proxy no-proxy
exit
time-zone-settings
offset 0
standard-time-zone-name UTC
exit
summertime-option disabled
ntp-option disabled
```

```
exit
service global-correlation
network-participation full
exit


[0] Go to the command prompt without saving this config.
[1] Return to setup without saving this config.
[2] Save this configuration and exit setup.
[3] Continue to Advanced setup.

Enter your selection[3]: 2
Warning: Global correlation inspection and reputation filtering have been
disabled because
there is not a current license installed.  Obtain a new license from
http://www.cisco.com/go/license.


--- Configuration Saved ---


Complete the advanced setup using CLI or IDM.
To use IDM,point your web browser at https://<sensor-ip-address>.
```

Command and Control Access for the Cisco IDSM-2

After the Cisco IDSM-2 has been initialized, it is important to configure command and control access so that the Cisco IDSM-2 can be managed remotely, as outlined in the following steps:

Key Topic

Step 1.   Log in to the switch console.

Step 2.   Enter global configuration mode:
configuration terminal

Step 3.   Put the command and control port into the correct VLAN using this syntax:
intrusion-detection module *module_number* management-port access-vlan
vlan_number

The configuration will look like this:
rack-6503(config)# **intrusion-detection module 2 management-port
access-vlan 1**

Step 4.   Test connectivity by initiating a session to the IDSM-2 and ping a known IP address.

Redirecting Traffic to the Cisco IDSM-2

The Cisco IDSM-2 can be configured to start analyzing traffic now that it has been initialized. The next steps will be as follows:

■   Configuring the interfaces to receive traffic

■   Configuring the IDSM-2 for inline or promiscuous operation

For the inline operation, you can also configure multiple virtual sensors and assign VLAN pairs to them, as outlined in these steps:

Step 1.   Log in to the router.

Step 2.   Enter privileged EXEC mode on the router and subsequently enter configuration mode.

Step 3.   Create two VLANs if not in existence, one for each side of the inline IDSM-2, repeating the following steps for each VLAN:
```
vlan vlan_number
name vlan_name
exit
```

Step 4.   Configure an access port for each interface if you have not done so already:
```
interface interface_name
switchport access vlan vlan_number
switchport mode access
exit
```

Step 5.   Configure each IDSM-2 data port to be one of the VLANs:
```
intrusion-detection module slot_number data-port {1 | 2}
access-vlan vlan_number
exit
```

Step 6.   Verify the configuration.
```
show running | include intrusion-detection
```

The **show running | include intrusion-detection** command helps you validate the configuration, and the output is shown in Example 24-3.

Example 24-3   *Verifying Module VLANs*

```
rack-6503# show running | include intrusion-detection
intrusion-detection module 2 data-port 1 access-vlan 10
intrusion-detection module 2 data-port 2 access-vlan 20
```

The configuration defining the management port VLAN might not be visible when this command is issued because it is using the default VLAN 1. If shown, it will look like this:

```
intrusion-detection module 2 management-port access-vlan 1
```

Because the management port configuration was not visible, to further validate and verify your configuration, issue the **show intrusion-detection module 2 management-port state** command, with the output shown in Example 24-4.

Example 24-4   *Verifying the Management Port Configuration*

```
rack-6503# show intrusion-detection module 2 management-port state
Intrusion-detection module 2 management-port:


Switchport: Enabled
Administrative Mode: dynamic desirable
Operational Mode: static access
Administrative Trunking Encapsulation: negotiate
Operational Trunking Encapsulation: native
Negotiation of Trunking: On
Access Mode VLAN: 1 (default)
Trunking Native Mode VLAN: 1 (default)
Trunking VLANs Enabled: ALL
Pruning VLANs Enabled: 2-1001
Vlans allowed on trunk: 1
Vlans allowed and active in management domain: 1
Vlans in spanning tree forwarding state and not pruned:
    1
Access Vlan = 1
```

Also, further verify that the data ports are configured correctly by issuing the **show intrusion-detection module 2 data-port 1 state** command, with the output as shown in Example 24-5.

Example 24-5   *Verifying the Data Port Configuration*

```
rack-6503# show intrusion-detection module 2 data-port 1 state
Intrusion-detection module 2 data-port 1:


Switchport: Enabled
Administrative Mode: static access
Operational Mode: static access
Administrative Trunking Encapsulation: dot1q
Operational Trunking Encapsulation: native
Negotiation of Trunking: Off
Access Mode VLAN: 10 (VLAN0010)
Trunking Native Mode VLAN: 1 (default)
Trunking VLANs Enabled: NONE
Pruning VLANs Enabled: 2-1001
Vlans allowed on trunk: 10
Vlans allowed and active in management domain: 10
Vlans in spanning tree forwarding state and not pruned:
    10
Administrative Capture Mode: Disabled
Administrative Capture Allowed-vlans: empty
Autostate mode: excluded
Portfast mode: default
```

Data port 2 will have a similar output but in VLAN 20. To ensure that you have the desired ports in VLAN 10 and 20, respectively, issue the **show vlan id 10** and **show vlan id 20** commands, respectively. The IDSM-2 ports must be access ports. The **show vlan id 10** command is issued in Example 24-6.

Example 24-6   show vlan *Command Output*

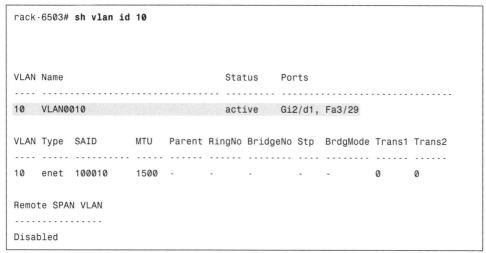

```
rack-6503# sh vlan id 10



VLAN Name                          Status    Ports
---- ------------------------------ --------- ------------------------------
10   VLAN0010                       active    Gi2/d1, Fa3/29


VLAN Type  SAID       MTU   Parent RingNo BridgeNo Stp  BrdgMode Trans1 Trans2
---- ----- ---------- ----- ------ ------ -------- ---- -------- ------ ------
10   enet  100010     1500  -      -      -        -    -        0      0


Remote SPAN VLAN
---------------
Disabled
```

This completes the switch configuration for the IDSM-2 in inline mode. The next step is to configure the IDSM-2 virtual sensor and assign the two ports int7 and int8 to it. This can be accomplished using the CLI or IDM.

For promiscuous operation, a span is configured on the switch and the destination is the Cisco IDSM-2 module. Example 24-7 shows what the output of the **show monitor** command will look like.

Example 24-7   *Verifying a Span Session for the Cisco IDSM-2 Promiscuous Operation*

Key
Topic

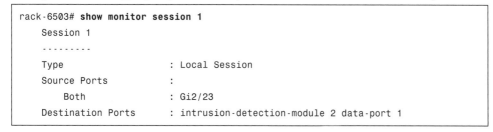

```
rack-6503# show monitor session 1
    Session 1
    ---------
    Type                  : Local Session
    Source Ports          :
        Both              : Gi2/23
    Destination Ports     : intrusion-detection-module 2 data-port 1
```

VACLs can also be used to redirect traffic for promiscuous operation. You can look up the configuration for that at the link provided in the "References" section, later in this chapter.

Maintaining the Cisco IDSM-2

The maintenance of the Cisco IDSM-2 is centered on three procedures, depending on the situation at hand:

- Upgrade
- Password recovery
- Re-image

Upgrade Procedure

The IDSM-2 upgrade procedure is used to apply Cisco IPS Sensor software upgrade files to the Cisco IDSM-2. During the course of the process, the configuration and signature settings of the Cisco IDSM-2 are retained. The **upgrade** command is issued to start the process when applying upgrades and updates, such as

- Major version upgrades
- Minor version upgrades
- Engine updates
- Service packs
- Signature updates

Recovery Procedure

The IDSM-2 has a unique architecture that differentiates it from other sensors regarding the recovery process and procedure. The Cisco IDSM-2 has two partitions:

- **Application partition:** This stores the IDSM-2 application.
- **Maintenance partition:** This is where the re-image process is launched.

A re-image of the Cisco IDSM-2 is launched from the maintenance partition. An embedded installation script in the Cisco IDSM-2 image performs the re-image procedure. The script is only executed from the maintenance partition.

When there is a new maintenance image, you can re-image the maintenance partition from the application partition.

Upgrading the Application Partition

To re-image or upgrade the Cisco IDSM-2 application partition, follow these steps:

Step 1.   Download the Cisco IDSM-2 image file from the software center. An example is the IPS-IDSM2-K9-sys-1.1-a-7.0-4-E4.bin.gz file. Store the image on an FTP server that will be accessed by the Cisco IDSM-2 later.

Step 2.   Log in to the switch CLI.

Step 3.   Boot the IDSM-2 to the maintenance partition:

```
hw-module module 2 reset cf:1
```

Step 4.   After the module reboots, session to the maintenance partition CLI and log in using the username guest and password cisco:

```
session slot 2 processor 1
```

Step 5.   Verify reachability to the FTP server by pinging the IP address of the server and verifying that the FTP service is running on the server.

Step 6.   Copy the image to start the installation process:

```
upgrade ftp://cisco@10.10.10.210/IPS-IDSM2-K9-sys-1.1-a-7.0.2-E4.bin.gz
```

Step 7.   Specify the FTP server password and the download starts; you are prompted to install. Enter **y** to continue:

```
Password for cisco@10.10.10.210: cisco
Do you want to proceed installing it [y|N]: y
```

Step 8.   Exit the maintenance partition CLI and return to the switch CLI.

Step 9.   Reboot the IDSM-2 to the application partition:

```
hw-module module 2 reset hdd:1
```

Step 10. Verify that the Cisco IDSM-2 is online, the software version is current, and the status is OK using the **show module** command.

Step 11. Session to the IDSM-2 application partition CLI.

Step 12. Initialize the Cisco IDSM-2 using the **setup** command.

Example 24-8 shows the output of the upgrade process from an IDS Software version 4.1(4)S91 to an IPS Software version 7.0(4).

Example 24-8   *Upgrade Process Output from IDS to IPS Software*

```
rack-6503# show module
Mod Ports Card Type                                Model              Serial No.
--- ----- ------------------------------------    ----------------   -----------
  1    2  Supervisor Engine 720 (Active)           WS-SUP720-3B       SAD090108S1
  2    8  Intrusion Detection System               WS-SVC-IDSM-2      SAD081407EY
  3   48  48-port 10/100 mb RJ45                    WS-X6148-45AF      SAL08321X2H

Mod MAC addresses                       Hw    Fw            Sw            Status
--- ---------------------------------   ----  ----------    ----------    -------
  1 0011.21a1.6f7c to 0011.21a1.6f7f    4.1   8.1(3)        12.2(18)SXF5  Ok
  2 000f.905c.606e to 000f.905c.6075    4.0   7.2(1)        4.1(4)S91     Ok
  3 0012.0150.3c0c to 0012.0150.3c3b    1.1   5.4(2)        8.5(0.46)RFW  Ok

Mod  Sub-Module               Model          Serial       Hw     Status
---- ------------------------ -------------- ------------ ------- -------
  1  Policy Feature Card 3     WS-F6K-PFC3B   SAD085205MA  1.1     Ok
  1  MSFC3 Daughterboard       WS-SUP720      SAD085208Z5  2.2     Ok
```

```
  2  IDS 2 accelerator board    WS-SVC-IDSUPG    ADEI4131283  2.3    Ok
  3  IEEE Voice Daughter Card   WS-F6K-FE48-AF   SAL08311DZU  1.1    Ok


Mod  Online Diag Status
----  -------------------
  1  Pass
  2  Pass
  3  Pass
rack-6503#


rack-6503# hw-module module 2 reset cf:1
Device BOOT variable for reset = <cf:1>
Warning: Device list is not verified.


Proceed with reload of module?[confirm]
% reset issued for module 2
rack-6503#
2d09h: SP: The PC in slot 2 is shutting down. Please wait ...
2d09h: SP: PC shutdown completed for module 2
2d09h: %C6KPWR-SP-4-DISABLED: power to module in slot 2 set off (Reset)
rack-6503#
2d09h: SP: OS_BOOT_STATUS(2) MP OS Boot Status: finished booting
2d09h: %DIAG-SP-6-RUN_MINIMUM: Module 2: Running Minimal Diagnostics...
2d09h: %DIAG-SP-6-DIAG_OK: Module 2: Passed Online Diagnostics
2d09h: %OIR-SP-6-INSCARD: Card inserted in slot 2, interfaces are now online


rack-6503# session slot 2 processor 1
The default escape character is Ctrl-^, then x.
You can also type 'exit' at the remote prompt to end the session
Trying 127.0.0.21 ... Open


Cisco Maintenance image



login: guest
Password: cisco


Maintenance image version: 2.1(1)


guest@localhost.localdomain#


guest@localhost.localdomain# upgrade ?
Usage: upgrade [ftp-url] [device:partition-num]  -  upgrade application
                                                     on the specified
                                                     device-partition
```

```
        upgrade [ftp-url] --install           -   factory installation
        upgrade [ftp-url]                      -   default installation
guest@localhost.localdomain#


guest@localhost.localdomain# upgrade ftp://cisco@10.10.10.240/IPS-IDSM2-K9-sy>
Downloading the image. This may take several minutes...
Password for cisco
ftp://cisco@10.10.10.240/IPS-IDSM2-K9-sys-1.1-a-7.0-4-E4.bin.gz (29007K)
/tmp/upgrade.gz          [#######################]   29007K ¦ 10384.20K/s
29704121 bytes transferred in 2.79 sec (10383.83k/sec)


Upgrade file ftp://cisco@10.10.10.240/IPS-IDSM2-K9-sys-1.1-a-7.0-4-E4.bin.gz is
downloaded.
Upgrading will wipe out the contents on the storage media.
Do you want to proceed installing it [y¦N]: y



Proceeding with upgrade. Please do not interrupt.
If the upgrade is interrupted or fails, boot into
Maintenance image again and restart upgrade.


Creating IPS application image file...


Initializing the hard disk...
Applying the image, this process may take several minutes...
Performing post install, please wait...
Application image upgrade complete. You can boot the image now.
guest@localhost.localdomain#


guest@localhost.localdomain# exit
logout

[Connection to 127.0.0.21 closed by foreign host]
rack-6503# hw-module module 2 reset hdd:1
Device BOOT variable for reset = <hdd:1>
Warning: Device list is not verified.


Proceed with reload of module?[confirm]
% reset issued for module 2
rack-6503#
2d10h: SP: The PC in slot 2 is shutting down. Please wait ...
2d10h: SP: PC shutdown completed for module 2
2d10h: %C6KPWR-SP-4-DISABLED: power to module in slot 2 set off (Reset)
rack-6503#
2d10h: %DIAG-SP-6-RUN_MINIMUM: Module 2: Running Minimal Diagnostics...
```

```
2d10h: %DIAG-SP-6-DIAG_OK: Module 2: Passed Online Diagnostics
2d10h: %OIR-SP-6-INSCARD: Card inserted in slot 2, interfaces are now online
rack-6503#
rack-6503# show module
Mod Ports Card Type                              Model               Serial No.
--- ----- -------------------------------------- ------------------- -----------

  1    2  Supervisor Engine 720 (Active)         WS-SUP720-3B        SAD090108S1
  2    8  Intrusion Detection System             WS-SVC-IDSM-2       SAD081407EY
  3   48  48-port 10/100 mb RJ45                 WS-X6148-45AF       SAL08321X2H


Mod MAC addresses                        Hw    Fw          Sw            Status
--- -------------------------------- ------ ----------- ----------- -------

  1  0011.21a1.6f7c to 0011.21a1.6f7f  4.1   8.1(3)      12.2(18)SXF5 Ok
  2  000f.905c.606e to 000f.905c.6075  4.0   7.2(1)      7.0(4)E4     Ok
  3  0012.0150.3c0c to 0012.0150.3c3b  1.1   5.4(2)      8.5(0.46)RFW Ok


Mod  Sub-Module                  Model               Serial      Hw    Status
---- ------------------------ ------------------- ----------- ------- -------

  1  Policy Feature Card 3      WS-F6K-PFC3B        SAD085205MA 1.1    Ok
  1  MSFC3 Daughterboard        WS-SUP720           SAD085208Z5 2.2    Ok
  2  IDS 2 accelerator board    WS-SVC-IDSUPG       ADEI4131283 2.3    Ok
  3  IEEE Voice Daughter Card   WS-F6K-FE48-AF      SAL08311DZU 1.1    Ok


Mod  Online Diag Status
---- ------------------

  1  Pass
  2  Pass
  3  Pass
rack-6503#
rack-6503# show module 2
Mod Ports Card Type                              Model               Serial No.
--- ----- -------------------------------------- ------------------- -----------

  2    8  Intrusion Detection System             WS-SVC-IDSM-2       SAD081407EY


Mod MAC addresses                        Hw    Fw          Sw            Status
--- -------------------------------- ------ ----------- ----------- -------

  2  000f.905c.606e to 000f.905c.6075  4.0   7.2(1)      7.0(4)E4     Ok


Mod  Sub-Module                  Model               Serial      Hw    Status
---- ------------------------ ------------------- ----------- ------- -------

  2  IDS 2 accelerator board    WS-SVC-IDSUPG       ADEI4131283 2.3    Ok


Mod  Online Diag Status
---- ------------------

  2  Pass
```

Re-imaging the Maintenance Partition

The re-imaging procedure for the maintenance partition is similar to the procedure you just completed for re-imaging the application partition. The only difference is that you stay in the current operating mode of the Cisco IDSM-2 and the image type downloaded has "mp," which stands for maintenance partition embedded in it. Follow these steps to re-image the maintenance partition:

Step 1.   Download the IDSM-2 maintenance partition image to a directory on the FTP server.

Step 2.   Log in to the switch CLI.

Step 3.   Session in to the Cisco IDSM-2.

Step 4.   Upgrade the maintenance partition using this command:

```
upgrade ftp://user@ftp_server_ip_address/directory_path/image
```

Step 5.   Specify the FTP server password when prompted, after which you are prompted whether you want to continue.

Step 6.   Enter yes to continue.

Troubleshooting the Cisco IDSM-2

The Cisco IDSM-2 runs the same software architecture as the Cisco IPS 4200 Series sensors. Thus, the same troubleshooting methodology applies in most cases, and in other cases, there are some troubleshooting procedures specific to the Cisco IDSM-2. The following switch commands are useful when troubleshooting. Most can be used extensively in verifying configuration or status, as the case might be:

- show module

- show version

- show intrusion-detection module

- show monitor

- show vlan access-map

- show vlan filter

If you cannot communicate with the Cisco IDSM-2, you will need to issue a reset to re-initialize the module. Use the **hw-module module** *module_number* **reset** [**hdd:1** | **cf:1**] command. If you do not specify the hdd:1 or cf:1, the switch will use the default boot variables.

Password Recovery

The password of the Cisco IDSM-2 can be recovered by performing a system image upgrade. The upgrade resets only the password; the rest of the other configuration remains intact. This is done by booting the switch to the maintenance partition and executing the **upgrade** command to install a new image.

Password recovery can be disabled in the host configuration. You will actually be able to run the commands to clear the password, but if password recovery is disabled on the Cisco IPS Sensor, the sensor detects that password recovery is not allowed and rejects the external request.

You can check the state of the password recovery by following these steps:

Step 1.   Log in to the CLI.

Step 2.   Session in to the IDSM-2.

Step 3.   Enter the service host submode:
Configure terminal
Service host

Step 4.   Issue the **show settings | include password** command.

Example 24-9 shows the output as detailed in Steps 3 and 4.

Example 24-9   *Verifying the Password Recovery State*

```
idsm(config)# service host
idsm(config-hos)# show settings | include password
  password-recovery: allowed <defaulted>
idsm(config-hos)#
```

The password recovery procedure is similar to the application partition re-image. Follow these steps to carry out the password recovery procedure:

Step 1.   Download the password recovery image from http://www.cisco.com.

Step 2.   Place the file on an FTP server that will be accessed later through the recovery process.

Step 3.   From the switch CLI, boot to the maintenance partition using the **hw-module module** *module_number* **reset cf:1** command.

Step 4.   Session in to the Cisco IDSM-2 after it reboots and log in as guest with a password of cisco.

Step 5.   Proceed with the upgrade procedure as described previously.

Summary

This section highlights the key topics discussed in this chapter:

- The Cisco IDSM-2 is a service module for the Cisco Catalyst 6500 Series switches.

- The Cisco IDSM-2 runs the same code as the Cisco IPS 4200 Series sensors.

- Sensor initialization tasks specific to the Cisco IDSM-2 include

  - Assigning the command and control port to the proper VLAN

  - (a) Configuring the switch for inline intrusion detection and ensuring that the data ports int7 and int8 are in the correct VLAN or (b) configuring the switch to capture traffic and send to data port 1 for promiscuous modes

  - Obtaining the time setting from either the host switch or an NTP server

- You can use the CLI **upgrade** command to apply an upgrade to the Cisco IDSM-2 sensor software without losing your configuration.

- You can recover the password of the Cisco IDSM-2 without losing the configuration on the switch.

- You can use the **show module** command to display the module status and information.

- You can recover the application partition image of the Cisco IDSM-2 by booting to the maintenance partition and using the **upgrade** command to install the image. When you install the image, you lose all your configuration.

References

More information can be found at the following URLs:

Installing the Cisco IDSM-2 in the Cisco Catalyst 6500 Series Switch, at www.cisco.com/en/US/docs/security/ips/7.0/installation/guide/hw_installing_idsm2.html.

Configuring the Cisco Catalyst 6500 Series Switch and Cisco IDSM-2 for Promiscuous Mode Using the CLI, at www.cisco.com/en/US/docs/security/ips/7.0/configuration/guide/cli/cli_idsm2.html#wp1030752.

Configuring VACL Capture, at www.cisco.com/en/US/docs/security/ips/7.0/configuration/guide/cli/cli_idsm2.html#wp1181521.

Configuring the Cisco Catalyst 6500 Series Switch and Cisco IDSM-2 Using IDM, at www.cisco.com/en/US/docs/security/ips/7.0/configuration/guide/idm/idm_interfaces.html.

Exam Preparation Tasks

Review All the Key Topics

Review the most important topics from the chapter, noted with the Key Topic icons in the margin of the page. Table 24-5 lists a reference of these key topics and the page numbers on which each is found.

Table 24-5   *Key Topics for Chapter 24*

Key Topic Element	Description	Page Number
Table 24-3	Comparing the IDSM-2 with the IPS 4200 Series	558
Table 24-4	Cisco IDSM-2 Features—Promiscuous Versus Inline Mode	560
Step list	Initializing the Cisco IDSM-2	565
Step list	Command and Control Access Configuration	568
Step list	Configuring the Cisco IDSM-2 for Inline Operation	569
Example 24-3	Verifying Module VLANs	569
Example 24-4	Verifying the Management Port Configuration	570
Example 24-7	Verifying a Span Session for the Cisco IDSM-2 Promiscuous Operation	571
Step list	Cisco IDSM-2 Application Partition Upgrade	572
Step list	Cisco IDSM-2 Maintenance Partition Re-image	577
Step list	Password Recovery	578

Complete the Tables and Lists from Memory

Print a copy of Appendix C, "Memory Tables" (found on the CD), or at least the section for this chapter, and complete the tables and lists from memory. Appendix D, "Memory Tables Answer Key," also on the CD, includes completed tables and lists to check your work.

Definitions of Key Terms

Define the following key terms from this chapter, and check your answers in the glossary:

promiscuous mode, inline mode

Part VIII: Final Exam Preparation

Chapter 25: Final Preparation

Final Preparation

The first 24 chapters of this book cover technologies, protocols, commands, and features required to pass the 642-627 IPS exam. Although these chapters supply detailed information, most people need more preparation than simply reading the first 24 chapters of this book. This chapter details a set of tools and a study plan to help reader(s) complete their preparation for the exams.

This short chapter has two main sections. The first section lists the exam preparation tools that are useful at this point in the study process. The second section lists a suggested study plan now that reader(s) have completed all the earlier chapters in this book.

Note: Appendixes C and D, referred to in this chapter, exist as soft-copy appendixes on the CD included in the back of this book.

Tools for Final Preparation

The following sections list some information about the available tools and describe how to access the tools.

Pearson Cert Practice Test Engine and Questions on the CD

The CD in the back of the book includes the Pearson IT Certification Practice Test Engine—software that displays and grades a set of exam-realistic, multiple-choice, drag-and-drop, fill-in-the-blank, and testlet questions. Using the Pearson IT Certification Practice Test Engine, you can either study by going through the questions in study mode, or take a simulated ICND1 or CCNA exam that mimics real exam conditions.

The installation process requires two major steps. The CD in the back of the book has a recent copy of the Pearson IT Certification Practice Test Engine. The practice exam—the database of ICND1 and CCNA exam questions—is not on the CD.

Note: The cardboard CD case in the back of this book includes the CD and a piece of paper. The paper lists the activation code for the practice exam associated with this book. *Do not lose the activation code.* On the opposite side of the paper from the activation code is a unique, one-time-use coupon code for the purchase of the *CCENT/CCNA ICND1 640-822 Official Cert Guide, Premium Edition* eBook and Practice Test.

Install the Software from the CD

The Pearson IT Certification Practice Test is a Windows-only desktop application. You can run it on a Mac using a Windows Virtual Machine, but it was built specifically for the PC platform. The minimum system requirements are as follows:

- Windows XP (SP3), Windows Vista (SP2), or Windows 7

- Microsoft .NET Framework 4.0 Client

- Microsoft SQL Server Compact 4.0

- Pentium-class 1-GHz processor (or equivalent)

- 512 MB RAM

- 650 MB disk space plus 50 MB for each downloaded practice exam

The software installation process is pretty routine as compared with other software installation processes. If you have already installed the Pearson IT Certification Practice Test software from another Pearson product, there is no need for you to reinstall the software. Simply launch the software on your desktop and proceed to activate the practice exam from this book by using the activation code included in the CD sleeve. The following steps outline the installation process:

Step 1.   Insert the CD into your PC.

Step 2.   The software that automatically runs is the Cisco Press software to access and use all CD-based features, including the exam engine and the CD-only appendixes. From the main menu, click the **Install the Exam Engine** option.

Step 3.   Respond to Windows prompts as with any typical software installation process.

The installation process will give you the option to activate your exam with the activation code supplied on the paper in the CD sleeve. This process requires that you establish a Pearson website login. You will need this login to activate the exam, so register when prompted. If you already have a Pearson website login, there is no need to register again. Just use your existing login.

Activate and Download the Practice Exam

After the exam engine is installed, you should then activate the exam associated with this book (if you did not do so during the installation process), as follows:

Step 1.   Start the Pearson IT Certification Practice Test (PCPT) software from the Windows Start menu or from your desktop shortcut icon.

Step 2.   To activate and download the exam associated with this book, click the **Activate** button from the My Products or Tools tab.

Step 3.   At the next screen, enter the activation key from the paper inside the cardboard CD holder in the back of the book. After the key is entered, click the **Activate** button.

Step 4.   The activation process will download the practice exam. Click **Next**, and then click **Finish**.

After the activation process is completed, the My Products tab should list your new exam. If you do not see the exam, make sure that you have selected the My Products tab on the menu. At this point, the software and practice exam are ready to use. Simply select the exam and click the **Open Exam** button.

To update a particular exam that you have already activated and downloaded, simply select the Tools tab and click the **Update Products** button. Updating your exams will ensure that you have the latest changes and updates to the exam data.

If you want to check for updates to the Pearson Cert Practice Test exam engine software, simply select the Tools tab and click the **Update Application** button. This will ensure that you are running the latest version of the software engine.

Activating Other Exams

The exam software installation process, and the registration process, only has to happen once. Then, for each new exam, only a few steps are required. For example, if you buy another new Cisco Press Official Cert Guide or Pearson IT Certification Cert Guide, extract the activation code from the CD sleeve in the back of that book—you don't even need the CD at this point. From there, just start the exam engine (if not still up and running) and perform Steps 2 through 4 from the previous list.

Premium Edition

In addition to the free practice exam provided on the CD-ROM, you can purchase additional exams with expanded functionality directly from Pearson IT Certification. The Premium Edition eBook and Practice Test for this title contains an additional two full practice exams, as well as an eBook (in both PDF and ePub format). In addition, the Premium Edition title also has remediation for each question to the specific part of the eBook that relates to that question.

Because you have purchased the print version of this title, you can purchase the Premium Edition at a deep discount. There is a coupon code in the CD sleeve that contains a one-time-use code as well as instructions for where you can purchase the Premium Edition.

To view the Premium Edition product page, go to the following URL:

www.informit.com/title/9780132748346

Cisco Learning Network

Cisco provides a wide variety of CCNP Security preparation tools at a Cisco Systems website called the Cisco Learning Network. This site includes a large variety of exam preparation tools, including sample questions, forums on each Cisco exam, learning video games, and information about each exam.

To reach the Cisco Learning Network, go to www.cisco.com/go/learnnetspace, or just search for "Cisco Learning Network." To access the Cisco Learning Network pages, readers/users need to log in with the Cisco.com credentials (login ID and password). If they don't have such a login, they can register for free. To register, go to http://www.cisco.com, click **Register** at the top of the page, and supply some information.

Memory Tables

Like most Official Cert Guides from Cisco Press, this book purposefully organizes information into tables and lists for easier study and review. Rereading these tables can be very useful before the exam. However, it is easy to skim over the tables without paying attention to every detail, especially when you remember having seen the table's contents when reading the chapter.

Instead of simply reading the tables in the various chapters, this book's Appendixes C and D give the reader another review tool. Appendix C, "Memory Tables," lists partially completed versions of many of the tables from the book. Readers can open Appendix C (a PDF file on the CD that comes with this book) and print the appendix. For review, readers can attempt to complete the tables. The exercise can help readers focus on the review. It also exercises the memory connectors in the reader's brain, which forces a little more contemplation about the facts.

Appendix D, "Memory Tables Answer Key," also a PDF file located on the CD, lists the completed tables for the reader(s) to check their answers. Readers can also just refer to the tables as printed in the book.

Chapter-Ending Review Tools

Chapters 1–24 have several features in the "Exam Preparation Tasks" section at the end of each chapter. Many readers have probably reviewed each chapter using these tools. Readers might have used some or all of these tools. It can also be helpful to use these tools again as readers make their final preparations for the exam.

Suggested Plan for Final Review/Study

This section lists a suggested study plan from the point at which readers finish reading Chapter 24 until they take the 642-627 IPS exam. Certainly, you can ignore this plan, use it as is, or just take suggestions from it.

The plan uses five steps. If readers are following the plan verbatim, proceed by part through these steps as listed. That is, starting with Part I ("Introduction to Intrusion Prevention and Detection, Cisco IPS Software, and Supporting Devices"), do the following five steps. Then, for Part II ("Installing and Maintaining Cisco IPS Sensors"), do the following five steps, and so on. The steps are as follows:

Step 1. Review the key topics and the "Do I Know This Already?" questions. You can use the table that lists the key topics at the end of each chapter, or just flip the pages looking for Key Topic icons. Also, reviewing the "Do I Know This Already?" questions from the beginning of the chapter can be helpful review.

Step 2.   **Complete the memory tables.** Open Appendix C on the CD and print the entire appendix, or print the tables by major part. Then, complete the tables. The answers are shown in Appendix D.

Step 3.   **Do hands-on practice.** Most people practice configuration and verification before the exam. Whether readers use real gear, a simulator, or an emulator, practice the configuration and verification commands.

Step 4.   **Build configuration checklists.** Glance through the Table of Contents, looking for major configuration tasks. Then, from memory, create individual configuration checklists for the various configuration commands.

Step 5.   **Use the Pearson Cert Practice Test Engine to practice.** The Pearson Cert Practice Test Engine on the CD can be used to study using a bank of several unique exam-realistic, multiple-choice questions available only with this book.

The following sections describe the steps in more detail.

Step 1: Review the Key Topics and the "Do I Know This Already?" Questions from the Beginning of the Chapter

This review step focuses on the core facts related to the 642-627 IPS exam. The exam will certainly cover other topics as well, but the DIKTA questions and the key topic items attempt to focus attention on the more important topics in each chapter.

As a reminder, if the reader follows this plan after reading the first 24 chapters, working a major part at a time helps the reader pull each major topic together.

Step 2: Complete the Memory Tables

The memory tables are an additional tool that can be used for exam preparation. An incomplete version of these tables (Appendix C) is designed to be printed and completed to test the topic knowledge. The complete version of these tables (Appendix D) can also be used as a crib sheet for important facts from each chapter.

Step 3: Do Hands-On Practice

Although this book shows readers many different configuration commands and specific configuration examples, there is no substitute for hands-on practice. This short section provides a couple of suggestions regarding readers' efforts at practice from the command-line interface (CLI).

Most people use one or more of the following options for hands-on skills:

■   **Real gear:** Either purchased (often used), borrowed, or rented

■   **Simulators:** Software that acts like real gear

■   **Emulators:** Software that acts like router hardware, with IOS running inside that environment

For real gear, this book makes no attempt at suggesting how to go about getting, borrowing, or renting gear. There are a number of different available outlets for used Cisco equipment that can be used to obtain a reasonably priced lab for practice.

As of this writing, there are no comprehensive CCNP Security simulators. Although Cisco IOS simulators exist that simulate many basic functionalities at the associate level, they come up short on more advanced configurations.

The last option is to use an emulator, of which there are two noteworthy options. For the general public, a group of two free software offerings cooperate to allow readers to run multiple instances of IOS: Dynagen (see www.dynagen.org) for the CLI interface and GNS3 (see www.gns3.net) for the graphical interface. All of these tools rely on another tool called *dynamips*, which emulates Cisco hardware. The Dynagen and GNS3 software provides different configuration methods for utilizing this functionality (GNS3 actually uses Dynagen as a back end). There are legal questions about utilizing these emulators with Cisco IOS Software, and they are simply mentioned in this book as available options without condoning or recommending their use.

Step 4: Build Configuration Checklists

This book contains a number of different configuration commands and configuration examples. Review those commands that are the least well known and practice them. After this is complete, write down these configuration checklists from memory to ensure a thorough understanding. In conjunction with this certification guide, it is highly recommended to review the references listed at the end of every chapter, especially the configuration guides found on Cisco.com. There are additional configuration examples and case studies on Cisco.com that will enhance the reader's understanding and knowledge in preparation for the IPS exam.

Step 5: Use the Exam Engine

The Pearson Cert Practice Test Engine on the CD includes a database of questions created specifically for this book. The Pearson Cert Practice Test Engine can be used in either study mode or practice exam mode, as follows:

- **Study mode:** Study mode is most useful when readers want to use the questions for learning and practicing. In study mode, readers can select options such as whether they want to randomize the order of the questions, automatically view answers to the questions as they go, test on specific topics, refer to specific sections of the text that resides on the CD, and so on.

- **Practice exam mode:** This mode presents questions in a timed environment, providing readers with a more exam-realistic experience. It also restricts readers' ability to see their score as they progress through the exam, view answers to questions as they are taking the exam, and refer to sections of the text. These timed exams not only allow readers to study for the actual 642-627 IPS exam, but they also help readers to simulate the time pressure that can occur on the actual exam.

Summary

The tools and suggestions listed in this chapter have been designed with one goal in mind: to help readers develop the skills required to pass the 642-627 IPS exam. This book has been developed from the beginning to not just teach the technologies but also to understand the reason for their specific uses and the configuration steps to be taken when implementing them. Regardless of the readers' experience level leading up to taking the exams, it is our hope that the broad range of preparation tools, and even the structure of the books, will help readers pass the exams with ease. We hope readers do well on the exam.

Part IX: Appendixes

Appendix A: Answers to the "Do I Know This Already?" Quizzes

Appendix B: CCNP Security IPS 642-627 Exam Updates, Version 1.0

Glossary

Appendix C: Memory Tables (CD Only)

Appendix D: Memory Tables Answer Key (CD Only)

Answers to the "Do I Know This Already?" Quizzes

Chapter 1

1. B. There are four commonly known security controls, but the one that represents an error, generally caused by too tight proactive or too relaxed reactive controls, is called a false positive.

2. B. A vulnerability is a weakness in a system that can result in harm to the system or its operations. This can be exploited by another system, either in conjunction with a particular event or circumstance.

3. C. An intrusion detection system (IDS) is a countermeasure that has the capability to detect, alert, and monitor misuse and abuse of, and unauthorized access to, networked resources. An intrusion prevention system (IPS) is a countermeasure that has the same capabilities as an IDS in addition to the capability to act or prevent if necessary.

4. D. There can be several factors that influence the addition of sensors to include performance capabilities of the sensor, exceeded traffic capacity, and network implementation. Because the sensor is often a separate device from the host system, the host performance capabilities are not relevant.

5. A. There are several network intrusion prevention approaches, but only anomaly-based network IPS devices observe network traffic and act if a network event outside the normal (or baseline) network behavior is detected.

6. E. All the items mentioned are major limitations of endpoint security controls.

7. A. API interception, also known as API hooking, is used by Cisco Security Agent (CSA) to control access to files, processes, Windows Registry, Windows Component Object Model (COM) interprocess communications, host firewalling (network), local media devices, the clipboard, and the kernel.

8. B. Antivirus or antispyware are both file-based antimalware software that is primarily designed to prevent file-based malware threats and use content scanning to identify known patterns of malware.

9. E. Some of the major endpoint security controls include cryptographic data protection, antimalware agents, host-based firewalls, and native operating system access controls.

10. C. In most cases, a single device can't provide a complete security solution; thus, a defense-in-depth solution attempts to provide as close to a complete security solution as possible through layers. The network-focused technology provides detection and prevention of denial of service (DoS) attacks, network reconnaissance attacks, and many other attacks against network-facing applications and operating systems.

Chapter 2

1. D. The Cisco IPS 4270 sensor has a maximum throughput of 4 Gbps.

2. E. All the listed modules are supported in the ASA 5500 Series.

3. A. The Cisco IDAPI provides the communications between the applications.

4. E. The Sensor app is supported by all the processors listed.

5. A. The maximum number of IDSM-2 modules supported in a 6500 is 8.

6. C. The maximum throughput supported by an NME-IPS module on an ISR Series router is 75 Mbps.

7. C. The Cisco SDEE uses a secure connection leveraging HTTPS in the pull communications model.

8. B. The IME can support up to 10 IPS devices.

9. A, B, and D. The Cisco Security Intelligence Operations consist of the Cisco SensorBase, Cisco Threat Operations Center, and Dynamic Updates.

10. E. All the options listed are online security resources.

Chapter 3

1. C. False positives with malware identification are a common limitation of packet header matching.

2. D. A known limitation of stateful content matching is false positives because of lack of context.

3. E. All of the listed options are benefits of protocol decoding as a method of IPS traffic analysis.

4. A. The most granular method of IPS traffic analysis is protocol decoding.

5. B. Reconnaissance attacks are the attacks mainly detected through the method of traffic analysis known as traffic correlation.

6. A. The IPS evasion technique where the attacker splits malicious traffic in an effort to avoid detection or filtering is known as traffic fragmentation.

7. D. When double encoding is utilized, it is the worst-case scenario with regard to unique ways that a single character can be encoded.

8.   C. The IPS evasion technique that causes the IPS sensor to ignore traffic that should not be ignored is protocol-level misinterpretation.

9.   E. The encrypted portion of network traffic can't be analyzed by an IPS for content and, as a result, an attacker can leverage the ability to use an encrypted protocol, like the ones shown here, to evade an IPS device.

10. A. By summarizing an attack that involved many sources, sending multiple attacks at the same time, the administrator can be provided summary alerts, instead of hundreds or thousands of alerts, for the same set of attacks. As a result, the system and the people managing the alerts will have less data to process.

Chapter 4

1.   E. All the options discussed are things an administrator should consider when deploying a network IDS or IPS sensor.

2.   D. Although memory is something to consider in any computer system, for the purposes of this exercise, which is to evaluate criteria considerations when deploying a network IDS or IPS sensor, the other three answers are more critical.

3.   A. Multiple network segments can be inspected without policy virtualization being configured.

4.   A. Of the listed network infrastructure or designs, the Internet edge is defined as a policy-facing network infrastructure exposed to a large array of external networks.

5.   B and C. Typically, the "trusted" interfaces are the inside and DMZ (less-trusted) interfaces when integrating a firewall with an IPS architecture.

6.   B. A WAN is defined as a network with geographically dispersed remote sites with access to the same services at central sites.

7.   D. All three options are threats that are addressed in the WAN edge IPS architecture.

8.   C. A data center typically hosts most of the critical applications and data for an enterprise or provider.

9.   A and D. Both RSPAN and ERSPAN are supported in a Cisco centralized campus sensor deployment.

10. B. A centralized campus architecture involves deploying network IPS sensors to inspect traffic on ports that are located on multiple remote network switches.

Chapter 5

1.   B. The main limitation of promiscuous mode on a Cisco IPS sensor is the lack of rich real-time preventive capabilities.

2.   E. All the deployment options listed are supported on the Cisco IPS sensor.

3.   C and D. The Catalyst 3560-E and 3570-E Series switches support the FSPAN feature.

4. A. The Cisco Catalyst 6500 Series switches support the VACL capture feature.

5. C. The multi-interface analysis feature can be connected to the same analysis engine and treated as the same traffic source.

6. C. All of these options, except for network availability, are benefits of an inline interface pair deployment on a Cisco IPS sensor.

7. E. All the features listed are specific to the mode on a Cisco IPS sensor.

8. B. VLAN pair mode on a Cisco IPS sensor acts as a wire between two VLANs on the same interface.

9. A. In an inline VLAN group deployment, no VLAN can be a member of more than one VLAN group subinterface.

10. E. All the listed ASA models with supporting modules support Cisco IPS selective inline analysis mode.

Chapter 6

1. C. Cisco IPS Sensor Software version 7.0 permits 10 concurrent CLI sessions.

2. D. The commands **session**, **ssh**, and **telnet** are all commands that are used to access the CLI for a given sensor.

3. B. An administrator/user can end configuration mode and return to the EXEC prompt using the Ctrl-Z key combination.

4. A. When initializing a Cisco IPS sensor appliance, the only access available is through the console port or service module session.

5. E. All the choices shown are present by default on the Cisco IDM home page.

6. A and C. The two required fields when configuring/creating inline interface pairs on the Cisco IPS sensor through IDM are the Interface Pair Name and Select Two Interfaces fields.

7. A, B, and C. The Interface Name, Subinterface Number, and VLAN Group are the required fields when configuring/creating an inline VLAN group on the Cisco IPS sensor.

8. B. Having both of the physical interfaces on a different interface card is *not* a condition for the sensor to fail-open with hardware bypass.

9. A. There is no command to interrupt a **ping** or **trace** command on the Cisco IPS sensor.

10. E. All the answers are common reasons for sensor management not being accessible on the Cisco IPS sensor.

11. A

Chapter 7

1. A. Telnet isn't a secure access service because it uses clear text; thus, it's recommended to use a secure method of access such as SSH or HTTPS, which is encrypted.

2. E. Under the Sensor Setup pane, the IDM GUI includes Network and Time settings as well as Reboot and Shutdown hot buttons.

3. B. The operator role permits the user access to most features on the Cisco IPS Sensor except reconfiguration of basic sensor settings.

4. A. Only one user can log in to a sensor at a time through the Cisco IDM.

5. C. The status of the license key can be seen at login through the CLI, the IDM Licensing pane, and the IDM Home window Licensing section on the Health tab.

6. A, B, and C. The Application, System, and Recovery images are valid types of sensor images.

7. D. In partnership with Trend Micro, Cisco pushes signature updates to sensors within 2 hours of the new signatures being created.

8. A and C. When performing password recovery on the Cisco IPS Sensor, the administrator or user can use the Esc or Ctrl-R key combination to interrupt the boot process.

9. E. The UDI includes the product version traceability, can be retrieved through the CLI or SNMP MIB, is guaranteed to be unique for all Cisco devices, and is a deliverable of the Cisco PEP.

10. B. The **show statistics** command displays the current state of sensor devices.

11. E. The Health Dashboard pane displays the Disk, CPU, and Memory Usage as well as the Inspection Load.

Chapter 8

1. A. A virtual sensor includes signature policy, event action policy, and anomaly policy.

2. B. The default virtual sensor on all IPS sensors is named vs0.

3. A and D. The two modes currently available on the Cisco IPS sensor for traffic normalization include Strict Evasion Protection and Asymmetric Mode Protection.

4. C. Clear nodes, clear inspectors, and clear alerts are options available in the Clear Flow States pane.

5. E. All the options listed are modes of IP fragment reassembly.

6. D. The virtual sensor, interface and VLAN, and VLAN only are TCP session tracking modes supported on the Cisco IPS sensors.

7.   D. There are three engines typically used to inspect IPv6 traffic that include ATOM-IC IP, ATOMIC IP ADVANCED, and ATOMIC IPv6.

8.   D. The Cisco IPS Manager Express (IME) elements that support IPv6 include filtering, grouping, and reporting.

9.   A. Typically, bypass mode is meant to be used only with inline paired interfaces.

10. B. The auto bypass mode enables traffic to flow through the sensor, even if the monitoring process of the sensor is down.

Chapter 9

1.   D. The Cisco IPS Sensor distinguishes among three types of signatures: Default, Custom, and Tuned.

2.   B. A signature engine is comprised of a parser and an inspector.

3.   D. All of these devices can pull alerts from the Cisco IPS Sensor using the Security Device Event Exchange (SDEE) protocol.

4.   B. Retiring inactive signatures enhances sensor performance because there will be more memory available.

5.   C. Deny Attacker Inline denies current and future packets from a single attacker address.

6.   A and B. The Cisco IPS Sensor will have a session into the blocking device using Telnet or SSH and will configure the device when necessary.

7.   D. All the devices listed can be configured as blocking or shunning devices.

8.   B. The Miscellaneous tab applies to Sig0 only here and not all signature sets; thus, it is not global.

9.   D. The logs have to be a *.cap file to be viewed through network protocol analyzers like Wireshark.

10. D. All of these are components of risk rating and they all influence it. Global correlation also influences the calculation of risk rating if enabled on the Cisco IPS Sensor.

Chapter 10

1.   D. The Cisco IPS signature engine enables you to tune built-in signatures and create new signatures. It also uses its parameters to provide the configuration of signatures.

2.   B. The ATOMIC signature engines support signatures that are triggered by matching the header or payload contents of a single packet.

3.   A. All the options except ATOMIC STRING are STRING signature engines.

4.   C. The SERVICE engines analyze application ports.

Chapter 11

1. C. The three anomaly detection operational modes are detect, inactive, and learn.

2. D. Anomaly detection is looking for scans based on TCP, UDP, and non-TCP non-UDP unidirectional flows with no return packets.

3. C. Anomaly detection is triggered when a single host exceeds a threshold, or a group of computers exceed the limits specified in a histogram.

4. D. Unidirectional flows, with return traffic not showing up within 15 seconds, would be considered a scan event.

5. C. Histograms are used to identify a group of scanners; the initial histogram relies on the knowledge base, which takes 24 hours initially to be built.

Chapter 12

1. C. When looking to match on specific traffic generated by an in-house application, it is unlikely that one of the default signatures could be used, and a custom signature would have to be created.

2. D. The String Engine will look for a string of text within a specific packet or within a specific session.

3. C. Using regular expressions inside a single signature that can identify a string of text with multiple variations can be used instead of creating multiple signatures, each looking for a specific string of text.

4. D. The advanced options in the wizard include Event Count and Summarization, but not the service port, which is located as another property of the signature.

5. C. Generating network traffic to verify that the custom signature is both active and working is a good way to test the signature.

Chapter 13

1. C. When the matching criteria is too strict for a signature, anything outside the parameters of the signature will not trigger the signature.

2. D. A false negative is when an attack did occur but the sensor failed to recognize it as an attack.

3. C. By removing the harmful actions during the tuning phase, we can have visibility to all the triggered signatures, without implementing countermeasures. This is important so that false positives don't interrupt production network traffic.

4. D. The default IP reassembly option for the sensor is NT.

5. D. Tuning options to correct a false positive include disabling the signature, using event action filters, and making a match criteria more strict within the signature itself.

Chapter 14

1. B. Properties of a signature that are related to the risk rating include signature fidelity rating and attack severity rating. WLR and TVR are not properties of a signature.

2. A. Watch list ratings are based on information from Management Center for CSA. The connectivity between the sensor and the Management Center is done through the external product interface.

3. C. The three primary factors that make up the risk rating are SFR, ASR, and TVR.

4. D. Dynamic DNS is not part of the learning process between the IP address of a device and the underlying operating system.

5. C. DNS services, as a client, are required by the sensor to use global correlation.

Chapter 15

1. B. Cisco IPS Manager Express supports up to 10 IPS sensor devices.

2. B. The troubleshooting tools built into Cisco IME are ping, whois, DNS lookup, and traceroute.

3. C. Cisco IME runs on Windows operating systems only.

4. D. To add a Cisco IPS sensor to Cisco IME, you need the following: sensor name, sensor IP address, sensor username and password, and a sensor web server port.

5. A. To ensure that the connectivity is secure and a trust is established, the sensor offers a certificate when connecting through Cisco IME for the first time. After it is accepted, the management session is established. Refusing the certificate terminates the session.

6. D. When an event occurs on the IPS sensor, the time on both management host and Cisco IPS sensor must be no more than 5 minutes apart to be able to track the chain of events for forensic processes.

7. C. Cisco IME comes with three default risk categories, which have risk thresholds of 90, 70, and 1. They are HIGHRISK, MEDIUMRISK, and LOWRISK, respectively.

8. A. Cisco IME comes preconfigured with two dashboards: Health Dashboard and Event Dashboard.

9. B. Adding dashboards is a simple process where from the Home view, you click the Dashboards subview and click Add Dashboard.

10. E. Cisco IME comes prepopulated with 14 gadgets. Clicking the Add Gadget button reveals gadgets that can be double-clicked to add to the dashboard.

Chapter 16

1. D. Cisco IME has one other view—the Real-Time Colored view—apart from answers A, B, and C.

2. C. Custom views are created by clicking **New** under **Event Monitoring > Event Monitoring** and are listed under My Views after they are created.

3. C. There are five tabs under the View settings: Filter, Group By, Color Rules, Fields, and General.

4. D. The Filter drop-down box provides two options: Add To Filter and Create Filter. The Add To Filter option further provides three options to filter by, while the Create Filter option uses the event parameters to create a filter from the event.

5. C. The Event details can be seen through **Event Monitoring** > **Event Monitoring** > **My Views** > *view_name* > **Event Details**.

6. D. Cisco IME does not have capabilities to create IPS sensor signatures but can edit signatures.

7. C. Cisco IME has features for importing or exporting the database as well as archiving old data to improve the performance of the database.

Chapter 17

1. B. Cisco IME has six built-in report categories in the Report tree (left side of the reporting pane). There is also a My Reports category, where newly added customized reports are listed. The My Reports category is not included in the six built-in categories. The six report categories expand into 18 individual reports.

2. B. The likely cause is that DNS is not configured on the IPS.

3. C. Cisco IME allows you to share reports as PDF and RTF files or through printing.

4. D. The Top N gadgets are Top Attacker, Top Victims, Top Signatures, and Top Applications.

5. A. The required email settings for notification are From address, Recipient address, and mail server.

Chapter 18

1. C. Cisco CSM manages all the other devices listed except MARS. It does have some significant degree of collaboration with MARS, though.

2. B. FTP is not a prerequisite and not required for managing an IPS sensor, so it is the wrong answer. The other answers are the basic requirements for managing a device through CSM.

3. D. These are all features of Cisco MARS.

4. A. SDEE is the protocol that CS-MARS uses to pull events from IPS.

5. A. Cross-launch capability in CS-MARS and CSM allows the launching of CSM within CS-MARS and launching CS-MARS within CSM.

Chapter 19

1. A. The Security Intelligence Operations portal does not have risk rating as a core section in the portal.

2. B. The Cisco Security IntelliShield Alert Manager Service provides alert information for various devices and applications and is not limited to Cisco devices and applications.

3. C. The IPS Threat Defense Bulletin is an alert that you can subscribe to for information on signature updates.

4. D. All the options listed are correct.

5. B. The virtual user is created to just receive notifications created by a registered user.

6. C. Notifications are sent through email, pager, and cell phone.

Chapter 20

1. C. The Cisco ASA AIP SSC-5 supports only one sensor instance and therefore does not support virtualization.

2. D. The maximum number of sensors supported is four.

3. C. All answers except C are benefits of sensor virtualization, which allows you to run multiple virtual sensors within the same hardware and have similar policies.

4. D. All the options listed in A, B, and C are correct.

5. C. The virtual sensor configuration and operation status has to be verified.

Chapter 21

1. D. A well thought-out design must be available before you venture into configuring the IPS sensors.

2. C. The maximum number of IPS sensors supported is 8.

3. B. All the other answers are correct except for B.

4. B. In the inline mode, the IPS sensor sits in the path of data traffic and all data passes through it.

5. D. D is the correct answer because all the answers can be used to redirect traffic to the IPS sensor.

Chapter 22

1. B. When the AIP is deployed in a manner as described here, all traffic is analyzed to ensure that malicious traffic does not get to its intended destination.

2. B. The Cisco ASA AIP can be deployed in two modes of operation.

3. D. The modes of operation are inline and promiscuous.

4. A. The Modular Policy Framework and access control lists are used to identify and redirect traffic to the AIP module in the Cisco ASA.

5. B. When applied to a VLAN interface, the **allow-ssc-mgmt** command permits management of the AIP-SSC through that VLAN. By default, VLAN 1 is the management VLAN.

6. C. The **boot** option in the command initiates the recovery or upgrade process.

7. A. The **configure** parameter in the command initiates the process to configure the image name and TFTP server address and image location.

8. B. After a session has been established to the CLI of the Cisco ASA, to further establish a session with the AIP module, the **session 1** command is used, which connects to give the CLI access to the AIP.

9. The **setup** command is used to initiate the menu-driven configuration of the AIP.

10. B and C. The AIP has two failure modes. They are fail-close, which will prevent the flow of traffic, and fail-open, which will allow traffic to flow unchecked.

11. D. Identifying the traffic with a class map, directing the traffic through a policy map, and implementing the policy map are all required steps for redirecting traffic to the module.

12. B. The **class** command is missing in this configuration.

13. B. The **show module** command lists the serial number, product ID, and software version of the AIP module.

Chapter 23

1. D. The IPS AIM card has no external interfaces.

2. C. The IDS-Sensor 0/0 interface is a valid logical interface to the IPS AIM.

3. D. The modes of operation are inline and promiscuous.

4. A. The modules connect to the router backplane interface to monitor traffic and do not need two interfaces to be inline.

5. B. The **show inventory** command provides details in this regard.

6. A. The **service-module ids-sensor 0/0 status** command is required to view the status of the module, which shows details on its working condition.

7. B. The **service-module ids-sensor 0/1 session** command is used to virtually console in the modules.

8. C. The correct answer is C because it is not a valid command. An access list can be used to specify traffic meant for captures, whereas the **ids-service-module monitoring** command is used to enable monitoring on an interface, specify the mode, and bind the access list.

9. The Router Blade Configuration Protocol (RBCP) is used.

10. E. All the options listed are carried out by the router to restore service to the IPS AIM or IPS NME in a failure situation.

11. B. The **clear password** command is used at the end of the password recovery process to clear the old password, after which the module reboots.

Chapter 24

1. D. The Cisco IDSM-2 has no external interfaces.

2. C. The IDSM-2 has a TCP reset interface, command and control interface, and two sensing interfaces that can be used inline or in promiscuous mode.

3. D. The modes of operation are inline and promiscuous.

4. Application and maintenance partitions.

5. B. The **show module** command is the correct answer; the **show inventory** command does not show the sensor software version.

6. A. The **show settings** filtering to include only password under the service host submode provides the status to see whether password recovery is enabled or disabled.

CCNP Security IPS 642-627 Exam Updates, Version 1.0

Over time, reader feedback allows Cisco Press to gauge which topics give our readers the most problems when taking the exams. To assist readers, authors can create new materials clarifying and expanding upon those troublesome exam topics. This additional content about the exam will be posted as a PDF document on this book's companion website, at www.ciscopress.com/title/1587142554.

This appendix is intended to provide you with updated information if Cisco makes minor modifications to the exam upon which this book is based. When Cisco releases an entirely new exam, the changes are usually too extensive to provide in a simple update appendix. In those cases, you will need to consult the new edition of the book for the updated content.

This appendix attempts to fill the void that occurs with any print book. In particular, this appendix does the following:

- Mentions technical items that might not have been mentioned elsewhere in the book

- Covers new topics if Cisco adds new content to the exam over time

- Provides a way to get up-to-the-minute current information about content for the exam

Always Get the Latest at the Companion Website

You are reading the version of this appendix that was available when your book was printed. However, given that the main purpose of this appendix is to be a living, changing document, it is important that you look for the latest version online at the book's companion website. To do so, follow these steps:

Step 1. Browse to http://www.ciscopress.com/title/1587142554.

Step 2. Select the **Updates** option under the More Information box.

Step 3. Download the latest Appendix B document.

Note: The downloaded document has a version number. Comparing the print version of this Appendix B (version 1.0) with the latest online version of this appendix, you should do the following:

■ **Same version:** Ignore the PDF file that you downloaded from the companion website.

■ **Website has a later version:** Ignore this Appendix B in your book, and read only the latest version that you downloaded from the companion website.

If there is no appendix posted on the book's website, that simply means there have been no updates to post and version 1.0 is still the latest version.

Technical Content

The current version of this appendix does not contain any additional technical coverage.

Glossary

ad0 The default anomaly detection policy.

administrator The user role for the Cisco IPS Sensor Software that has the highest level of privileges. The administrator role has unrestricted view access and can perform enabling and disabling of physical interfaces, assigning physical monitoring interfaces to a virtual sensor, modifying sensor address configuration, adding and deleting users and modifying passwords, modifying the list of hosts allowed to connect to the sensor, tuning signatures, and managing blocking devices.

anomaly The deviation from the common rule, baseline, or norm.

anomaly detection Identifies individual scanners on the network and can identify whether multiple devices are infected with a worm.

ARR (Attack Relevancy Rating) This is configured as a property of a signature. If the person who wrote the signature indicates that the signature match is only relevant if the operating system is UNIX, and the IPS sensor knows that the destination address for a signature match is also UNIX, it will increase the value of the risk rating.

ASR (Attack Severity Rating) This is assigned as a property of the signature to indicate how serious an attack, in the mind of the person who created the signature, is happening when this signature is matched.

asymmetric As it applies to networking, this is the imbalance of inbound and outbound traffic traversing one link or links and returning on a different link or links.

attack An operation focused on disrupting or rendering an information system unusable, which can also destroy or devalue the information if obtained.

Attack Response Controller (ARC) The blocking application on the sensor.

Cisco IntelliShield Service Provides a comprehensive, cost-effective solution for delivering the intelligence that organizations need.

Cisco Security Intelligence Operations A service that provides global threat intelligence.

Cisco Security IntelliShield Alert Manager (SIAM) Provides a comprehensive solution for delivering the security in mission-critical environments to prevent and remediate attacks.

Cisco Security Manager (CSM) An enterprise-class security management software application designed for scalable operational, management, and policy control for a wide variety of devices.

Cisco Security Monitoring, Analysis, and Response System (CS-MARS or MARS)
An appliance-based, all-inclusive solution that provides insight into events to help administrators monitor, identify, isolate, and remedy security issues or incidents.

custom signature   A signature that is not a default signature and did not come included with the sensor by default.

decode   The process by which information/code is converted back into information understandable by the receiver or host.

deobfuscation   The practice that is used to simplify something such as code that was intentionally made more difficult to understand to evade detection.

DST (daylight saving time)   Also known as summertime. The practice of temporarily advancing clocks during the summertime so that evenings have more daylight and mornings have less.

encode   The process by which information/code from a source is converted to another code to be communicated to a particular receiver or host.

ERSPAN (Encapsulated Remote Switched Port Analyzer)   An enhanced and encapsulated version of the RSPAN feature.

evasion   The act or instance of avoiding, escaping, or shirking something.

event correlation   Monitoring events from different devices at the same time to determine patterns of events that might be malicious.

exploit   The mechanism used to leverage a vulnerability to compromise the security functionality of a system.

false negative   Malicious traffic that did not trigger any alerts.

false positive   Nonmalicious traffic that triggers an alert.

From address   Address from which the message is sent to the SMTP server; for example, ips@cisco.com.

FTP (File Transport Protocol)   Typically uses the well-known TCP port 21.

global correlation   The collection and analysis of network attacks used to protect other Cisco IPS–protected networks from being attacked by the known threat.

GRE (generic routing encapsulation)   A tunneling protocol developed by Cisco Systems that can encapsulate a wide variety of network layer protocol packet types inside IP tunnels.

high availability   The ability of a system to limit or avoid network disruption when a network component fails.

histogram   A method used by the sensor to identify multiple devices that as a group exceed thresholds.

HTTPS (Hypertext Transfer Protocol Secure)   A combination of the Hypertext Transfer Protocol (HTTP) with the SSL/TLS protocol to provide encryption communications and secure identification of a network web server or host. TCP port 443 has been assigned for HTTPS.

IDM (Cisco IPS Device Manager)   The Java-based GUI that enables the administrator/user for that single IPS sensor to configure, monitor, and troubleshoot through a GUI interface.

inline mode   The configuration that allows an IPS to be in the pathway of packets flowing into and out of a device so that it can analyze and drop any malicious packets.

IPsec (Internet Protocol Security)   Provides a method of authentication and encryption for each IP packet of a communications session. IPsec leverages protocols such as AH (Authentication Header) for integrity and authentication; ESP (Encapsulating Security Payload) for confidentiality, authentication, integrity, and antireplay; and ISAKMP (Internet Security Association and Key Management Protocol) for a framework for authentication and key exchange.

jitter   The variation in the time between packets arriving from a given source or sources often caused by network congestion, timing drift, or path/route changes.

knowledge base   A baseline of normal traffic, related to scans, that is built to establish histograms and group thresholds.

LAN (local-area network)   The connectivity of two or more computer systems in the same geographic area, often in the same building or location.

mail server (SMTP Host)   An SMTP server address; for example, smtp.cisco.com.

MDIX   Medium dependent interface crossover.

MPF (Modular Policy Framework)   Provides a consistent and flexible way to configure security appliance features in a manner similar to the Cisco IOS Software QoS command-line interface.

NIC   Network interface card.

NMS   Network management system.

NTP (Network Time Protocol)   The protocol for synchronizing the clocks of hosts over a network. This can be either manually configured (typically) or automatically generated by a connected GPS/Stratum clock.

operator   This user role for the Cisco IPS Sensor Software that has the second-highest level of privileges. The operator role can view all configuration events and can change his or her own user password, tune signatures, and manage blocking devices.

PD (promiscuous delta)   If the sensor has a signature match and is in promiscuous mode, and if the given signature that was matched includes a promiscuous delta value, the risk rating will be reduced by that value.

promiscuous mode   The configuration that makes an interface pass all traffic it receives to the central processing unit rather that just packets sent directly to it.

Recipient address   Email address(es) to which notifications will be sent by the SMTP server; for example, admin@cisco.com.

reconnaissance attack   A common method by which a user or users maliciously gather information about a target network or system to be used for subsequent access or denial of service attacks.

regular expression   A method of using variables and meta-characters to effectively represent a string that can have multiple variations, such as uppercase and lowercase text.

risk   The likelihood that a particular threat using a specific attack will exploit a particular vulnerability of an asset or system that results in an undesirable consequence.

RR (risk rating)   This is the final risk rating result.

RSPAN (Remote Switched Port Analyzer)   An advanced feature of a switch that is used to monitor source ports available all over in the switched network. All SPAN features are typically supported in RSPAN.

rules0   The default event action rules policy.

scanner   A single host that has exceeded the scanner threshold.

SCP (Secure Copy Protocol)   Typically uses SSH (TCP port 22) to securely transfer files between two hosts.

Security Device Event Exchange (SDEE)   A specification for the message formats and the messaging protocol used to communicate the events generated by security devices. It replaces the Remote Data Exchange Protocol (RDEP).

Security Intelligence Operations (SIO)   A cloud-based service that connects global threat information, reputation-based services, and sophisticated analysis to Cisco network security devices to provide stronger protection with faster response times.

service   A special role for the Cisco IPS Sensor Software that allows the user to log in to a native operating system shell.

SFR (Signature Fidelity Rating)   Assigned as a property of the signature to indicate how accurate the signature is, in the mind of the person who created the signature, regarding matching ability of the signature.

sig0   The default signature definitions policy.

signature   A rule configured in a network IPS or IDS device that describes a pattern of network traffic that is used to detect and respond to malicious or suspicious activity.

SNMP (Simple Network Management Protocol)   Typically uses the well-known UDP port 161.

SPAN (Switched Port Analyzer)   Sometimes called port mirroring or port monitoring. Selects network traffic for analysis by a network analyzer.

SSH (Secure Shell)   A network protocol that allows data to be exchanged using a secure channel between two networked devices. TCP port 22 has been assigned for the SSH protocol.

SSL (Secure Socket Layer)   A commonly used protocol for managing the security of a message transmission on the Internet. SSL has been succeeded by Transport Layer Security (TLS), which is based on SSL. Thus, when SSL is used in text, it's assumed that TLS/SSL is being used. SSL uses a program layer between Hypertext Transfer Protocol (HTTP) and Transport Control Protocol (TCP) layers.

symmetric   As it applies to networking, this is the balance of inbound and outbound traffic that traverses a link or links and returns on that link or links.

Telnet   A network protocol used on the Internet or local-area networks to provide bidirectional interactive text-oriented communications using a virtual terminal connection. TCP port 23 has been assigned for the Telnet protocol.

threat   Any circumstance or event with the expressed potential for the occurrence of a harmful event to an information system in the form of destruction, disclosure, adverse modification of data, or denial of service.

TLS (Transport Layer Security)   A protocol that provides communications securely over the Internet. TLS uses symmetric cryptography for privacy and a keyed message authentication code for message reliability.

tuned signature   A default signature that has had at least one attribute modified.

tuning   The process of modifying the sensor settings, policies, and/or signatures to adapt them for a given network, including the reduction of false positives and false negatives.

TVR (Target Value Rating)   This is configured in the set of rules that is assigned to a virtual sensor. The more critical the device is, based on its IP address, and the higher the Target Value Rating will be, the higher the final risk rating will be.

UDI   Unique Device Identifier

UDLD (UniDirectional Link Detection)   A Layer 2 protocol that enables devices connected through fiber-optic or twisted-pair Ethernet cables to monitor the physical configuration of the cables and detect when a unidirectional link exists.

URL (Uniform Resource Locator)   A Uniform Resource Identifier (URI) that specifies where a known resource is available and indicates the mechanism for retrieving it, such as a website URL (for example, http://www.cisco.com).

UTC (Coordinated Universal Time)   The time standard by which the world regulates clocks and time.

VID   Version identifier.

viewer   The user role for the Cisco IPS Sensor Software that has the lowest level of privileges. The viewer role can view configurations and events. A viewer cannot modify any configuration data except his or her own passwords.

virtual sensor   A collection of data that is defined by a set of configuration policies that is applied to a set of packets through groups of interfaces.

VPN (Virtual Private Network)   A method of communicating securely using IPsec, SSL/TLS, and so on over a public or shared untrusted telecommunications infrastructure.

vs0   The default virtual sensor.

vulnerability   A weakness that compromises either the security or the functionality of a system.

WAN (wide-area network)   The connectivity between two or more sites over a geographic area, often connecting local-area networks.

WLR (Watch List Rating)   If the Cisco Security Agent Manager has been configured, and has notified the sensor that a specific IP address is under attack, the Watch List Rating will be added to the risk rating.

Index

D

I

J-K-L

M

Q-R

S

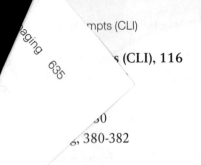

FREE Online Edition

CCNP Security IPS 642-627

DAVID BURNS
ODUNAYO ADESINA, CCIE® No. 26695
KEITH BARKER, CCIE No. 6783

Your purchase of **CCNP Security IPS 642-627 Official Cert Guide** includes access to a free online edition for 45 days through the Safari Books Online subscription service. Nearly every Cisco Press book is available online through Safari Books Online, along with more than 5,000 other technical books and videos from publishers such as Addison-Wesley Professional, Exam Cram, IBM Press, O'Reilly, Prentice Hall, Que, and Sams.

SAFARI BOOKS ONLINE allows you to search for a specific answer, cut and paste code, download chapters, and stay current with emerging technologies.

Activate your FREE Online Edition at www.informit.com/safarifree

STEP 1: Enter the coupon code: QKMMNVH.

STEP 2: New Safari users, complete the brief registration form. Safari subscribers, just log in.

If you have difficulty registering on Safari or accessing the online edition, please e-mail customer-service@safaribooksonline.com

Addison Wesley | Adobe Press | ALPHA | Cisco Press | FT Press | IBM Press | lynda.com | Microsoft Press | New Riders

O'REILLY | Peachpit Press | PRENTICE HALL | Que | Redbooks | SAMS | SAS Publishing | Sun microsystems | WILEY

Cisco Learning Network

Free Test Prep and Beyond.

☑ Access review questions
☑ Watch Quick Learning Modules (QLMS)
☑ Search for jobs and network with others
☑ Take self-assessments
☑ Participate in study groups
☑ Play online learning games

Register for a free membership
and get started now.
www.cisco.com/go/learningnetwork

Cisco Learning Network
A social learning site brought to you by Learning@Cisco

FREE Online Edition

Your purchase of **CCNP Security IPS 642-627 Official Cert Guide** includes access to a free online edition for 45 days through the Safari Books Online subscription service. Nearly every Cisco Press book is available online through Safari Books Online, along with more than 5,000 other technical books and videos from publishers such as Addison-Wesley Professional, Exam Cram, IBM Press, O'Reilly, Prentice Hall, Que, and Sams.

SAFARI BOOKS ONLINE allows you to search for a specific answer, cut and paste code, download chapters, and stay current with emerging technologies.

Activate your FREE Online Edition at www.informit.com/safarifree

> **STEP 1:** Enter the coupon code: QKMMNVH.

> **STEP 2:** New Safari users, complete the brief registration form.
> Safari subscribers, just log in.

If you have difficulty registering on Safari or accessing the online edition, please e-mail customer-service@safaribooksonline.com

Addison Wesley   Adobe Press   ALPHA   Cisco Press   FT Press   IBM Press   lynda.com   Microsoft Press   New Riders

O'REILLY   Peachpit Press   PRENTICE HALL   Que   Redbooks   SAMS   SAS Publishing   Sun microsystems   Wharton School Publishing   WILEY